REGESTA REGUM SCOTTORUM

VOLUME IV Pt I

The Acts of Alexander III

KING OF SCOTS

1249–1286

edited by
CYNTHIA J. NEVILLE
and
GRANT G. SIMPSON

EDINBURGH UNIVERSITY PRESS

REGESTA REGUM SCOTTORUM

I. ACTS OF MALCOLM IV, 1153–1165
edited by G. W. S. Barrow (1960)

II. ACTS OF WILLIAM I, 1165–1214
edited by G. W. S. Barrow with the collaboration of W. W. Scott (1971)

III. ACTS OF ALEXANDER II, 1214–1249
edited by Keith J. Stringer

IV. PT 1 ACTS OF ALEXANDER III, 1249–1286
edited by Cynthia J. Neville and Grant G. Simpson (2012)

IV. PT 2 ACTS OF THE GUARDIANS AND JOHN, 1286–1306
edited by Alan Young

V. ACTS OF ROBERT I, 1306–1329
edited by Archibald A. M. Duncan (1988)

VI. ACTS OF DAVID II, 1329–1371
edited by Bruce Webster (1982)

www.euppublishing.com/series/rrs

Edinburgh University Press Ltd
22 George Square, Edinburgh EH8 9LF
www.euppublishing.com

Typeset in Plantin by Koinonia, Manchester, and
printed and bound in Great Britain by
CPI Group (UK) Ltd, Croydon CR0 4YY

A CIP record for this book is available from the British Library

ISBN 978 0 7486 2732 5 (hardback)
ISBN 978 0 7486 3144 5 (webready PDF)
ISBN 978 0 7486 4932 7 (epub)
ISBN 978 0 7486 4931 0 (Amazon ebook)

Published with the support of the Edinburgh University
Scholarly Publishing Initiatives Fund.

PREFACE

This volume had a long gestation. It was conceived many years ago as Volume IV of the *Regesta Regum Scottorum* series and thus part of the editors' original plan to bring into print all the written acts of the Scottish kings before 1424. As so conceived, it was intended that it include documents issued under the seals of Alexander III, the Guardians and John Balliol, that is, acts dated to the period 1249 to 1306. Grant Simpson agreed to take on the task of editing the volume, and as many will know, his *Handlist* duly appeared in 1960. He had no idea then that his compilation would remain a standard, and indeed the only, reference work on the royal acts of that period for as long as it did.

By 1999, and despite heavy teaching and postgraduate supervisory commitments, Grant Simpson had made good progress on collecting and transcribing most of the documents that survive as originals. When he had to set aside his work on the *RRS*, the editors of the earlier volumes in the series approached Cynthia Neville and Alan Young to ask if they might take up the challenge of completing the project that Simpson had laboured so long to produce. Both readily agreed, and for much of the following decade, although each was heavily involved in teaching and other scholarly obligations, they worked part-time on the project, Neville on the *acta* of Alexander III, Young on those of the Guardians and John. A decade later, Volume IV was divided into two Parts: a first including the acts of Alexander III and a second with the acts issued between 1286 and 1306. The current volume, then, represents the culmination of a sustained effort spread over several decades on the part of Simpson and Neville. Academic collaborations of this kind sometimes test even the strongest of friendships and the most courteous of professional relationships, but at every step of the way ours has been a most collegial and fruitful partnership.

It remains for the editors to thank the many people who made other, equally important contributions to this editorial project. These include the original *Regesta Regum Scottorum* editorial board: Geoffrey Barrow, Archie Duncan, Bruce Webster, Athol Murray and Keith Stringer; the host of colleagues, friends and acquaintances who made regular and tireless contact with the editors over the years in order to bring to their attention references to unknown or otherwise untraced documents, and research assistants on both sides of the Atlantic, including Trevor Chalmers, Nick Wilkinson and Chris McKelvie. The editors wish to express particular thanks to the people who have staffed the offices of what is now known as the National Records of Scotland, and before that the National Archives of Scotland and for many years less formally as the Scottish Record Office; as well as the staff of the National Library of Scotland and of a range of private muniment collections in Scotland, England and abroad. Without the helpfulness of all these persons the task of assembling this widely scattered collection would have been impossible. Several scholars provided advice about transcriptions, place names or other matters related to the editorial notes attached to each entry; still others agreed to examine sources to which we did not have ready access. The names here would fill a volume in and of themselves, but we would like to single out for thanks Keith Stringer, Dauvit Broun and, for their very generous assistance with place names, Simon Taylor, Thomas Owen Clancy, Peter McNiven, Peter Drummond, Matthew Hammond and Gilbert Márkus.

The editors are also grateful for the financial support that they have enjoyed over the years from a range of bodies, including the Carnegie Trust for the Universities of Scotland, the Society of Antiquaries of Scotland, the Anderson Dunlop Fund of the Scottish Medievalists, the Strathmartine Trust and the Social Sciences and Humanities Research Council of Canada.

Last, but by no means least, we would like to thank our respective spouses. Neither Anne Turner Simpson nor Stephen Bloom ever set out to become an intimate acquaintance of Alexander III, but over the many years that it took to bring this project to fruition, both have been made to spend a great deal of time with him. In its closing stages the volume benefited immensely from Anne's assistance and the very generous provision of her time. We hope that when they finally see this volume in print both Stephen and Anne will consider their time well spent.

GRANT G. SIMPSON, Aberdeen

CYNTHIA J. NEVILLE, Halifax, NS

CONTENTS

Preface v
List of Abbreviations viii

INTRODUCTION
Analysis of the Acts of Alexander III 3
I. Diplomatic analysis 3
II. Classification and subject matter 6
III. The hands 22
IV. The king's seals 30
V. Place dates in the acts of Alexander III 34
Appendix I. The Inventory of 29 September 1282 37
Methods of Editing 40
List of Sources 44
Notes to the Introduction 48

THE ACTS OF ALEXANDER III
Dated Acts, Full Texts, 1–163 57
Undated Acts, Full Texts, 164–175 193
Calendar of Lost Acts, 176–330 201
Unattributable Acts: Alexander II or Alexander III 234

Index of Persons and Places 237
Index of Subjects 262
Map of Places at which Alexander III's Acts were Issued *at end*

LIST OF ABBREVIATIONS

Aberdeen-Banff Illustrations *Illustrations of the Topography and Antiquities of the Shires of Aberdeen and Banff* (Spalding Club, 4 vols, 1847–69).

Aberdeen Registrum *Registrum episcopatus Aberdonensis* (Spalding and Maitland Clubs, 2 vols, 1845).

Aberdeen Burgh Chrs *Charters and Other Writs Illustrating the History of the Royal Burgh of Aberdeen*, ed. P. J. Anderson (Aberdeen, 1890).

Anderson, *Diplomata Scotiae* J. Anderson, *Selectus Diplomatum et Numismatum Scotiae Thesaurus*, ed. T. Rudderman (Edinburgh, 1739).

Anderson, *ES* *Early Sources of Scottish History, A.D. 500 to 1286*, ed. A. O. Anderson (Edinburgh, 2 vols, 1922).

APS *Acts of the Parliaments of Scotland*, ed. T. Thomson and C. Innes (Edinburgh, 11 vols, 1814–24).

Arbroath Liber *Liber S. Thome de Aberbrothoc* (Bannatyne Club, 2 vols, 1848–56).

Ayr Burgh Chrs *Charters of the Royal Burgh of Ayr* (Ayrshire and Wigtonshire Archaeological Society, 1883).

Ayr Friars Chrs *Charters of the Friars Preachers of Ayr* (Ayrshire and Wigtonshire Archaeological Society, 1881).

Balmerino Liber *Liber Sancte Marie de Balmorinach* (Abbotsford Club, 1841).

Barrow, *Kingdom of the Scots* G. W. S. Barrow, *The Kingdom of the Scots: Government, Church and Society from the Eleventh to the Fourteenth Century*, 2nd edn (Edinburgh, 2003).

Bateson, 'The Scottish King's Household' 'The Scottish King's Household and Other Fragments, from a Fourteenth Century Manuscript in the Library of Corpus Christi College, Cambridge', ed. M. Bateson, *SHS Miscellany*, vol. II (Edinburgh, 1904), 3–43.

BL British Library

Cal. Charter Rolls *Calendar of the Charter Rolls preserved in the Public Record Office* (London, 6 vols, 1923–7).

Boardman, *Campbells* S. Boardman, *The Campbells, 1250–1513* (Edinburgh, 2006).

Cal. Inqu. Misc. *Calendar of Inquisitions Miscellaneous (Chancery) preserved in the Public Record Office, London* (London, 1916–75).

CCR *Calendar of the Close Rolls preserved in the Public Record Office* (London, 1892–1963).

CDS *Calendar of Documents relating to Scotland preserved in Her Majesty's Public Record Office, London*, ed. J. Bain, G. G. Simpson and E. L. G. Stones (Edinburgh, 5 vols, 1881–8, 1986).

Chron. Fordun *Johannis de Fordun Chronica Gentis Scotorum*, ed. W. F. Skene (Edinburgh, 2 vols, 1871–2).

Chron. Lanercost (Stevenson) *Chronicon de Lanercost*, ed. J. Stevenson (Maitland Club, 1839).

Chron. Wyntoun *The Original Chronicle of Andrew of Wyntoun*, ed. F. J. Amours (STS, 6 vols, 1903–14).

Close Rolls *Close Rolls of the Reign of Henry III* (London, 1902–75).

Coldingham Correspondence *The Correspondence, Inventories, Account Rolls, and Law Proceedings of the Priory of Coldingham* (Surtees Society, 1841).

Coldstream Chartulary *Chartulary of the Cistercian Priory of Coldstream* (Grampian Club, 1839).

Coupar Angus Chrs *Charters of the Abbey of Coupar Angus*, ed. D. E. Easson (SHS, 2 vols, 1947).

CPR *Calendar of the Patent Rolls preserved in the Public Record Office* (London, 1891–).

David I Chrs *The Charters of David I: The Written Acts of David I King of Scots,*

1124–53, and of his Son Henry, Earl of Northumberland, 1139–52, ed. G. W. S. Barrow (Woodbridge, 1999).

Diplom. Norveg. *Diplomatarium Norvegicum* (Oslo, 1847–).

DOST *Dictionary of the Older Scottish Tongue*, ed. W. A. Craigie et al. (London and Aberdeen, 12 vols, 1937–2002).

Douglas, *Baronage* R. Douglas, *The Baronage of Scotland* (Edinburgh, 1798).

Dowden, *Bishops* J. Dowden, *The Bishops of Scotland* (Glasgow, 1912).

Dryburgh Liber *Liber S. Marie de Dryburgh* (Bannatyne Club, 1847).

Duncan, *Kingship of the Scots* A. A. M. Duncan, *The Kingship of the Scots, 842–1292: Succession and Independence* (Edinburgh, 2002).

Duncan, *Making of the Kingdom* A. A. M. Duncan, *Scotland: The Making of the Kingdom* (Edinburgh, 1975).

Dunfermline Registrum *Registrum de Dunfermelyn* (Bannatyne Club, 1842).

East Lothian Deeds *Deeds Relating to East Lothian*, ed. J. G. Wallace (Haddington, 1899).

Edward I and the Throne of Scotland *Edward I and the Throne of Scotland 1290–1296: An Edition of the Record Sources for the Great Cause*, ed. E. L. G. Stones and G. G. Simpson (Glasgow, 2 vols, 1978).

ER *Rotuli Scaccarii regum Scotorum. The Exchequer Rolls of Scotland*, ed. J Stuart et al. (Edinburgh, 23 vols, 1878–1908).

Foedera *Foedera, conventiones, litterae etc.*, ed. T. Rymer (Record Commission, 4 vols in 7 parts, 1816–69).

Frag. Scoto-Monastica *Fragmenta Scoto-Monastica*, ed. W. B. D. D. Turnbull (Edinburgh, 1842).

Fraser, *Carlaverock* W. Fraser, *The Book of Carlaverock* (Edinburgh, 2 vols, 1873).

Fraser, *Douglas* W. Fraser, *The Douglas Book* (Edinburgh, 4 vols, 1885).

Fraser, *Facsimiles* W. Fraser, *Facsimiles of Scottish Charters and Letters* (Edinburgh, 1903).

Fraser, *Grant* W. Fraser, *The Chiefs of Grant* (Edinburgh, 3 vols, 1883).

Fraser, *Lennox* W. Fraser, *The Lennox* (Edinburgh, 2 vols, 1874).

Fraser, *Menteith* W. Fraser, *The Red Book of Menteith* (Edinburgh, 2 vols, 1880).

Fraser, *Pollok* W. Fraser, *Memoirs of the Maxwells of Pollok* (Edinburgh, 2 vols, 1863).

Fraser, *Southesk* W. Fraser, *History of the Carnegies, Earls of Southesk, and of their Kindred* (Edinburgh, 2 vols, 1867).

Fraser-Mackintosh, *Invernessiana* C. Fraser-Mackintosh, *Invernessiana: Contributions toward a History of the Town & Parish of Inverness from 1160 to 1599* (Inverness, 1875).

Glasgow Registrum *Registrum Episcopatus Glasguensis* (Bannatyne and Maitland Clubs, 2 vols, 1843).

Glasgow Friars Munimenta *Liber Collegii Nostre Domine ... Munimenta Fratrum Predicatorum de Glasgu* (Maitland Club, 1846).

Goss, *Chron. Reg. Manniae* *Chronica regum Manniae et insularum*, ed. F. A. Munch, rev. A. Goss (Manx Society, 1859).

Hamilton, *Lanark and Renfrew* W. Hamilton, *Descriptions of the Sheriffdoms of Lanark and Renfrew* (Maitland Club, 1831).

Handbook of British Chronology E. B. Fryde et al., eds, *Handbook of British Chronology*, 3rd edn (London, 1986).

Hartshorne, *Feudal and Military Antiquities* C. H. Hartshorne, *Feudal and Military Antiquities of Northumberland and the Scottish Borders* (London, 1858).

Hay, Sainteclaires R. A. Hay, *Genealogie of the Sainteclaires of Rosslyn* (Edinburgh, 1835).

Highland Papers *Highland Papers*, ed. J. R. N. Macphail (SHS, 4 vols, 1914–34).

HMC *Reports of the Royal Commission on Historical Manuscripts* (London, 1870–).

HN J. C. Hodgson, *A History of Northumberland in Three Parts* (Newcastle-upon-Tyne, 7 vols, 1820–58).

Holford and Stringer, *Border Liberties* M. L. Holford and K. J. Stringer, *Border Liberties and Loyalties: North-East England, c.1200 to c.1400* (Edinburgh, 2010).

Holm Cultram *Register and Records of Holm Cultram*, ed. F. Grainger and W. G. Collingwood (Cumberland and Westmorland Antiquarian and Archaeological Society, 1929).

Inchaffray Chrs *Charters, Bulls and Other Documents relating to the Abbey of Inchaffray*, ed. W. A. Lindsay, J. Dowden and J. Maitland Thomson (SHS, 1908).

Inchcolm Chrs *Charters of the Abbey of Inchcolm*, ed. D. E. Easson and A. Macdonald (SHS, 1938).

Kelso Liber *Liber S. Marie de Calchou*, ed. C. Innes (Bannatyne Club, 1846).

L&I, vol. xlix *List of Diplomatic Documents, Scottish Documents and Papal Bulls preserved in the Public Record Office* (List and Index Society, 1923).

Laing Chrs *Calendar of the Laing Charters, A.D. 854–1837*, ed. J. Anderson (Edinburgh, 1899).

Laing, *Seals*, i H. Laing, *Descriptive Catalogue of Impressions from Ancient Scottish Seals ... from A.D. 1054 to the Commonwealth* (Bannatyne Club, 2 vols, 1850).

Laing, *Seals*, ii H. Laing, *Supplemental Descriptive Catalogue of Ancient Scottish Seals, Royal, Baronial, Ecclesiastical, and Municipal, Embracing the Period from A.D. 1150 to the Eighteenth Century* (Edinburgh, 1866).

Le Glay, *Inventaire-sommaire* *Inventaire-sommaire des archives départementales antérieures à 1790* (4 vols, Lille, 1863).

Lennox Cart. *Cartularium comitatus de Levenax* (Maitland Club, 1833).

Lindores Cart. *Chartulary of the Abbey of Lindores 1195–1449*, ed. J. Dowden (SHS, 1893).

Lindores Liber *The Chartularies of Balmerino and Lindores*, ed. W. B. B. D. Turnbull (Abbotsford Club, 1841).

Macfarlane, *Genealogical Collections* *Genealogical Collections concerning Families in Scotland made by W. Macfarlane, 1750–1751*, ed. J. T. Clark (SHS, 1900).

Macnaghten, *Clan Macnachtan* A. I. J. Macnaghten, *The Chiefs of Clan Macnachtan and their Descendants* (Windsor, 1951).

MacQueen, *Common Law* H. L. MacQueen, *Common Law and Feudal Society in Medieval Scotland* (Edinburgh, 1993).

Melrose Liber *Liber Sancte Marie de Melros*, ed. C. Innes (Bannatyne Club, 2 vols, 1837).

Midlothian Chrs *Registrum domus de Soltre, necnon ecclesiae Collegiate S. Trinitatis prope Edinburgh ... Charters of the Hospital of Soltre, of Trinity College, Edinburgh, and other collegiate churches in Mid-Lothian*, ed. D. Laing (Bannatyne Club, 1861).

Milne, *Blackfriars of Perth* *The Blackfriars of Perth: The Chartulary and Papers of their House*, ed. R. Milne (Edinburgh, 1893).

Moncreiffs F. C. Moncreiff, *The Moncreiffs and the Moncreiffes* (Edinburgh, 1929).

Moray Registrum *Registrum episcopatus Moraviensis e pluribus codicibus consarcinatum circa A.D. MCCC, cum continuatione diplomatum recentiorum usque ad A.D. MDCXXIII*, ed. C. Innes (Bannatyne Club, 1837).

Morton Registrum *Registrum honoris de Morton*, ed. T. Thomson, A. Macdonald and C. Innes (Bannatyne Club, 2 vols, 1853).

MRHS I. B. Cowan and D. E. Easson, *Medieval Religious Houses, Scotland*, 2nd edn (London, 1976).

Nat. MSS. Scotland *Facsimiles of National Manuscripts of Scotland* (Southampton, 3 vols, 1867–71).

NCH Northumberland County History Committee, *A History of Northumberland* (Newcastle-upon-Tyne, 15 vols, 1893–1940).

Newbattle Registrum *Registrum S. Marie de Neubotle: abbacie Cisterciensis Beate Virginis de Neubotle chartarium vetus, 1140–1528*, ed. C. Innes (Bannatyne Club, 1849).

Northumb. and Durham Deeds *Northumberland and Durham Deeds from the Dodsworth MSS. in Bodley's Library, Oxford*, ed. A. M. Oliver (Newcastle-upon-Tyne Records Committee, 1929).

NLS National Library of Scotland

NRS National Records of Scotland

OPS *Origines parochiales Scotiae: The Antiquities Ecclesiastical and Territorial of the Parishes of Scotland*, ed. C. Innes (Bannatyne Club, 3 vols, 1850–5).

Paisley Registrum *Registrum monasterii de Passalet cartas privilegia conventiones aliaque munimenta complectens a domo fundata A.D.MCLXIII usque ad A.D.MDXXIX, etc.*, ed. C. Innes (Maitland Club, 1832).

Palgrave, *Antient Kalendars* *The Antient Kalendars and Inventories of the Treasury of His Majesty's Exchequer*, ed. F. Palgrave (Record Commission, 1836).

Palgrave, *Docs. Hist. Scot.* *Documents and Records Illustrating the History of Scotland*, ed. F. Palgrave (London, 1837).

Peebles Chrs *Charters and Documents relating to the Burgh of Peebles*, ed. W. Chambers (SBRS, 1872).

Place-Names of Fife Simon Taylor with Gilbert Márkus, *The Place-Names of Fife* (Donington, 4 vols, 2006–10).

PROME *The Parliament Rolls of Medieval England, 1275–1504*, ed. C. Given-Wilson et al. (Woodbridge, 16 vols, 2005).
Pryde, *Burghs* G. S. Pryde, *The Burghs of Scotland* (Oxford, 1965).
PSAS *Proceedings of the Society of Antiquaries of Scotland*
Raine, *North Durham* J. Raine, *The History and Antiquities of North Durham* (London, 1852).
Records of Elgin *The Records of Elgin, 1234–1800*, ed. W. Cramond (New Spalding Club, 2 vols, 1903–8).
Records of Lanark *Extracts from the Records of the Royal Burgh of Lanark*, ed. R. Renwick (SBRS, 1872).
Records of Peebles *Charters and Documents relating to the Burgh of Peebles*, ed. W. Chambers (SBR, 1872).
Reg. Halton *The Register of John de Halton, Bishop of Carlisle, A.D. 1292–1324*, ed. W. N Thompson (Canterbury and York Society, 2 vols, 1906–13).
Reid and Barrow, *Sheriffs* *The Sheriffs of Scotland: An Interim List to c.1306*, ed. N. H. Reid and G. W. S. Barrow (St Andrews, 2002).
Reiffenberg, *Monuments* *Collection de chroniques belges: monuments pour servir à l'histoire des provinces de Namur, de Hainaut et de Luxembourg*, ed. Baron de Reiffenberg (8 vols, Brussels, 1844–74).
RMS *Registrum magni sigilii regum Scottorum*, ed. J. M. Thomson et al. (Edinburgh, 11 vols, 1882–1914).
Rot. Scot. *Rotuli Scotiae in turri Londoniensi et in domo capitulari Westmonasteriensi asservati*, ed. D. MacPherson et al. (London, 2 vols, 1814–19).
RPS *Records of the Parliaments of Scotland*, http://www.rps.ac.uk.
RRS, i *The Acts of Malcolm IV King of Scots, 1153–1165, Regesta Regum Scottorum*, vol. I, ed. G. W. S. Barrow (Edinburgh, 1960).
RRS, ii *The Acts of William I King of Scots, 1165–1214, Regesta Regum Scottorum*, vol. II, ed. G. W. S. Barrow (Edinburgh, 1971).
RRS, v *The Acts of Robert I King of Scots, 1306–1329, Regesta Regum Scottorum*, vol. V, ed. A. A. M. Duncan (Edinburgh, 1988).
RRS, vi *The Acts of David II King of Scots 1329–1371, Regesta Regum Scottorum*, vol. VI, ed. B. Webster (Edinburgh, 1982).
RS Rolls Series
SBRS Scottish Burgh Records Society
Scone Liber *Liber ecclesie de Scon munimenta vetustiora monasterii Sancte Trinitatis et Sancti Michaelis de Scon*, ed. C. Innes (Bannatyne Club, 1843).
Scotichronicon *Scotichronicon* by Walter Bower, in Latin and English, ed. D. E. R. Watt et al. (Aberdeen, 9 vols, 1987–98).
Scoular, *Handlist* J. M. Scoular, *Handlist of the Acts of Alexander II 1214–1249* (Edinburgh, 1959).
SHR *Scottish Historical Review*
Shirley, *Royal Letters* *Royal and Other Historical Letters Illustrative of the Reign of Henry III*, ed. W. W. Shirley (RS, 1828–66).
SHS Scottish History Society
Simpson, *Handlist* G. G. Simpson, *Handlist of the Acts of Alexander III, the Guardians and John 1249–1296* (Edinburgh, 1960).
Simpson, 'Kingship in Miniature' G. G. Simpson, 'Kingship in Miniature: A Seal of Minority of Alexander III, 1249–1257', in A. Grant and K. J. Stringer, eds, *Medieval Scotland: Crown, Lordship and Community: Essays presented to G. W. S. Barrow* (Edinburgh, 1993), pp. 131–9.
Simpson, *Scottish Handwriting* G. G. Simpson, *Scottish Handwriting 1150–1650* (Aberdeen, 1973).
SP *The Scots Peerage*, ed. J. Balfour Paul (Edinburgh, 9 vols, 1904–14).
Spalding Misc. *Miscellany of the Spalding Club* (Spalding Club, 5 vols, 1841–52).
SRS Scottish Record Society
St Andrews Liber *Liber cartarum prioratus Sancti Andree in Scotia*, ed. T. Thomson (Bannatyne Club, 1841).
Statistical Account (1791) Sir John Sinclair, ed., *The Statistical Account of Scotland, 1791–1799* (Edinburgh, 20 vols, 1791–9).
Statuta Ecclesiae Scoticanae *Concilia Scotiae ecclesiae Scoticanae statuta tam provincialia*

quam synodalia quae supersunt, MCCXXV–MDLIX, ed. J. Robertson (Bannatyne Club, 2 vols, 1866).

Stevenson, *Documents* *Documents Illustrative of the History of Scotland 1286–1306*, ed. J. Stevenson (2 vols, Edinburgh, 1870).

Stevenson and Wood, *Seals* J. H. Stevenson and M. Wood, *Scottish Heraldic Seals: Royal, Official, Ecclesiastical, Collegiate, Burghal, Personal* (Glasgow, 3 vols, 1940).

Stones, *Anglo-Scottish Relations* *Anglo-Scottish Relations 1174–1328: Some Selected Documents*, ed. E. L. G. Stones (Oxford, 1965).

Talbot, *Priory of Whithern* T. Talbot, *The Priory of Whithern and its Lands and Churches in Mann* (Douglas, 1900).

Templaria *Templaria: Papers relative to the History, Privileges, and Possessions of the Scottish Knights Templar, and their successors the Knights of Saint John*, ed. J. Maidment (Edinburgh, 1828).

Teulet, *Inventaire* J. B. A. T. Teulet, *Inventaire chronologique des documents relatifs à l'histoire d'Écosse conservés aux Archives du royaume à Paris* (Abbotsford Club, 1839).

Theiner, *Monumenta* *Vetera monumenta Hibernorum et Scotorum historiam illustrantia*, ed. A. Theiner (Rome, 1864).

TRHS *Transactions of the Royal Historical Society*

Uredius, *Genealogia* Olivario Uredius, *Genealogia comitum Flandriae à Balduino Ferreo, usque ad Philippum IV. Hisp. Regem* (Bruges, 2 vols, 1642–3).

Watt, *Graduates* D. E. R. Watt, *A Biographical Dictionary of Scottish Graduates to AD1410* (Oxford, 1977).

Watt and Shead, *Heads of Religious Houses* D. E. R. Watt and N. F. Shead, eds, *The Heads of Religious Houses in Scotland from Twelfth to Sixteenth Centuries* (SRS, 2001).

Watt, 'Minority' D. E. R. Watt, 'The Minority of Alexander III of Scotland', *TRHS*, 5th ser. 21 (1971), 1–23.

INTRODUCTION

The edition of Alexander III's charters presented here consists of some 330 documents, of which 175 survive in full or almost full texts. Some ninety-six of these are single parchment sheet originals; another seventy-nine are preserved in medieval cartularies or more recent transcriptions. A handful of deeds survive in more than a single copy, produced either in duplicate, or as original parchment sheets that were copied into cartularies in the medieval period. In a few other cases the originals have been lost and the editors have had to depend on post-medieval transcriptions of their contents. The edition includes also a calendar of a further 155 deeds, described below as 'lost acts', that survive only as fragments or in incidental references. Details about the arrangement of the volume are found below, 42–3.

ANALYSIS OF THE ACTS OF ALEXANDER III

I. DIPLOMATIC ANALYSIS

Geoffrey Barrow's exhaustive work on the diplomatic practices of the royal chancery in the late twelfth and early thirteenth centuries has shed valuable light on the stages by which royal clerks experimented with, then gradually established, the several elements that collectively came to characterise the Scottish charter of the later medieval period. By the closing years of the reign of William I, he has argued, royal charters were already beginning to acquire a 'stereotyped form'.[1] In the thirteenth century, two of the consequences of a vigorous land market were the rapid development of the law of real property and a sharp rise in the demand for sophisticated instruments of conveyance. During the long and, for the most part, stable reign of Alexander II (1214–49) the scribes of the king's writing chapel made intensive study of the diplomatic practices then current in the English chancery and began to adapt the conventions associated there with charters, writs and other documents to the requirements of Scottish royal government. Closer contact still with England after Alexander III's marriage in 1251 to the daughter of Henry III helped to perpetuate fruitful intellectual exchange between the royal writing offices, and in the course of the later thirteenth century Scottish royal charters developed a series of constituent parts that were to remain standard features of diplomatic for the rest of the medieval period and well beyond. Already in 1249, for example, the king's scribes were demonstrating a marked preference for the royal style *Alexander Dei gratia rex Scottorum* in the introductory clause, for a general address and salutation worded as *omnibus probis hominibus suis tocius terre sue salutem*, for a witness list introduced by the ablative term *testibus* and, finally, for a concluding clause that included both a place name and a date designated by month and regnal year. The latter was deemed to have commenced on 7 July, 1249, the day after the death of Alexander II. Well before 1200, moreover, scribes were using almost exclusively a notification clause that expressed the king's will by means of the verb *scire*, which they rendered in his charters as *sciatis nos* ... or *sciant presentes et futuri* ..., both forms using the accusative and infinitive cases.

There are remarkably few exceptions to these general lexical and structural rules among the charters that record new gifts and confirmations among Alexander III's acts. The exceptions, moreover, are found largely in texts that represent late medieval or early modern copies of lost originals. Thus, the king is designated *rex Scocie* in only ten of 175 extant full texts, but only two of these survive as originals, leaving open the possibility of mistakes of transcription, rather than deviation from what was clearly the standard form 'king of Scots' (*rex Scottorum*).[2] Likewise, after 1249, so prevalent was the *omnibus probis hominibus* style of address that the clerk responsible for the single example of a French-language charter, no. 73, took pains to ensure that his text should include an exact translation of the phrase: *a tuz les prudes homes de tute sa terre saluz*.[3] Similarly, the clerks responsible for drawing up royal charters in the reign of Alexander III demonstrated a clear preference for the succinct verb *scire* in the notification clause, to the exclusion of virtually all other word choices. The imperative *noverit* that opens the clause in no. 157 may represent an interpolation, either by the cleric responsible for compiling the (now lost) register of Whithorn priory or the attorney responsible for the notarial deed of 1504 into which the surviving version of the grant was copied. No. 164 also has *noverit* in place of *sciant* or *sciatis*, but this act survives in a copy that is later still, in this case a register of deeds datable to 1565–6. King Alexander II's scribes had used *scire* predominantly, but not exclusively; it was only, therefore, in the reign of his son that it became the verb of choice in Scottish royal charters.

The contents of charter witness lists suggest that in the latter half of the thirteenth century professional scribes both within and beyond the royal chancery shared a set of assumptions and drew on a stock of social conventions common to British and European practice more generally. As had been customary since the late twelfth century, churchmen normally occupy the highest rank in the lists, with bishops preceding abbots and priors; thereafter, there follow the names of lay administrative officials (as appropriate), noblemen who had achieved the status of knights and, finally, lay persons of lesser rank. Scribal custom in the matter of attestation, however, was by no means firmly fixed in this period, and the composition of witness lists continued to reflect a variety of influences, some the consequence of clerical inclination, others of specific circumstance. The former, for example, clearly discouraged the inclusion of women's names in royal witness lists, including that of the queen, though there can be little doubt that on some occasions Alexander III's first wife, Margaret, was present to witness proceedings and, perhaps, to offer testimony *viva voce* or by means of an attorney.[4] Likewise, although the king's elder son, Prince Alexander, played an increasingly active role both at court and in the governance of the former kingdom of Man from the later 1270s, he is never named as an attestor to his father's acts. The absence of the prince's name from testing clauses stands in marked contrast to earlier Scottish practice in this regard. In the twelfth century, Henry earl of Northumberland frequently witnessed the acts of his father, David I; moreover, he was often accorded the status of co-donor with the king.[5] There is other evidence, too, of a change of attitude concerning the office of heir to the Scottish throne in the latter half of the thirteenth century. Altogether, it suggests an effort on the part of the crown and its advisors to elevate the position to a status commensurate with that enjoyed by royal and imperial heirs elsewhere in contemporary Europe.

During the period of his minority between 1249 and 1258, of course, Alexander's acts required the consent of council, and the text of no. 1, for example, reveals the scribe's awareness of these circumstances.[6] Thereafter, scribes occasionally took care to make formal note of royal acts performed at meetings of the king's council. The conveyance described in no. 41, for example, is dated at Forfar in December 1262, but the judgement that preceded it occurred several months earlier in Edinburgh, before a group of named magnates. The persons identified as councillors, moreover, are not the same as those whose names and offices are carefully listed in order of importance in the testing clause of the deed. Here, clerical preoccupation with ensuring that the ceremonies in which one royal tenant renounced his claim to an estate of land and another secured new title be recorded accurately had a direct influence on the form and content of an otherwise simple charter of infeftment. Similar concerns are apparent in the texts of nos 115, 152 and 153, in which witnesses to acts of quitclaim are carefully distinguished from the persons who attested the king's subsequent conveyance of the same lands to new tenants. There are no examples among Alexander III's charters of the overt tampering with witness lists that a recent study by Dauvit Broun has found in the testing clauses of private charters,[7] and no examples of dead witnesses 'rubbing shoulders' with the living. Nonetheless, Broun's study serves as a useful reminder that in some circumstances witnesses and scribes alike played a significant role in shaping the testing clauses of medieval charters.

By the second half of the thirteenth century it is rare to find a royal deed that does not include a clause identifying the place and date of a royal act. By this time, moreover, the formula for conveying this information had acquired a standard form consisting of a day of the month and regnal year. So routine was this aspect of royal diplomatic practice that the handful of exceptions are readily explicable, either as omissions committed in error at the time of transcription or as the predictably irregular features of unusual document styles.[8] Thus, the dating clauses of the documents produced in the Flemish chancery (nos 133–5, 141) have an *anno domini* date, but as noted elsewhere,[9] they were not drafted in Alexander's chancery, but rather in Flanders.

Collectively, the diplomatic features of the acts of Alexander III bear witness to a series of widely acknowledged and well-tested conventions for the routine production of instruments of conveyance. The brief diplomatic analysis that follows reveals some intriguing similarities between the development and subsequent refinement of chancery practices in England and Scotland, even if each unfolded at a different pace .[10] One of the most striking is the inclination of royal scribes in both realms to abandon altogether traditional document forms – notably the diploma – in favour of instruments that more effectively and more efficiently gave expression to the will of their respective kings. Another is the readiness of the kings' scribes to combine the clauses traditionally associated with one type of document with the features of another and thus to create unique, hybrid instruments.

Such, for example, were the writ-charters of twelfth-century England and their thirteenth-century Scottish counterparts.

Developments in English diplomatic practice occurred over a very substantial period, stretching roughly from the eighth century through the early thirteenth. In Scotland, the shift on the part of royal government from 'memory to written record', in Michael Clanchy's famous expression,[11] began much later and took place much more rapidly. The acts produced at the behest of Alexander III offer incontestable support, should any be needed, for viewing the professional scribes of the period as 'experienced draftsmen', skilled in adapting the practices associated with the technical language of deeds of conveyance to the myriad needs of their king and attentive to the legal implications of the terminology they chose to use in such documents.[12] The demands of thirteenth-century Scottish society, moreover, required that chancery scribes deploy their professional skills in a host of contexts beyond that of simple conveyance, and the chancery of the years 1249–86 is remarkable above all for the great variety of its output and the ability of its employees to give written expression to the full range of the crown's authority.

II. CLASSIFICATION AND SUBJECT MATTER

By the end of Alexander III's reign the organisation and operation of the royal household were much more complex and sophisticated than they had been under his twelfth-century predecessors. The treatise generally referred to as 'The Scottish King's Household', probably written in the early 1290s to provide guidance to John Balliol and his advisors, discusses at considerable length the duties assigned to a host of royal officials. The care that its author devoted to his task has enabled scholars to reconstruct in minute detail the role that each of these officials – and the army of clerks and servants whom they employed – fulfilled in the governance of the realm.[13] The treatise makes it clear that the chancery was the most important of the royal offices and that the professional skills of the chancellor were critical to the effective implementation of the king's will the length and breadth of the realm.

The variety and number of the acts that the chancellor issued in the name of King Alexander III offer another, equally revealing perspective from which to understand the sophistication of the later thirteenth-century chancery. There can be little doubt that the 175 full texts and 155 notices of other texts in this collection represent only a small fraction of the total output of written deeds produced there. Just how much material has been lost to the ravages of time and careless storage is impossible to establish, but the sheer number of documents attested in the long list of 'lost acts' compiled here suggests that Scottish landholders, great and small, lay and clerical, male and female, had regular recourse to the services that chancery clerks offered and that the king himself depended heavily on staff there for the conduct of all kinds of routine business.

The demand for written documents, moreover, underwent something of a sea change over the course of the thirteenth century. Professor Barrow's examination of the full-text charters and deeds surviving from the reigns of Malcolm IV and William I has shown that the clerks who staffed the king's writing office put pen to parchment overwhelmingly in favour of ecclesiastical beneficiaries.[14] Recent research into charter-writing in medieval Scotland, however, has made it clear that, despite the better survival rate of documents issued in favour of the church well into the thirteenth century, the numbers and types of deeds issued to, and on behalf of, secular clients increased markedly after 1200.[15] By the reign of Alexander III, in fact, lay persons and burgh corporations were as likely to be the clients of chancery scribes as were members of the church.

Recent scholarship, moreover, has made a compelling argument for understanding the production of written acts, in Scotland as elsewhere in the British Isles, as a form of 'dialogue' between donor and beneficiary,[16] a process in which subjects played as significant a role in shaping the output of the royal chancery as did the king himself. Here, too, the long period covered by Alexander III's reign offers an important opportunity to trace such developments at first hand. The years between 1249 and 1286 and, even more, those that followed the end of the royal minority in 1258, saw a steady expansion in the variety of documents emanating from chancery. Thus, in addition to the rich body of correspondence noted above and to the writ-charters and confirmations that first became common in the twelfth century, the chancery began to issue a variety of new brieves as well as early examples of the letters patent and close that would become standard features of the reformed writing office of Robert I in the fourteenth century. Many of the documents in this collection, moreover, defy rigid categorisation: an act recording a new gift of land or privilege, for example, might incorporate into its narrative an account of the circumstances that preceded the grant or instructions about its implementation. In no. 41, a long preamble describing a meeting of the royal council before which a tenant of Alexander III surrendered his title to lands in Tillicoultry precedes the dispositive clause by which the king infefts a new tenant. Following the latter, but before the witness list, the scribe has inserted a clause prohibiting the felling of trees or the hunting of animals without the licence of the new tenant. No. 115, likewise, begins with notice of a ceremony of quitclaim before proceeding to describe the bestowal of the land in question on the monks of Dunfermline. Before the attestation clause, the scribe has included a statement rendering null and void any charters that might in future threaten the monks' claim. Still again, no. 163 is ostensibly a gift of burghal privileges to the inhabitants of Lanark, but includes also a long list of prohibited legal actions against the burgesses. Other examples of such hybrid deeds might be cited.[17] Collectively, they suggest that while a traditional analysis of the diplomatic of Alexander III's acts remains a useful exercise, a sound understanding of the chancery of the later thirteenth century ultimately requires the rejection of a rigid system of classification in favour of an appreciation of the many social and legal contexts that generated a demand for written records in the Scotland of his day. Accordingly, the introductory remarks below offer a brief analysis of the main diplomatic features of the 175 full texts that survive from the reign and an examination of the types of deed that the king's clerks produced. There follows a fuller discussion of the functions that each kind of deed fulfilled in the increasingly literate – and litigious – world of the later thirteenth-century kingdom.

Charters

By the later thirteenth century the clerks of the royal chancery appear to have viewed as archaic the once popular instrument of conveyance known as the diploma, its long clauses of invocation needlessly cumbersome. Yet features of this style might on occasion still serve a useful purpose. The monks of Dunfermline abbey had long been partial to the solemnity associated with the pious language and prolixity of the royal diploma,[18] and in 1277 again opted for this style of document in Alexander III's general confirmation of their possessions and privileges.[19] Nevertheless, the basic charter form familiar to Alexander III's predecessors remained the medium of choice both as a standard deed of conveyance and a formal record of new royal grants of land, property and privilege. Among the 175 acts that survive as full texts, no fewer than twenty-eight include the features that scholars associate with charters that effected gifts *de novo*, that is, a collective address to all the king's law-worthy men, a dispositive formula that usually includes the verbs *dare* (to give), *concedere* (to licence, to establish) and *confirmare* (to make firm), and a list of attestors representing witnesses who were normally present at the gifting ceremony.[20] The exercise of good lordship on the part of the king regularly brought into his orbit new tenants, secular and ecclesiastical, to whom he gave gifts of land or privilege. As it had been for a hundred years and more already,[21] the charter was admirably suitable as a record of such acts, its narrative, dispositive and holding clauses sufficiently flexible to accommodate virtually any gift. To take but one example, when in 1285 Alexander assigned to the canons of Whithorn the advowson of the church of the Holy Trinity at Ramsay, he did so by means of a simple charter of infeftment.[22] When a tenant formally relinquished 'by rod and staff' title to land or revenues as a consequence of failure to perform the required service or for any number of other reasons, the king often made a gift of such property to a new tenant. Here, too, the charter style served a simple and effective purpose as a formal record of the conveyance.[23]

Grants and Confirmations

Some years ago Professor Barrow observed that in the twelfth century it was customary for the great monastic and episcopal lords of Scotland to seek formal confirmation of their possessions and privileges soon after the succession of a new ruler.[24] By the middle years of the following century, developments in Scottish law had endowed the church with greater security of tenure and the security of lawful title once associated with such deeds diminished. Nevertheless, the forty-two confirmations found among the acts of Alexander III – defined here as acts that include the dispositive verbs *concedere* and *confirmare* – demonstrate that his subjects continued to generate a healthy demand for such deeds among both ecclesiastical and secular tenants.[25] Some beneficiaries sought explicit recognition of recent or newly made grants, many more of estates and possessions that had been the subject of litigation. The abbots of Melrose were particularly careful stewards of the church's wealth and remained avid consumers of the Scottish chancery's record producing services throughout the reign, but confirmations were also sought by, and granted to, the bishops of Glasgow and St Andrews, the abbots of Paisley, Dunfermline and Lindores, and the priors of Lesmahagow, Coldingham and Whithorn, among others. Meanwhile, secular lords, great and small, and royal burghs the length and breadth of the realm continued to find royal confirmation a useful validation of their claims to property and privilege. Some sought confirmations in an effort to guarantee titles acquired as a consequence of inheritance or sale,[26] others as a mark of social status. In no. 19, for example, King Alexander III confirmed to David de Graham a long list of lands, possessions and privileges that the latter had amassed over the course of a successful career as an adventurer and opportunist. The list of magnates whom he acknowledged as lords approximates a social register of the greatest magnate families in the kingdom. The king's charter was thereafter carefully preserved in the family archives as a tangible expression of Graham's admission to the rarified world of the upper aristocracy and demonstrable evidence of his access to the exclusive society of the king's court.

In a recent study of twelfth- and thirteenth-century Scottish charters Richard Sharpe and John Reuben Davies have made a compelling case for linking the dispositive language of charter texts to the duty to perform warrandice.[27] More specifically, they argue, scribes reserved the use of the verb *dare* to gifts in which the donor assumed full legal responsibility for warranting title to land, property or privilege. The verbs *concedere* and *confirmare* in a clause of disposition, by contrast, signalled a donor's 'affirmation, confirmation and corroboration' of a tenant's title, but such deeds carried no implicit duty to vouchsafe title.[28] By and large, the language of the charters issued under Alexander III's seal conform to the observations of Sharpe and Davies, and it is interesting to note that the triple combination of *dare*, *concedere* and *confirmare* appears consistently in acts that represented new gifts in perpetuity (for example, no. 1) or acts by which title to property or privilege passed from the hands of one tenant into those of another (e.g. no. 41). Similarly, the king normally expressed his reassertion of already existing privileges with the use of the latter two terms only (e.g. no. 54), often, it would seem, at the behest of ecclesiastical beneficiaries. Yet, an examination of the proliferation of new brieve styles under Alexander III serves as a reminder that while the rules governing the redaction of instruments of conveyance may indeed have become increasingly rigid in the course of the thirteenth century, they did not simplify the laws governing tenure, nor did they substantially reduce levels of land-based litigation in the royal courts. Moreover, after 1249, as before, there remained ample opportunity for scribes to use the clauses of royal charters as a medium for the expression of creative licence. No. 139, for example, describes the transfer of a widow's dower estate to Sir Nicholas de Hay. The scribe responsible for drafting a record of the transaction chose to narrate the king's act with the phrase *infeodasse et homagium suum inde recepisse*.

Brieves

Several years ago Alan Harding and Geoffrey Barrow noted the enthusiasm with which the writing chapel of the twelfth-century kings of Scotland adopted and adapted to their own uses the English administrative document known as the writ.[29] A century after the reign of David I, the brieve (as it was known in Scottish parlance) remained a favourite instrument for conveying simple instructions from the royal court to the localities. Indeed, a generation and more before the momentous reforms that Robert I effected to the Scottish chancery, the term *brevia* had come to encompass a 'full and diverse range of documents' for expressing the king's will to subjects great and small, corporate and individual, and for ensuring the implementation of decisions made in curial or conciliar settings. So numerous were the types of brieves emanating from chancery that, well before the death of Alexander III in 1286, working lawyers began to compile formularies in which they sought to distinguish the legal from administrative, the pleadable from the non-pleadable, the retourable from the non-retourable, brieves *de cursu* from brieves *de gratia* and the brieve *tout court* from more general 'judicial letters'.[30] This collection includes thirty-one documents identifiable as brieves.

In the second half of the thirteenth century Alexander III used brieves in both familiar and novel contexts: to extend his peace and protection to his religious subjects (no. 8), to initiate inquests of various kinds (nos 32, 36), to proclaim new law (no. 49), to direct or enforce the payment of allowances and annuities (nos 14, 154), to remedy the wrong done to an aggrieved tenant,[31] or, increasingly, to accomplish two or more of these aims with simplicity and efficiency in a hybrid brieve-charter. No. 3, for example, in which the king grants freedom from poinding to the burgesses of Inverness is framed in the style of a charter, but concludes with a general prohibition against breaching the terms of his deed.[32] No. 49 begins with a narration of the circumstances under which royal officials reviewed the claims (i.e. presumably the charters) of the monks of Melrose in respect of the 'ancient customs' governing hospitality (wayting), and concludes with an injunction against any who would violate their rights; no. 53 combines a grant in free forest with a prohibition against felling timber. A single document such as no. 45 might accomplish simultaneously the extension of the king's protections to the nuns of Coldstream, their labourers and all their possessions; a prohibition against unlawful poinding; a provision requiring the payment of outstanding debts owed the nuns and, finally, a warning against breach of any of the convent's rights and privileges. Still again, no. 60 combines an affirmation of the right of the master and brethren of Soutra hospital to pursue serfs and fugitive men with what looks very much like a traditional brieve of neyfty. Older still was the notion of breach of the king's peace, which in some brieves is linked to 'full forfeiture' and in others to 'full forfeiture of £10'.[33] Under Robert I this offence became the subject of specific legislation, but Alexander III's brieves, and those of his predecessors, show that the concept was already by then well developed in Scotland.[34]

Alexander addressed some of his missives to specific officials, including sheriffs and bailies north of the Mounth (no. 3), the provost of Perth (no. 10), the justiciar of Scotia (no. 27) and the bailiff of Tynedale (no. 82), but others more comprehensively to 'all his justiciars, sheriffs, provosts and bailies' (no. 44) or, simply, 'all his law worthy men' (no. 101). While the legal implications associated with verbs of disposition may have limited the lexicology available to professional scribes in the drafting of charter texts in the later thirteenth century, fewer such conventions bound them in the redaction of brieves. Deeds referred to above as hybrid brieve-charters normally include witness lists, though these are for the most part decidedly truncated, consisting of only two or three names, compared to the eight to twelve persons recorded in the testing clauses of more traditional charters. A handful (nos 36, 40, 67, 70, 75, 76) have no named witnesses at all, the relevant clause appearing rather as a simple statement that the deed is attested by the king alone (*teste me ipso*).[35]

Hector MacQueen has shown that the actions that would later become staples of the Scottish courts of common law – the brieves of mortancestry, dissasine and right – all had their origins in the period before the redaction of the earliest extant formularies of Scots law in the late thirteenth century.[36] The uniformity of style and the homogeneity of language evident in these sources, however, are in many respects illusory, a consequence of the requirements of the formulary style itself. In Alexander III's time it was precisely the lack of rigid lexicological rules that made the brieve both a favourite medium for expressing the king's will and an indispensable instrument of judicial administration.

Letters

Among the 175 full texts that survive from the reign of Alexander III, some forty-four fall under the general category of royal correspondence. Alexander III's marriage to the English princess Margaret in 1251 brought the Scottish royal court directly into the political, social and cultural ambits of the kingdom of England, first under Henry III, then under his son Edward I. This proximity accounts for the very substantial body of extant correspondence between the royal families, over and above the sort of routine documentation of a diplomatic and political nature that relations between the realms had traditionally generated. The letters defy easy categorisation: they range from personal expressions of good will and friendship between the crowns (e.g. nos 146, 150), to politely worded petitions (nos 125, 144), to thinly veiled demands for payment of debts (nos 35, 37), to formal requests for information or attention of the kind that any ruler of a sovereign realm might send to one of his peers (no. 138).

Alexander III used his privy seal to authenticate two of the letters (nos 86, 116), both drafted while he was outwith Scotland, but whether or not he used the personal seal on his other missives is, frustratingly, unknowable. Evidence relating to the diplomatic of the deeds, which might be expected to shed light on chancery practice in this context, is inconclusive. Noteworthy, for example, is the method that the king and his clerks used to attach the seal to his letters. In all but two cases it was invariably by means of a tongue cut from the bottom right corner of the parchment piece, rather than by means of a strip of parchment passed through slits cut into the folded foot of the sheet (that is, *sur double queue*). Alexander used the first of these methods on the privy seal letter that he wrote to Queen Eleanor (no. 86), and it might be expected that expediency alone would dictate that he use the lighter-weight privy seal with this flimsy style of parchment tongue. But that does not seem to have been the case. Two letters directed to Guy count of Flanders (nos 142, 143), both with a tongue cut from the bottom of the parchment sheet, bear fragmentary but clear evidence of the king's great seal. The physical condition of the remaining examples of original letters precludes any firm statements about the method used to append the seal: most, though, appear to have employed the simpler style of tongue.

Intriguing also is the fact that virtually all the king's letters employ the brief phrase *teste me ipso* in the testimonial clause, followed by the simple *apud* ... to introduce the place and date.[37] The exceptions here merit attention. No. 24 is a letter to King Henry III attested with the terms *teste Patricio comite de Dunbar*; it dates to the period of Alexander III's minority, when the young king was still under the tutelage of a baronial council. Nos 145 and 170 end in a terse and none-too-friendly greeting: both are letters directed to Edward I complaining of the unlawful activities of English bailiffs within the Scottish king's lordship of Tynedale. Although a small number of Alexander II's deeds were attested by the king alone,[38] the specific phrase *teste me ipso apud* ..., so familiar to scholars as a 'peculiarity' of the English chancery,[39] was new to the Scottish chancery in the second half of the thirteenth century and represents yet another example of the easy movement of ideas and practices from one writing office to the other. Scribes in the employ of Henry III and Edward I, it is worth emphasising, used more than one style of testimonial clause and more than one method for applying the rulers' large and small seals. After this period of experimentation under Alexander III, however, the chanceries of Robert I and David II, in fact, abandoned almost altogether this form of testimonial clause.[40]

Letters patent

Borrowing from English chancery practice is apparent also in a series of deeds that includes both the sealing clause 'in testimony of which' and specific reference to the status of a deed as 'letters patent'. Among the 175 full texts dating from Alexander III's reign, some eighteen incorporate into their texts the phrase *in cuius rei testimonium has litteras nostras fieri fecimus patentes*, or some close variant of it.[41] Another six have *in cuius rei testimonium*, but make no reference to letters patent; the clause concludes, rather, with a reference to the act of appending the royal seal: *sigillum nostrum apponi fecimus.*[42] Of these, only eight deeds survive as originals, and inspection of these shows that the king's great seal was appended both *sur double queue* and by means of tongues cut from the right side of the parchment sheet. The eight extant originals, moreover, represent the work of several different scribes; in short, preference for one method over another cannot be attributed merely to clerical idiosyncrasy. Earlier in the thirteenth century Alexander II's chancery had also experimented with English-inspired letters patent and letters close; in the early fourteenth, by contrast, Robert I's stopped using them.[43] The lack of discernible pattern in the structure of these letters and in the purposes for which they were intended offers still more evidence of a keen interest on the part of Alexander III's scribes in contemporary developments in English chancery practice and a readiness to imitate English practice, but a reluctance to adhere slavishly to models that they considered unsuitable in the Scottish context.

Notifications

Several of Alexander III's acts fall into no easily defined category: they are, in the most general sense, notifications. No. 22 is a unique document in every respect. Embedded in a letter addressed to King Henry III, it sets out the terms under which a new council of fifteen magnates would govern the realm until the king should come of age.[44] The arrangements were manifestly not of Alexander's making, though the letter was issued under the seal of the young king and attested, in the manner of letters patent, with the formula *in huius autem rei testimonium presenti scripto sigillum nostrum fecimus apponi. Teste me ipso*, and dated at Roxburgh in September 1255. Alexander's original letter (if it ever existed) was never returned to him as the arrangements promised; instead, it was conveniently lost in the aftermath of the minority, but only after 'copies' had been carefully engrossed in two different series of English records.[45]

No. 133 represents an equally remarkable deed: here, on the eve of the marriage of Prince Alexander to Marguerite of Flanders, the now ageing (and widowed) Alexander III announced that after consultation with the barons of his council, he intended to establish anew 'the ancient customs and practices of the kingdom of Scotland in use since time immemorial ... for the succession to the throne'. The document should be read in conjunction with a clause of the treaty of marriage with the king of Norway that had been agreed just a few months earlier in 1281. Here, too, Alexander sought to make provision for succession to the kingdom in the event of his death without heirs. Both nos 22 and 133 include clauses of notification addressed in general terms 'to all who shall see and hear them', and in both the king refers to his written deeds using the term 'letters', but each of the documents concludes with an attestation and sealing clause on the part of several named magnates. As discussed elsewhere,[46] the deed is not a product of the Scottish chancery; its peculiarities reflect not only its unusual contents, but the circumstances under which it came to be drafted and sealed.

Equally exceptional are the contents of four other deeds relating to the prince's marriage (nos 134, 135, 140, 141). These, too, include introductory clauses framed in the style of general notifications, but they do not refer to the terms 'letters patent' (which in any case would have been unfamiliar to the Flemish chancery). All four include versions of the *in cuius rei testimonium* formula that appears in other royal letters (though the first three are written in Picard French), and while all four are dated (the first three by *anno domini*, the last by regnal year), neither no. 134 nor 135, drafted in Flanders rather than Scotland, includes a place date. In nos 140 and 141 the concluding clauses introduce the authorial voice of Prince Alexander in succession to that of the king, in order to accommodate a statement of attestation on the latter's part and reference to his use of his father's seal. The first three deeds relate to arrangements for the payment of Marguerite's tocher. In an elaborate fashion entirely suited to such weighty matters of state, the king's great seal is attached to all three by means of delicately braided crimson silk cords passed through slits in the folded parchment foot; several other seals, including that of Prince Alexander, are appended to nos 135 and 140 in the same fashion. No. 141 is a simple notification that Count Guy has made an initial payment of the bride's tocher. A product of the Scottish chancery, drafted in Latin and sealed *sur double queue*, it is framed in the style of a general notification in recognition of its status as a diplomatic document of more than usual significance.

Treaties

Pierre Chaplais's observation that in the drafting of solemn treaties European scribal custom of this period demonstrated a preference for the indenture or chirograph and the structure of the formal concord holds true for Scotland as well.[47] The treaty of 1266 by which Alexander III took possession of the kingdom of Man (no. 61) and the contract of marriage that in 1281 he sealed with the king of Norway (no. 132) used these features to good effect, endowing both agreements with the gravity and authority that civilian tradition considered appropriate. In a style reminiscent also of the diplomas of old, each of the documents begins with an invocation of the Holy Trinity. If, as suggested elsewhere, the scribe responsible for drafting no. 132 was the high-ranking cleric William de Dumfries,[48] his university training will have provided him with sufficient training in technical language and diplomatic to ensure that treaties produced in the chancery of the king of Scots achieved the rigid standards required of civilian law elsewhere in Europe.

Conclusion

The collection of documents edited in this volume leaves little doubt that the chancery of Alexander III's time represented a busy and sophisticated operation. Examination of the 175 deeds that survive as full texts suggests that while demand on the part of both the king and his subjects for deeds executed in the form of the traditional writ-charter remained high, the rapidly developing economic conditions, increasingly complex fiscal demands of central government and growing intricacy of land-based litigation characteristic of the period compelled chancery clerks to draw on a varied repertoire of documentary styles. The 155 additional deeds that survive as *notitiae* confirm the impression of a chancery staff whose members readily experimented with instruments ranging from simple brieves through more elaborate warrants for payment, from formal letters patent to elaborately framed charters of infeftment. Some styles they abandoned as outdated or incompatible with their needs, others they altered or refined to suit Scottish circumstances.

Any lingering doubt about the ability of Alexander III's chancellors and their staff to respond in efficient fashion to the documentary requirements of central government must surely be obviated with a glance at the inventories that were made of the royal archives in 1282, 1292 and 1296.[49] The first listed the several classes of deeds stored in the treasury at Edinburgh castle, carefully distinguishing original charters from papal bulls, exchequer rolls from rolls of chancery, engrossments and diplomatic documents from administrative ephemera. The inventory was sophisticated enough to suit the requirements of Scottish chancery clerks during the years of the Guardianship following the king's death in 1286, and impressive enough to earn one of the clerks responsible for drafting it the position of Keeper of the Rolls of Scotland and, eventually, promotion to chancellor.[50] Subsequent inventories, compiled in 1292 and 1296 at the command of Edward I, were more comprehensive still: in addition to schedules, accounts, letters, charters, rolls, large and small, as well as jewels, relics and other valuables, they identify boxes, leather bags, sacks, chests, coffers and other containers, all carefully organised for ease of access.

Some years ago Geoffrey Barrow likened scholarly efforts to classify the written deeds of the twelfth-century kings of Scotland to an exercise in frustration, a chase of the will o' the wisp.[51] That observation is no longer appropriate with regard to the period after 1249. In many of their endeavours the chancery clerks charged with drafting written acts in the name of Alexander III enjoyed much less creative licence than had those who worked in the writing chapels of Malcolm IV and William I. Not yet in evidence, however, are the 'prolix style', the 'wearisome repetition' and the 'labouring of synonyms' that make the reading of late medieval and early modern instruments of conveyance such a test of scholarly endurance.[52] The long reign of Alexander III made it possible for the king's clerks to experiment widely with the language of royal acts, to adapt English chancery practices to the requirements of Scottish usage, to shape the form and content of brieves to suit the peculiarities of Scots law. The customs, practices and conventions that they refined in the decades after 1249 in turn proved instrumental in ensuring the success of the Guardians' rule in the dark days following Alexander's unexpected death in March 1286.

Lost Acts

The sources of the 'lost' acts that constitute nos 176 to 330 in this collection range from reliable, often contemporary, acts of confirmation (e.g. no. 2), to oblique references to the issue of a brieve, charter or letter patent within the body of an extant full text, to inventories and calendars of the archives of noble families drafted well after the medieval period containing items that have subsequently disappeared. Of particular value as sources of *notitiae* for the period of Alexander's rule are the voluminous records of the English chancery and exchequer, for in his capacity as a tenant in chief of the English crown in Northumberland and Cumberland, Alexander frequently authorised his representatives to appear in his stead before agents of Henry III and Edward I. Examination of the records arising from the work of the justices in eyre, in particular, has yielded a substantial number of new references to acts of Alexander III. The full texts of almost all of these, unfortunately, are lost, but occasionally (e.g. no. 72) the eyre records cite a royal deed that was later lost or destroyed.

In a number of instances it has been difficult to determine whether a reference qualifies as a genuinely 'lost' act or if the existence of a written deed is merely implicit or conjectural. The examples here are numerous. What is to be made, for example, of the many references among the close and patent rolls to Henry III's exercise of royal mercy 'at the instance of King Alexander'? The presence at the English court of the Scottish royal couple offered rich opportunities for both Henry and his successor Edward I to exercise this most solemn of royal prerogatives on their behalf. Over the course of the week-long festivities at Christmas 1251 that celebrated the knighting of the young Alexander III and his marriage to the princess Margaret, for example, a host of outlaws secured formal pardon of their transgressions when Alexander himself pleaded their cause before his new father-in-law.[53] The public ceremonies that accompanied the Scottish couple's visit late in 1260, timed to coincide with the birth of their first child, prompted a similar display of royal mercy at the behest of King Alexander.[54] As a tenant in chief, moreover, Alexander himself regularly discharged the lordly obligation of interceding with the English crown on behalf of his men or, indeed, anyone else fortunate enough to catch his ear. Thus, several miscreants accused of breaching forest law in Inglewood (Cumberland) found in him a willing advocate,[55] as did a man who sought and obtained respite from having to perform military service when he set off on pilgrimage to Santiago de Compostella.[56] On some occasions

King Alexander may well have presented entreaties of this sort to Henry III or Edward I *viva voce*, either in person or by the mouths of envoys, but on others, clearly, they were the subject of written communications now lost. Requests on the part of Alexander for a host of other favours were no doubt sent to the English king in missives that escaped archiving by otherwise diligent chancery clerks in London and Westminster. Thus, Henry III appointed protégés of the Scottish king to clerical livings,[57] relaxed demands on visiting merchants,[58] arranged formal perambulations of disputed border territory,[59] and even ordered a commission of oyer and terminer to put to trial a man accused of assaulting one of Alexander III's household servants as the royal entourage progressed through Durham,[60] all presumably in response to written letters the texts of which have since suffered the ravages of time and poor storage. Diplomatic convention, moreover, must have dictated that correspondence of a personal nature (like the letter recorded in no. 150 and the communication that c. 1281 Prince Alexander sent to his uncle, Edward I, enquiring politely after the latter's health)[61] receive formal, written acknowledgement. So, too, must have memoranda generated from business of a routine nature. In many cases these materials have perished.[62] On the occasion of his marriage to Princess Margaret, for example, the young king accepted from his father-in-law a handsome grant of armour and harness as well as a set of new bedding; less than a decade later, he received the sum of fifty merks of silver.[63] Both gifts will have prompted formal notes of acknowledgement and thanks, but neither has left any trace in the records of the Scottish chancery or exchequer. Neither did Alexander's appointment in 1279 of attorneys to represent him in the court of King's Bench, though the nomination must have been carried out in response to written instructions of some sort from Scotland.[64] In similar fashion, examples of the everyday concerns that engaged Alexander's time and efforts back in Scotland were undoubtedly the stuff of ephemeral documents that did not survive the passage of time.

The very substantial collection of documents currently housed in the National Archives of the United Kingdom under the series code SC 8 and recently edited in the *Parliament Rolls of Medieval England* includes a series of petitions presented to the English parliament by Alexander III's subjects, first in the decade following Edward I's conquest of the kingdom in 1296 and again, a generation later, during the turbulent rule of Edward Balliol.[65] Some make reference to gifts of land, revenue and privilege that beneficiaries claimed Alexander III had made them over the long course of his reign; others, more ambiguously, to possessions that the petitioners argued they had held 'in the time of the late King Alexander'. On rare occasions the petitions reproduce in detail the terms of such grants, as did, for example, John de Swinburne's request for restoration of the annual pension of ten merks that Alexander had given him (no. 168). More often, the petitions offer less comprehensive but nonetheless reliable evidence about the gift in question. All such grants are listed among the lost acts found below, in nos 176 to 330.

The texts of still other petitions, however, offer more ambiguous information about the claimants' title to lands, privileges or revenues, and the editors have had to make judgements about the wisdom of including such *notitiae* in this collection. In the Westminster parliament of autumn 1295, for example, Hugh de Flotterton appeared to argue his title to a house in Berwick of which he had been seised 'in the time of King Alexander', but which he had subsequently lost to a rival.[66] Likewise, in 1337 the burgesses of the same town sought relief from the obligation to pay gauge and tronage on cloth and wine on the basis of an exemption they had enjoyed in the time of King Alexander.[67] In neither case is it possible to confirm unambiguously an original grant on the part of the Scottish king; in neither case, in consequence, have such claims been considered in this collection as genuinely 'lost' acts.

Of uncertain status also are several other kinds of extant documents all of which infer, but by no means bear clear witness to, the existence of written deeds of Alexander III. Thus, the National Archives of the United Kingdom preserves the (badly damaged) text of a letter to the king dated 10 November 1264 in which the 'community' of Aberdeen argued against the grant of trading privileges to nearby Kildrummy.[68] The petition must have prompted some sort of formal reply, but if so, the latter has since perished. Into this general category of presumed, but by no means certain, royal *acta* fall a wide range of other documents that requested, and sometimes prompted, action on the part of Alexander's household, administrative or judicial agents. Among them are a petition of c. 1268 complaining about the plunder of a Catalan ship by Scottish pirates, which in turn became the subject of a formal inquest, and a monitory letter from the conservators of Reading abbey concerning the king's interference in the affairs of May priory, for which the king later made amends.[69] The lost act referred to in no. 304, a confirmation of a gift of land in Fife by Richard de Kilmaron to his kinsman, Alexander son of Colin son of Carun of Cupar, is in this respect noteworthy. The text of the act is unremarkable, but the document offers a rare example of the circumstances that preceded the issue of many royal acts of confirmation. The deed was prompted by a petition that the donor submitted to his king, in which he specifically requested formal corroboration of his gift:

> Richard de Kilmaron, his liege, writes to the magnificent prince and his most reverend lord, Alexander, illustrious king of Scots, informing his reverend lordship that he has given in free feuferme and granted and by his charter confirmed to Alexander son of Colin son of Carun of Cupar, his kinsman, his land of Kinmult, namely the land of Woddeflatter which is called 'Lillockisfeyld' with all its pertinents and bounds, according to the tenor of the charter that he made out to Alexander regarding the said land. Hence it is that he considered it appropriate to call upon his reverend lordship to confirm his said donation and grant.[70]

On this occasion Alexander responded favourably to the petition by authorising the chancellor to issue a deed of confirmation. Similar petitions from other subjects must have been the genesis of many other similar acts in this collection.

Alexander III's lands in Tynedale and Cumberland generated a steady business for the agents who safeguarded his lordly interests there.[71] Many of their activities were of a routine nature, executed as a matter of course and probably without need of close or formal contact with the king. Such business involved, most notably, actions relating to the tenure and transmission of estates in these parts, the giving of seisin,[72] or the summoning of an inquest to determine traditional renders from tenants who held their lands in drengage.[73] More numerous still were the dozens of actions (of novel disseisin, mort d'ancestor, terce, etc.) that tenants brought before justices in eyre when these officials travelled the northern circuit in 1257, 1279–80 and 1293.[74] Alexander III proved adept at defending his jurisdictional rights within these lands and English justices in eyre duly surrendered their authority to Scottish bailies when their travels took them to Tynedale.[75] In order to initiate action of any kind, then, demandants of all ranks had to sue out original writs with the officials who acted on Alexander's behalf in Northumberland and Cumberland. Unfortunately, almost all these ephemeral deeds have perished; where they do survive, they are numbered below among the lost acts.

Another category of actions for which no distinct deeds survive relates to rulings, appointments and decisions of a routine administrative nature that Alexander III made arising in consultation with members of his council and/or household. These defy simple categorisation, but all must have been carried out in response to formal directives the texts of which have long since perished. A few examples, all relating to the king's son, Prince Alexander, will suffice. The *Scotichronicon* notes that in 1270, following the death of Colban earl of Fife, the king gave the earldom lands in wardship to his son until the heir should come of age; within a few years he had also endowed the prince with an appanage that consisted of the entire island of Man and had assigned his trusted friend, William de St Clair, as the prince's guardian. In another example, the chronicler Andrew of Wyntoun notes the king's judgement in the settlement of a suit in 1285 concerning rival claims to the earldom of Menteith.[76] Soon after Lord Alexander's wedding in 1282, moreover, the king wrote to the pope requesting formal approval of the terms that had been agreed for Princess Marguerite's tocher, as he had undertaken to do in the marriage agreement.[77] Each of these actions will have been preceded by the drafting of a formal act, its authentication with the royal seal and perhaps also the engrossment of copies in the Scottish chancery. None, however, has left any notice in written record, and none is counted among the lost acts of Alexander III.

No discussion of the lost acts of any of Scotland's twelfth- and thirteenth-century kings would be complete without reference to the inventories that Cosmo Innes included in the first volume of the *Acts of the Parliaments of Scotland* or to the abundance of archival material to which they bear witness. The earliest of these was compiled in 1282 at the command of King Alexander III by the keeper of the rolls, Thomas de Charteris, his chief clerk, William de Dumfries and a third chancery clerk, Ralph de Bosco. Two others were carried out in 1292 and 1296 when Edward I ordered a survey of the archives of the Scottish treasury and exchequer in the course of his deliberations concerning the succession to the Scottish throne.[78] Bruce Webster long ago warned against blaming Edward I entirely for the subsequent loss of the national records of Scotland,[79] but there remains good reason to lament the king's actions, for the inventories attest both the sophistication of the later thirteenth-century Scottish administration and the extent to which contemporaries, great and small, lay and clerical, had come to depend on the authority of the king's writing office for ratification and authentication of their written deeds. In many instances it has been possible to link a document listed in one of the inventories with extant originals,[80] in others, to identify an inventoried deed with a lost act,[81] but there is no escaping the fact that among the rolls of 'recognitions', 'inquests', 'perambulations', 'extents', and the records of 'plaints', 'pleas' and 'settlements' once stored in Edinburgh there lay an untold wealth of now lost source materials relating to the operation of the exchequer and chancery under King Alexander III.[82]

Spurious acts

Research into the written deeds of Alexander III has brought to light a handful of documents of undoubtedly spurious provenance, none of which is included in this edition. Several are found in the later medieval register of the bishopric of Aberdeen, which includes a number of entries that, in the words of G. W. S. Barrow, were 'concocted' in order to make good the loss of genuine documents of earlier provenance.[83] Thus, an act said to have been issued under the king's seal on 10 May 1256, gifted to the bishop of Aberdeen the teinds of all the royal rents raised in the lands between the Dee and Spey rivers.[84] The lack of a witness clause in this document is suspicious, the form and contents of the dating clause are unusual and the use of some terms is uncharacteristic of the period. The circumstances of the grant, said to have occurred during the king's minority, are equally questionable. In his history of the see of Aberdeen, John Dowden treated the act as genuine,[85] and for a decade and more after 1296 Bishop Henry le Cheyne used the claim to the teinds as leverage in negotiations with the English crown.[86] Professor Barrow long ago opined that the fourteenth-century bishops of Aberdeen were not above 'tampering' with their records in defence of their claims to lands and privileges,[87] and it looks very much as if the deed of May 1256 represented a creative revision of the cathedral register intended to offset losses that the recent war had inflicted on the archives of the see. The source of the act, in short, is not trustworthy and the gift is not included among the authentic royal deeds relating to Aberdeen.

Another charter of Alexander III in favour of an ecclesiastical beneficiary that must be classified as spurious is found at fo. 20^v in the fourteenth-century cartulary of Balmerino abbey.[88] It purports to confirm to the monks several estates that they had acquired from the Revel family in the 1230s, and which King Alexander II had subsequently included in the abbey's foundation charter.[89] The spurious confirmation is dated to the month of August in the twentieth year of the reign of Alexander III (1268), but closer investigation reveals that its address is characteristic of the later thirteenth century, its contents lifted largely from the text of the earlier royal deed of Alexander II, but with the witness list of the latter altered so as to include the names of persons who were alive in the later 1260s and to omit those long dead. The act is quite clearly a fabrication, intended to lend weight to the abbey's claim to a cluster of estates that had been the subject of considerable dispute only a generation earlier.[90]

A group of other spurious deeds is deserving of mention here, if only because the documents managed for so many years to pass muster among Scottish archivists and antiquarians as authentic. Among the muniments of the duke of Montrose now stored in the National Records of Scotland are several charters relating to members of the Graham family, including David lord of Dundaff, whom scholars have dubbed both an ambitious 'new' man of the thirteenth century and a 'rapacious speculator'.[91] To those sobriquets might be added yet another, that of creative forger. In 1253 David sought royal confirmation of the several estates in Lothian, Stirlingshire, Carrick and Cunningham that he had amassed on his scramble up the social ladder and Alexander III was pleased to oblige (no. 19). Around the year 1260 David further acquired lands in Perthshire as a tocher, on the occasion of his marriage to Annabella, sister of Earl Malise II of Strathearn.[92] When the earl died in 1271, David must have worried that the lands might slip from his grasp, for in that same year he concocted a second, forged, royal confirmation of his title to the estates.[93] The son of the marriage, Patrick, seems to have shared his father's concerns. He, too, requested, and in November 1285 received, from Alexander III a charter confirming his title to the Perthshire lands of Foswell, but like his father he must have been concerned about his claim to other nearby estates, for he, too, commissioned a spurious royal confirmation of all the recently acquired Perthshire lands, this one identifying as a beneficiary of royal favour his long-dead father![94] Clearly, by the later years of the thirteenth century some questions had arisen either about the Grahams' title to the lands or to the obligation to offer warrandice for them. The long lapse of time between original grant, real or alleged, and subsequent voucher to warrant, moreover, must have tempted some land holders to make good the consequences of careless archival practice. This observation may explain the entry found in an early Register of Deeds in which a sixteenth-century hopeful laid claim to lands in Kincardineshire by producing a charter of Alexander III which purported to have carved out of the forest of Clunie (Perthshire) an estate for his servant, Richard de Straiton.[95] The alleged beneficiary is indeed attested in the thirteenth-century royal household,[96] and the witness list of the deed is contemporary with the middle years of the king's reign, but other features of the charter text, notably its address and tenurial clauses, are characteristic of later medieval deeds, as is the render in cash. There are good reasons for treating the grant as an authentic act of Alexander III, but it may be that other acts were crafted later in the medieval period, when tenants sought to protect their title to the lands from sweeping acts of revocation, such as those that David II's parliament authorised in November 1357 and September 1367.[97]

Unattributables

In a small number of cases, it has proved impossible for the editors to decide whether a lost act is attributable to Alexander III or represents a much earlier deed, issued under the authority of his father, King Alexander II. In the years since Grant Simpson first began to assemble the handlist of royal acts datable to the second half of the thirteenth century, archival work has made it possible to assign several such acts reliably to the reign of Alexander II or that of his son, Alexander III, but the circumstances that produced some eleven deeds remain unclear. These 'unattributable' acts are listed both in this volume and in *Regesta Regum Scottorum*, Volume III.

III. THE HANDS

Among the ninety-six acts that survive as original parchment sheets there are distinguishable some twenty-one different hands. All but three scribes were responsible for writing two or more of the king's documents. They are identified in the apparatus to each text with a letter from A to U, though no attempt is made here to discuss the peculiarities associated with each hand.

The texts associated with each scribe are listed below. The dates that appear in brackets after each entry designate the period within which that scribe was active.

Scribe A: nos 2, 3, 7, 11, 12, 13, 14, 16, 19, 25, 31, 56 (1250–65).
Scribe B: nos 23, 26, 62, 82 (1257–73).
Scribe C: nos 27, 29, 32, 34, 36, 40 (1260–2).
Scribe D: nos 35, 37, 38, 39 (1262).
Scribe E: nos 41, 45 (1262, 1263).
Scribe F: nos 49, 51, 52, 53, 55, 59 (1264–6).
Scribe G: nos 65, 66, 67, 139 (1267–8, ?1282).
Scribe H: no. 69 (1268).
Scribe I: nos 70, 73, 75 (probably), 80 (1269–72).
Scribe J: no. 71 (1269).
Scribe K: nos 63, 74, 78, 83, 84, 86 (1267–73).
Scribe L: nos 87, 120 (1272, 1279).
Scribe M: nos 90, 92, 94, 95, 96, 99, 101, 106, 109, 112, 113, 114, 116, 117, 118, 119, 121, 125 (1274–9).
Scribe N: nos 98, 131 (1276, 1280).

Scribe O: nos 107, 136, 137, 144, 145, 146, 147, 150, 151, 155, 160, 161 (1272–85).
Scribe P: nos 123, 138, 170 (1275–86).
Scribe Q: no. 124 (1279).
Scribe R: no. 132 (1281).
Scribe S: nos 133, 134, 135, 140 (1281–2).
Scribe T: nos 141, 142, 143 (1282).
Scribe U: no. 162 (1285).

The number and variety of hands invite several observations about the royal chancery during the reign of Alexander III. Some men dedicated most of their adult years to service there. With some twelve documents attributable to his hand and a record of royal service spanning fifteen years, for example, Scribe A was clearly a dedicated member of the royal entourage, both sufficiently skilled to undertake a range of clerical tasks on behalf of his king and politically astute enough to survive the tumultuous events of the minority period between 1249 and 1258. Scribe O was equally hard working, though his professional career as a chancery clerk was slightly briefer: he joined the stable of chancery clerks rather later than did Scribe A, but between 1272 and 1285 he wrote another dozen of Alexander's extant *acta*. A third scribe, M, was responsible for casting into proper diplomatic language most of the personal letters that Alexander III directed to Edward I in the decade of the 1270s. The king's teenage children, Margaret and Alexander, shared their father's enthusiasm for this man's craftsmanship and entrusted Scribe M with the task of writing the king of England on their behalf.[98]

The texts of the king's extant acts identify more than a dozen clerks (*clerici*) in the king's employ, though the term, of course, applied to a wide range of persons and did not designate chancery scribes exclusively. Some of these clerics must have served under Alexander II and simply continued in the employment of Chancellor Robert de Kenleith, who remained in office in the early years of the minority. The names of William 'our chaplain' and Alexander *de capella*, for example, appear in the witness list of a charter of Alexander II dated April 1248;[99] they may be the same 'William the chaplain and Alexander de Corbridge, our clerks' whose names were included in the witness list of a deed issued early in the reign of Alexander III (no. 18). Other clerics were undoubtedly mere birds of passage, present in the royal household in the train of a dignitary visiting court when an act of gift or confirmation was executed, or called upon at the site of a royal ceremony of conveyance to record the proceedings in a formal charter. Under the first of these categories might fall the scribe who penned no. 124, a confirmation issued in favour of the knight William Dallas, a royal tenant in Moray, whose distinctive hand is not found again among the extant originals of the period 1249–86. Under the second, perhaps, was the clerk who penned no. 69, a grant of guild privileges to the burgesses of Elgin that Alexander bestowed on the occasion of his visit there in November 1268. His hand, too, is unique.

Several extant documents appear to have been executed at the instance of beneficiaries who supplied their own scribe and perhaps also their own parchment and sealing wax, a practice that was already well established in Scotland, and one that would continue well into the fourteenth century.[100] Nos 49, 51, 52, 53 and 59, for example, were all issued in favour of the Cistercian abbey of Melrose between 1264 and 1266, two of them at Traquair on the same day in 1264, suggesting that on this latter occasion, at least, an agent of Abbot Adam sought out the justiciar's court that had assembled there under the presidency of Alexander III, prepared to record in official fashion the business that he transacted there.[101] The Cistercians enjoyed a strong reputation as careful archivists, and their chancery at Melrose was among the most sophisticated in the kingdom. They had little need, then, to call upon the personnel of the royal writing office, and indeed, good reason to entrust the redaction of important legal instruments to their own scribes. More intriguing is the hand of no. 162, which records Alexander III's confirmation of an act of Earl Malise II of Strathearn in favour of Sir Patrick de Graham. It is not found elsewhere among extant royal acts of the period, but it is almost certainly the same as that of the scribe who, around the same time, penned several other deeds in which the Graham family were (or sought to portray themselves as) beneficiaries of royal and comital patronage.[102] The household of Malise II (d. 1271), although modest in size, is known to have been sophisticated enough to employ at least two scribes;[103] his household counted among its members the man who executed no. 162.

All but a handful of the ninety-six originals are written in the cursive 'court' or 'chancery' hand that had become dominant in the king's chapel in the closing years of the twelfth century.[104] The quality of the hands and the care that clerks took to achieve clarity of design and composition vary not only from one scribe to the next, but also within the repertoire of a single clerk's output. Scribe A's documents, for example, range from the beautifully executed no. 7, written in an even hand with a carefully prepared pen nib on a cleanly cut piece of expensive vellum, through nos 3, 19 and 31, all less tidily drafted. Likewise, Scribe M was capable of writing in a bold, elegant hand a formal charter such as that in which the king granted his protection to the burgesses of Aberdeen (no. 101); yet, the several letters for which he was responsible are written in a smaller, more workaday script (e.g. nos 90, 96). By the later thirteenth century, the court hand was sufficiently commonplace to permit scribes to develop a range of easily discernible idiosyncrasies, and these in turn often make it possible to distinguish one hand from another.

In the latter half of the reign royal scribes tended to signal a distinction between ephemeral documents such as brieves or letters close and deeds recording confirmations or new grants. Generally, the former are written in a small, cramped, hurried-looking hand on parchment of rough grade; to the latter they tended to allocate greater parchment surface and more care and attention to the appearance of the handwriting. Collectively, the patterns discernible in the hands over the course of the period 1249–86 suggest that well before the reign of Robert I, the clerks of the king's writing office were making use of a 'hierarchy of scripts', one that reflected both the contents of individual documents and the purposes for which they were intended.[105]

Closer examination of some of the unusual deeds extant in original form reinforces the impression that scribes made deliberate choices about handwriting styles. No. 132 is a record of the marriage agreement made at Roxburgh in the summer of 1281 in which Eric II king of Norway, represented by four highly ranked envoys, agreed to accept as his wife Alexander III's daughter, Margaret. The agreement, here referred to as a final concord, was drawn up in the form of an elaborately executed indenture, handsomely written in a small but tidy book hand that, by the late thirteenth century, European scribes otherwise reserved to expensively bound works such as illuminated bibles. This half of the indenture was intended to remain in the hands of the Scottish ruler and his chancellor: its closing clauses state this clearly, as does one of the contemporary endorsements, and it bore the seals of each of Eric's four envoys (although these are now lost). The care taken to ensure the consistency of the hand throughout the lengthy 2,500-word text and to adhere to clearly delineated margins in each of the document's forty-three lines without benefit of guiding lines or pricking bear eloquent testimony to the talents of a senior scribe, aware of the solemnity of the agreement and skilled in the use of visual cues appropriate to such a deed. The backward-leaning riser of the letter 'd', the squared shape of the capital letters A, E, N and R, the stylised symbol for contractions and abbreviations: all are distinct features of this scribe's hand, and it is not found anywhere else among the ninety-six acts that survive in original form issued under Alexander III's seals. This same scribe, however, was the man responsible for drafting the inventory of muniments deposited in the treasury of Edinburgh castle that the king commissioned in the autumn of 1282. He is probably the William de Dumfries who identified himself in the text of the inventory.[106] If this is indeed the case, it suggests that William's skills as a scribe were of very high calibre and his hand reserved for only the most important of royal acts.

There seems little reason to doubt that the documents relating to the marriage on 15 November 1282 of Prince Alexander and Marguerite of Flanders (nos 133, 134, 135, 140) were neither written nor sealed in Scotland, but rather in the chancery of Guy de Dampierre count of Flanders (d. 1305). The diplomatic of the acts is unique. The hand of Scribe S, who drafted all four, is stylistically distinct from the hands of the other clerks who penned Alexander III's Scottish deeds. His Picard French is characteristic of the dialect used in the count's writing office in the later thirteenth century.[107] That dialect, moreover, is markedly different from the Norman French of other contemporary Scottish documents, notably no. 73 (1270) and the ordinances of 1304 for the governance of the realm.[108]

The structure of each of the documents is also unusual. No. 133 begins as a simple notification: Alexander addresses all who shall see or hear his letters, then goes on to cite the customs used since time immemorial to determine succession to the Scottish throne. Towards the end of the document, however, the king disappears, and the narrative voices become those of his envoys, lay and clerical, who collectively swear to observe these arrangements and who conclude the act with the statement that 'together with the seal of our dear lord the king, we have set our seals to these letters'. In no. 134, more customarily, the authorial voice of both the notification and the sealing clauses is that of the king alone. In no. 135 there is yet another change: the address and much of the text of the notification are in the king's voice, but in the latter part of the document Prince Alexander becomes the speaker, swearing to observe the terms of the tocher payment that his father has laid out, and it is he who appends both his seal and that of his father to the document. All three of these deeds include a month date (December), but they do not mention the place where Scottish and Flemish envoys met, though this must have been the court of Guy de Dampierre. Finally, in no. 140 the king and his son again share the authorial voice, with Prince Alexander noting, as he had done in no. 135, that he affixes to the act his own seal and the great seal of Scotland. This last document is unusual, too, in that it includes both a date and note of the place, Roxburgh, where it was drawn up.

The diplomatic of the documents makes it clear that the king entrusted a matrix of his great seal to the keeping of his envoys, and perhaps specifically to his chancellor, William Fraser bishop of St Andrews, with instructions to deploy it as necessary. It is probably no accident that the examples of the great seal that adorn nos 134 and 135 are in near perfect condition: if William did travel with a matrix it may have been used only on the occasion of the visit to Flanders. The prince did not accompany the envoys when they set off for Flanders late in 1281 to arrange the details of the marriage. Thus, he, too, must have entrusted a matrix to the chancellor's keeping; the condition of his seals, too, support the suggestion of a device otherwise little used. In fact, the dispatch of the embassy on this business marked the occasion for the design of a distinct seal for the young Alexander: in a letter that he wrote to his uncle, Edward I, earlier that same year he had remarked that he did not own a seal, and in its absence was using the device of his guardian, William de St Clair.[109] In the end, the marriage did not take place as early as planned, probably owing to the prince's illness, and by November 1282, when in no. 140 the king confirmed afresh the arrangements for Marguerite's tocher, the prince had commissioned a second seal. Intriguingly, both were small in size; both were surely intended to evoke the memory of the seal of minority that his father had used in the 1250s.

While chancery clerks in Flanders and France were already practised in the use of French as a language of formal communication, Latin remained the language of choice in Scottish royal acts throughout the reign of Alexander III and indeed well beyond then. All but one of the acts issued in Scotland or England under the seal of Alexander III are in Latin. No. 73 stands out as the sole exception to this rule. It is an unusual document in all respects. Drafted and sealed in the style of a charter dated 28 March 1270, it narrates the circumstances of a recent dispute between the king and Robert Bruce lord of Annandale over rights of presentation to benefices during the vacancy of the see of Glasgow. Summoned to appear before a meeting of the great council, Bruce conceded that such appointments belonged to the crown, but in return he secured confirmation in this act of the other franchises he enjoyed in his lands. Many years ago, Joseph Robertson accurately noted that the charter represents 'probably the earliest [writ] in the French tongue extant under the great seal of Scotland'.[110] It may have been penned in Norman French at the request of Bruce, whose considerable landed possessions and political interests in England will have acquainted him with the language, but the scribe (Scribe I) who wrote it was based in Alexander III's chancery rather than Bruce's, for he also set his hand to nos 70, 75 and 80. The unique linguistic features of the charter of 1270 offer important evidence about the use of French as a language of government in Scotland in the later thirteenth century. It was also the language in which Princess Margaret addressed her uncle, Edward I, when in 1280 she wrote to send him her good wishes.[111] Latin may have retained its status as the most appropriate medium for the expression of the royal will in Scotland, but the multilingual skills of royal scribes show that the kingdom was in close touch with English and European cultural trends and well able to accommodate them.

In the second half of the century the royal chancery enjoyed a reputation as a useful stepping stone for ambitious career churchmen. Several of the clerics and scribes employed in the production of the king's charters, brieves and letters spent only a brief period in the entourage of the chancellor or chamberlain before moving on to more lucrative office. Such a man, perhaps, was Reginald de Rihill: he is identified in no. 113 (May 1278) as the friend (*socius*) of Bishop William of St Andrews, but thereafter served as a trusted envoy of Alexander III in embassies to the English court (nos 114, 123, 125). More certainly, among the clerics who used their chancery experience and proximity to the king as a springboard to preferment were Andrew de Gartly, Ralph de Dundee and, if in rather different fashion, the Tynedale cleric-turned-grandee William de Swinburne. Andrew began his professional life in the employ of the bishop of Moray, went on to study canon law on the continent, then moved into royal service in the 1270s, eventually securing a grant of the church of Fordyce in Aberdeenshire.[112] Ralph's progress up the social ladder was more impressive still and certainly more unusual: after a university education at Bologna he served as a *clericus* in the household of Alexander III, acquiring a handful of rich benefices in the process as well as a gift of land from the king himself, before abandoning the clerical world altogether for life as a family man in the western reaches of the kingdom.[113] William de Swinburne's career achievements were noteworthy, too. By means of a skilful exploitation of his Tynedale connections with the wealthy Comyn family he parlayed a modest prebend south of the border into employment at the heart of the Scottish court as treasurer of Alexander III's queen; thereafter, he used his influence as a courtier to build a rich lordship based the length and breadth of Northumberland.[114]

The careers of three other chancery employees suggest, moreover, that the Scottish royal chancery was a highly sophisticated organ of government after 1250, its business sufficiently complex to require a wide range of administrative, intellectual and political expertise. Alexander III was fortunate to be served by a succession of well educated and capable chancellors. Robert de Kenleith abbot of Dunfermline continued in office following the sudden death of Alexander II in the summer of 1249. Well versed in the world of papal politics, he has been credited with leading the successful campaign to have Queen Margaret of Scotland canonised in 1249–50.[115] The turbulent years of the king's minority saw the office occupied by three different men, each a candidate of the political party then in power: Gamelin bishop of St Andrews from 1252 to 1255, Richard de Inverkeithing from 1255 through 1257 and, from 1259 to 1273, William Wischard bishop of Glasgow.[116] In the later years of the reign William Fraser bishop of St Andrews (1273–9) and Thomas de Charteris (1285–91) held the office in succession.[117] The vicissitudes of factional politics during the early years of the reign made the office of chancellor a precarious prize. Frequent turn-around at the highest echelons of the chancery, however, did not have a deleterious effect on the operation of the king's chapel, for each of the chancellors came to office with a good deal of clerical administrative experience behind him. Robert, as noted, was a veteran of the papal curia and in 1249 enjoyed a strong reputation as a vigorous advocate of the privileges of Dunfermline abbey.[118] His four successors were all university men and all brought to Alexander's chancery experience in curial service: Gamelin as a protégé of William de Bondington in the later years of the latter's chancellorship, Richard as royal chamberlain, William as a clerk under Chancellor Gamelin and Thomas as Clerk of the Rolls. Under Gamelin, in fact, the episcopal household at St Andrews became something of a nursery for royal public servants. The three chancery clerks responsible in 1282 for compiling an inventory of the king's muniments, Thomas de Charteris, William de Dumfries and Ralph de Bosco, were all recruited to royal court from the bishop's *familia*. All, significantly, were graduates of the universities of Paris or Bologna, and all three rose to prominence in the Scottish chancery after serving in the *familia* of Bishop Gamelin of St Andrews.[119]

Keith Stringer's study of the written acts of King Alexander II has led him to posit the existence, by the 1230s, of a sophisticated and efficient chancery well able to cope with the demands of royal government and equally well placed to respond to the myriad needs of the crown's secular and ecclesiastical subjects.[120] The professionalism that characterised the conduct of routine business in the two decades before 1249 in turn ensured the smooth functioning of the chief organ of government through the period of political upheaval that troubled the realm between 1249 and 1258. The twenty-six full texts and dozen-odd notices of royal acts that survive from the first decade of Alexander III's reign may not constitute a plentiful output, but neither do they suggest a bureaucracy incapable of serving the needs of the crown or its subjects. Moreover, the fact that after 1258 there was no headlong rush into chancery by ecclesiastical or secular tenants intent on securing confirmations of acts of conveyance, sale or excambium effected during the period of the minority speaks to the confidence of land holders great and small in the enduring authority of the chancellor's office even in the absence of a legally competent monarch.

The efficiency of the Scottish chancery is difficult to measure, but there is good reason to argue that the well staffed office of central government portrayed in the late thirteenth-century treatise 'The Scottish King's Household' represents more than an abstract ideal. The treatise suggests that the royal archives were by then sufficiently abundant to require the attention of a specialist whom it identified as the Clerk of the Rolls, whose chief responsibility was 'to counter-roll all the charters and muniments issuing forth from the chancery'.[121] The inventory of 1282 further reveals that among the tasks assigned to that clerk, Thomas de Charteris, and his staff was the design of a system of classification that would make it possible to separate materials such as old exchequer accounts, papal bulls and treaty texts from deeds more likely to be of immediate relevance in the day-to-day conduct of business in the royal court: charters of confirmation, records of quitclaim and surrender, judicial decisions. The justiciars charged with determining royal pleas, moreover, appear to have had ready access to records that they required in their deliberations. Thus, when in 1267 the abbot of Kelso appeared before Alexander III to complain that an annuity payable from the ferme of the burgh of Perth had been withheld, it was a simple matter for the king to command an inspection of 'the charters of his ancestors and the rolls of his chapel' and to find in favour of the monks (no. 64). The efficient organisation of the royal chancery must in turn have made royal justice swifter and more satisfactory. Here again, there is slight but important evidence in favour of portraying Alexander's administration as well organised and responsive to the needs of his subjects: in early November 1262 an inquest into an alleged deforcement in Peebles was summoned and a report of its findings delivered to chancery less than a month after the king had commanded it.[122]

Alexander III's own acts make mention of the engrossment of deeds frequently enough to suggest that after 1250 the practice had become customary,[123] and it is not surprising that in 1289 the Guardians of Scotland should have assigned William de Dumfries, recently promoted to the position of Clerk of the Rolls, to represent the estate of the late king in litigation with of his chief creditors.[124] The inventories that Edward I commissioned in 1292 and 1296 were more elaborate versions of William's initial effort, with several of the items they list readily identifiable among the lists compiled in the document of 1282.[125] If the treatise was composed as a *vademecum* for John Balliol –

and that would certainly appear to be the case – the brevity and clarity of its passages served the inexperienced king very well indeed, for the overall impression conveyed by the acts issued under his authority is of a central administrative office well able to cope with the several demands made of it.

IV. THE KING'S SEALS

The sigillography of the early part of Alexander III's reign is in all respects remarkable and bears eloquent witness to the potency of heraldic imagery as an expression of thirteenth-century identity. Many years ago the scholarly work of antiquarians brought to light a highly unusual seal of the minority period (1249–58), of a design and function hitherto unknown in Scottish, British or continental sigillography. The small size of the seal, which measures a mere 4.0 centimetres in diameter, led them to posit that it was in fact a privy, or secret, seal,[126] unique in the sense that unlike other examples of such seals from Scotland, it bears an image on both the obverse and reverse sides; unique, too, in that in the three surviving examples the seal is attached to the deed it authenticates by means of a tag hanging from a slit cut into the centre of the foot of the fold, that is, in the style common for large seals, rather than to a tongue cut along the foot of the document.[127] Recently, Archibald Duncan has drawn attention to the fact that there survive, in fact, two slightly different versions of the small seal, the first appended to a deed of June 1250 (no. 2), the other to two later acts of June 1252 and June 1257 (nos 16 and 25).[128] Two of the seals appear to be of yellow wax, the third white, although it is possible that poor preservation has darkened what was once white sealing wax to dull yellow.

The obverse of the first small seal, which survives in a single example (no. 2), shows the king wearing a crown, the first such representation of the royal figure in Scotland since 1107.[129] He is seated on a simple throne, both arms crooked, grasping in his right hand the pommel of a sword laid horizontally across his knees and in his left a sceptre the end of which terminates in a foliated ornament, reminiscent of the flowering rod of the biblical Aaron. The legend, surrounded by beaded borders, reads ESTO PRVDENS VT SERPENS ET SIMPLEX SICVT COLUMBA, 'be ye wary as a serpent and innocent as a dove', an adaptation of the New Testament passage found in the gospel of St Matthew: 'be wary as serpents, innocent as doves'.[130] On the reverse is a heater-shaped shield bearing the royal arms of Scotland, here portrayed for the first time as a lion rampant within a double tressure, the latter evocative of the young king's affinity, through his mother, with the French royal house.[131] Two years later, perhaps in anticipation of a favourable response to a recent request that the pope grant the privileges of anointing and coronation to the rulers of Scotland,[132] the king's chancery crafted a new version of the small seal (nos 16, 25). It is in most respects identical to the first, with the important difference that on the obverse, surrounding the figure of the seated king, there appear the additional and, in Scottish sigillography most unusual, words DEI GRA' REX SCOTT'. Here, writ small but indelibly, were the aspirations of the young king to parity with other European rulers of his day proclaimed.

The unusual characteristics of the small seals continue to fascinate historians, and long after they were first noted by antiquarians they remained the subject of close analysis. Grant Simpson has demonstrated not only that they were not privy seals at all, but rather scaled-down – though no less authoritative – versions of the traditional-looking great seal that Alexander would use exclusively after 1260. He argues that the imagery and legend call to mind simultaneously 'a royal figure who could not in person dispense justice, because he was a child', but also 'a young king who has to learn to grow up into the realm of harsh political reality as he reaches maturity'. Together, the imagery and the biblical quotation constitute a unique exemplar of the subtlety and complexity characteristic of medieval sigillography.[133]

The second version of the small seal remained in use until at least 1257, when it was appended to a deed issued in favour of William de Swinburne,[134] but noteworthy also about the small seals is the fact that during the years of the minority between 1249 and 1258 neither was used exclusively, but rather in alternation with a third, great, seal.[135] Thus, a document dated December 1250 (no. 3) and four others dated 1251 (nos 7, 11, 12, 13) were all authenticated by a great seal of traditional size and appearance. It was presumably this item that was at the centre of one of the first crises to disturb the early part of the reign, when the chancellor, Robert de Kenleith abbot of Dunfermline, sought to put the king's great seal to treasonable use in aid of his colleague and ally, Alan Durward. The author of an anonymous St Andrews chronicle that recounts the story notes, however, that the abbot's machinations were soon revealed. He was made to surrender the seal to the king and his magnates, and the latter 'was straightaway broken up in the people's sight; while a smaller seal was given to Gamelin [bishop of St Andrews], who became the king's chancellor'.[136] It was in these circumstances, then, as much as it was in the context of the (ultimately fruitless) request to the pope, for the privilege of coronation that the design and legend of the second small seal were conceived.

Grant Simpson and Archibald Duncan have both suggested that the small seals of the minority period were emblematic of a ruler whose actions might later be subject to review or rejection.[137] There is good sigillographic and paleographical precedence to support these arguments, not least the fact that all three of the acts that they authenticate were confirmations of transactions, the circumstances of which the crown might, especially in the aftermath of the royal minority, be called upon to warrant.[138] That will have been the case also, of course, with respect to any act of the minority, notably the five deeds sealed with the first great seal, and there is no indication that the legal value of the small seal was in any way inferior to that of the king's great seals. Interestingly, all three of the deeds authenticated by the small seal are drafted in the same hand, that of Scribe A. His identity is not known; he did, however, boast sharp political acumen, for he managed to survive the tumult of the 1250s and to continue in the king's service until well into the following decade.[139]

The two great seals that Alexander used, the first until the end of his minority, the second thereafter, resemble more generally those of his father, Alexander II, and, in the early fourteenth century, of Robert I. The symbolism of both was also modelled more closely on sigillographic practice then current in England and on the continent. The first measures some 9.0 centimetres in diameter. One side shows the king on an elaborately caparisoned horse, wearing a square helmet decorated with a plume, chain mail that covers him from head to foot and, over this, a surcoat.[140] In his right hand he holds aloft a sword; from his left shoulder is suspended a shield bearing the royal arms of Scotland, here again within a double tressure; the lion rampant appears also on the horse's caparisons.[141] The other side depicts Alexander III, once again crowned, seated on a bench-shaped throne the front of which is decorated with quatrefoil panels enclosing lions' faces. His feet rest lightly on a footboard, and he is clad not in mail but in a tunic and a mantle lined with ermine. Both arms are extended: in the right he holds a sword and in his left a flowering sceptre. There are five surviving examples of the seal (nos 3, 7, 11, 12, 13); all, unfortunately, are in such fragmentary condition as to make it impossible to read the legend.

Alexander probably began to use the second of his great seals soon after his minority had drawn to a close in 1258, but the earliest extant example dates only from July 1264 (no. 49). The numismatist Henry Laing described the rich design of this seal as a vibrant exemplar of the 'advanced state of the Arts in this period' in Scotland, and with good reason.[142] It survives in multiple versions,[143] one or two in such flawless condition that the design and workmanship are preserved in wondrous detail.[144] The king's new status as a sovereign prince of full age and one, moreover, who had aspirations to the ceremonies of coronation and unction, dominates both sides of this seal, which measures almost 10 centimetres in diameter. Here again, the king appears on one side in the guise of a helmeted knight mounted on horseback, outfitted in chain mail and surcoat, his right arm thrusting backwards holding a sword, his left hidden behind a shield adorned with the arms of Scotland and suspended around his neck. The arms are repeated on the caparisons of the horse, and a field of trefoils fills the entire space behind the figure. On two of the extant examples the king's left hand is visible clutching the reins, on two others the fine feathers of the horse's panache are clearly discernible. The artist's painstaking attention to detail is equally apparent on the other side of the seal. Clearly, no expense was spared in the crafting of this device. The king sits in majesty on a throne that is richly carved, the back raised and divided into three distinct sections marked by four finials ending in fleur-de-lys points, the sides and front decorated with arcades, quatrefoils and trefoils. His feet rest on the necks of two small wyverns placed on a cushioned footboard, itself balanced on an arcaded corbel. He wears a crown topped with fleurs-de-lys. This king is no boy, but a full grown, virile man: he has long, curly hair, a full beard and moustache.[145] He wears a tunic and over it a loose mantle, its broad sleeve hanging below his elbows. His right arm rests on his right knee, the hand holding upright a royal sceptre, its point decorated with foliations. His left arm is bent so that his hand can grasp the cords of his mantle before his chest. The background space is filled with elaborate trefoils. The same legend appears on each of the two sides, between delicately beaded borders: ALEXANDER . DEO . RECTORE . REX . SCOTTORVM . The words signalled a return to the designation that had appeared on Scottish royal seals since the time of Alexander I in the early twelfth century,[146] visual cues that made a bold statement about the lineage of this latest of the kingdom's rulers that was in every respect as powerful as were the ceremonies that had marked his inauguration.[147] The crown, the mantle, the sword, the sceptre, the facial hair: collectively, these details will have communicated to all who saw the seal Alexander III's God-given right to rule and, by extension, the authority of his acts.

Archibald Duncan's meticulous study of the written deeds of Robert I has revealed a variety of circumstances under which the king made use of a privy seal.[148] Such sophistication was but one feature of a wider programme on the part of Robert I to reform the governmental machinery of Scotland along an English model, but he was not the first to own a privy seal, for Alexander III also had one (as did John Balliol). The author of the treatise 'The Scottish King's Household' not only recommended that such a seal be struck, but also that it be reserved to the king's special use.[149] Unfortunately, no example of Alexander III's has survived – a consequence, no doubt, of the fact that such devices were usually small and fragile – and the king makes specific reference to its use only twice in extant documents. Precisely how it was attached cannot now be known, but the traces left by folds and the remnants of a tongue on no. 86 suggest that it was placed at the far right tip of a tongue cut from the right bottom of the parchment sheet, then folded up and around the top of the letter, in much the same way as the clerks of Robert I's chancery later applied his device.[150] On at least one of the occasions when he specifically mentioned using his secret seal, Alexander was travelling on pilgrimage to the shrine of St Cuthbert in Durham and was therefore at some distance from the person of his chancellor: in the letter to which he affixed the seal he informed his mother-in-law rather peevishly that a complaint about an ongoing dispute with an English forest official had interrupted his prayers.[151] The king had his privy seal on his person again in October 1278, while en route to meet Edward I in order to perform homage for his English lands (no. 116); this time, he affixed it to a letter because, he explained, he did not have his great seal with him. The evidence of these two missives, although limited, suggests that the passage in the treatise 'The Scottish King's Household' which recommended that the chancellor should, at the king's direction, stay 'in a suitable place and for the convenience of the people' reflected real and significant change within the administrative heart of government.[152] The chancellor remained at the beck and call of the king and was wont for many years yet to set up operations in the larger burghs of the realm as the royal court moved around, but the availability of a privy seal confirms the impression conveyed in other sources that in the later thirteenth century the chancery and its (increasingly large) staff was less peripatetic than they had once been. The existence of two royal seals, one securely and permanently lodged with the chancellor, as the treatise-writer recommended, the other on the king's person, both reflected and accommodated the movements of a ruler whose kingdom extended over very considerable terrain and whose regular contact with England often took him out of his own realm.

V. PLACE DATES IN THE ACTS OF ALEXANDER III

Some years ago John Maitland Thomson warned of the dangers of associating too closely the place names identified in the texts of Robert I's charters with the location of the king himself.[153] Archibald Duncan's partial reconstruction of the king's itinerary after 1314 and Dauvit Broun's analysis of charter witness lists have both, if from different perspectives, demonstrated how apt was this admonition.[154] Thomson's observation is equally relevant with respect to the written acts of Alexander III. Several of his deeds describe ceremonies of conveyance that occurred on an occasion and in a setting different from those identified in the dating clause of the relevant charters. In no. 41, for example, a royal tenant who had failed to render the service owed for the lands of Tillicoultry resigned his claim in the king's presence and 'before a great number of the king's magnates' in Edinburgh on 4 June 1262; Alexander's charter assigning new title to the estate to William earl of Mar is dated at Forfar on 21 December later that same year. This case, and others,[155] lend support to the argument that the drafting and sealing of some charters sometimes occurred at a place and on a date quite distinct from those that are identified as the setting for royal acts of infeftment. They lend credence, moreover, to the suggestion that charter place names probably reveal more about the movements of the chancellor than they do those of the king or his court. On the other hand, there were occasions when the business conducted in meetings of the royal council and of the colloquia that were the precursors of parliament were clearly the setting for ceremonies of conveyance. No. 56 records the gift of an annual rent to Hugh de Abernethy made at Scone on 31 March 1265, soon after a 'parliament' (colloquium) had convened there; likewise, only six days elapsed between the resignation of a small plot of Perthshire land made before the king at Dundee in July 1284 and its grant to a new tenant by means of a charter also dated at the burgh (no. 153).[156] It is not unreasonable to posit the proximity of the chancellor and his king on both occasions.

While the dating clauses of charters must therefore be used with caution, the place dates of the acts issued under the seal of Alexander III plotted on the map at the end of this volume nevertheless reveal some interesting patterns in the peregrinations of the royal court. This is particularly the case in comparison with those discernible for the reigns of William I and Alexander II, on the one hand, and of Robert I, on the other.[157] In the second half of the thirteenth century, however, the movements of the royal court were still confined largely to the eastern regions of the kingdom, much as they had been under William I and Alexander II. Like his father and grandfather, Alexander III did not regard the Firth of Forth as a barrier of any kind, administrative, political or cultural, and he moved easily from the southern reaches of the kingdom to the north through the chief burghs of the east. Thus, some fourteen of the king's acts are dated at Roxburgh, thirteen at Edinburgh, and nine at Haddington. The long service of Bernard abbot of Arbroath as chancellor of the realm under King Robert I (1308–28) helps to explain the prominence of the north-eastern burgh in the dating clauses of this king's acts.[158] Alexander III's six successive chancellors, by contrast, came to office from various locations,[159] and cannot be assigned so confidently to one or the other of the greater religious houses of Scotland. Surprisingly, some of the more important burghs of the realm appear on the map only occasionally (Perth, for example, only three times) or not at all (Glasgow, Aberdeen, Arbroath).

Some eight of Alexander II's written instruments were dated at Cadzow and another six at Ayr, a reflection, surely, of his well documented efforts to exert strong royal control over the region. In the early fourteenth century, likewise, the location of the Bruce family's patrimonial estates in Scotland and, from the mid-1320s, Robert I's active interest in a new manor house at Cardross in Dunbartonshire account for the dating of a good number of his written deeds at various sites west of Glasgow. Alexander III's seldom documented appearances in the western reaches of his kingdom are in this respect noteworthy. There may be several reasons for this apparent anomaly other than the vagaries associated with the survival of source materials, among them a readiness to delegate the day-to-day governance of this part of the realm to trusted servants but also a tendency, posited above, for chancellors and their writing staff to become more sedentary in the later thirteenth century and thus more easily accessible to their clients. Of equal interest are the many appearances of Scone in the dating clauses of Alexander III's charters: at twenty-three, it was by far the most frequently named site on the king's travels around his realm. The Augustinian priory (and later abbey) had, of course, long been popular with the descendants of Malcolm III and St Margaret, but there are good reasons for believing that from the time of his inauguration as a boy Alexander III actively promoted the reputation of the moot hill at Scone as a cultic site and to emphasise its distinct status as both the physical and symbolic centre of the Scottish royal landscape.[160] An agenda such as this certainly helps to explain why he should have favoured Scone quite as much as he did over other larger and more heavily populated burghs in the realm.

The king's personal interests may account for several other sites identified in the place dates of Alexander's acts. Some forty-two deeds are dated at Stirling (ten), Traquair (ten), Selkirk (five), Kintore (four), Kincardine (three), Kinross (three), Durris (three), Elgin (two), Inverness and Jedburgh (one each). In the later thirteenth century all were either actively in use as hunting grounds or well on the way to being developed for such purposes. There are other, albeit incidental, indications of genuine enthusiasm for the sport on the part of the king. In 1284, for example (no. 150), he made a gift of falcons to his brother-in-law, Edward I. Exchequer accounts from the 1260s make references to the maintenance of several kettles of birds of prey and to the establishment of mews and kennels at Forfar, Forres, Dunipace and Kincardine.[161] Alexander devoted considerable expense to the expansion or improvement of royal parks at Stirling, Kincardine and Clunie,[162] and was a vociferous critic of efforts to encroach on his rights in the forest lands that he controlled in northern England.[163] If these various references do attest an unusual enthusiasm on the part of Alexander III for contemporary hunt culture, they suggest also that much of the business conducted as a consequence of decisions made in the royal entourage had become so routine that it could easily be left in the hands of a competent staff of chancery officials.

APPENDIX I
THE INVENTORY OF 29 SEPTEMBER 1282

Although the inventory has long been familiar to scholars and its contents readily available in print, the document itself has not been the subject of close scrutiny. Examination of its physical features and diplomatic, however, offers a series of valuable insights into the professional world of the later thirteenth-century Scottish chancery, and important information about the function of the king's writing office.

The text of Alexander's commission to survey the contents of the treasury is no longer extant, but the opening lines of inventory reveal that the task of 'viewing', that is, organising, examining, counting and listing documents of all kinds – papal bulls, charters, royal letters, diplomatic correspondence, treaties and indentures – fell to the three most experienced clerks in the king's employ. All came into the king's service after extensive training in the household of Bishop Gamelin of St Andrews.[164] In 1282 Thomas de Charteris was the most senior in rank under the current chancellor, William Fraser. He had acted as an envoy to England for Alexander III (no. 99) and by the early 1280s had achieved the rank of Clerk of the Rolls; in 1284 he would go on to assume the office of chancellor of the realm. William de Dumfries, like Charteris, was an Annandale man; in September 1282 he was a senior clerk and later would assume the position of Clerk of the Rolls following de Charteris's promotion. Ralph de Bosco, canon of Dunkeld, was fairly new to royal service, but like his fellows destined for a successful career at the heart of Scottish government.

Of the three, as Clerk of the Rolls Thomas is the most likely to have assumed chief responsibility for opening and viewing the several deed boxes, coffers and leather sacks mentioned in the inventory, and it was probably William de Dumfries who undertook the task of compiling and listing the treasury's contents. He did so on two large parchment sheets, each carefully scraped to offer a clean surface. In a small but neat hand, under a series of simple, well spaced headings, he listed in roughly chronological order papal bulls, documents concerning negotiations with England, negotiations touching on Flemish business, negotiations with Norway (two series, one relating to the treaty of 1266, the other to the recent marriage of Princess Margaret to King Eric II), a long list of (cancelled) charters that had been returned to the chancellor over the preceding century and, finally, a miscellany of unspecified writings, each of which the inventory-takers said they had inspected but were not important enough to merit specific mention. John Maitland Thomson long ago surmised, no doubt correctly, that these items included the several rolls of chancery and exchequer deeds which later thirteenth-century inventories identify among the Scottish royal muniments,[165] and which are mentioned in passing in some of Alexander III's own acts.[166]

Among the deeds and documents relating to negotiations with England was a cancelled letter. It clearly touched on a matter of some sensitivity, for the entry that refers to it notes cryptically that the surveyors 'declined to describe it (*non vidimus*) because William de Dumfries wished first to show its contents to the king'.[167] The nature of this mysterious letter has long generated speculation among Scottish historians. Its location in the list of documents relating to negotiations with England is interesting: it comes after an entry that refers to 'letters of Robert de Ros and Eustace de Vescy' but before 'letters of Louis son of the king of France confirming the barons' charter' and a series of other deeds datable to 1212, including reference to a payment of 3,750 merks as part of the settlement of 1209. If this section of the inventory lists documents in genuinely chronological order – and that certainly looks to be the case – then the date of the 'cancelled letter' falls between April 1209 and January 1212;[168] right at the heart, then, of the Anglo-Scottish negotiations that led to William's formal submissions in 1209 and 1212.[169] The next two entries in the inventory, moreover, make reference to 'another agreement between the Scots and the English' and to the payment of an instalment of the sum of £4,000 that William had agreed to remit to John, both clearly linked to the Anglo-Scottish agreements between the kings.[170] It is tempting to link the 'cancelled letter' that William de Dumfries was so determined to reserve to the king's eyes with the texts of one or both of the lost treaties of 1209 and 1212. Contemporary observers and modern scholars alike have always regarded the submissions of 1209 and 1212 as humiliating and disadvantageous to King William.[171] The documents recording them are believed to have been among the 'writings and documents' that were returned to the Scottish crown according to the terms of the treaty of 1237.[172] Professor Duncan is of the opinion that they were 'doubtless destroyed' soon thereafter,[173] but if that surmise is correct, the suppression of the records of a shameful peace need not have occurred in 1237.

A date of September 1282, in fact, might be equally likely. Over the course of the previous summer the king's son, Prince Alexander, had fallen gravely ill. On 3 July he wrote to Edward I requesting that the physician Adam de Kirkcudbright, who controlled several benefices south of the border, be given licence to remain in Scotland for an indefinite period. The physician, he claimed, had restored him to health 'from the point of death',[174] and he wished Adam to continue indefinitely in his service lest he suffer 'irreparable damage' to his well being. This illness, coming as it did only a year after the death of Alexander III's younger son, David,[175] appears to have been the reason for delaying the prince's marriage to Marguerite of Flanders, which did not take place as planned in the autumn of October 1282, but rather in mid-November.[176] By then, moreover, Queen Margaret was also dead.[177] A growing sense of alarm over the future of the royal line at a period when its continued existence was under threat may have prompted an assessment of the kingdom's archival strengths and potential weaknesses. If the 'cancelled letters' that William de Dumfries considered so sensitive were, in fact, one or both of the notorious treaties of 1209 and 1212, the unsettled dynastic circumstances of the autumn of 1282 may well have required their disposal.[178]

METHODS OF EDITING

GENERAL REMARKS

In general the methods of editing adopted here are those found in other volumes in the *Regesta Regum Scottorum* series, with a few modifications. The collection begins with a list of 175 full texts, each numbered in chronological order. The task of ordering these is rendered simple by the fact that by the middle years of the thirteenth century it had become customary to include in royal acts a clause identifying both the place and the date of issue. Each full text is introduced by a substantial English-language summary. The names of beneficiaries are given here in modern form. Similarly, modern place names are used where possible, the exceptions being sites that no longer exist or that the editors have been unable to trace on a map. The name of the pre-1974 county is provided for each site. The Index of Persons and Places includes entries for both the medieval and modern versions of personal names and place names, as well as a National Grid Reference number for each site. In nos 1 to 333 the English-language summaries conclude with a date and, where it may be identified, a place name.

There is a critical apparatus of varying length associated with each entry. For deeds that survive as original parchment sheets this includes, first, under the heading of 'Notes', variant readings of the original text as these appear in cartulary copies, later medieval or early modern (to c. 1700) transcriptions or printed versions. Where a deed survives in more than one contemporary copy the two versions are closely collated and, if needed, explanations are offered for the choice of one version over the other. Original copies are carefully collated with medieval cartulary copies, where these survive. A description of the physical features of the document and, if appropriate, information about endorsements and sealing methods, appears next. A third heading identifies the scribe responsible for drafting the deed. The fourth ('Source') and fifth ('Printed') headings provide information about the provenance of each text, then the location of printed versions of the document, both full texts and English-language summaries (indicated by the words 'cal.' for a calendared version, 'note' for a simpler, briefer notation or 'facs.' for a reproduction in facsimile). Any additional information relating to the deed, its provenance or its context is placed in a 'Comments' section. For acts that survive only in cartulary or other copies, in place of the sections on description and hand, the critical apparatus includes a note of any rubrication associated with the document, but otherwise retains the sections headed 'Notes', 'Source', 'Printed' and 'Comments'.

As noted above, recent research on the language of English and Scottish charters offers compelling arguments in favour of distinguishing writ-charters that conveyed new gifts of land, revenue or privileges from those that merely confirmed, clarified or amplified existing grants. It shows that by Alexander III's time royal clerks were making careful use of the dispositive verbs *dare*, *concedere* and *confirmare*, choosing one, two or all three in an effort to define unambiguously the beneficiary's legal rights in relation to the obligations of the donor.[179] The editors concur, *grosso modo*, with the suggestions for revised terminology that these scholars have proposed. Thus, the English-language summaries accept the new practice of translating *dare* as 'to give', that is, to effect a gift *de novo*; *concedere* as 'to grant', in the sense of 'to allow', 'to concede' or 'to licence'; and *confirmare* as 'to confirm', with the understanding that this last should be interpreted as meaning 'to establish firmly', 'to make firm' or 'to strengthen' an earlier act.

EDITORIAL CONVENTIONS

The printed texts are intended to make the contents of Alexander III's acts available to as wide a readership as possible. The chief aim of the English-language summaries is to offer a comprehensive synopsis of the contents and purpose of each document; accordingly, these vary in length and detail. The Latin transcriptions preserve the spellings found in the originals, but some licence has been taken with punctuation and capitalisation. Medieval scribes observed few of the rules of punctuation familiar to modern readers and sometimes wrote texts that run to several lines and many dozens of words. On occasion, then, notably in the transcription of texts that survive in cartulary and other post-medieval versions, the editors have inserted a full stop to indicate the end of one section of a document and the beginning of another. Where documents survive as single parchment sheets, however, an attempt is made to insert full stops where these appear and to respect the spacing of words as the scribes laid them out. Full stops also signal other punctuation marks found in the originals, including commas, colons, inverted semi-colons and strokes. Medieval writers likewise used capital letters in a much more casual way than do modern writers, applying a full capital in one instance, a semi- or small capital in another and none at all in a third. The transcriptions that follow use capital letters in all proper nouns, including that of God, but otherwise follow the text of the original.

Thirteenth-century orthography knew few standard rules. The Latin texts here normally follow the spelling of the original, notably in the use of the letters 'c' and 't', 'u' and 'v'. The letters ' j' and 'i', minuscule and majuscule, were virtually interchangeable in this period, and here, too, the editors have tended to aim for clarity, using 'i' as a vowel and 'j' as a consonant where this is deemed appropriate, with the exception of a handful of words that begin in the modern vernacular with 'j': thus: justice, justiciar, January, June, July, Janet,

James. In French-language texts or endorsements the spelling appears as it does in the original.

Medieval scribes were inveterate abbreviators, and clerical idiosyncrasies in the use of symbols indicating contractions and abbreviations often make it possible for editors to differentiate one man's hand from that of another. Anyone who has ever had occasion to use the nineteenth- and early twentieth-century editions of medieval documents published by antiquarian and local history societies, however, will acknowledge that these textual features render it difficult to navigate medieval deeds, particularly those that run to more than a few sentences. In this edition, words in which the expansion is clear are printed extended. Where the names of persons or places end with a mark of suspension and it is difficult or impossible to posit a certain reading of the last few letters, that mark is preserved. Otherwise, the words are extended and declined in accordance with the appropriate case ending. A testing clause that begins with the word *testibus*, for example, requires the ablative case; thus, *Robert'* or *Jac'* in such a witness lists appears as *Roberto* or *Jacobo* respectively. Where the last few letters of a word are doubtful or conjectural, however, the text prints the suspended or abbreviated letters in italics. Square brackets surround words that the editors have supplied by conjecture. Gaps are indicated by three dots or empty brackets, as appropriate. In all such cases textual notes explain the length of the lacuna or suggest possible readings. Words or phrases inserted into a text by a contemporary scribe are printed between oblique strokes; deleted words are omitted in the printed text with the fact of deletion clearly indicated in the accompanying textual notes. Throughout the edited texts the full word 'et' is used in place of its abbreviated form.

ARRANGEMENT OF THIS EDITION

The contents of the book are divided into five sections.

Section one includes the full texts of acts that include a firm dating clause; these appear in chronological order. A few acts have been assigned dates that differ from those appearing in Simpson, *Handlist*. In the years since the latter was compiled, moreover, new documents have come to light. There are 163 full, dated texts in the edition.

Section two includes a further twelve acts that survive in full or almost full texts but lack a clear dating clause. In almost all cases the omission is a consequence of copyists' errors or carelessness on the part of copyists. The documents are arranged in roughly chronological order, with the earlier of the date ranges dictating the position that each act occupies in the list. Notes in the apparatus offer a rationale for the date ranges assigned to each document.

A calendar of some 155 lost deeds begins in Section three. These are acts known only from references, contemporary, early modern or modern, which make reliable mention of a deed datable to the reign of Alexander III but that has since disappeared. Section three presents a brief narrative describing some 128 such deeds, listed according to the date range that the editors have assigned to each. At the end of each entry there appear notes about the source of the information concerning the dating and a brief explanation of the provenance and context of the document.

In Sections four and five there appear acts for which no firm date range between 1249 and 1286 may be assigned. Nineteen deeds relating to secular beneficiaries are listed first, alphabetically by beneficiary, followed by eight deeds issued (or probably issued) on behalf of ecclesiastical beneficiaries, also listed alphabetically by beneficiary. Here again, editorial notes explain the reason for positing the existence of a written deed.

Last of all, the calendar notes eleven, unnumbered, 'unattributable' lost acts. Despite their best efforts the editors of this volume and Keith Stringer, the editor of *Regesta Regum Scottorum*, Vol. III, have been unable to identify these as acts belonging clearly to King Alexander III or his father Alexander II. For this reason, notices of these eleven lost acts, with a brief series of accompanying notes, appear both in this volume and in *Regesta*, Vol. III.

There is no formal bibliography, but the List of Abbreviations at the beginning of the volume offers information about the chief printed sources used in this edition, and there is a full list of all the manuscript sources of the 175 extant full texts. The comments in the critical apparatus of each document cite full bibliographical references for items that are not listed in the Abbreviations.

LIST OF SOURCES

(*a*) ORIGINALS

ABERDEEN
Aberdeen City Archives, Aberdeen City Muniments **87, 101**

AYR
Carnegie Library, Ayr Burgh Charters, B.6 **31**

BERKELEY CASTLE
Berkeley Castle, BSN **80**

DURHAM
Muniments of the Dean and Chapter, Miscellaneous Charters **98**

EDINBURGH
Edinburgh University Library, Laing Charters **12**

National Records of Scotland
GD 26 Papers of the Leslie family, Earls of Leven and Melville **10**
GD 55 Melrose Charters **16, 49, 51, 53, 71**
GD 86 Sir William Fraser Charters **7**
GD 90 Yule Collection, Charters **2**
GD 124 Papers of the Erskine Family, Earls of Mar and Kellie **41**
GD 190 Papers of the Smythe Family of Methven, Perthshire **26**
GD 212 Coldstream Charters **74**
GD 220 Montrose Muniments **19**
GD 248 Seafield Papers **65, 66**
RH 5 Documents transferred from the Public Record Office, London **27, 32, 36, 40, 67, 70, 124**
RH 6 Register House Charters **14, 45, 62**

National Register of Archives
No. 258 Moncreiffe of Moncreiffe Family, Baronets, Perthshire **13**
No. 859 Douglas-Home Family, Earls of Home **55**
No. 925 Hay Family, Earls of Erroll **11**

ELGIN
Moray District Council Record Office, Elgin Burgh Charters **69**

HADDINGTON
Colstoun House, Coalston Muniments **79**

INVERNESS

Inverness Library and Museum, Inverness Burgh Charters **3**

LONDON

British Library

Additional Charters **56**

Campbell Charters **52**

Cotton Charter XVIII **59**

The National Archives

DL 25 Duchy of Lancaster: Deeds, Series L **73**

SC 1 Special Collections: Ancient Correspondence of the Chancery and the Exchequer **29, 34, 35, 37, 38, 39, 75, 78, 86, 90, 94, 95, 96, 99, 106, 107, 112, 113, 114, 116, 117, 118, 119, 121, 123**

NEWCASTLE

Northumberland Collections Service, Swinburne (Capheaton) estate records, ZSW/ 1 **3, 25, 63, 82, 83, 84**

PERTH

Messrs Condie, Mackenzie and Co., Kinnoull Muniments **120**

(*b*) MANUSCRIPT COPIES

CAPRINGTON CASTLE

Lindores Cartulary **33, 47**

CARLISLE

Cumbria Record Office, Carlisle D and C Muniments, Register of Holm Cultram Abbey **129**

COPENHAGEN

Danish National Archives, NKR 2958 **61**

DARNAWAY CASTLE

Moray Muniments **128**

EDINBURGH

National Library of Scotland

Adv. Ch. A.4 **10**

Adv. MS. 16.1.10, Register of the Cathedral Church and Bishopric of Aberdeen **21, 28, 105**

Adv. MS. 34.4.1 Chartulary of the Hospital of the Holy Trinity, Soutra **43, 46, 48, 60, 85**

Adv. MS. 34.1.3A Register of Dunfermline Abbey **18, 20, 102, 103, 104, 115**

Adv. MS. 34.4.2 Chartulary of Arbroath Abbey **89, 127**

Adv. MS. 34.4.13 Chartulary of Newbattle Abbey **111**

Adv. MS. 34.4.14 Chartulary of Paisley Abbey **1, 76**

Adv. MS. 34.5.1 Chartulary of Kelso Abbey **50, 64**
Adv. MS. 34.5.3 Chartulary of Balmerino Abbey **30**
Adv. MS. 34.6.24 Genealogical Notes **6**
Adv. MS. 34.7.1 Chartulary of Lindores Abbey **9, 54, 58**
MS. 72 Morton Cartulary **68, 100**

National Records of Scotland
C 1 Great Seal Rolls **97**
C 2 Great Seal Register **91**
GD 45 Muniments of the Earl of Dalhousie **4, 5**
GD 90 Yule Collection, Charters **2**
GD 220 Montrose Muniments **81**
PA 5/4 Manuscript Collections of early Scottish laws etc. **61**

Scottish Catholic Archives
MS. JB1, no. 3, Registrum vetus of Glasgow **8, 17**
MS. JB1, no. 4, Liber ruber ecclesiae **108, 122**

GLASGOW
Glasgow University Library
GUA 12354, Blackhouse Charters **15**
MS. Gen 198, Red Book **108**

INVERKEITHING
Inverkeithing Burgh Records, B34 **44**

LONDON
British Library
Add. MS. 33245 **127**
Harleian MS. 3960 **42**
Harleian MS. 4693 **6**
Lansdowne MS. 326 **63**

The National Archives
C 47 Chancery Miscellanea **92, 106, 109, 125**
C 53 Charter Rolls **22**
C 66 Chancery and Supreme Court of Judicature: Patent Rolls **22, 110**
C 145 Chancery: Miscellaneous Inquisitions **88**
E 32 Justices of the Forest: Records formerly in the Treasury of the Receipt of the Exchequer **72**

MUSSELBURGH
Pinkie Castle, Fyvie Castle Muniments **77**

OXFORD
Bodleian Library
MS. Dodsworth XLV **63, 93**
MS. Lansdowne 326 **93**

(*c*) PRINTED TEXTS

Diplom. Norveg., viii, no. 9 **61**
Foedera, I. i. 353 **24**
Hay, *Sainteclaires*, 41–2 **126, 130**
Milne, *Blackfriars of Perth* **57**
Newbattle Registrum, App., Cartae Originales, App. 1, no. 6 **126, 130**

NOTES TO THE INTRODUCTION

1. *RRS*, ii, 69.
2. Nos 15, 24, 49, 72, 76, 78, 82, 93, 111, 170. Only nos 49 and 82 survive as originals.
3. See here G. W. S. Barrow, '*Omnibus probis hominibus [suis]*: the Scottish Royal General Address (*inscriptio*), c. 1126–1847', in T. Kölzer, F.-A. Bornschlegel, C. Friedl and G. Vogeler (eds), *De litteris, manuscriptis, inscriptionibus* (Wien, 2007), 58–64.
4. See, for example, no. 18.
5. Barrow, *Charters of David I*, 5–8.
6. See also nos 18, 22.
7. See here D. Broun, 'The Presence of Witnesses and the Writing of Charters', in idem (ed.), *The Reality Behind Charter Diplomatic in Anglo-Norman Britain*, ed. D. Broun (Glasgow, 2011), 235–88.
8. Nos 93, 164, 165, 166, 169, 170, 171, 172, 173, 174, 175. The texts of these acts have all been recovered or reconstructed from later medieval or early modern copies. The damage to no. 168 has rendered much of its testing clause illegible.
9. See below, 25–6.
10. The history of document-writing in England has been the subject of extensive scholarly analysis. A concise recent treatment of the evolution of charters and other instruments of conveyance may be found in J. M. Kaye, *Medieval English Conveyances* (Cambridge, 2009).
11. M. T. Clanchy, *From Memory to Written Record: England 1066–1307* (2nd edn, Oxford, 1993).
12. R. Sharpe, 'People and Languages in Eleventh- and Twelfth-century Britain and Ireland: Reading the Charter Evidence', in Broun (ed.), *The Reality Behind Charter Diplomatic*, 104.
13 Bateson, 'The Scottish King's Household', 3–43; see also Duncan, *Making of the Kingdom*, 595–610.
14. Of 161 full texts extant from Malcolm IV's reign, no fewer than 150 were issued in favour of ecclesiastical clients; there are a further thirty-two among the fifty-two deeds for which notices alone survive. The figures for William's reign demonstrate the ongoing prevalence of ecclesiastical beneficiaries: the latter account for 425 of 596 full or partial texts. *RRS*, i, 57–8; *RRS*, ii, 68–9.
15. See here the online database 'The Paradox of Medieval Scotland', available at http://www.poms.ac.uk/db/faceted/. The database includes many more acts issued in favour of secular beneficiaries than is apparent in an examination of Scoular, *Handlist* (for Alexander II) and Simpson, *Handlist* (for Alexander III).
16. D. Bates, 'Charters and Historians of Britain and Ireland: Problems and Possibilities', in M.-T. Flanagan and J. A. Green (eds), *Charters and Charter Scholarship in Britain and Ireland* (Basingstoke, 2005), 8.
17. See also nos 81, 131, 148.
18. *David I Chrs*, nos 33, 147, 172; *RRS*, i, no. 118; *RRS*, ii, no. 30; *Dunfermline Registrum*, no. 74.
19. No. 102.
20. Nos 1, 41, 42, 55, 56, 58, 81, 84, 87, 88, 91, 111, 115, 124, 126, 127, 130, 131, 139, 148, 152, 153, 157, 163, 164, 166, 168, 169. The dispositive language of charters is discussed at greater length below, 9–10.

21. *RRS*, i, 60–1; *RRS*, ii, 69–70.
22. No. 157 and, for the gift of an annual income from the ferme of Tannadice in Angus, no. 56.
23. The examples here are numerous, but see nos 41, 55, 112, 127.
24. *RRS*, i, 61.
25. Nos 2, 4, 5, 6, 7, 11, 12, 13, 16, 17, 18, 19, 25, 26, 33, 47, 51, 52, 59, 63, 65, 66, 68, 74, 79, 80, 93, 97, 100, 102, 103, 104, 105, 108, 120, 122, 128, 149, 162, 165, 171, 174.
26. E.g. nos 2, 4, 7, 12.
27. J. R. Davies, 'The Donor and the Duty of Warrandice: Giving and Granting in Scottish Charters', in Broun (ed.), *The Reality behind Charter Diplomatic*, 122–30.
28. Ibid., 130–1.
29. A. Harding, 'The Medieval Brieves of Protection and the Development of the Common Law', *Juridical Review*, new ser. 11 (1966), 115–16; *RRS*, i, 62.
30. *RRS*, v, 104.
31. Nos 27, 40.
32. See also no. 20.
33. Full forfeiture: nos 3, 49, 60, 163. Full forfeiture of £10: nos 9, 14, 41, 53, 54, 81, 156.
34. Harding, 'Medieval Brieves of Protection', 130–1, 137; *RRS*, v, 405–6, 412; *Formulary E: Scottish Letters and Brieves, 1286–1424*, ed. A. A. M. Duncan (Glasgow, 1976), 21; G. W. S. Barrow, *Robert Bruce and the Community of the Realm of Scotland* (4th edn, Edinburgh, 2005), 387–8.
35. See also below, 12–13.
36. H. MacQueen, 'The Brieve of Right in Scots Law', *Journal of Legal History*, 3 (1982), 53; idem, *Common Law and Feudal Society*, 35–214; *The Register of Brieves as contained in the Ayr MS., the Bute MS. and Quoniam Attachiamenta*, ed. T. Cooper (Stair Soc., 1946), 28–32. For the dating of the earliest extant formulary, the Berne Manuscript, see H. MacQueen, 'Scots Law under Alexander III', in N. H. Reid (ed.), *Scotland in the Reign of Alexander III 1249–1286* (Edinburgh, 1990), 77, 86–92.
37 Nos 29, 34, 35, 37, 38, 39, 78, 90, 92, 94, 95, 96, 99, 106, 107, 109, 110, 112, 113, 114, 117, 118, 119, 121, 123, 125, 146, 147, 150, 151, 155, 160, 161.
38. *Foedera*, I, i, 135; *Scone Liber*, no. 65; *Nat. MSS. Scot.*, i, no. 51; NRS, GD1/203/1; *Kelso Liber*, ii, no. 396. The text of the fourth document, from the National Records of Scotland, survives only in a transumpt of 1450 and may have been altered.
39. T. F. Tout, *Chapters in the Administrative History of England: The Wardrobe, the Chamber and the Small Seals* (6 vols, Manchester, 1920), i, 135–6n, 211n; v, 124–6; H. F. M. Prescott, 'The Early Use of *Teste me ipso*', *English Historical Review*, 35 (1920) 214–17.
40. *RRS*, v, 108–9; *RRS*, vi, 26–8.
41. Nos 15, 30, 43, 46, 48, 56, 62, 64, 78, 82, 83, 88, 89, 111, 131, 159, 167, 168. There are also indirect references to letters patent of Alexander III in nos 35 and 78. No. 142 reads *in cuius rei testimonium has nostras litteras vobis mittimus* ..., but is illegible thereafter. In no. 172, which survives only in a sixteenth-century transumpt, the copyist notes the phrase *in cuius rei testimonium*, but abbreviates the final words with the unhelpful contraction 'etc'.
42. Nos 1, 85, 132, 141, 143, 164.
43. Scoular, *Handlist*, nos 91, 116, 219, 246, 253, 306, 328; *RRS*, v, 88.
44. The circumstances leading up to the crisis of 1255 are discussed in A. Young, 'The Political Role of Walter Comyn, Earl of Menteith, during the Minority of Alexander III of Scotland', in K. J. Stringer (ed.), *Essays on the Nobility of Medieval Scotland* (Edinburgh, 1985), 139–41.
45. See below, comments to no. 22.
46. See below, 25–6.

47. P. Chaplais, *English Diplomatic Practice in the Middle Ages* (2 vols, London, 1982), i, 40, 44; see also P. Wormald, 'Charters, Law and the Settlement of Disputes', in W. Davies and P. Fouracre (eds), *The Settlement of Disputes in Early Medieval Europe* (Cambridge, 1986), 162.
48. See above, 25.
49. See also an indenture listing the muniments taken to Berwick in 1291. All are printed in *APS*, i, 107–12, 113–18 and discussed, if briefly, in J. Fergusson, 'The Public Records of Scotland (II)' *Archives*, 9 (1953), 4–5; J. M. Thomson, *The Public Records of Scotland* (Glasgow, 1922), 3–6, 28–9, 78–9, and J. Hunter, 'King Edward's Spoliations in Scotland in A.D. 1296', *Archaeological Journal*, 13 (1856), 245–9.
50. Stevenson, *Documents*, i, 73, 276–7; *APS*, i, 111; A. L. Murray, 'The Lord Clerk Register', *SHR*, 53 (1974), 124–5.
51. Barrow, 'The Scots Charter', 157.
52. Ibid., 150; see also *RRS*, vi, 19–23.
53. *CPR, 1247–58*, 121, 122.
54. *CPR, 1258–66*, 128.
55. *Close Rolls, 1251–53*, 83; *Close Rolls, 1259–61*, 368; TNA, PRO JUST 1/618 m. 23d.
56. *Close Rolls, 1259–61*, 216; see also ibid., 238.
57. *Close Rolls, 1259–61*, 278–9; *Close Rolls, 1264–68*, 202.
58. *Close Rolls, 1264–68*, 65, 88–9.
59. *CPR, 1281–92*, 211.
60. *Foedera*, i, 565.
61. TNA, PRO SC 1/20/170; *Nat. MSS Scotland*, i, no. 65.
62. The examples here are numerous: nos 90, 92, 94–6, 99, 106, 107, 109, 110, 112–14, 116–18, 121, 123, 136–8, 144, 145, 147, 151, 155, 160, 161, 170.
63 *Close Rolls, 1251–53*, 13; *Close Rolls, 1259–61*, 124.
64. *CCR, 1272–79*, 575; *CPR, 1272–81*, 327.
65. The petitions presented to parliament in England in both periods are discussed at some length in G. Dodd, 'Sovereignty, Diplomacy and Petitioning: Scotland and the English Parliament in the First Half of the Fourteenth Century', in G. Dodd, A. King and M. Penman (eds), *England and Scotland in the Fourteenth Century: New Perspectives* (Woodbridge, 2007), 175–92.
66. TNA, PRO SC 8/9/432. For a petition of 1334 in which a couple claimed that they had lost possession of another Berwick tenement following their forfeiture by Robert Bruce, see TNA, PRO SC 8/310/15492.
67. TNA, PRO SC 8/93/4612; see also *Rot. Scot.*, i, 493–4.
68. TNA, PRO SC 8/195/9734.
69. NRS, RH 5/37, 38; BL, Add. Ch. 19630.
70. NRS, RH 1/2/681. 'Kinmult' is now The Mount, 'Lillockisfeyld' is Lilac, 'Woddeflatter' is Woodflat, all in Monimail parish, Fife. *Place-Names of Fife*, iv, 592, 597–8, 607. Alexander went on to renown as standard bearer, first for the Guardians, and later for Bruce. See Barrow, *Robert Bruce*, 209.
71. See now Holford and Stringer, *Border Liberties*, 235–8.
72. Nos 198, 200, 208, 269, 322.
73. *HN*, III, ii, 288.
74. TNA, PRO JUST 1/649, JUST 1/657. The roll of the 1257 eyre does not survive. See also TNA, PRO SC 8/60/2983.
75. Holford and Stringer, *Border Liberties*, 235–7; TNA, PRO JUST 1/653, m. 25.
76. *Scotichronicon*, v, 381; no. 171; Duncan, *Making of the Kingdom*, 588; TNA, PRO SC 1/20/169; *Chron. Wyntoun*, v, 138.
77. No. 133 below; Theiner, *Monumenta*, no. CCXCVII.
78. NRS, RH 5/8, printed *APS*, i, 107–18; *Foedera*, i, 615–17.
79. B. Webster, *Scotland from the Eleventh Century to 1603* (Cambridge, 1975), 45, 124–5.

80. E.g. nos 61, 132, 313.
81. E.g. no. 293.
82. *APS*, i, 114.
83. *RRS*, i. 83.
84. NLS, Adv. MS. 16.1.10, fo. 50^{v}–51^{r}, printed in *Aberdeen Registrum*, i, 18.
85. J. Dowden, *The Bishops of Scotland* (Glasgow, 1912), 106.
86. TNA, PRO SC 8/10/452, 455; see also an early fourteenth-century rental that lists in detail the second teinds owing from secular and ecclesiastical estates throughout the north-east (*Aberdeen Registrum*, i, 55–8), showing that by this time these had become a regular part of the bishops' income.
87. *RRS*, ii, 287.
88. *Balmerino Liber*, no. 56, listed in Simpson, *Handlist* as no. 69.
89. *Balmerino Liber*, no. 1. The confirmation was copied into later versions of the cartulary, i.e. NLS, Adv. MS 33.2.5 (sixteenth century), fos 35^{r-v}; NLS, Adv. MS 35.3.13 eighteenth century, fo. 8^{v}; NLS, Adv. MS 9A.1.4 (nineteenth century), fos 371^{v}–372^{r}.
90. Ibid., no. 7. The topic is discussed briefly in G. Márkus, 'Reading the Place-Names of a Monastic Landscape: Balmerino Abbey', in R. D. Oram et al., *Life on the Edge: The Cistercian Abbey of Balmerino, Fife (Scotland)* (Pontigny, 2008), 121–4, 136–43.
91. Duncan, *Making of the Kingdom*, 563; C. J. Neville, *Native Lordship in Medieval Scotland: The Earldoms of Strathearn and Lennox, c. 1140–1365* (Dublin, 2005), 50n, 56.
92. NRS, Montrose Muniments, GD 220/1/A1/3/3, /4, both original and authentic.
93. NRS, Montrose Muniments, GD 220/1/A1/3/5, dated 22 June 1271. While a small fragment of wax remains attached to the parchment tongue of the deed, it is so defaced as to be illegible. More suspiciously still, the parchment surface of the document appears to have been scraped clean before being reused, hardly a practice one might expect in the royal writing office or a nobleman of the status of the Grahams. Some years ago, the document was photographed using ultrasensitive plates; later still, it was examined under ultraviolet light, in the hope that one of these methods might reveal the script that appears to underlie the present text. No such script was positively identified on either occasion. Altogether, the peculiarities of the document suggest that it is of dubious authenticity. The charter is noted also in Alexander Nisbet, *A System of Heraldry, Speculative and Practical*, new edn (2 vols, Edinburgh, 1916), ii, Appendix, 184, where it is misdated to the reign of Alexander II. David was also responsible for commissioning a forged charter by which King William purported to give him the lands of Kinnaber, near Montrose. *RRS*, ii, 68.
94. NRS, Montrose Muniments, GD 220/1/A1/3/6. This deed has equally peculiar features. It is dated at Scone, 13 November 1285, the same day as no. 162, long after David's death around 1272. The seal and tag are both missing. All six of the Graham documents, that is, the two authentic acts of Alexander III, the two authentic acts of Earl Malise II of Strathearn and the spurious confirmations of 1271 and 1285 (NRS, GD 220/1/A1/2–7) are in the same hand, that of the unidentified Scribe U.
95. No. 164.
96. Nos 110, 160, 282.
97. *RPS*, 1357/11/9 and /11; *RPS*, 1367/9/2.
98. TNA, PRO SC 1/20, 170, a letter of Prince Alexander inquiring after his uncle's health, dated c. 1281, and PRO, SC 1/20/171, a letter of Princess Margaret, in French, to the same effect, dated 1280. Another letter of Prince Alexander to Edward, dated March 1279, was written by Scribe O; PRO, SC 1/20/169.
99. *Melrose Liber*, no. 237.
100. See, for example, *RRS*, v, 177; *RRS*, vi, 13.

101. Nos 52, 53.
102. NRS, Montrose Muniments, GD 220/1/A/1/3/3, GD 220/A/1/3/4; both around the same date, and both genuine. NRS, Montrose Muniments, GD 220/1/A/1/5 and /6, both purporting to be near contemporary royal confirmations in favour of Sir David de Graham, are spurious. All five documents were written by the same scribe.
103. C. J. Neville, 'The Earls of Strathearn from the Twelfth to the Early Fourteenth Century, with an Edition of their Written Acts (2 vols, PhD thesis, University of Aberdeen, 1983), i, 172–200, 333; ii, 112–13.
104. *RRS*, ii, 84; G. G. Simpson, *Scottish Handwriting, 1150–1650: An Introduction to the Reading of Documents* (Edinburgh, 1973), 5–6.
105. *RRS*, v, 170.
106. *APS*, i, 107–10; *Foedera*, I, ii, 615–17. See also below, Appendix, for a discussion of the inventory.
107. See, for example, *Foedera*, I, ii, 514, 850–1. For the use of the French of Picardy in this period, see S. Lusignan, 'Langue et société dans le nord de la France: le Picard comme langue des administrations publiques (XIIIe-XIVe s.)', *Académie des inscriptions et des belles-lettres Comptes-rendus des séances*, 3 (2007), 1282–5.
108. S. Lusignan, *La langue des rois au Moyen Âge* (Paris, 2004), 181–2, 185–6, 200–1; Tout, *Chapters*, v, 116; *APS*, i, 119–23.
109. TNA, PRO SC 1/20/170. Prince Alexander was already by then lord of Man, and there are a few written acts issued under his authority dating from the years after 1275. In none of these cases, however, did he have a seal of his own. In No. 171 below, in fact, his father states quite clearly that the charter recording Prince Alexander's gift of land to the canons of Whithorn was authenticated by the royal seal, because as still a minor the prince did not yet have a seal of his own.
110. *Statuta Ecclesiae Scoticanae*, i, lxxiii, n2.
111. TNA, PRO SC 1/20/171.
112. No. 167; Watt, *Graduates*, 214–15.
113. Ibid., 162–3; no. 153.
114. Holford and Stringer, *Border Liberties*, 254, 264–5.
115. Anderson, *ES*, ii, 87; discussed in *The Miracles of St Æbbe of Coldingham and St Margaret of Scotland*, ed. R. Bartlett (Oxford, 2003), xxxv–xxxviii.
116. Watt, *Graduates*, 210–12, 280–1, 590–3.
117. Watt, *Graduates*, 85–6, 203–4; see also *Handbook of British Chronology*, 181.
118. James Tait, 'Kenleith, Robert (*d.* 1273)', rev. Norman H. Reid, *Oxford Dictionary of National Biography* (Oxford, 2004).
119. Watt, *Graduates*, 58, 85–6, 166.
120. K. J. Stringer, 'The Scottish "Political Community" in the Reign of Alexander II (1214–49)', forthcoming. We wish to thank Professor Stringer for his permission to cite this work in advance of its publication.
121. Bateson, 'The Scottish King's Household', 32. Bateson's translation of the Anglo-Norman term *countrerouler* as 'control' is inaccurate; the passage makes it clear that the author of the treatise had in mind the formal engrossing of copies of royal acts.
122. NRS, RH 5/25, 26.
123. Nos 64, 166, 214, 216; see also nos 189, 196, 271, 287, 292, 293, 305, 324.
124. Stevenson, *Documents*, i, 73–8.
125. *APS*, i, 112, 113–17.
126. See, for example, Laing, *Seals*, i, 5; Stevenson and Wood, *Seals*, i, 25; J. H. Stevenson, *Heraldry in Scotland* (2 vols, Glasgow, 1914), i, 134. Even that most careful of paleographers, John Maitland Thomson, made this error; he did, however, correctly note its use in nos 86 and 116; Thomson, *Public Records of Scotland*, 62.

127. Simpson, 'Kingship in Miniature', 133, which discusses the use of the small seal.
128. Duncan, *Kingship of the Scots*, 151.
129. Ibid., 137–8.
130. Duncan, *Making of the Kingdom*, 556, discussed in Simpson, 'Kingship in Miniature', 137.
131. L. Larchey, *Ancien armorial équestre de la toison d'or et de l'Europe au 15e siècle* (Paris, 1890), 256.
132. See no. 181 below; Duncan, *Kingdom of the Scots*, 558–9.
133. Simpson, 'Kingship in Miniature', 136–7, an interpretation preferable to that offered in Duncan, *Kingship of the Scots*, 152–3.
134. No. 25.
135. Nos 3, 7, 11, 12, 13, all dated before the end of 1252.
136. *Chron. Fordun*, i, 296; Watt, *Graduates*, 211. The various strands that make up Fordun's chronicle and the dates assigned to each of these are unravelled in D. Broun, 'A New Look at *Gesta Annalia* Attributed to John of Fordun', in B. E. Crawford (ed.), *Church, Chronicle and Learning in Medieval and Early Renaissance Scotland: Essays Presented to Donald Watt on the Occasion of the Completion of the Publication of Bower's* Scotichronicon (Edinburgh, 1999), 9–30 and, more recently still, in *Scottish Independence and the Idea of Britain from the Picts to Alexander III* (Edinburgh, 2007), esp. 215–68.
137. Simpson, 'Kingship in Miniature', 139; Duncan, *Making of the Kingdom*, 556.
138. See here Davies, 'The Donor and the Duty of Warrandice', 120–65.
139. See above, 23.
140. Laing, *Seals*, ii, 3–4; W. de G. Birch, *History of Scottish Seals* (2 vols, Stirling and London, 1905–7), i, 27–8 and plates 10–11; Stevenson and Wood, *Seals*, i, 5.
141. Simpson, 'Kingship in Miniature', 131. B. A. McAndrew, *The Historic Heraldry of Scotland* (Woodbridge, 2006), 24; and C. Campbell, 'The Royal Arms in the Grunenberg Roll', *Scottish Genealogist*, 14, pt 2 (1967), 48; see also Birch, *History of Scottish Seals*, i, 27–8 and plates 10–11.
142. Laing, *Seals*, i, 4–5; see also Stevenson and Wood, *Seals*, i, 5, and Birch, *History of Scottish Seals*, i, 28–9.
143. Nos 49, 51, 53, 55, 69, 71, 73, 74, 80, 87, 98, 101, 131, 133–5, 139–43 and, apparently, 148. These include a magnificent detached seal, now TNA, PRO SC 13/H 22, probably from no. 52, and a fine cast, NRS RH 17/1/14, from no. 53, both in favour of Melrose abbey.
144. None is more striking than the two examples appended to documents produced in the Flemish chancery, nos 135, 140.
145. See here P. Stafford, 'The meanings of hair in the Anglo-Norman world: masculinity, reform, and national identity', in M. van Dijk and R. Nip (eds), *Saints, Scholars, and Politicians: Gender as a Tool in Medieval Studies* (Turnhout, 2005), 155–71; R. Bartlett, 'Symbolic Meanings of Hair in the Middle Ages', *TRHS*, 6th ser., 4 (1994), 43–60.
146. Laing, *Seals*, i, 3; Stevenson and Wood, *Seals*, i, 3; Duncan, *Making of the Kingdom*, 553–4; *RRS*, i, 87; *RRS*, ii, 91–2.
147. J. Bannerman, 'The King's Poet and the Inauguration of Alexander III', *SHR*, 68 (1989), 120–49; Duncan, *Kingship of the Scots*, 131–49.
148. *RRS*, v, 119–26.
149. Bateson, 'The Scottish King's Household', 31–2. Bateson's argument that the mention of the privy seal is anachronistic (ibid., 6–7) is clearly in need of revision.
150. See the illustrations in *RRS*, v, 194–5.
151. No. 86.
152. Bateson, 'The Scottish King's Household', 31; see also Tout, *Chapters*, v, 150–1.
153. Thomson, *Public Records of Scotland*, 61.
154. *RRS*, v, 135–57.

155. See also nos 115, 152.
156. *RPS*, A1265/1; no. 153.
157. For William I and Robert I, see the map at the end of the volume in *RRS*, ii and *RRS*, v; see also McNeill and MacQueen (eds), *Atlas of Scottish History to 1707* (Edinburgh, 1996, repr. 2000), 161–8.
158. McNeill and MacQueen (eds), *Atlas of Scottish History*, 167.
159. Kenleith from Dunfermline, Gamelin and William Fraser from St Andrews, Inverkeithing from Dunkeld, Wischard from Glasgow and Charteris from East Lothian.
160. S.T. Driscoll, 'The Archaeological Context of Assembly in Early Medieval Scotland – Scone and its Comparenda', in A. Pantos and S. Semple (eds), *Assembly Places and Practices in Medieval Europe* (Dublin, 2004), 73–6, 81–91; D. Broun, 'The Origin of the Stone of Scone as a National Icon', in R. Welander et al. (eds), *The Stone of Destiny: Artefact and Icon* (Edinburgh, 2003), 183–4.
161. *ER*, i, 7, 8, 15, 24; see also *APS*, i, 100.
162. J. M. Gilbert, *Hunting and Hunting Reserves in Medieval Scotland* (Edinburgh, 1979), 24, 82, 85, 215; see also no. 164.
163. See no. 273 and the several references cited in the Comments section.
164. Above, 28.
165. Thomson, *Public Records of Scotland*, 3.
166. Nos 166, 214, 216.
167. *Foedera*, I, ii, 616.
168. King John's letter to William, noting that he sends Eustace de Vescy, Robert de Ros and others to escort the king of Scots southward, is found in *Rotuli litterarum patentium in Turri Londinensi asservati, Vol. 1, 1201–1216*, ed. T. D. Hardy (London, 1835), 91; Louis's oath is found in *Foedera*, I, i, 104.
169. See here A. A. M. Duncan, 'John King of England and the Kings of Scots', in S. D. Church (ed.), *King John: New Interpretations* (Woodbridge, 1999), 255–64; idem, *Making of the Kingdom*, 241–6.
170. *Foedera*, I, ii, 616; Duncan, *Making of the Kingdom*, 245.
171. *Chron. Fordun*, i, 275–8; Duncan, *Making of the Kingdom*, 248, 252; G.W. S. Barrow, *Kingship and Unity: Scotland 1000–1306* (2nd edn, Edinburgh, 2003), 63.
172. Stones, *Anglo-Scottish Relations*, lxv–lxvii, 48n.
173. Duncan, 'John King of England', 259.
174. *Foedera*, I, ii, 611.
175. June 1281; *Chron. Fordun*, i, 307.
176. No. 135. Marguerite was already by then on her way to Scotland for the wedding; *Foedera*, I, ii, 613.
177. She died in May 1275; *Chron Fordun*, i, 305.
178. Although he cannot have known, William's caution proved salutary: in January 1284 Prince Alexander, the last of Alexander III's three children, died. By March 1286, of course, so had the king, and the last of his line, Margaret the Maid of Norway, perished in the autumn of 1291. Among the earliest of Edward I's acts in the determination of what became known as the Great Cause was a command to search the archives of English and Scottish monasteries for evidence of English claims to lordship over the Scots.
179. Davies, 'The Donor and the Duty of Warrandice', 120–65; see, in particular, the discussion of the findings of Richard Sharpe at 122–32. More generally, see the Paradox of Medieval Scotland website, http://www.poms.ac.uk/index.html.

THE ACTS OF ALEXANDER III

Dated Acts, Full Texts, 1–163

Undated Acts, Full Texts, 164–175

Lost Acts, 176–330

Unattributable Acts: Alexander II or Alexander III

DATED ACTS

1 Announces that, on the advice of his magnates, he gives licence to the abbot and convent of Paisley to repair the fishpond which they have customarily had on the River Leven near Dumbarton, and afterwards to use it to their advantage, on condition that they leave free entry and exit to the thread of the stream in accordance with the laws and assizes of the kingdom. Edinburgh, 1 June a.r. 1 [1250].

Alexander[a] Dei gr*ati*a rex Scottorum om*n*ib*us* probis homi*n*ib*us* tocius terre sue salutem. Sciatis nos de consilio magnatum nostroru*m* dedisse abbati et co*n*uentus de Passelet dilectis et fidelib*us* nostris licenciam et plenariam potestatem reficiendi et reparandi stagnum piscarie sue quam habere solebant super aquam de Leuen iuxta Dunbertan et exinde suum commodum faciendi ita tamen quod relinquat in filo aque eiusdem piscarie liberum et exitum secundum leges et assisas regni nostri. In cuius rei testimoniu*m* sigillum nostrum apponi fecim*us* huic scripto. Testibus venerabili patre epis*copo* Wilelmo Glasgwen'. Waltero Cumyng' Wilelmo de Menteth Alexandro senescallo Roberto de Ross et Roberto de Merness' Apud Edynburg' primo die Junii anno regni nostri primo.

NOTE. [a] Decorated initial.
RUBRIC. Littera licencie et plenarie potestatis reficiendi stagnum piscarie sue in Leuen per Alexandrum regem.
SOURCE. NLS, Adv. MS. 34.4.14, Chartulary of Paisley Abbey, fo. cxxxi^r.
PRINTED. *Paisley Registrum*, 215; *APS*, i, 425. There is a transcript at NLS, Adv. MS. 35.4.9, fo. 163.

2 Grants and by this charter confirms to John de Pitcairn the gift that his kinsman Hugh de Abernethy made him of the whole land of Innernethy on the west side of the pow. To be held in feu and heritage, as Hugh's charter to John bears witness, saving the king's service. Edinburgh, 3 June a.r. 1 [1250].

A .[a] D*e*i gr*ati*a rex Scott*orum*[b] om*n*ibus p*r*obis ho*min*ib*us* toci*us* t*er*re sue salutem . Sciant p*rese*ntes et futuri nos co*n*cessisse et hac carta n*ost*ra co*n*firmasse donac*io*nem illa*m* qua*m* Hug*o* de Abernithyn'[c] fecit Joh*ann*i de Petcarn'[d] consaguineo[e] suo p*ro* homagio et s*er*uic*io* suo de tota t*er*ra de Inn*er*nith'[f] ex occidentali p*ar*te polli[g] . Tenend*am* et habend*am* eidem Joh*anni*[h] et h*er*edib*us* suis de p*redict*o Hug*one* et h*er*edib*us* suis in feodo et h*er*editate p*er* rectas diuisas suas et cu*m* om*n*ibus p*er*tin*en*ciis suis ita lib*er*e quiete plenarie et honorifice sicut carta d*ict*i Hug*onis* inde p*re*fato Joh*ann*i pleni*us* conf*ec*ta iuste testatur saluo n*o*stro s*er*uic*io* . Test*ibus* . Rob*er*to de Ros'[i] . Rob*er*to de Meyn*ers*[j] . Gilbert*o* de Haya . Joh*ann*e de Vallib*us* . Ric*ardo* marescall*o*'. Thom*a* fil*io* Ranulf*i* ap*u*d Castr*um* Puell*arum* t*er*c*io* die Junii . Anno regni d*omi*ni reg*is* primo.

NOTES. [a] Initial A only in B. [b] Scotorum in B. [c] Abernethyn' in B. [d] Petcarn in B. [e] Sic, consanguineo; corrected in B. [f] Innernithyn' in B. [g] Gaelic *poll*, 'pool, pond, inlet'. [h] Interlined over caret in B. [i] Ross' in B. [j] Meyns in B.

ENDORSED. Carta *con*firmacionis d*om*ini Regis de Innarnethy (fifteenth-century hand, probably the same as in B (see below).

DESCRIPTION. 17.3 cm x 5.1 cm; fold, 1.4 cm. Sealing: a tag, 0.6 cm broad, is passed through a single slit and bears a fragment of the first version of the king's small seal, 3.7 cm in diameter, in white wax. Only a small central portion of the seal is now visible.

HAND. Scribe A.

SOURCE. Original. NRS, Yule Collection, Charters, GD 90/1/18/1 = A; GD90/1/18/2 = B, a notarial transumpt of the act dated 5 Oct. 1415. Transcribed here from A.

COMMENT. The endorsement on B reads: 'Transsumptum carte confirmationis domini regis super terra de Innernethey 1415'.

3 Grants to his burgesses of Inverness that no one may take poinds of them save for their own debts, forfeitures or pledges. Commands his sheriffs and bailies north of the Mounth to distrain those who owe debts to the burgesses of Inverness and strictly forbids all from poinding the said burgesses or initiating suits against them in violation of this grant on pain of his full forfeiture. Scone, 3 December a.r. 2 [1250].

Alex*ander* Dei gratia rex Scott*orum* . omnib*us* probis hominib*us* tocius terre sue salutem . Sciatis qu*od* concessimus burgensib*us* nost*ris* de Inuernis vt nullus eorum nametur in regno n*ost*ro pro aliquo nisi pro suo p*ro*prio debito forisf*ac*to aut plegiagio . Pret*er*ea mandamus et p*re*cipimus vicecomitib*us* n*ost*ris et balliuis ex aquilonali p*ar*te de Moneth' constitutis vt om*n*es illos in eo*rum* balliis qui debita d*ic*tis burgensib*us* nostris debuerint . que r*at*ionabilit*er* p*ro*bare potuerint . ad eadem debita eis iuste et sine dilacione reddend*a* iuste distringant . Firmit*er* aut*em* inhibemus ne quis debita que eis debet iniuste detinere aut sectam ip*s*os contr*a* pred*ic*tam concessionem n*o*stram qua*m* eis fecimus de namis suis iniuste uexare presumat . sup*er* n*ost*ram plenariam forisf*ac*turam . Testibus . R . electo Dunkeldens'. R . ab*ba*te de Neubotil' . Alano hostiario just*iciario* Scocie et Gilb*er*to de Haya . apud Schona*m* t*er*c*i*o die Decembris anno regni d*omi*ni reg*is* se*cun*do.

ENDORSED. A charter for the burgh of Invernes re fredom (fourteenth or fifteenth century).

DESCRIPTION. 18.8 cm x 6.6 cm. Sealing: the fold is now torn away and the tag missing. A detached fragment of the first great seal in white or yellow wax survives, showing only a portion of the obverse side: the king seated on a throne.

HAND. Scribe A.

SOURCE. Original. Inverness Library and Museum, Inverness Burgh Charters, B1/1/18/3.

PRINTED. Fraser-Mackintosh, *Invernessiana,* 31 (trans.); *RMS*, ii, no. 804 (cal.); *Appendix to the General Report together with Local Reports of the Commissioners on the Municipal Corporations of Scotland, 1836* (London, 1836, repr. London, 1969), 97 (note). These sources mistakenly assign the act to the reign of Alexander II.

COMMENT. A modern transcript appears in NRS, RH 1/1/1.

4 Grants and by this charter confirms to Roger Wyrfaut the gift that Richenda daughter of Winfred (Humphrey) de Berkeley made him of the land that belonged to Hugh son of Waltheof in the territory of Conveth (now Laurencekirk), with the common pasture of

Scotston (both in Kincardineshire). To be held in feu and heritage, as Richenda's charter bears witness, saving the king's service. Crail, 9 March a.r. 2 [1250].

Alex*ander* D*ei* gra*ti*a rex Scott*orum* om*n*ibus probis hominib*us* tocius te*rr*e sue. sal*ute*m. Sciatis nos *con*cessisse et hac carta n*os*tra *con*firmasse donac*ion*em illam q*ua*m Rychenda filia Wynfridi de Berkeley fecit Rogero Wyrfaut' de tota te*rr*a illa que fuit Hugonis filii Waldeui in te*rr*itorio de Cuneueth'. Tenenda et h*abe*nda eidem Rogero et heredib*us* suis v*e*l ei*us* assignatis de p*re*dic*t*a Richenda et h*er*edib*us* suis in feodo et h*er*editate p*er* rec*t*as diuisas suas cu*m* co*m*muni pastura de Scottistun'. et cu*m* omnib*us* iu*s*tis p*er*tinenciis suis. lib*er*tatib*us* et aysiame*n*tis ad d*ict*am te*rr*am spe*c*tantibus. adeo lib*ere*. Q*u*iete. Plenarie. et honorifice. sicut carta *dict*e Richende p*re*d*ict*o Rogero exinde co*n*fe*c*ta pleni*us*. iuste testatur. saluo s*er*uic*i*o n*os*tro. Tes*tibus* Walt*er*o Byseth. Dauid de Hadington'. Joh*anne* de Hyrdmannistoun' et Will*elm*o de Haya. Apud Karal. nono die Marcii anno regni d*omi*ni reg*is* sec*un*do.

SOURCE. NRS, Register of the Priory of St Andrews, GD 45/27/8, fo. xlix[r].
PRINTED. *St Andrews Liber*, 334–5.

5 Grants and by this charter confirms to the priory of St Andrews the gift that Simon son of Simon of Kinnear made them of five oxgangs of land and four acres in the territory of Kedlock (Fife), which start from the acre of the brethren of St Lazarus and stretch as far as a syke on the south side and thence extend to the land that belonged to the late Reginald, towards the west side, up to the boundary of the land of Matthew, late brother of John of Kinnear, and thus northwards to a path that lies near the hill that is called Adkar, together with the toft that lies next to the same land. Further grants three other oxgangs of land that start on the north side of the same toun and extend as far as the muir in length, and in breadth, from the west side of the muir to the east side of the same in circumference. To be held in perpetual alms, as Simon's charter bears witness, saving the king's service. Haddington, 25 April a.r. 2 [1251].

Alexand*er* Dei gr*ati*a rex Scott*orum* *om*nibus p*ro*bis hominib*us* tocius te*rr*e sue sal*ute*m. Sciatis nos concessisse et hac carta n*os*tra co*n*firmasse donacione*m* illa*m* q*ua*m Simo*n* filius Simonis de Kyn' fecit Deo et ecclesie beati sancti Andree apostoli . et canonicis ibide*m* Deo seruientib*us* et i*n* posterum s*er*uituris de quinque bouatis te*rr*e et q*ua*tuor acris i*n* te*rr*itorio de Kathlath. scilicet de duab*us* bouatis et quatuor acris qu*e* i*n*cipiu*n*t ab acra fratru*m* sancti Lazari. et se extendunt usq*ue* ad unu*m* siket. ex p*ar*te australi. et inde se extendunt ad te*rr*am q*ue* fuit quonda*m* Reginaldi u*er*sus p*ar*tem occidentale*m* usq*ue* ad metas te*rr*e Mathei quonda*m* f*ra*tris Joh*an*nis de Kyn'. et sic u*er*sus aq*ui*lonem usq*ue* ad qu*a*md*a*m simita*m* q*ue* iacet iuxta monte*m* q*ue* uocat*ur* Adkar' cu*m* tofto ad eande*m* te*rr*a*m* adiacente. Et de t*ri*bus aliis bouatis te*rr*e q*ue* i*n*cipiu*n*t ex p*ar*te boriali ei*us*de*m* ville. et se exte*ndu*n*t* usq*ue* ad mora*m* i*n* longitudine. Et i*n* latitudine ab occidentali p*ar*te more usque ad orientalem partem eiusdem more per circuitum. Tenenda et habenda eisde*m* cano*n*icis in puram et perpetua*m* elemosina*m* adeo lib*er*e. quiete. plenarie. et honorifice sicut carta d*ic*ti Symonis p*re*d*ic*tis cano*n*icis exin*de* co*n*fecta plenius. iuste testatur. saluo s*er*uicio n*os*tro. Test*ibus* Rob*erto* Meyn*er*is camer*ario*. Gilb*er*to de Haia. Joh*anne* de Vallib*us*. et Dauid de Meyners. Apud Hadingt*un*. xx°. q*ui*nto die Ap*ri*lis anno regni d*omi*ni regis s*ecun*do.

RUBRIC. Confirmacio de Kathlac (in red).
SOURCE. NRS, Register of the Priory of St Andrews, GD 45/27/ 8, fos lxxxij[r–v].
PRINTED. *St Andrews Liber*, 294.
COMMENT. 'Adkar' is now lost.

6 Grants and by this charter confirms to William de Hay the gift that his brother Gilbert de Hay made him of two ploughgates in the feu of Errol (Perthshire), one of which Thomas Segan held of Gilbert, and the second of which formerly belonged to the monks of Cupar, in exchange for twelve acres that Gilbert's cottars hold and the oxgang that John de Kinninmonth now hold. To be held in feu and heritage, as Gilbert's charter bears witness, saving the king's service. Roxburgh, 29 April a.r. 2 [1251].

Alexander Dei gratia rex Scottorum omnibus probis hominibus totius terre sue etc. Sciatis nos[a] concessisse et hac carta nostra confirmasse donationem illam quam Gilbertus de Haya fecit Willielmo de Haya fratri suo. de duabus carrucatis[b] terre in feodo[c] de Eroll[d]. de una[e] quam quondam Thomas Segan tenuit de parte eiusdem Gilberti. et de illa[f] carrucata[g] terre quam aliquando monachi de Cupro tenuerunt propter duodecem acras quas cottarii dicti Gilberti tenent. et propter unam bovatam terre quam Johannes de Kynman tenet[h]. Tenendum et habendum eidem Willielmo et heredibus suis de predicto Gilberto et heredibus suis. in feodo et hereditate. per suas rectas divisas. cum libertatibus et asiamentis ad dictas duas carrucatas[i] terre \pertinentibus/[j]. adeo quiete libere plenarie et honorifice sicut carta dicti Gilberti predicto Willielmo exinde[k] confecta plenius testatur. saluo seruitio n*os*tro. Testibus[l] Roberto de Wymes[l] camerario nostro, Johanne de Vallibus et Johanne Airdmanston[m]. Apud arcem[n] de Roxbrugh[o]. 29 Aprilis. anno regni n*os*tri 2[do].

NOTES. [a] Nobis in B. [b] Carucitis in B. [c] Feodo suo in B. [d] Erole in B. [e] Word missing in both A, B. [f] Illo in B. [g] Carucita in B. [h] Tenuit in B. [i] Carucitas in B. [j] Word not interlineated in A. [k] Ex inde in B. [l] Sic, for Meners. [m] Birmanstone in B. [n] Arcem nostram in B. [o] Roxburghe in B.
RUBRIC. In margin of A: Carta originaria de Layes (late seventeenth century).
SOURCE. NLS, Adv. MS. 34.6.24, Genealogical Notes, pp. 430–1 = A; BL, Harleian MS. 4693, fo. 34[v] = B. The original, believed to have been among the muniments of the Hay family of Leys, is now lost. A is a handwritten MS collection of several hundred pages of excerpts concerning genealogies, collected between 1707 and 1717. It includes various materials relating to Fife, St Andrews priory and Aberdeen, but also other items. B is found among transcripts and copies of early charters compiled by James Balfour of Kinnaird, Lord Lyon. This transcription is from A.
COMMENT. A modern transcript appears in NRS, RH 1/1/1.

7 Grants and by this charter confirms to Malcolm son of Duncan and Eva sister of Maldouen earl of Lennox the gift that the earl made them of the lands of 'Glaskhel' and Barnego (Stirlingshire) and of a ploughgate and a half in Kilsyth (Stirlingshire), together with the advowson of the church of Moniabrock. To be held by Malcolm and Eva in feu and heritage, as the earl's charter bears witness, saving the king's service. Roxburgh, 30 April a.r. 2 [1251].

Alex*ander* Dei gr*ati*a rex Scott*orum* omnib*us* probis hominib*us* toci*us* t*er*re sue sal*ute*m . Sciatis nos concessisse et hac carta n*ost*ra confirmasse donac*i*onem illam q*ua*m Maldouen*us* comes de Leuenax fecit Malcolmo filio Duncani et Eue sorori ips*i*us comitis de t*er*ris de Glaskhel' . Brengoen' . et de vna carucata t*er*re et dimidia de Kelnasydhe . cum donac*i*one ecc*les*ie de Moniabrocd' . Tenenda*s* et habenda*s* d*ict*is Malcolmo et Eue et eor*um* heredib*us* de p*re*dic*t*o comite et he*re*dibus suis in feodo et *he*reditate p*er* suas r*ec*tas diuisas . et c*um* om*ni*b*us* iustis p*er*tine*n*ciis suis lib*er*tatib*us* et asiame*n*tis ad d*ic*tas t*er*ras et ecc*le*siam p*er*tine*n*tib*us* . adeo *li*bere quiete . plenarie et honorifice . sicut carta d*ic*ti comit*is* p*re*dictis Malcolm*o* et Eue exinde conf*ec*ta pleni*us* . iuste testat*ur* . saluo s*er*uici*o* n*ost*ro . Test*ibus* Alex*andro* senescall*o* . Walt*er*o Byseth' . Eym*er*o de Macusuuell' . Joh*anne* de Vallib*us* et Will*el*mo de Hawden' Apud Rok*is*burc' . tricesimo die Ap*ri*lis anno regni *domini* reg*is* sec*und*o .

DESCRIPTION. 18.6 cm x 7.6 cm; fold 2.4 cm. Sealing: a tag, 1.2 cm broad, is passed through a single slit and bears a fragment of the first great seal, 5.9 cm in diameter, in white wax. Only a small central portion of the seal is now visible. At the top right side of the fold, in a contemporary hand, there appear the letters 'Rai'.
HAND. Scribe A.
SOURCE. Original. NRS, Sir William Fraser Charters, GD 86/2.
PRINTED. Fraser, *Carlaverock*, ii, 405–6 (facs.); Fraser, *Lennox*, ii, 405–6 (facs.); Fraser, *Pollok*, i, 123; Fraser, *Facsimiles*, no. 51.
COMMENT. Modern transcripts appear in NRS, RH 1/1/1; NRS, GD 212/1/126, item 5. 'Glaskhel', once located in the parish of Campsie, is now lost.

8 Takes under his firm peace and protection William bishop of Glasgow, his men and all his lands, and strictly prohibits anyone from causing them injury or harm, on pain of his full forfeiture. Roxburgh, 30 April a.r. 2 [1251].

Alexander Dei gratia rex Scottorum omnibus probis hominibus tocius terre sue salutem. Sciatis nos venerabilem patrem Willelmum episcopum Glasguensem. terras suas et homines suos et uniuersas eorundem possessiones sub firma pace et protectione nostra iuste suscepisse. Quare firmiter prohibemus ne quis eis malum iniuriam molestiam aut grauamen aliquid[a] inferre presumat iniuste super nostram plenariam forisfacturam. Test*ibus* Patricio comite de Dunbar'. Alexandro senescallo. et Roberto de Meyners camerario. apud Rokesburg' tricesimo die Aprilis anno. regni. regis. secundo .

NOTE. [a] Sic, aliquod.
SOURCE. SCA, MS. JB 1, no. 3, Registrum vetus of Glasgow, fo. 56^{v}.
PRINTED. *Glasgow Registrum*, i, no. 202.

9 Grants to the abbot and convent of Lindores that they should hold the whole of their woods in the feu of Fintray (Aberdeenshire) in free forest. Strictly prohibits anyone from felling timber or hunting there without their licence, on pain of his full forfeiture of £10. Kinghorn, 20 May a.r. 2 [1251].

Alexander Dei gratia rex Scotorum omnibus probis hominibus tocius terre sue salutem. Sciatis quod concessimus abbati et conuentui de Lundor'[a] ut habeant et teneant totum boscum suum in feodo de Fyntreth in liberam forestam. Quare firmiter prohibemus ne quis in dicto bosco. sine eorum licencia secet aut venetur super nostram plenariam foresf\ac/turam decem librarum. Testibus Gilberto de Haya, Johanne de Vallibus et Johanne de Hyrdmanston'. Apud Kingorne xx° die Maii anno regni domini regis secundo etc.

NOTE. [a] Printed version has Lundoris.
RUBRIC. Liberta (sic) foreste de Fyntre.
SOURCE. NLS, Adv. MS. 34.7.1, Chartulary of Lindores Abbey, fo. 8v.
PRINTED. *Lindores Liber*, no. 8.

10 Commands the provosts of Perth to cause the Friars Preachers of Perth to have from the fermes of the burgh one wey of good wax annually on the Feast of the Nativity of John the Baptist, which his father, King Alexander II, gave them when the church was dedicated. Scone, 31 May a.r. 2 [1251].

Alexander Dei gratia rex Scotorum prepositis suis de Perth salutem. Mandamus vobis et precipimus. quatinus de firmo burgi nostri de Perth habere faciatis fratribus predicatoribus de Perth quolibet anno vnam pisam bone cere die natiuitatis sancti Johannis Baptiste quam inclite[a] recordacionis[b] dominus rex Alexander pater noster eis dedit ad luminare ecclesie sue in dedicacione[c] eiusdem. facientes de eisdem firmis dictos fratres pas[si][d] singulis septimanis vno die. Testibus. Roberto de Ros'. Roberto de Meyners camerario et Dauid[e] de Louthor'[f] vicecomiti de Pert' apud Scon'[g] vltimo die Maii anno regni domini regis secundo.

NOTES. [a] Inclyte in B. [b] Recordationis in B. [c] Dedicatione in B. [d] Tear in A; letters supplied from B. [e]Adam (sic) in B. [f]Louchoir in B. [g] Sconam in B.
RUBRIC. Carta de firmis regis Alexandri de Craigy et Maler et de firmis ville de Pert (fifteenth-century hand, contemporary with the transumpt); vnam pisam cere (sixteenth century).
SOURCE. NLS, Adv. Ch. A.4, item ii, a fifteenth-century transumpt by Bishop Wardlaw of St Andrews of three royal grants to the Friars Preachers = A; NRS, Papers of the Leslie family, Earls of Leven and Melville, GD 26/3/1109 = B. See also no. 57 below.
PRINTED. Milne, *Blackfriars of Perth*, no. 2; *HMC*, vi, 713 (where it is noted but misdated).

11 Grants and by this charter confirms to Gilbert de Hay the gift that his brother, William earl of Mar, made him of the whole of the land of Dronley (Angus). To be held as the earl's charter bears witness, saving the king's service. Scone, 26 July a.r. 3 [1251].

Alexander Dei gratia rex Scottorum . omnibus probis hominibus tocius terre sue salutem . Sciatis nos concessisse et hac carta nostra confirmasse donationem illam quam Willelmus comes de Mar' fecit Gilberto de Haya de tota terra sua de Drunlav . Tenendam et habendam predicto Gilberto et heredibus suis de prefato comite et heredibus suis adeo libere . quiete . plenarie et honorifice sicut carta dicti comitis predicto Gilberto exinde confecta plenius . iuste testatur saluo seruicio nostro . Test*ibus* W . Cumyn com*ite* de Meneth' . Alano host*iario* justi*ciario* Scocie, Joh*a*nne de Bayol' et Rob*erto* de Meyners camerario apud Schon' . vicesimo sexto die Julii anno regni d*omini* regis tercio .

ENDORSED. De Dronley (contemporary hand).
DESCRIPTION. 18.5 cm x 6.1 cm; fold 1.8 cm. Sealing: a tag, 2.3 cm broad, is passed through a single slit, and bears a fragment of the first great seal, 4.2 cm in diameter, in natural wax varnished brown. Only the central portion of the seal is now visible.
HAND. Scribe A.
SOURCE. Original. Old Slains, Erroll Muniments, Easter Moncreiffe, no. 11; photographic copy in NRS, RH1/6/11.
PRINTED. *Spalding Misc.*, ii, 307–8; *Aberdeen-Banff Illustrations,* iv, 696 (abridged).

12 Grants and by this charter confirms to Alexander de Montfort the gift that his brother, John de Montfort, made him of fifty acres of land in the territory of Athelstaneford (East Lothian) from his demesne called 'Dremmesfeld', as far as the stream that is the boundary between Drem (East Lothian) and Athelstaneford; of ten acres of land of his demesne, that is, of the ploughland that lies on the north side of the church; of the two cottars' tofts next to the nunnery of Haddington; and of six oxgangs of land in the same toun, with three tofts pertaining to the said six oxgangs of land; together with three bondmen who formerly held the said six oxgangs at ferme under the same John, with all their chattels and household. To be held in feu and heritage, as John's charter bears witness, saving the king's service. Kincardine, 19 August a.r. 3 [1251].

Alex*ander* Dei gracia rex Scott*orum* omnib*us* probis hominib*us* toci*us* terre sue sal*ut*em . Sciatis nos concessisse et h*ac* carta n*ost*ra confirmasse donac*io*nem illam q*ua*m Joh*an*nes de Monte Forti fecit Alex*andro* de Monte Forti frat*ri* suo p*ro* homagio et s*er*uic*i*o suo de qu*in*q*ua*ginta ac*ri*s t*er*re in t*er*ritorio de Elstaneford' de dominio suo quod uocat*ur* Dremmesfeld' . et usq*ue* ad riuulu*m* q*ui* est diuisa int*er* Drem' et Elstaneford' . et de decem ac*ri*s t*er*re de suo d*omini*o . scil*ice*t de cult*ur*a sua que iacet ex aquilonari parte eccl*es*ie et de duob*us* toftis cottari*orum* iuxt*a* domos monialiu*m* de Hadyngton' u*er*sus occidente*m*. et de sex bouatis t*er*re in eadem villa cu*m* t*ri*b*us* toftis ad d*ic*tas sex bouatas t*er*re p*er*tine*n*tib*us* . et eciam cu*m* t*ri*b*us* bondis qui d*ic*tas sex bouatas t*er*re q*uo*ndam ad firma*m* de ip*s*o Joh*ann*e tenueru*n*t cu*m* om*n*ib*us* catallis et sequela eo*rum* . Tenenda et habenda eidem Alex*andro* et h*er*edib*us* suis de p*re*dic*t*o Johanne et h*er*edib*us* suis in feodo et h*er*editate cu*m* om*n*ib*us* suis p*er*tine*n*ciis lib*er*tatib*us* et asiame*n*tis ad ip*s*as t*er*ras sp*e*ctantib*us* . adeo lib*ere* . quiete . plenarie . et honorifice . sicut carta p*re*dicti Joh*ann*is p*re*fato Alex*andro* exinde conf*e*cta pleni*us* . iuste testat*ur* . saluo s*er*uicio n*ost*ro . Test*ibus* Alex*andro* Cumyn' comite de Buchan'. Rob*erto* de Meyn*er*s cam*erari*o . Will*elm*o de Brethyn' . Gilb*er*to de Haya et Joh*ann*e de Vallibus . apud Kyncard' . nonodeci*m*o die Aug*us*ti . ann*o* regni d*omini* reg*is* ter*ti*o .

ENDORSED. 1. Adilstanfurd gevin be kyng Alex'. 2. Carta Alex[ri]3.[tij] 1252 terrarum de Elstanford (both sixteenth century).
DESCRIPTION. 15.8 cm x 13.5 cm; fold 2.0 cm. Sealing: a tag, 2.1 cm broad, is passed through a single slit, and bears a fragment of the first great seal, 6.5 cm in diameter, in white wax. Only a portion of the seal is now visible on both obverse and reverse sides.

A small parchment tie has been cut from the right side of the tag.
HAND. Scribe A.
SOURCE. Original, Edinburgh University Library, Laing Charters, no. 12, Box 1.
PRINTED. *Laing Chrs*, no. 7 (cal., where it is misdated to 1252); *East Lothian Deeds*, 5–6.
COMMENT. A modern transcript appears in NRS, RH 1/1/1.

13 Grants and by this charter confirms to Matthew de Moncreiffe the gift that Roger de Mowbray made him of the whole land of Moncreiffe and the whole land of Balgonie (Perthshire), for which Roger has remitted and quitclaimed to Matthew the ancient ferme customarily rendered to him from those lands. To be held for homage and service, that is, for the twentieth part of the service of one knight, as Roger's charter bears witness, saving the king's service. Edinburgh, 20 October a.r. 3 [1251].

Alexander Dei gratia rex Scottorum omnibus probis hominibus tocius terre sue salutem . Sciatis nos concessisse et hac carta nostra nostra[a] confirmasse donacionem illam quam Rogerus de Mubray fecit Matheo de Muncref' et heredibus suis de tota terra de Muncref' et de tota terra de Balconathin' per suas rectas diuisas pro homagio et seruicio suo scilicet vicesima parte seruicii vnius militis pro qua idem Rogerus pro se et heredibus suis remisit et quietum clamauit dicto Matheo et heredibus suis veteram firmam quam de dictis terris sibi reddi consueuit . Tenendam et habendam dicto Matheo et heredibus suis de predicto Rogero et heredibus suis per suas rectas diuisas cum omnibus libertatibus pertinenciis et aisiamentis ad predictas terras spectantibus adeo libere quiete plenarie et honorifice sicut carta predicti Rogeri predicto Matheo exinde confecta plenius iuste testatur saluis seruiciis nostris . Testibus venerabili patre Ricardo episcopo Dunkeld'. Roberto de Ros. Roberto de Meiners' camerario. Johanne de Vallibus et Johanne de Hirdmaniston'. Apud Castrum Puellarum vicesimo die Octobris anno regni domini regis tertio.

NOTE. [a] Word is repeated in original.
ENDORSED. Carta confirmationis regis de Muncreff (contemporary hand).
DESCRIPTION. 21.6 cm x 8.1 cm; fold 1.8 cm. Sealing: a tag, 3.8 cm broad, is passed through a single slit, with a fragment of the first great seal, measuring 6.1 cm in diameter, in natural wax, still visible. Attached to the front left of the fold is a small parchment tie, once attached to the seal.
HAND. Scribe A.
SOURCE. Original. Moncreiffe of Moncreiffe Family, Moncreiffe Writs, Bundle 1, no. 7.
PRINTED. *Moncreiffs*, i, opp. p. 12 (facs.); ii, 636–7. A modern transcript appears in NLS, Adv. MS. 34.3.25, fo. 244.

14 Commands the sheriff and bailies of Linlithgow, when it should be necessary, to compel the provosts and collectors of fermes of his burgh of Linlithgow, on pain of his full forfeiture of £10, to pay to the nuns of Manuel (West Lothian) annually at Pentecost and St Martin the fermes and renders from the burgh and bailie of Linlithgow which they have by gift of the king's ancestors. Linlithgow, 21 April a.r. 3 [1252].

A . Dei gr*ati*a rex Scott*orum* . vicecom*iti* et ball*iu*is suis de Linlithq[v] sal*utem* . Mandam*us* vob*is* et firmiter p*re*cipim*us* quatinus p*re*positos burgi n*os*tri de Linlithq^{v} et firmarios n*os*tros in ballia v*es*tra cu*m* necesse fuerit arti*us* compellatis . ut sine occasione aliqua et sup*er* n*os*tram plenaria*m* forisf*ac*turam decem librar*um* . singulis annis ad t*er*minos Pentecost*en* . et s*anc*ti Martini . u*e*l saltem infra octo dies a p*redic*tis t*er*minis . satisfacia*n*t monialibus de Manuel' de firmis et redditib*us* quos h*abe*nt ex donis an*te*cess*orum* n*os*tror*um* in burgo et ballia de Linlithq^{v}. Q*uo*d si qui eor*um* hoc facere noluerint . forisf*ac*-t*u*ram decem librar*um* ad opus n*os*tr*u*m ab eis capiatis nich*il*omin*us* ip*s*os p*er* possessiones et bona sua co*m*pellentes ad satisfaciend*um* sine dilac*i*one d*ic*tis monialib*us* sup*er* memoratis firmis et redditibus . q*uo*s r*ati*onabi*li*ter monstr*ar*e pot*er*unt s*ibi* ab omnis deb*iti* . Test*ibus* Walt*er*o Cumyn' com*ite* de Meneth' . W . com*ite* de Mar' camerar*io* et Alex*andro* senescall*o* . apud Linlithq^{v} vicesimo p*ri*mo die April*is* . anno regni nost*ri* tert*i*o.

ENDORSED. Vicecomiti . et balli*vi* . de Linlitq^{v} (contemporary hand; probably the same as the scribe's).
DESCRIPTION. 16.3 cm x 6.2 cm, L x 4.8 cm, R. Sealing: formerly sealed on a tongue cut from right to left across the bottom of the deed, now torn away.
HAND. Scribe A.
SOURCE. Original. NRS, Register House Charters, RH 6/49.
PRINTED. *Fragmenta Scoto-monastica*, App., xlii.
COMMENT. A modern transcript appears in NRS, RH 1/1/1.

15 Commands the provosts of Dumbarton to give the Friars Preachers of Glasgow £10 annually from the fermes of the said burgh, one half at Martinmas and the other at Pentecost. Edinburgh, 23 April a.r. 3 [1252].

Alexander Dei gracia rex Scocie prepositis suis de Dunbretan salutem. Mandamus vobis et precipimus quatinus pro die quo in qualibet septimana caritatiue pascimus fratres predicatores de Glasgu eisdem fratribus vel eorum certo attornato habere faciatis singulis annis de firmis burgi [nostri][a] de Dunbretan decem libras medietatem. videlicet ad festum sancti Martini et aliam medietatem ad Pentecosten. In cuius rei testimonium has nostras literas patentes vobis transmittimus. Testibus venerabilibus patribus Dauid et W. Sancti Andree et Glasguensis episcopis. W. Cumyn comite de Menethet, W. comite de Marr camerario. Apud Edinburgum vicesimo tercio die Aprilis anno regni domini regis tercio.

NOTE. [a] MS rubbed away; word supplied by conjecture.
RUBRIC. 1. Carta Regis ... ta (some letters illegible) in litera capitula Glasguen' de decem librorum de firme de Dumbarton' (contemporary with transumpt). 2. This is about 1240 that King Alexander granted this charter (sixteenth century).
SOURCE. Glasgow University Library, GUA 12354, Blackhouse Charters, no. 1, a transumpt dated 21 October 1304, sealed by the Dean and Chapter.
PRINTED. *Glasgow Friars Munimenta*, no. 3; Hamilton, *Lanark and Renfrew*, 190–1.

16 Grants and by this charter confirms to the abbot and convent of Melrose the sale by Richard Bernard de Fairnington, knight, of the meadow of Fairnington (Roxburghshire) that is called East Meadow. To be held as Richard's charter bears witness, saving the king's service. Newbattle, 8 June a.r. 3 [1252].

Alex*ander* Dei gr*ati*a rex Scott*orum* . om*n*ibus probis hominibus tocius terre sue sal*ute*m . Sciatis nos concessisse et hac carta n*ost*ra confirmasse vendic*io*n*e*m illam q*ua*m Ricardus Burnard de Farningdun miles . fecit abb*a*ti et conuentui de Melros' de prato de Farni*n*gdun q*uo*d vocat*ur* Estmedu . Tenendum et habendum d*ic*tis abb*a*ti et conuentui de Melros' . adeo lib*er*e . quiete . plenarie . et honorifice . sicut carta pred*ic*ti Ricardi Burnard eisdem abb*a*ti et conuentui exinde confecta plenius . iuste testatur . saluo s*er*uic*i*o [nostro][a]. Test*ibus* . [W][1] . Cumyn com*ite* de Meneth' . Alex*andro* Cumyn com*ite* de Buchan' . W . comite de Mar' camerar*io* . Rob*er*to de Ros' . et Eymero de Macc*us*well apud Neubotil octauo die Junii . anno regni nost*ri* tert*io* .

NOTE. [a] MS torn; letters supplied by conjecture.

ENDORSED. Confirmac*i*o prati de Fa[rni]ngdun (contemporary hand; probably the same as the scribe's).

DESCRIPTION. 17.8 cm x 7 cm; fold 2.2 cm. Sealing: on a tag, 11.0 cm broad, is appended the second version of the king's small seal, 4.2 cm in diameter, in white wax. The image is slightly damaged at the edges, but the words DEI GRATIA REX SCOTTORUM around the enthroned figure of the king are clearly visible. There are casts of the obverse and reverse of this seal in NRS, RH 1/17, Drawer 2, nos 15, 16.

HAND. Scribe A.

SOURCE. Original. NRS, Melrose Charters, GD 55/336.

PRINTED. *Melrose Liber*, i, no. 336.

17 Grants and by this charter confirms to St Kentigern and the church of Glasgow the gift that Isabella de Valognes, lady of Kilbride, made them of fifteen librates of land in the feu of Kirkpatrick (Kirkcudbrightshire), namely the whole of her forest called Dalquhairn, by the bounds that were drawn on the day the gift was made, or by the bounds that the bishop shall determine by inquest if he so chooses. If, by such an extent, the fifteen librates cannot be determined, Isabella will assign another fifteen librates elsewhere from other lands. To be held in free, pure and perpetual alms, as Isabella's charter and its confirmation by John de Balliol bear witness, saving the king's service. Roxburgh, 12 November a.r. 5 [1253].

Alex*ander* Dei gratia rex Scott*orum* omnibus probis hominibus tocius terre sue salutem. Sciant presentes et futuri nos concessisse et hac carta nostra confirmasse donacionem illam quam Isabella de Valloniis domina de Killebrid' fecit pro salute anime sue parentum et successorum suorum et pro anima Dauid comitis[a] mariti sui Deo et beato Kenteg' et ecclesie Glasg' de quindecim libratis terre in feodo de Kirkepatric scilicet de tota foresta sua que vocatur Dalkarn' prout extenta fuit die huius donacionis uel secundum visum proborum virorum extendi poterit si venerabilis pater Willelmus episcopus Glasg' hoc elegerit. Ita videlicet quod si quid deerit de quindecim libratis terre in terra predicta de Dalkarn' dicta Isabella illud ei assignabit in proxima terra sua eidem terre coniuncta in loco competenti. Tenendam et habendam dicte ecclesie Glasg' et predicto episcopo et successoribus suis inperpetuum in liberam puram et perpetuam elemosinam ita libere quiete plenarie et honorifice sicut carta domine Isabelle et confirmacio Johannis de Balliolo eis inde plenius confecte iuste testantur saluo seruicio nostro. Test*ibus*. M. abbate de Melros'. Willelmo comite de Mar' camerario. Roberto de Ros. Waltero de Morauia. Eymero de Maxwelle et Ricardo Mariscallo. Apud Rokeburg'. xii die Nouembris anno regni nostri quinto .

NOTE. [a] Sic, Comin.
SOURCE. SCA, MS. JB 1, no. 3, Registrum vetus of Glasgow, fo. 67^{v}.
PRINTED. *Glasgow Registrum*, i, no. 201; ii, no. 503, the latter a transumpt dated 14 January 1544.
COMMENT. The feu of Kirkpatrick was located in the present-day parish of Irongray.

18 Announces that in the year 1253, on the Wednesday before the feast of St Thomas the Apostle, at Stirling, Emma daughter and heiress of the late Gilbert de Smeaton, widow, in the presence of the king and the magnates of his council, willingly acknowledged that the land of Smeaton (Midlothian), in the feu of Musselburgh, which her ancestors at one time held of Dunfermline abbey, and about which she brought suit by royal letters of mortancestry, was the proper land of Dunfermline abbey, and had been unjustly alienated from it, the land having been given in free and perpetual alms to it by King David. The king has seen David's charter and had it read in his presence; the abbot and convent also have confirmations of the charter from his ancestors. Therefore, Emma has renounced forever all rights and claim to the land and has quitclaimed it to the use of the monastery. The king confirms the rights and pertinents of the monastery in the land of Smeaton and commands that every year, while Emma is alive, the abbot and convent of Dunfermline should pay her twenty merks for her maintenance; after her death, however, her heirs shall have no right to this payment. The abbot and convent have pledged themselves to observe this agreement. Stirling, 17 December a.r. 3 [1253].

A[a] Dei gr*ati*a rex Scott*orum* om*n*ibu*s* probis ho*min*ibu*s* tociu*s* te*r*re sue. p*re*sentibu*s* et futur*r*etis[b] ad quos p*re*sentes litt*er*e p*er*uen*er*int sal*utem*. Sciatis q*uo*d anno gr*ati*e. M°. CC°. L iii°. die M*er*curi*e* p*roxim*a an*te* fest*um* s*anc*ti Thome ap*osto*li ap*u*d St*ri*uelin Emma filia et h*er*es q*uo*ndam Gilb*er*ti de Smythetun'. vidua et i*n* sua potestate lib*er*a et ligia *con*stituta. in pre\sencia/ n*os*tra et magnatum de n*os*tro *con*silio sponte recognouit q*uod* terra de Smythetun' i*n* feodo de Muskelb' cu*m* p*er*tinenciis q*ua*m an*te*cessores sui aliq*uo* temp*or*e tenuerant de domo de Dunf'. et q*ua*m ip*s*a pecierat p*er* litte*r*as regias de morte an*te*cessoris. fuit et e*ss*e debuit p*ro*p*ri*a te*r*ra monast*er*ii de Du*n*f' et a d*ic*to monast*er*io alienata iniuste. tanq*ua*m te*r*ra q*ue* data fuit i*n* lib*er*am et p*er*petua*m* elemosinam eidem monast*er*io. ab antecessore n*os*tro clare memorie Rege Dauid cui*us* cartam exinde *con*fectam *con*speximu*s*. et q*ua*m fecimus in p*re*sencia n*os*tra legi. et de q*ua* abb*as* et conu*entus* ei*us*de*m* monast*er*ii h*ab*ent confirmac*i*ones an*te*cesso*rum* nostro*rum* vnde d*ic*ta Emma pro se et h*er*edibu*s* suis i*n* p*er*petuum renu*n*ciauit cora*m* nobi*s* et p*re*dictis magnatibu*s* n*os*tris toti iuri et clamio q*uod* ip*s*a u*e*l sui aliq*uo* te*m*p*or*e habueru*n*t et h*ab*ere potuerunt i*n* eade*m* te*r*ra. Et d*ict*um ius tale q*ua*le fuit p*ro* se et h*er*edibu*s* suis p*er* fustu*m* et bacculu*m* total*iter* nob*is* ad opus d*ict*i monast*er*ii. reddidit. Resignauit.

et q*ui*etum clamau*it*. p*ro*mittens fidel*ite*r quod sup*er* d*ict*a t*er*ra. ip*s*a aut heredes sui *contra* d*ictu*m monast*er*ium n*u*llo temp*ore* quomodo mouebunt. Hoc aut*em* terra ex *con*cessione d*i*cte Emme q*ua* ex tenore d*i*ctaru*m* cartaru*m* an*te*cessoru*m* no*s*troru*m* ius d*i*cti monast*er*ii i*n* d*i*cta t*er*ra de Smithetun' liq*ui*de p*er*pen*d*entes. ea*m* cu*m* p*er*tinenciis d*i*cto monast*er*io de Dunf' ad exemplu*m* an*te*cessoru*m* no*s*troru*m* duxim*us* confirmandam. Precepim*us* insup*er* *con*patientes i*n*edie d*i*cte mulieris abb*a*ti et conue*n*tui d*i*cti monast*er*ii de Dunf'. ut sing*u*lis annis q*ui*bus d*i*cta mulier uix*er*it xx[ti]. m*a*rcas ei ad suam sustentac*io*nem p*er*soluant. ita q*uo*d ip*s*a defuncta. h*er*edes sui nichil iuris in ip*s*is. xx[ti]. m*a*rcis valeant uendicare. Et hoc iidem abb*a*s et con*uentus* taliter. Fac*ere*. fidelit*er* manucep*er*unt. Test*ibus*. ven*er*ab*i*li p*at*re. C. ep*iscop*o Dunblan'. Ric*ardo* abb*a*te de Camb*us*kin'. Walt*er*o Cumi*n* comit*e* de Meneth'. Alexandro Cumin comite de Buch'. justici*ario* Scoc*ie*. Will*elm*o comit*e* de Mar'. cam*er*ar*io*. Alex*andro* senescall*o*. Rob*er*to de Ros. Nich*olao* de Soulis'. D*aui*d de Graha*m*. mag*istro* Gamellin'. Will*el*mo cap*e*ll*a*no et Alex*andro* de Correbrig' cl*er*icis no*str*is. Joh*anne* Blundo. et Joh*anne* Saluain. ap*ud* Str*i*uelin. xvii°. die Decemb*ris*. anno regni nostri. V°.

NOTES. [a] Decorated initial. [b] Sic, futuris.
RUBRIC. Alexander rex filius Alexandri regis (in red and blue).
SOURCE. NLS, Adv. MS. 34.1.3A, Register of Dunfermline Abbey, fo. xvij[r].
PRINTED. *Dunfermline Registrum*, no. 82, including a partial facsimile, ibid., after p. 48.
COMMENT. A modern transcript appears in NRS, RH 2/2/5. See also no. 182, below.

19 Grants and by this charter confirms to David de Graham the gifts made to him by several others, namely, by Malcolm earl of Fife of lands in the barony of Earl's Calder (Midlothian); by Patrick earl of Dunbar of the land of Dundaff (Stirlingshire); by Roger de Quincy earl of Winchester of land in the territory of Dalcove and Mertoun (Berwickshire); by Maldouen earl of Lennox of the lands of Mugdock and Strathblane (Stirlingshire); by Duncan earl of Carrick of land in the territory of Girvan (Ayrshire); by Alexander the steward of the land in Strathgryfe that is called Spango (Renfrewshire); by Roger de Mowbray of lands in Cunningham (Ayrshire); by Malcolm son of the earl of Lennox of the land of Strathblane in Lennox (Stirlingshire); by Henry de Graham of the toun of Clifton (Midlothian); by William Galbraith of a part of the land in the territory of Kincaid (Stirlingshire); by Henry de Ashkirk of the land in the barony of Oliver Castle (Peeblesshire) called 'Minnauer'; by Alwin de Callendar of a part of the land in the territory of 'Varia Capella' (Stirlingshire); by John de Carrick of two pennylands in Carrick; by Adam de Polwarth of the land of Catscleugh (Stirlingshire); by Maurice son of Galbraith of land in the territory of Kincaid; by Richard brother of Geoffrey of land in Hillington (Renfrewshire); by Philip de Hillington of land in the territory of Hillington (Renfrewshire); by Geoffrey brother of Richard of a part of the land of Hillington; and by John Machudri of land in the territory of Kincaid. To be held by David and his heirs in feu and heritage, as the infeftors' charters bear witness, saving the king's service. St Andrews, 27 December a.r. 5 [1253].

. Alex*ander*[a] Dei gr*ati*a rex Scott*orum* . om*n*ibus probis ho*minib*us toc*ius* terre sue sal*ute*m . Sciant presentes et futuri nos concessisse et hac carta n*ost*ra confirmasse donac*ione*m illam q*ua*m Malcolm*us* com*es* de Fyf' fecit Dauid de Graham' de quib*us*dam t*er*ris in baronia de Caledou*er* cum p*er*tinenciis suis . Et donac*ione*m illam q*ua*m Pat*ricius* comes de Dumbar' fecit eid*e*m Dauid de t*er*ra de Dundaf' . cu*m* p*er*tinenciis suis . Et donac*ione*m illam q*ua*m Rog*er*us de Quency com*es* Wynton' fecit eid*e*m D*aui*d . de quadam p*ar*te t*er*re in t*er*ritorio de Dalcoue et de M*er*ton' cu*m* p*er*tinenciis suis . Et donac*ione*m illam q*ua*m Maldoueny com*es* de Leuenax' fecit eid*e*m D*aui*d de t*er*ris de Mucraw . et de Stratblachan' cu*m* ear*um* p*er*tinenciis . Et donac*ione*m illam q*ua*m Duncan*us* com*es* de Carrik' fecit eid*em* . D*aui*d . de q*ua*dam t*er*ra in territorio de Innirgarvan' . cu*m* p*er*tinenciis suis . Et donac*ione*m illam q*ua*m Alex*ander* Sen*escallus* fecit eid*em* Dauid de q*ua*dam t*er*ra in Stratgrif' . que vocat*ur* Spangok' . cu*m* p*er*tinenciis suis . Et donac*ione*m illam q*ua*m Rog*er*us de Mubray fecit eid*e*m Dauid de quib*us*dam t*er*ris in Cunin*g*ham' cu*m* p*er*tinenciis suis . Et donac*ione*m illam q*ua*m Malcolm*us* filius comitis de Leuenax' fecit eid*em* . D*aui*d . de t*er*ra de Stratblacha*n* in Leuenax' cu*m* p*er*tinenciis suis . Et donac*ione*m illam q*ua*m Henr*icus* de Graham' fecit eid*e*m . Dauid . de villa de Cliftu*n* cu*m* p*er*tinen*ciis* suis . Et donac*ione*m illam q*ua*m Will*elmus* Galbrath' fecit eid*em* . Dauid . de quadam p*ar*te terre in t*er*ritorio de Kyncath' cu*m* p*er*tin*enciis* suis . Et donac*ione*m illam q*ua*m Henr*icus* de Haschirch' fecit eide*m* . Dauid . de q*ua*dam t*er*ra in baronia Castri Oliueri . que vocat*ur* Minnau*er* cu*m* p*er*tin*enciis* suis . Et donac*ione*m illam q*ua*m Alewin*us* de Kalentyr' fecit eid*e*m Dauid de q*ua*dam p*ar*te t*er*re in t*er*ritorio Varie Capelle' . cu*m* p*er*tin*enciis* suis . Et donac*ione*m illam q*ua*m Joh*annes* de Carrik' fecit eid*em* . Dauid . de duab*us* denariatis t*er*re in Ca[rrik'][b] cu*m* p*er*tin*enciis* suis . Et donac*ione*m illam q*ua*m Adam de Poulwrth' fecit eide*m* . Dauid . de t*er*ra de Cattiscloch' cu*m* p*er*tin*enciis* suis . Et donac*ione*m illam q*ua*m Mauricius filius Galbrath' fecit eid*em* . Dauid . de q*ua*dam t*er*ra in t*er*ritorio de Kincath' cu*m* p*er*tin*enciis* suis . Et donac*ione*m illam q*ua*m Ricard*us* frat*er* Galfridi fecit eid*em* . D*aui*d . de q*ua*dam t*er*ra in Hyliniston' cu*m* p*er*tin*enciis* suis . Et donacione*m* illam q*ua*m Philipp*us* de Hyliniston' fecit eid*em* .Dauid . de quadam t*er*ra in t*er*ritorio de Hy[linist]on'[c] . cu*m* p*er*tin*enciis* suis . Et donac*ione*m illam q*ua*m Galfridus frat*er* Ricardi fecit eid*em* Dauid de q*ua*dam p*ar*te t*er*re in Hyliniston' cu*m* p*er*tin*enciis* suis . Et donac*ione*m illam q*uam* Joh*anne*s Machudri fecit eidem D*aui*d de quadam t*er*ra in t*er*ritorio de Kincath' cu*m* p*er*tinenciis suis . Tenendas et habendas eid*e*m Dauid et heredib*us* suis u*e*l suis assignatis . de p*re*dictis infeudatorib*us* et eorum heredib*us* . in feodo et hereditate p*er* suas r*e*ctas diuisas . et cu*m* om*n*ib*us* iustis p*er*tinenciis suis . in bosco et plano . in t*er*ris et aquis . in pratis et et pas[cui]s[b] . in moris et maresiis . in stagnis et molendinis . et cu*m* om*n*ib*us* aliis ad d*i*ctas t*er*ras iuste p*er*tinentib*us* . ita lib*ere* . quiete . plenarie et honorifice . sicut carte pred*ictorum* infeudantiu*m* prefato Dauid exinde confecte pleni*us* . iuste testant*ur* . saluo seruic*i*o n*ost*ro . Test*ibus* . ven*er*abili pat*r*e . C . ep*iscop*o Dumblan' .W . Cumyn' com*ite* de Meneth' . Alex*andro* Cumyn' com*ite* de Buchan' just*iciari*o Scoc*ie*. W . com*ite* de Marr' camer*ari*o . Rob*er*to de Ros' . Nich*olao* de Soulis' . Thom*a* filio Ranulph' . Dauid de Louchor'. et Joh*anne* Blundo ap*ud* S*anc*tum Andr*eam*' . xx° vij° . die Decembr*is* . anno regni n*ost*ri q*ui*nto .

NOTES. [a] Decorated initial. [b] MS surface is rubbed away; letter supplied by conjecture. [c] Hole in MS; letters supplied by conjecture.
ENDORSED. King Allexander his chairtour \confirmacoun/ to David llord Graeme of Dundaf and many other landis (seventeenth century). There is possibly one other (early modern?) endorsement, which is now obscured by an attempt to repair the parchment.
DESCRIPTION. 19.8 cm x 16.8 cm; fold 2.0 cm. Sealing: only a fragment of the tag, 1.5cm broad, inserted through a single slit, remains.
HAND. Scribe A.
SOURCE. Original. NRS, Montrose Muniments, GD 220/2/1/12.
PRINTED. Fraser, *Lennox*, ii, 13–15; *HMC*, iii, 386, no. 12 (cal.).
COMMENT: 'Minnauer' is a problematic place name: it is possibly Castlehill of Manor in Peeblesshire, but is not the same site as the 'Meners' of no. 166. W. J. Watson, *The History of the Celtic Placenames of Scotlan*d (Edinburgh, 1926, repr. 1993), 383; but see also ibid., 399–400.

20 Grants to the abbot and convent of Dunfermline that no one may take poinds of them or the men dwelling on their land of Dunduff (Fife) for any reason save for their own debts, forfeitures or pledges, saving the rights of the royal burghs. Strictly forbids anyone from disturbing them in defiance of this grant, on pain of his full forfeiture. Edinburgh, 4 February a.r. 5 [1254].

A[a] Dei gr*ati*a rex Scott*orum* om*n*ibus p*r*obis ho*min*ibus toci*us* t*er*re sue s*al*ut*em*. Sciatis q*uo*d concessim*us* abb*at*i et con*uen*tui de Dunf' ut nullus namos suos u*e*l ho*minum* suor*um* mantiu*m*[b] in t*er*ra de Dunduf' u*e*l in aliis t*er*ris suis capiat p*ro* alicui*us* debito forisf*ac*to v*e*l plegiagio nisi pro eor*un*de*m* p*r*op*r*io debito forisf*a*cto pleg*iagi*o saluis burgis n*os*tris. Quare firmit*er* p*ro*hibemus ne quis cont*ra* hanc[c] *con*cessione*m* n*ost*ram eos vexare p*re*sumat i*n*iuste sup*er* nos*tr*am plenariam forisfacturam. Testi*bus* W. Cumi*n* comit*e* de Men'h. Alex*andro* Cumi*n* comite de Buch' justic*iario* Scoc*ie* et Rob*erto* de Ros apud Castr*um* Puell*arum* iiii° die Februar*ii* anno regni n*ost*ri V°.

NOTES. [a] Decorated initial. [b] Sic, manentium. [c] Nostram crossed out here.
RUBRIC. Vt nullus capiat namos nostros uel hominum nostrorum manencium in terra nostra pro alicuius debito forisfacto vel plegiagio' nisi pro eorundem proprio debito forisfacto vel plegiagio.
SOURCE. NLS, Adv. MS. 34.1.3A, Register of Dunfermline Abbey, fo. xvii^{v}.
PRINTED. *Dunfermline Registrum*, no. 84.
COMMENT. A modern transcript appears in NRS, RH 2/2/5.

21 Commands John his chamberlain and Fergus justiciar of Scotia and the sheriffs of Aberdeen and Banff to cause payment to be made to Peter bishop of Aberdeen of the teinds of the royal fermes from the thanages in these sheriffdoms and second teinds from the royal profits of justice there, to which the bishop has a right by gift of King Alexander II. Edinburgh, 12 May a.r. 5 [1254].

Alex*ande*r Dei gr*ati*a rex Scott*orum* Joh*ann*i cam*er*ario suo et Fergusio justic*iario* suo ex parte boreal*i* Scocie vicicom*i*tib*us*q*ue*[a] de Ab*er*den' et de Banff sal*ut*em. [Quam][b] intelleximu*s* p*at*rem n*ost*r*um* dedisse d*omi*no Petr*o* e*pisco*po Ab*er*donen' et ecc*les*ie eiusdem deci*m*as de om*nibus* firmis thanagior*um* *nost*rorum et exitib*us* curiar*um* n*ostr*ar*um* ma*n*dam*us* vobis et p*re*cipim*us* q*ua*ten*us* p*re*d*ic*to d*omi*no epi*scop*o et eius successorib*us* de p*re*dictis decimis re*spo*nderi faciat*is*. Datum ap*ud* Edynburgh' iiii[to] yd*us* Maii anno regni n*ost*ri q*ui*nt*o*.

NOTES. [a] Sic, vicecomitibusque. [b] Word missing; supplied here by conjecture.
RUBRIC. A late (sixteenth-century) hand has (mistakenly) added *Anno domini 1219*.
SOURCE. NLS, Adv. MS. 16.1.10, Register of the Cathedral Church and Bishopric of Aberdeen, fos 50[r]-50[v].
PRINTED. *Aberdeen Registrum*, i. 17–18, 55–8.
COMMENT. Several aspects of this charter are problematic, but in balance the decision here is to treat it as genuine. John the chamberlain and Fergus the justiciar are not otherwise attested, and the form and contents of the dating clause are unusual. No original charter of Alexander II is extant, but in 1360, King David II commanded the sheriffs of Aberdeen and Banff to pay the bishop second teinds based on his review of 'letters' of his predecessors, Alexander II and Alexander III (*RRS*, vi, no. 234). Earlier still, William I confirmed similar gifts made by his brother Malcolm IV and grandfather David I (*RRS*, ii, no. 251). In the opening years of the fourteenth century, Bishop Henry Cheyne of Aberdeen petitioned King Edward I of England for restoration of these payments, claiming that 'he, his church and his predecessors have been in full sasine of second tithes from time immemorial, and notably in the time of King Alexander and more recently in the time of the present King Edward', but that the chamberlain of Scotland was now withholding payment (PRO, TNA, SC 8/10/452; see also SC 8/10/455). The text of the act of William I noted above has been described as 'inflated or tampered with to say the least' (*RRS*, ii, 287), much as this document appears to have been. It may be the case that the muniments of the bishopric were lost, destroyed or dispersed in the aftermath of the war that began in 1296, and that Bishop Henry sought confirmation of the cathedral church's possessions and privileges so that valuable property rights would not be threatened in future. A rental contemporary with the cathedral register lists in detail the second teinds owing from secular and ecclesiastical estates throughout the north-east (*Aberdeen Registrum*, i, 55–8), suggesting that by the fourteenth century these were still (or had now become), a regular part of the bishops' income.

22 Announces changes in the membership of the Scottish royal council by reciting how, with the advice of twenty-five of his magnates (named), together with 'many other barons', he removed twenty-six persons (named) from his council and their offices owing to lack of merit. He undertakes not to admit these men, their accomplices or their supporters to his counsels, to the conduct of the business of the realm, to his grace or to any sort of intimacy until they have made full amends, by concord or judgement, for their offences, which he shall compel them to do by every lawful means. He further states that if the kingdom of Scotland should be invaded by a foreign prince he is to be allowed to admit and invoke the assistance of the magnates thus removed from his council, and any others as he sees appropriate, to come to his aid. Commands, with the advice of King Henry and his magnates, that at least fifteen of the first group (named), who have been appointed to his council, the government of his realm and the guardianship of his body and that of his queen, shall remain in office for a full seven years beginning at the feast of the translation of St Cuthbert next. If one or more of them should be removed from office as unworthy or should die, then, with the advice of the remaining councillors, one or more others shall be substituted in his or their place. If sheriffs, foresters and other officials are removed from office owing to misconduct he will place others in their stead, again with the advice of his councillors. He undertakes not to remove custody of royal castles from persons to whom they are now entrusted except with the common counsel of his advisors. He also promises King Henry that he will treat the queen with the affection and consideration that befit her, and he ratifies and agrees to the undertakings and concessions that his bishops and magnates have made with King Henry. Patrick earl of Dunbar swears on his behalf that he will faithfully and inviolably observe all these provisions and Alexander subjects himself to papal discipline and ecclesiastical censure should he fail to do so. When the period noted above is complete, King Henry is to restore this letter to him or his heirs in good faith and thenceforth it is to have no weight. Roxburgh, 20 September a.r. 7 [1255].

Vniuersis Christi fidelibus ad quos presens scriptum peruenerit Alex*ander* Dei gratia rex Scottorum salutem. Nouerit vniuersitas vestra quod cum karissimus pater noster et dominus H*enricus*[a] rex Angl*ie* illustris pro honore et vtilitate nostra et regni nostri ad marchiam regnorum Angl*ie* et Scot*ie* sui gratia personaliter accessisset nos ad instanciam ipsius regis et de consilio magnatum nostrorum scilicet venerabilium patrium in Christo. W. Glasg'. R. Dunkeld'. et P. Abberden'[b] episcoporum et domini. G. electi Sancti Andree de Dunfermel'. de Kelchou'. de Geddewurth'. et de Neweboltle[c] abbatum. H [d]. comitis de Fif'. P. comitis de Dunbar[e]. N. comitis de Carrik [f]. H.[g] comitis de Strathern'. Alex*andri* senescalli Scot*ie*. Roberti de Brus. Alani hostiar*ii*. Walteri de Morruia[h]. Dauid de Lindes'. Willielmi[i] Brechyn'[j]. Hug*onis* Giffard. Rogeri de Mumbray[k]. Gilb*erti*[l] de Haya. Roberti de Meyn*ers*[m]. Willelmi de Duneglas. Johannis de Vallibus. Willelmi de Rammes'[n]. et aliorum plurium baronum nostrorum amovimus[o]. W. Glasg'. C. Dumblan'. episcopos. G. electum Sancti Andr*ee*. W. Comyn comitem de Menetye . Alex*andrum* Comyn. comitem de Bochan'[p]. Willielmum[q] comitem de Mar. Johannem de Bayllol[r] Robertum de Ros. Aymerum de Makeswell'[s] et Mariam uxorem eius. Johannem Comyn. Nicholaum de Sules. Thomam de Normanuill[t]. Alex*andrum* Vuiet. Johannem de Dundemor[u]. Dauid de Graham. Johannem le Blund. Thomam filium Ranulfi[v]. Hug*onem* Gurle. Et. Willielmum[q] fratrem eius. Willielmum[q] Whischard[w] archidiaconum Sancti Andree. fratrem Ricardum elemosinarium de ordine Milicie Templi. Dauid de Louchor'. Johannem Whyschard[x]. Willielmum[q] de Cadyhou[y] et Willielmum[q] quondam capellanum nostrum meritis eorum exigentibus ut dicitur. a concilio[z] nostro. et balliis suis. et ipsos aut complices vel[aa] fauctores[bb] suos ad concilia[cc] nostra et negotia[dd] regni nostri tractanda seu ad graciam nostram uel ad[ee] familiaritatem aliquam nequaquam admittemus. donec ipsi predicto Henrico et nobis excessus eis impositos[ff] et imponendos concordia uel iudicio ad plenum emendauerint. Ad quod faciendum modis omnibus quibus iustum fuerit eos si necesse fuerit compellendum. Illud quoque condictum et utriumque[gg] concessum est quod si principem extraneum regnum Scot*ie* inuadere uel impugnare contingit. liceat nobis predictos[hh] magnates a nostro consilio iam amotos[ii] et alios quoscumque ad nostrum auxilium admittere et inuitare. Ad hec[jj] autem mediante predicti[kk] H*enrici*. consilio et dictorum magnatum nostrorum ordinauimus quod venerabiles patres. Ricardus et Petrus Dunkeld'[ll] et Abberden'[mm] episcopi'. H[d]. comes de Fif'. P. comes de Dunbar[nn]. M. comes de Strathern'. N. comes de Carrik[f]. Alex*ander* sen*escallus* Scot*ie*[oo]. Robertus de Brus[pp]. Alanus hostiar*ius*. Walterus de Moreuya[qq]. Dauid de Lindes'. Willielmus[rr] de Brechin[j]. Robertus de Meyner'[ss]. Gilbertus de Haya. et Hugo Giffard ad consilia nostra et gubernacionem regni nostri et custodiam corporis nostri et regine sponse nostre sint[tt] deputati. a consilio nostro et balliis suis citra terminum septem annorum completorum et incipientium[uu] ad festum translacionis sancti Cutberti[vv] anno Domini M. CC °. LV[ww]. uel terminum breuiorem in quem dictus dominus rex uel eius heredes et nos communiter duxerimus consentiendum[xx] nullatenus amouebuntur[yy] nisi manifeste demeruerint quominus nostris[zz] conciliis[aaa] et regni nostri negotiis[bbb] debeant interesse. Quod si ipsorum aliquem uel aliquos ex causa huiusmodi amoueri[ccc] uel in fata concedere infra dictum tempus contigerit alii[ddd] uel alii loco ipsius uel ipsorum de consilio predictorum episcoporum. comitum et baronum consiliariorum nostrorum uel eorum qui ex ipsis superstites extiterint substituentur. Preterea de feodalibus custodiis uel escaetis nostris nichil fiet nisi de consilio. et consensu dictorum consiliariorum nostrorum[eee] eisdem modo predicto substituendorum et nostro[fff]. Si vero uice\comites/[ggg] forestarii et ceteri minores balliui deliquerint[hhh] per quod debeant a suis balliis amoueri[iii] nos per supradictum consilium nostrum alios loco eorum[jjj] substitui faciemus. Nec castra nostra ab eis quibus tempore confectionis presencium commissa fuerint resumemus. nisi per consilium commune eorundem consiliariorum nostrorum ad custodiam et gubernationem[kkk] regni nostri et corporis nostri et regine nostre assignatorum. Promisimus eciam bona fide prefato domino regi quod filiam suam reginam nostram affectu maritali cum honorificentia omnimoda que filiam tanti principis et nostram decet reginam tractabimus et custodiemus et eidem a regno nostro honores debitos et conuenientes in omnibus et per omnia exhiberi faciemus. Obligaciones eciam et concessiones racionabiles quas predicti episcopi et magnates nostri fecerunt prefato domino regi. ratas habemus et acceptas et eas que de mandato nostro et voluntate processerunt. Et ad omnia predicta fideliter et inuiolabiliter obseruanda. Iurare. fecimus in animam nostram Patricium comitem de Dunbar[nn]. subicientes nos cohertioni domini pape vt si contra predicta in aliquo quod absit veniamur. ipse per censuram ecclesiasticam absque strepitu iudiciali nos ad plenam premissorum obseruacionem compellat. Presenti scripto completo predicto termino ut predictum est nobis uel heredibus nostris bona fide restituendo. nec postmodum aliquo tempore valituro[lll]. In huius autem rei testimonium presenti scripto sigillum nostrum fecimus apponi. Teste[mmm] me ipso apud Rokesburg' vicesimo[nnn] die Sept*embris* anno regni nostri[ooo] septimo.

NOTES. These record only variant readings between Texts A and B. [a] . H . in B. [b] Abbirden' in B. [c] Newebolt' in B. [d] Sic. B has the correct initial, M., for Malcolmi. [e] Dumbar in B. [f] Carric' in B. [g] Sic. B has the correct initial, M., for Malisii. [h] Morauia in B. [i] Willelmi in B. [j] Brechyn in B. [k] Munbray in B. [l] Gileberti in B. [m] Meyner' in B. [n] Rameshey in B.

[o] ammouimus in B. [p] Bocham' in B. [q] Willelmum in B. [r] Baylol' in B. [s] Makyswell' in B. [t] Normanvill' in B. [u] Dundemar in B. [v] Ranulphi in B. [w] Wyschard' in B. [x] Wyscard' in B. [y] Cadihau' in B. [z] consilio in B. [aa] uel in B. [bb] fautores in B. [cc] consilia in B. [dd] negocia in B. [ee] Word omitted in B. [ff] B adds 'et' here. [gg] B has the word 'vtriusque' interlined over a caret here. [hh] dictos in B. [ii] ammotos in B. [jj] hoc in B. [kk] Word omitted in B. [ll] Dunkelden' in B. [mm] Abbirden' in B. [nn] Dumbar' in B. [oo] Scocie in B. [pp] Bruis in P. [qq] Morauia in B. [rr] Willelmus in B. [ss] Meyners in B. [tt] Word omitted in B. [uu] incipiencium in B. [vv] Cuthberti in B. [ww] quinquagesimo quinto in B. [xx] consenciendum in B. [yy] ammouebuntur in B. [zz] ipsis in B here. [aaa] consiliis in B. [bbb] negociis in B. [ccc] ammoueri in B. [ddd] Sic. B has the correct 'alius'. [eee] B inserts 'seu' here. [fff] In B the words 'et nostro' are inserted above a caret. [ggg] vicoemites in B. [hhh] delinquant in B. [iii] ammoueri in B. [jjj] ipsorum in B. [kkk] gubernacionem in B. [lll] valituro in B. [mmm] B has 'Regis' here, crossed out. [nnn] The number appears as . xx . in B. [ooo] Anno ipsius domini Regis in B, with the last three words crossed out.

RUBRIC. Inserted into the margin are the following comments, in a contemporary hand: quod ista littera facta fuit et concessa domini regi Scocie per preceptum domini Regis Anglie apud Karham per consilium et voluntatem R . comitem Glouc' . G . de Lezign' . W de Valenc' fratrum regis J . Maunsell' prepositi Beuerl' . R. le Bigod comitis Norf' marescalli Anglie . J . de Warenne comitis Surr' . W. de Fortibus comitis Albermarl' . Edmundi de Lacy . J . de Plessetis comitis Warr' . Hugonis le Bigod . Rogeri de Monte Alto . Elye de Rabbayne . J . de Grey . R. Walerand' . Willelmi Clare et multorum aliorum baronum et consiliariorum regis tunc ibidem.

SOURCE. The king's original letter is now lost. Transcripts appear in both the Patent Rolls (Text A) and Charter Rolls (Text B). TNA, C 66/69, m 3^r = A; C 53/46A, m. 8, schedule = B. Transcribed here from A.

PRINTED. *RPS*, A1255/1; *Anglo-Scottish Relations,* ed. Stones, no. 10 (both from B). Stones's transcription includes the memoranda noted below in the Comments section; *Foedera*, I, i, 329 (from A); *APS*, i. 419–20 (from A); *Cal. Charter Rolls, 1226–57*, 438 (cal.); *CPR, 1247–1258*, 426 (cal.); *CDS*, i. no. 2013 (cal.).

COMMENT. The schedule stitched to the Charter Roll text (B) includes a series of memoranda that issued from the English chancery in the three days that followed. These included copies of letters patent of Henry III directing Richard de Clare earl of Gloucester and Hereford and John Mansel, provost of Beverley, to ensure that the arrangements made for the new Scottish royal council were put into effect, letters empowering Gloucester and Mansel to act with full authority in Henry's place in their dealings with Alexander, and letters of protection for Ewen of Argyll, who had recently returned to Scotland after being restored to the peace of the king of Scots. The schedule further notes Henry's command that copies of all these instruments be enrolled in the Patent Rolls, 'as required by the meeting of the king's council convened at Carham', and that official transcripts of Henry's letters patent be sent to Alexander. The clerk who wrote the schedule noted carefully, however, that 'the letter of Alexander III to King Henry concerning a forthcoming meeting, written at Wark, is to remain in the keeping of John of Mansel'. The contents of that letter, unfortunately, remain unknown. See also below, no. 184.

23 Takes William de Swinburne parson of Fordun (Kincardine) together with his lands and his men under his firm peace and protection and strictly prohibits anyone from causing them injury or harm, on pain of his full forfeiture. He also grants to William and his men that no one shall poind them for any reason except for their own debts, saving the rights of the royal burghs. Roxburgh, 3 February a.r. 8 [1257].

A . D*ei* gr*a*t*ia* rex Scott*orum* om*n*ib*us* p*ro*bis hominib*us* tocius t*er*re sue sal*ut*em . Sciatis nos Will*el*m*um* de Swynebu*r*n p*er*sonam de Fordun' . terras suas . homines suos . et vniu*er*sas eoru*n*dem possessiones sub firma pace et proteccio*n*e no*st*ra iuste suscepisse . Quare firmit*er* *p*rohibem*us* ne quis eis . malum . iniuriam molestiam . aut gr*a*uamen aliq*uo*d i*n*iuste p*re*sumat i*n*ferre . sup*er* no*st*ram plenariam forisfacturam . Concessim*us* ecciam[a] eidem Will*elm*o . vt nullus namos suos v*el* hominu*m* suor*um* capiat pro alicui*us* debito . plegiagio . vel forisf*ac*to . nisi p*ro* eor*um* p*ro*prio debito . plegiagio . vel forisf*ac*to . saluis burgis n*ost*ris firmit*er* inhibentes . ne quis eos cont*ra* hanc co*n*cessione*m* n*ostr*am vexare presumat iniuste . sup*er* nos*tr*am plenariam forisfacturam . Test*ibus* . P . com*ite* de Dumbar' . Rob*erto* de Meners' . Hugon*e* Giffard . apud Rokesburg' . iii[o] . die Februar*ii* . anno *regni* n*ost*ri . octauo .

NOTE. [a] Sic, eciam.

ENDORSED. The charter has long been bound in a volume, its dorse unavailable for examination.

DESCRIPTION. 18.0 cm x 7.5 cm. Sealing: formerly sealed on a tongue cut from right to left across the bottom of the deed. The tongue, 1.0 cm wide, is intact, but all traces of a seal are gone.

HAND. Scribe B.

SOURCE. Original. Northumberland Collections Service, Swinburne (Capheaton) Estate Records, ZSW/1/13.

24 Writes to Henry III king of England accrediting his envoys, Master Robert de Stuteville dean of Dunkeld, and Adam de Morham. Informs him that the earls of Menteith, Buchan and Mar, John Comyn and certain other magnates of his realm have been incessantly petitioning him, they say for the benefit and tranquility of the realm, concerning the complaints he has made about them. Requests that he give credence to the envoys, who will convey these and other matters to him. Roxburgh, 4 February a.r. 8 [1257].

Magnifico principi domino, ac patri suo karissimo, domino H. Dei gratia, illustri Regi Angliae, domino Ybernie duci Normannie et Aquitannie et comiti Andegavie Alexander eadem gratia, Rex Scociae, salutem et cum omni reverentia et honore, paratam ad beniplacita voluntatem. Statum nostrum, et statum Reginae karissimae sponsae nostrae, per Dei gratiam, prosperum esse et jocundum dominationi vestrae nunciamus; quod de faelici statu vestro, utinam! semper prospero et salubri, et de statu Reginae consortis vestrae, dilectae matris nostrae, ac faelicium liberorum vestrorum, intimo cordis desiderio scire et audire plurimum affectantes; Excellentem dominationem vestram precamur affectuose, quatinus caris et fidelibus nostris, magistro Roberto de Stutevill, decano Dunkeldensis et Ade de Morham latoribus praesentium (quos ad vestrae magnificentiae praesentiam destinamus super quadam forma , de qua comites de Menech' de Buchwan' de Marr' et Johannes Cumyn, una cum caeteris regni nostri magnatibus, pro bono pacis et regni nostri tranquilitate, nobis instanter supplicarunt; de querelis, quas contra ipsos habemus, et etiam super aliis quae vestrae serenitati ex parte nostra pleniùs intimabunt) fidem, si placet, adhibeatis indubitatam; statum vestrum, una cum vestro beneplacito, nobis saepius, ad cordis nostri gaudium et solamen non modicum, si placet, significare curetis. Teste Pat*ricio* com*ite* de Dunbar', apud Rokburc', iv die Febr*uarii* anno regni nostri octavo.

SOURCE. *Foedera*, I. i. 353. The original has not been traced.

PRINTED. *CDS*, i. no. 2077 (cal.).

25 Grants and by this charter confirms to William de Swinburne the gift that Reginald Prat, knight, made him of the lands (all in Tynedale) of Haughton, of all of Reginald's land in 'the Huntland', of the manor of Williamston in the fee of Knarsdale and of the lands that John Hok and Robert Darybald held of Reginald in Slaggyford in said fee. To be held by the same boundaries as are contained in Reginald's charter, saving the king's service, and according to the terms laid out in the final concord made between them before John de Eslington and Richard de Bickerton, justices itinerant in Tynedale. Stirling, 24 June a.r. 8 [1257].

Alex*ander* Dei gratia rex Scottorum . omnibus p*ro*bis hominibus tocius t*er*re sue sal*ute*m . Sciatis nos concessisse et hac p*re*senti carta n*ost*ra confirmasse . donacio*n*em illam quam Reginaldus Prat' miles fecit Will*elm*o de Swyneburn' p*ro* homagio et s*er*uitio suo de t*er*ris de Halutoun' cu*m* p*er*tinenciis . et de tota t*er*ra cum pertinenciis quam idem Reginaldus habuit in Le Huntland' tam in dominicis q*ua*m in s*er*uitiis . et de toto manerio de Wyllamestun cu*m* p*er*tinenciis in feodo de Knarisdal' . et de tota t*er*ra illa cu*m* pertinenciis q*ua*m Joh*anne*s Hok' . et Rob*er*tus Darybald' de p*redic*to Reginaldo tenuerunt infra diuisas de Slaghingford'. ex occidentali p*ar*te de Tyna . in d*ic*to feodo de Knarisdall' . Tenendas et habendas eidem Will*elm*o . et h*er*edibus suis . uel asignatis[a] . et eor*um* h*er*edibus . de p*redic*to Reginaldo et h*er*edibus suis u*e*l assignatis de Knarisdall' . ita libere . quiete . plenar*ie* . et honorifice . p*er* easdem diuisas cu*m* p*er*tinenciis sicut carte p*redic*ti Reginaldi p*re*fato . Will*elm*o exinde confecte plen*ius* iuste testa*n*tur saluo s*er*uicio n*ost*ro . et sec*und*um q*uod* in finali concordia super t*er*ris p*re*nominatis cu*m* pertinenciis facta . coram Joh*ann*e de *Exlingtun'* . et Ric*ardo* de Bygertun' justic*iariis* itin*er*antibus in Tindall' . anno gr*atie* mill*esimo* . duc*entesimo* . quinquag*esimo* . septim*o* . plen*ius* continetur . Test*ibus* . Rog*er*o de Quency . com*ite* Wynton' . constabul*ario* Scoc*ie* . Pat*ricio* com*ite* de Dunbarr' . M . com*ite* de St*ra*thern' . Walt*er*o de Morau*ia* . just*iciario* Laodon' . et Will*elm*o de Breych'. apud Striuely*n*' . vicesimo quarto die Junii . ann*o* regni n*ost*ri viii°.

NOTE. [a] Sic, assignatis.

ENDORSED. The charter has long been bound in a volume, its dorse unavailable for examination.

DESCRIPTION. 22.7 cm x 19.0 cm; fold 2.8 cm. Sealing: on a tag, 2.0 cm broad, is appended the second version of the king's small seal, diameter 3.5 cm, in white wax. The images and lettering are clear on obverse and reverse, though the seal is quite damaged at the edges.

HAND. Scribe A.

SOURCE. Original. Northumberland Collections Service, Swinburne (Capheaton) Estate Records, ZSW/1/16.

PRINTED. *HN*, III, i, 12–13; *Northumb. and Durham Deeds*, 200 (cal.).

COMMENT. 'The Huntland' represents the moorland that lay south-west of Wark.

This document was reissued on 1 May 1267; see no. 63, below. Both versions are noted in Bodleian Lib., MS. Dodsworth XLV, fo. 49^v and BL, MS Lansdowne 326, fo. 134^v. These consist of summaries, in Latin, of deeds belonging to several Northumberland families, written in 1638–9 by the antiquary Roger Dodsworth. The final concord mentioned in the document is recorded in ZSW/1/12, dated 16 April 1257. Swinburne's acquisition of these estates from Reginald Prat was not uneventful. The eyre held at Wark in 1257 found that both parties had made arrangements for the transfer of titles without regard for the rights of Alexander III, from whom the estates were held. The king's bailiff seized them; thereafter, 'for the good will and licence and confirmation of the king and to have peaceful seisin of the lands and on account of the above claim of the bailiff, William gave 20 merks of silver' to the king. Alexander's deed of confirmation – and the good will that it represented - thus came at a price.

26 Grants and by this charter confirms to John Sparetunt, burgess of Perth, the gift that Roger de Quincy earl of Winchester, constable of Scotland, made him of 24s of rent from various holdings in the burgh of Perth. To be held by John for homage and service, as the earl's charter bears witness, saving the king's service. Perth, 16 October a.r. 10 [1258].

Alex*ander* Dei gr*ati*a rex Scott*orum* . omnib*us* probis hominib*us* tocius te*rr*e sue salutem . Sciatis nos concessisse . et h*ac* p*re*senti carta n*ost*ra confirmasse donac*i*onem illam q*ua*m Roge*ru*s de Q*ue*ncy com*es* Wynton' constab*ularius* Scoc*ie* fecit Joh*ann*i Sparetunt burgensi n*ost*ro de Perth' pro homagio et s*er*uicio suo . de viginti et quatuor [solidis de redditu][a] in uilla de Perth' . videlic*et* in capitali mesuagio in [ ][b] et de decem solid*is* et [ ][c] conuent' de Scon' tenenti [ ][d] u*er*sus orientem int*er* ecclesia[m] ...[e] go . tenet p*er* cartam [ ][b] octo denar*ios* . et in te*rr*a que iacet coram capitali messuagio [consta?]bular*ii*[f] u*er*sus austr*alem* q*ua*m Will*elmu*s de Lenn dedit in maritagiu*m* cu*m* Claricia filia sua . de sex solid*is* et octo denar*iis*. Tenend*a* et habenda d*ic*to Joh*ann*i Sparetunt et h*er*edib*us* suis de p*redic*to Rog*er*o et h*er*edib*us* suis . ita lib*ere* . quiete . plenarie . et honorifice . sicut carta d*ic*ti Rog*er*i p*redic*to Joh*ann*i exinde confecta . pleni*us* iuste testatur . saluo s*er*uicio n*ost*ro. Testibus . Walt*er*o Cumyn' com*ite* de Meneth' . W. com*ite* de Marr' . et Hugone de Berkeley just*iciario* Laodon*ie*. apud Perth' . xvi^{to} die Octobr*is* . anno regni n*ost*ri decimo .

NOTES. [a] Words supplied by conjecture. [b] Three–four words missing. [c] Six–seven words missing. [d] Five–six words missing. [e] Seven–eight words missing. [f] Constabularii?

ENDORSED. C*onfirmacio* reg*is* Alexa*n*dry sup*er* te*rr*am Rogerii de Qwyncy. The first word is penned in a different ink, and is contemporary with the document. It is probably in the same hand as the scribe's. The rest of the endorsement is in a fourteenth-century hand.

DESCRIPTION. 20.0 cm x 8.3 cm; fold 1.4 cm. Sealing: single slits for a seal tag, but neither tag nor seal remains. The document is disfigured by a series of holes and tears which appear to have been made before the abbey's cartulary was drafted.

HAND. Scribe B.

SOURCE. Original. NRS, Papers of the Smythe Family of Methven, Perthshire, GD 190/3/64.

27 Commands Alexander Comyn earl of Buchan, justiciar of Scotia, and his bailies of Carrick to hold an inquest to determine whether Hector son of Hector de Carrick, knight, was vested and seised of five pennylands of the land of Auchensoul (Ayrshire) and how he was ejected from them. He is to return the record of the inquest, together with this brieve, to the king. Kilwinning, 21 May a.r. 11 [1260].

. A . Dei gr*ati*a rex Scott*orum* . Alexandro Cumyn' . comit*i* . de Buchan' . just*iciario* . Scoc*ie* . dil*ec*to et fideli suo et balliuiis suis de

Karric' . salutem . Mandam*us* vob*is* et p*re*cipim*us* q*ua*tinus p*er* sac*ra*mentum p*ro*bor*um* et fideliu*m* hominu*m* patrie diligent*er* et fidelit*er* inquiri faciatis si Hector filius Hectoris de Karric' . militis fuit vestit*us* et saysit*us* per dies et annos de q*ui*nq*ue* denariatis t*er*re de Ackinsauhil' et q*ua*lit*er* de eisdem fuit eiectus . Et d*ic*tam inquisi*tione*m diligent*er* et fidelit*er* factam sub sigillo v*es*tro et sub sigillis eor*um* qui dicta inquisi*tioni*[a] faciende int*er*eru*n*t nob*is* qu*am*cici*us* t*ra*nsmitti faciatis et hoc breue . Et hoc n*u*llaten*us* omittatis . Test*o* Henr*ico* de Graham . apud Kilwynyn' . xxi . die . Maii . anno . regni . nostri . vndecimo .

NOTE. [a] Sic, inquisitione.

DESCRIPTION. 17.8 cm x 4.0 cm. Sealing: formerly sealed on a tongue cut from right to left across the bottom of the deed, now torn away.

HAND. Scribe C.

SOURCE. Original. NRS, Documents transferred from the Public Record Office, London, RH 5/42.

PRINTED. *CDS*, i, no. 2193 (cal.); *L & I,* vol. xlix, 184 (note). A modern transcript appears in NRS, RH 2/2/13, item 10 (3).

28 Commands his sheriffs, provosts and the rest of his bailies on the north side of the Scottish Sea to hold an inquest to determine the hospices and lodgings belonging to the bishop of Aberdeen, both in the burghs and in the king's other manors. Inverness, 18 August a.r. 12 [1260].

[*A*]lex*ander*[a] Dei gr*ati*a rex Scottor*um* vic*ecomitibus* p*re*po*s*itis et cet*er*is balliuis suis ex aq*ui*lonali p*ar*te maris Scocie salutem. Mandam*us* vobis firmit*er* precipientes q*ua*tinus p*er* probos et fideles homines balliuar*um* v*es*trar*um* diligent*er* et fidelit*er* inq*ui*ri faciatis que sunt hospicia et hostilagia ven*erabilis* patris ep*iscop*i Ab*er*donen' vel de iure et r*ati*o*n*e esse debent tam in burgis q*uam* in cet*er*is maneriis n*ost*ris et q*ue* per dictam inquisic*ione*m dilige*n*ter et fidelit*er* factam suam esse i*n*uen*er*itis eisdem ipsum gaudere decet*er*o faciatis. Testibus Alano hostiar*io*. Eymerio de Maxwell' cam*er*ario. Apud Inu*er*ness' decim*o* octauo die Augusti anno. regni n*ost*ri duodecimo.

NOTE. [a] Space left blank for initial A.

RUBRIC. A later hand has (mistakenly) added *Anno Domini 1226*.

SOURCE. NLS, Adv. MS. 16.1.10, Register of the Cathedral Church and Bishopric of Aberdeen, fo. 50[v].

PRINTED. *Aberdeen Registrum*, i. 27.

29 Writes to Henry III king of England requesting that he grant respite from distraint of knighthood to Walter de Lindsay until the latter returns from his intended pilgrimage to Santiago. Durris, 28 August a.r. 12 [1260].

Excellentissimo p*ri*ncipi d*omi*no ac patri karissimo d*omi*no H . Dei gr*ati*a regi Angl*ie* illustri . d*omi*no Hib*er*nie et duci Aquitann*ie* . A . eadem gr*ati*a rex Scott*orum* sal*ute*m et cumulum felicitatis et*er*ne cu*m* augmento honoris et glorie . pro Walt*er*o de Lindesey fideli n*ost*ro v*est*re celsitudinis serenitate*m* affecti*us* duxim*us* implorand*um* quatin*us* compulsione*m* q*ua*m eidem fieri fecistis ad arma milicie recipiend*a* quousq*ue* de s*anc*to Jacobo vbi p*er*egre proficisci p*ro*ponit redierit . pro nostris p*ar*tib*us* et amore eidem relaxare dignemini . ip*s*um si placet ad n*ost*re peticionis instanciam cingulo militari a nobis p*er*mittentes accingi . p*re*ces n*ost*ras in hac p*ar*te talit*er* si placet exaudientes . vt ide*m* Walt*er*us eas sibi senciat profuisse . p*er* quod ad ea que vestre d*omin*ac*i*onis excellencie beneplacita fu*er*int et accepta obnoxi*us* m*er*ito temporib*us* oportunis debeam*us* astringi . Teste me ip*s*o apud Durres' . xx°viii° . die Augusti ann*o* regni nostri . xii° .

DESCRIPTION. 19.0 cm x 4.2 cm. Sealing: formerly sealed on a tongue cut from right to left across the bottom of the deed, now torn away.
HAND. Scribe C.
SOURCE. Original. TNA, Special Collections: Ancient Correspondence of the Chancery and the Exchequer, PRO SC 1/5/31.
PRINTED. *Nat. MSS. Scotland*, i, no. 62 (facs.); *CDS*, v, pt. 2, no. 19 (cal.).

30 Grants and by this charter confirms to the monks of Balmerino the gift that Simon de Kinnear made them of half the land in the feu of Kinnear (Fife) and of the land that lies next to it to the east of Kinnear. To be held by the monks in perpetuity, as Simon's charter bears witness, saving the king's service. Selkirk, 21 September a.r. 12 [1260].

Alexander[a] D*e*i gr*ati*a rex Scott*orum*. om*n*ib*us* p*ro*bis ho*min*ib*us* toci*us* t*er*re sue salutem. Sciatis nos co*n*cessisse et hac carta n*ost*ra *con*firmasse D*e*o et beate Marie et monachis de Balm*ur*ynach in Fyf' D*e*o seruientib*us* et inp*er*petuu*m* seruituris donac*ion*em illam quam Symon de Kynn*er* fecit eisdem de medietate toci*us* t*er*re in feodo de [ ][b] Kynher et de t*er*ra p*ro*xi*m*a adiacente ex p*ar*te orientali de Kynner. Tenend*am* et habend*am* eisde*m* monachis et suis successorib*us* in p*er*petuu*m* adeo lib*er*e. quiete. plenarie. et honorifice sicut carta dicti Symonis eisd*em* monachis exinde co*n*fecta pleni*us* iuste testatur. saluo seruicio n*ost*ro. In cui*us* rei test*imonium* eisde*m* super hoc has l*itte*ras n*ost*ras fieri fecim*us* pate*n*tes. Test*ibus* Alex*andro* Cumyn. com*ite* de Buchan justiciar*io* Scoc*ie*. P. com*ite* de Dunbar. et Alex*andro* senescallo ap*ud* Selekyrke. vicesimo p*ri*mo die Septembr*is* ann*o* regni nostri duodecimo.

NOTES. [a] Capital initial letters rubricated (in red). [b] Blank space in MS here.
RUBRIC. Confirmacio regis de terris de Kyner'.
SOURCE. NLS, Adv. MS. 34.5.3, Chartulary of Balmerino Abbey, fos. 6^{v}–7^{r}.
PRINTED. *Balmerino Liber*, no. 15.

31 Grants and by this charter confirms to the burgesses of Ayr an annual fair on the feast of the nativity of St John the Baptist and for the following fortnight. To be held by the burgesses with all the liberties and customs associated with fairs, as freely and quietly as other burghs in the kingdom enjoy. Grants also to the burgesses freedom from all captions and suits both within and beyond the town, excepting only the king's own captions and prises and those of the queen. Strictly forbids anyone from disturbing them in defiance of this grant, on pain of his full forfeiture. Traquair, 12 December a.r. 12 [1260].

Alex*ander* D*e*i gr*ati*a rex Scottor*um* omnib*us* probis hominib*us* tocius
te*r*re sue sal*ute*m . Sciant p*re*sentes et fut*uri* nos concessisse et hac
carta n*ost*ra confirmasse burgensib*us* n*ost*ris de Ar' . vt ip*s*i ad meliora-
c*i*on*e*m burgi n*ost*ri de Ar' h*a*beant quolibet anno apud Ar' nundinas
ad festum natiuitatis s*an*cti Joh*ann*is baptiste . durantes p*er* qu*i*ndecim
dies sequentes . Tenend*as* et habend*as* eisd*em* burgensib*us* cum
om*n*ib*us* libertatib*us* . et consuetudinibus nundinar*um* adeo libe*re* et
quiete sicut alii burgenses regn*i* nostri in aliis burgis n*ost*ris libe*r*tat[es]
a et consuetudines nundinar*um* libe*r*ius et quieti*us* habent et possident
volum*us* eciam et concedimus eisdem burgensib*us*. vt ip*s*i libe*r*i sint ab
om*n*imodis capc*i*onib*us* et [ ]*a* p*er* que*m*cum*que* tam extra villam de Ar'
q*uam* infra capiendis . exceptis n*ost*ris propriis capc*i*onib*us* et prisis .
regine sponse n*ost*re . Et firmite*r* p*ro*hibem*us* ne quis eos cont*ra* hanc
concessionem n*ost*ram iniuste uexare presumat sup*er* n*ost*ram plenariam forisfac*tu*ram decem librarum . Test*ib*us . Alex*andro* Cumyn'
. com*ite* de Buchan' . justic*i*ario Scoc*ie* . P . com*ite* de Dumbar' .
Eyme*r*o de Maccu*s*well' . came*r*ario . Hugon*e* de Abbe*r*nythyn' . et
Walt*er*o senescall*o* . apud Tr[oue]q*uer*'*a* . duodecimo die Decembris
ann*o* regni nostri duodecimo .

NOTE. *a* Hole in MS here.
DESCRIPTION. 18.8 cm x 8.6 cm; fold 1.5 cm. Sealing: a tag, 1.3 cm broad, is passed
through a single slit; seal lost.
HAND. Scribe A.
SOURCE. Original. Ayr, Carnegie Library, Ayr Burgh Charters, B.6/30/11.
PRINTED. *Ayr Burgh Charters*, no. 11.

32 Commands Alexander de Montfort sheriff of Elgin to hold an
inquest to determine the right that Robert the crossbowman
claims to have to the king's garden at Elgin by reason of his wife
Margaret. He is to return the record of the inquest, together with this
brieve, to the king's chapel. 'Ratthen', 13 August a.r. 13 [1261].

. A . D*e*i gr*ati*a rex Scottor*um* . A . de Monte Forti . vic*e*comiti de Elgyn'
. dilec*t*o et fideli suo sal*ute*m. Mandam*us* uobis et firmite*r* precipimus .
quatin*us* p*er* probos . fideles . et libe*r*os homines pat*ri*e . et p*er* meliores
et fideliores de burgensib*us* n*ost*ris de Elgyn' . diligentem et fidelem
inquisic*i*on*e*m fieri faciatis sup*er* iure quod Robe*r*tus Balistarius lator
p*re*sencium dicit se habere racione Margarete vxoris sue ad gardin*um*
n*ost*rum de Elgyn' . et te*r*ram ad dic*t*um gardin*um* pertinentem et
dic*t*am inquisic*i*onem diligente*r* et fidelite*r* *f*ac*t*am vna cum hoc brevi*a*
. ad cap*e*llam n*ost*ram defe*r*ri faciatis . Teste . Hugon*e* de Abbe*r*nythyn'.
Apud Ratthenec' . xiii° . die Augusti . ann*o* *regni* nostri . xiii° .

NOTE. *a* Sic, breve.
DESCRIPTION. 19.1 cm x 2.8 cm. Sealing: formerly sealed on a tongue cut from right
to left across the bottom of the deed, now torn away.
HAND. Scribe C.
SOURCE. Original. NRS, Documents transferred from the Public Record Office,
London, RH 5/44.
PRINTED. *APS*, i, 99; *CDS*, i, no. 2272 (cal.); *L & I*, vol. xlix, 184 (note).
COMMENT. The inquisition held on 27 August 1261 in pursuance of this brieve is
recorded in NRS, RH 5/43. The thanage of 'Ratthen' or 'Rathenec' lay between Elgin
and the river Spey; it now survives in the name Rapenache Manor, near Meft in Moray;

see A. Grant, 'Thanes and Thanages, from the Eleventh to the Fourteenth Centuries', in A. Grant and K. J. Stringer (eds), *Medieval Scotland: Crown, Lordship and Community – Essays presented to G. W. S. Barrow* (Edinburgh, 1993), 40n. Note the single attestor.

33 Grants and by this charter confirms to the abbot and convent of Lindores the gift that Robert de Bruce made them of his land called Williamston in Garioch (Aberdeenshire), which lies between the convent's lands of 'Lethgaven' and Wrangham; and also of his land of Boynds near Caskieben in the parish of Inverurie, in exchange for the second teinds which the abbot and convent were accustomed to receive annually and the profits, pleas, escheats and all other things that the said Robert had within his land and beyond, above the Mounth, in Garioch, by gift of Earl David [of Huntingdon]. The abbot and convent are to hold these lands in perpetuity, as Robert's charter bears witness, saving the king's service. Kinross, 29 August a.r. 13 [1261].

Alex*ander*[a] Dei gr*ati*a rex Scott*orum*. omnib*us* p*ro*b*is* ho*min*ib*us* toci*us* te*rr*e sue sal*ute*m. Sciatis nos co*n*cessisse et hac p*re*senti carta n*ost*ra *confir*masse donac*ione*m illam q*ua*m Rob*er*tus de Brus'. fecit religiosis viris. abb*a*ti et con*u*entui de Lundors' de te*rr*a sua qu*e* d*icitur* villa Will*elm*i i*n* Garuiach qu*e* iacet int*er* te*rr*as eoru*n*dem abb*at*is et co*n*uentus de Lethgauen et de Wrangham. et de te*rr*a sua de Bondes iuxt*a* Caskyben i*n* pa*r*ochia de Inuerury i*n* escambium s*ecun*dar*um* decimar*um* qu*a*s idem abbas et co*n*uent*us* co*n*su*er*unt[b] p*er*cipe[c] annuatim de te*rr*is ei*us*dem Rob*er*ti et lucris. placitis. eschaetis. et om*n*ib*us* aliis reb*us* dic*ti* Rob*er*ti infra te*rr*am sua*m* et extra ultra Moneth i*n* Garuiach ex dono comitis. D*aui*d. Tenend*am* et habend*am* eisdem abb*a*ti et conuentui et suis successorib*us* in pe*r*petuu*m* adeo lib*er*e. quiete. plenarie et honorifice sicut carta eiusde*m* Rob*er*ti d*ic*tis abb*ati* et co*n*uentui exi*n*de co*n*fecta plenius iuste testatur. saluo seruic*i*o n*ost*ro. Test*ibus*. Willelmo archid*iacono* S*anc*ti Andree. Cancellar*io*. Joh*anne* de Dundemor' Joh*anne* de Parco. et Will*elm*o de Sancto Clar*o*. apud Kynros'. vicesimo nono die Augusti. anno regni n*os*tri tercio decimo.

NOTES. [a] Initial A written outwith the margin. [b] Sic, consueuerunt. [c] Sic, percipere.
RUBRIC. Item de eadem terra Will*el*mi de Letgauen de Wr*a*ngham et de te*rr*a de Bondes item nota de s*ecundis* de decimis (Bruce's grant precedes this one) (fourteenth century).
SOURCE. Caprington Castle, Kilmarnock, Lindores Cartulary, fos 81^{v}–82^{r}.
PRINTED. *Lindores Cart.*, no. 117.
COMMENT. 'Lethgaven' is probably G. *Leth gamhainn*, later Ledingham, probably now Little Ledikin in Culsalmond parish, Aberdeenshire; see J. B. Johnston, *Place-names of Scotland* (London, 1934), 236. Wrangham is nearby.

34 Writes to Henry III king of England accrediting his clerk John de Lindores. Newbattle, 12 February a.r. 13 [1262].

Serenissimo p*r*incipi [et] p*at*ri suo in *Chris*to carissimo d*omi*no Henr*ico* Dei gr*ati*a regi Angl*ie* illustri do*mino* Hyb*ernie* et duc*i* Aquitan*nie* Alex*ande*r eadem gr*ati*a rex Scott*orum* sal*ute*m [et] perp*e*tue felicitates augmentum cum parata ad b*ene*placita voluntate. Johanne*m* de Lundors' cl*er*icum n*os*trum latorem [presenciam] destinamus [ ][a] [de] p*u*tantes quamcicius eidem Joh*anni* in hiis q*uam* vobis [ ][b] parte [ ][c] fiodem si placet exhibeatis indubitam [ ][d] paternitatis v*est*re affec*tione*m erga nos purum et integrum [ ][d] firmius astringamur . valeat pat*er*nitas v*est*ra per temp*or*a longiora . Test*e* me ip*s*o apud Neubotell xii° die Februar*ii* . ann*o* r*egni* n*ostri* xiii° .

NOTES. [a] One or two words illegible. [b] One word illegible. [c] Two words illegible. [d] Several words illegible.
ENDORSED. A[nn]o 13 . Henr . 3 (fourteenth century).
DESCRIPTION. 16.3 cm x 4.1 cm. Sealing: formerly sealed on a tongue cut from right to left across the bottom of the deed, now torn away. The document is in a very poor state of preservation: the middle portion is badly stained and the right side faded, though the bottom left corner is clear. The stain does not completely obscure the text, but much is illegible, even under ultraviolet light.
HAND. Scribe C.
SOURCE. Original. TNA, Special Collections: Ancient Correspondence of the Chancery and the Exchequer, PRO SC 1/5/32.
COMMENT. The business that John de Lindores was accredited to treat was clearly the dowry of Princess Margaret; see the next entry.

35 Writes to Henry III king of England noting that a payment of 1,000 [merks] has been made to his clerk, William de Swinburne, in part settlement of the £1,000 that Henry is due to give him on the feast of St Botulf next by reason of the marriage contracted between him and Henry's daughter, Margaret. Reminds Henry that the king of England promised to return the letters patent by which Alexander agreed to the above-mentioned sum when he supplied a receipt for the 1,000–merk payment, and requests that Henry now give these letters to his clerk, John de Lindores. Traquair, 14 February a.r. 13 [1262].

Serenissimo p*r*incipi d*omi*ni et p*at*ri suo in *Christ*o carissimo d*omi*no H . Dei gr*ati*a regi Anglie . domino Hyb*ernie* et duc*i* Aquitan*nie* Alex*ander* eadem gr*ati*a [rex Scottorum salutem et semper augmentum]. Cum Will*elmu*s de Swyneburn' cl*ericus* nost*er* a vobis recepit ad opus n*ost*r*u*m mille [marcarum sterlingorum in partem solutionis] mille librarum st*er*lingor*um* q*ua*s nobis solu*er*e p*ro*misistis in nundinis s*anc*ti Botulphi p*ro*ximo pret*er*itis in partem [ ][a] in quo nobis tenemini rac*io*ne mat*ri*monii cont*ra*cti inter nos et Margaretam consortem n*ost*ram filiam v*est*ram primoge[nitam . Et idem Willelmus litteras nostras] patentes soluc*ion*em d*ic*tar*um* mille libr*arum* testificantes carissime d*omi*ne et m*at*ri n*ost*re d*omi*ne Alyen[ore Dei gratia regine consorti vestre commiserit ut in] equa manu quas quidem litteras nobis restitu*ere* p*ro*misistis q*ua*mcito vobis litt*er*as n*ost*ras [solut*ion*em dictar*um* mille marcarum testificantes] mitteremus . Attenti*us* vos rogam*us* . q*ua*tinus Johanni de Lundors' cl*er*ico latori p*re*senci*um* dic*tas* [litteras nostras patentes de dictis mille marcis] def*er*enti p*re*fatas litt*er*as n*ost*ras mille librar*um* restitui faciatis . Test*e* me ip*s*o apud Tra[... anno regni nostri] [b] nostri xiii°.

NOTES. Words in brackets here are supplied from printed edition. [a] Three–four words illegible. [b] The concluding sentence in the printed version reads: 'Teste meipso, apud Sna ... xvii. die Februarii anno nostri decimo tertio'.
ENDORSED. I. Hen 3 [struck through; Alex inserted above] (near-contemporary hand).

DESCRIPTION. 18.8 cm x 4.8 cm. Sealing: formerly sealed on a tongue cut from right to left across the bottom of the deed, now torn away. The document is in a very poor state of preservation: a large stain on the left edge obscures much of the writing, even under ultraviolet light. Staining in the centre and right does not totally obscure the writing, and a section in the middle (representing about half the total width) is relatively clear. Serious damage to the parchment did not become visible until after the Record Commission had completed its work on Rymer's *Foedera*: that edition reproduces a number of words that are now completely illegible.
HAND. Scribe D.
SOURCE. Original. TNA, Special Collections: Ancient Correspondence of the Chancery and the Exchequer, PRO SC 1/5/33.
PRINTED. *Foedera*, I, i, 380 (where it is misdated); *CDS*, i, no. 2290 (cal.).
COMMENT. The payment and receipt noted above were the subject of a letter to Alexander III dated 30 July 1261; see *CPR, 1258–1266*, 170. Margaret's unpaid dowry remained a source of tension between Alexander III and his father-in-law; see also below, no. 213.

36 Commands Robert de Monte Alto sheriff of Forfar and his bailies of Forfar to hold an inquest to determine whether Margaret, Agnes, Suannoch, Christine and Marion, daughters of the late Simon, door-keeper of Montrose, are the nearest lawful heirs of his land of Inyaney (in Kirkden, Angus) and of his office of door-keeper. He is to return the record of the inquest, together with this brieve, to the king. Montrose, 21 March a.r. 13 [1262].

A . Dei gr*ati*a rex Scott*orum* Rob*er*to de Monte Alto dil*ect*o et fideli suo vicecom*iti* et balliuis . suis de Forfar' sal*ute*m . Mandamus vob*is* et p*re*cipim*us* quatin*us* p*er* probos et fideles homines p*at*rie diligent*er* et fidelit*er* inquir*i* faciatis si Margaret*a* . Angnes . Suannoch' . Cristiana . et Mariota filie quonda*m* Symonis janitoris \ de Monros' / sint legitim\e/ et p*ro*pinquiores . h*er*edes d*ic*ti \ quonda*m* / Symonis de t*er*ra de Inyaney et de officio janue cast*ri* n*os*tri de Monros' . et si dict*us* quondam Symo*n* obiit vestit*us* et seisit*us* vt de feodo \ de / dictis \ t*er*ra / et officio . et hec omnia diligent*er* et fidelit*er* inquisita vna cu*m* valore et ra*tio*nabili extenta t*er*re p*re*nom*inate* quamcici*us* pot*er*itis nob*is* mitti faciatis et hoc breue . Test*e* me ip*s*o ap*u*d Monros' xxi° . die Martii anno regni n*os*tri . xiii° .

DESCRIPTION. 14.0 cm x 4.4 cm. Sealing: no evidence of a tongue or tag for a seal.
HAND. Scribe C.
SOURCE. Original. NRS, Documents transferred from the Public Record Office, London, RH 5/23.
PRINTED. *APS*, i, 100; *CDS*, i, no. 2294 (cal.).
COMMENT. NRS, RH 5/24 records an inquisition *post mortem* in pursuance of this brieve. See also *RRS*, ii, no. 556.

37 Writes to Henry III king of England requesting that he pay a debt owed to Peter de Tilliol, knight. Stirling, 10 April a.r. 13 [1262].

Excellentissimo p*r*incipi . d*omi*no[a] . ac p*at*ri [Deo gracia domini regi][b] Angl*ie* d*omi*no Hybern*ie* et duc*i* Aquit*annie* . Alex*ander* . eadem gr*ati*a rex Scott*orum* . sal*ute*m [et felices ad uota successus cum][c] incremento gl*or*ie et honoris . Pro Petro de Tilloloy milite dilecto et fideli nostro [ ][d] dilectissimo affectuose[e] supplicam*us* q*u*atinus eidem de debito quod ei debetis pro [ ] [f] nostris precibus et amore . satisfieri faciatis taliter si placet eundem cui*us* [ ] [f] H. q*uod* preces n*ostr*as per effectu*m* sibi sentiat profuisse . ac ad n*ostr*um festinant*ur* [ ][g] [Teste me] ip*s*o apud Striuelin . x . die Aprilis . ann*o* . r*egni* . nostri . xiii° .

NOTES. The central portion of the document is obscured by a large water stain, its legibility further compromised by a series of deep creases running across its face.[a] Two letters, struck through. [b] Words supplied by conjecture. [c] Words here supplied by conjecture, based on similar sentence structures found in nos 38, 92, 94, 96 and 99. [d] Four–five words illegible. [e] Both words are largely hidden in a crease. [f] Five–six words illegible. [g] Three–four words illegible.
DESCRIPTION. 16.0 cm x 4.6 cm. Sealing: no evidence of a tongue or tag for a seal.
HAND. Scribe D.
SOURCE. Original. TNA, Special Collections: Ancient Correspondence of the Chancery and the Exchequer, PRO SC 1/5/34.

38

Writes to Henry III king of England stating that he cannot spare Roger de Mowbray at present, because the latter is engaged in urgent business concerning the kingdom. Requests an adjournment of the suit that Robert son of Adam de Bassenthwaite and Ralph de Lonsdale have brought against Roger before the sheriff of Cumberland until the fortnight after the feast of St Michael next. Traquair, 10 June a.r. 13 [1262].

Excellentissimo p*r*incipi d*omi*no ac pat*ri* p[re]*co*rdialissimo[a] d*omi*no H . D*ei* g*rati*a regi Angl*ie* illust*ri* d*omi*no Hybern*ie* et duci Aquitann*ie* Alex*ander* ead[*em*][b] [grati]a rex Scott*orum* sal*ute*m et felices ad vota successus cu*m* omni reverentia et honore . Statum n*ostr*um et regiu*m* filie [v]*es*tre[c] consortis n*ost*re k*arissi*me ac filie n*ost*re dilecte diuine mediante fauore prosp*er*um e*ss*e et iocundum v*est*re celsitudini nunc[ia]m*us*[d] q*uod* de vobi*s* et regina consorte v*est*ra matre n*ost*ra dilectissima ac de lib*er*is v*est*ris p*r*eclaris vehementi cordis aff*ec*tu scire des[id]*er*amu*s*[d] et q*ua*m p*r*esencia Rog*er*i de Mubray dil*ec*ti et fidelis n*ost*ri propt*er* ardua negocia n*ost*ra nos et regnu*m* n*ostru*m tangencia que de nouo emerserunt ad presens comode carere no*n* valem*us* v*est*re sublimitatis magnificenciam de qua vehemente*m* g*er*im*us* fiduciam et deberi parte qua possumus imploram*us* quatinus loquelas quas Rob*er*tus fili*us* Ade de Baste\nes/wayth' et Radulphus de Vlnesdal' mouent contra eundem coram vicecom*ite* v*est*ro Cumb*er*land' pon*ere* velitis in respectum . vsq*ue* in quindenam p*o*st festum s*anc*ti Michael*is* proximo futurum . velle v*est*rum super hoc dicto vicecom*ite* v*est*ro \per v*est*ras litt*er*as/ si placet significantes . p*r*eces n*o*stras in hac p*ar*te talit*er* exaudientes . prout v*est*ras in casu consimili vel maiori nos velletis exaudire \cum effectu/ . Test*e* me ip*s*o apud Trouequayr' . x° . die Ju*n*ii . ann*o* regni n*ost*ri . xiii° ·.

NOTES. [a] Letters in brackets in this word and the one immediately following it are lost in a tear. [b] This word and the one immediately following are largely obscured by a tear. [c] Letter in square brakets lost owing to the tear. [d] Medial letters lost in tear.
DESCRIPTION. 16.3 cm x 7.1 cm. Sealing: formerly sealed on a tongue cut from right to left across the bottom of the deed, now torn away. Some staining on the left side restricts legibility, though examination under ultraviolet light clarifies some portions. Small tear at top left corner.
HAND. Scribe D.

SOURCE. Original. TNA, Special Collections: Ancient Correspondence of the Chancery and the Exchequer, PRO SC 1/5/35.
PRINTED. Shirley, *Royal Letters*, ii, 211–12; *CDS*, i, no. 2306 (cal.).

39 Writes to Henry III king of England accrediting Richard de Castle, his bailiff of Cumberland, whom he has instructed in the matter of his suit concerning Wheatley (Nottinghamshire) and whom he sends to Henry's court to request a favourable outcome of the case. Traquair, 13 June a.r. 13 [1262].

Magnifico principi . d*omi*no ac p*at*ri p*re*cordialissimo d*omi*no . H . Dei gr*ati*a regi Angl*ie* illustri . d*omi*no Hybern*ie* . et duc*i* Aquitann*ie* . Alex*ander* eadem gr*ati*a rex Scott*orum* sal*u*tem et utri*us*q*ue* vice felicitatem cum filial*is* dil*ec*cionis aff*ec*c*i*one . V*est*re celsitudinis s*er*enitatem p*re*ce qua possu*m*us imploramus ampliori quatinus Ricardum de Castilkayroch' balliuum n*ost*rum Cumb[er]'[a] qui in causa n*ost*ra de Weteley est instr*u*ctus et que*m* ob causam p*re*dictam ad curi*am* v*est*ram destinam*us* sicut comodum[b] n*ost*r*u*m ac iuris n*ost*ri hereditarii care diligitis saluat*ion*em h*abe*re dignemini recomendatum[c] . et cum comodum[b] n*ost*r*u*m tanqua*m* p*ro*priu*m* si placet cum fauoris gr*ati*a nos prosequi velle debeatis . eundem p*ro* n*ost*ris p*re*c*ib*us et amore in d*ic*te cause nostre execuc*i*one fauorabilit*er* admittatis et benigne . licet erga ips*u*m aliquo modo com*m*oti fu*er*itis per emulor*um* suggestionem . saluum et securu*m* conductu*m* v*est*r*u*m ibidem accedendi et pro n*ost*ris negotiis expediendis co*m*morandi . ac illinc saluo recedendi ad instanciam n*ost*ram eidem concedentes . per quod v*est*re sublimitatis magnificencie ad g*ra*tes teneam*ur* ub*er*iores . Test*e* me ipso apud Trouequayr' . xiii° . die Jun*ii* . anno . regni . nostri . xiij° .

NOTES. [a] Letters in brackets are obscured by a tear. [b] Sic, commodum. [c] Sic, recommendatum.
DESCRIPTION. 17.5 cm x 5.1 cm. Sealing: formerly sealed on a tongue cut from right to left across the bottom of the deed, now torn away. There is a small hole in the upper left side of the MS, which does not, however, affect legibility of text.
HAND. Scribe D.
SOURCE. Original. TNA, Special Collections: Ancient Correspondence of the Chancery and the Exchequer, PRO SC 1/5/36.
PRINTED. Shirley, *Royal Letters*, ii, 212–13; *CDS*, i, no. 2307 (cal.).
COMMENT. Alexander III acquired an interest in the dower lands of his aunt Margaret, sister of Alexander II, when she died in 1259, predeceased by her only child Megotta. Wheatley lay in the honour of Tickhill. Alexander was still involved in litigation about the land as late as 1275; see below, no. 199. He was, however, careful to keep a record of the proceedings.

40 Commands Aymer de Maxwell sheriff of Peebles and his bailies of Peebles to hold an inquest to determine whether Robert Cruik has deforced the burgesses of Peebles of the peat moss of Waddenshope (Peeblesshire), which his father, King Alexander II, gave them and he himself confirmed to them. They are also to determine whether Robert farmed the common pasture or otherwise unlawfully occupied it. He is to return the record of the inquest, together with this brieve, to the king. Lanark, 7 October a.r. 14 [1262].

. A . Dei gr*ati*a rex Scott*orum* Eym*ero* de Mackisuuell' dil*ecto* et fideli suo vicecom*iti* et balliuis suis de Pebblys' sal*ute*m . Mandam*us* vob*is* firmit*er* p*re*cipientes quatin*us* p*er* probos \ fideles / . liberos . et legales homines p*at*rie diligent*er* et fidelit*er* inquiri faciatis si Rob*er*tus Cruik' deforciet burgensib*us* n*ost*ris de Pebblys' petariam n*ost*ram de Waltanishop' ab bone[a] memorie d*omi*no . \ rege / A . patre \ n*ost*ro ut dicunt et postmodum a nobis sibi concessam . / et si idem . R . t*er*ram n*ost*ram et communem pasturam d*ic*tor*um* burgens*ium* n*ost*ror*um* arrauerit *vel* aliqu*o* alio modo iniuste occupau*er*it et d*ic*tam inquisit*ione*m diligent*er* et fide*li*ter f*ac*tam . s*u*b sigillo v*est*ro vna cu*m* sigill*is* aliq*uorum* qui d*ic*te inquisit*ioni* int*er*erunt faciende . nob*is* qu*am*cicius pot*er*itis mitti faciatis et hoc breue . Test*e* me ip*s*o apud Lanark' . vii° . die Octobr*is* . ann*o* . r*egni* . n*ostri* . xiiii° .

NOTE. [a] The MS has been erased here and the following sentence and its interlineations added.

DESCRIPTION. 16.5 cm x 3.2 cm. Sealing: formerly sealed on a tongue cut from right to left across the bottom of the deed, now torn away.

HAND. Scribe C.

SOURCE. Original, NRS, Documents transferred from the Public Record Office, London, RH 5/25.

PRINTED. *APS*, i, 100–1; *Peebles Chrs*, no. 2; *CDS*, i, no. 2313 (cal.); *L & I*, vol. xlix, 184 (note).

COMMENT. NRS, RH 5/26 is an inquest held on 6 November 1262 in pursuance of this brieve.

41 Gives, grants and by this charter confirms to William earl of Mar the land of Tillicoultry in the feu of Clackmannan, with all the neyfs that were resident on the land on the day that it was first bestowed on Alwin de Mes, son and heir of Alwin de Mes. Recites how Alwin junior held the land heritably of him but, owing to default of service, resigned it and quitclaimed all right in it to the king at Edinburgh on Trinity Sunday, before a great number of the king's magnates (several are named). To be held in feu and heritage and in free forest, with sake and soke, with gallows and pit, with toll, team and infangentheof, by the same bounds as Walter son of Alan the steward, then justiciar of Scotia, and Roger Avenel, then sheriff of Stirling, first gave it to Alwin senior at the command of the late King Alexander II, for the service on one knight, saving the king's alms. Strictly prohibits anyone from felling timber or hunting there without licence, on pain of his full forfeiture of £10. Forfar, 21 December a.r. 14 [1262].

Alex*ander* Dei *gra*tia rex Scottor*um* omnib*us* probis hominibus tocius terre sue sal*ute*m . Sciant presentes et futuri quod cum Aleuin*us* de Mes' filius et heres quondam Aleuini de Mes' totam t*er*ram suam de Tulicultry cum p*er*tinenciis in feodo de Clacmanan' quam de nobis tenuit h*er*editarie p*er* def*ec*tum s*er*uicii de dicta t*er*ra nobis debiti coram plurib*us* regni n*ost*ri magnatib*us* scilicet . Alex*andro* Cumyn' com*ite* de Bouchan' tunc just*iciario* Scot*ie*. Hugon*e* de Abyrnith' . mag*ist*ro . W . Wischard tunc cancellar*io* Ferg*usio* Cumyn . Will*elmo* . de Abernyth' . Will*elmo* de Lysurs' et Nich*olao* de Rutyrford' . ac multis aliis die sanct*e* Trinitatis . anno *grat*ie millesim*i* ducents*imi* sexagesimi p*ri*mi apud Castru*m* Puellar*um* per fustum et baculu*m* nobis reddidisset . et totum jus suum q*uo*d h*ab*uit in dicta t*er*ra cum p*er*tinenciis vel h*ab*ere potuit pro se et heredib*us* suis imp*er*petuu*m* quietu*m* clamasset . Nos totam dictam t*er*ram de Tulicultry cum p*er*tine*n*ciis Will*elmo* comiti de Marr' dilecto n*ost*ro et fideli pro homagio et seruicio suo dedim*us* concessimus et hac presenti carta n*ost*ra confirmauimus sine aliquo retenemento . Tenend*am* et habend*am* eid*em* Will*elmo* et heredib*us* suis de nobis et heredib*us* n*ost*ris in feodo et hereditate p*er* easdem diuisas p*er* quas Walterus filius Alan*i* senescall*i* tunc justiciar*ius* Scoc*ie* et Rogerus Auenel' tunc vicecomes de St*ri*uelyn pred*ic*to Aleuino patri dicti Aleuini ex precepto inclite recordac*i*onis d*omi*ni Alex*andri* reg*is* p*at*ris nostri carissimi assignauerunt et tradiderunt cum incremento quod p*er* eosdem Walterum fil*ium* Alan*i* et Rog*erum* Auenel' . f*ac*tum fuit Math*e*o cl*er*ico de Tulycultry . in nemore . in saltib*us* . in planis et asp*er*is . in t*er*ris et aquis . in p*ra*tis et pascuis . in moris et maresiis . in stagnis et molendinis . cum socco et sacca . cum furca et fossa . cum tol et them . et infangandethef' . et cum omnib*us* aliis iustis p*er*tinenciis suis . et cum omnib*us* natiuis eiusdem t*er*re . qui die collac*i*onis f*act*e predicto Aleuino p*at*ri dicti Aleuini[a] in dicta t*er*ra manentes fuerunt . libere . quiete . plenar*ie* et honorifice . p*er* s*er*uicium vnius militis . saluis n*ost*ris elemosinis . Concessimus eciam eid*em* Will*elmo* vt ip*s*e et heredes sui habeant et teneant dictam t*er*ram in liberum forestum . Q*ua*re firmi*t*er prohibemus ne quis s*in*e eor*um* licencia in pred*ic*ta t*er*ra secet . aut venetur sup*er* nostram plenariam forisfacturam decem librarum . Test*ibus* venerabili p*at*re Gamelino . e*pisco*po S*an*c*t*i Andr*ee* . Alex*andro* Cumyn' comite de *Bouchan* . justiciario Scoc*ie* . Walt*er*o com*it*e de Menetht' . Joh*anne* Cumyn' . Will*elmo* . de Brechyn' . Eustach*io* de Turrib*us* . Reginaldo le Chen' apud Forfar' . vicesimo primo die Decembr*is* anno regni n*os*tri qu*ar*todecimo .

NOTE. [a] The transcript that appears in *Aberdeen-Banff Illustrations* has dicti Alewini extiterant and omits the next ten words. The transcript in *HMC Mar and Kellie*, however, reproduces the clause as it appears in the original document.

ENDORSED. 1. Carta de Tulycult*er* (contemporary hand). 2. Tullecultre 1261 (fourteenth century). 3. King Alexanders charter of Tillicultre to William Earle of Marr (sixteenth century).

DESCRIPTION. 22.6 cm x 20.3 cm; fold 3.6 cm. Sealing: a tag, 2.0 cm broad, is passed through a single slit; seal lost.

HAND. Scribe E.

SOURCE. Original. NRS, Papers of the Erskine Family, Earls of Mar and Kellie, GD 124/1/513.

PRINTED. *HMC Mar and Kellie Supp. Report*, 1–2; *Aberdeen-Banff Illustrations*, iv, 697–8; *Statistical Account* (1791), xv, 211–12. A modern transcript appears in NLS, Adv. MS. 34.3.25, fo. 217.

42 Grants and by this charter confirms to the monks of Melrose abbey the gift that Nicholas Corbet made them of all his fisheries in the river Tweed, near his land of Makerstoun (Roxburghshire), that is, from the boundary of Dalcove all the way to the boundary of Broxmouth. To be held by the monks in free, pure and perpetual alms, with free entry and exit to the fisheries, as Nicholas's charter bears witness, saving the king's service. Notes that Nicholas, in the king's own presence in the refectory of Melrose abbey, undertook responsibility to render any service that might in future be required from the land. Selkirk. 6 February a.r. 14 [1263].

Alexander[a] Dei gr*ati*a rex Scott*orum* . om*n*ib*us* probis hominib*us* t*er*re sue salutem . Sciant p*rese*ntes et futuri nos concessisse et hac p*rese*nti carta n*ost*ra confirmasse donac*ione*m illam qua*m* Nicholai*us* Corbet pro salute a*n*i*me* n*ost*re et p*ro* a*nim*ab*us* patris et m*at*ris et *omnium* antecessor*um* et successor*um* suor*um* et p*ro* salute a*n*ime sue et spo*ns*e sue Margarethe et o*mni*um amicor*um* suor*um* fecit Deo et b*ea*te Marie de Melros et monachis ibidem Deo seruientib*us* et inp*er*petuum seruituris specialiter et p*ro*p*re* augmentu*m* et emendacione*m* et sustentac*i*onis et recreacionis eor*und*e*m* de om*n*ib*us* piscariis suis quas idem Nicholaius h*ab*uit in flumine de Tuede adiace*n*tes t*er*re sue de Malkaruyston' . videlicet a marchia de Dalcoue co*n*tinue usq*ue* ad marchiam de Brokismuthe sine aliquo retineme*n*to et aliquo jure uel potestate quouismodo piscandi in eisdem. Tenendu*m* et h*ab*endum eisdem monachis in lib*er*am puram et p*er*petua*m* elemosinam adeo libere q*ui*ete plenarie honorifice et solute cu*m* lib*er*o intr*o*itu et exitu ad dictas piscarias sicut carta predicti Nicholay eisdem monachis sup*er* hoc confecta plenius testatur . saluo s*er*uicio n*ost*ro si q*uod* nobis debetur de dictis piscariis quod idem Nicholai*us* in p*rese*ncia n*ost*ra in refectorio de Melros nobis p*ro* se et heredibus suis manucepit inp*er*petuu*m* soluere pro monachis memoratis . Testibus Patricio comite de Dunbar . Henrico abbate de Kalchow . Eusthach*i*o de Turrib*us* . Will*elm*o de Mo*n*te Alto . et multis aliis apud Selekyrk . vi° . die Febr*uarii* anno regni n*ost*ri . xiii° . etc.

NOTE. [a] Initial 'A' is shared by the words 'Alexander' in both the rubric text and the charter text.

RUBRIC. Confirmac*i*o regis Alexandri de dono Nicholai Corbet sup*er* piscaria de Tuede.

SOURCE. BL, Harleian MS. 3960, fos 105v–106r.

PRINTED. *Melrose Liber*, i, no. 243.

COMMENT. Nicholas Corbet made the gift to the monks elsewhere than in the king's presence at Selkirk on 6 February 1263. Corbet's grant (fo. 95) is undated and has no witness list, but this royal charter reveals that the king, too, was in attendance on that earlier occasion, when the grant was made in the refectory at Melrose.

43 Announces to his worthy men on the south side of the Scottish Sea that he has granted and by this charter confirmed to the brethren of Soutra hospital one thrave of corn annually from each plough of his demesne lands on the south side of the sea, as in the time of his grandfather, King William and his father, King Alexander II. Strictly commands all his fermers on that side of the sea to answer to the brethren every year for the corn and to ensure that the hospital's envoys are assisted. Edinburgh, 14 February a.r. 14 [1263].

Alex*ander* Dei gr*ati*a rex Scottor*um* om*n*ib*us* p*ro*bis hom*in*ib*us* suis ex aust*r*ali p*ar*te maris Scottor*um* salu*te*m. Sciat*is* nos caritat*is* intuitu concessisse et hac p*resen*ti carta n*ost*ra conf*ir*masse Deo et s*anct*e T*r*i*n*itat*is* hospitali de Soltr' ac f*r*at*r*ib*us* ibid*e*m imp*er*petuu*m* commorantibus in om*n*ib*us* dominiis n*ost*ris ex aust*r*ali p*ar*te maris Scott*ie* singulis annis de qualibet caruca vna*m* t*r*auam bladi s*ecundu*m q*uod* temp*or*ib*us* felic*is* recordac*ion*is d*omi*ni Will*elm*i aui n*ost*ri et d*omi*ni Alex*and*ri pat*r*is n*ost*ri carissimi regu*m* Scoc*ie* illustriu*m* pleni*us* p*er*cipe[a] consueueru*n*t iuxta tenore*m* carte d*ic*ti d*omi*ni reg*is* Will*elm*i q*ua*m inde h*abe*nt. Quar*e* om*n*ib*us* firmariis n*ost*ris ex p*re*d*ic*ta p*ar*te maris Scocie fi*r*mit*er* precipim*us* quatinus de sing*u*lis caruc*is* in d*ict*is dominiis n*ost*ris eisd*em* *fr*atri*bus* vel eor*um* ce*r*tis attornatis latorib*us* p*rese*nciu*m* sing*u*lis annis efficacit*er* sint r*espo*ndentes vos eciam[b] similit*er* rogam*us* affectuose q*ua*tin*us* caritatis intuitu et n*ost*ra mediante petic*io*ne vnusquisq*ue* v*est*rum de sing*u*lis carucis suis eis faciat tantu*nd*em. Et nuncios suos p*ro* collecta illius bladi int*er* se venentes benigne suscipiatis p*er* quod a Deo remuneraci*o*nem et a nob*is* grates m*er*ito recip*er*e debeatis. In cui*us* rei testi*m*oniu*m* has n*ost*ras litt*er*as fieri fecimus patentes. Testibus Willelmo comite de Marr' camerario Will*elm*o de Monte Alto. Will*elm*o de Sancto Claro. Fergusio Cumyne et Joh*ann*e de Lamm*er*ton'. ap*u*d Castr*um* Puellar*um* xiiii die Febr*uarii* anno regni n*ost*ri xiiii°.

NOTES. [a] Sic, percipere. [b] MS repeats vos eciam. For a discussion of the authenticity of this act, see *RRS*, v, no. 529.

RUBRIC. Confirmacio regis in larga forma (sixteenth century).

SOURCE. NLS, Adv. MS. 34.4.1, Chartulary of the Hospital of the Holy Trinity, Soutra, fos 17v–18r, a confirmation by King Robert I, dated Berwick 14 February 1325, of three charters to the hospital granted by kings William I and Alexander III. This text represents the second of these grants. See also no. 48, below.

PRINTED. *Midlothian Chrs*, Soutra, no. 52; *RRS*, v, no. 266.

44 Grants to the burgesses of Inverkeithing that they may impose toll and customs and all dues pertaining to the burgh between the river Leven and the river Devon, on water and land and from boats and ships. Strictly prohibits anyone from taking toll or trading within these boundaries without the burgesses' licence, on pain of the king's full forfeiture, as the charters of his grandfather, King William I, and his father, King Alexander II, bear witness. Further grants to the burgesses all the customs, rights and liberties that the burgesses of Perth and Aberdeen enjoy. Scone, 19 March a.r. 14 [1263].

Alexander Dei gracia rex Scottorum, justiciariis, vicecomitibus, prepositis, ministris, et omnibus probis hominibus tocius terre sue, salutem. Sciatis nos concessisse burgensibus nostris de Inuyrkethine ut capiant tolneum et consuetudines et omnes rectitudines ad burgum pertinentes inter aquam de Levene et aquam de Douane, in aquis et terris, tam de batellis quam de nauibus. Et firmiter prohibemus, ne quis tolneum aut aliquam consuetudinem ad predictum burgum pertinentem, aut in aquis aut in terris, infra predictas diuisas, absque eorum licencia, capiat, aut aliquam mercaturam extra burgum exerceat, super nostram plenariam forisfacturam, sicut carte domini regis Willelmi, aui nostri, et domini regis Alexandri, patris nostri, inde facte predictis burgensibus plenius testantur. Concessimus vero eisdem burgensibus nostris aut omnimodis consuetudinibus rectitudinibus et libertatibus gaudeant quibus gaudent burgi nostri de Perth, et de Abirdene, ac vtuntur. Testibus venerabili patre G episcopo Sancti Andree, Malcolmo comite de Fyf , A . Cumyn comite de Buchane, justiciario Scocie, W. comite de Marr', camerario, Johanne Cumyn, Roger de Moubray, et Waltero de Moravia. Apud Scone, decimo nono die mensis Marcii, anno regni nostri decimo [quarto?].

SOURCE. NRS, Inverkeithing Burgh Records, B34/20/349, with an exact duplicate in B34/20/350. The text is cited an inspeximus of Robert III, dated Edinburgh 24 April 1399 of various royal charters to the burgh, which refers to (among others) a charter of Alexander III, authenticated with the great seal. The original act is now lost.
PRINTED. *Municipal Corp. Scotland*, App. 8.
COMMENT. The printed version gives a.r. 10, i.e., 1259. But William earl of Mar, chamberlain, who witnesses the act, held that office 1251 x 1255 and 1260 x 1267. Maitland Thomson (NRS, GD 212/1/38, 28) gives a.r. 14, possibly from knowledge of the MS source, and on the whole this date is the more likely. A modern transcript appears in NRS, RH 9/11/16/6.

45 Takes the nuns of Coldstream, their lands, their men and all their possessions, movable and immovable, ecclesiastical as well as worldly, under his firm peace and protection, strictly forbidding anyone from causing any harm or injury to them, on pain of his full forfeiture; also grants that no one may take poinds from them or their men for any debt, pledge or forfeiture other than for their own debts, pledges or forfeitures, except in his burghs, and again strictly forbids anyone from disturbing them in defiance of this grant, on pain of full forfeiture. Commands his justices, sheriffs, provosts and their bailies to compel all those in their burghs or bailiaries who owe a debt to the nuns to pay them without delay. Further grants to the nuns that that they should enjoy all the liberties they were accustomed to have under his ancestors and, for a third time, strictly forbids anyone from disturbing them in defiance of this grant, on pain of full forfeiture. Roxburgh, 3 May a.r. 14 [1263].

Alex*ander* Dei gr*ati*a rex Scottor*um* omnib*us* probis hominib*us* toti*us* t*er*re sue sal*ut*em . Sciatis nos s*anc*timoniales de Kaldestrem' t*er*ras suas . homines suos et vniu*er*sas eorumdem possessiones ac bona sua mobilia et immobilia tam eccl*es*iastica q*ua*m mundana s*u*b fi*r*ma pace et proteccione nostra iuste suscepisse . Q*ua*re fi*r*miter inhibemus ne quis eis malum . molestiam . iniuriam seu . g*ra*uamen aliquod inf*er*re presumat iniuste sup*er* n*ost*ram plenariam forisf*ac*turam . Concessim*us* etiam eisdem vt nullus namos suos . v*el* ho*min*u*m* suoru*m* capiat pro alicui*us* debito . plegiagio . v*el* forisf*ac*to . nisi pro eorumdem p*ro*prio debito . plegiagio . v*el* forisf*ac*to saluis burgis n*ost*ris . firmit*er* inhibentes ne quis cont*ra* hanc concessione*m* n*ost*ra*m* ips*os* vexare presumat iniuste sup*er* n*ost*ram plenariam forisf*ac*turam . Mandam*us* insup*er* et firmit*er* p*re*cipim*us* justiciar*iis* . vicecomitib*us* . p*re*positis et eor*um* balliuis ad quos p*re*sentes littere p*er*uen*er*int vt omnes illos in balliis suis seu burgis qui debita debent eisdem monialib*us* que ip*s*e v*el* eor*um* c*er*tus atornat*us* lator p*re*sencium eis ab eisdem deb*ita* r*ati*onabilit*er* probare pot*er*unt *vel* pot*er*it . ad eadem debita eis iuste et sine dila*ti*one reddenda prout iustum fu*er*it comp*e*llant . ita . ne pro eor*um* defe*c*tum amplius inde iustam querimoniam audiam*us* . Concessim*us* eciam eisdem monialib*us* vt omnib*us* lib*er*tatib*us* gaudeant . quib*us* temporib*us* antecess*orum* n*ost*rorum regu*m* Scoc*ie* illust*ri*um et n*ost*ris hactenus vse sunt et gauise . firmiter prohibentes ne quis eas super hiis contra hanc concessionem nostram vexare presumat iniuste super nostram plenariam forisfacturam . Testibus venerabili patre . J . episcopo Glasg' . P . comite de Dunbarr' Johanne Cumyn' . et Hugone de Abrnitthyn' apud Rokisburch' tertio die Maii . anno regni nostri . xiiii°.

DESCRIPTION. 20.1 cm x 12.1 cm; fold 2.4 cm. Sealing: a tag, 2.1 cm broad, is passed through a single slit; seal lost.
HAND. Scribe E.
SOURCE. Original. NRS, Register House Charters, RH 6/30.
PRINTED. *Coldstream Chartulary*, App., no. 3.
COMMENT. A modern transcript appears in NRS, RH 2/2/15, item 11.

46 Commands Simon Fraser sheriff of Traquair and his bailies every year at Easter to allow the master and brethren of the hospital of Soutra to have the half-chalder of oatmeal from the mill of Peebles which his father, King Alexander II, bestowed on them. Melrose, 21 July a.r. 15 [1263].

Alexander Dei gratia rex Scottorum Symoni Fraser' vicecomiti et balliuis suis de Tracquar' singulis annis ad Pascha habere faciatis magistro et fratribus domus hospitalis de Soltr' vnam dimidiam celdram farine auene quam ex collacione inclite recordacionis domini Alexandri regis Scocie illustris patris nostri percipere consuerunt de molendino de Peblis. Et nos dictam dimidiam celdram farine in compotis vestris singulis annis faciemus plenius allocari. In cuius rei testimonium has nostras litteras fieri fecimus patentes. Testibus Gwydon' de Balliolo Willelmo Cumyne de Kirbrid Johanne de Lammerton. Apud Melros vicesimo primo die Julii anno regni nostri quintodecimo.

RUBRIC. Molendinum de Peblis (fifteenth century).
SOURCE. NLS, Adv. MS. 34.4.1, Chartulary of the Hospital of the Holy Trinity, Soutra, fos 3v–4r.
PRINTED. *Midlothian Chrs*, Soutra, no. 41.

47 Grants and by this charter confirms to the abbot and convent of Lindores the gift that Roger de Quincy earl of Winchester, constable of Scotland, made them of the church of Collessie (Fife). To be held in free, pure and perpetual alms as the earl's charter to them bears witness. Linlithgow, 25 December a.r. 15 [1263].

Alexander Dei gratia rex Scottorum omnibus probis hominibus tocius terre sue salutem. Sciatis nos concessisse et hac presenti carta nostra confirmasse donacionem illam quam Rogerus de Quency' comes Winton'. constabularius Scocie fecit caritatis intuitu pro salute anime sue et pro animabus antecessorum et successorum suorum Deo et beate Marie et ecclesie Sancti Andree de Lundors' et abbati et conuentui ibidem Deo seruientibus et inperpetuum seruituris de ecclesia de Cullesin' cum omnibus suis pertinenciis. Tenenda et habenda eisdem abbati et conuentui et eorum successoribus inperpetuum in liberam puram et perpetuam elemosinam adeo libere quiete plenarie et honorifice sicut carta dicti comitis eis inde confecta plenius iuste testatur. Testibus Gamelino episcopo Sancti Andree. Ricardo episcopo Dunkeldens'. Roberto episcopo Dunblanens'. Willelmo comite de

Marr' camer*ario*. Joh*anne* Cumyn. Hugone de Abirnethyn. Hug*one* de Berklay justic*iario* Laudonie et Joh*anne* de La*m*be*r*to*u*n apud Linlithg[v] vicesi*m*oquinto die Decembr*is* anno regni n*ostr*i quintodecimo.

SOURCE. Caprington Castle, Kilmarnock, Lindores Cartulary, fo. 6[r].
PRINTED. *Lindores Cart.*, no. 132.

48 Announces that he has inspected the charter by which his father, King Alexander II, gave and granted to the hospital of Soutra and its brethren a half-chalder of oatmeal annually at Easter from the mill of Peebles. The meal that was customarily given is now being rendered at ferme in cash; he wills and grants that henceforth they should receive the half-chalder every year from his mill at Traquair, as freely and quietly as the terms of his father's charter bear witness. Newbattle, 10 March a.r. 15 [1264].

Alex*ander* Dei gr*ati*a rex Scott*orum* om*n*ib*us* p*ro*bis hom*in*ib*us* suis ad quos p*rese*ntes litt*ere* p*er*uen*er*int sal*ute*m. Scia*tis* q*uod* inspexim*us* cartam inclite recordac*ion*is Alex*and*ri regis Scott*orum* p*at*ris n*ost*ri p*er* qua*m* ip*s*e dedit et concessit Deo et eccl*es*ie sancte T*r*initatis de Soltr' et f*ra*tribus in ead*e*m eccl*es*ia s*er*uientib*us* et imp*er*petuu*m* s*er*uitu*r*is vnam di*mi*diam celdri farine auene in puram et p*er*petuam eli*mo*sinam[a] an*n*uatim p*er*cipiendam ad Pascha de molendino n*ost*ro de Peblis que farinam redder*e* solebat iam dat*ur* ad fi*r*mam in denariis. Volum*us* et concedim*us* eisd*e*m f*ra*tribus vt ip*s*i et eor*um* successores imp*er*petuu*m* d*ic*ta*m* di*mi*diam celdre farine auene decet*er*o sing*u*lis annis p*er*cipiant ad Pascha de molendino n*ost*ro de Trecquar' p*er* manu*m* illi*us* qui p*ro* te*m*p*or*e fu*er*it fi*r*marius d*ic*ti molendini de Trecquar' adeo lib*er*e et q*ui*ete sicut d*ic*ta carta p*at*ris n*ost*ri eis inde confecta in d*ict*o molendi*no* de Peblis pleni*us* iuste testat*ur*. In cui*us* rei testi*moniu*m has l*itt*eras n*ost*ras fieri fecim*us* patentes. Test*ibus* Gam*el*ino e*pisco*po S*anc*ti Andr*e*e. Malcolmo Comite de Fyf'. Patricio comite de Dunbar. Willelmo Comyn[b] de Marr' cam*er*ar*io*. Joh*anne* Cumyne. Hugone de Ab*er*nethy. Hugon*e* de Berclay justiciar*io* Laudo*n*ie et Joh*anne* de Lamb*er*ton' apud Neubotil decimo die Marcii anno regni n*ost*ri qui*n*todeci*mo*.

NOTES. [a] Sic, elemosinam. [b] Sic, comite.
RUBRIC. De molendino de Treqwar' (sixteenth century).
SOURCE. NLS, Adv. MS. 34.4.1, Chartulary of the Hospital of the Holy Trinity, Soutra, fos 18[r]–18[v], a confirmation by King Robert I, dated Berwick 14 February 1325, of three charters to the hospital granted by kings William I and Alexander III. This text represents the second of these grants. See also no. 43, above, and the comments in *RRS*, v, no. 529 about the authenticity of this grant.
PRINTED. *Midlothian Chrs*, Soutra, no. 52; *RRS*, v, no. 266.

49 Announces that, as he understands from the instruments and charters of his ancestors, by ancient custom and common law any religious persons travelling through the country with carts may remain and pasture their animals in any feu for one night. Wishing to observe custom and common law and under pain of his full forfeiture, he strictly prohibits anyone from harming, injuring or in any way obstructing the monks of Melrose, or any other religious travelling with beasts and carts, in violation of this custom and law. Melrose, 21 July a.r. 16 [1264].

Alex*ander* Dei gra*ti*a rex Scoc*ie* . omnibus p*ro*bis hominibus tocius t*er*re sue . sal*ute*m . Sciatis q*uo*d cum temporibus antecessorum n*ostr*or*um* . regum Scoc*ie* illustrium et n*ost*ris hactenus ex antiqu*a* consuetudine approbata et iure co*m*muni p*er* regnum n*ost*rum Scoc*ie* . ita fu*er*it vsitatum . q*uo*d tam viri religiosi q*ua*m alie p*er*sone p*er* patr*ia*m t*ra*nseuntes cum cariagiis suis in quemcumq*ue* feodum ven*er*int p*er* vnam noctem moram cont*ra*here licite possint in eodem . animalia sua ibidem ext*ra* segetes et prata pascendo s*ecundu*m q*uo*d p*er* instrumenta et sc*ri*pta dicto*rum* antecesso*rum* n*ost*ro*rum* satis euident*er* intelleximu*s* . Nos eandem consuetudinem . et ius co*m*mune firmit*er* obseruari volentes . firmit*er* inhibemus ne quis cont*ra* hanc consuetudine*m* et ius com*m*une monachis de Melros uel aliis viris religiosis p*er* q*ua*scumq*ue* partes ip*s*os t*ra*nsire contigerit malum inferat . iniuriam aut impedimentum . quo minus cum auerijs suis et cariagijs ext*ra* segetes et p*ra*ta pascendo libere possint t*ra*nsire sup*er* n*ostr*am plenariam forisfacturam . Test*ibus* . Hugone de Abirnithin . Will*elm*o Comin de Kellebride . Joha*nn*e . de Lambirton'. ap*u*d Melros' . xxi . die Julii . ann*o* regni n*ost*ri sextodecimo .

ENDORSED. De passagiis (contemporary hand).
DESCRIPTION. 22.0 cm x 10.6 cm; fold 3.1 cm. Sealing: a tag, 2.2 cm broad, is passed through a single slit and bears a fragment of the second great seal 9.0 cm in diameter, in white wax. The seal is rubbed and extensively damaged at the edges, the legend almost completely illegible, but the figure of the seated king on the obverse and the equestrian pose on the reverse are both clear.
HAND. Scribe F.
SOURCE. Original. NRS, Melrose Charters, GD 55/309.
PRINTED. *Melrose Liber*, i, no. 309; *Nat. MSS. Scotland*, i, no. 60 (facs.).
COMMENT. This is the first surviving example of the king's second great seal.

50 Takes the prior and monks of Lesmahagow, their lands, their men and all their possessions, movable and immovable, ecclesiastical as well as worldly, under his firm peace and protection, strictly forbidding anyone from causing any harm or injury to them, on pain of his full forfeiture. Machan,[a] 7 August a.r. 16 [1264].

Alex*ander* Dei gra*ti*a rex Scott*orum* om*n*ibu*s* p*ro*bis hominibu*s* tocius t*er*re sue sal*utem* . Sciatis nos p*r*iore*m* et monachos de Lesmahag' t*er*ras suas ho*min*es suos ac vniu*er*sas eor*undem* possessiones et bona sua mobilia et inmobilia[b] ta*m* eccl*es*iastica q*uam* mu*n*dana sub firma pace et p*r*otecc*i*one n*ostr*a iuste suscepisse . Quare fi*r*mit*er* p*ro*hibemus ne q*ui*s eis malu*m* iniuria*m* molestia*m* aut g*ra*uamen inf*er*re p*r*esumat iniuste sup*er* n*ostr*am plenar*iam* forisfactura*m* . Test*ibu*s Will*elm*o Cumyn' de Kelbride . Joh*ann*e d*e* Dundemor' Joh*ann*e de Lambirtun' ap*ud* Machan' . septi*m*o die Augusti anno regni n*ost*ri sexdecimo .

NOTES. [a] Near Larkhall. [b] Sic, immobilia.
RUBRIC. Top of folio: Lesmahag'; alongside this entry: Ite*m* littera pacis et p*r*oteccio*n*is p*r*ioris et monachor*um* de Lesmahag' (in red, with most of the capital initials in the text also rubricated).
SOURCE. NLS, Adv. MS. 34.5.1, Chartulary of Kelso Abbey, fos. 75^{v}–76^{r}.
PRINTED. *Kelso Liber*, i, no. 185.

51 Grants and by this charter confirms to the abbot and convent of Melrose all the charters, confirmations, rights and liberties that his royal predecessors have granted them. To be held in perpetuity as freely, quietly, fully and honourably as his predecessors' charters bear witness. Selkirk, 9 December a.r. 16 [1264].

Alex*ander* Dei gr*at*ia rex Scott*orum* omnibus probis hominib*us* tocius t*er*re sue sal*ut*em. Cum int*er* cet*er*a monast*er*ia regni n*ost*ri monast*er*ium de Melros specialius diligamus patris n*ost*ri k*arissi*mi vestigiis inherentes . concessimus et hac p*re*senti carta [con]f[irm]auim*us* . abb*at*i et conuentui eiusdem monast*er*ii . omnes cartas confirmationes . libertates et iura p*re*decessorum n*ost*ror*um* regum Scot*ie* illust*ri*um eisdem concessa . Tenend*as* et habend*as* eisdem abb*at*i et conuentui et eor*um* successoribus in p*er*petuu*m* sec*und*um tenorem d*ictorum* cartar*um* confirmationu*m* et iuriu*m* ac lib*er*tatum . adeo lib*ere* quiete plenar*ie* . et honorifice . sicut carte et confirmationes d*ictorum* lib*er*tatum et iuriu*m* p*re*dictor*um* p*re*decessor*um* n*ost*ror*um* eisdem confecte . plenius iuste testantur . Test*ibus* Hug*one* de Berkeley just*iciario* Laod*onie* . Eym*er*o de Maxwell' just*iciario* Galwath' Nichol*ao* Corbetth . Guydone de Balliol' et Johanne de Lamberton' apud Selekirk' nono die Decembr*is* anno regni n*ost*ri sextodecimo .

ENDORSED. Carta regis A. junioris de confirmacione omnium libertatum una cum clausula ista, cum inter cetera rengni [sic] nostri etc.
DESCRIPTION. 24.7 cm x 7.5 cm; fold 2.6 cm. Sealing: a tag, 1.7 cm broad, is passed through double slits and bears a fragment of the second great seal 10.4 cm in diameter, in white wax. The seal is rubbed and extensively damaged at the edges, the legend almost completely illegible.
HAND. Scribe F.
SOURCE. Original. NRS, Melrose Charters, GD 55/310.
PRINTED. *Melrose Liber*, i, no. 310.

52 Grants and by this charter confirms to the monks of Melrose abbey the gift that Alexander steward of Scotland made them of all right and claim that he or his heirs might have in the lands and pastures of Mauchline (Ayrshire) and Cairn Table (Lanarkshire) on both sides of the river Ayr, given to them by Alexander's ancestors, in return for one annual pittance, to be made in perpetuity on the feast of St James the Apostle. To be held by the monks in free, pure and perpetual alms as Alexander's charter bears witness. Traquair, 12 December a.r. 16 [1264].

. Alex*ander* . Dei gr*at*ia rex Scott*orum* . omnib*us* p*ro*bis hominib*us* tocius t*er*re sue sal*ut*em . Sciant presentes et futuri nos concessisse et hac carta n*ost*ra confirmasse donac*io*nem illam . quam Alex*ander* . senescall*us* Scoc*ie* . fecit Deo et eccl*esie* s*anc*te Marie de Melros' . et monachis ibid*em* s*er*uientib*us* et inpost*er*um s*er*uituris p*ro* salute sua . vxoris sue . et omnium antecessorum et successorum suorum de omnimodo iure et clamo . quod idem Alex*ander* . v*el* heredes sui h*ab*uerunt . v*el* h*ab*ere pot*er*unt in t*er*ris et pasturis de Mauhelyn' . et de Carnetabell' et p*er*tinenciis suis ab antecessoribus eius eisd*em* monachis datis et concessis ex vt*raque* p*ar*te fluminis de Ar' . sine aliquo retenem*en*to . ad vnam pitanciam annuam conuentui de Melros' in*per*petuu*m* faciendam . die s*anct*i Jacobi ap*ost*oli . Concedim*us* etiam et confirmam*us* concessione*m* illam q*ua*m idem Alex*ander* fecit eisd*em* monachis de eisd*em* t*er*ris et pasturis tenendis et possidendis cum om*n*ibus iurib*us*. lib*er*tatib*us* et p*er*tinenc*iis* suis in lib*er*am . puram et p*er*petuam elemosinam in bosco et plano . in p*ra*tis et pascuis . in viis et semitis . in moris et maresiis . aquis . stagnis et molendinis . tam aquariis . q*ua*m ventoriis . cum feris . auib*us* . piscib*us* . et omnib*us* aliis que infra d*ic*tas t*er*ras et pasturas inuenta su*n*t . vel poterunt inueniri . tam subt*us* t*er*ram . quam supra . ad ip*sum* Alexan*drum* et heredes suos spectancia . uel spectare debencia . ita lib*er*e . quiete . plenarie et honorifice . sicut carta eiusd*em* Alex*andri* . q*ua*m d*ic*ti monachi de eisd*em* t*er*ris et pasturis habent pleni*us* iuste testat*ur* . saluo s*er*uic*i*o nostro . Test*ibus* . P . com*ite* de Dunbarr' . Hug*one* de Berkeley justic*i*-*ario* Laodon*ie* . Walt*er*o de Morauia . Joh*ann*e de Lambirtun' . Simone Fraser' . et Bernardo de Monte Alto . apud Traquayr' duodecimo die Decembr*is* . anno regni nostri sextodecimo .

ENDORSED. *Con*firmacio reg*is* Alex*andri* juni*o*ris de carta Alex*andri* senescalli de lib*er*-tatib*us* de Kule (contemporary hand).
DESCRIPTION. 22.0 cm x 13.3 cm. The portion that was once folded up measures 4.5 cm. Sealing: formerly on a tag, through double slits. Seal and tag now missing; see below for further comments concerning the seal.
HAND. Scribe F.
SOURCE. Original. BL, Campbell Charters, XXX, no. 8. There are several early modern and modern transcripts of the document, including one by Matthew Hutton, NLS, Adv. MS. 22.1.13, fo. 211[v]. In the eighteenth century the archivist and collector Thomas Astle (BL, MS Stowe 551, fos 40–3), made copies of this deed and several other charters then in his possession. All had been published in 1739 in J. Anderson's *Diplomata Scotiae*. Still another transcription was made in 1837 (BL, Add. MS. 11545, fos 22–3).
PRINTED. *Melrose Liber*, i, no. 323; Anderson, *Diplomata Scotiae*, pl. 36 (facs.).
COMMENT. Astle added to his transcript brief notes about the king and his untimely death; more important, he made a beautifully detailed coloured engraving of the royal seal that was then still appended to the act. The seal was still attached in 1814, when Lord Frederick Campbell deposited the document in the British Museum, but by the time that the transcript of 1837 was made it had disappeared. It is probably the seal now found in The National Archives as TNA, Special Collections: Seals, PRO SC 13/H 22.

53 Grants that the monks of Melrose abbey should hold their lands and pastures of Mauchline (Ayrshire) and Cairn Table (Lanarkshire) in free forest. Strictly prohibits anyone from felling timber or hunting there without their licence, on pain of his full forfeiture of £10. Traquair, 12 [December] a.r. 16 [1264].

. Alex*ander* . Dei gr*ati*a rex Scott*orum* . omnibus p*ro*bis hominib*us* tocius t*er*re sue sal*ut*em . Sciatis . q*uo*d concessimus abb*at*i et conuentui de Melros' . ut *hab*ean*t* et teneant om*n*es t*er*ras suas et pasturas de Machelyn' et Carnetabell' ex vt*raque par*te fluminis de Ar' cum suis p*er*tinenc*iis* in lib*er*am forestam . Q*ua*re firmit*er* p*ro*hibemus . ne quis in dictis t*er*ris . uel pasturis sine licencia d*ict*orum abbatis et conuent*us* secet . aut venet*ur* . sup*er* n*ost*ra*m* plenariam forisf*act*uram decem libr*arum* . Test*ibus* . P . com*ite* de Dunbarr' . Hug*one* de Berkeley justic*iario* Laodonie [Waltero de] Morauia . Johanne de Lambirtun' et Simone Fraser' apud Traquayr' . duodec[imo die mensis Decembris[a] anno] regni nostri sextodecimo .

NOTE. [a] The month name is obscured by a large stain, but the witness list and date of the charter reveal that it was granted on the same day – and probably in the same venue – as no. 52, above.
ENDORSED. Conf*irmacio* reg*is* Alex*andri* de libera foresta t*er*re de Kule (contemporary hand; probably the same as the scribe's).
DESCRIPTION. 17.3 cm x 8.8 cm; fold 2.5 cm. Sealing: a tag, 1.8 cm broad, is passed through double slits and bears the second great seal 10.0 cm in diameter, in darkened white wax. The seal is almost entire, although a few words of the legend are missing. The seal is slightly rubbed at the edges, but is otherwise well preserved.
HAND. Scribe F.
SOURCE. Original. NRS, Melrose Charters, GD 55/324.
PRINTED. *Melrose Liber*, i, no. 324.

54 Grants that the abbot and convent of Lindores should hold all the wood and land of Lindores in free forest. Strictly prohibits anyone from felling timber or hunting there without their licence, on pain of his full forfeiture of £10. Lindores, 14 March a.r. 16 [1265].

Alexand*er* Dei *gra*tia rex Scott*orum* om*n*ib*us* p*ro*bis ho*min*ib*us* toci*us* t*er*re sue sal*u*te*m*. Sciatis quod *con*cessim*us* abb*at*i et *co*nue*n*tui de Lundor' ut h*ab*eant et tenea*n*t tot*um* boscu*m* suu*m* cu*m* t*er*ra de Lu*n*dors'[a] in libera*m* foresta*m*. Quar*e* firmit*er* p*ro*hibem*us* ne quis sine eoru*m* licencia in p*redict*o bosco secet aut venet*ur* sup*er* n*ost*ram plenaria*m* forisfacturam dece*m* librar*um*. Testib*us* Alexand*r*o Cumyn'. co*m*ite de Buchane. justiciar*io* Scoc*ie* Will*elm*o co*m*ite de Mare camer*ario* et Eustachio de T*ur*rib*us*. Apud. Lu*n*dors quarto deci*m*o die M*ar*cii anno regni n*ost*ri sexto decimo etc.

NOTE. [a] Lundoris in printed version.
RUBRIC. Libertas foreste de Lundoris (sixteenth century).
SOURCE. NLS, Adv. MS. 34.7.1, Chartulary of Lindores Abbey, fo. 8^{v}.
PRINTED. *Lindores Liber*, no. 9.

55 Gives, grants and by this charter confirms to Hugh de Abernethy the whole land of Lour (Angus), which Henry de Nevay, knight, resigned and quitclaimed for default of service owed to the king for that place, saving to Henry and his heirs the land of Nevay. To be held in feu and heritage, with gallows and pit, soke and sake, toll, team and infangentheof, for the service of one knight, which is owed for the lands of Nevay and Lour. Perth, 19 March a.r. 16 [1265].

Alex*and*er Dei gr*ati*a rex Scott*orum* . omnib*us* p*ro*bis hominibus tocius t*er*re sue sal*u*tem . Nou*er*itis nos dedisse . concessisse . et hac *presenti* carta n*ost*ra confirmasse Hugoni de Abirnith' p*ro* homagi*o* et *s*eruicio suo totam t*er*ram de Lur' cum p*er*tinenc*iis* . q*ua*m Henricus de Neuith' miles p*er* defectum seruicii n*ost*ri nobis inde debiti . p*er* fustum et baculum nobis reddidit . et resignauit . ac p*ro* se et heredibus suis quietam clamauit inp*er*petuum . saluis d*ict*o Henr*ico* et heredibus suis t*er*ris de Neuith' cum iustis p*er*tinenc*iis* suis adeo libere . quiete et plenarie . sicut eas die resignac*io*nis t*er*re de Lur' cum suis p*er*tinenc*iis* q*ua*m p*ro* se et heredibus suis nobis reddidit p*er* fustum et baculum resignauit . ac inp*er*petuum quiete clamauit . lib*er*ius . quietius et plenarius tenuit et possedit saluo s*er*uicio n*ost*ro q*ua*ntum p*er*tinet ad s*er*uicium vnius militis quod nobis debe*tur* p*ro* t*er*ris de Neuith' . et de Lur' cum suis p*er*tinenciis . Tenend*am* et habend*am* eidem Hugoni et heredibus suis de nobis et heredibus n*ost*ris in feodo et hereditate tam in dominiis q*ua*m in homagiis et seruiciis . libere . quiete . plenarie et honorifice . cum furca et fossa . socc*o* et sacco . toll' et them' . et infangandethef' . et cum omnibus libertatib*us* et aisiamentis ac cet*er*is p*er*tinenc*iis* ad dictam t*er*ram de Lur' . iuste spectantib*us* v*e*l spectare valentib*us* de iure . Faciendo inde nobis et heredib*us* n*ost*ris ip*s*e et heredes sui qua*ntu*m p*er*tinet ad eandem t*er*ram de s*er*uicio vnius militis q*uo*d nobis de d*i*cta t*er*ra de Lur' . et de t*er*ra de Neuith' debetur . Test*ibu*s venerabilib*us* patrib*us* Gamel*ino* . Johanne . Ricardo et Roberto . S*anc*ti Andr*ee* . Glasguens' . Dunkeldens' . et Dunblanens' e*pisco*pis . Alexandro Cvmyn' com*ite* de Buchan' justici*ario* Scocie . W . com*ite* de Marr' camer*ario* . P . com*ite* de Dunbarr' . D . com*ite* Atholie . Alex*andro* Sen*escallo* Sco*cie* . Alano Host*iario* . Hug*one* de Berkeley just*iciario* Laodon*ie* . apud Perth decimo nono die Marcii . anno regni n*ost*ri sextodecimo' .

ENDORSED. 1. Carta de Lowres (fifteenth century). 2. King Alexander his chartour to Hew Abirnethye of the landis of Lowr 19 Marcii qhairin the namis and styllis off ye comminis ar seit doun (sixteenth century).
DESCRIPTION. 26.7 cm x 15.7 cm; fold 3.0 cm. Sealing: on a tag, 2.5 cm broad, attached through double slits, there appears a fragment of the second great seal, 5.8 cm in diameter, in green wax, with traces of natural wax also apparent. The fragment is in a poor state of preservation, with only a small portion of the centre visible.
HAND. Scribe F.
SOURCE. Original. Douglas Charters, Douglas-Home Family, earls of Home, NRAS 59/85/1/3.
PRINTED. Fraser, *Douglas*, iii, 3 (facs.); Fraser, *Southesk*, ii, 479; Fraser, *Facsimiles*, no. 60.

56 Gives, grants and by this charter confirms to Hugh de Abernethy £50 sterling annually to be taken from the ferme of Tannadice (Angus) until the king makes another provision of the same amount to him by wardship, marriage, escheat or other means. Scone, 31 March a.r. 16 [1265].

Alex*ander* Dei gracia rex Scott*orum* omnib*us* probis homini*b*us toci*us* t*er*re sue salutem . Sciatis nos dedisse . concessisse . et hac p*re*senti carta n*ost*ra confirmasse Hugoni de Abrinithyn' dil*ect*o n*ost*ro et fideli quinquaginta libras sterlingor*um* singulis annis de firma nostra de Thanethes' p*er* manus firmarii n*ost*ri de Thanethes' qui pro tempore fu*er*it p*er*cipiendas donec eidem Hugoni in warda . maritagio . eschaetta . v*e*l aliquo alio modo in tantum v*e*l vberius fec*er*imus p*ro*uideri . In c*ui*us rei testimonium has n*ost*ras litt*er*as eidem Hugoni fi*er*i fecim*us* patentes . Test*ibu*s . A . Cumyn' com*ite* de Bouchan' just*iciario* Scoc*ie* . P. com*ite* de Dunbarr' . M . com*ite* de Strathern' . W . com*ite* de Marr' camer*ario* . et W . com*ite* de Meneteth' . apud Schon' vltimo die Marcii . anno regni nostri . sexto decimo .

DESCRIPTION. 22.7 cm x 11.8 cm. The portion that was once folded up measures 2.3 cm. Sealing: a tag, 2.2 cm broad, through single slits. The seal is missing.
HAND. Scribe A.
SOURCE. Original. BL, Add. Ch. 66979.

57 Commands his provosts of Perth and his fermers of Craigie and St Magdalen's (Perthshire) to allow annually to the Friars Preachers of Perth five chalders of corn and ten chalders of malt from the fermes of these places, £7 16s from the ferme of the burgh of Perth, and one wey of wax. Scone, 10 October a.r. 17 [1265].

ALEXANDER,[a] Dei gratia, rex Scotorum, prepositis suis[b] de Perth, et firmariis suis de Cragyn,[c] et de Malhen, uni vel pluribus, qui pro tempore fuerint, salutem. Mandamus vobis, et precipimus, quatinus de firmis nostris de Cragyn,[c] et de Malhen, habere faciatis singulis annis, fratribus predicatoribus de Perth quinque celdras boni frumenti et bene vannati, et decem celdras boni brasii,[d] et similiter habere faciatis eisdem fratribus, singulis annis, de firma nostra burgi de Perth, septem libras et sexdecim solidos, pro procuratione[e] sua annua, et unam pisam cere, [cum m]elius[f] forum cere fuerit in anno, et solucion[em omnium][f] predictorum, singulis annis, quousque super hoc a nobis aliud receperitis in mandatis, dictis[g] fratribus ita bene fieri faciatis, ne ipsi de vobis iustam habeant materiam conquerendi, per quod ad vos graviter capere merito debeamus . Et nos omnia praedicta vobis in compotis vestris faciemus plenius allocari . Testibus Malcolmo, comite de Fyf,[h] Willelmo, comite de Marr', camerario, et Johanne de Parco . Apud Sconam, decimo die Octobris, anno regni nostri septimo decimo.

NOTES. [a] In small capitals in A. [b] Word omitted in B. [c] Crengyn in B. [d] Brasei in B. [e] Presentationes in B. [f] Solutionem fratrum in B. [g] Predictis in B. [h] Fyfe in B.

RUBRIC. Carta eiusdem domini Alexandri Scotorum regis [in capitals] fillii fundatoris de decem celdris brasii et quinque celdris frumenti de Cragy et Malhen (fifteenth-century hand contemporary with the transumpt).

SOURCE. NLS, Adv. Ch. A.4, item iii, a fifteenth-century transumpt by Bishop W[ardlaw] of St Andrews of three royal grants to the Friars Preachers = A; NRS, GD 26/3/1109 = B. See also no. 10, above.

PRINTED. Milne, *Blackfriars of Perth*, no. 3; *HMC*, vi, 713 (noted and misdated).

COMMENT. Milne, *Blackfriars of Perth*, 2, notes that: 'Craigie and St Magdalen's are well known and contiguous places in the neighbourhood of Perth – the latter, now a farm, marking the site of a hospital of an early date. Some think that the reference in the charter is to Mailer, also a property in the same neighbourhood, but Mr. Scott reads the word, more correctly it seems, Malhena, a softened form, he says, of Magdalena.'

58 Gives, grants and by this charter confirms to the abbot and convent of Lindores that they should have the toun that is called Newburgh, near the abbey, in free burgh and a market in that burgh every Tuesday, with the liberties of burgh and market, saving the rights of the king's burghs. Stirling, 4 March a.r. 17 [1266].

Alexand*er* Dei gr*ati*a rex Scott*orum* om*n*ib*us* probis ho*min*ibus tocius t*er*re sue sal*ut*em. Sciatis nos caritatis intuitu dediss*e* concessisse et hac p*rese*nti carta n*ost*ra *con*firmasse religios*is* viris abbati et *con*uentui de Lundor'[a] vt ip*s*i et eoru*m* successores in p*e*rpetuu*m* habea*n*t villam eoru*m* que dicit*ur* Nouo Burgus iuxta mo*na*sterium de Lundor' in lib*e*rum burgu*m* et foru*m* in eod*em* burgo quolibet die Martis cu*m* libertatib*us* burgi et fori saluis in om*n*ib*us* burgoru*m* n*o*strorum libertatibus. Test*ibus* Will*el*mo comite de Mare camer*ario* Joh*anne* de Lamberton' Joh*anne* de Lyndes' Joh*anne* de Hay et Gillascopp'

Ca*m*bell et Will*el*mo Biseht. Apud Striuelyn' quarto die Marcii anno regni n*ost*ri septimo deci*mo*, etc.

NOTE. [a] Lundoris in printed version.
RUBRIC. Concessio domini Regis sup*er* lib*er*tate Noui Burgi.
SOURCE. NLS, Adv. MS. 34.7.1, Chartulary of Lindores Abbey, fo. 6r.
PRINTED. *Lindores Liber*, no. 3.

59 Grants and by this charter confirms to the abbot and convent of Melrose the confirmation by which Alexander steward of Scotland confirmed to them the gift by Richard le Waleys, tenant of Alexander the steward, of the lands of Barmuir (Ayrshire) and Galdenoch (Wigtonshire). Also confirms the grant and quitclaim that Alexander made to the monks of suit of his court, freedom to buy, sell and levy toll, to hold courts and pleas in their lands of Cairn Table (Lanarkshire), Mauchline (Ayrshire) and Barmuir and to take the fines, amercements and escheats of these pleas. To be held as Alexander's charter bears witness, saving the king's service. Scone, 14 April a.r. 17 [1266].

Alex*ander* Dei gr*ati*a rex Scott*orum* omnibus probis hominib*us* toci*us* t*er*re sue salut*em* . Sciatis nos concessisse et hac carta n*ost*ra confirmasse concessionem et confirm*a*cionem illam quam Alexander senescallus Scocie fecit Deo et ecc*le*sie s*anc*te Marie de Melros' . et monachis ibidem Deo s*er*uientib*us* [super] donac*i*one*m* illa*m* quam Ricardus le Waleys tenens ip*s*ius Alexandri fecit eisdem monachis de t*er*ra sua de Barmor et de Godeneth' p*er* rectas diuisas suas . vna cum concessione et quietaclamac*i*one quas idem Alexander fecit eisdem monachis et hominibus eor*un*dem de sequela curie eiusdem Alex*andri* et de lib*er*tate emendi uendendi et tholoneii ac curie et placita sua tenendi in tenemento ip*sorum* de Carentabel . et de Mauchlyn' et de Barmor et forisf*ac*ta amerciamenta et eschaetas eor*un*dem placitor*um* capiendi . adeo libere . quiete . plenarie et honorifice in omnibus sicut scriptum ip*s*ius Alexandri eisdem monachis inde confectum pleni*us* iuste testatur . saluo s*er*uicio n*ost*ro . Test*ibus* Alexandro Cumyn' comite de Buchan' justiciari*o* Scoc*ie* . Patric*i*o comite de Dumbar' . et Rob*er*to de Brus' apud Scon' quartodecimo die Aprilis anno regni n*ost*ri septimodecimo .

ENDORSED. Confirmac*i*o libertatis de Kale (contemporary hand).
DESCRIPTION. 25.9 cm x 17.1 cm. The portion that was once folded up measures 1.1 cm. Sealing: formerly on a tag, through double slits. Seal and tag now missing.
HAND. Scribe F.
SOURCE. Original. BL, Cotton Ch. XVIII, no. 3.
PRINTED. *Melrose Liber*, i, no. 326.

60 Announces that he has granted to the master and brethren of the hospital of Soutra that wherever they or their men are able to find neyfs and fugitives who are theirs by right and reason outside the king's demesnes, they should have them. Strictly forbids anyone from unlawfully withholding such persons, under pain of his full forfeiture. Edinburgh, 20 May a.r. 17 [1266].

Alex*ander* Dei gr*ati*a rex Scott*orum* om*n*ib*us* probis hom*in*ib*us* tocius t*er*re sue sal*utem*. Sciat*is* q*uod* concessim*us* mag*istro* et frat*r*ib*us* domus de Soltr' vt vbicumque ipsi vel homines sui latores presencium inuenire poterunt extra dominia nostra natiuos et fugitiuos homines ipsorum magistri et fratrum qui sui de iure et ratione esse debent eos iuste habeant et firmiter inhibemus ne quis eos eis iniuste detinere presumat[a] super nostram plenariam forisfacturam. Testibus Willelmo comite de Marr' camerario Hugone de Berclay justiciario Laudonie et Thoma Ranulphi. apud Edynburgh vicesimo die Maii anno regni nostri septimodecimo.

NOTE. [a] Printed version has presumant (sic).
RUBRIC. Homini de Soltr'.
SOURCE. NLS, Adv. MS. 34.4.1, Chartulary of the Hospital of the Holy Trinity, Soutra, fo. 4[r].
PRINTED. *Midlothian Chrs*, Soutra, no. 42.

61 Announces a final concord with Magnus king of Norway for the cession of Man and the Isles made on the Friday following the feast of saints Peter and Paul, in the church of the Friars Preacher at Perth. The agreement is made between Magnus's envoys, his chancellor Asketin and his baron, Andrew son of Nicholas, on the one hand, and King Alexander III himself, together with his clergy and the greater magnates of his realm, on the other, to the effect that Magnus has granted, resigned and quitclaimed to Alexander Man and the rest of the Sudrey islands and all the other islands to the west and south of the Great Sea, with all the rights which he and his progenitors had of old therein. The islands are forever to be held, had and possessed by the said Alexander and his heirs, with all the demesne lands, homages, renders, services and all rights and pertinents belonging to them, together with the advowson of the bishopric of Man, saving, however, the right, jurisdiction and liberty which the church of Trondheim has in the bishopric of Man and his church, and excepting the islands of Orkney and Shetland with their lordships, homages, renders, services, rights and pertinents, which the king of Norway has specially reserved to his domain. Henceforth, all the inhabitants greater as well as lesser, of the said islands are to be subject to the laws and customs of the realm of Scotland and shall be judged and treated according to these, though they are not to be punished or troubled in their heritages for any misdeeds or injuries and damage which they have committed down to this day, while they adhered to the said king of Norway, but shall stand peacefully therein under the lordship of the king of Scots, as other free men and lieges of the said king do. If they choose to remain in the islands under the lordship of the king of Scots they may remain freely and in peace; if they choose to leave they may do so with their goods, lawfully, freely and in peace, so that they shall not be compelled either to remain or to leave against their will, contrary to the laws and customs of the realm of Scotland. In consideration of this grant, resignation and quitclaim and for the blessing of peace, King Alexander undertakes to pay to the king of Norway and his heirs and assigns, within the octave of the nativity of St John the Baptist, in Orkney, that is, in the land of the king of Norway, in the church of St Magnus, into the hand of the bishop of

Orkney or the bailie of the king of Norway specially deputed by him for the purpose or, if the bishop or bailie are not to be found, shall deposit in the custody of the canons of the said church, the sum of 100 merks sterling annually and in perpetuity, for which the bishop or bailie shall give letters of quittance and receipt and, in addition, 4,000 merks within the coming four years, namely 1,000 merks within the octaves of St John the Baptist in the year 1267 and 100 merks of the said pension, the same in 1268, 1269 and 1270. Thereafter Alexander shall pay only the 100 annual merks. Asketin and Andrew take an oath on behalf of King Magnus that he will observe this agreement; Adam earl of Carrick and Robert de Meyners swear a similar oath on behalf of King Alexander. Both parties also bind themselves to a penalty of 10,000 merks sterling if either should withdraw from this agreement; they also subject themselves and their heirs to the jurisdiction of the apostolic see for its observance. Both parties agree to remit all offences and injuries committed by either side down to this day and to release all hostages taken or detained on either side. If an enemy of one king flees to the other the latter is not to offer refuge unless the fugitive be restored to his own king's favour, excepting, however, persons who have committed high treason, who are not to be received by either king. If men of the king of Norway suffer shipwreck in the kingdom or domain of the king of Scotland, or contrariwise, it shall be lawful for them, either in person or by others, to gather their ships, broken or shattered, together with their goods, and to dispose of these without any claim made against them, as long as they have not abandoned them. If anyone seizes anything fraudulently or violently from such ships or goods in violation of this agreement and is found guilty, he is to be punished as a plunderer and breaker of the peace. Persons found and convicted of violating this agreement are to be chastised by the king in whose dominions they are found so that their punishment may be the terror of others. Perth, 2 July 1266.

In nomine Patris et Filii et Spiritus Sancti amen .Vt certitudo presencium det veram et euidentem memoriam preteritorum eternaliter est sciendum quod anno gracie millesimo ducentesimo sexage*s*imo sexto die Veneris pr*oxima* post f*estu*m apostolorum Petri et Pauli in ecclesia fratrum predicatorum apud Perth' inita fuit hec composicio et finalis concordia super contencionibus querimoniis[a] dampnis et iniuriis ac discordiis insularum Mannie et Sodorensium ac iurium earundem sopiendis diuina operante[b] prouidencia inter magnificos et illustres principes dominos[c] Magnum quartum Dei gracia regem Norwagie illustrem per sollempnes nuncios[d] Askatinum cancellarium suum et Andream filium Nicholai baronem suum super hiis illuc specialiter destinatos ac legitime constitutos comparentes ibidem ex parte vna et dominum Alexandrum tercium eadem gracia regem Scocie illustrem ibidem cum clero et proceribus regni sui maioribus personaliter comparentem ex altera sub hac forma. Videlicet quod dictus dominus Magnus rex Norwagie tanquam amicus pacis et cultor iusticie ad Dei reuerenciam et mutue dileccionis ac pacis obseruanciam diligencius confouendam et animarum periculum propulsandum ac strages hominum cicius euitandas ad instanciam et honorem domini Alexandri regis Scocie memorati Manniam cum ceteris insulis Sodoren' et omnibus aliis insulis ex parte occidentali et australi Magni Haff' cum omni iure quod in eis ipse et progenitores sui habuerunt ab antiquo tempore vel ipse et heredes sui habere poterunt in futurum per predictos viros discretos dominos Askatinum cancellarium ipsius domini Magni regis Norvagie et Andream filium Nicholai baronem suum habentes ab ipso rege plenam auctoritatem componendi et concordandi super ipsis amicabiliter et socialiter concessit resignauit et quietas clamauit tam in petitorio quam in possessorio pro se et heredibus suis inperpetuum . Tenendas et[e] habendas et possidendas dicto domino Alexandro tercio regi Scocie et suis heredibus cum dominiis homagiis redditibus seruiciis et omnibus iuribus et pertinenciis dictarum insularum sine retinemento[f] vna cum iure patronatus episcopatus Mannie saluis iure iurisdiccione ac libertate Nithdrosen' ecclesie[g] in omnibus et per omnia quod vel quas habet in episcopatu Mannie[h] et exceptis insulis Orcadie[i] et Yhetlandie[j] quas idem rex Norwagie cum dominiis homagiis redditibus seruiciis et omnibus iuribus et pertinenciis suis infra easdem contiguis dominio suo specialiter reseruauit. Ita quod omnes homines dictarum insularum que prefato domino regi Scocie sunt concesse resignate et quiete clamate tam minores quam maiores[k] subiaceant legibus et consuetudinibus regni Scocie et secundum eas ex nunc in posterum iudicentur et tractentur[l] . Pro hiis autem forisfactis vel iniuriis et dampnis que fecerunt vsque in hodiernum diem dum memorato regi[m] Norvagie adheserunt[n] nullatenus puniantur nec querelentur super hereditatibus suis in illis insulis sed pacifice stent in eisdem sub dominio regis Scocie sicut alii liberi et ligii dicti domini regis[o] qui liberiori iusticia gaudere dinoscuntur nisi aliquid de cetero faciant propter quod iuste puniri debeant iuxta leges et consuetudines regni Scocie approbatas . Et si in dictis insulis sub dominio dicti domini regis Scocie morari voluerint morentur in dominio libere et in pace et si recedere voluerint recedant cum bonis suis licite et libere et in plena pace itaque[p] nec morari nec recedere contra leges et consuetudines regni Scocie et suum libitum compellantur . Dominus itaque Alexander rex Scocie memoratus veritatis zelator et pacis et concordie amator et heredes sui imperpetuum pro istis concessione et resignacione ac quieta clamacione[q] et precipue pro bono pacis et vt fatigaciones et labores redimantur dabunt et reddent imperpetuum sepedicto regi[r] Norvagie et heredibus suis et eorum[s] assignatis imperpetuum infra octauas natiuitatis sancti Johannis Baptiste in Orcadia[t] / terra scilicet domini Regis Norvagie in ecclesia sancti Magni in manu episcopi Orcadie[i] seu balliui ipsius domini regis Norvag*ie* ad hoc per ipsum specialiter deputati vel in eadem ecclesia deponent ad opus ipsius domini regis Norvagie sub custodia canonicorum eiusdem ecclesie si episcopus vel balliuus non inueniantur ibidem qui dabunt eis litteras adquietacionis et facte solucionis centum marcas bonorum et legalium sterlingorum secundum modum et vsum curie Romane ac regnorum Francie Anglie et Scocie numerandas annuatim et nichilominus quatuor milia marcarum sterlingorum dicto modo numerandorum infra proximum quadriennium loco et termino prenotatis videlicet mille marcas infra octauas natiuitatis sancti Johannis Baptiste anno gracie millesimo ducentesimo sexagesimo septimo et centum marcas de predicta pensione . Et anno gracie millesimo ducentesimo sexagesimo octauo[u] ad eosdem locum et terminum mille marcas et centum marcas de pensione prefata et anno gracie millesimo cc° sexagesimo nono[v] dictis loco et termino mille marcas et centum marcas de pensione memorata[w] et vltimo anno gracie millesimo cc° septuagesimo[x] eisdem loco et termino mille marcas et centum de eadem pensione inposterum autem dictis loco et termino duntaxat centum marcas de pensione predicta predicto modo numerandas imperpetuum pro omnibus annuatim . Et ad hec omnia et singula vt prenominata sunt fideliter et firmiter obseruanda dicti A . cancellarius et A . baro pro domino suo Magno illustri rege Norvagie et heredibus suis et assignatis in animam ipsius regis de cuius voluntate eis super hiis constabat ad plenum et in animas suas proprias iurauerunt[y] publice in ecclesia fratrum predicatorum apud Perth' tactis evangeliis sacrosanctis et dictus dominus Alexander rex Scocie per nobiles viros Adam comitem de Carryk et Robertum de Meygners eodem modo in animam suam et in animas eorum pro se et heredibus suis fecit iurare solemniter in presencia nunciorum eorundem . Et ad maiorem huius rei securitatem vtraque pars se obligauit ad penam decem milium marcarum soluendam de plano et absque strepitu iudiciali a parte resilire volente parti composicionem istam et finalem concordiam obseruanti composicione ipsa et finali concordia nichilominus imperpetuum in pleno robore duraturis . Dominus insuper Magnus rex Norvagie per suos nuncios supradictos seipsum et heredes ac successores suos et dominus Alexander rex Scocie se et heredes suos subiecerunt in hoc iurisdiccioni sedis apostolice vt vnica admonicione[z] premissa per sentencias excommunicacionis in personas nullius persona excepta et interdicti in regna absque strepitu iudiciali et cause cognicione aliqua[aa] compellat partem resilientem a composicione et finali concordia predictis ad soluendam[bb] parti ipsas composicionem et finalem concordiam obseruanti dictam penam decem milium marcarum integre et plenarie et nichilominus ad ipsas composicionem et finalem concordiam in omnibus et singulis articulis obseruandas non relaxandas quousque dicta pena vt dictum est plenarie fuerit persoluta ipsis composicione et finali concordia in suo robore in omnibus et per omnia duraturis et imperpetuum valituris . Renunciauit itaque vtraque pars in hoc facto omni excepcioni fraudis et doli accioni in factum et priuilegio fori et specialiter restitucioni in integrum et omnibus litteris inter eosdem reges ac[cc] antecessores suos hucusque habitis et optentis cuiuscunque tenoris existant et omnibus litteris et indulgenciis apostolicis impetratis et impetrandis et omni remedio iuris canonici et ciuilis per que dicte composicio resignacio quieta clamacio et finalis concordia[dd] impediri diferri vel destrui valeant seu aliquo modo eneruari. Adiectum est eciam huic concordie et statutum communi consensu inter reges et regna Norvagie et Scocie vt omnes transgressiones et delicta inter eos et antecessores suos et homines eorum vsque in hodiernum diem perpetrata ex vtraque parte penitus sint remissa quoad ecclesias sicut et regna nullo ex hiis mali ire vel vindicte tramite remanente et vt obsides dictorum insulanorum hincinde capti et detenti plene libertati restituantur . Et si inimicus ipsorum regum[ee] Scocie scilicet et Norvagie ad alterum ipsorum confugiat ipsum in regno suo vel dominio ad grauamen eius a quo effugerit non receptet nisi forte ad tempus vt graciam sibi impetret si graciam meruerit et si graciam domini sui offensi habere non poterit ipsum statim post annum non differat a se et suo dominio remouere exceptis illis qui crimen lese maiestatis commiserunt qui nullo modo hinc inde recipientur. Insuper si contingat homines regis[ff] Norvagie quod absit in regno vel dominio Regis Scocie pati naufragium[gg] vel e conuerso liceat \ eos / libere et quiete naues suas fractas vel collisas vna cum rebus suis omnibus[hh] per se vel per alios colligere[ii] et habere et[jj] vendere et alienare absque omni calumpnia quam diu eas non habuerint pro derelicto[kk]. Et siquis contra hoc statutum communis[ll] concordie de rebus vel nauibus huiusmodi quicquam[mm] fraudulenter vel violenter surripuerit[nn] et super hoc conuictus fuerit tanquam raptor et pacis violator prout demeruerit puniatur consuetudine siqua sit contraria non obstante . Siquis autem repertus fuerit et conuictus perturbator pacis istius et finalis concordie inter predictos reges et regna eorum et regnicolas habite et confirmate per regem in cuius dominio repertus fuerit qui talia presumpserit sic acriter puniatur vt pena illius metus fiat aliorum . In cuius rei[oo] testimonium parti huius scripti in modum cirographi[pp] confecti penes dominum regem Norvagie illustrem remanenti[qq] sigillum dicti domini regis Scocie vna cum sigillis venerabilium patrum Gamelini Sanctiandree et Johannis Dei gracia Glasguen' episcoporum[rr] et nobilium virorum Alexandri Comyn' comitis de Buchan. Patricii de Dunbar. Willelmi de Marre. Ade de Carric comitum. et Roberti de Meygners baronis est appositum et alteri parti eiusdem scripti per[ss] modum cirographi confecti penes dictum dominum regem Scocie remanenti sigillum excellentis dicti domini regis Norvagie vna cum sigillis venerabilium patrum Petri Berngen'[tt]. Thorgils[uu] Stauangren'. Dei gracia episcoporum et nobilium virorum Gunter[vv] de Mel[ww] Kynsiti[xx] filii Johannis Fynij filii Gunter[yy], Andree filii Nicholai[zz] et Askatyni[aaa] cancellarii dicti domini regis Norvag*ie* est appensum.

NOTES. [a] In margin here, in a fourteenth-century hand: Mannie Sodorensie. [b] Cooperante in B. [c] Dominoum in B. [d] Muncios suos dominum in B. [e] Et omitted in B. [f] Aliquo retenemento in B. [g] Ecclesie Nithdrosen' ecclesie in B. [h] In episcopum et ecclesiam Mannie in B. [i] Orchadie in B. [j] Hietlandie in B. [k] Tam maiores quam minores in B. [l] Tractentur et iudicentur in B. [m] Domino regi in B. [n] Adherebant in B. [o] Regis Scocie in B. [p] Ita quod in B. [q] Concessione resignacione ac quieta clamacione in B. [r] Domino regi in B. [s] Eorndem in B. [t] Orchadia in B. [u] Mcclx octauo in B. [v] Mcclx nono in B. [w] Memorata pensione in B. [x] Mclxx in B. [y] Et animas suas iurarunt in B. [z] Ammonicione in B. [aa] Aliqua omitted in B. [bb] Soluendum in B. [cc] Et in B. [dd] Predicte concessio resignacio quieta clamacio composicio et finalis concordia in B. [ee] Alterius regum ipsorm in B. [ff] Regni in B. [gg] In margin here, in a fourteenth-century hand: naufragium. [hh] Omnimodis in B. [ii] Recolligere in B. [jj] Et omitted in B. [kk] The letters 'dili' are crossed out here before derelicto. [ll] Commune statutum in B. [mm] Huiusmodi periclitatis in B. [nn] Sic, surrepuerit. [oo] Et in huius rei in B. [pp] Cyrographi in B. [qq] Remanenti penes dictum dominum regem

Norvagie illustrem in B. [rr] Gamelini Sancti Andree et Johannis Glasguen' Dei gracia episoporum in B. [ss] In, in B. [tt] Bergen' in B. [uu] Thorgilsi in B. [vv] Gauti in B. [ww] Mele in B. [xx] Brvnolui in B. [yy] Gouti in B. [zz] Nicholae in B. [aaa] Assketini in B.

RUBRIC. Factum Norwagie concordia inter Alexandrum regem Scotie et Magnum eius nominis 4 super insulis regni Scotie.

SOURCE. NRS, Black Buik, PA 5/4, fos. 7^{r}–8^{v} = A; *Diplom. Norveg.*, viii, no. 9 = B. The original treaty is now lost: A represents a late fourteenth-century copy, preserved in a renewal of the treaty by Robert I effected on 29 October 1312; B is a copy of this confirmation preserved in a letter of 29 July 1426, now in the Danish National Archives, Copenhagen, NKR 2958. Transcribed here from A.

PRINTED. *RRS*, v, no. 24; *APS*, i, 420–1; *Diplom. Norveg.*, viii, nos 9, 275, 276; *Norske Middelalderdokumenter*, ed. S. H. Bagge (Bergen, 1973), no. 25; Goss, *Chron. Reg. Manniae*, ii, 323–33 (trans.); D. Donaldson, *Scottish Historical Documents* (Edinburgh, 1970), 34–6 (summary); Anderson, *Early Sources*, ii, 655–6 (cal.).

COMMENT. Payment of the 4,000 merks did not proceed on schedule – the final instalment was not made until after the marriage of Princess Margaret with King Eric II of Norway in 1281. A thorough study of the text of the treaty and its implications is offered in R. I. Lustig, 'The Treaty of Perth: A Re-examination', *SHR*, 58 (1979), 35–57.

62 Grants to Gillcrist MacNachdan and his heirs custody of the castle and isle of Fraoch Eilean (in Loch Awe). Gilchrist is to maintain the castle in good repair and to be prepared to offer hospitality to the king whenever he should wish to visit the castle. Scone, 12 February a.r. 18 [1267].

Alexander Dei gr*at*ia rex Scotor*um* omnibus probis hominib*us* toci*us* t*er*re sue sal*ute*m . Sciatis q*uod* concessimus Gillecrist [Mac Nachdan] et h*er*edib*us* suis vt ips*i* h*ab*eant custodiam castr*i* n*ost*ri et insule de Frechelan' . ita q*uod* d*ict*um castrum su*m*ptib*us* n*ost*ris construi faciant et reficiant quociens opus fu*er*it et saluo custodiant . ad op*us* [n*ost*rum et quociens ibidem venerimus dictum] castru*m* honeste p*ar*atum nob*is* lib*er*abit*ur* . ad hospitand*um* et ibid*em* morand*um* pro voluntate n*ost*ra . In cui*us* rei testimoniu*m* has n*ost*ras litt*er*as eide*m* Gillecr*is*t et suis h*er*edibus fieri fecim*us* patentes . Testib*us* Alexandro Comin comite de Buchan' justic*iario* Scoc*ie* W . com*ite* de Marr' cam*erario*, M . comit*e* de Strathern' . A . comit*e* de Carric' et Alan*o* hostiario apud Scon' . xii die Februarii [anno regni nostri xviii^{o}].

DESCRIPTION. 20.0 cm x 13.0 cm; fold 4.8 cm. Sealing: formerly on a tag, through double slits. Seal and tag now missing. Part of the fourth line is erased; words in brackets are supplied by conjecture.

HAND. Scribe B.

SOURCE. Original. NRS, Register House Charters, RH 6/55.

PRINTED. Douglas, *Baronage*, 419n; Macnaghten, *Clan Macnachtan*, 15–16; *Origines Parochiales*, II, i, 145 (cal.); *Highland Papers*, i, 107 (cal.).

COMMENT. Although some scholars have suggested that the charter is spurious, it is treated as genuine in Boardman, *Campbells*, 28n. A facsimile and transcript, dated 1753, may be found in NRS, GD 112/16/7/2/34. Modern transcripts appear in NRS, RH 1/1/1 and NRS, RH 2/2/13, item 13.

63 Grants and by this charter confirms to William de Swinburne the gift that Reginald Prat, knight, made him of the lands (all in Tynedale) of Haughton, of all of Reginald's land in 'the Huntland', of the manor of Williamston in the fee of Knarsdale and of the lands that John Hok and Robert Darybald held of Reginald within the boundaries of Slaggyford in said fee. To be held by the same boundaries as are contained in Reginald's charter, saving the king's service, and according to the terms laid out in the final concord made between them before John de Eslington and Richard de Bickerton, justices itinerant in Tynedale. Jedburgh, 1 May a.r. 18 [1267].

Alex*ander* Dei g*ra*tia rex Scott*oru*m omnibus probis hominib*us* tocius terre sue sal*ute*m . Sciatis nos concessisse et hac presenti carta n*ost*ra confirmasse donat*i*on*em* illam quam Reginaldus Prath' miles fecit Will*elm*o de Swyneburn' pro homagio et seruitio suo de t*er*ris de Haluchton' cum p*er*tinenciis . et de tota t*er*ra cum pertinenciis quam idem Reginaldus habuit in le Huntland . et de tota terra de Williamiston' cum p*er*tinenciis in feodo de Knarisdal'. et de tota t*er*ra illa cum pertinenciis q*ua*m Joh*ann*es Hok' et Rob*ertus* Darybald' de predicto Reginaldo tenu*er*unt inf*ra* diuisas de Slaggingford' ex p*ar*te occidentali de Tyna in feodo de Knarisdal' . Tenend*as* et habend*as* eidem Will*elm*o et heredib*us* suis *vel* assignatis et eor*um* heredib*us* de p*re*d*ict*o Reginaldo et heredib*us* suis v*e*l assignatis de Knarisdal' adeo lib*er*e . quiete . plenarie . et honorifice p*er* easdem diuisas cu*m* p*er*tinenciis . sicut carte predicti Reginaldi prefato Will*elm*o exinde confecte . pleni*us* iuste testant*ur* saluo s*er*uitio nostro . et s*ecund*um quod in finali concordia sup*er* t*er*ris p*re*nominatis cu*m* p*er*tinenciis f*ac*ta coram Joh*ann*e de Exlington' et Ricardo de Bykirton' justiciar*ii*s itin*er*antibus in Tyndal' ann*o* g*ra*tie m*illesim*o . ducentes*imo* . quinquages*imo* . septimo . pleni*us* continet*ur* . Test*ibus* ven*er*abilib*us* p*at*ribus Gamel*ino* S*anct*i Andr*ee* . et Joh*anne* Glasgu' e*piscop*is . Pat*ri*cio com*ite* de Dunbarr' . Rob*er*to de Meyners' . Hugon*e* de Abrinitthyn' . Nichol*ao* Corbeth' . et Will*elm*o de Som*er*uill' . apud Jeddewrth' primo die Maii . anno regni n*ost*ri . xv^{o}iii .

ENDORSED. The document has long been bound in a volume, its dorse unavailable for examination.

DESCRIPTION. 23.0 cm x 16.0 cm; fold 3.1 cm. Sealing: a tag, 3.0 cm broad, is passed through double slits. Most of the tag and the seal are missing.

HAND. Scribe K.

SOURCE. Original. Northumberland Collections Service, Swinburne (Capheaton) Estate Papers, ZSW/1/22. See also Bodleian Library, Oxford, MS. Dodsworth XLV, fo. 49^{v} and BL, Lansdowne MS. 326, fo. 134^{v}. These volumes consist of summaries, in Latin, of deeds belonging to several Northumberland families, written in 1638–9 by the antiquary Roger Dodsworth.

PRINTED. *HN*, III, i, 13–14; *Northumb. and Durham Deeds*, 200 (cal.).

COMMENT. This is a reissue of no. 25, above. The final concord that is the subject of this confirmation was sealed at Nunwick on 16 April 1257; see ZSW/1/12.

64 Notifies the provosts of Perth that inspection of the charters of his ancestors and the rolls of his chapel has revealed that the monks of the holy Trinity of Tiron (Kelso) should receive three merks annually on the feast of St John the Baptist from the ferme of his burgh of Perth in place of the cain of one ship, which King David I gave them in free alms. Commands them to ensure that the abbot and monks of Kelso receive the three merks as above. Scone, 1 June a.r. 18 [1267].

Alex*ander* Dei g*rat*ia rex Scott*orum* p*re*positis de Perth' q*ui* p*ro* temp*ore* fu*er*int sal*ute*m. Q*ua*m *p*er inspecc*ione*m cart*arum* p*ro*genitor*um* n*ostr*or*um* reg*um* Scott*orum* illust*ri*um et insp*eccion*em rotulor*um* capelle n*ostr*e nobis *con*stat ad plen*um* q*uod* monachi s*anct*e T*ri*nitatis Tyron' solebant et debent p*er*cip*ere* et h*ab*ere annuati*m* die s*anct*i Johannis Bapt*iste* tres marcas st*er*ling*orum* de firma burgi n*ostr*i de Perth'. p*ro* cano vni*us* nauis q*uo*d inclite recordac*ion*is Dauid rex Scoc*ie* illust*ri*s eis dedit in lib*er*am elemosina*m*. Id*eo* vob*is* mandam*us* et p*re*cipim*us* q*ua*tin*us* abb*a*ti et monach*is* de Kelch' p*ro*curatorib*us* d*ictorum* monach*orum* Tyron' tres marcas st*er*lingor*um* de f*ir*ma d*ict*i burgi nostri de Perth' die s*anct*i Joh*ann*is Bapt*iste* annuatim h*ab*ere faciatis. Et nos eas vobi*s* i*n* v*estr*is compotis faciem*us* sing*u*lis annis pleni*us* allocari. In cui*us* rei testimon*ium* has n*ostr*as l*itt*eras fieri fecim*us* patentes. Test*ibus*. Symone abb*a*te de Dunf*er*mel'. Colbano com*ite* de Fife. Alano Host*iario*. et Hug*one* de Berkel' just*iciario* Laod*onie*. apud Scona' primo die Junii. anno regni nostri. xvii^{o}j.

RUBRIC. Conf*ir*macio s*uper* tres marc*as* p*er*cipiend*as* annuati*m* de burgo de Perth'. Top of folio: ^{cc}Kelsou; bottom of folio: Alexander Dei. Initial capitals in first line are all slightly rubricated.
SOURCE. NLS, Adv. MS. 34.5.1, Chartulary of Kelso Abbey, nos 147^{v}–148^{r}.
PRINTED. *Kelso Liber*, ii, no. 398.

65

Grants and by this charter confirms to Gilbert de Glencarnie, junior and his wife, Marjory, the gift that Marjory's brother, John Prat, knight, made them of the whole of his land of Daltulich in Moray. To be held by Gilbert and Marjory in feu and heritage, as John's charter bears witness, saving the king's service. Aboyne, 14 August a.r. 19 [1267].

. Alex*ander* Dei g*ra*tia rex Scott*orum* . omnibus probis hominibus tocius t*er*re sue sal*u*tem . Sciatis nos concessisse . et hac p*re*senti carta n*ostr*a confirmasse . donationem illam quam Johannes Prat miles fecit Gilberto de Glennegerni juniori et Mariorie sponse sue sorori d*ic*ti Johannis . et eor*um* heredibus de ip*s*is p*ro*creatis de tota t*er*ra sua de Daltely in Morauia cum p*er*tinenciis . sine aliquo retinemento . Tenend*am* et habend*am* ei*s*dem Gilberto et Mariorie sponse sue et eor*um* heredibus de ip*s*is p*ro*creatis . de p*re*dicto Johanne et heredibus suis . in feodo et hereditate p*er* rectas diuisas suas . et cum omnibus p*er*tinenciis suis . libertatib*us* et aysiamentis ad p*re*dictam terram p*er*tinentibus . adeo lib*ere* . et quiete plenarie . et honorifice . sicut carta ip*s*ius Johannis exinde confecta plenius iuste testat*ur* . saluo s*er*uitio n*ostr*o . Test*ibus* Colbano com*ite* de Fif' . Alano Hostiar*io* . Hugon*e* de Abirnith' . Eustach*io* de Turribus . Reginald*o* le Chen' et Alex*andro* de Morauia apud Obeyn' q*ua*rtodecimo die Aug*us*ti . anno regni n*ostr*i nonodecimo .

ENDORSED. Chartour of confirmacione be King Alex' of ane chartour granted be John Prast knicht to Gilbert of Glencharnich and his spows of the land of Daltely 3rd year of the kingis raigne (sixteenth century).
DESCRIPTION. 21.3 cm x 8.4 cm; fold 2.0 cm. Sealing: a tag, 2.1 cm broad, through single slits. There are no traces of the seal.
HAND. Scribe G.
SOURCE. Original. NRS, Seafield Papers, GD 248/4/8.
PRINTED. Fraser, *Grant*, iii, 6 (facs.); Fraser, *Facsimiles*, no. 61.

66 Grants and by this charter confirms to Gilbert, son of Gilbert de Glencarnie the gift that, with the consent and agreement of his wife Mary, countess of Menteith, Walter the steward earl of Menteith made him of half the toun of Brackland, that is, the half that lies on the east side towards the boundaries of 'Eglysdissentyn' (both in Perthshire). To be held by Gilbert and his heirs of Walter and Mary and their heirs in feu and heritage, as freely, quietly, fully and honourably as Earl Walter's charter bears witness, excepting the king's service. Aboyne, 14 August a.r. 19 [1267].

. Alex*ander* Dei gr*at*ia rex Scott*orum* . omnibus probis hominibus tocius t*er*re sue sal*ute*m . Sciatis nos concessisse . et hac p*re*senti carta n*ost*ra confirmasse donacionem illam quam Walt*er*us Senescallus comes de Meneteth fecit Gilberto fil*io* Gilberti de Glenkerny militi de consensu et voluntate Marie sponse sue comitisse de Meneteth . de medietate ville de Broculy cum p*er*tinenciis . videlicet [illa] medietate que iacet in p*ar*te orientali u*er*sus marchias de Eglysdissentyn' . Tenend*am* et habend*am* eidem Gilberto et heredibus suis de p*re*dictis Walt*er*o com*ite* et Maria sponsa sua et eor*um* heredibus in feodo et hereditate . p*er* rectas diuisas suas . et cum omnibus iustis p*er*tinenciis suis libertatibus et aysiamentis ad p*re*dictam medietatem ville de Broculy p*er*tinentibus . adeo lib*er*e et quiete . plenarie . et honorifice . sicut carta p*re*dicti Walt*er*i comitis eidem Gilberto exinde confecta plenius iuste testat*ur* . saluo s*er*uitio n*ost*ro . Test*ibus* Colban*o* com*ite* de Fif' . Alano hostiari*o* . Hug*one* de Abirnith' . Eustach*io* de Turribus . Reginaldo le Chen' . et Alex*andro* de Morauia . apud Obeyn' qu*ar*todecimo die Aug*us*ti anno regni n*ost*ri nonodecimo .

ENDORSED. 1. *Con*firmacio regis Al[ex' de] donacione de [1 word, illegible] de Menethet (fourteenth century). 2. Broculy (fifteenth century; so faded as to be almost illegible). 3. Chart*our* of confirmacione be Alex' king of Scots of a don[acione] made be the earle of Mentethe and his ladye to Gilberte of Glen[charnich] of half of Brocule 13 August 19th year of that king's reign (sixteenth-century hand, though partly obliterated by the tear described below).
DESCRIPTION. 19.6 cm x 10.2 cm. Sealing: the bottom portion of the document, including what remains of the fold, is torn away, obliterating all evidence of a tag or seal.
HAND. Scribe G.
SOURCE. Original. NRS, Seafield Papers, GD 248/4/9.
PRINTED. Fraser, *Grant*, iii, 6–7; Fraser, *Menteith*, ii, 217 (facs.); Fraser, *Facsimiles*, no. 62.
COMMENT. 'Eglysdissentyn' in Menteith, now obsolete, is noted as 'Eglisdisdane' in an exchequer account of 1480; *ER*, ix, 564. The name may recall an obscure saint of the area: Gaelic *do* + *Iastan*. See also G. W. S. Barrow, 'The Childhood of Scottish Christianity: A Note on some Place-name Evidence', *Scottish Studies*, 27 (1983), 12. 'Broculy' is Brackland, in Callander parish.

67 Commands Simon Fraser sheriff of Traquair to go to the land near the Gala Water that belongs to the abbot and convent of Melrose and to hold an inquest into the diversion of the course of the water there. He is to return the record of the inquest, together with this brieve, to the king. Berwick, 13 April a.r. 19 [1268].

. A . Dei gr*at*ia rex Scott*orum* . Symon*i* Fras*er* vic*ecomiti* de Treuequair' [ ][a] et fid[el]ibus suis sal*ute*m . Mandamus vobis et p*re*cipimus quatinus ac [ ][a] accedatis ad terram abb*at*is et conuentus de Melr*os* iuxta aquam de Galu vt [ ]^a dicta aqua occupant [ ]^b terram eor*undem* abb*o*tis et conuentus p*er* nouu*m* cursum suu*m* . et illud quod p*er* sacramentu*m* dic*torum* proborum [virorum] ibidem inuen*eritis* nob*is* sub sigill*is* ves*t*ris qu*am* cicius mitti faciatis et hoc breue . Teste me ip*so* apud Berewik' . xiii° die April*is* ann*o* . regni . n*ostri* . xix°.

NOTES. ^{a} Seven–eight words missing. ^{b} Two–three words missing.
DESCRIPTION. 20.0 cm x 3.4 cm. Sealing: no evidence of a tongue, tag or seal. The surface on which the first two lines of the document appear is rubbed away almost completely.
HAND. Scribe G.
SOURCE. Original. NRS, Documents transferred from the Public Record Office, London, RH 5/34.
PRINTED. *Melrose Liber*, ii, app., no. 13; *CDS*, i, no. 2679 (cal.); *L & I*, vol. xlix, 185 (note).

68 Grants and by this charter confirms to Herbert de Maxwell, son of the late Aymer de Maxwell, knight, the gift that William de Conisbrough, son of the late William de Conisbrough, knight, made him of the feu ferme of one ploughgate in Langholm and half a ploughgate of land in Brackenwrae (both in Dumfriesshire). To be held in feu ferme, for an annual render of twelve pence, as William's charter bears witness, saving the king's service. Berwick, 16 April a.r. 19 [1268].

Alexender^a Dei gr*a*tia rex Scottorum om*n*ibus p*ro*bis hom*in*ibus toci-us te*r*re sue sal*ute*m. Sciatis nos concessisse et hac p*re*senti carta n*ost*ra confirmasse donacionem illam q*uam* Will*elm*us de Cunygb*ur*g filius quond*am* Will*elm*i de Cunygburg' militis fecit Herberto de Maxwell'. filio et h*er*edi Eymericy de Maxwell'. militis no*m*ine feodofirme de vna carucata te*r*re in Langholm' et de vna dimidi*a* carucata te*r*re in Bra-ca*n*wra. Tene*n*dam et habend*am* eodem Herberto et h*er*edibus suis uel suis assign*atis* de p*re*di*c*to Will*elm*o et h*er*edibus suis in feodo firmam cum om*n*ibus p*er*tinenciis suis libertatib*us* et aysiamentis ad d*i*ctas terras ce*r*te p*er*tinentib*us*. adeo libere et quiete plenarie et honorifice sicut carta p*re*fati Will*elm*i eid*em* Herberto exinde confecta. plenius iuste testatur . saluo s*er*uicio n*ost*ro. Et reddendo inde annuatim eid*em* Will*elm*o et h*er*edibus suis. duodecim denarios videlic*et* sex denarios ad P*enthec*osten et sex denarios ad festum *sancti* Martini in hyeme. Testibus Hugone [Ber]keley^b justiciario Laudon*ie*. Thomam^c Ranul-phy Bernardo de Monte Alto. P*at*ricio [Berkel]ey.^{b} Symon*e* Fraser' et Henrico de Haliburton'. apud Berewiko. sexto decimo die. [Aprilis] anno regni n*ost*ri nonodecimo.

NOTES. ^{a} Sic, Alexander. ^{b} MS stained; letters supplied from printed version. ^{c} Sic, Thome.
RUBRIC. Confirmacio prescripte carte per regem Alexandrum lxxxiiii.
SOURCE. NLS, MS. 72, Morton Cartulary, fos 70^v–71^r.
PRINTED. *Morton Reg.*, ii, no. 8.

69 Grants and by this charter confirms to the burgesses of Elgin that, for the improvement of the burgh, they should have their merchant guild as freely as his other burghs have theirs. Elgin, 28 November a.r. 20 [1268].

Alexander Dei gratia rex Scottorum . omnibus probis hominibus totius terre sue salutem . Sciatis nos concessisse . et hac carta nostra confirmasse burgensibus nostris de Elgyn' . vt ipsi ad melioracionem burgi nostri de Elgyn' habeant in eodem burgo gildam suam mercatricem adeo liberam . sicut aliquis burgorum nostrorum in toto regno nostro gildam suam habet liberiorem . Testibus .Alano hostiario . Reginaldo le Chen camerario . Hugone de Abbernyth' . Willelmo et Bernardo de Monte Alto . Alexandro de Morauia . et Willelmo Byset . apud Elgyn' . vicesimo octauo die Nouembris . anno regni nostri . vicesimo .

DESCRIPTION. 19.1 cm x 10.2 cm; fold 2.0 cm. Sealing: on a tag, 2.5 cm broad, through single slits, there remains a fragment of the second great seal, in natural wax, 2.8 cm in diameter. Little of the surface is visible.
HAND. Scribe H.
SOURCE. Original. Moray District Council Record Office, Elgin Burgh Charters, no. 2.
PRINTED. *Records of Elgin,* i, no. 8 (facs.), wrongly attributed here to Alexander II.
COMMENT. Modern transcripts appear in NRS, RH 1/1/1 and NLS, Adv. MS. 34.5.3, fo. 20^{v}.

70 Commands Thomas Randolph sheriff of Roxburgh and his bailies to hold an inquest to determine by which persons, and at whose order or instigation, the land of Horndean (Berwickshire), currently in the hands of James Giffard and his farmer, was plundered, and whether the plundered goods have been brought to anyone in their bailiary. He is to return the record of the inquest, together with this brieve, to the king's chapel. Kelso, 6 January a.r. 20 [1269].

Alexander Dei gratia rex Scottorum Thome Ranulphi dilecto. et fideli suo vicecomiti et balliuis suis de Rokesburch' salutem . Mandamus vobis et precipimus . quatinus per sacramentum proborum et fidelium \ hominum / patrie diligenter et fideliter inquiri faciatis . per quas personas et ad cuius iussionem seu procuracionem terra de Horneden' que est in ma[nibus Ja]cobi[a] Giffard et firmarii sui depredata fuit . et si bona dicte predacionis ad aliquos uel aliquam [infra] balliam vestram deuenerunt . Et dictam inquisicionem diligenter et fideliter factam \ et in scriptis red[uctam] sub/ sigillis [vestris] et illorum qui dicte inquisicioni faciende intererunt ad capellam nostram . mitti faciatis quamcicius et hoc breue . Teste me ipso apud Kelchou vi^{to} . die Januarii . anno . regni . nostri . xx^{o} .

NOTE. [a] A piece of the document is torn away here; letters supplied by conjecture.
DESCRIPTION. 17.4 cm x 4.7 cm. Sealing: no evidence of a tongue, tag or seal.
HAND. Scribe I.
SOURCE. Original. NRS, Documents transferred from the Public Record Office, London, RH 5/35.
PRINTED. *CDS*, i, no. 2680 (cal.); *L & I*, vol. xlix, 185 (note).
COMMENT. A modern transcript appears in NRS, RH 1/1/1.

71 Commands his justiciars, sheriffs, provosts and their bailies to ensure that the monks of Melrose, their lands, their men, and all their possessions, rights, and goods movable and immovable, ecclesiastical and worldly, to be found in the addressees' bailiaries and burghs are lawfully maintained and defended and that no one disturb them in violation of their charters and muniments. If there are any forfeitures to be made to the monks they are to cause these to be paid without delay. Kelso, 7 January a.r. 20 [1269].

Alex*ander* Dei *gra*tia rex Scott*orum* justiciariis . vicecomitibus . prepositis et eor*um* balliuis ad quos p*re*sentes litt*ere* p*er*uen*er*int salutem . Mandamus vobis et p*re*cipimus . quatinus monachos de Melros' . t*er*ras suas homines suos . ac vniu*er*sas eor*un*dem possessiones . iura et bona sua om*n*ia mobilia et im*m*obilia eccl*e*siastica et mundana in v*est*ris balliis et burgis . iuste manuteneatis et defendatis non p*er*mittentes ip*s*os contra cartar*um* et munimentor*um* suor*um* ac p*ro*teccio*n*is n*ost*re tenores [quos] habent . sup*er* pred*ic*tis ab aliquibus indebite molestari . Et si quid eis forisfac*tum* fu*er*it . id eis iuste et sine dilac*i*one emendari faciatis mis*er*icordiam nos contingentem de i*n*iuriatoribus ip*s*is de pace et p*ro*tec*t*ione n*ost*ra fracta ad opus n*ost*rum capientes . Et hoc nullatenus omittatis p*er* q*uod* ad vos de negligencia v*est*ra grauit*er* cap*er*e debeam*us* . Test*ibus* . P . com*ite* de Dumbar' . Walt*er*o de Morauia . et Walt*er*o de Lyndes' apud Kelchou septimo die [Janu] arii anno regni nostri vicesimo .

ENDORSED. Proteccio Allixandri regis a. (contemporary hand).
DESCRIPTION. 19.3 cm x 8.2 cm, L x 5.9 cm, R. Sealing: on a tongue cut from the left bottom portion of the parchment, 2.2 cm broad, there appears the second great seal, 7.0 cm in diameter, in white wax. Much of the seal surface is now effaced; there remains only a small central portion, also badly rubbed.
HAND. Scribe J.
SOURCE. Original. NRS, Melrose Charters, GD 55/311.
PRINTED. *Melrose Liber*, i, no. 311.
COMMENT. A modern transcript appears in NRS, RH 2/2/13, item 10 (15).

72

Commands Richard de Bickerton sub-bailiff of the forest of Inglewood (Cumberland) to ensure that no one erects fences there. If he finds any of these they are to be thrown to the ground, lest the (value of) the king's commonty in the forest be diminished. Edinburgh, 4 March a.r. 20 [1269].

Alex*ander* Dei gr*at*ia rex Scot*torum* Ricardo de Bykerton' dil*ec*to et fideli et ball*iv*is suis de Penreth' et de Cumberlaund' sal*utem*. Mandam*us* vob*is* et firmit*er* precipim*us* q*uo*d n*u*llo modo p*er*mittatis q*uo*d aliquis aliq*u*am sepem erigat infra forestam n*ost*ram de Engelwod'. Et si quis aliquam erex*er*it illa*m* vsq*ue* in t*er*ram p*ro*sterni fac*iat*is. N*em*o p*er*mittentes q*uo*d d*ic*ta com*m*unia n*ost*ra in aliq*uo* diminiat*ur* p*er* q*uo*d ad vos *g*ravit*er* cape*re* debeam*us*. Teste P. comite de Dunbar. Joh*ann*e Comyn et Hug*one* de Abernyth'. apud Castrum Puell*arum*. iiii[to] die Marcii anno r*egni* n*ost*ri xx[o].

RUBRIC. In the right hand margin at membrane 36 the following words appear (MS is badly damaged on this side; lacunae indicated here by square brackets): Alex*ander* Dei gr*at*ia rex Scoc*ie* Ric*ardo* de Kyrketon dil*ect*o et fideli et ball*iv*is suis de Penreth' et Cumberlaund'. P*re*cipim*us* q*uo*d n*u*llo modo p*er*mittatis q*uo*d aliquis aliq*uam* sepem erigat infra com*m*unam n*os*tram de Engelwod' [ ] usque in t*er*ram p*ro*sterni faciatis N*em*o p*er*mitt*en*tes q*uo*d d*ict*a com*m*una n*ost*ra in aliquo diminiat*ur* p*er* q*uo*d ad vos [ ] de Dunbar. Joh*ann*e Comyn et Hugone de Ab*er*nyth' apud Castrum Puellarum iiii[to] die Marcij anno r*egni* [ ]. In the left margin: Vacat' ne quia alibi.

SOURCE. TNA, Justices of the Forest: Records formerly in the Treasury of the Receipt of the Exchequer, PRO, E 32/5, mm. 35d-36, included in the record of a plea heard at the Cumberland Forest eyre of November 1285.
COMMENT. See also below, nos 86, 255.

73 Recites how a dispute arose between Robert Bruce and the king concerning the advowsons and fruits of the benefice of churches in Annandale during the vacancy of the see of Glasgow, the king claiming right to them, and Robert unlawfully withholding them. On the Friday next after the Annunciation of Our Lady 1270, at Scone, Robert appeared in the presence of the king and his magnates and acknowledged that the aforesaid rights and franchises belong to the king without contradiction by him or his heirs. The king announces that this acknowledgement shall in no way be damaging to Robert's other franchises in Annandale, which he has by right and reason. Scone, 28 March a.r. 21 [1270].

Alysandre par la grace de Deu roy Descoce . a tuz les prudes homes de tute sa terre saluz . Contek ew entre nos e Robert de Brus le pere noster feel e noster leel . sur auoweysoun e fruz de benefice de eglise . e dreitures e franchises a nos apurtenanz en le val de Anand . par voidance de leglise de Glasg' . la warde de la quele . a nos apartent par reson de nostre reale poeste . oue tutes ses dreytures . appurtenances . e franchises . Tant au Vendresdy procheyn apres lannu*n*ciation nostre dame lan de grace millime . deucentime settantime a Schon' apara*n*t le auandit Robert en nostre presence e de nos granz genz . rec*unu*ht e otria tutes les auand dites choses . dreitures e franchises estre noster dreit . e a nos apartenyr heritablem[en]t . et sanz contradiccion de luy e de ses heirs a nul j*ou*r . E des amendes del empeschement . et de la detenance fete par luy par hubliance des choses auandites e franchises . se mist il de haut e de bas a nostrre volente . les queles amendes de tut luy pardonames . a la priere de luy e de ses amys . E volons e grantons . ke lauand dite reconoysance e otreyement a nul j*ou*r or soit damaiouse a ses franchises de val de Anand . ke il doit auer par droit e par reson . ke il e ses heyrs ne le puyssent franchementes joir par droit e par reson . Tesmoyn' Richard eueske de Dunkeldyn . Alysandre Cumyn conte de Buchan' justice Descoce . Willame conte de Marr' . Gilberd de Humfrancuile conte de Aneg*us* . Johan Cumyn' le pere . e Hwe de Berkeley justice de Loenesse a Schon' le vint e vtime jor de Marz . lan de noster regne vint e vn.

ENDORSED. De valle Anandie (contemporary hand).
DESCRIPTION. 21.0 cm x 18.0 cm; fold 3.5 cm. Sealing: A tag, 2.7 cm broad, is passed through single slits. Attached is a remnant of the king's second great seal, 4.0 cm in diameter, in natural wax, much deteriorated along the edges.
HAND. Scribe I.
SOURCE. Original. TNA, Duchy of Lancaster: Deeds, Series L, PRO, DL 25/80.
PRINTED. *Statuta Ecclesiae Scoticanae*, ed. J. Robertson (2 vols, Bannatyne Club, 1866), i, lxxiii, n2,which also discusses the context of the king's claim to dispose of episcopal benefices during a vacancy; *Nat. MSS. Scotland*, i, no. 61 (facs.).
COMMENT. There is a modern transcript in NRS, RH 1/1/1.

74 Grants and by this charter confirms to the nuns of Coldstream the gift that Patrick earl of Dunbar made them of the whole of his land in the toun of Lennel (Berwickshire), namely, the Southtoun of Lennel. To be held in free and perpetual alms, as the earl's charter bears witness, saving royal service. Haddington, 21 June a.r. 21 [1270].

Al*ex*ander Dei gr*at*ia rex Scott*orum* . omnibus probis hominibus toci*us* terre sue sa*lut*em . Sciatis nos concessisse et hac presenti carta n*o*stra confirmasse donac*i*onem illam quam Patrici*us* comes de Dumbar' fecit Deo et eccl*e*sie beate Marie de Caldestrem' et monialib*us* ibidem Deo s*er*uientibus . et in p*er*petuu*m* s*er*uituris de tota t*er*ra sua in villa de Laynhal' scilicet del Suthtun' de Laynhal' cum p*er*tinenciis . Tenend*am* et habend*am* eisdem monialib*us* de *dict*o comite et heredib*us* suis cum om*n*ib*us* lib*er*tatib*us* aisiamentis et p*er*tine*n*ciis suis tam infra u*i*llam q*ua*m extra sine aliqua reten*c*ione . subtrac*t*ione vel diminuc*i*one . in lib*er*am puram et p*er*petuam elemosinam adeo libere . quiete . plenar*ie* et honorifice . sicut aliqua elemosina in toto regno n*ost*ro lib*er*ius . quietius plenius et honorificenci*us* ab aliquo tenetur et possidetur et sicut carta d*ict*i comitis eisdem monialib*us* exinde confecta pleni*us* iuste testatur . saluo s*er*uicio nostro de d*ict*o comite et heredibus suis . Test*ib*us . Hugon*e* de Berkeley justic*iario* Laudon*ie* . Hug*one* de Abernyth' . Alex*andro* de Balliolo de Cau*er*es . Alex*andro* de Vallibus . Ricardo Syward . Will*el*mo de Valoniis . Bernardo de Monte Alto . Ricardo Fras*er* . et Will*el*mo Byseth . apud Hadyngton' vicesimo p*ri*mo die Junii . anno regni n*ost*ri vicesimo primo .

ENDORSED. Confirmacio Alexandri tercij super donacione Patricij etc. de terra Laynhale scilicet Southtun de Laynell. The last four words are in a different, but still contemporary, hand.
DESCRIPTION. 23.2 cm x 14.5 cm, fold 2.7 cm. Sealing: through single slits, on a tongue 2.2 cm wide, there appears a fragment of the second great seal, in white wax. Attached to the front left of the fold is a small parchment tie, once attached to the seal.
HAND. Scribe K.
SOURCE. Original. NRS, J. Maitland Thomson Collection, GD 212/2/1/29.
PRINTED. *Coldstream Chartulary*, no. 56.

75 Commands Ralph de Lascelles sheriff of [Fife] and his bailies to hold an inquest. He is to return the record of the inquest, together with this brieve, to the king. Dumfries, 28 August a.r. 22 [1270].

A[lex' Dei] gratia Rex Scott*orum* . Radulfo de Lasceles' [ ] suo vicecomiti et balliuis suis [ ] . per probos [ ]homines patrie [ ] ad terram [ ] all [ ] vt dictam [ ] em diligenter et fideliter [ ] ad nos [ ] faciatis . Et [ ] . Et hoc nullo modo omittatis . Teste [me] ip*s*o apud Dunfr' . xxviii die Augusti [anno regni nostri] . xxij .

DESCRIPTION. 19.8 cm x 4.6 cm. Sealing: no evidence of a tongue, tag or seal.
HAND. Scribe I (probably). The document is so badly damaged that is is almost wholly illegible, even under ultraviolet light.
SOURCE. Original. TNA, Special Collections: Ancient Correspondence of the Chancery and the Exchequer, PRO SC 1/11/92A.
PRINTED. *CDS*, v, pt. 2, no. 26 (cal.).

76 Commands Walter earl of Menteith, sheriff of Dumbarton and his bailies to hold an inquest to determine whether Mary wife of John Wardrop, Elena wife of Bernard de Airth and Forveleth wife of Norrin de Monorgan, the three daughters of the late Finlay de Campsie, are the legitimate and true heirs also of the late Dougal, brother of Earl Maldouen of Lennox. He is to return the record of the inquest, together with this brieve, to the king's chapel. Kinclaven, 24 April a.r. 22 [1271].

Alexander Dei gratia rex Scocie Waltero comiti de Menthet dilecto et fideli suo vicecomiti et balliuis suis de Dunbretan salutem. Mandam*us* vobis et precipimus quatinus per probos et fideles hom*in*es patrie diligenter et fideliter inquiri faciatis si Maria sponsa Johan*n*is de Wardroba. et Elena sponsa Bernardi de Erth. ac Forueleth sponsa Norrini de Monorgund. filie quondam Finlai de Camsi. sint legittime et vere heredes quondam Dufgalli fratres[a] Maldoueni comitis de Leuenax et dictam inquisitionem diligenter factum et inscriptis redactam sub sigillo nostro et sigillas[b] eorum qui dicte inquisitioni faciende intererint ad capellam nostram mitti faciatis. et hoc breue. Teste meipso apud Kynclewyn' xxiiii die Aprilis. anno regni n*os*tri xx. s*ecun*do.

NOTES. [a] Sic, fratris. [b] Sic, sigillis.
RUBRIC. Littera domini regis et vicecomiti de Dunbartan' de inquicitione.
SOURCE. NLS, Adv. MS. 34.4.14, Chartulary of Paisley Abbey, fos cxiiii^{r-v}, cited in the record of the inquisition convened pursuant to the brieve on 15 May 1271.
PRINTED. *Paisley Registrum*, 191–2.

77 Takes the abbot and convent of Dunfermline, their lands, their men and all their possessions, movable and immovable, ecclesiastical as well as worldly, under his firm peace and protection, strictly forbidding anyone from causing any harm or injury to them, on pain of his full forfeiture. Also grants that no one may take poinds from them or their men for any debt, pledge or forfeiture other than for their own debts, pledges or forfeitures, except in his burghs, and again strictly forbids anyone from disturbing them in defiance of this grant, on pain of full forfeiture. Commands his justices, sheriffs, provosts and their bailies to compel all those in their burghs or bailiaries who owe a debt to the nuns to pay them without delay. Newbattle, 3 October a.r. 23 [1271].

Alexander Dei gracia rex Scotorum omnibus probis hominibus totius terre sue salutem. Sciatis nos abatem[a] et conventum de Dumfermleine terras suas hominos suos et uniuersas eorundem possessiones et omnia bona sua mobilia et immobilia tam ecclesiastica quam undana[b] sub firma pace et protectione nostra iuste suscepisse. Quare firmiter prohibemus ne quis eis malum molestiam iniuriam seu gravamen aliquod inferre presumat iniuste super nostram plenarium forisfacturam. Concessimus eisdem abate[a] et conventue[c] ut nullus namos suo uel hominum suorum capiatt[d] pro alicuius debito plegiagio uel forisfacto nisi pro eorumdem proprio debito pleggiagio[e] uel forrisfacto[f] saluis burgis nostris firmiter inhibentes ne quis eos contra hanc concessionem nostram vexare presumat iniuste super nostram plenariam forisfacturam. Mandamus insuper et firmiter precipimus justiciariis uicecomitibus prepositis et eorum balliuis ad quos presentis[g] littere pertenerint[h] ut omnes illos in eorum balliuis seu burgeis[i] cui[j] debita debent eisdem abbati et conuentui ad eadem debita eis uel certo eorum attornato latorum[k] presencium iuste et sine dilacione reddenda sed in quod[l] ipsi uel dictus eorum actornatus dicta debita sibi deberi ad eisdem racionabiliter probare poterint[m] uel poterit coram eis prout iustum fuerit compellant ita ne pro eorum defectum amplius inde iustum querimoniam audiemus[n]. Testatur Johannes Cummynge presente[o] Willelmo de Sancto Cleir et Johanne de Fentoun. Apud Newbottill tertio die Octobris anno regni nostri uicesimo tertio.

NOTES. [a] Sic, abbati. [b] Sic, mundana. [c] Sic, conventui. [d] Sic, capiat. [e] Sic, plegiagio. [f] Sic, forisfacto. [g] Sic, presentes. [h] Sic, peruenerint? Maitland Thomson's transcript corrects the copyist, preferring 'pertenerint'. [i] Sic, burgis. [j] Sic, qui. [k] Sic, latori. [l] Sic, quantum. [m] Sic, poterunt. [n] Sic, audiamus. [o] This must be an error for 'patre'; Maitland Thomson's transcript (see below), however, treats it as 'presente'.

SOURCE. Pinkie Castle, Musselburgh, Fyvie Castle Muniments, bundle 289–97, item 295 (a gathering of six folios), fo. 4^{v} (top); a typed transcript made in 1624. There is another typed transcript in NRS, GD 212/1/126, made by J. Maitland Thomson. Here, Thomson corrected – not always accurately – the errors of the seventeenth-century copyist.

COMMENTS. We are grateful to Professor Dauvit Broun for making a copy of this MS for us.

78 Writes to Henry III king of England concerning a dispute over common land at Langley (Northumberland) and Staward (Tynedale). Recites that Nicholas de Boltby holds the barony of South Tynedale of King Henry in chief by the law of England, by reason of the children whom Nicholas has produced by Philippa, daughter and heiress of Adam of Tynedale, who formerly held the barony. Adam of Boltby, son and heir of Philippa, has come before King Henry complaining that William of Swinburne, who holds the toun of Staward within King Alexander's liberty of North Tynedale, has attempted to appropriate the common land of the toun of Staward to himself and his men, to the manifest disinherison of Nicholas and Adam. Adam asserts that Philippa's ancestors granted the tenants of the toun of Staward free common within their manor of Langley, which is, in turn, within the county of Northumberland and is the caput of the barony of South Tynedale; Swinburne maintains that the land lies in North Tynedale. King Alexander therefore announces that he is sending William de Swinburne to King Henry armed with letters patent on the fortnight after the feast of St Hilary next. He requests that a perambulation of the bounds of the disputed land be made by a local jury, composed half of men of the county of Northumberland and half of men from his own liberty of North Tynedale, and that the sheriff of Northumberland be instructed accordingly. He undertakes to ensure that his bailiff of North Tynedale makes similar arrangements. Kinross, 7 January a.r. 23 [1272].

Excellentisimo principi et p*atr*i in *Christo* k*arissimo* . domino . H . Dei g*r*atia illustr*i* regi Angl*ie* . d*omi*no Ybern*ie* et duc*i* Acquietann*ie*

. Alex*ander* eadem gr*at*ia rex Scoc*ie* sal*ut*em . in ips*o* qui dat salute*m* regib*us* . Cu*m* Nich*olaus* de Bolteby . baro v*este*r de vob*is* teneat in capite baronia*m* de SuthTyndall' p*er* lege*m* Angl*ie* r*atio*n*e* prolis q*ua*m idem Nich*olaus* procreauit de Phi*lippa* filia et h*er*ede . Ad*e* de Tyndall' . qui eande*m* baron*iam* cu*m* lib*er*tatib*us* et consuetudinib*us* . et om*n*ib*us* aliis jurib*us* et p*er*tine*n*ciis suis de vob*is* tenuit . et Ad*am* de Bolteby fil*ius* et h*er*es p*redic*t*e* Ph*ilippe* de baron*ia* p*redic*t*a* cora*m* vob*is* ven*er*it . et vob*is* intimau*er*it . quod Will*elmu*s de Swyneburn' r*atio*n*e* ville de Staworth . que est inf*ra* lib*er*tate*m* *nos*tram de NorthTindall' . et q*ua*m tenet hereditarie . cui*us* ville tene*n*tib*us* . antecessores p*redic*t*e* Ph*illipe* concesseru*n*t lib*er*am com*m*unam inf*ra* com*m*unam man*er*ii sui de Langeley . sicut pred*ic*tus Adam filius et h*er*es p*redic*t*e* Ph*ilipp*e vob*is* intimauit quod est *inf*ra comitatum Northumbr*ie* et caput baron*ie* p*redic*t*e* . et q*uo*d de vob*is* tenet*ur* in capite . solum ei*us*dem com*m*une ad se et ad ho*min*es suos de Staworth' ap*ro*priare nitit*ur* . in ips*orum* Nich*ol*a*i* . et Ad*e* exh*er*edac*io*nem manifesta*m* . vt dicunt . Et quia p*er*ic*ulu*m exh*er*ed*it*ac*io*n*i*s t*em*pore custodie vob*is* et h*er*edib*us* v*est*ris ex hoc posset p*ro*uenire te*mp*or*ibus* fut*ur*is . si ita fuisset . sup*er* hiis excellencie v*est*re sig*nifica*mus quod illud solum p*redic*t*e* com*m*une de quo co*n*tent*io* mouet*ur* int*er* p*ar*tes p*redic*t*as* . no*n* est de solo de Langeley . quod est man*er*iu*m* predicti Nicholai de SothTindall' . et infra comitatum Northumbrie . s*ed* de solo de Staworthe . quod est man*er*ium Will*elm*i de Swyneburn' inf*ra* lib*er*tate*m* *nostrum* de Northtindall' . sicut p*er* p*re*d*ictum* Will*elm*um . et alios fideles n*os*tros intelleximu*s* . Nos v*ero* petit*io*ni v*est*re adquiescentes et p*er*icul*um* v*est*rum et nostru*m* ac p*redic*t*arum* partiu*m* vitare volentes . perp*en*dentes quod pax et t*ra*nquilitas int*er* p*redic*t*as* p*ar*tes p*er* alia*m* via*m* q*uam* p*er* p*er*ambulac*io*nem fieri no*n* potest . sicut nob*is* p*er* l*itte*ras v*est*ras significastis . rogantes vt p*er*ambulac*io*ni p*redic*t*e* assensu*m* preberem*us* p*er* l*itte*ras n*os*tras patentes . et quod nos i*n*iungeremus p*redic*t*o* Will*el*mo ad ponendu*m* se in p*er*ambulac*io*nem illam . et ip*sum* Will*elmu*m ad vos . mitte*mus* cu*m* l*itte*ris n*os*tris patentib*us* assensum n*ostru*m sup*er* hoc testificantib*us* in q*ui*ndena s*anc*ti Hillar*ii* pro*x*im*a* futur*a* . Et *cum* p*redic*t*e* ville de Langeley . et Staworth' site sint in confinio comitatus Northumbr*ie*. et lib*er*tatis n*os*tre Northtindall' . et *per* illam p*er*ambulac*io*nem c*er*te diuise fi*er*i debe*n*t int*er* p*redic*t*u*m comitatu*m*. et p*redic*t*a*m lib*er*tate*m* n*os*tram ipsi p*er*ambulac*io*ni assensum n*os*trum prebemus . Ita q*uod* medietas ips*orum* . p*er* quo*s* ip*s*a p*er*ambulac*i*o fi*er*i debet . sit de comitatu Northumbr*ie* . et alia medietas de lib*er*tate nostra Northtindall . Et ma*n*dabim*us* ball*iuo* n*os*tro Northtindall' . quod ip*s*e venire faciat . tot . et tales . de lib*er*tate n*os*tra Northtindall' ad c*er*tam die*m* et ad p*redic*t*um* locum vbi co*n*tenc*i*o mou*eretur* . sec*un*d*u*m quod vic*ecomes* v*est*er Northumbr*ie* et ball*ivus* n*os*t*e*r Tindall' sup*er* hiis int*er* ips*os* p*ro*uidebu*n*t . Ita quod p*er*ambulac*i*o illa no*n* remaneat p*ro* defec*t*u jurator*um* lib*er*tatis n*os*tre Tindall' . In cui*us* rei testimon*ium* has l*itte*ras nostras assensum n*os*trum sup*er* hoc testificantes vob*is* t*ra*nsmittim*us* patentes . vna cu*m* l*itte*ris *pre*dic*t*i Will*elm*i de Swyneburn' patentib*us* assensum suu*m* forma *pre*dic*t*a testificantib*us* . si ad diem p*redic*t*a*m cora*m* vob*is* p*er*sonalit*er* int*e*resse no*n* pot*er*it . Test*e* meip*s*o apud Kynros' vii° . die Januar*ii* . ann*o* . *regni* . *nostri* . xxiij° .

DESCRIPTION. 28.4 cm x 12.1 cm. Sealing: no evidence of a tongue, tag or seal.
HAND. Scribe K.
SOURCE. Original. TNA, Special Collections: Ancient Correspondence of the Chancery and the Exchequer, PRO SC 1/5/37. There is a partial copy of this letter in a seventeenth-century hand in Northampstonsire Record Office, Finch Hatton (Kirby) collection, FH 2538.
PRINTED. Shirley, *Royal Letters*, ii, 340–2; *CDS*, i, no. 2627 (cal.); HMC, 6th Report, pt 1, App., 244 (note)
COMMENT. See also *CDS*, v, pt 2, no. 31. Swinburne's agreement to the perambulation, noted in Alexander's letter, is recorded in TNA, PRO SC 1/5/52. The letter is mistakenly identified as an act of Alexander II in Scoular *Handlist*, no. 360.

79 Grants and by this charter confirms to the monks of Holyrood abbey the gift that David Broun, knight, made them of that part of his land in the territory of Coalston (East Lothian) that William Wyppot, burgess of Haddington, held of him in feu ferme. To be held in pure and perpetual alms, as Broun's charter bears witness. Haddington, 26 January a.r. 23 [1272].

Alexander Dei gracia rex Scotorum omnibus probis hominibus tocius terre sue salutem. Sciatis nos concessisse et hac presenti carta nostra confermasse[a] donacionem illam quam David Broun miles fecit[b] divine charitatis intuitu pro animabus antecessorum nostrorum et suorum[c] Deo et ecclesie sancte crucis de Edinburgh et canonicis ibidem[b] Deo seruientibus et imperpetuum seruituris de illa parte [terre][d] sue in territorio de Cumbircolstoun quam Willelmus Wyppot burgensis de Hadingtoun' quondam de ipso tenuit ad firmam . Tenenda et habenda predictis canonicis in puram et perpetuam elemosinam sine omni onere et exactione seculari cum omnibus pertinenciis libertatibus et asiamentis ad dictam terram spectantibus ita[e] libere et quiete plenarie et honorifice sicut predicta carta de predictis canonicis exinde confecta plenius iuste testatur. Saluo seruicio nostro. Testibus Johanne Cumyn filio Johannis de Keth, Simon Frauser, Ricardo Frauser et Willelmo Byseth apud Hadingtoun xxvi° die Januarii anno regni nostri vicesimo tercio.[f]

NOTES. [a] Sic, confirmasse. [b] The word domino is crossed out here. [c] The words suo et are crossed out here. [d] MS stained; word supplied by conjecture. [e] The word sine is crossed out here. [f] The word secundo is crossed out here.
SOURCE. Colstoun House, Haddington, Coalston Muniments, no. 2, a seventeenth-century transcript of an original that is now lost.
COMMENT. Modern transcripts appear in NRS, RH 1/1/1 and NRS, GD 212/1/127.

80 Grants and by this charter confirms the gift that Cristiana de Mowbray, wife of the late Roger de Mowbray, knight, and daughter and heiress of the late Bernard Fraser, knight, made to the brethren of the order of the Holy Trinity and the Captives when she founded the religious house called Grace of God in the territory of her manor of Houston (Renfrewshire), that is, of the whole of the manor of Houston, the whole land in the tenement of Houston which is called East Linton (East Lothian), the whole land that belonged to the hospital of Fortune, the whole land that belonged to Thomas de Lessuden in the toun of Fortune, and the land of Crauchie (all in East Lothian). To be held in pure and perpetual alms, as Christina's charter bears witness, saving the king's service. Haddington, 26 January a.r. 23 [1272].

Alex*ander* Dei gratia rex Scott*orum* . omnibus probis hominibus tocius terre sue salut*em* . Sciatis nos concessisse et hac presenti carta n*ost*ra confirmasse donac*i*onem illam . quam Cristiana de Mubray sponsa quondam Rogeri de Mubray militis filia et heres quondam Bernardi Fraser militis . in legittima viduitate et libera potestate sua constituta fecit f*ratri*bus ordinis s*anc*te Trinitatis et captiuor*um* . de domo que dicitur Gracia Dei . quam ead*em* Cristiana fundauit in teritorio[a] manerii sui de Huwystun' . et de toto eodem man*er*io et de tota t*er*ra que vocatur Lyueryngham' . in tenem*en*to de Huwystun' . et de tota t*er*ra que fuit hospitalis de Fortun' . et de tota t*er*ra que fuit quondam Thome de Lessedwyn' . in villa et in t*er*itorio[a] de Fortun' . et de tota t*er*ra de Crauchot' . Tenendas et habendas f*ra*tribus p*redic*ti ordinis et eor*um* successoribus in p*er*petuu*m* de d*ic*ta Cristiana et h*er*edibus suis in puram et perpetuam elemosinam . cu*m* om*n*ibu*s* lib*er*tatib*us* et aisiamentis ad d*ic*tas t*er*ras p*er*tinentib*us* . adeo lib*er*e quiete . plenarie . et honorifice sicut carta p*redic*te Cristiane eisdem f*ra*tribus exinde confecta . plenius iuste testatur saluo s*er*uic*i*o n*ost*ro . Testibus Joh*anne* Cumyn' . Reginaldo le Chen' . Symone Fras*er* . Ricardo Fras*er* et Dauid Brun' . apud Hadyngtun' . vicesimo sexto die Januar*ii* . anno . regni nostri . vicesimo terc*i*o .

NOTE. [a] Sic, territorio.
ENDORSED. A deed from the kinge of Scotland (sixteenth century).
DESCRIPTION. 21.5 cm x 11.5 cm; fold 2.4 cm. Sealing: on a tag, 3.1 cm broad, through a single slit, there survives part of the second great seal, 6.0 cm in diameter, in white wax. Most of the obverse and reverse sides are rubbed away.
HAND. Scribe I.
SOURCE. Original. Berkeley Castle, BSN D/5/99/1.
PRINTED. B. Wells-Furby, *A Catalogue of the Medieval Muniments at Berkeley Castle* (2 vols, Bristol: Bristol and Gloucestershire Archaeological Association, 2004), ii, 820–1 (cal.); F. W. F. Jeayes, *Descriptive Catalogue of the Charters and Muniments in the possession of the Rt. Hon. Lord Fitz-Hardinge, at Berkeley Castle* (Bristol, 1892), 137–8 (transl.).

81 Gives, grants and by this charter confirms to Malcolm earl of Lennox all the lands lying within the following bounds: from 'East Douglas' to Shian (Stirlingshire), from Shian to 'Keryne' (Carron?) and as the 'Keryne' descends to 'Phale', and from there to the water called 'Gall' and as the same 'Gall' descends to the loch, from the 'Gall' to 'Fynnovhyne' as it descends to the Forth, and from the 'Fynnovhyne' to the eastern boundary of Cremannan, from the same boundary to the burn called the 'Melach' and from the 'Melach' burn to 'Keryn'. To be held in free forest and in feu and heritage as freely and quietly as any lands in Scotland are given and granted in free forest. Strictly prohibits anyone from felling timber or hunting there without the earl's licence and in violation of the free forest, on pain of his full forfeiture of £10. Kintore, 1 July a.r. 23 [1272].

Alex*ander* Dei gr*at*ia rex Scottorum omnibus probis hominibus totius terre sue clericis et laycis salutem. Sciant presentes et futuri nos dedisse concessisse et hac presenti carta nostra confirmasse di[lecto et fideli] nostro Malcolmo comiti de Leuenax totas[a] terras cum pertinenciis videlicet ab Est' Douglas vsque ad Sehynne' et ab Sehynne' vsque ad Keryn' et sicut Keryn' descendit [in Phale et][b] deinde vsque ad aquam quod dicitur Gall' et sicut idem Gall' descendit in lacu et ab idem Gall' vsque ad Fynnovhyn' sicut descendit in Forth' et ab idem [Fynnovhyn' vsque ad metam][b] orientalem. de Cramenane et ab eadem meta vsque ad riuulum qui dicitur Melach' et a dicto riuulo de Melach' vsque ad Keryn' in liberam forestam. Tenendas et habendas [totas dictas][b] terras cum pertinentiis dicto Malcolmo et heredibus suis de nobis et heredibus nostris in liberam forestam in feodo et hereditate adeo libere et quiete in omnibus et per omnia sicut alique terre [in toto][b] regno Scocie in liberam forestam alicui mortali liberius dari possunt vel concedi. Quare firmiter prohibemus ne quis in eadem terra predicta sine ipsius Malcolmi et su[orum heredum][b] licencia speciali secet aut venetur aut faciat in contrario [iuri][b] dicte libere foreste super [nostram][b] plenariam forisfacturam [decem librarum][b] Testibus Alexandro Cumyn comite de [Buchan][c] Donaldo de Marr' Willelmo Cumyn Bernardo de Monte Alto Willelmo Bysseth' et aliis. Apud Kyntor primo die Julii anno regni nostri vicesimo tercio.

NOTES. [a]Totas illas terras in B. [b]Words supplied from B. [c]Words supplied by conjecture.

SOURCE. NRS, Montrose Muniments, GD 220/1/F/5/2/1, an inspeximus of David II, dated 2 May 1361 = A; NRS, GD 220/2/202 = B, fifteenth-century Lennox cartulary. Transcribed here from A, with lacunae supplied by B.

PRINTED. *RRS*, vi, no. 258 (from A, with lacunae filled in by B); Fraser, *Lennox*, ii, 29–30 (from A); *Lennox Cart.*, 2–4, from a transcript of B made in the eighteenth century by Walter Macfarlane.

COMMENTS. The loss of the original grant is particularly regrettable, since it is clear that by the fourteenth century familiarity with Gaelic place names was not a normal feature of the royal chancery. Scribal difficulty with the names is apparent already in 1321, when Robert I confirmed Alexander III's grant to Earl Malcolm (*RRS*, v, no. 194). Here, the 'Duueglas' of the early to mid-thirteenth century (Fraser, *Lennox*, ii, nos 204, 207), a fair rendering of the Gaelic *Dubhghlais*, had already become Douglas. The clerk who drafted this inspeximus of David II further obscured other place names: the 'Sehymmie' (originating in the Gaelic *sìthean*?) of 1321, for example, became 'Sehynne', the 'Fynnovhne' of 1321 the equally garbled 'Fynnovhyn' (originally *fionn* + *abhainn*?). Most of the place names now defy identification, but it would appear that Alexander's grant incorporated a very considerable territory in the region north and east of Loch Lomond.

82

Commands William de Swinburne, his bailiff of Tynedale, to enclose all the lands, meadows and pastures taken into the king's hands by itinerant justices in their most recent eyre, and to put these to ferme in accordance with the extents that were made of them and the customs of the kingdom of England. Scone, 15 March a.r. 24 [1273].

A . Dei gr*at*ia rex Scoc*ie* . Will*elm*o de Swynebur*n*' balli*uo* suo Tyndall' sal*utem* . Mandam*us* tibi et p*re*cipim*us* q*ua*tinus om*n*es t*er*ras . prata et pasturas . in [manu]m[a] *nost*ram captas per justic*iarios nost*ros vlti*mo* in Tyndall' itin*er*antes ad com*m*od*um* *nost*rum appruar[i] facias [et ad][a] firmam dimittas s*ecun*d*um* exte*n*tas de eisd*em* te*rr*is . p*ra*tis . et pasturis coram p*re*di*ct*is justic*iariis* [ ][b] con[s]uetudines regni Anglie . In cui*us* rei testimoniu*m* has litt*er*as n*os*tras t*ibi* mittim*us* patentes [Teste m]e[a] ip*s*o apud Scon'. xv . die Marc*ii* anno r*egni* n*ostri* xxiiii^to .

NOTES. [a] The document is damaged by a large tear; letters supplied by conjecture. [b] Two words here rendered illegible by the tear.

ENDORSED. The document has long been bound in a volume, its dorse unavailable for examination.

DESCRIPTION. 20.3 cm x 5.9 cm, L x 4.9 cm, R. Sealing: formerly sealed on a tongue cut from right to left across the bottom of the deed, now torn away.

HAND. Scribe B.

SOURCE. Original. Northumberland Collections Service, Swynburne (Capheaton) estate records, ZSW 1/20.

PRINTED. *HN*, III, ii, 22.

COMMENT. This would appear to be a brieve issued in consequence of the agreement recorded above at no. 78. The rights and privileges that the king enjoyed within his Tynedale lands remained a source of much contention between the crowns.

83 Grants to William de Swinburne, at the instance of Queen Margaret, for his lifetime, freedom from being placed on any assizes, juries or inquests, and that he shall not be made the king's sheriff, coroner, escheator, forester, verderer, agister, regarder or other bailiff against his will. Scone, 15 March a.r. 24 [1273].

Alex*ander* Dei g*ra*tia rex Scott*orum* . om*n*ibus balli*u*is et fidelib*us* suis Tyndalie ad quos p*re*sentes litt*ere* p*er*uene*r*int sal*u*tem . Sciatis q*uo*d ad instanciam carissime sponse n*ost*re Margarete regine Scoc*ie* . conces-sim*us* dil*ect*o nob*is* Will*elm*o de Swyneburne q*uo*d toto temp*ore* vite sue h*ab*eat hanc lib*er*tatem . videlicet . q*uo*d no*n* ponat*ur* in assisis juratis . vel recogniti*on*ib*us* aliquib*us* . et q*uo*d non fiat vicecomes . coronator . escaetor . forestarius . viridari*us* . agistator . regardator . aut ali*us* balliuus n*oster* cont*ra* voluntatem suam . In cuius rei testimonium has litteras n*ost*ras eidem Will*elm*o fieri fecimus patentes . Teste me ip*s*o apud Scon' . xv die Martii . anno regni n*ost*ri . vicesim*o* . quarto .

ENDORSED. The document has long been bound in a volume, its dorse unavailable for examination.

DESCRIPTION. 19.5 cm x 7.6 cm, L x 4.8 cm, R. Sealing: formerly sealed on a tongue cut from right to left across the bottom of the deed. The tongue, 2.0 cm wide, is intact, but all traces of a seal are gone.

HAND. Scribe K.

SOURCE. Original. Northumberland Collections Service, Swynburne (Capheaton) estate records, ZSW 1/15.

PRINTED. *HN*, III, ii, 23.

84 Gives, grants and by this charter confirms to William de Swinburne, at the instance of Queen Margaret, the lands of Haughton Strother in Tynedale, together with the demesnes lying nearby between Haughton and Nunwick, in free forest, with right of vert and venison. To be held quit of all suits of court, wardships, reliefs, marriages, aids and all other demands due from the land for an annual render of a pair of white gloves or 2d at Wark in Tynedale, saving the common of herbage to all those who have right to it. Scone, 15 March a.r. 24 [1273].

Alex*ande*r Dei gr*at*ia rex Scott*orum* . om*n*ib*us* probis hominib*us* toci*us* t*er*re sue [salutem . Noueritis] nos ad i*n*stanciam Margarete regine carissime co*n*sortis n*ost*re dedisse co*n*cessisse . et hac p*re*senti [carta nostr]a confirmasse . Will*elm*o de Swyneburne dil*ect*o et fideli n*ost*ro Halutonstrother in Tyndal' vna cum [dominiis] c*ir*cu*m*adiacentibus int*er* Haluton' et Nunewych' i*n* lib*er*a foresta . cum virida et venatione [ ][a] toto iure n*ost*ro quod in eadem h*abe*mus uel h*abe*re pot*er*im*us* . Habend*a* et tenend*a* d*ict*o Will*elm*o . et h*er*edib*us* u*e*l ass[ignatis suis de] nob*is* et h*er*edib*us* n*ost*ris lib*er*e . qui[ete plenarie] . et honorifice in om*n*ib*us* . q*ui*ete de sectis om*n*imodar*um* [curie et wardis releuiis mari]tagiis . auxiliis et de om*n*ib*us* reb*us* aliis . et demand*is* que ab aliq*ui*b*us* exigere [ ][b] [red]dend*um* inde [annua]tim nobis et h*er*edib*us* n*ost*ris ip*s*e et h*er*edes u*e*l assig*n*ati sui vnu*m* par alba[rum cyrothecarum] v*e*l duos denar[ios] apud Werk i*n* Tyndal' ad Pentecosten' . p*ro* om*n*ib*us* s*er*uitiis . co*n*suetudinib*us* exact[ionibus] u*e*l vexac*ion*ib*us* . et [deman]dis . salua tamen om*n*ib*us* illis com*m*una herbagii . qui pro te*m*p*or*e i*n* eodem de iure com*m*unicare . debent. Test*ibus* . Alex*andro* Cumin . com*ite* de Buchan' . justic*iario* Scoc*ie* . Joh*ann*e Cumyn' . Alex*andro* [sen*escallo*] Scoc*ie* . Gilb*er*to de Haya Will*elm*o de Montealto . Reginald*o* le Chen' . Bernardo de M[ontealto et] Joh*ann*e de Lamberton apud Schon' . xv^{o} . die Marcii . ann*o* regni n*ost*ri vicesimo . quarto .

NOTES. The document is in a poor state of preservation, with several holes obliterating the text. Some of the words in brackets are supplied by conjecture; others from TNA, PRO JUST 1/657, m 9d (see below). [a] Two–three words missing owing to document damage. [b] Three–four words missing.

ENDORSED. The document has long been bound in a volume, its dorse unavailable for examination.

DESCRIPTION. 20.0 cm x 11.0 cm; fold 2.5 cm. Sealing: a tag, 1.8 cm broad, is passed through a single slit.

HAND. Scribe K.

SOURCE. Original. Northumberland Collections Service, Swynburne (Capheaton) estate records, ZSW1/24.

PRINTED. *HN*, III, i, 15–17; *Northumb. and Durham Deeds*, 242 (cal.).

COMMENT. This charter represents a second grant of the lands of Haughton Strother to Swinburne: he had an earlier charter dated 10 February 1264; see below, no. 230. The earlier grant, however, did not include free warren. The terms of the royal charter were the subject of an inquiry on the part of the justices eyre who visited Wark in the spring of 1293, when William de Swinburne's widow sought to avoid paying a marriage fine to the new lord of Tynedale, Edward I (TNA, PRO JUST 1/657, m 9d). The text of the charter was clearly recited *viva voce*, although the eyre clerk recorded only the portion relating to the Swinburne claim to freedom from feudal incidents. That portion of the charter, interestingly, corresponds to part of the text that was lost over the years owing to poor preservation.

85

Sends to Robert bishop of Glasgow a copy of an inquisition made at his own command at Roxburgh regarding a dispute between the master and brethren of the hospital of Soutra and Walter de Moravia, knight. Narrates the record of the inquest by Richard James, suitor of the barony of Eckford and four other suitors of that barony, Hugh, suitor of the barony of Upper Crailing and four other suitors of that barony and Richard, suitor of the barony of Heton and four other suitors of that barony, held to determine whether the late Sir Walter Olifard and Sir David de Olifard, ancestors of Walter de Moravia, were accustomed to giving to the house of Soutra one thrave of corn annually from every plough in the land of Crailing and of Smailholm (all in Roxburghshire), not only from their own but also those of their bondmen. The suitors returned that the brethren of the house of Soutra and their attorney had long been accustomed to receiving the corn, and that they should receive it from Sir Walter de Moravia and his men. Kelso, 15 April a.r. 24 [1273].

Alex*ander* Dei *gra*tia Rex Scott*orum* ven*er*abili pat*ri* in *Christ*o R eade*m* *gra*tia e*piscop*o Glasg' sal*ute*m. Mittim*us* de v*er*bo ad v*er*bum inquisi*cio*nem f*act*am ap*u*d Roxb*urg*h sup*er* contenc*io*ne mota int*er* mag*istrum* et fratres de Soltr' ex vna p*a*rte et Walterum de Morauia militem ex alt*era* que talis est. Inquisic*io* f*act*a p*er* p*re*ceptum d*omi*ni regis in pleno comitatu comitat*us* de Roxb*urg*h die Mart*is* p*roximo* post vicesimu*m* diem natal*is* Do*mi*ni anno etc. septuagesim*o* p*ri*mo p*er* antiq*ui*ores pat*rie* qui melius v*er*itatem sup*er* hoc nou*er*int scilic*et* p*er* Ricardum Jambis sectatore*m* baronie de Ecfurde et p*er* quatuor de fideliorib*us* ho*min*ib*us* tocius baronie et p*er* Hugone*m* sectatorem baro*n*ie de sup*er*iori Cralyng' et p*er* quatuor de fideliorib*us* ho*min*ib*us* to*cius* d*ict*e baronie et p*er* Ricardu*m* sectatorem baro*n*ie de Heton et per quatuor fideliorib*us*[a] eiusd*e*m baro*n*ie si quo*n*d*a*m d*omin*us Walt*er*us Olifard et d*omin*us Dauid Olifard an*te*cessores d*omi*ni Walt*er*i de Morauia de sing*u*lis caru*c*is inf*ra* t*er*ram de Cralyng' et de Smalh*a*m tam de p*ro*p*r*iis caruc*is* q*uam* de caruc*is* bondor*um* vna*m* thravam bladi domui de Soltr' sing*u*lis annis dar*e* solebant. Qui om*n*es iurati dixeru*n*t q*uo*d f*ra*tres d*ict*e dom*us* de Soltr' et attornati eor*um* hoc p*er* m*ul*ta temp*or*a recip*er*e consuerunt et de d*omi*no Walt*er*o de Mora*u*ia et de ho*min*ib*us* suis dic*tu*m bladum recep*er*unt . In cui*us* rei testi*moniu*m sigillu*m* n*ost*rum apponi fecim*us* p*re*senti sc*r*ipto. Test*ibus*[b] meips*o* apud Calcov quinto decim*o* die Ap*r*il*is* anno regni n*ost*ri vicesimo quarto.

NOTES. [a] Sic, de fidelioribus. [b] Sic, teste.
RUBRIC. Inq*ui*sici*o* (fourteenth century).
SOURCE. NLS, Adv. MS. 34.4.1, Chartulary of the Hospital of the Holy Trinity, Soutra, fos 6v–7r.
PRINTED. *Midlothian Chrs*, Soutra, no. 44.

86 Writes to Eleanor queen of England reminding her that Henry late king of England granted his father, King Alexander II, all the amercements, fines, escheats and pertinents arising from pleas of the forest or other pleas relating to the men who reside in his Cumberland manors, and that when the steward of Inglewood forest, in violation of this agreement, prevented his officers from collecting these sums Alexander sent envoys to King Henry to complain. King Henry in turn commanded Geoffrey de Neville justiciar of the forests north of Trent and the said steward to allow Alexander's bailiffs the sums. Now, however, the current steward of the forest, William de Leybourne, is again withholding the fines and amercements in violation of the agreement. He requests that Eleanor advise the council once more to send a justice itinerant to the region so that he may plead his suit. Notes that he is on pilgrimage to the shrine of St Cuthbert at Durham and that he appends his privy seal to these letters. Durham, [22 April] a.r. 23 [1273].

[ ][a] suam in Christo karissime Eleanore Dei gracia regine Angl*ie* domine Hibern*ie* et ducisse Aquit*annie* . Alex*ande*r eadem *gra*tia rex Scott*orum* sal*ute*m . Cum . H . quondam rex Angl*ie* [ ][b] Alex*andri* q*uo*ndam regi Scott*orum* pa*tr*i nostri et heredibus siue regibus Scott*orum* dudum concessit omnia am*er*ciamenta . finibus . eschaete et p*er*tinenciis de man*er*iis. t*er*ris . et ho*min*ibus suis inp*er*petuum [ ][a] Cumb*er*land ex q*ua*cu*m*que causa p*ro*uedencia tam de placitis foreste q*ua*m de om*n*ibu*s* aliis placitis ip*s*a man*er*ia t*er*ras et ho*m*ines p*re*dictos ta*n*gentibu*s* tam coram justic*iariis* com*m*unium placit*or*um q*ua*m foreste aliis [ ][b] balli*u*is quibu*s*cu*m*q*ua* . secu*n*d*um* q*uo*d in forma coneunc*io*nis int*er* pred*ic*tum . H . q*uo*ndam regem Angl*ie* et . A . q*uo*ndam regem Scott*orum* pa*tr*em no*s*trum iuste plenius co*n*tinet*ur* [ ][c] nos p*er* q*uo*sdam ministros foreste de Inglewode aliquot te*m*pore impediti fuimus q*uo*minus ip*s*e am*er*ciame*n*ta p*re*dicta man*er*ia t*er*ras et ho*min*es tange*n*tes coram senescallum foreste p*re*dicte [ ][d] percipere peteremur . Super q*uo*d nuncios pred*ict*o . H . q*uo*ndam regi Angl*ie* destinauim*us* co*n*querentes nos de hui*us*modi am*er*ciame*n*tis p*er* senescallum foreste p*re*d*ic*te fore i*m*peditos *con*tra forma*m* co*n*uenc*io*nis p*re*d*ic*te nobis [ ][e] mandauit Galfrido de Neuill' justic*iario* foreste vltra Trentam et senescallo foreste de Inglewod q*uo*d om*n*es fines et am*er*ciamenta ad q*uo*s ho*min*es [ ][d] de p*re*d*ic*tis man*er*iis et t*er*ris coram ip*s*ius senescallo r*ati*one p*re*d*ic*te foreste am*er*ciati fu*er*int balli*u*os no*s*tros s*ine* impedime*n*to et contradict*i*one percipere et h*abe*re p*er*mitterint ad [ ][f] h*er*edibu*s* d*ic*ti . H . q*uo*ndam regis Angl*ie* d*ict*o justic*iario* et aliis senescallis et balli*u*is foreste p*re*d*ic*te inde destinat plenius *con*tinet*ur* q*uo*rum infrasc*r*ipta [ ][f]mam inspicienda . Et balli*ui* no*s*tri p*re*d*ict*oru*m* man*er*ioru*m* p*er* execuc*i*onem p*re*d*ic*toru*m* mandatoru*m* p*er* p*re*d*ic*ti . H . q*uo*ndam regis Angl*ie* fines et [ ][f] coram justic*iariis* senescallis et aliis balli*u*is foreste p*re*d*ic*te de Inglewod ad [ ][d] no*s*trum sine i*n*pedime*n*to uel *con*tradict*i*one alicui*us* balli*u*oru*m* p*re*d*ict*oru*m* [ ][e] Will*el*mus de Layburn' nunc senescallus foreste p*re*d*ic*te et balli*ui* sui ei*us*dem ho*min*es man*er*ioru*m* nost*rorum* q*ui* finibus et am*er*ciame*n*tis coram ip*s*is factis de foreste p*re*d*ic*te [ ][d] distringu*n*t et tam *con*tra forma*m* co*n*uenc*io*nis p*re*d*ic*te q*ua*m contra seysina*m* no*s*trum p*er* longu*m* tempus . pacifice et sine om*ni* i*m*pedime*n*to [ ][b] et ad exh*er*edac*i*one*m* no*s*trum manifesta*m* . huic *est* q*uo*d v*es*tram exp*er*tissima*m* dilect*io*ne*m* de q*uo* ad plenu*m* confidem*us* . affectuose rogam*us* q*ua*tinus amore n*os*tro vna cu*m* [ ][b] consiliu*m* sane consilias d*om*ini regis Angl*ie* *im*pendere velitis q*uo*d ip*s*i de consilio d*ic*ti d*om*ini regis mandare vel*i*nt itin*er*ac*i*one ex p*ar*te [ ][a] si placet amore n*os*tro sup*er* his facientes me oporteneat alia vice p*ro* hui*us*m*od*o ad curia*m* Angl*ie* destinare. Et q*ui*a de p*re*d*ic*tis [ ][f] n*os*tris p*er* senescallu*m* p*re*d*ic*tum foreste de Inglewode nobis non [ ][d] anteq*ua*m *p*eregr*i*nante*m* ad s*an*ctu*m* Cuthb*er*ti de Dunelm' venebam*us* in q*ua* p*er*egrinat*i*o*ne* [ ][g] p*re*sentibu*s* priuatu*m* sigillu*m* no*s*trum apposuim*us*.

Statum vestrum quod dominus per longum tempus prosperum custodiat vna cum beneplacito vestro si [ ][g] Datum apud Dunelm . x. kalendas Maii anno regni nostri . xx . tertio.

NOTES. [a]Two–three words. [b]Two words. [c]Three–four words. [d] One word. [e]Four words. [f] Four–five words. [g] Five–six words.

DESCRIPTION. 19.3 cm x 7.9 cm. Sealing: formerly sealed, with the privy seal, on a tongue cut from right to left across the bottom of the deed, now torn away. The seal is missing. The very poor state of preservation makes the document almost illegible, even under infrared light and using digital photography software.

HAND. Scribe K.

SOURCE. Original. TNA, Special Collections: Ancient Correspondence of the Chancery and the Exchequer, PRO SC 1/31/10.

COMMENT. The dating of this document is problematic but not impossible to establish. The text refers to Henry III as deceased; although gravely ill in April 1272, he did not die until November of that year and it is unlikely that Alexander should have committed the diplomatic indiscretion of referring to him as *quondam* while he was still alive. Moreover, William de Leybourne, who is identified here as steward of the forest of Inglewood, did not take seisin of the office until after 2 September 1272 (*CCR, 1268–72*, 569–70). Alexander's presence in the border region on 15 April 1273 (no. 85, above) makes it likely that his pilgrimage to Durham and the writing of this letter took place in this year, rather than 1272. The letter to Queen Eleanor followed the unsuccessful conclusion of litigation initiated by King Alexander in the autumn of 1271 against Leybourne's predecessor, Roger de Lancaster, for encroachments on his rights in Inglewood forest (TNA, PRO SC 1/2/98, PRO C 47/12/1/4, 5). Disputes about the Scottish crown's rights and privileges in its English estates were frequent thereafter (see below, nos 123, 170, 222, 250, 252, 253, 254, 255, 260, 273, 285, 328) and remained unresolved at Alexander's death in 1286. The king's decision to travel on pilgrimage without his great seal reflects pious intent, if ultimately misplaced optimism. Affairs of state, especially those related to the lands of the Scottish king in England, seldom lay quiescent for long.

87

Grants, gives and by this charter confirms to the burgesses of Aberdeen an annual fair on the feast of the Holy Trinity and for the following fortnight, with all the liberties and customs associated with fairs, as freely and quietly as other burghs in the kingdom enjoy. Kintore, 2 December a.r. 25 [1273].

. Alexander Dei gratia rex Scottorum omnibus probis hominibus tocius terre sue salutem . Noueritis nos concessisse dedisse . et presenti carta nostra confirmasse . burgensibus nostris de Aberden' dilectis et fidelibus nostris ut habeant singulis annis a die sancte Trinitatis nundinas in burgo nostro de Aberden' per duas septimanas continue sequentes . duraturas . cum omnibus iuribus . libertatibus . rectitudinibus . et consuetudinibus ad alias nundinas nostras in burgis nostris per regnum nostrum constitutas iuste pertinentibus . Testibus Willelmo Cumyn' de Kylbryde . Thoma Ranulphi tunc . camerario . Reginaldo le Chen' . Roberto de Cambrun' . Willelmo de Sancto Claro . Patricio de Graham' . et . Willelmo Byseth . apud Kyntor' secundo die Decembris . anno regni nostri . vicesimo quinto .

ENDORSED. 1. Concessio nundinarum (contemporary). 2. Carta Alexandri regis scotorum de priuilegio nundinarum post diem sante Trinitatis prespicimus (?) quatuor dierum (sixteenth century).

DESCRIPTION. 20.8 cm x 10.2 cm; fold 3.6 cm. Sealing: on a tag, 2.0 cm broad, through single slits, there remains a small fragment 4.6 cm in diameter, of the second great seal, in natural wax. Only a small central portion of the seal is now visible.

HAND. Scribe L.

SOURCE. Original. Aberdeen City Archives, Aberdeen City Muniments, no. A[1]5.
PRINTED. *Aberdeen Burgh Chrs*, 8–9.

88 Gives, grants and by this charter confirms to John de Swinburne, for his faithful service, ten merks sterling annually from the king's chamber and two suits of clothes annually such as the king's servants receive. Roxburgh, 20 March a.r. 25 [1274].

Alexander Dei gracia rex Scottorum omnibus probis hominibus totius terre sue salutem . Sciatis nos pro nobis et heredibus nostris dedisse concessisse et hoc presenti carta nostra confirmasse[a] Johanni de Swynburn decem marcas sterlingorum annuatim de camera nostra sibi perpetuo percipiendas pro fideli seruitio suo nobis inpenso. et duas robas tales quales seruientes nostri p*er*cipere annuatim. videlicet quinque marcas et vnam robam ad Pentecosten et quinque marcas ad festum sancti Martini in hyeme et[a] aliam robam ad natale Domini quolibet anno in tota vita sua. In cuius rei testimonium litteras nostras predicto Johanni de Swynburn fieri fecimus patentes. Testibus Alex*andro* Comyn comite de Buchan' justiciario Scocie. Waltero senescallo comite de Minethey. Gilberto de Vmfranuill' comite de Anegos. Hugone de Berclay justiciario Laodon*ie*. Willelmo Comyn de Kilbride[b] et Simone Fraser. Apud Rokesburg' anno regni nostri vicesimo quinto.

NOTES. [a] Word omitted in B. [b] Kirkibride in B.
SOURCE. TNA, Chancery: Miscellaneous Inquisitions, PRO C 145/66/24, the record of an inquest *post mortem* held in February 1307 = A; Bodleian Library, MS. Dodsworth XLIV, fo. 329 (sixteenth-century copy) = B. Transcribed here from A.
PRINTED. Text B was printed in *Northumb. and Durham Deeds*, 285.
COMMENT. The Dodsworth volume, dated 1638, belongs to a large series of transcriptions compiled by the antiquary Roger Dodsworth. It consists of Latin-language summaries and, occasionally, full transcripts of several charters then in the possession of various Northumberland families. While John apparently enjoyed the gift unencumbered during the lifetimes of kings Alexander III and John, payments ceased after the Tynedale estates passed into the hands of Bishop Anthony Bek of Durham, apparently 'under pretense of anger against John'. In 1307 Swinburne petitioned Edward I successfully for a restoration of the payments, but they were still being withheld in 1311. See *CDS*, ii, no. 1917; TNA, PRO SC 1/45/156 (*CDS*, v, no. 556).

89 Announces that he wills and grants to the abbot and convent of Arbroath that the aid which their men of Tarves offered to the king shall not prejudice the abbey in future. Haddington, 1 August a.r. 26 [1274].

Alexand*er*[a] Dei gratia rex Scott*orum* om*n*ib*us* p*ro*bis ho*min*ib*us* toci*us* t*er*re sue sal*u*tem. Sciatis q*uod* volum*us* et *con*cedim*us* abb*a*ti et co*n*uentui de Abirbr*oth*oc q*uod* ill*u*d auxiliu*m* q*uo*d ho*min*es sui de Tarvays nob*i*s hac vice de g*rat*ia p*re*stit*er*u*n*t eis i*n* p*re*iudiciu*m* vel g*ra*uame*n* cedere n*on* valeat i*n* futu*r*um. In cui*us* rei testi*mo*ni*um* has n*ost*ras l*itt*eras fieri fecim*us* pate*n*tes. Test*ibus* Alex*andro* Cvmyn comit*e* Buchan'. Will*el*mo comite de Marr. Rob*e*rto de Bruys comit*e* de Karryk. Will*el*mo Cvmyn de Kelbryd'. Symone Fras*er*. Ap*u*d Hadi*n*gton' p*ri*mo die Augusti. anno regni n*ost*ri . xxvi.

NOTE. [a] Initial in red.
RUBRIC. *Quod non preiudicet auxilium factum* de Taruays (in red) (fourteenth century).
SOURCE. NLS, Adv. MS. 34.4.2, Chartulary of Arbroath Abbey, fo. xxi^{v}.
PRINTED. *Arbroath Liber*, i, no. 246.

90 Writes to Edward I king of England informing him that Cristiana, formerly the wife of Walter de Lindsay, has bound herself to Walter de Percy, to which marriage Alexander has given his consent. 'Lochcumberay' [Great Cumbrae?], 23 September a.r. 26 [1274].

Excellentissimo principi . et fratri suo in *Christo* k*arissi*mo . d*omi*no Edwardo D*ei* g*ra*tia regi Angl*ie* d*omi*no Hybernie et duci Aquitann*ie* illustr*i* . Alex*ander* eadem g*ra*tia rex Scott*orum* sal*ut*em . et sincere dilec*ti*onis semper augmentum . Quoniam pium est u*er*itati testimoniu*m* p*er*hibere . tenore p*re*sentium vobis significamus q*uo*d Cristiana quondam sponsa Walt*er*i de Lyndesay matrimonio se copulauit[a] Waltero de Percey infra regnum n*ost*rum . cui matrimonio g*ra*tiosum . p*re*buim*us* assensum . T*este* . me ip*s*o apud Lochcumberay . xxiii° die Septembris . anno regni n*ost*ri xx° . sexto .

NOTE. [a] Cum missing?
DESCRIPTION. 20.8 cm x 4.6 cm. Sealing: formerly sealed on a tongue cut from right to left across the bottom of the deed, now torn away.
HAND. Scribe M.
SOURCE. Original. TNA, Special Collections: Ancient Correspondence of the Chancery and the Exchequer, PRO SC 1/20/143.
PRINTED. *Nat. MSS Scotland*, i, no. 63 (facs.); *CDS*, ii, no. 23 (cal.).

91 Gives, grants and by this charter confirms to the Friars Preachers of Inverness a portion of the highway lying from the river Ness to the land that the abbot and convent of Arbroath bestowed on them in perpetuity, and the land across from it lying between the churchyard of the parish church and the wall of the said friars' house and the island of royal land on the north side of the friary and on the south side of the river Ness; together with a fishery as far as 'Scurry'. Berwick, 20 May a.r. 26 [1275].

Alexander Dei gracia rex Scotorum omnibus probis hominibus totius terre sue salutem. Sciatis nos dedisse concessisse et hac presenti carta nostra confirmasse fratribus predicatoribus de Inuernys ibidem Deo seruientibus et seruituris illam viam regiam nostrum jacentem in longitudine ab aqua de Nys vsque ad terram illam quam abbas et conuentus de Abirbrothok eis perpetue contulerunt et in latitudine inter cimiterium ecclesie parochialis et murum dictorum fratrum et illam insulam terre nostre jacentem ex parte boreali eorundem fratrum ex parte australi aque de Nys cum integra aqua et piscatione a prefata via fratrum vsque ad Scurry in puram et perpetuam elemosinam cum omnibus commoditatibus libertatibus et asiamentis inhabitandis libere quiete honorifice bene et in pace imperpetuum sicut aliqua terra viris religiosis in regno nostro datur vel conceditur. Testibus Alexandro Comyne comite Buchanie constabulario et justiciario Scotie Donaldo comite de Mar Ingeramo de Genes et Reginaldo de Schen patre militibus. Apud Beruicum vicesimo die mensis Maii anno regni nostri vicesimosexto.

SOURCE. NRS, Great Seal Register, C 2/24, no. 27.
PRINTED. *RMS*, iii, no. 962 (cal.). Fraser-Mackintosh, *Invernessiana*, 17, offers a translation of the document, but mistakenly assigns it to the reign of Alexander II.
COMMENT. The act is narrated in a confirmation of James V, dated 31 August 1530. A note in the Register suggests that already in 1530 the original document was in poor condition. Scurry is now obsolete.

92 Writes to Edward I king of England informing him that the men of Alexander of Argyll, putting into the port of Bristol, were arrested there with their ship and goods on suspicion of piracy. In order that King Edward may see that they are his liegemen, he is sending the names of some of them, namely Master Alan, the captain of the ship, Gilfolan Kerd and those of others who, on the day of the writing of this letter, he himself does not know. Requests that the king order his bailiffs of Bristol to permit the men freely to come back to Scotland with their goods. Elgin, 15 August a.r. 27 [1275].

. Excellentissimo p*r*incipi . et fratri suo in *Christ*o k*arissi*mo . d*omi*no . E . Dei g*rat*ia illustri regi Anglie d*omi*no Ibernye et duci Acquietannie . Alex*ander* eadem g*rat*ia rex Scott*orum* . salutem . et felices ad vota successus cum incremento gl*or*ie et honoris . Celsitudini v*est*re regie tenore p*re*sencium innotescimus quod \ sicut intelleximus / quidam homines cui*us*dam baronis n*ost*ri Alexandri de Argadia nomine ad portum v*est*rum de Bristov cum naui sua applicantes ibidem cum omnib*us* bonis suis arestati sunt . pro eo quod eis inpositum erat q*uod* raptores in mari existebant . S*e*d ut celsitudini v*est*re liquidius constet ips*o*s in d*ic*ta naui existentes n*ost*ros fideles ho*min*es esse . q*uorum*dam ips*orum* nomina mittim*us* hic notata . primus magister Adam qui est d*ic*te nauis gub*er*nator . alius Gilfolan Kerd . et eor*um* consortes . quor*um* nomina confec*ti*o*n*e p*re*sentium nob*is* erant ignota . Quare serenitatem v*est*ram affectuose requirimus et rogamus q*ua*tinus p*er* litt*er*as v*est*ras precipere velitis . balliuis v*est*ris de Bristov ut d*ict*os homines n*ost*ros vna cum om*n*ib*us* bonis suis delib*er*ent et . libere p*er*mittant eosdem cum d*ict*is bonis suis ad terram n*ost*ram remeare . Tantum si placet ad instanciam n*ost*ram in hac p*ar*te facientes ut celsitudini v*est*re m*er*ito assurgere debeamus ad grates . T*este* . me ip*s*o apud Elgyn' . xv . die Augusti . ann*o* . reg*ni* . nostri . xxvii^{o} .

DESCRIPTION. 19.8 cm x 7.6 cm. Sealing: formerly sealed on a tongue cut from right to left across the bottom of the deed, now torn away. The document is slightly stained.
HAND. Scribe M.
SOURCE. Original. TNA, Chancery Miscellanea, PRO C 47/22/9/11.
PRINTED. *CDS*, ii, no. 55 (cal.); *L & I*, vol. xlix, 185 (note).

93 Grants and by this charter confirms to John de Swinburne the gift and grant that Ranulf de Haughton made him of all his lands in Hindlaw and Humshaugh, together with the mill of Humshaugh, all the suits of court from both lands and the wood called Midhow (all in Tynedale). Roxburgh, 12 September a.r. 27 [1275].

Alexander rex Scotie omnibus probis hominibus totius terre sue salutem. Sciatis nos concessisse et hoc litera nostra confirmasse donacionem et concessionem \ illam / quam Ranulfus de Haludon fecit Johanni de Swynneburne et heredibus suis de omnibus terris et tenementis que habuit in Huntelaw et in Homisale cum molendino eiusdem et cum tota secta tam de Hauton quam de Homishaule et cum bosco quod vocatur Midhoue. Testibus Patricio comite de Dunbar Hugone de Berkeley etc. Datum apud Rokisburg 12 Septembris xx° septimo regni nostri anno.

SOURCE. Bodleian Library, Oxford, MS Dodsworth XLV, fo. 89r; BL, MS Lansdowne 326, fo. 146v. These volumes, dated 1638–9, belong to a large series of transcriptions compiled by the antiquary Roger Dodsworth. Each consists of Latin-language summaries and, occasionally, full transcriptions of several dozen charters then in the possession of various Northumberland families; this document was included among the muniments of Sir William Widdrington of Widdrington. This collection is now lost.

PRINTED. The summary of this charter found in MS Dodsworth XLV was published in *Northumb. and Durham Deeds*, 243.

COMMENT. The king's charter was produced at the eyre sessions convened at Wark in 1293, when the presiding justices summoned the current holder of the lands, Sir John Swinburne, to explain by what warrant he claimed the right to operate gallows on the estates of Haughton and Humshaugh and to collect the chattels of condemned felons. The confirmation of King Alexander III, he argued successfully, gave him the authority to exercise these lordly prerogatives 'just as all other English knights and free tenants do'. See TNA, PRO JUST 1/657, m. 5. The terminology here recalls that of the holding clause that must surely have been included in the lost original: it would appear that Swinburne prudently brought the charter to court with him and read it aloud there.

94 Writes to Edward I king of England acknowledging receipt of his letter concerning the plunder of some merchants by pirates who are said to have taken refuge in Scotland. Informs him that he sent letters of his own to his justiciars, sheriffs and others to hold an inquest into the matter. He has nothing to report at present, but will do justice on the offenders when found, according to the laws and customs of his realm. Stirling, 24 October a.r. 27 [1275].

Excellentissimo p*ri*ncipi et f*rat*ri suo in *Christ*o k*arissi*mo d*omi*no Edwardo D*e*i *grat*ia regi Anglie d*omi*no Ibernie et duci Acquietanni*e* Alex*ander* eadem g*rat*ia rex Scott*orum* . sal*ut*em . et felices ad uota successus cum incremento gl*ori*e et honoris . Sup*er* eo quod nobis p*er* litt*er*as n*ost*ras significatis q*uo*d quidam m*er*catores ad regnum n*ost*rum declinantes quedam bona sua incursu rapta et in mari amiserunt . qui quidam m*er*catores ad t*er*ram n*ost*ram recursum ut dicebatur habuerunt . vobis duximus certificandum . quod ser[ ][a] litt*er*e v*est*re plenius intellecta [ ][b] docuit recepimus reu*er*ent*er* et p*re*cepimus p*er* litt*er*as n*ost*ras . justiciariis vicecomitib*us* et cet*er*is balliuis n*ost*ris quod sup*er* p*re*missis diligenter facerent inquisit*ion*em . verum quia tempore confec*ti*onis p*re*sentium nichil certitudinis d*ic*ti f*ac*ti balliui n*ost*ri \ prout intelleximus / requirendum potuerunt . Excellencie v*est*re tenore p*re*sentium significamus q*uo*d si quid certum d*ic*ti f*ac*ti scire pot*er*imus scelerem [emendari?][c] ad instanciam v*est*ram prout debemus . et s*ecundum* quod iuxt*a* leges et consuetudines regni n*ost*ri fac*er*e pot*er*imus de [terminari?][c] apponemus . valeat excellentia v*est*ra semper in

D*omi*no . T*este* . me ip*s*o apud Striuelyn' . xxiiii^{to} . die Octobr*is* . anno . r*egni* . nostri . xxvii^{o}.

NOTES. The document is crumpled and rubbed clear in places, with some loss of legibility. [a] Rest of word obliterated. [b] Two words illegible. [c] Words supplied by conjecture.
DESCRIPTION. 21.8 cm x 7.4 cm. Sealing: no evidence of a tongue, tag or seal.
HAND. Scribe M.
SOURCE. Original. TNA, Special Collections: Ancient Correspondence of the Chancery and the Exchequer, PRO SC 1/20/144.
PRINTED. *CDS*, ii, no. 59 (cal.).

95

Writes to Edward I king of England requesting that he show favour to Alexander steward of Scotland concerning matters that his envoys will relate to the king *viva voce*, and about which he has already sent him letters. Roxburgh, 14 November a.r. 27 [1275].

. Magnifico principi et f*rat*ri suo dilectissimo d*omi*no Edwardo Dei g*rat*ia illust*ri* regi Angl*ie* . d*omi*no Hybernye . et duci Aquitan*nie* . Alex*ander* eade*m* gratia rex Scott*orum* . *salutem* . et sincere dilec*t*ionis semp*er* incrementu*m* . Pro Alexandro senescallo Scocie dil*ec*to et fideli n*ost*ro serenitati v*est*re preces porrigimus affectuosas attentius exorantes quatinus eide*m* in negociis suis que nuncii sui latores p*re*senciu*m* vobis intimabunt voce viva . et pro quibus litt*er*as n*ost*ras deprecatorias celsitudini v*est*re meminim*us* \ nos / alias direxisse . solita moti bonitate . fauorabiles amore n*ost*ri et benignos vos dignemini exhibere . Tantu*m* inde ad instanciam n*ost*ram si plac*et* facientes . quod ip*s*e de n*ost*ro letari possit interuentu . p*er* quod excellencie v*est*re ad grates vb*er*imas teneamur . T*este* . me ip*s*o apud Roxburg' . xiiii^{o} . die Nouembr*is* . anno . regni . n*ost*ri . xx^{o} septimo .

DESCRIPTION. 22.9 cm x 4.1 cm. Sealing: no evidence of a tongue, tag or seal.
HAND. Scribe M.
SOURCE. Original. TNA, Special Collections: Ancient Correspondence of the Chancery and the Exchequer, PRO SC 1/20/147.
PRINTED. *CDS*, ii, no. 60 (cal.).

96

Writes to Edward I king of England acknowledging receipt of his letter concerning the collection of his aid in the liberty of Tynedale. Informs him that he is unable to reply until he has consulted his magnates. Brechin, 29 December a.r. 27 [1275].

. Excellentissimo p*r*incipi et f*r*atri suo in *Christ*o k*ariss*imo . d*omi*no . E . D*e*i g*rat*ia regi Angl*ie* d*omi*no Ib*er*nie et duci Acquitann*ie* . Alex*andro* [ea]d[em] gratia rex Scott*orum* sal*ut*em . et felices ad vota successus cum incremento gl*o*rie et honoris . L*itt*eras v*est*re excellencie [ ][a] tas sup*er* auxilio v*est*ro infra lib*er*tatem n*ost*ram de Tyndall' colligendo recepim*us* ut decuit reu*erent*er verum quia s*up*er d*ict*o [ ][a] antequ*am* cum magnatibus regni n*o*stri tractatum habuerim*us* serenitati v*est*re liquido respondere non possumus . excellencie v[estre significa]mus[b] . quod d*ict*is magnatib*us* n*ost*ris cong*r*egatis et consultis q*uo*d erit Deo annuente q*uam*cici*us* com*m*ode pot*er*imus . vobis liquid[ ][a] d*ict*o mandato v*est*ro curabimus respondere . T*este* . me ip*s*o apud Brechyn' . xxix . die Decembr*is* . ann*o* regni n*ost*ri vices*imo* septimo .

NOTES. The writing is stained away down the entire right side, obliterating some of the text. Ultraviolet lighting and digital software were able to reveal only one or two words. [a] Two–three words. [b] Words supplied by conjecture.
DESCRIPTION. 22.1 cm x 5.3 cm. Sealing: no evidence of a tongue, tag or seal.
HAND. Scribe M.
SOURCE. Original. TNA, Special Collections: Ancient Correspondence of the Chancery and the Exchequer, PRO SC 1/20/148.
PRINTED. *CDS*, ii, no. 62 (cal.).

97 Grants and by this charter confirms to Roland de Carrick the gift and grant that Neil earl of Carrick made him, namely that Roland and his heirs shall be chiefs of all their kindred in matters relating to the kindred, with the office of bailie and the right of leading the men under whoever shall be the earl at the time. To be held heritably, as Neil's charter bears witness. Stirling, 20 January a.r. 27 [1276].

Alexander Dei gracia rex Scottorum omnibus probis hominibus tocius terre sue salutem. Sciatis nos concessisse et hac presenti carta nostra confirmasse concessionem illam et donacionem quam Nigellus comes de Carryk fecit Rolando de Carrik et heredibus suis videlicet vt dictus Rolandus et heredes sui sint capud tocius progeniei sue tam in calumpniis quam in aliis articulis et negociis ad kenkynoll'[a] pertinere valentibus vna cum officio balliui predicte terre et hominum ipsius duccione in omnibus sub comite qui pro tempore fuerit adeo libere et quiete sicut in carta ipsius Nigelli prefato Rolando et heredibus suis exinde confecta plenius continetur salvo jure cuiuslibet . Hiis testibus Alexandro senescallo Scocie, Jacobo filio suo et Ricardo de Straton'[b] . Datum apud Strivelyne . xx^{o}[c] die Januarii . anno regni nostri vicesimo septimo.

NOTES. [a] Kenkynolle in printed version. [b] Stratona in printed version. [c] Vicesimo in printed version.
RUBRIC. Confirmacio Johannis Kenedy.
SOURCE. NRS, Great Seal Rolls, C 1/3, no. 6.
PRINTED. *RMS*, i, no. 508.
COMMENT. The act is narrated in a royal confirmation in this same office of James Kennedy of Dunure, dated at Ayr, 1 October 1372.

98 Grants to the prior and convent of Coldingham that they should hold all their lands of Coldinghamshire in free warren. Strictly prohibits anyone from felling timber or hunting there without their licence, on pain of his full forfeiture. Selkirk, 16 June a.r. 27 [1276].

Alex*ander* D*e*i gr*at*ia rex Scott*orum* . omnibus probis hominib*us* tocius t*er*re sue sal*ute*m . Sciatis quod concessimus priori et conuentui de Coldingham . quod iuste habeant t*er*ras suas de Coldinghamscyr' . in liberam warennam et liberam forestam . et firmiter inhibemus . ne quis in d*ic*tis t*er*ris sine ip*sorum* prioris et conuent*us* licencia secet aut venetur . sup*er* n*os*tram plenariam forisfacturam . Testibus Hugone de Berkeley . Joh*anne* Cumyn' filio . et Symone Fras*er* . apud Selkirk'. xvi^{to} . die Junii . anno regni n*os*tri vices*im*o septimo .

ENDORSED. 1. Carta Alexandri regis de warenna (contemporary hand). 2. Carta Alexandri de warenna in Coldynghamchyr' dupplicatur (fourteenth century). 3. E (fourteenth century, part of the press mark). The remainder of this last endorsement may have been on the part of the tongue that has been torn away.
DESCRIPTION. 19.8 cm x 3.9 cm. The portion that was once folded up measures 2.8 cm. Sealing: no tag remains, though there are double slits for its insertion. Detached from the document is the second great seal, 9.9 cm in diameter, in natural wax varnished brown. The seal is badly damaged at the edges, the surface cracked and rubbed.
HAND. Scribe N.
SOURCE. Original. Durham, Muniments of the Dean and Chapter, Misc. Ch. 630.
PRINTED. Raine, *North Durham*, no. 76.

99 Writes to Edward I king of England requesting that he give his attention to the matter that his envoys, William bishop of Brechin, his chancellor Master Thomas son of Ranulph and his clerk Master Thomas de Charteris or any two of them carrying these letters, will more fully reveal to him *viva voce*. Scone, 18 August a.r. 28 [1276].

Excellentissimo pr*in*cipi et fr*at*ri suo in *Christ*o Carissimo d*omi*no . E . D*ei* gr*at*ia regi Anglie d*omi*no Ibern*i*e et duci Acquitann*ie* illustri . Alex*ander* eadem gr*at*ia rex Scott*orum* . sal*ut*em . et felices ad vota successus cum incremento gl*or*ie et honoris . Sciatis nos et lib*er*os nostros disponente altissimo bona prosp*er*itate et sanitate gaudere quod de vobis et v*est*ris scire cupimus incessanter . vos attentius exorantes quatinus venerabili p*at*ri in *Christ*o . Will*elm*o *episco*po Brechennens*e* . Thome Ranulph' cam*er*ario n*ost*ro . et magistro Thome de Carnoto . cl*er*ico n*ost*ro dilectis et fidelibus n*ost*ris . u*e*l eor*um* duobus latoribus[a] p*re*sentium in hiis que vobis ex p*ar*te n*ost*ra dux*er*int[a] viua voce plenius exprimenda . fidem adhibere velitis indubitatam . voluntatem v*est*ram sup*er* hiis et aliis . vna cum statu v*est*ro vtinam p*ro*sp*er*o et jocundo nobis frequentius ad maiorem annui nostri recrea*ti*on*e*m \ si placet / significantes . T*este* . me ip*s*o apud Schon' . xviii° . die Augusti ann*o* . regni n*ost*ri . xxviii° .

NOTE. [a] Erasure and space in MS here, filled in with a line.
DESCRIPTION. 17.3 cm x 5.3 cm. Sealing: no evidence of a tongue, tag or seal. There is a hole in the top left portion of the document.
HAND. Scribe M.
SOURCE. Original. TNA, Special Collections: Ancient Correspondence of the Chancery and the Exchequer, PRO SC 1/20/149.
PRINTED. *CDS*, ii, no. 96 (cal., where it is misdated).
COMMENT. There can be little doubt about the subject matter that the bearers of these letters were 'more fully' to reveal to Edward I. Already by the summer of 1276 tensions had flared up among the inhabitants of the area around Berwick regarding the precise location of the border between the realms, when the bishop of Durham complained to Edward I that agents of the Scottish crown had violated episcopal prerogatives and, ultimately, those of the English crown. Edward I wrote to the sheriff of Northumberland on 26 October commanding the arrest of 'all Scottish persons travelling through' the region until the matter should be settled (TNA, PRO SC 1/13/155; C 47/22/9/5); he wrote to Alexander no fewer than three times in the autumn and winter of 1277–8 (see here the Comment below, no. 106). The question of the border line was not satisfactorily settled; by the spring of 1278 it was, however, temporarily eclipsed by arrangements for Alexander III to perform homage to Edward for his English lands. As early as 1279 a jury of Northumberland men reported to justices in eyre that Scotsmen from Berwick were still violating the 'true boundary' between the kingdoms, mid-stream in the River Tweed (TNA, PRO JUST 1/645, m 14).

100 Gives, grants and by this charter confirms to William de Douglas the gift that his father, Andrew, made him of the land of Hermiston (Midlothian) in the feu of Earl's Calder. To be held as Andrew's charter bears witness. Stirling, 8 September a.r. 28 [1276].

Alexander[a] Dei gr*at*ia rex Scotorum om*ni*b*us* p*ro*bis hominib*us* tocius te*rr*e sue salutem. Sciatis nos dedisse co*n*cessisse et hac p*rese*nti carta nostra co*n*firmasse illam donac*io*nem q*ua*m Andreas de Douglas dedit Will*elm*o filio suo de Douglas[b] de te*rr*a de Hirdmanyston' cum p*er*tine*n*c*iis* in feodo de Caldor' Comitis. Tenend*am* et habend*am* adeo libere q*ui*ete plenarie et honorifice p*ro*ut carta d*ict*i Andree inde conf*ec*ta pleni*us* iuste testatur saluo s*er*uic*io* nostro. Testibus Johanne de Lambyrton' Pat*ric*io de Graha*m* Roberto Biset, Vuill*el*mo de S*anct*o Claro apud Str*iu*elyn octauo die Septembris anno regni n*ost*ri xx^{o}. octauo.

NOTES. [a] Lightly decorated initial. [b] Printed version omits 'de Douglas'.
RUBRIC. Confirmac*io* de Hirdmanyston'.
SOURCE. NLS. MS 72, Morton Cartulary, fo. 50.
PRINTED. *Morton Registrum*, ii, no. 10.

101 Takes under his firm peace and protection his burgesses of Aberdeen, their lands, their men and all their possessions, movable and immovable, strictly prohibiting anyone from causing them injury or harm, on pain of his full forfeiture. Grants also that no one may take poinds of them or any of their men for any reason save for their own debts, pledges or forfeitures. Kincardine, 27 January a.r. 28 [1277].

Alex*ander* Dei gr*at*ia rex Scott*orum* omnib*us* probis hominib*us* toci*us* te*rr*e sue ad quos presentes littere p*er*uen*er*int . sal*u*t*e*m . Sciatis nos burgenses n*ost*ros de Abirden te*rr*as suas homines suos et vniu*er*sas eoru*n*d*em* possessiones ac om*n*ia bona sua mobilia et im*m*obilia sub fi*r*ma pace et p*ro*tect*i*one n*ost*ra iuste suscepisse . Q*ua*re firmiter p*ro*hibem*us* . ne quis eis malum . molestiam . iniuriam seu gr*a*uamen aliquod inferre p*re*sumat iniuste sup*er* n*ost*ram plenariam forisfactura*m* . Concessim*us* e*tiam* eisdem vt nullus namos suos vel alicuius ips*orum* seu hominu*m* suo*rum* capiat p*ro* alicui*us* debito . plegiagio vel forisfacto . nisi p*ro* suo p*ro*p*ri*o debito plegiagio vel forisfacto . firmit*er* inhibentes . ne quis eos vel aliqu*e*m ips*orum* cont*ra* hanc concessionem n*ost*ram vexare p*re*sumat iniuste sup*er* n*ost*ram plenaria*m* forisfacturam . Test*ibus* . Will*elm*o Cumyn de Kelebrid . Will*elm*o de S*anct*o Claro . Symone Fras*er* . Pat*ric*io de Graham' ap*ud* Kyncardyn vicesimo septimo die Januari[a] anno regni n*ostri* vicesimo octauo .

NOTE. [a] Sic, Januarii.
ENDORSED. 1. Littera protectionis regis Alexandri (contemporary hand). 2. ane protectioun of King Alexander (sixteenth century).
DESCRIPTION. 24.1 cm x 12.2 cm; fold 3.6 cm. Sealing: on a tag, 3.0 cm broad, through double slits, there is a fragment of the second great seal, 7.6 cm in diameter, in natural wax. The fragment is much defaced, with only the central portion visible.
HAND. Scribe M.
SOURCE. Original. Aberdeen City Archives, Aberdeen City Muniments, no. A^{1}6.
PRINTED. *Aberdeen Burgh Charters*, 9–10.

102 Grants and confirms in perpetual peace to the church of Dunfermline, with the agreement of his bishops, earls and barons and the agreement of his clerics and people, all the gifts and rights that the church has received from his ancestors, namely, from King Malcolm and Queen Margaret Broomhill, Urquhart, Pitbauchlie, Pitcorthie, Pitliver, (Wester) Bogie, the shire of Kirkcaldy and 'Little Inveresk' (all in Fife); from King Duncan two touns called Luscar (Fife); from King Edgar the shire of Gellet (Fife); from Æthelred Hailes (Midlothian); from King Alexander Primrose, the shire of Goatmilk, Pitconmark, Balwearie (Fife), 'Drumbernin' and Keith (Humbie, East Lothian); from Queen Sybil Beath (Fife). Also confirms the gifts that the church had from his great-great-grandfather, King David, on the day of its dedication, namely, Dunfermline on this side of the water, where the abbey is to be found, Kinghorn and its dependent estates, which is nearer Dunfermline (Wester Kinghorn, now Burntisland), Fod, 'Greater Inveresk' with its mill and fishery (all in Fife), Smeaton, Carberry, the church of Inveresk, Woolmet (all in Midlothian), Fetters near St Andrews (Fife), Penick (Nairn), a ploughgate of land at Pitteuchar, Newburn with its dependent estates and Balchrystie (all in Fife), saving the customary services that the Culdees have there. Also confirms to the church a series of other possessions: a dwelling in Berwick, another in Roxburgh, another in Haddington, another in Edinburgh, another in Linlithgow, another in Stirling, and in the latter two churches and a ploughgate of land adjacent to the church itself; every teind of the king's demesne, in crops and livestock, in fish from their own nets, and in money; the teind of the king's cain of all occupants of castles in the province (of Fife?); the dwellings of Roger the priest as he held them; one and a half nets and a dwelling in the burgh of Dunfermline, every teind of the burgh ferme, the teind of the mill and of all his demesnes of Dunfermline; a dwelling in the burgh of Perth, the church there and the chapel of the castle there; a dwelling that belongs to the church itself; every teind of his demesne, and every eighth part of all royal pleas and profits in Fife and Fothrif; every teind of gold that comes to him from Fife and from Fothrif, and every teind of his cain and malt of Fife and Fothrif, except the rights of the abbot of Dunkeld therein; the teind of all deer caught between Lammermuir and Tay; and half of all hides, tallow and fat of beasts slaughtered at feasts held in Stirling and between the Forth and Tay. Grants also that the church and its men should have in his forests everything necessary for fire and their building, just as the king and his men do; that they should have all oblations offered at the high altar of the abbey church; the seventh part of the seals that are caught at Kinghorn after these have been teinded; every teind of salt and iron brought to Dunfermline for his use; the whole parish of Fothrif (Fife); and the tract of Aldstell (now Calot Shad) in Berwick. He strictly forbids the taking of poinds in respect of the land or men of the abbey and further grants that all the rights to fugitive serfs and their property which the church has had since the time of King Edgar be restored, forbidding on pain of his forfeiture that any such fugitive serfs be withheld. Confirms to the church the teind of all his wild mares of Fife and Fothrif and that the church and its men be quit throughout the king's whole land of toll on everything traded for their own needs. Also [confirms to them] the passage and ferry of Inverkeithing, on condition that pilgrims, envoys travelling to and from the king, and the men of his court, should cross in that ferry without charge; undertaking further to remit to the abbot any losses he may incur concerning the ferry. Grants that the abbot and monks need not respond to anyone laying claim to the men who belonged to the (above named) lands on the day when these were offered and given. Also grants the teind of his cain of Clackmannan and that each Saturday at court the abbot and monks should have from the royal jurisdiction this side of Lammermuir one hide and on the sixth Saturday, two hides, two parts of the tallow, and the sixth hide of rams and lambs; half of the king's teind from Argyll and Kintyre and a fishery in Perth. Confirms to the abbot and monks other gifts from his predecessors, namely, from King Malcolm Lethmacdunegil (Mastertown, Fife), as Master Ælric the mason held it, which Malcolm offered to the abbey on the day when King David I was buried; near Dunfermline twenty-three *iugera* of land [approximately 15 acres] and a meadow which King Malcolm formerly had in his demesne; and the whole head, except the tongue, of every whale which comes to shore or is caught on the Scottish side of the Forth; half the fat of all the whales caught between the Forth and the Tay to which he is entitled for lighting the altars of the church. Grants also that their men should be free from all labour service on bridges, castles and other works. Grants to the abbey the church of the Holy Trinity of Dunkeld, with its lands and pertinents, but only after the death of Andrew bishop of Caithness, to whose see King David gifted the said church. Grants also a toft in Edinburgh which Robert of London held; one full toft with a croft in the toun of Clackmannan; the church of Kellie and the chapel of Abercrombie (both in Fife). From King William a rent of 100s. from the ferme of Edinburgh, which he gave to the abbey on the day of his brother Malcolm's funeral and twenty acres of land and a toft in Dunfermline, which Walter the steward confirmed to the abbey on the day that the said King Malcolm was buried. Grants and confirms to the monks all these gifts and possessions just as they are set out in the church's authentic charters; these are to be preserved whole and unaltered for ever. Cupar (Fife), 10 March a.r. 28 [1277].

In[a] no*mine* sancte T*ri*nitatis ego Alex*ander* Dei *gra*tia rex Scott*orum* filius Alexandri illustris regis Scott*orum* auctoritate regia. ac potestate e*pisco*porum comitum. baronu*m*q*ue* regni mei co*n*sensu atque testimonio. clero ettiam adq*ui*esce*n*te et populo. ecclesie s*anct*e T*ri*nitatis de Dunf*er*melyn' p*re*decessor*um* meor*um* pietatis studio et largi*t*ionis initiate. om*n*ia s*u*bsc*ri*pta concedo. et pace perpetua confirmo. attaui itaq*ue* mei reg*is* Malcolmi et regine ei*us*dem bone memorie Margarete dona s*u*bseq*ue*ncia propono. hec scilic*et*. Pardusin. Petnarcha. Petbachlakin. Petcorthin. Lauer. Bolgin. sciram de Kercaledin. Inuirese minorem. dona Du*n*cani regis.duas uillas nomine Luscher, de dono

Edgari regis sciram de Gelland, de dono Ætheldredi. Hales de dono Alexandri reg*is*. Primros. sciram de Gatmilk. Petco*n*marthin.[b] Belecherin. Drunbernin. Cleth'. de dono Sybille reg*ine*. Beth. hec p*re*dicta p*re*decessor*um* meor*um* dona co*n*cedo liberalit*er* p*re*fate eccl*esi*e cu*m* om*n*ib*us* appenciis[c] suis et rectis diuisis de dono abaui mei excellentissimi reg*is* Dauid. Du*n*fe*r*melyn' citra aqua*m* in q*ua* eccl*esi*a sita est eade*m*. Kyngorn cu*m* suis append*i*ciis q*ue* p*ro*pinq*ui*or est Du*n*f*er*mel*yn*'. Foeth. Inuiresk maiore*m* et molendin*um* et piscinam et Smetheby. et Crebarrin et eccl*esi*am de Inueresk et Wymeth' cu*m* suis rectis diuisis et Fothros iuxta S*anct*um Andream cu*m* suis rectis diuisis et Pethenac cum rectis suis diuisis et vna*m* carucatam terre Petioceher.[d] et Nithebren cu*m* suis appendiciis et Balcristyn cum suis rectis diuisis in p*ra*tis et pascuis excepta rectitudine q*ua*m celedei inde habere debent. cum om*n*ib*us* reb*us* iuste ad eam p*er*tinentib*us* sicut date fueru*n*t p*re*d*i*c*t*e eccl*esi*e in dotem ab abauo meo regie Dauid die q*ua* dedicata fuit. Et p*re*terea vna*m* ma*n*suram in Berwych. aliam in Rokesburg'. aliam in Hadigton'. aliam in Edinburg'. aliam in Linchithcu aliam in St*ri*uelyn. et in eadem uilla duas eccl*esi*as. et vnam carucatam t*er*re q*ue* adiacet ip*s*i eccl*esi*e. et omne*m* decima*m* meor*um* dominior*um* in frugib*us* in a*nim*alib*us* et in pisscibus[e] de p*ro*priis retib*us* et ecciam in denariis. et decimam mei can toci*us* castrens*is* p*rou*i*n*cie et mansiones Rog*er*i p*re*sbiteri. ita plene sicut ip*s*e san*us* et incolumis tenuit. Et vnu*m* rete et dimidiu*m*. et vna*m* mansione*m* in burgo de Dunfermely*n* lib*er*am et q*ui*etam et omne*m* decimac*i*one*m* firme burgi. et decimac*i*one*m* molendini. et de om*n*ib*us* dominiis meis de Du*n*fermely*n* et vnam ma*n*sione*m* in \ burgo /[f] de Perth' et eccl*esi*am ei*us*de*m* uille et capella*m* de castello cum om*n*ib*us* appendiciis ut*ri*us*que* et vnam mansione*m* q*ue* p*er*tinet ipsi ecclesie. et omne*m* decima*m* de dominio meo. et omne*m* octaua*m* pa*r*tem de om*n*ib*us* placitis et luc*ri*s meis de Fyf' et de Fotherif' et omne*m* decimam de auro q*uod* m*ihi* eueniet de Fyf' et de Fotheryf' et omne*m* decima*m* toci*us* mei can. et brasei de Fyf' et de Fotheryf' exceptis rectitudinib*us* q*ue* abbathie de Dunkeldyn' p*er*tinent. Et decimam om*n*ium uenac*i*onu*m* q*ue* capiu*ntur* int*er* Lambirmor et Thaei. et medietatem om*n*ium corior*um* et sepor*um* et sagiminis om*n*ium bestiar*um* que occidentur ad festiuitates tenendas de St*ri*uely*n*. et inter Forth et Thaie. et ut habeant i*n* nemorib*us* meis om*n*ia n*ecessari*a ad igne*m* et ad edificia sua sicut ego ip*s*e et ho*m*ines eor*um* sicut et mei. et ut o*m*nes oblac*i*ones que ad mai*us* altare eiusde*m* eccl*esi*e offerent*ur* s*i*ne calu*m*pnia lib*e*rali*ter* h*ab*eant et de selyhes que ad Ky*n*gorn capie*ntur* p*ost*q*uam* decimati fuerint omnes sept*im*os selyhes h*abe*ant salis q*uoque* et ferri q*uod* ad op*us* meu*m* ad Du*n*fermely*n* allata fueri*n*t omne*m* dec*i*ma*m* concede. Et p*a*rochiam tota*m* Fotheref' et in Berwyc' tractu*m* de Aldstel. et om*n*em quod ei iuste p*er*tinet . P*ro*hibeo ecci*am* ne aliquod nam capiat*ur* sup*er* t*er*ram u*e*l super ho*m*ines s*anct*e T*ri*nitatis p*ro* forisf*a*cto alicui*us* n*e*c p*ro* p*ro*p*ri*o forisf*a*cto eorum. Concedo e*ciam* quod iuste redda*ntur* eccl*esi*e s*anct*e T*ri*nitatis om*ne*s serui sui quod attau*us* me*us* et abau*us* meus Dauid et f*ra*t*r*es sui ei dederunt et om*ne*s sui cumelahe a temp*o*r*e* Edgari reg*is* u*s*q*ue* nu*n*c cu*m* tota pecunia sua ubicu*m*q*ue* inue*n*iant*ur*. Et p*ro*hibeo sup*er* meu*m* forisfactum ne iniuste retineantur. et ut habeant omnes homines cum omni pecunia eorum in cuiuscunque terra fuerint qui fuerunt in terris die qua fuerunt oblate et date ecclesie sancte Trinitatis et decimam de omnibus meis siluestribus equabus de Fif' et de Fotherif'. Et ut habeant per totam terram meam theloneum quietum de cunctis rebus quas mercati fuerint ad propria eorum necessaria. et passagium et nauem de Inuirkethin sicut habui in do\mi/nio meo tali condițione quod peregrinantes et nuncii ad me uenientes et a me redeuntes et homines curie mee transeant in eadem naui sine precio. Et si contingat aliquem istorum sine precio transire non posse[g] et abbas clamorem inde audieret et ille non emendauerit ego ipse illud emendabo sine abbatis et fratrum ecclesie molestia. Et abbas et monachi \ ecclesie / sancte Trinitatis non respondeant aliter calumpnianti de hominibus qui fuerunt in terris die qua oblate et date fuerint ecclesie sancte Trinitatis . Concedo \ eciam / eidem ecclesie decimam tocius mei can de Clacman'. et ut citra Lambirmor in tota regia prestate singulis sabbatis in curia habeant vnum corium et si in sexto sabbatis duo coria et duas partes de sepo. et sextam pellem arietum et agnorum. et dimidiam partem decimi mei de Ergathyl' et de Kentyr. et quandam piscaturam apud Perth' ita libere et quiete sicut meas ibi habeo. De dono regis Malcolmi patrui patris mei Lethmacdunegil[h] cum suis rectis diuisis sicut magister Eilricus cementarius illam tenuit quam in die sepulture predicti abaui mei eidem ecclesie obtulit. Et viginti et tria iugera[i] terre et quodam pratum prope Dunfermelyn qui prius in dominio suo habuit. et quodcunque cete ex parte Scocie applicuerit seu captum fuerit totum capud preter linguam eidem ecclesie remaneat et dimedietatem tocius sagiminis omnium cetuum qui capiuntur inter Forth' et Thay ad luminaria coram altaribus ecclesie et omnes homines eorum sint liberi ab omni operacione pontium et castellorum et omnium aliorum operum. Et ecclesiam sancte Trinitatis de Dunkeldyn cum terris ad illam pertinentibus et cum aliis rectis pertinenciis suis. optinendam in perpetuam elemosinam. post decessum Andree episcopi Catinensis pro salute anime mee et omnium predecessorum meorum. cum omni libertate et rectitudine cum quibus idem episcopus eam unquam melius tenuit et dono regis Dauid possedit et vnum tofth in Edinburg' quod Robertus de Londoniis habuit. et vnum plenarium tofth cum crofto in villa de Clacman'. et ecclesiam de Kellyn et capellam de Abyrcrombin cum omnibus ad eas iuste pertinentibus. Ex dono uero aui mei regis Willelmi redditum centum solidorum de firma burgi de Edinburg' quos dedit in die exequiarum fratris sui regis Malcolmi. et viginti acras terre et vnum tofth in Dunfermelyn quas Walterus dapifer dedit concessione aui mei die sepulture predicti regis Malcolmi. Omnia autem sicut prenominata sunt que a bonis antecessoribus meis scilicet rege Malcolmo et regina eiusdem bone memorie Margarita. Duncano rege. Edgaro rege. Ethelredo fratre eius. Alexandro rege. Sybilla regina eiusdem. Dauid excellentissimo Malcolmo rege. Willelmo rege. Alexandro rege ecclesie sancte Trinitatis de Dunfermelyn data. concessa sunt et confirmata sicut in auctenticis eorum scriptis continentur cum omni illa plenitudine et integritate auctoritate regia consilio proborum hominum meor*um* pre*d*ic*t*e eccl*esi*e et frat*r*ibus ibid*em* s*er*uientibus concedo et in p*er*petuu*m* integ*ra* et illibata co*n*seruanda confirmo. Testib*us* Will*elm*o abb*at*e de Abirbroth*oc*'. Joh*anne* p*ri*ore Sancti Andree. magistro Will*elm*o Fraser cancellario n*ost*ro. Dauid de Louchor. Joh*anne* de Lambirton' Henrico de Dundemor. Will*el*mo Byset. Th*om*a de Clenhill'. Eduardo de Pethglassyn. ap*u*d Cupir in Fyf' decimo die Marcii. anno regni n*ost*ri vicesimo octauo.

NOTES. [a] Rubric and initial in red. [b] Petcomarthy in printed version. [c] Sic, appendiciis. [d] Petiocher in printed version. [e] Sic, piscibus. [f] The word uille is struck out here and burgo written over it. [g] Sic, posset. [h] For an argument in favour of 'Lethmacdunegil' rather than 'Lethmacduuegil', see S. Taylor with G. Márkus, *The Place-Names of Fife*, Vol. I (Donington, 2006), 331. [i] A measure of land: one *iugum* was equal to two-thirds of an acre.

RUBRIC. Confirmacio domini regis (thirteenth century).

SOURCE. NLS, Adv. MS. 34.1.3A, Register of Dunfermline Abbey, fos xviii[v]–xix[v].

PRINTED. *Dunfermline Registrum*, no. 81.

COMMENT. 'Drumbernin' may be Dumbarrow (Perthshire), formerly a part of Fife, but possibly also Dunbarney in Perthshire. See *Place-Names of Fife*, i, 41. For Aldstell, now Calot Shad, see *RMS*, ii, no. 429 and *Dunfermline Reg.*, no. 461. A modern transcript appears in NRS, RH 2/5/5.

103 Grants and by this charter confirms to the monks of Dunfermline the gift that his father, King Alexander II, made them of the land of Dollar in the feu of Clackmannan, in exchange for the alms in grain and coin that the monks were accustomed to receive in his demesne of Kinghorn and Crail, and in exchange for the dues that they were accustomed to receive from the royal kitchens. To be held in free and perpetual alms by the same boundaries and customs as Alexander II infeft them, with the monks nonetheless obliged to render the forinsec service owing from the land of Dollar. Cupar (Fife), 10 March a.r. 28 [1277].

Alex*ander* D*e*i g*ra*tia rex Scott*orum* fili*us* Alex*andri* illustris reg*is* Scott*orum* om*n*ib*us* p*ro*b*is* h*om*inibus toci*us* t*er*re sue sal*ute*m. Sciant p*re*sentes et futuri nos *con*cessisse et hac p*re*senti carta n*ost*ra *con*firmasse Deo et eccl*esi*e s*anc*te T*r*initatis de Dunfermely*n* et monach*is* ibid*em* Deo s*er*uientib*us* et in p*er*petuu*m* s*er*uitur*is* . donac*i*one*m* illam q*ua*m pie memorie Alex*ander* rex Scott*orum* pat*er* noster eisd*em* fecit de t*er*ra de Dolar' in feodo de Clacmanan' in excambiu*m* elemosinar*um* quas p*re*dicti monachi de Dunfer*melyn* p*er*cip*er*e consueueru*n*t in dominiis nostris de Kyngorn' et de Karal' tam in frumento . farina auene . braseo . p*re*be*n*da quam in denariis et simil*iter* in excambiu*m* r*ec*titudinu*m* quas p*er*cip*er*e *con*sueueru*n*t in coq*ui*nis n*ost*ris et regine sponse n*ost*re . Tenend*um* et habend*um* eisd*em* monach*is* in lib*er*am et p*er*petuam elemosinam p*er* easd*em* rectas diuisas et co*n*suetudines p*er* quas dict*us* pat*er* nost*er* eosdem monachos de dicta terra de Dolar infeodauit lib*er*e q*ui*ete . plenarie et honorifice . faciendo forinsecu*m* s*er*uiciu*m* q*uo*d p*er*tinet ad dictam t*er*ram de Dolar'. Testib*us* . Will*elm*o abb*at*e de Abyrbroth*oc* . Joh*anne* p*ri*ore Sanc*t*i Andree Dauid de Louchor' . Joh*anne* de Lambyrton' . Henrico de Du*n*demor' . Thom*a* de Clenhill' . Will*elm*o Byseth militib*us* apud Cupyr in Fyf' decimo die Martii. anno regni nost*ri* vicesimo octauo.

RUBRIC. Confirmatio illustris regis Alexandri tercii de terre de Doler (thirteenth century).
SOURCE. NLS, Adv. MS. 34.1.3A, Register of Dunfermline Abbey, fo. 18[r].
PRINTED. *Dunfermline Registrum*, no. 88.
COMMENT. A modern transcript appears in NRS, RH 2/5/5.

104 Grants and by this charter confirms to the monks of Dunfermline the gift that Malcolm de Moravia, knight, made them of the land of Wester Beath (Fife), which he held heritably of Alexander de Moravia, knight. To be held in free and perpetual alms, as Malcolm's charter bears witness. Cupar (Fife), 10 March a.r. 28 [1277].

Alex*ander*[a] Dei *gra*tia rex Scott*orum* filius Alexandri illust*ri*s reg*is* Scott*orum* om*n*ib*us* pro*bis* hominib*us* toci*us* ter*re* sue sal*ute*m. Sciant p*re*sentes et fut*uri* nos co*n*cessisse et h*ac* presenti carta nostra confirmasse Deo et eccl*esi*e s*anc*t*e* T*ri*nitatis de Du*n*fermely*n* et monachis ibid*em* Deo seruientib*us* et imp*er*petu*um* s*er*uitu*ri*s donac*io*ne*m* illam q*ua*m Malcolm*us* de Morauia miles eisd*em* fecit de t*er*ra de Beth' Occidentali q*ua*m de Alex*andro* de Morauia milite tenuit h*ere*ditar*io*. Tenend*um* et habend*um* eisd*em* monach*is* de Dunfermelyn in lib*er*am et p*er*petuam elemosinam cu*m* om*n*ib*us* asiame*n*tis et iustis p*er*tine*n*ciis et lib*er*tatib*us* ad dictam t*er*ram p*er*tine*n*cib*us*. adeo lib*er*e q*ui*ete et plenarie et honorofice[b] sicut carta p*re*dicti Malcolmi milit*is* eisd*em* monach*is* inde confecta plenius testatur iuste et p*ro*portat. Testibus Will*elm*o abb*a*te de Abirbroth*oc*. Joh*anne* priore Sancti Andree. Dauid de Louchor'. Joh*anne* de Lambyrton'. Henrico de Du*n*demor'. Th*oma* de Clenhill'. Will*elm*o Byseth militib*us*. ap*ud* Cupyr in Fyf'. decimo die M*ar*cii. an*n*o regni vices*imo* octauo.

NOTES. [a] Initial rubricated. [b] Sic, honorifice.
RUBRIC. Confirmac*i*o domini regis de Beeth Occidentali (in red) (thirteenth century).
SOURCE. NLS, Adv. MS. 34.1.3A, Register of Dunfermline Abbey, fos 18[r-v].
PRINTED. *Dunfermline Registrum*, no. 89.
COMMENT. A modern transcript appears in NRS, RH 2/5/5.

105 Grants and by this charter confirms the gift or collation that the late Ralph bishop of Aberdeen, with the agreement of the chapter of his church, made to the brethren of the Knights Templar of the church of Aboyne with its chapels, lands, teinds, offerings, and everything else belonging to it. To be held of the king by the terms laid out in the chapter's charters to the brethren, saving to them the appointment of a perpetual vicar. Accordingly, he ratifies the brethren's presentation to the vicarage church of his chaplain, John de Annan. Forfar, 15 April a.r. 28 [1277].

Alex*ander* Dei *gra*tia rex Scott*orum* om*n*ib*us* p*ro*bis hom*i*nib*us* totius terre sue sal*ute*m. Sciatis nos co*n*cessisse. et hac p*rese*nti carta n*ostr*a confirmasse donacio*ne*m illam seu collac*io*nem qua*m* bone memorie q*uo*nda*m* Radulphus e*pisco*pus Ab*er*donen' de consensu et assensu cap*it*uli eccl*es*ie Ab*er*donen' fecit intuitu caritatis Deo et beate Marie et *fra*tribus milicie templi Salomonis de Ier*usa*lem de eccl*es*ia de Obeyne cu*m* capellis. t*er*ris decimis oblac*io*nib*us* et cet*er*is om*n*ib*us* p*er*tine*n*-

ciis. Tenend*as* et h*abe*nd*as* eisd*em* f*ra*trib*us* qui p*ro* temp*ore* fuerint in p*ro*p*ri*os vsus in p*er*petua*m* de nobis et h*er*edib*us* n*os*tris s*ecundu*m q*uod* in instrument*is* cartis et muni*men*tis dictor*um* et capituli eisd*em* f*ra*trib*us* exinde *con*fect*is* plenius *con*tinet*ur*. saluo perpetuo vicar*io* p*er* eosdem f*ra*tres p*rese*ntato debita et co*n*sueta porcione sua in \ ip*s*a / ecc*le*sia. Ratificam*us* ecia*m* p*rese*ntac*io*nem p*er* p*re*dictos f*ra*tres facta*m* de Joh*ann*e de Anandia capellano n*os*tro. ad vicariam d*ic*te ecc*le*sie de Obeyne vacantis de iure et de facto. quap*ro*pt*er* plen*um* ius patr*o*nat*us*[a] memorate ecc*le*sie de Obeyne cu*m* o*mn*ib*us* suis iurib*us* et p*er*tine*n*-*ciis* eisdem f*ra*trib*us* *con*tulim*us* et co*n*firmauim*us*[b] inp*er*petuu*m* intuitu caritat*is*. Testib*us* Alex*andro* Comy*n* comite de Buchane. Co*n*stabu-lar*io*. Scocie. Hugone de Ab*ir*nethy. Dauid de Lochore. Symone Fras*er* et Will*elm*o de S*an*c*t*o Claro apud Forfar quindecimo die Ap*ri*lis anno regni n*os*tri vicesimo octauo.

NOTES. [a] Patronatus is missing in printed version. [b] Printed version has 'conservauimus', incorrectly.

RUBRIC. Ecc. de Obeyn (in margin, in a sixteenth-century hand).

SOURCE. NLS, Adv. MS. 16.1.10, Register of the Cathedral Church and Bishopric of Aberdeen, fos 69^{v}–70^{r}.

PRINTED. *Aberdeen Registrum*, ii, 272–3.

106 Writes to Edward I king of England informing him that although troublesome matters have prevented him from doing so until now, he will soon attend to Edward's recent letters and, on Sunday next after the feast of the Holy Trinity, will send an envoy to discuss the controversies that have arisen of late in the marches of the kingdoms. The matter will be treated according to the laws of the march, that is by the usages, liberties and customs that hitherto were approved and maintained, saving to himself his long-standing sasine [of lands in the region]. Forfar, 18 April a.r. 28 [1277].

Serenissimo principi et fratr*i* suo k*arissi*mo d*omi*no . Edwardo Dei gr*at*ia regi Anglie illust*ri* . d*omi*no Ib*er*nie . et duci Acquitanie . Alex*ande*r eade*m* gr*at*ia rex Scott*orum* . sal*utem* . et felices ad vota successus cum p*a*rata ad beneplacita voluntate . De amicabili et curiali mandato v*es*tro p*er* litt*er*as v*es*tras nob*is* nup*er* directas . celsitudini v*est*re gr*at*es multi-plices et graciar*um* referimus acciones . excellencie v*est*re p*ro* certo nu*n*ciantes . q*uod* libertates et iura v*es*tra sicut n*os*tra p*ro*p*ri*a illesa co*n*seruari q*ua*mplurimu*m* affectamus . Et mittemus aliquem fidelem de n*o*stris dominica p*roxima* post festum s*anc*te T*ri*nitatis . quoniam citra d*icta*m diem p*ro*pt*er* ardua negocia n*os*tra com*m*ode mitt*ere* no*n* valemus . quod si placet tediose non feratis . ad tractandum sup*er* co*n*trou*er*siis in marchya subortis s*ecundu*m leges marchye p*r*out ratio sua debit vsib*us* . libertatib*us* . co*n*suetudinib*us* hactenus app*ro*batis et optentis . et n*os*tra saysina diutina nob*is* saluis . Sublimitate*m* v*es*tram attencius exorantes . q*ua*tinus s*u*b festinac*io*ne nob*is* remandare velitis si p*re*d*ict*am diem dux*er*itis acceptare . Nec est intenc*io*nis n*os*tre aut erit p*er* Dei graciam in futuru*m* . aliquid fac*ere* . q*uo*d possit aut debeat in aliquo v*es*tre culmen ledere magestatis . Test*e* . me i*p*so apud Forfar' . xviii . die . Aprilis . anno regni nostri . xx . octauo .

DESCRIPTION. 17.8 cm x 7.9 cm. Sealing: no evidence of a tag, tongue or seal.
HAND. Scribe M.
SOURCE. Original. TNA, Special Collections: Ancient Correspondence of the Chancery and the Exchequer, PRO SC 1/20/150. There are near-contemporary partial copies also in TNA, Chancery Miscellanea, PRO C 47/22/9/15 and PRO SC 1/13/155 (see below).
PRINTED. *CDS*, ii, no. 90 (cal.).
COMMENT. The contents of the chancery enrolments noted above confirm that the nature of the 'border-related controversies' to which Alexander's letter refers included the precise location of the easternmost boundary line between the realms. It was said to lie 'mid-stream' in the river Tweed; as noted above (see above, Comments at no. 99), men from Scotland had allegedly violated the line and done 'grave and serious' injury to the prerogatives of the bishop of Durham, whose Norhamshire lands lay on the English side of the river. Edward did not treat the matter lightly: the chancery enrolments include the texts of two letters admonishing Alexander for his presumption and requiring a meeting between royal envoys for the formal (and 'amicable') settlement of the 'true boundary'. Alexander's agreement to send envoys, recorded here, did little to ease Edward's concerns about the threat that Scottish activities in the area represented to his authority. A third letter, dated 8 May, rehearsed afresh the outrages that the inhabitants of Berwick had committed against the bishop's men (see here also *Chron. Fordun*, i, 306; *Scotichronicon*, v, 409).

107 Writes to Edward I king of England informing him that he has received the latter's letter informing him that Alexander Comyn earl of Buchan and his wife Elizabeth, one of the co-heiresses of the late Roger de Quincy earl of Winchester, have asserted that Helen la Zouche, another of the said heirs, had received a larger share of their father's lands than lawfully fell to her, and have sued her before the Scottish king's officials and bailies, to Helen's damage and to the injury of Edward's dignity and that of the English crown. Alexander assures him that he has not heard of the matter to date, but that he will make full inquiry of the earl and, in accordance with the laws of his own kingdom, will prevent him and others from disturbing or disquieting Helen or Edward in future. Kincardine, 20 April a.r. 28 [1277].

Magnifico principi et f*ra*tri suo carissimo d*om*ino . Edward*o* D*e*i gr*at*ia illustri regi Anglie d*omi*no Hybern*ie* . et duci Aquytan*nie* . Alex*ander* eade*m* gr*at*ia rex Scott*orum* salute*m* et fraterne dil*e*ccionis sinceros amplexus . Serenitatis v*est*re litt*er*as nobis nup*er* directas . recepimus int*er* cet*er*a continentes . quod Alex*ander* Cumyn' comes de Buchan' . et Elizabet vxor eius vna h*er*edum et participum h*er*editatis que fuit q*uo*ndam Rog*er*i de Quency com*itis* Wynton' asserentes Elenam la Zuche coheredem et p*ar*ticipem hereditatis ip*s*ius quondam Rog*er*i plus habere ad partem suam de t*er*ris et teneme*n*tis que fu*er*unt p*re*d*ic*ti quondam Rog*er*i quam ad ipsam pertinet de iure . trahunt ip*s*am inde in placitum coram minist*r*is et balliuis n*ost*ris in regno n*ost*ro in graue da*m*pnu*m* ip*s*ius Elene et in manifestam v*est*re regie dignitatis ac corone v*est*re lesionem . sicut a relatu multor*um* intellexistis . Sup*er* quo celsitudini v*est*re dignu*m* duximus significandum . Nos ante p*redic*t*arum* litt*erarum* v*est*rarum recepcionem quicquam de p*redic*t*o* negocio nullatenus audiuisse . verumpt*amen* n*ost*ram regiam dignitatem ac iura vestra utpote n*ost*ra p*ro*pria in om*n*ib*us* cons*er*uari cupientes illesa . pred*ic*t*e* rei veritatem a p*redic*t*o* comite diligent*er* inquiremus . et si intellex*er*imus pred*ic*tum comitem seped*ic*tam

Elenam hui*us*modi occasione in regno n*ost*ro vexasse et inquietasse . ip*su*m ab hui*us*modi inq*ui*etac*io*ne desistere faciem*us* . et simil*iter* quoscumq*ue* alios de regno n*ost*ro quos intellig*ere* pot*er*imus corone v*est*re ac dignitati adu*ers*antes i*n* modum p*re*d*ict*um . efficaci animo compescemus iuxta leges et co*n*suetudines regni n*ost*ri . Nec e*tiam* displiceat v*est*re serenitati q*uod* nos tam tarde s*uper* tenore p*re*d*ict*ar*um* litt*er*ar*um* u*est*rar*um* vobis ad presentes respondem*us* . c*um* ips*a* licet m*ul*to temp*or*e elapso fu*er*it impetrata et *con*fecta . nob*is* uix q*ui*ndena p*re*terita exstitit exhibita . T*este* me ips*o* . ap*ud* Kyncard' .xx° . die Ap*ri*lis . anno . r*egni* . n*ostri* . xx° . octauo .

DESCRIPTION. 17.8 cm x 8.4 cm. Sealing: no evidence of a tag, tongue or seal.
HAND. Scribe O.
SOURCE. Original. TNA, Special Collections: Ancient Correspondence of the Chancery and the Exchequer, PRO SC 1/20/149.
PRINTED. *CDS*, ii, no. 91 (cal.).

108 Grants and by this charter confirms to St Kentigern and the church of Glasgow the gift that Devorguilla de Balliol, daughter and heir of Alan of Galloway, made them of the land and pasture of Tourgill in her holding of Cunningham, of the land and pasture of Ryedale, of eighty acres of land from her demesne of Largs commonly called 'Bayllolfislandys' (all in Ayrshire) and of one oxgang of land in her holding of Largs which formerly belonged to Thomas Seysil. To be held in pure and perpetual alms, as Devorgilla's charter bears witness. Haddington, 18 May a.r. 28 [1277].

[*A*]lexand*er*[a] Dei g*ra*tia[b] rex Scottor*um* om*n*ibu*s* probis[c] ho*min*ibu*s* toci*us* t*er*re sue sal*utem*. Sciatis nos concessisse et hac presenti carta n*ost*ra co*n*firmasse donac*io*nem illam quam Deruorguilla de Balliolo filia et vna hered*um* q*uo*nd*am* Alani de Galwathya[d] in legittima viduitate[e] sua co*n*stituta et i*n* ligia potestate sua fecit Deo et beati[f] Kenteg*er*no et ecc*les*ie Glasguen.'[g] necno*n*[h] et ven*erabili* p*at*ri Rob*er*to[i] e*pisc*opo Glasguen'[g] suisq*ue*[j] successoribu*s*. et capit*u*lo eiu*s*d*em* loci. de tota t*er*ra sua et pastura de Torhgil[k] cu*m* p*er*tinenciis[l] in teneme*n*to suo de Cuny*n*gham. et de tota t*er*ra sua et pastura de Ryesdale[m] cu*m* p*er*tine*n*ciis.[l] et de quat*uor* viginti acris t*er*re de dominieo[n] suo de Larges que vulgarit*er* appellant*ur* Bayllolfislandys'. et de vna bouata t*er*re in teneme*n*to suo de Larges'[o] cu*m* pertine*n*ciis[l] q*ue* fuit q*uo*nda*m* Thome Soysit[p]. Tenendas et habendas eid*em* Rob*er*to e*pisc*opo Glasguen'[g] et eius successoribu*s* capit*u*loq*ue*[q] eiusd*em* loci in pura*m* et p*er*petua*m* elemosina*m* inp*er*petuum.[r] cum omnibus pertinentiis. juribus. libertatibus et aysiamentis adeo libere. quiete plenarie et honorifice sicut carta predicte Dervorguille eidem Roberto Glasg' episcopo et suis successoribus exinde confecta plenius testatur. Testibus Patricio comite de Dumbar'. Gilberto de Emfrayvyl comite de Anegus. Waltero de Moravia. Willelmo de Culer. Hugone de Berkeley. Thoma Raulfi et Bertramo de Kerdener. Apud Hadyngton' 18 die Maii anno regni nostri 28.

NOTES. [a] Space for initial A, which is missing in Text A. Text B spells the king's name out in full in bold, enlarged letters, possibly recreating scribal embellishment in the original deed. [b] Gratia in B. [c] Omitted in B. [d] Galwachia in B. [e] Viduitate legitima in B. [f]

Letter 'B' only in B. [g] Glasg^{se} in B. [h] Nec non in B. [i] Omitted in B. [j] Suis in B. [k] Porghyl in B. An annotator of Text B has inserted into the margin here the suggestion that 'Porghyl' should be replaced with 'Torkgill'. [l] Pertinentiis in B. [m] Reysdale in B. [n] Sic, dominio. [o] The words vulgariter … Larges are omitted in B, although the annotator of this text has inserted them in pencil into the margin here. [p] Seysil in B. [q] Capitulo que in B. [r] Text A ends abruptly here. The concluding clauses are supplied here from B. There are substantial variations in spelling between the personal names as they appear in the witness list of Text B and in the list reproduced in Cosmo Innes's printed text. The latter did not have access to the original charter; the names he printed, which are much more accurate than those of the eighteenth-century author of Text A, must be derived from one of several exemplars of Glasgow documents still missing. See Comments below.

RUBRIC. Carta Alexandri regis III qua confirmat donationem factam per Deruorgillam de Balliolo ecclesie Glasg^{se} (B only).

SOURCE. SCA, MS. JB1, no. 4, fo. lxi^{r}, Liber ruber ecclesiae = A; Glasgow University Library, MS. Gen 198, fo. 259^{r} = B. Transcribed here largely from A.

PRINTED. *Glasgow Registrum*, i, no. 230.

COMMENT. Text A is that of a fifteenth-century cartulary. Text B is a collection of full transcripts of several hundred original documents relating to Glasgow cathedral which were taken to the Scots College in Paris at the Reformation and subsequently lost. This cartulary is a late production: it was drafted in 1766 by the College principal, John Gordon. It is, however, of considerable value. Gordon was meticulous in noting which of his transcripts – including this one – were made from original documents; he even went so far as to identify the site that each deed had occupied within the cathedral muniments room before its removal. The care that he took in reproducing the scribal features of his exemplars is evident throughout the manuscript, and there is reason to suggest that the rubrics he assigned to each document represent original endorsements. Alexander's confirmation is noted briefly also (in an English summary) in Glasgow University Library, MS Gen 1245, Item 1, fo. 279. This is a *mélange* of English-language notes and partial transcripts, made early in the nineteenth century by John Dillon, a member of the Maitland Club; still another transcript may be found at NRS, RH 2/2/5. The complicated history of the Glasgow archives subsequent to their removal to Paris is carefully reconstructed in G. G. Simpson and B. Webster, 'The Archives of the Medieval Church of Glasgow: An Introductory Survey', *Bibliotheck*, 3 (1962), 195–201. The place name 'Bayllolfislandys' survives in the Baillieland Burn, north of Largs. 'Ryedale' is a composite name, taken from the Rye Water, which flows through the parish of Dalry, the 'haugh' or 'dale' of the Rye. See *Topographical Account of the District of Cunningham, Ayrshire, compiled about the year 1600, by Timothy Pont, with notes and an appendix*, ed. J. Fuller (Maitland Club, 1858), 163.

109 Writes to Edward I king of England informing him that on Sunday in the octave of the Holy Trinity just past he sent envoys fully empowered to discuss the contents of the letter that he had recently sent. On the same day Master Roger de Béthune and Sir Alexander of Kirkton arrived in Scotland bearing more letters, which he received at Roxburgh on the following Monday. From these he learned that Edward had been given to understand that matters were not as he thought; informs him that he told the messengers that he would once more send envoys and speedily return an answer on these matters. Urges Edward not to believe any sinister reports he may receive. Roxburgh, 5 June a.r. 28 [1277].

Excellentissimo principi amico et fratri suo k*arissi*mo d*omi*no Edwardo Dei gr*at*ia regi Anglie illustri . d*omi*no Ibernie . duci Acquitann*ie* . Alex*ander* eadem gr*at*ia rex Scott*orum* sal*ut*em . et inc*re*mentum glorie et honoris . cum plenitudine dilecc*i*onis sinc*ere* . Nou*e*rit excellencia v*est*ra q*uo*d die D*omin*ico in octabis s*an*cte T*r*initatis p*ro*ximo p*re*terito . misim*us* q*uo*sdam fideles n*ost*ros habentes ex p*ar*te n*ost*ra potestatem tenendi d*ic*t*u*m diem et faciendi ea que dies exigebat . s*ecundum* tenorem litt*erarum* nostrar*um* quas p*ri*us v*est*re magnificencie destinauim*us* . quo die ibid*em* venerunt magist*er* Rog*er*us de Betun et d*omin*us Alex*ander* de Kirketun' portantes litt*er*as v*est*ras clausas quas die Lune sequente recepim*us* apud Roxburg' cum reu*er*encia qua decebat . ex quarum tenore et p*er* quedam alia verba que d*ic*t*i* nuncii v*est*ri extra tenorem d*ic*t*arum* litt*erarum* . nob*is* dixerunt . intelleximus q*uod* aliqui sublimitati v*est*re ded*er*unt aliqua intellig*er*e . alio modo q*uam* res se habent . propt*er* q*uod* d*ic*t*i*s nunciis v*est*ris respondim*us* quod vos p*ro*p*r*ios nuncios n*ost*ros mitt*er*em*us* . et p*er* eosd*em* nuncios tale responsum sup*er* hiis et aliis que d*ic*t*i* nuncii v*est*ri nob*is* dix*er*unt v*est*re celsitudini sub festinacione qua poterimus nunciabimus in quod ult*er*ius non op*or*tebit v*est*ram excellenciam solicitari ex inde in aliquo seu moueri . V*estre* magnificencie om*n*i affectione n*ost*ra p*re*sum*us* supplicantes q*ua*tinus aliquib*us* sinistra vob*is* super p*re*d*ic*t*i*s de nob*is* referentib*us* . cred*er*e non velitis . cum p*ar*ati sumus semp*er* et fu*er*im*us* lib*er*tates et iura v*est*ra tanq*uam* n*ost*ra quia illesa in om*n*ib*us* cons*er*uare . sicut v*est*ri g*ra*t*i*a nup*er* nob*is* significastis q*uod* velletis n*ost*ra iura illibata cons*er*uari . sup*er* quo celsitudini v*est*re quantus [ ] [a] g*ra*t*i*arum referimus acc*i*o*n*es . T*este* . me ips*o* apud Roxb*ur*g q*ui*nto die Junii . anno . r*egni* . n*ostri* . vices*imo* octauo .

NOTES. [a] Two words, illegible owing to stain on bottom right corner of manuscript surface.

DESCRIPTION. 24.4 cm x 7.6 cm. Sealing: no evidence of a tag, tongue or seal. The document is stained in places.

HAND. Scribe M.

SOURCE. Original. TNA, Chancery Miscellanea, PRO C 47/22/5/21.

PRINTED. *CDS*, ii, no. 93 (cal.); *L & I*, vol. xlix, 186 (note).

COMMENT. A modern transcript appears in NRS, RH 2/2/13, item 10 (14).

110 Writes to Edward I king of England informing him that he is sending his envoys, W[illiam] bishop of St Andrews, R[obert] bishop of Dunblane, Robert de Bruce earl of Carrick and Richard of Straiton, and asking him to trust what they will relate to him. Cupar (Fife), 10 July a.r. 29 [1277].

Excellentissimo principi et fratri suo karissimo domino . Edwardo . Dei gracia regi Anglie illustri . domino Hybernie . et duci Acquitanniae . Alexander eadem gracia rex Scottorum salutem . et perpetuum honoris . et glorie incrementum . cum plenitudine dileccionis sincere . Ad sublimitatis vestre presenciam venerabiles patres . W . et . R . Sancti Andree et Dumblanens' episcopos . Robertum de Brus comitem de Carric' . et Ricardum de Strattun . dilectos et fideles nostros destinamus . excellenciam vestram attentius exorantes quatinus hiis que ipsi seu eorum aliqui latores presencium ex parte nostra serenitatis vestre auribus intimabunt fidem plenariam adhibere velitis . Et per ipsos nobis vestra beneplacita remandare . que parati sumus amicabiliter adimplere . Teste me ipso apud Cuper in Fyf' . x . die Julii . anno regni nostri . xx. nono .

RUBRIC. Patent Roll entry headed Litterae de credentiâ ab Alexandro Rege Scotiae.

SOURCE. TNA, Chancery and Supreme Court of Judicature: Patent Rolls, PRO C

66/96, m. 7, schedule 1.
PRINTED. *Foedera*, I, ii, 543; *CPR 1272–1281*, 225 (cal.); *CDS*, ii, no. 94 (note).
COMMENT. The original letter is now lost; but as this copy was executed by a clerk of the English chancery probably soon after its receipt, it should be considered reliable. The envoys were reporting to King Edward about the ongoing quarrel concerning the eastern portion of the Anglo–Scottish border line.

111 Gives, grants and by this charter confirms to Malcolm de Lamberton the land that Thomas de Duddingston resigned and quitclaimed to the king, that is, Easter Craig of Gorgie (Midlothian), by the following boundaries: beginning in the south at the boundaries between Braid and the aforesaid land of the Craig and from there towards the west as far as the boundaries of the Craig, which Stephen Lockhart, knight, held, and from there towards the north, as far as the boundaries of Merchiston, and from there towards the west as far as the boundaries between Merchiston and Braid. To be held in feu and heritage in return for an annual render, at the fair of Haddington, of one pound of pepper; saving to the king all the services customarily owing from the said land. Traquair, 2 December a.r. 29 [1277].

Alex*ander* Dei gr*at*ia rex Scoc*ie* om*nibus* p*ro*bis ho*min*ibus toci*us* te*rr*e sue sal*utem*. Cu*m* Tho*ma*s de Dodyngston nobis resignauerit p*er* fustu*m* et baculu*m* totu*m* ius et clamiu*m* q*uo*d h*ab*uit v*e*l hab*er*e potuit . in te*rr*a de Estcrag' de Gorgyn cu*m* p*er*tinenc*iis*. sciant p*re*sentes et fut*ur*i nos dedisse. co*n*cessisse et hac presenti carta n*ost*ra *con*fir*ma*sse. Malcolmo de Lamberton' filio Will*elm*i filii d*om*ini Alex*andri* de Lamb*er*ton' totam illa*m* te*rr*a*m* de Estircrag de Gorgyne p*ro* homagio et *ser*uicio suo cu*m* om*nibus* p*er*tinenc*iis* suis p*er* has di*ui*sas scil*icet* *i*ncipie*n*do in austro ad di*ui*sas int*er* Bradd'. et p*re*d*ic*tam te*rr*a*m* de le Krag' et inde v*er*sus occidente*m* vsq*ue* ad di*ui*sas te*rr*e illi*us* Crag' q*ua*m Steph*anu*s Loccard miles tenuit. et inde uersus aquilone*m* vsque ad di*ui*sas de Merhammesto*n* et inde uersus occidente*m* usque ad di*ui*sas int*er* Merham*m*esto*n* et Bradd'. sine aliq*uo* retineme*n*to. Tene*n*dam et h*abe*ndam p*re*d*ict*o Malcolmo. et h*er*edib*us* suis vel assig*na*tis.[a] de nob*is* et h*er*edib*us* n*ost*ris in feodo et hereditate. libere quiete plenarie et honorifice. cu*m* om*n*ib*us* lib*er*tatib*us* et aysiam*en*tis ad p*re*d*ic*tam te*rr*a*m* p*er*tine*n*tib*us*. Redde*n*do inde an*n*uati*m* nob*is* et h*er*edib*us* n*os*tris. temp*or*e nu*n*dinar*um* de Hadi*n*gton vna*m* libra*m* pip*er*is. saluis t*am*en nob*is* s*er*uiciis debitis et consuetis de d*ic*ta te*rr*a. In cui*us* rei test*imonium* has litt*er*as nostras fieri fecim*us* pate*n*tes. T*estibus* Patr*ic*io co*m*ite de Donbarr'. Joh*anne* Cumyn. Filio. Will*elm*o de S*anct*o Claro et Symone Fras*er*. apud T*r*aueqr' i*n* s*ecun*do die Decembr*is*. anno reg*ni* n*ost*ri vicesimo nono.

NOTES. [a] The word assign is scraped off here in the MS.
RUBRIC. A. resigna' (on fo. x[v]); continued on fo. 11[r]: vicecomitat de Edor'; in ista posteriori carta del Krag exprimuntur diuise terre ipsius et non in priori (fourteenth century).
SOURCE. NLS, Adv. MS. 34.4.13, Chartulary of Newbattle Abbey, fo. x[v].
PRINTED. *Newbattle Registrum*, no. 42.
COMMENT. See no. 152, below, for another charter concerning these lands.

112 Writes to Edward I king of England informing him that he is sending his envoys, William bishop of St Andrews and William de Soules, knight, asking him to trust what they will relate to him and requesting a reply. Scone, 20 February a.r. 29 [1278].

. Excellentissimo principi et f*ra*tri suo k*arissi*mo d*omi*no . E . Dei g*ra*tia regi Angl*ie* illust*ri* . d*omi*no Hybern*ye* . et duci Aquytan*nie* . Alex*ander* ead*em* g*ra*tia rex Scott*orum* . salut*em* et continuum honoris et gl*or*ie increme*n*tum . Mittimus ad serenitatis v*est*re presenciam ven*er*abilem p*at*rem . Will*elmu*m e*pisco*pum S*anc*ti Andr*ee*. et Will*elmu*m de Sules' milit*em* dil*ec*tos et fideles n*ost*ros . quib*us* si plac*et* in hiis que celsitudini v*est*re ex p*ar*te n*ost*ra plenius intimabunt . fid*em* adhibere velitis indubitatam . Et si qua penes nos uolu*er*itis . nob*is* ea dignemini significare . Teste me ip*s*o apud Schon' . xx° . die Februarii . anno regni n*ost*ri xx° . nono .

DESCRIPTION. 17.8 cm x 3.6 cm. Sealing: no evidence of a tag, tongue or seal.
HAND. Scribe M.
SOURCE. Original. TNA, Special Collections: Ancient Correspondence of the Chancery and the Exchequer, PRO SC 1/20/150.
PRINTED. *CDS*, ii, no. 104 (cal.).

113 Writes to Edward I king of England informing him that he has received the king's answer on the matters between them from his own envoys, W[illiam] bishop of St Andrews and William de Soules, knight. He and his council have replied in letters which they are sending via Reginald, the bishop's clerk and friend. Yester, 24 May a.r. 29 [1278].

. Magnifico principi et f*ra*tri suo k*arissi*mo . d*omi*no . Edw*ardo* . D*e*i g*ra*tia illust*ri* regi Angl*ie* . d*omi*no Hyb*er*nye . et duci Aquytan*nie* . Alex*ander* eadem g*ra*tia rex Scott*orum* . salut*em* et quicquid pot*er*it amicitie et honoris . Responsum excellencie v*est*re quod sup*er* negociis n*ost*ris p*er* ven*er*abilem patre*m* . W . e*pisco*pum S*anc*ti Andree . et .W . de Sules' milit*em* nunc*i*os . dil*ec*tos et fideles n*ost*ros . nobis nup*er* remandastis . intellexim*us* euidenter . quib*us* . prout nobis et consilio n*ost*ro . melius et decencius visum fu*er*at dignu*m* duximus respondere sup*er* eisdem . quod q*uide*m responsum n*ost*rum p*redic*ti nuncii n*ost*ri in l*itt*eris suis p*er* Reginaldum cl*er*icum et sociu*m* memorati e*pisco*pi lator*es* p*re*senc*ium* magnificencie v*est*re t*ra*nsmittunt . sicut firmit*er* credimus et speramus . Stat*um* v*est*rum vtina*m* iocu*n*dum et prosp*er*um . nob*is* ad leticie n*ost*re cumulum . vna cu*m* ben*e*placitis v*est*ris in om*n*ibus remandare velitis . securi . q*uod* nos D*e*o propicio sum*us* incolumes atq*ue* sani . T*este* . me ip*s*o apud Yhestryth' . xxiiii^to^ . die . Maii . anno . r*egni* . nostri . xx° . nono .

DESCRIPTION. 20.1 cm x 5.1 cm. Sealing: no evidence of a tag, tongue or seal.
HAND. Scribe M.
SOURCE. Original. TNA, Special Collections: Ancient Correspondence of the Chancery and the Exchequer, SC 1/20/151.
PRINTED. *CDS*, ii, no. 119 (cal.).

114 Writes to Edward I king of England informing him that he is sending his envoys, Richard Fraser, knight and Reginald the clerk, and asking him to trust what they will relate to him *viva voce*. Traquair, 3 September a.r. 30 [1278].

. Excellentissimo principi et f*ra*tri suo carissimo d*omi*no . Edwardo Dei g*rat*ia regi Angl*ie* illust*ri* d*omi*no Hybernye . et duci Aquytanye Alex*ander* eade*m* g*rat*ia rex Scott*orum* . salute*m* et continuum honoris et gl*ori*e increme*n*tum . Serenitati v*est*re reuerende affectuose supplicamus quatinus Ricardo Fras*er* militi . et Reginaldo Clerico . dil*ec*tis et fidelib*us* n*ost*ris latorib*us* p*re*sencium in hiis que vobis dicent voce viua ex p*ar*te n*ost*ra ce*r*tam fide*m* dignemini adhibere. Velle v*est*rum sup*er* eisd*em* vna cum statu vestre vtinam prosp*er*o et iocundo nob*is* si plac*et* remandantes p*er* eosd*em* . Teste me ipso ap*ud* Treuequayr . iii^{o} . die Septembr*is* anno regni nostri . t*ri*cesimo .

DESCRIPTION. 23.6 cm x 3.6 cm. Sealing: no evidence of a tag, tongue or seal. The right side of the document is stained.
HAND. Scribe M.
SOURCE. Original. TNA, Special Collections: Ancient Correspondence of the Chancery and the Exchequer, PRO SC 1/20/152.
PRINTED. *CDS*, ii, no. 125 (cal.).

115 Gives, grants and by this charter confirms to the monks of Dunfermline abbey the moiety of the land of Beath Waldeve (Fife) that was formerly held of him by John de Strachan, son and heir of the late Ralph de Strachan, knight, which the said John resigned and quitclaimed to the king at Edinburgh on the Saturday after the feast of St Dunstan in May 1278, before William de St Clair sheriff of Edinburgh, the chamberlain John de Lindsay (and several others, named). To be held as John and his ancestors held it, with the monks nonetheless obliged to render the forinsec service owing from the land. Any charters that might in future appear to threaten the monks' title are hereby declared void and of no value. Roxburgh, 2 October a.r. 30 [1278].

Alex*ander* Dei g*rat*ia rex Scotto*r*um om*n*ib*us* p*ro*b*is* ho*min*ibus tocius terre sue sal*utem*. Sciant p*re*sentes et futuri nos dedisse co*n*cessisse et hac carta n*ost*ra confirmasse Deo et monasterio b*eat*e Margarite regine de Dunfermely*n* et monach*is* ibidem Deo seruientib*us* et inpe*r*petuu*m* se*r*uitur*is* totam illam medietatem t*er*re de Beth Waldef' que quond*am* fuit Johan*n*is de Strathethyn' filii et hered*is* quond*am* Ranulphi de Strathechyn' milit*is* q*ua*m de nob*is* et p*ro*genitoribus nostris. idem Joh*anne*s et p*re*decessores sui iure h*er*editario tenueru*n*t cum om*n*ib*us* hominib*us* ligiis ad dictam terram pertinentibus et cum omnibus pertinentiis et rectitudinibus ad eandem terram p*er*tinentibus. Q*ua*m quide*m* medietatem terre de Beth Waldef' idem Joh*anne*s de Strathechyn' nob*is* die Sabb*a*ti p*roxima* p*ost* festum s*anc*ti Dunstani archie*pisc*opi in mense Maio. anno g*rat*ie m^{o} . cc^{o}. lxx^{o}. octauo ap*ud* Castrum Puellar*um* de Edenburg' in cam*er*a n*ost*ra que d*icitur* cam*er*a b*eat*e Margarite regine p*er* fustum et baculu*m* p*ro* se et h*er*edib*us* suis reddidit. resignauit. et q*u*ietam clamauit. et om*n*i iuri et clamo \ quod /

habuit u*el* h*ab*ere potuit in p*er*petuu*m* renu*n*ciauit coram Will*elm*o de S*anct*o Claro tu*n*c vicecom*iti* de Edenburg'. Joh*ann*e de Lyndes' cam*er*ario n*os*tro. Ric*ardo* de Stratu*n*. Will*elm*o Byseth Pat*ri*cio de Lemeton' cl*er*ico n*os*tro de lib*er*at*i*one mag*ist*ro Joh*ann*e de Muxilburg' cl*er*ico n*os*tro de p*re*bend*a*. Willelmo de Caraumund cl*er*ico de warderoba. Will*elm*o cl*er*ico tu*n*c *con*stabular*io* castri de Edenburg'. Joh*ann*e de Rames'. Symone de Eskendi. Symone de Leselly'. Randino de warde*r*oba. Alex*andro* de Melgedru*m*. Alano de Walchoup'. Will*elm*o de Morauia. Wil*lelm*o de Maist*er*tun'. Th*om*a de Logyn'. Alano de cam*er*a et aliis fidedignis. Tenendam et h*ab*endam eisd*em* monachis in lib*er*am et p*er*petuam elemosinam. lib*er*e. q*ui*ete. plenarie. et honorifice p*er* easd*em* diuisas et r*e*ctitudines p*er* quas idem Joh*anne*s et an*te*cessores sui eandem t*er*ram tenu*er*unt u*el* ten*er*e dubueru*n*t faciendo forinsecu*m*[a] q*ua*ntu*m* ad dictam t*er*ram p*er*tinet . Et si alique carte seu ettiam aliq*ua* instr*u*menta inue*n*iant*ur* q*ue* p*re*dictis monachi*s* noc*er*e pot*er*unt u*el* obuiare. volum*us* et decernim*us* q*uo*d om*n*ino iurib*us* careant in p*er*petuu*m* cassa fuit irrita. et uacua. et de cet*er*o nulli*us* ualore existant. Test*ibus* magistro Will*elm*o Fras*er* cancellar*io* n*os*tro. Joh*ann*e de Lindes' cam*er*ario n*os*tro. Will*elm*o ep*isc*opo Sancti Andree. Roberto episcopo Glasguens'. Alex*andro* Cum*in* com*ite* de Buch*an*. Pat*ri*cio comite de Dunbar. Rob*er*to com*ite* de Carr'. Will*elm*o de Sulys'. Dauid de Louchor'. Will*elm*o Cum*in* de Kylbrid'. Symone Fras*er*. Will*elm*o de Sancto Claro. Pat*ri*cio de Gram'. et multis aliis ap*u*d Rokesburg'. secundo die Octobr*is*. anno regni n*os*tri tricesimo.

NOTES. [a]Word seruicium missing.
RUBRIC. Carta d*omi*ni regis de Beethwaldef (fourteenth century).
SOURCE. NLS, Adv. MS. 34.1.3A, Register of Dunfermline Abbey, fo. xviii[r].
PRINTED. *Dunfermline Registrum*, no. 87.
COMMENT. A modern transcript appears in NRS, RH 2/2/5.

116 Writes to Edward I king of England requesting that he show favour to Richard de [obliterated], who is delayed in his service. Since he does not have [his great seal] he is using here his privy seal. October a.r. 30 [1278].

. Magnifico p*r*incipi et f*rat*ri suo k*arissi*mo domino Eduardo dei gr*at*ia regi Angl*ie* d*omi*no Ibern[ie duci Aquitannie Alex*ander* eadem gratia] rex Scott*orum* . sal*ute*m . et sinc*er*e dilectionis se*mper* [incrementum] pro Ricardo de [ ][a] seruicio moratur vos rogam*us* et req*ui*rimus q*ua*tinus unde negociis [ ].[a] exspedire[b] pa*r*tibus n*ost*ris e*ss*e velitis fauorabiles et in sui iure [ ][a] no*n* habuim*us* . sigill*um* n*ost*rum sec*re*tu*m* p*re*sentibus apponi ma*n*dauimus [ ][a] die Octobris anno regni nostri . xxx[o].

NOTES. The right side of the MS is torn off and badly stained; letters in brackets supplied by conjecture. [a]Three-four words missing. [b]Sic, expedire.
DESCRIPTION. 15.7 cm x 4.1 cm. Sealing: no evidence of a tag, tongue or seal.
HAND. Scribe M.
SOURCE. Original. TNA, Special Collections: Ancient Correspondence of the Chancery and the Exchequer, PRO SC 1/20/153.
PRINTED. *CDS*, ii, no. 132 (cal.).
COMMENT. The Richard referred to here may be Richard de Straiton, who acted as an envoy of Alexander III on several other occasions; see above, no. 110 and below, nos 160, 164, 282.

117 Writes to Edward I king of England informing him that after Easter he intends to send envoys to relate to him *viva voce* the recent actions of Edward's bailiffs in the Scottish marches and to obtain from him a solution to the problem. Edinburgh, 26 March a.r. 30 [1279].

. Magnifico principi et f*ra*t*r*i suo k*arissi*mo d*omi*no . E . Dei g*ra*t*i*a . illust*ri* regi Angl*ie* d*omi*no Hybernye . et duci Aquitan*nie*[a] . Alex*ander* ead*em* g*ra*t*i*a rex Scott*orum* . sal*ut*em . et sincere dilect*i*onis affect*u*m . cum augm*en*to gl*o*r*i*e et honoris . De statu v*est*ro . d*omi*ne regine sponse v*est*re sororis n*ost*re carissime lib*erorum*q*ue* v*est*ror*um* . bonos rumores continue audire ac scire . efficaci desid*er*io affectantes . Excellencie v*est*re duximus suplicandu*m*[b] . quatinus statum vestrum et eor*um* vtinam semp*er* prosp*er*um et iocundu*m* nobis ad maiorem animi n*ost*ri recreac*i*onem . velitis frequencius significare . Et quia credimus vos vice u*er*sa auditis de statu n*ost*ro et lib*erorum* nostror*um* rumoribus prosp*er*is vb*er*iorem in mente velle concip*er*e letitiam . celsitudini v*est*re tenore p*re*sencium duxim*us* i*n*sinuandum nos et ips*o*s disponente Altissimo optata hiis dieb*us* p*er*frui sanitate . P*ro*ponimus et*iam* q*uam*cicius pot*er*i*mus* \ com*m*ode / post instans festum Pasch*e* prox*imo* venturu*m* nunc*i*os n*ost*ros sollempnes ad p*re*senciam serenitatis v*est*re destinare . vt ea que p*er* balliuos v*est*ros nup*er* acta fu*er*unt in marchia n*ost*ra per que sentimus nos indebite grauari . quod non credimus v*est*re frat*er*nitatis beniuolenciam nobis velle . sic*ut* accepimus et exp*er*ti sum*us* v*est*ri gratia experie*n*tia freq*ue*nti . viua voce plenius exponant . et a vobis remediu*m* optineant sup*er* eisd*em* . T*este* . me ips*o* apud Castr*um* Puellar*um* . xxvi . die Martii . anno regni n*ost*ri . xxx^{o} .

NOTES. [a] The letter q has been altered. [b] Sic, supplicandum.

DESCRIPTION. 20.3 cm x 5.6 cm. Sealing: formerly sealed on a tongue cut from right to left across the bottom of the deed, now torn away.

HAND. Scribe M.

SOURCE. Original. TNA, Special Collections: Ancient Correspondence of the Chancery and the Exchequer, PRO SC 1/20/154.

PRINTED. *Foedera*, I, ii, 531 (where it is misdated); *CDS*, ii, no. 154 (cal.).

118 Writes to Edward I king of England requesting that he show favour to Ingram de Umfraville, knight, who is petitioning to have the hereditary lands of his late father, Robert de Umfraville. Traquair, 29 March a.r. 30 [1279].

. Excellentissimo principi et f*ra*t*r*i suo carissimo d*omi*no Edwardo D*e*i g*ra*t*i*a illust*ri* regi Angl*ie* . d*omi*no Hybern*ie* et duci Aquitan*nie* . Alex*ander* . ead*em* g*ra*t*i*a rex Scott*orum* . salut*em* . et sincere dilecc*i*onis *con*tinuos amplexus . Pro Ingerramo de Humfrauyle milite latore . p*re*sentium celsitudinem v*est*ram reu*er*endam . affect*u*osissime exoramus . q*ua*tinus eid*em* i*n* suis iustis petic*i*onibus serenitati v*est*re sup*er* t*er*ris . hereditariis quondam Rob*er*ti de Humfrauyl' p*at*r*i*s sui . humil*iter* faciendis . vos amore n*ost*ri exhibere velitis fauorabiles et benignos . T*a*men inde si plac*et* fac*er*e dignetur v*est*ra excellencia . quod ips*e* de n*ost*ro int*er*uencio*n*i commodum se senciat assecutu*m* . p*er* q*uo*d fraternitati v*est*re per amande ad amplas grates et g*ra*t*i*as assurg*ere* debeamus . Teste . me ip*s*o apud Treuequayr' . xxix . die . Marcii . anno . r*egni* . nostri . xxx°.

DESCRIPTION. 20.3 cm x 3.3 cm. Sealing: no evidence of a tag, tongue or seal.
HAND. Scribe M.
SOURCE. Original. TNA, Special Collections: Ancient Correspondence of the Chancery and the Exchequer, PRO SC 1/20/155.
PRINTED. *CDS*, ii, no. 155 (cal.).
COMMENT. Umfraville's claim to his father's estate was the subject also of a letter dated around the same time that Prince Alexander, the king's son, addressed to Edward I; TNA, PRO SC 1/20/169, printed in *Chron. Lanercost* (Stevenson), 473–4. The prince's patronage proved successful, with Umfraville and his wife assigned 100 merklands in Carrick and an annual pension of £40 from the royal chamber; see *RPS*, 1293/2/15.

119 Writes to Edmund earl of Cornwall informing him that he is sending W[illiam] bishop of St Andrews, R[obert] bishop of Dunblane and Patrick de Graham, knight, as envoys to the English court and asking him to trust what they will relate to him *viva voce*. Edinburgh, 10 April a.r. 30 [1279].

. Alex*ander* Dei gr*ati*a rex Scott*orum* k*arissi*mo amico suo d*omi*no Edmundo de Almann' . com*iti* Cornub*ie* . sal*utem* . et sinc*ere* dil*ecci*onis plenitudinem . Sciatis nos atq*ue* liberos n*ost*ros D*omi*no an*n*uente hiis dieb*us* sanos esse et iocundos . q*uod* de vob*is* et v*est*ris scire cupimus incessant*er* . Mittimus et*iam* ad curi*am* d*omi*ni reg*is* Angl*ie* illust*ri*s pro negociis n*ost*ris in ead*em* p*ro*ponend*is* . et expediend*is* . ven*er*abiles in *Christo* pat*r*es . W . et . R . *Sancti* Andr*ee* . et Dunblan' e*pisco*pos . et P*at*ricium de Graham mil*it*em . dil*ec*tos et fideles n*ost*ros . Rogantes vos attencius et req*ui*rentes . quatinus eis omnib*us* u*e*l duob*us* eorum . in hiis que vobis dicent plenius viua voce ex p*ar*te n*ost*ra . fide*m* adhib*ere* velitis indubitatam . T*este* . me ip*s*o apud Castr*um* Puellar*um* . x° . die . Aprilis . anno regni n*ost*ri . xxx° .

DESCRIPTION. 16.3 cm x 4.3 cm. Sealing: no evidence of a tag, tongue or seal.
HAND. Scribe M.
SOURCE. Original. TNA, Special Collections: Ancient Correspondence of the Chancery and the Exchequer, PRO SC 1/31/11.
PRINTED. *CDS*, ii, no. 157 (cal.).

120 Grants and by this charter confirms to Walter Edgar, son of the late Patrick Edgar, knight, the gift that Gilbert de Ruthven, knight, made him of the land of Easter [and Wester?] Cultmalundie (Perthshire). To be held as Gilbert's charter bears witness, saving the king's service. Haddington, 6 May a.r. 30 [1279].

Alex*ander* Dei gr*ati*a rex Scott*orum* . omnib*us* p*ro*bis hominib*us* tocius t*er*re sue sal*utem* . Sciatis nos concessisse et hac p*re*senti carta n*ost*ra confirmasse Walt*er*o Edger' filio q*uo*ndam Pat*ri*cii Edger militis donacionem illam q*ua*m Gilb*er*tus de Rothewen' miles fecit sibi de t*er*ra de duob*us*[a] Cultemelyndis cum p*er*tinenciis. Tenend*am* et habend*am* eidem Walt*er*o et suis heredib*us* u*e*l assignatis de p*re*fato Gilb*er*to et eius heredibus adeo lib*ere* . quiete . plenarie . et in pace . sicut carta p*re*dic*ti* Gilb*er*ti eidem Walt*er*o et suis heredib*us* u*e*l assignatis exinde confecta . pleni*us* iuste testat*ur* . saluo s*er*uicio n*ost*ro .

Testib*us* . Pat*ri*cio comit*e* de Dunbar' . Symone Fras*er* . et Will*elm*o de S*anct*o Claro . apud Hadingtun' sexto die Maii . anno regni n*ost*ri t*ri*cesimo.

NOTE. [a]The manuscript surface has been scraped here and the word duobus added to the empty space.
ENDORSED. Confirmacio Alexandri regis de duobus Culltmelyndeys (fifteenth century).
DESCRIPTION. 20.8 cm x 6.9 cm; fold 2.3 cm. Sealing: a tag, 2.0 cm broad, is passed through single slits. The seal is now missing.
HAND. Scribe L.
SOURCE. Original. Kinnoull Muniments, *penes* Messrs Condie, Mackenzie and Co., Perth, Green deed box, no. 8, Dupplin Charters, no. 76.
COMMENT. A later royal confirmation of Gilbert de Ruthven's grant, dated 1369, has been tampered with, much as appears to have been the case here, perhaps in an effort to ensure that the descendants of the Edgar family had firm title to the two portions of the estate. Modern transcripts appear in NRS, RH 1/1/1 and NRS, GD 212/1/6, fo. 15 and GD 212/1/127.

121 Writes to Edward I king of England requesting that he give a favourable hearing to the envoys he is sending to the English court and that none of Edward's subjects be permitted to diminish his liberties. Selkirk, 25 May a.r. 30 [1279].

. Excellentissimo principi et f*rat*ri suo k*ariss*imo d*omi*no E . D*e*i g*rat*ia illust*ri* regi Angl*ie* . d*om*ino Hybern*ie* . et duci Aquitan*nie* . Alex*ander* ead*em* g*rat*ia rex Scott*orum* . salut*em* cum gl*or*ia et honore . et sincere affecc*i*onis *con*tinuu*m* increme*n*tum . Sciatis v*es*tra serenitas amabilis nos et lib*er*os n*ost*ros bona hiis dieb*us* corp*or*is sanitate gaudere altissimo annuente . quod de vobis d*omi*na regina spo*n*sa v*est*ra sorore n*ost*ra dilectissima p*ro* c*er*to scire cordialit*er* affectamus . Mansuetudini v*est*re affectuose suplicantes .[a] q*ua*tin*us* negocia nost*ra* pro quib*us* nunc*i*os n*ost*ros modo sicut alias ad curiam v*est*re magnificencie transmittim*us* . auribus equitatis et benivolentie dignemini exaudire . Non permittentes si placet sicut nobis sepius l*itter*atorie v*est*ra gratia sc*ri*psistis q*uod* lib*er*tatib*us* n*ost*ris p*er* aliquos de v*est*ris in aliquo indebite derogetur . Statum v*est*rum d*omi*ne regine *con*sortis v*est*re lib*erorum*q*ue* v*est*rorum . vtina*m* semp*er* prosp*er*um et iocundu*m* . nob*is* ad augmentum letitie n*ost*re velitis si placet frequencius significare . T*este* . me ip*s*o apud Selek' . xx^{o}v^{o} . die Maii . anno . r*egni* . nostri . xxx^{o} .

NOTES. [a] Sic, supplicantes.
DESCRIPTION. 17.8 cm x 4.8 cm. Sealing: no evidence of a tag, tongue or seal. The document is badly stained.
HAND. Scribe M.
SOURCE. Original. TNA, Special Collections: Ancient Correspondence of the Chancery and the Exchequer, PRO SC 1/20/156.
PRINTED. *Foedera*, I, ii, 533 (where it is misdated); *CDS*, ii, no. 159 (cal.).

122 Grants and by this charter confirms to St Kentigern and the church of Glasgow the gift that John Cumyn lord of Bedrule made them of the whole land of Rulehaugh (Roxburghshire) that lies on the north side of the river Teviot. To be held in pure and perpetual alms, as John's charter bears witness. Dumfries, 19 July a.r. 31 [1279].

[A]lex*ander*[a] Dei gr*at*ia rex Scott*orum* o*mn*ibus p*ro*bi*s* ho*min*ibus suis ad quos p*re*sentes l*itt*ere p*er*uenerint sal*u*tem. Sciatis nos *con*cessisse et hac p*rese*nti carta n*ost*ra *con*firmasse donac*io*nem illa*m* qua*m* Joh*ann*es Cumyn. d*omin*us de Rulebethok' fecit Deo et beato Kenteg*er*no ac ecc*lesi*e Glasg'. et ven*er*ab*i*li p*at*ri Rob*er*to Glasg' e*pisco*po. ac successorib*us* suis Glasg' e*pisco*pis inp*er*petuu*m* de to*ta* t*er*ra de Rulehalch' cu*m* p*er*tinenciis. ex aquilonali p*ar*te aque de Teuyoth. Tenend*as* et habend*as* eidem R e*pisco*po Glasg' et successorib*us* suis episcopis Glasg' inp*er*petuu*m*. in lib*er*am. pura*m*. et p*er*petua*m* elemosinam p*er* om*ne*s re*c*tas diuisas suas et cum omnib*us* iustis p*er*tinenciis suis. Adeo. lib*ere* q*ui*ete plenar*ie*. et honorifice sicut carta p*re*dicti Joh*ann*is Cumy*n* eid*em* R episcopo inde confecta pleni*us* iuste testat*ur*. Testib*us*. P*at*ricio comite de Dunbar Hugo*ne* de Ab*er*nyth'. Will*elm*o Cumy*n* de Kilbryde. Simo*ne* Fras*er* et. W de S*anct*o Claro. Apud Du*m*fres'. xix°. die Julii. anno regni nostri. xxxi°.

NOTES. The bottom portion of the manuscript is torn and crumpled. [a] Space for initial A, which is missing.
RUBRIC. Conf*ir*macio reg*is* super terra de Rulehalch (fifteenth century).
SOURCE. SCA, MS JB1, no. 4, Liber ruber ecclesiae, fos. lvi^v–lvii^r.
PRINTED. *Glasgow Registrum*, i, no. 233.
COMMENT. For a note about the sources, see above, no. 108.

123 Writes to Edward I king of England informing him that some of his own men, who recently appeared before Edward's itinerant justices in Cumberland, Westmorland and York, have given him to understand that the said justices have injured him contrary to English law. He sends his envoys, John de Swinburne, knight and Reginald de Rihill, clerk, to explain the matter to him *viva voce*, and to obtain redress. Durris, 28 July a.r. 31 [1279].

Excellentissimo principi et f*ra*tri suo carissimo d*omi*no . E . Dei gr*at*ia illust*ri* regi Angl*ie* . d*omi*no Hyb*erni*e . et duc*i* Aquitan*nie* . Alex*ander* eadem gr*at*ia rex Scot*torum* . salute*m* et f*rat*erne dileccionis sinceros amplexus . Excellencie v*est*re suplicamus[a] aff*e*ct*u*ose . quatinus statu*m* v*est*rum d*omi*ne regine sponse v*est*re sororis n*ost*re k*arissi*me ac lib*er*-or*um* v*est*ror*um* . vtinam semp*er* prosp*er*um et iocundu*m* . nob*is* ad vb*er*iorem animi n*ost*ri recr*e*ac*i*oni . dignemini frequencius significare . sciturі nos atq*ue* lib*er*os n*ost*ros hiis dieb*us* bona sanitate gaudere altissimo concedente . quod de vob*is* et v*est*ris scire cupimus desid*er*io efficaci . Quia vero quidam fideles n*ost*ri nup*er* constituti in p*re*sencia justiciar*iorum* v*est*ror*um* itinerancium in comitat*ibus* Cumberland' . Westmerland' et Ebor' . nob*is* dederunt intellegi q*uod* iid*em* justic*i*-*arii* quasdam diu*er*sas duricias et gr*a*uamina nob*is* inf*er*unt . cont*ra* leges et consuetudines regni v*est*ri . Joh*ann*em de Swyneburn' milit*em* et Reginald*um* de Rihill' cl*er*icum . dil*e*ctos et fideles n*ost*ros lator*es* p*re*sencium . ut ipsas duricias et grauamina serenitati v*est*re viua voce ostendant . et remedium sup*er* eisd*em* nob*is* a v*est*ra regia discrec*i*one reportent . ad vestre celsitudinis p*re*senciam duxim*us* destinandos. Q*ua*re serenitat*em* v*est*ram de qua plene *con*fidimus attencius exoramus . quatin*us* p*re*dic*t*is Joh*ann*i et Regin*aldi* . uel eor*um* alt*er*i .

in p*re*missis nomi*ne* n*ost*ro fidem adhib*ere* dignantes . remedium sup*er* eisd*em* quale decet equitatem regiam . nob*is* concedere velitis . voluntatis v*est*re b*ene*placita nob*is* volentes cum frequencia significare . T*este* . me ip*so* apud Durrys' . xxviii° . die Julii . anno . r*egni* . n*ostri* . xxxi° .

NOTES. [a] Sic, supplicamus.
DESCRIPTION. 19.8 cm x 6.9 cm. Sealing: no evidence of a tag, tongue or seal.
HAND. Scribe P.
SOURCE. Original. TNA, Special Collections: Ancient Correspondence of the Chancery and the Exchequer, PRO SC 1/20/157.
PRINTED. *CDS*, ii, no. 162 (cal.).

124 Gives, grants and by this charter confirms to William de Dallas, knight, the land of Meikle Dallas (Moray), by the same boundaries as his grandfather, King William, infeft his ancestor, William de Ripley. To be held in feu and heritage, with soke and sake, gallow and pit, with toll, team and infangenthef for the service of one-quarter of a knight, saving to the bishop of Moray the two-shilling teinds that he is accustomed to receive annually from the land. Stirling, 5 September a.r. 31 [1279].

Alex*ander*[a] Dei g*ra*tia rex Scott*orum* . om*n*ib*us* prob*is* hom*in*ib*us* toci*us* t*er*re sue sal*ut*em . Sciatis nos dedisse . co*n*cessisse et h*ac* p*re*senti carta n*ost*ra *con*firmasse Will*elm*o de Dolays militi p*ro* homagio et s*er*uic*i*o suo t*er*ram de Dolaysmykel' p*er* easd*em* diuisas p*er* quas bone memorie q*uo*ndam . W . auus n*ost*er infeodauit q*uo*ndam Will*elmu*m de Rypeley p*ro*genitore*m* suu*m* . Tenendam et h*abe*ndam sibi et h*e*redib*us* suis de nob*is* et h*e*redib*us* n*ost*ris in feodo et h*e*reditate in bosco et plano . in t*er*ris et aq*ui*s . in p*ra*tis et pascuis . in moris et marisiis . i*n* stagnis et molendinis . cu*m* socco et sacca . cu*m* furco et fossa . cu*m* tol et them . et infanganthef' . et cu*m* om*n*ib*us* aliis iustis p*er*tine*n*tiis suis . libere et q*ui*ete . plenarie et honorifice p*er* s*er*uiciu*m* q*ua*rte p*ar*tis vni*us* militis . saluis ep*isco*po Morauiens*is* illis duob*us* solidis . quos de d*ic*ta t*er*ra pro decima sua annuati*m* p*er*cipere co*n*sueuit . Testib*us* . Rob*er*to e*pisco*po Glasguens' . Alex*andro* Cumyn' comite de Buchan' . Will*elm*o de Morauia . Joh*ann*e de Lyn[des'][b] . Hug*one* de Ab*ir*nith' . Will*elm*o Cumyn' de K[i]lbride Reginaldo le Chen' p*at*re . Galfrido de Mubray Will*elm*o de S*anc*to Claro . Symone Fraser' . Pat*ric*io de Graham' . et multis aliis . apud Striuelyn' . q*ui*nto die Septembr*is* anno regni n*ost*ri tricesimo . primo .

NOTES. [a] Initial A highly decorated. [b] Small hole in MS; letters supplied by conjecture.
DESCRIPTION. 23.0 cm x 9.1 cm. The portion that was once folded up measures 4.1 cm. Sealing: formerly on a tag, through double slits. Seal and tag now missing.
HAND. Scribe Q.
SOURCE. Original. NRS, Register House Charters, RH 6/58.

125 Writes to Edward I king of England informing him that he is sending his envoys, Robert bishop of Dunblane, John de Swinburne, knight and Reginald de Rihill and asking him to trust what they will relate to him *viva voce*. Edinburgh, 10 September a.r. 31 [1279].

Excellentissimo p*r*incipi ac f*ra*tri in *Christ*o . k*arissi*mo d*omi*no . E . Dei g*ra*tia regi Angl*ie* . d*omi*no Hyb*erni*e et duc*i* Aquit*annie* . Alex*ander* eadem g*ra*tia rex Scott*orum* salutem . et p*ro*sp*er*os ad singula vota successus . cu*m* om*n*i incremento honoris et glorie . Excellentissima[m] d*omi*nac*io*n*e*m ves*t*ram ac fraternitatem in *Christ*o k*arissi*mam requirim*us* et affectuose rogamus q*ua*tinus ven*er*abili [Roberto Dei][a] g*ra*tia Dunblanen' e*pisc*opo . Joh*anni* de Swyneburn' militi . et Reginaldo de Rihille cl*er*ico dilectis et fidelib*us* n*os*tris [ ][b] vobis ex parte n*os*tra viua voce intimabunt fidem adhibere velitis . Et ea si placet amore n*os*tri [ ][b] ac grac*i*oso effectui mancipare . statum v*es*trum . ac liberor*um* v*es*tror*um* quem scire desideramus p*ro*sp*er*um et [ ][b] nobis vna cum b*e*n*e*placitis v*est*ris significare velitis . valeat excellencia v*es*tra semp*er* in D*omi*no . T*este* meip*s*o [apud] Castru*m* Puellar*um* . x . die Septemb*ri*s . ann*o* . r*egni* . n*ostri* . xxx° . p*ri*mo.

NOTES. [a] Illegible owing to tear in manuscript. [b] A few letters missing.

DESCRIPTION. 18.3 cm x 4.8 cm. Sealing: formerly sealed on a tongue cut from right to left across the bottom of the deed, now torn away. The document is torn away on the right side, obliterating some letters.

HAND. Scribe M.

SOURCE. Original. TNA, Chancery Miscellanea, PRO C 47/22/9/12.

PRINTED. *CDS*, ii, no. 164 (cal.); *L & I*, vol. xlix, 186 (note).

126 Gives, grants and by this charter confirms to William de St Clair, knight, for his homage and service, the lands of Roslin and Catcune (Midlothian), which Henry de Roslin resigned and quitclaimed to him. To be held in feu and heritage with soke and sake, gallow and pit, with toll, team and infangenthef, as Henry held them, for the service of one-half of a knight. Traquair, 14 September a.r. 31 [1279].

Alexander Dei gracia rex Scottorum omnibus probis hominibus tocius terre sue salutem. Cum Henricus de Roskelyn tenens noster de terris de Roskelyn' et de Cattekon resignauerit per fustum et baculum in manu nostra et quietum clamauerit pro se et heredibus suis predictas terras de Roskelyn et de Cattekon cum omnibus suis iustis pertinentiis sciant presentes et futuri nos dedisse concessisse et hac presenti carta nostra confirmasse Willelmo de Sancto Claro militi pro homagio et seruicio suo et heredibus suis predictas terras de Roskelyn et de Cattekon. Tenendas et habendas predicto Willelmo de Sancto Claro et heredibus suis de nobis et heredibus nostris in feodo et hereditate cum socco et sacca et furco et fossa cum tol et them et infangandethef in boscis et planis pratis et pascuis molendinis et stagnis et omnibus aliis libertatibus et aisiamentis ad predictas terras pertinentibus adeo libere et quiete integre et pacifice sicut predictus Henricus de Roskelyn terras illas liberius quiecius aut melius aliquo tempore tenuit aut possedit faciendo inde nobis et heredibus nostris seruicium dimidii militis. Testibus Roberto episcopo Glasgu'[a], Willelmo[b] Fraser cancellario nostro, Gilberto comite de Anegus', Willelmo Cumyn de Kilbryd', Symone Fraser, Bernardo de Monte Alto, Willelmo Byseth', Patricio de Graham' et multis aliis. Apud Treuequayr' quartodecimo die Septembris anno regni nostri tricesimo primo.

NOTES. [a] Glasguens' in printed version. [b] W. in printed version.
ENDORSED. Carta de Roskelyn. This heading may represent the original endorsement.
SOURCE. NLS, Adv. MS 32.6.2, fos. 3^{v}–4^{r}, a little book of notes and transcripts of original charters made by Augustine Hay, probably between 1686 and 1690. In 1849 the original was said to be in the possession of W. E. Aytoun of Edinburgh; its present location is unknown.
PRINTED. *Newbattle Registrum*, App., Cartae Originales, App. 1, no. 6; Hay, *Sainteclaires*, 41–2.
COMMENT. See also below, no. 130.

127 Gives and grants to the abbot and monks of Arbroath 100s annually from the fermes of his manor of Forfar, in compensation for the 100s which the abbot and convent pay annually on his behalf to the prior and convent of Canterbury for feeding thirteen paupers. Coupar (abbey), 12 November a.r. 31 [1279].

Alex*ander* Dei gr*at*ia rex Scot*orum* om*n*ib*us* p*ro*bis ho*min*ibus toci*us* t*er*re sue sal*ute*m. Sciatis nos dedisse et concessisse p*ro* nob*is* et successorib*us* n*ost*ris abb*at*i de Ab*er*br'. et mo*na*chis ibide*m* Deo s*er*uientib*us* et in perpetuu*m* s*er*uituris centu*m* solidos sterlingor*um* sing*u*lis an*n*is p*er*cipiend*os* de firmis man*er*ii n*ost*ri de Forfar ad festu*m* Pentecost*en* p*er* man*us* vicecomitis et balliuor*um* n*ost*rorum q*ui* ibidem p*ro* temp*ore* fuerint. in reco*m*pensac*io*nem centu*m* solidorum quos dicti abb*as* et mo*na*chi soluu*n*t an*n*uati*m* pro nobis p*ri*ori et *con*uen*t*ui monasterii sancti Thome martiris de Ca*n*tuaria p*ro* refeccio*ne* tredeci*m* paup*erum* ibid*em* p*er*petuo pascendor*um*. donec eisd*em* abb*at*i et mo*na*chis[a] de Abirbr' p*er* nos vel successores n*ost*ros in eccl*es*iastico b*ene*ficio seu bonis temp*or*alib*us* vberi*us* fuerit p*ro*uisu*m*. Testib*us* Waltero senescallo comite de Meneteth.'[b] Will*el*mo de Brechyn et Pat*ri*cio de Berklay[c]. apud Cupru*m* Mo*na*chor*um* duodeci*mo*[d] die Nouembris. anno regni n*ost*ri tricesi*mo* primo.

NOTES. [a] Conuentui in B. [b] Menteth in B. [c] Berkelay in B. [d] xvii in B.
RUBRIC. Carta Regis de c. s' apud Forfar' (rubric and initial A in red).
SOURCE. NLS, Adv. MS 34.4.2, Chartulary of Arbroath Abbey, fo. xviii^{r} = A; BL, Add. MS 33245, fo. 124^{v} = B, an inspeximus dated 1292 by Bishop William of Dunblane and abbots Thomas and Andrew of Scone and Coupar of two earlier royal charters. Transcribed here from A, a fourteenth-century cartulary of Arbroath abbey. The B text is found in a sixteenth-century copy of the cartulary that was unknown to Cosmo Innes, editor of the published Bannatyne version.
PRINTED. *Arbroath Liber*, i, no. 265.
COMMENT. The king's gift is also mentioned in letters patent in which William abbot of Arbroath declares himself bound to pay the sum of 100s annually for the purpose of feeding the paupers 'on behalf of King Alexander III, in honour of St Thomas, for the sake of his soul and the souls of his predecessors and successors'. This document further reveals that the king's charitable act was to take place every Tuesday; Canterbury Cathedral Archives, CCA-DCc-ChAnt/C/168 and CCA-DCc-Register/B, fo. 304^{v}; *Nat. MSS. Scot.*, i, no. 3. See also below, nos 291 and 300.

128 Grants and by this charter confirms to the canons of Inchcolm abbey the gift that William Dod, burgess of Inverkeithing, and his wife, Matilda, made them of the mill of Fordell (Fife), with the whole land pertaining to it. To be held in perpetuity, as the charter of William and Matilda bears witness, saving royal service. Dunfermline, 1 December a.r. 31 [1279].

Alex*ander* Dei gr*at*ia rex Scottor*um* om*n*ib*us* prob*is* ho*min*ibus tocius te*rr*e sue salute*m*. Sciatis nos co*n*cessisse et hac p*rese*nti carta n*ost*ra co*n*firm*a*sse donac*i*one*m* illa*m* qua*m* Will*elmu*s Dod burgens*is* de Innerkethin et Matilda spo*n*sa sua feceru*n*t Deo et mon*aste*rio de insula s*anct*i Colu*m*be et canonic*i*s ibidem Deo se*r*uientib*us* et impe*r*petuu*m* Deo se*r*uituris de molendinis de Fordale cu*m* tota terra ad dicta molendina pe*r*tinente. Tene*n*da et h*abe*nda eisd*e*m canon*icis* et eor*um* successorib*us* i*m*pe*r*petuu*m* cu*m* om*n*ib*us* pe*r*t*inentiis* suis. libe*r*tatib*us* et asia*mentis* ad dicta mole*n*dina et d*ict*am te*rr*am pe*r*tin*en*tib*us* adeo libe*re*. quiete plenarie et hono*rifice*. sicut carta p*re*dicti Will*elm*i et Matilde spo*n*se sue dictis canon*icis* et eo*rum* succesorib*us* exinde confecta plenius iuste testatur. salvo se*r*uicio n*ost*ro. Testibus Pat*ri*cio de Berclay W de Megeldro*m* et Ric*ardo* de Straton. apud Dunfe*r*meline p*ri*mo die Dece*m*br*is* anno regni n*ostri* tricesimo p*ri*mo.

SOURCE. Darnaway Castle, Moray Muniments, box 42, no. 3, an early fifteenth-century transumpt of several Inchcolm charters.
PRINTED. *Inchcolm Chrs*, no. 31.

129 Takes under his firm peace and protection the abbot and convent of Holm Cultram, their lands, their men and all their possessions, movable and immovable, ecclesiastical as well as worldly, as well as their ships, sailors and goods, wherever these may be in the realm, strictly forbidding anyone from causing any harm or injury to them on pain of his full forfeiture. Gives leave for the lay brethren and servants of the abbey to purchase whatever is necessary for their own needs, but not as merchandise. Scone, 1 April a.r. 31 [1280].

Alex*ander* Dei gr*at*ia rex Scottor*um* om*n*ib*us*. p*r*obis ho*min*ibus toci*us* te*rr*e sue salutem. Sciatis nos abbatem et *con*uentu*m* de Holmcult*ran*. te*rr*as suas. h*omin*es suos. et vniue*r*sas eor*undem* possessiones. ac om*n*ia bona sua mobilia et im*m*obilia. ecclesiastica et mundana. que h*abe*nt infra regnu*m* n*ost*rum. naues e*tiam* suas cum nautis et cet*e*ris h*omin*ib*us* et bonis suis i*n* eisd*em* nauib*us* co*n*tentis et existentibus vbicu*mque* infr*a* regnu*m* n*ost*r*u*m applicuerint. et infr*a* limites regie n*ost*re potestatis. ta*m* in mari q*u*am ext*ra* sub firma pace et speciali p*r*oteccio*ne* n*ost*ra iuste suscepisse. Q*ua*re firmit*er* p*r*ohibem*us*. ne q*ui*s eis malum. molestia*m* i*n*iuriam. aut g*rau*ame*n* aliq*u*od infe*rr*e p*r*esumat i*n*iuste sup*er* nostram plenaria*m* forisf*ac*tura*m*. Dam*us* e*tiam* eidem abb*a*ti et *con*uentui licencia*m* n*ost*ram speciale*m* ubi*cumque* inf*ra* regnu*m* n*ost*r*u*m eme*n*di per conuersos et e*tiam* se*r*uientes suos ea q*ue* vsui p*ro*p*rio* s*ibi* fue*r*int nece*ssaria*. ita lib*er*e et plenarie sic*ut* cet*er*i viri religiosi de regno n*ost*ro n*ecessaria* sua infra regnu*m* n*ost*rum venant*ur*. Ex*ceptis*. modo et vsu m*er*candi. Testib*us*. Alex*andro* Cumyn com*ite* de Buchan constabular*io* et justic*iario* Scoc*ie*. Will*el*mo de Sules justic*iario* Laudon*ie*. Reginaldo le Chen p*at*re. Symone Fras*er*. Will*el*mo de S*anct*o Claro. ap*ud* Scon' primo die Aprilis. anno regni nostri. t*ri*cesimo primo.

SOURCE. Cumbria Record Office, Carlisle D and C Muniments Register of Holm Cultram Abbey, fos. 235–6.
PRINTED. *Holm Cultram*, no. 267 (cal.).

130 Gives, grants and by this charter confirms to William de St Clair the land of Inverleith (Midlothian), resigned and quitclaimed by Nicholas the baker, his former servant, who held it of the king's ancestors by a charter of William king of Scots. Also grants that William may freely grind the corn for his own house at the king's mill, but that his men must pay multure. Haddington, 8 April a.r. 31 [1280].

Alexander Dei gracia rex Scottorum omnibus probis hominibus totius terre sue salutem. Cum Nicholaus pistor quondam seruiens noster nobis resignauerit per fustum et baculum terram de Inuerlech[a] cum pertinentiis suis quam idem Nicholaus de antecessoribus nostris et nobis[b] quondam tenuit per cartam bone memorie Willielmi regis Scottorum illustris noueritis nos eandem terram de Inuyrlech[a] dedisse concessisse et hac presenti carta nostra confirmasse Willielmo de Sancto Claro militi et heredibus suis. Tenendam et habendam sibi et heredibus suis de nobis et heredibus nostris cum omnibus justis pertinentiis. Concessimus etiam eidem Willielmo et heredibus suis ut bladum suum de domo sua propria molant ad molendinum nostrum libere absque multura aliqua inde danda sed homines sui multuram dent. Testibus Willielmo de Soulys justiciario Laodonie, Hugone de Perisby, Thoma Ranulph', Simone Fraser, Nicholao de Haya et Nicholao de Veteri Ponte. Apud Hadington octauo die Aprilis anno regni nostri tricesimo primo.

NOTES. [a] Inuerleth in printed version. [b] The printed version omits et nobis'.
SOURCE. NLS, Adv. MS 32.6.2, fo. 4^{r}, a little book of notes and transcripts of original charters made by Augustine Hay, probably between 1686 and 1690. In 1849 the original was said to be in the possession of W. E. Aytoun of Edinburgh; its present location is unknown.
PRINTED. *Newbattle Registrum*, App., Cartae Originales, App. 1, no. 5; Hay, *Sainteclaires*, 43.
COMMENT. See also above, no. 126. Hay noted that the original had a seal in white wax, 'the king on horsback the hors covered wth a cloth upon which is seen a lyon rampan in a double tresshur floure and contriflour. The reverse the king in a seet of justice'.

131 Gives, grants and by this charter confirms to Henry, monk of Farne Island (Northumberland), and the monks who come after him 8s in free alms annually from the ferme of the king's mill at Berwick, in return for the half-chalder of wheat that he customarily received from the same source by the charter of the king's grandfather, William king of Scots. He commands the sheriff of Berwick and the tenants at ferme of the said mill to ensure that the said monks have the 8s annually without disturbance. Berwick, 4 July a.r. 31 [1280].

Alex*ander* Dei *gra*tia rex Scott*orum* . omnibus probis hominibus tocius terre sue sal*ute*m . Sciatis nos dedisse concessisse et hac carta n*ost*ra confirmasse Henrico monacho qui Deo et s*anct*o Cudhberto seruit in Farneland' et monachis ei ibidem successuris et Deo seruituris . octo solidos sterlingor*um* in liberam elemosinam recipiend*os* annuatim de fi*r*ma molendini n*ost*ri de Berewyc' . p*ro* dimidia celdra frumenti q*ua*m de firma d*ict*i molendini annuatim p*er*cipere consueuit p*er* cartam inclite recordat*i*onis d*omi*ni Will*elm*i regis Scocie aui n*ost*ri

. Quare p*r*ecipimus vicecomiti n*ost*ro de Berewyc' et firmariis n*ost*ris qui d*ict*um molendinum n*ost*rum de Berewyc' tenuerint ad f*ir*mam . quatin*us* p*r*edic*t*os octo solidos sine disturbat*i*one h*ab*ere faciant annuatim p*r*edic*t*is monachis ad Pentecosten . In cui*us* rei testimoniu*m* has n*ost*ras l*itt*eras fieri fecimus patentes . Testibus Joh*ann*e de Lyndesey cam*er*ario . Thoma Ranulph' et Bernardo de Monte Alto apud Berewyc' . quarto die Julii anno regni n*ost*ri . xxx . p*ri*mo.

ENDORSED. 1. De \Alexandro/ rege Scocie. De viii s. concessis monachis Farne commorantibus (contemporary). 2. Carta Alexandri regis etc. vt supra . O . secunda sexte. (fourteeth-century hand; the last three words referring to a press mark).

DESCRIPTION. 19.1 cm x 8.6 cm; fold 2.5 cm. Sealing: on a tag, 2.5 cm broad, through single slits, there appears the second great seal, 8.1 cm in diameter, in natural wax varnished brown. Although the edges are broken away and the surface is rubbed, the seal is in good condition, with the images clear on the obverse and reverse.

HAND. Scribe N.

SOURCE. Original. Durham, Muniments of the Dean and Chapter, Misc. Ch. 631.

PRINTED. Raine, *North Durham*, no. 77.

132 Announces that, at Roxburgh on the feast of St James the Apostle, 1281, a final agreement has been made on behalf of himself and his daughter, Margaret, with the assent of his son, Alexander, and all his council, on the one part, and Peter bishop of Orkney, the nobleman Bjarne, Master Bjarne the chancellor and Brother Maurice of the Friars Minor, envoys of Eric king of Norway, on the other, for the marriage of the said Margaret and Eric, as follows. King Alexander undertakes to give his daughter in marriage to Eric, together with a tocher of 14,000 merks sterling, payable at Bergen in several instalments, namely, the first quarter will be sent to Norway with Margaret, the second will be paid on the feast of St Peter in Chains in the year 1282, the third on the same day in 1283 and the last on the same day in 1284. King Eric's envoys agree, for his part, that he accepts the said Margaret as a bride and will contract marriage with her no later than the feast of the nativity of the Blessed Virgin Mary and, if legitimate business prevents this, no later than the feast of the beheading of St John the Baptist next following. On her wedding day Margaret shall be crowned queen and, if legitimate business prevents this, as soon as possible thereafter. The envoys further promise that King Eric shall assign to Margaret, by his own charter, an estate of land in Norway worth 1,400 merks as a wedding gift and that on the day of their marriage he will ratify *viva voce* her title to the lands; she is to have the said lands even if Eric should die before the wedding takes place. The king of Scotland is to have the option to pay the second half of the tocher in coined money or, if he so chooses, to assign annual land rents to Eric in its place, at the rate of one hundred merks of annual rent for every thousand merks outstanding on the tocher, such lands to be identified and assigned by Pentecost. Following her arrival in Norway, Margaret is to be offered a castle or secure place where she, her household and her dowry money may remain under safe custody until the wedding day. Eric and his chief noblemen promise to provide such custody and Eric in particular promises not to have carnal knowledge of the princess before the wedding. If it should happen that Eric die after the wedding has been celebrated, Margaret is to keep the 1,400 merks of Norwegian land promised her as a wedding gift; thereafter, the same lands are to become her dower. If she chooses not to remain in Norway, she is to be assigned from the Norwegian king's chamber an annual cash sum of 1,400 merks, payable at Bergen. Margaret is to have the right to choose how to collect the monies, either in the form of fermes assigned to her or in cash directly from the king's chamber, and if these are not forthcoming she is to have the right to take possession, once more, of the lands she received as a wedding gift. Within two years of the death of her husband, Margaret is to receive half the tocher that she was assigned, with a first payment due on the feast of St Peter in Chains, the second a year later on the same date, payable at Berwick in Scotland. After Margaret's death the 1,400-merk wedding gift is to be returned to the king of Norway. The first half of the tocher is to be paid after the marriage has been celebrated irrespective of circumstances, as if King Eric had reached the age of maturity, unless he refuses to go ahead with it; if Margaret should die before the tocher payments have been completed, the second half of those monies is to be assigned to her children. If Margaret should die without child or children, the second half of her tocher is to revert to the king of Scots and his heirs. If the king of Norway should die before the wedding and Margaret remains a virgin, she, her household and the portion of her tocher that she has brought with her are to be free to return to Scotland and the marriage agreement is to be considered dissolved, as long as she is not pregnant. If Margaret should die before the marriage the portion of the tocher that she brought with her to Norway is to be returned safely to Scotland. The risk that accompanies the sending back and forth of the various portions of the tocher and wedding gift is to be shared equally between the parties. If it should happen that the king of Scotland die without a legitimate son, and none of his sons leaves lawful issue and Margaret has children by the king of Norway, she and her children shall succeed the king of Scotland and his children, both in the kingdom and in other goods, or she alone shall, even if she is without children, according to Scottish law and custom; and the king of Scotland agrees generally that his daughter and all her descendants shall be freely admitted to all successions and all other rights which can belong to them according to Scottish law or the custom of the said realm. And if the said king of Norway has a daughter or daughters by Margaret they shall succeed to everything to which they have the right by Norwegian law and custom, including the kingdom itself, if this is the custom. The envoys of King Eric promise and offer pledges on his behalf to observe all the terms of this agreement until the king shall have reached the age of fifteen years, at which time he will ratify it himself. If he should contravene it in any way, they bind him, his heirs and the whole kingdom of Norway itself to pay the king of Scotland and his heirs at Berwick the sum of £100,000 by way of damages, expenses and interest. If Eric should refuse to undertake the marriage once he has reached the age of fifteen years, the envoys agree to surrender the payment of one hundred merks that the king of Scotland has been making annually to the king of Norway, together with the whole land of Orkney and all the rights that the king of Norway and his heirs enjoy in it, and all agreements relating to the king of Scotland's obligation to pay the said hundred merks annually shall be considered null and void. The envoys specify again that the above undertakings regarding Orkney and the hundred-merk annual rent are to be considered valid only for the period between Margaret's departure for Norway and Eric's fifteenth birthday, and only in the event that he should refuse to ratify and then consummate the marriage. The king of Scotland, his daughter and his magnates undertake to observe all of the above until the king of Norway reaches the age of fifteen years and likewise promise to pay the sum of £100,000 by way of damages, expenses and interest to the king of Norway at Bergen if the king or his daughter should in any way contravene it. If it should happen that Margaret refuse to go forward with the marriage, the king of Scotland undertakes to offer Eric, by way of damages, expenses and interest, the whole of [the isle of] Man and all claims that he or his heirs may ever have in it, in addition to the above said £100,000 fine, and all written instruments concerning Scottish title to said lands shall be considered null and void. These undertakings are to be valid only from the time that Margaret sets sail for Norway, and only in the event that she refuses to ratify the marriage once the king of Norway has reached the age of fifteen years. Both parties agree that the dangers of piracy and war may compel them to make other arrangements for the payment of monies; no prejudice is to be held against either if this should become necessary. Once the marriage has been formally undertaken, King Eric has reached the age of fifteen years, has ratified the marriage and then consummated it, none of the contingency-related obligations noted above is to have any validity. The envoys solemnly promise to observe all the arrangements made here and Berner de Bjarkey swears a personal oath on behalf of the king of Norway to do so; they make similar promises and pledges on behalf of the queen, the mother of the king of Norway, and all the magnates of the kingdom. The king of Scotland and his daughter, for their part, promise to observe the agreement, and their envoys in Norway, namely Robert Lupel, knight, and Master Godfrey, swear oaths to this effect. Present on this day and swearing oaths before the council of the king of Scotland and the envoys from Norway were Patrick earl of Dunbar, Donald earl of Mar, Gilbert de Umfraville earl of Angus, Walter earl of Menteith, Duncan earl of Fife, Alexander steward of Scotland, John Comyn, William de Soules justiciar of Lothian, William de Brechin and Patrick son of Patrick earl of Dunbar. Also swearing oaths by means of procurators are Alexander Comyn earl of Buchan and constable of Scotland and Malise earl of Strathearn, specially appointed by the king of Scotland to accompany Margaret to Norway to ensure that the terms of this agreement are observed until the king of Norway should reach the age of fifteen years. Vivenus, knight, brother of Bjarne the knight, John son of Finn, Isaac son of Gauton,

Andrew Petri, Elan Arufinn and Auduenus de Slindon stepped forward and, touching the holy gospels, offered themselves as hostages for the king of Norway's undertaking to observe the agreement, promising to remain in Scotland at the will of the king of Scots until the marriage should be completed and consummated. In return, the king of Scotland promised that he would release the hostages at that time, under pain of quitclaiming to the king of Norway the isle of Man and a further £100,000 in damages. To the part of this chirograph remaining in Scotland the envoys of the king of Norway appended their seals; to the part going back to Norway the king of Scotland appended his. Roxburgh, 25 July 1281.

IN[a] nomine p*at*ris et filii et sp*iritu*s sancti amen . Hec est finalis conuenc*io* f*act*a in festo s*anct*i Jacobi ap*osto*li anno D*omi*ni mille*simo* . ducent*esimo* . octages*imo* . primo apud Rokesburg' int*er* illustrem p*rin*cipem d*omin*um Alexandru*m* Dei g*rat*ia regem Scott*orum* no*mine* suo et no*mine* nobilis domicelle Margarete filie sue k*ariss*ime de consensu d*omi*ni Alex*andri* filii sui et toci*us* consilii d*ict*i d*omi*ni reg*is* ex p*ar*te una et venerabile*m* p*at*rem d*omin*um Petrum Orchadens' e*pisco*pum . et nobilem virum d*omi*ni Bernerium baron*em* mag*is*tr*u*m Bernardum cancellariu*m* et f*rat*rem Mauricium de ordin*e* minor*um* p*ro*curatores et nu*n*cios sollempnes et sp*eci*ales d*omi*ni Eryci Dei g*rat*ia regis Norwagi*e* illust*ri*s ex alt*era* . super sponsalib*us* cont*ra*ctis et mat*rimo*n*io* cont*ra*hendo int*er* prefatum d*omin*um rege*m* Norwag*ie* et d*ict*am nobilem domicellam Marga*reta*m . videlicet q*uo*d dom*in*us rex Scoc*ie* dat d*ict*am Margareta*m* filiam suam d*ict*o d*omi*no Eryco regi Norwag*ie* in vxorem. et p*ro*mittit et dabit cu*m* ea q*ua*tuordecim milia marcarum st*er*lingor*um* noue et vsualis monete in dotem . Ita qu*od* q*ui*nq*ui*es viginti marce p*ro* q*ui*buslibet centu*m* marc*is* computent*ur* et soluent*ur* apud Bergys' in Noruuag*ia* su*m*ptibus regis Scoc*ie* t*er*minis infra sc*ri*ptis . videlicet q*uo*d quarta pars p*redict*e sum*m*e portabit*ur* cum d*ict*a Margar*eta* in Noruuagi*am* . et s*ecun*da q*ua*rta p*redict*e sum*m*e ad festum b*eat*i Petri ad vinc*u*la anno D*omi*ni mill*esimo* ducent*esimo* octag*esimo* secundo . et tercia quarta in festo eodem anno D*omi*ni mill*esimo* . ducent*esimo* . octoges*imo* . tercio . et ultima quarta in eodem festo anno D*omi*ni mill*esimo* . ducent*esimo* . octogesimo . quarto . Et d*ict*i p*ro*curatores promittunt fidelit*er* p*ro* d*omi*no suo . ip*s*um s*u*b penis infra sc*ri*ptis arcius obliga*n*do . q*uo*d idem rex Norwag*ie* d*ict*am domicella*m* accipiet in uxorem et cu*m* ea mat*rimo*-*niu*m cont*ra*het et nupcias celeb*ra*bit ad tardius infra festum natiuitat*is* b*eat*e Virginis nisi legittimum int*er*uen*er*it impedime*ntu*m et tunc quamcici*us* fi*er*i pot*er*it et adcici*us* post crastinu*m* decollac*io*nis s*anct*i Johannis Baptiste . Et die nupciar*um* d*ict*a Margareta coronabit*ur* in reginam nisi legittim*um* *con*stit*er*it impedimentum . et tunc om*n*em apponent diligencia*m* rex Norwag*ie* et regni magnates . quod quam cicius fi*er*i pot*er*it coronet*ur* . Et promittunt d*ict*i p*ro*curatores q*uo*d d*omi*nus rex Noruuag*ie* mille et q*ua*dringentas marcatas t*er*re de moneta sua Norichana usuali nunc temp*or*is u*e*l ad eius valorem . si ip*s*a mutetur . cu*m* man*er*io co*m*petenti in donac*io*nem p*ropt*er nupcias d*ict*e domicelle Marg*arete* p*er* carta*m* d*ict*i regis eid*em* assignatas et prout ibi continetur die nupciar*um* viua uoce ratificabit et confirmabit . ita quod . si huma*n*itus de d*ict*o rege Noruuagi*e* contingat . q*uo*d absit . d*ict*a Margareta d*ict*ar*um* t*er*rar*um* possessionem p*ro*p*ri*a auctoritate p*er* p*re*d*ict*as l*itt*eras regias possit apprehend*er*e et tenere . Et sciendu*m* q*uo*d erit in opc*i*one d*omi*ni regis Scoc*ie* secu*n*dam medietate*m* dotis in pecunia num*er*ata solu*er*e u*e*l t*er*ras ex ea u*e*l ex parte ip*s*ius suis t*er*minis soluenda co*m*paratas assignare . ita q*uo*d ex illis terris p*ro* singulis mille marc*is* centu*m* marce no*min*e redditus p*er*cipiantur illo anno et sic ult*er*ius an*n*uatim opc*i*onem siquidem h*ab*et d*ict*us d*omi*nus rex Scoc*ie* du*m* tamen in festo Pentecost*en* ante tempus soluc*io*nis regi Norwagi*e* intimet*ur* q*uo*d t*er*ras velit om*n*es assignare loco competenti et simul u*e*l loco uiciniori et magis ydoneo q*uo* poterunt ad comparandum inueniri . d*ic*to regi Norwagi*e* constante matr*im*o*n*io lib*er*e tenendas et habendas . Dicte uera Margarete p*ost*q*ua*m t*er*ram Norwagi*e* fuerit ingressa certum castrum u*e*l securum man*er*ium prout ip*s*a et sui eleg*er*int statim assignabitur . in quo ip*s*a cu*m* familia sua et d*ict*a pecunia sub custodia regis Scoc*ie* et suor*um* sumptibus regis Norwagi*e* . q*uo*usq*ue* nupcie celebrent*ur* saluo et secure possint morari . Et rex Noruuagi*e* et regni magnates ip*s*am cu*m* familia sua et d*ict*a pecunia saluo et secure interim facient custodiri . ita quod nullum ad eam rex Norwagi*e* inhonestu*m* accessum int*er*im h*ab*eat u*e*l carnalem . Quod si rex Norwagi*e* post nupcias celebratas p*re*decedat d*ict*a Margar*eta* donac*io*nem illam p*ro*pt*er* nupcias eodem anno integr*e* p*er*cipiet . et [sic u]lt*er*ius[b] annuatim scilicet d*ict*as mille et q*ua*dringentas marcatas t*er*re s*ibi* assignatas si velit in t*er*ra Noruuagi*e* mora*m* fac*er*e . Si autem velit moram fac*er*e ext*ra* regnum Noruuagi*e* . mille et q*ua*dringentas marcas vbicu*m*q*ue* co*n*uer*s*etur de cam*er*a regis Norwagi*e* lib*er*e p*er*cipiet annuatim apud Bergys' . Ita quod erit in op*t*ione d*ict*e Margar*et*e fi*r*mas illar*um* t*er*rarum sibi assignatar*um* suis t*er*minis s*ecun*d*um* co*n*suetudi*n*em patr*ie* p*er* p*ro*cur*a*torem suu*m* in t*er*ra recip*er*e . vel de cam*er*a regis in festo Pentecost*en* anno seq*ue*nti et sic vlterius annuatim d*ict*am pecunia*m* p*er*cip*er*e apud Bergys' . veru*m*pt*am*en in def*ect*um soluc*io*nis recursum h*ab*eat ad t*er*ras s*ibi* assignatas r*ati*one donac*i*onis propter nupcias . Et nich*il*ominus debet h*ab*ere d*ict*a Margar*eta* q*ui*cq*ui*d regina du*m* vidua fu*er*it ibidem com*m*orans h*ab*ere debet s*ecun*d*um* [leges patrie et c][b]onsuetudi*n*em regionis approbata*m* . Et p*re*t*er*ea h*ab*ebit medietate*m* toci*us* dotis infra bienniu*m* proximo seq*ue*ns p*os*t morte*m* reg*is* . ita quod una medietas illi*us* medietatis p*ri*mo anno in festo sancti Pet*ri* ad vinc*u*la . et alia medietas s*ecun*do anno in eodem festo nisi p*ri*us in Norwagi*a* soluta fu*er*it . apud Berewic*um* in Scocia p*er*solu*etur* . D*ict*a u*er*o donac*i*o p*ro*pt*er* nupcias p*os*t morte*m* d*ict*e Margar*ete* ad rege*m* Noruuagi*e* redibit . p*ri*ma u*er*o medietas toci*us* . dotis suis t*er*minis solue*n*da post nupcias celebratas in o*mn*em euentu*m* regis Noruaggi*e* . nisi in illo casu si a matr*im*o*n*io resilierit cu*m* fu*er*it legitti*m*e etatis . pleno iure efficiet*ur* . alia u*er*o medietas toci*us* dotis u*e*l t*er*re pro ea in Scoc*ia* assignate p*ost* morte*m* d*ict*e Margar*ete* ad liberos suos siq*ui*s habu*er*it in o*mn*em euentu*m* p*er*tinebit . sup*er* quo regi Noruuagi*e* cauebitur ydonee p*ro*ut ipsa pot*er*it q*ua*ncu*n*q*ue* velit d*ict*am pecuniam ext*ra* regnu*m* Noruuag*ie* h*ab*ere si h*ab*eat liberos uel liberum in Norwag*ia* sup*er*stites u*e*l sup*er*stitem . ad q*uo*s u*e*l ad q*ue*m d*ict*a sum*m*a pecunie de iure debeat p*er*tinere . Si uero d*ict*a Margareta sine libero u*e*l lib*er*is moriat*ur* d*ict*a vltima dotis medietas ad rege*m* Scoc*ie* et ip*s*ius regis h*er*edes redibit . Si u*er*o d*omin*us rex Norwag*ie* an*te* nupcias celeb*ra*tas in fata decedat . d*ict*a Margar*eta* illibata et non cognita lib*ere* p*er* om*n*ibus de regno Norwag*ie* cu*m* tota pecunia secu*m* portata sumptib*us* regis Norwag*ie* et magnatu*m* suor*um* in Scociam reducet*ur* . Idem erit de d*ict*a Margar*eta* q*uo*d ip*s*a in o*mn*em euentu*m* nisi p*re*gnans fu*er*it lib*ere* possit reu*er*ti mat*ri*monio dissoluto . Si uero d*ict*a Margar*eta* ante nupcias celeb*ra*tas in fata decedat . tota d*ict*a pecunia nomine dotis secum portata eodem modo ut in clausula sup*er*iori d*ict*o regi Scoc*ie* ap*u*d Berewic*um* in Scoc*ia* reportabit*ur* . Et sciend*um* est q*uo*d in om*n*i portac*i*one et reportac*i*one dotis et cui*us*cumq*ue* p*ar*tis ei*us* q*uan*docu*m*q*ue* p*er*ic*ul*um *con*tig*er*it . com*m*une erit vt*raque* parti p*ro* equalib*us* porc*i*onibus . Si u*er*o *con*tingat q*uo*d d*omi*nus rex Scoc*ie* sine filio legitt*im*o infata decedat n*ec* aliq*ui*s filior*um* suor*um* p*ro*lem legittimam reliqu*er*it et d*ict*a Marg*areta* ex d*ict*o rege Norwag*ie* liberos h*ab*u*er*it . ip*s*a et lib*er*i sui succedent d*ict*o regi Scoc*ie* et lib*er*is suis . tam in regno q*ua*m in aliis bonis . uel ip*s*a eciam si fu*er*it absq*ue* lib*er*is s*ecundu*m legem et *con*suetudi*n*em Scoticana*m* . Et gen*er*al*iter* consensit d*ict*us rex Scoc*ie* q*uod* d*ict*a filia sua et om*n*es ex ea descende*n*tes admittant*ur* lib*er*e ad om*n*es successiones et ad o*m*nia alia iura q*ue* ip*s*os conting*er*e possint quoq*uo* modo s*ecund*um legem Scoticana*m* vel d*ict*e regionis *con*suetudi*n*em . Et si d*ict*us rex Norwag*ie* de d*ict*a Margar*eta* filiam u*e*l filias p*ro*creau*er*it . succedent in om*n*ib*us* que ip*s*am u*e*l ip*s*as conting*er*e possunt s*ecund*um leges et *con*suetudi*n*es Norichanas eciam in regno si consuetudo fu*er*it . D*ict*i uero nu*n*cii et p*ro*curatores no*min*e regis Norwag*ie* p*ro*miseru*n*t et manuceperunt ip*s*um regem arci*us* obligando q*uod* omnia et sing*u*la sup*er*ius *con*tenta ex nu*n*c rata et firma h*abe*buntur q*uo*usq*ue* d*ict*us rex Norwag*ie* fu*er*it q*ua*tuordecim anno*rum* co*m*pletor*um* et tu*n*c ea plene ratificabit . Et si *con*tingat q*uod* absit p*re*d*ict*um rege*m* Norwag*ie* in aliquo usq*ue* ad illud temp*us* u*e*l in illo temp*or*e *contra*uenire . d*ict*i p*ro*curatores obligant ip*s*um regem . heredes suos . et regnum Norwag*ie* . seip*s*os et h*er*edes suos ad soluend*um* et dandu*m* d*ict*o regi Scoc*ie* et h*er*edib*us* suis u*e*l assignatis centu*m* milli*a* librar*um* bonor*um* et legaliu*m* st*er*lingor*um* in villa de Be*re*wico in Scoc*ia* no*min*e et r*ati*one dampnor*um* . expensar*um* et int*er*esse . Obligau*er*unt e*tiam* d*ict*o regi Scoc*ie* illust*ri* p*ro* dampnis . exp*en*sis . et interesse . in illum casum ta*ntu*m . si rex Norwag*ie* non ratificau*er*it[c] mat*ri*mo*n*ium cum fu*er*it q*ua*tuordecim anno*rum* completor*um* sum*m*am centu*m* marcar*um* q*ua*m dic*t*us rex Norwag*ie* ab eo p*er*cipit annuatim . et totam t*er*ram Orchadie cu*m* om*n*i iure quod d*ict*us rex Norwag*ie* h*abe*t uel h*ab*ere pot*er*it in eade*m* . ita q*uod* predi*ct*e tam sum*m*a q*ua*m t*er*ra cu*m* p*er*tinenciis d*ict*o regi Scoc*ie* et h*er*edibus suis ex tunc . remaneant imp*er*petuu*m* in feodo et h*er*editate . cu*m* rex Norwag*ie* noluerit d*ict*um mat*ri*mo*n*i*um* ratificare u*e*l dampna . expensas . et int*eresse* . vno cu*m* pena p*re*d*ict*a cent*um* mille libr*arum* regi Scoc*ie* et h*er*edibus suis u*e*l assignatis resarcire . Et instrumenta q*ue* h*abe*t penes se d*ict*us rex Norwagie sup*er* d*ict*a sum*m*a pecunie cent*um* marcar*um* annuatim p*er*cipienda ex tu*n*c virib*us* careant et cassa sint et irrita ip*s*o iure . inst*ru*mentis q*ui*ete clamac*io*nis d*ic*ti regis Norwag*ie* sup*er* insulis penes regem Scocie residentib*us* . in suo nich*il*ominus robore duraturis . Et sciendu*m* e*ss*e quod obligac*i*o de te*r*ra Orchadie et de redditu cent*um* marcar*um* t*a*m h*abe*t locu*m* a temp*o*re t*ra*nsfretac*io*nis d*ic*te domicelle in Norwagia*m* . q*uo*usq*ue* d*ict*us rex Noruuagie fu*er*it q*ua*tuordecim annor*um* completorum . solu*m*modo in illu*m* casum si rex Norwag*ie* cu*m* fu*er*it q*ua*tuordecim annor*um* co*m*pletor*um* cont*ra* d*ict*um mat*r*imo*n*ium reclamauerit et illud nolu*er*it ratificare et co*n*sum*m*are . D*ict*us u*er*o rex Scoc*ie* nomi*n*e suo et filie sue ac magnates regni promiserunt se arci*u*s obligando . q*uod* o*m*nia et sing*u*la superi*u*s contenta ex nu*n*c . rata et firma habebun*t*ur q*uo*usq*ue* rex Norwag*ie* fu*er*it etatis q*ua*tuordec*i*m annor*um* . completor*um* . Et si *con*tingat q*uod* absit d*ict*um rege*m* Scoc*ie* u*e*l filiam suam usq*ue* ad illud temp*us* in aliquot *contra*uenire . obligat ip*s*e rex Scoc*ie* . se et h*er*edes suos et regnu*m* Scoc*ie* ad . soluendu*m* et dandu*m* dic*t*o regi Norwag*ie* et h*er*edib*us* suis uel suis assignatis cent*um* millia lib*ra*rum bonor*um* et legaliu*m* ste*r*lingor*um* ap*u*d ciuitatem Bergens'. in Norwag*ia* no*m*i*n*e et r*ati*one dampnor*um* . expensar*um* et inte*r*esse . Obligau*it* eciam d*ict*us rex Scoc*ie* . d*ict*o regi Norwag*ie* p*r*o dampnis . expe*n*sis . et inte*r*esse . in illum casum . ta*ntu*m si dic*t*a filia reg*is* Scoc*ie* a d*ict*o *con*tractu resilierit ant*e*quam d*ict*us rex Norwag*ie* fu*er*it q*ua*tuordecim annor*um* completor*um* et mat*r*imo*n*ium fu*er*it ratificatu*m* . totam Manniam cu*m* o*m*n*i* iure quod d*i*ctus rex Scoc*ie* h*abe*t uel habe*r*e pote*r*it in eadem . ita q*uod* p*r*ed*ict*a te*r*ra cu*m* pertinenciis d*ict*o regi Norwag*ie* et h*er*edib*us* suis ex tunc remaneat in feodo et h*er*editate . cu*m* d*ict*a filia regis Scoc*ie* d*ict*um mat*r*imo*n*ium nolu*er*it ratificare et co*n*sum*m*are . ve*l* dampna . expe*n*sis . et int*er*esse . vna cu*m* p*r*ed*ict*a pena cent*um* mill*ia* libr*arum* d*ict*o regi Norwag*ie* *u*el h*er*edib*us* suis u*e*l assignat*is* resarcire . Et inst*ru*menta q*ui*ete clamac*io*nis d*ict*i regis Norwag*ie* sup*er* d*ict*a insula Mannie que d*ict*us rex Scoc*ie* penes se h*abe*t extunc virib*us* careant et cassa sint et irrata ip*s*o iure . inst*ru*mentis d*ict*i regis Scoc*ie* sup*er* d*ict*a sum*m*a pecunie cent*um* marcar*um* annuatim p*er*cipienda . penes rege*m* Norwag*ie* residentib*us* in suo robore duraturis . Et sciend*um* est q*uod* obliga*t*io de te*r*ra Mannie ta*ntu*m h*abe*t locu*m* a temp*o*re t*ra*nsfretac*io*nis ip*s*ius Margarete et solu*m*modo in illu*m* casum . si d*ict*a Marga*reta* nolu*er*it mat*r*imo*n*i*u*m ratificare *cu*m d*ict*us rex Norwag*ie* fu*er*it q*ua*tuordecim annor*um* completor*um* . Et sciend*um* est q*uod* in om*n*ib*us* p*r*emissis saluu*m* est vt*r*iq*ue* pa*r*ti . q*uod* temp*us* q*uo* pecunia soluetur p*r*o q*u*olibet te*r*mino ex vt*r*aq*ue* pa*r*te pe*r* gwerra*m* pe*r* piratas u*e*l pe*r* aliquem casum fortuitu*m* et inopinatu*m* possit mutari seu p*r*orogari sine pe*r*iculo parcium circa premissa p*r*eiudicio u*e*l iactura . Post *contr*actum u*er*o mat*r*imo*n*ium et p*o*stq*ua*m rex Norwag*ie* fu*er*it q*ua*tuordecim annor*um* *com*pletor*um* . et mat*r*imo*n*ium ratificau*er*it et q*u*antum in ipso e*ss*e *con*summau*er*it . p*r*ed*ict*e . obligac*io*nes penales locu*m* no*n* h*abe*nt ne*c* in *duobus* casibus t*am* . scilic*et* q*uod* ipsa libere possit a Norwag*ia* recedere . Et si ip*s*a et lib*er*i ex ea descendentes ad successiones et ad alia iura libere non admittantur in qualibet uero solucione pecunie suo termino hinc inde soluende . tam ante matrimonium quam post si defectus aliquis fuerit tantum erit pena dupli illius quantitatis siue summe hinc inde soluende que suo termino solui debet . Et sciendum quod ad maiorem huius rei securitatem dicti procuratores habentes ad hoc plenum et speciale mandatum ratificant nomine domini regis Norwagie iuramentum a domino Bernerio de Berkrey in animam ipsius regis prestitum super isto contractu sponsalium et matrimonii et omnia alia in isto scripto cyrographato contenta . Item promittunt fideliter dicti procuratores et manucapiunt . quod domina regina mater dicti regis Norwagie et magnates regni Norwagie qui super hoc contractu iurauerunt quamcicius presentes haberi poterunt in presencia nunciorum regis Scocie . iuramenta sua prius prestita ratificabunt . et omnia alia hic contenta secundum huius scripture tenorem . Dicti uero dominus rex Scocie et domina Margareta filia sua in presencia nunciorum regis Norwagie similiter ratificauerunt sacramenta per procuratores suos uidelicet dominum Robertum Lupellum militem et magistrum Godefridum in animas ipsorum in Norwagia . prestita . Item ratificant omnia in hoc scripto contenta . Item iurauerunt in presencia prenominatorum nunciorum regis Norwagie . Patricius comes de Dunbar' . Douenaldus comes de Marr' . Gilbertus de Humfrauill' comes de Anegus' . Walterus comes de Menetheth' . Duncanus comes de Fif'. Alexander senescallus Scocie . Johannes Comin . Willelmus de Sulys tunc justiciarius Laudonie . Willelmus de Breyham' . et Patricius filius dicti Patricii comitis de Dunbar' personaliter qui tunc coram domino rege . consilio suo . et dictis nunciis regis Norwagie presentes fuerunt . Iurauerunt eciam Alexander Comyn comes de Bouchan' constabularius Scocie . necnon Malisius comes de Strathern' in presencia dictorum nunciorum regis Norwagie per procuratores suos habentes ad hoc speciale mandatum sicut patet in eorum litteris patentibus inde confectis . videlicet se curaturos et procuraturos . quod omnia et singula ex parte illustris principis domini Alexandri Dei gratia regis Scottorum[d] et nobilis domicelle Margarete filie sue super federe matrimonii inter dominum Erycum regem Norwagie et dictam domicellam premissa et conuenta firmiter et inuiolabiliter obseruentur . prout in isto instrumento plenius continetur . quousque dictus dominus rex Norwagie fuerit quatuordecim annorum completorum et matrimonium ratificauerit et consummauerit quantum in ipso est . Preterea sciendum est quod Vivenus miles frater Bernerii militis . Johannes filius Finni . Isaac filius Gautonis . Andreas Petri . Elanus Arufinni . Auduenus[e] de Slindon' . spontanee et expresse consencientes et tactis sacrosanctis euangeliis iurantes promittunt bona fide quod in Scocia stabunt tanquam obsides ad voluntatem dicti regis Scocie . nec a regno Scocie sine expressa licencia domini regis Scocie recedent . quousque rex Norwagie fuerit quatuordecim annorum completorum et matrimonium inter ipsum et dictam Margaretam ratificauerit et quantum in ipso est consummauerit . Obligauit eciam dictus dominus rex Scocie totam Manniam cum pertinentiis pro centum milibus librarum et dampnis . expensis et interesse . in illum casum si dictos obsides cum dictus rex Norwagie compleu*er*it q*ua*tuordecim annos et mat*ri*mo*niu*m q*ua*ntum in ipso est co*n*summau*er*it . apud Berewic*um* si eos p*ri*us ibidem recep*er*it nisi casus mortis *uel* alius casus legittim*us* p*ro*pedierit . u*e*l p*ro*pria voluntate recesserint . libere no*n* dimittat . In cui*us* rei testimo*niu*m p*ar*ti illius cyrographi penes dominum regem Scoc*ie* residenti . d*ic*ti procuratores regis Norwag*ie* . sigilla sua apposueru*nt* . P*ar*ti uero residenti penes *dictos* procuratores . sigillum d*ic*ti d*omi*ni regis Scoc*ie* . est appensum .

NOTES. [a] Decorated initial. [b] Hole in MS; word supplied from *Dipl. Norveg.* [c] Ratificauit, sic, in *Dipl. Norveg.* [d] Scocie, sic, in *Diplom. Norveg.* [e] Auduennus, sic, in *Diplom. Norveg.*

ENDORSED. 1. Scriptum cirographatum apud Berwyc'. 2. Duplicatum set alterum eorum fuit missum in Norwagiam set fuit reportatum et submersum cum nuncios regis (both contemporary hands).

DESCRIPTION. 52.3 cm x 29.0 cm; top edge of MS is cut into thirteen teeth (with half-teeth on left and right) with letters spelling out 'cyrographum' visible on some teeth. Initial I is decorated, though not coloured, and extends down six lines of text on left margin. No seals or tags, but there are double slits for four sets of tags. The parchment is torn away at three of the slits.

HAND. Scribe R. The document is written in a small, neat book hand, no doubt meant to emphasise the solemnity of the agreement.

SOURCE. Original. NRS, Documents transferred from the Public Record Office, London, RH 5/6.

PRINTED. *APS*, i, 421–4 (with several mistakes); *Foedera*, I, ii, 595–6; *Dipl. Norveg.*, xix, no. 305; *CDS*, ii, no. 197 (note); *L & I*, vol. xlix, 187 (note).

COMMENT. The endorsement makes reference to the loss at sea of the ship that carried the abbot of Balmerino (probably William de Perisby), Bernard Mowat and 'many others' back to Scotland following the marriage (*Chron. Fordun*, i, 307–8; *Scotichronicon*, v, 41). Recovered, but badly damaged, were several records relating to Scoto-Norse diplomatic relations. *APS*, i, 109–10. The lands assigned to Eric in place of the second half of the tocher were those of Rothiemay (Banffshire), Belhelvie (Aberdeenshire), Bathgate (West Lothian) and Ratho (Midlothian) and, if necessary to make up 700 merks per annum, Menmuir in Angus. Payment of the tocher instalments ceased even before Alexander III had died. In the summer of 1292, King Eric sent a petition to Edward I's Berwick parliament seeking a resumption of the payments: the latter granted him only a lifetime interest in them (*PROME*, i, 596–8). Eric's efforts to recover his lands are examined in K. Helle, 'Norwegian Foreign Policy and the Maid of Norway', *SHR*, 69 (1990), 148–50. The identity of the Norwegian envoys is discussed in J. Beveridge, 'Two Scottish Thirteenth-century Songs, with the Original Melodies, Recently Discovered in Sweden', *PSAS*, 73 (1938–9), 277: they included Bjarne Erlingsson, baron of Bjarkey, whose father had fought at the battle of Largs, and the Norwegian chancellor, Bjarne Lodinsson, who appears in the Latin text here as Bernardus.

133 Announces that, together with the barons of his council, he has reviewed the ancient customs and practices of the kingdom of Scotland in use since time immemorial and now still in use for the succession to the throne, with reference to the forthcoming marriage of his son, Alexander, to Marguerite, eldest daughter of Guy count of Flanders, marquis of Namur and Isabelle daughter of the count of Luxemburg, as follows. That if the son and heir male of a king of Scots has an heir and the former predeceases the king, the heir of this son remains and must remain heir to the kingdom of Scotland. Thus, if it should happen that Prince Alexander and his wife Marguerite should marry and have male issue, the latter shall be the lawful heir to the kingdom of Scotland. If Prince Alexander should predecease his father and he has brothers they shall not have any claim to the kingdom by reason of heritage. If Marguerite should predecease her husband before producing heirs male and the prince takes another wife from whom he has male issue, the latter shall become heir to the kingdom without prejudice. If the heirs male of the prince's second marriage should die without male heirs, the kingdom of Scotland shall revert and return in its entirety to the eldest female child of Prince Alexander and his wife Marguerite; the same shall happen if King Alexander should marry a second time and any heir male of that marriage fail to produce issue. Members of the royal council, and the king himself in the person of Simon Fraser, take an oath to abide by the ancient custom and practices set out here and renounce any custom or practice that might overturn them or might be prejudicial to Marguerite and her above-mentioned heirs. The king commands that all the barons of Scotland, that is, bishops, earls and others, as well as their heirs, swear an oath to observe these customs and practices; he also requests, by these letters, that the pope approve them. The following men, namely William bishop of St Andrews, William bishop of Brechin, Hugh bishop of Aberdeen, Robert bishop of Glasgow and Robert bishop of Strathern,[a] Alexander earl of Buchan called Comyn, Malise earl of Strathearn, Patrick earl of Dunbar, Duncan earl of Mar, Duncan earl of Fife, Robert de Bruce earl of Carrick, John Comyn, Alexander de Balliol, William de Moravia, William de Soules and William de St Clair, knight, members of the king's council, affirm that the arrangements set out above are and have been the custom and practice used in the kingdom since time immemorial and swear faithfully that they will recognise the heir of Prince Alexander as the lawful claimant to the kingdom of Scotland and forswear any arrangements to the contrary. They also ask that the pope confirm these matters, as the king has requested. c. 4 December 1281.

Alixandres par le grasse de Dieu rois Descoche a tous chiaus ki ces p*re*sentes lettres verront e oront . salut en n*ost*re Signeur . Com*me* il soit ensi ke Alixandres nos ainsnes fiex et nos oirs . ait p*ro*pos et volente . de prendre a femme . e a espeuse Margheritain . ainsnee fille de haut houme e noble Guion conte de Flandres e marchis de Namur ke il a de noble dame . Yssabiel se feme fille au conte de Lussenbourch . nous enseurte e pour lefforchement de chelui mariaghe . faisons sauoir a tous dou consel des barons de no rengne . e affermons en boin*ne* foi sans mauvais enghien ke coustume et vssaghes ont este tel ou roiaume Descoche de si lonch tans de coi il nest point de memoire . e sont encore . ke se fiez de roi Descoche et ses oirs malles . a oirs de se p*ro*pre char . e muire cil fiex ainscois . ke li rois ses pere. li oir ki seront issu de cel fil . demeurent . e doiuent demourer airete del roiame . Dont sil auenoit chose ke chius Alixandres nos fiex . et cele Margherite sasanbloient par mariaghe e eussent oirs malles de leur deus chars . chil oir ki diaus deus seroient issu demouroient airete del roiaume Descoche selonch le coustume et lussaghe deuantdis . tout fust il ensi ke chius Alixandres morust deuant nous . ne ne poroit oirs ki de nous issist riens demander au roiaume par raison diretaghe . Et est a sauoir ke se chele Margherite moroit ainscois ke chius Alixandres e de li ne demouroit oirs malles . e chius Alixandres prendroit autre fem*me* de le quele il eust oir malles nous ne volons ne nentendons ke a chelui oir malle soit nus prejudisses fais ke il nait se droite escanche el roiaume Descoche selonch le coustume et lussaghe devantdis . E si li oirs malles ki de chelui Alixandre seroit issus de sen secont mariaghe moroit sains oir de sa char li roiaumes Descoche tout entirement revenroit . et revenir deueroit a lainsnet oir femelle ki seroit issus e demoures Dalixandre e de Margheritain deuant noumes . Sensi nestoit ke nous eussiens oir malle de no char . e se chius oirs malles ki de nous seroit issus dautre mariaghe nauoit oir de se char nous volons ke li roiaumes revingnes a loir femelle ki seroit issus Dalissandre no fil et de Margheritain deuant noumes . Et nous le coustume e lussaghe devantdis loons et approuvons comme sires . et proumetons par no sairement fait en no nom e pour nous par no foiaule chev*alier* Simon Fresiel a cui nous donno*n*s plain pooir de faire cel sairement en nostre ame ke nous encontre ces coustumes et ces vssaghes ne venrons . ne venir par autrui ferons en nule maniere . ne art ne enghien querrons fraude ne boidie par coi ces coustumes ne chil usaghe soient enfraint . Et pour chou a tenir fermeme*n*t . oblighons nous nousmeismes e tous nos successeurs par ces p*re*sentes lettres saielees de no saiel . en toutes les manieres ke n*ous* poons . Et quant a chou renonchons nous a tout droit esc*ri*t et no*n* escrit a toute coustume cont*ra*ire a ces choses . a toutes indulgences a toutes grasses a tous p*ri*vileghes empetres pour nous a lapostole e a empetrer e generaume*n*t e especiaume*n*t a toutes exceptions . actions e cauillations ki a nous e a nos successeurs poroient aidier e a cheli Margheritain e a ses oirs greuer . Et mandons e p*ri*ons a tous les barons de no rengne ki sour chou seront requis . vesques . contes e autres ke il toutes ces coustumes e ces vssaghes tesmoignent . appreuvent e loent e proumethent pour iaus . pour leur successeurs . e pour leur oirs par leur fois e par leur sairemens loiaument a tenir toutes ces choses e si sen oblighent souffisaument par leurs saiaus . pour lavanchement del mariaghe deseuredit . et supploions par ces p*re*sentes letres a no saint pere n*ost*re sign*eur* lapostole ke il toutes ces choses daingne co*n*fermer de se autorite en n*ost*re absence e sans autre requeste . E nous par le grasse de Diu Willaumes . evesques de Saint Andriu . Willaumes . evesques de Breskin . Hues . evesques Dabredenne . Robers . evesques de Glascu . e Robers . evesque de Stradierne . nous Alixandres . conte de Bouscan . dis Commins . Malusens quens de Stradierne . Pat*ri*s quens de Donbar . Dounans quens de Mar . Donnekans quens de Fiffich . Robiers . de Bruis quens de Karruch . e nous Jehans Coumins Alixandres de Bailleul Willaumes de Moreve Willaumes de Soles Willaumes de Saint Cler chevalier dele vol*on*te et dou consel n*ost*re chier signeur le roi devantdit et a sen requeste de commun consel de nous tous e par grant deliberation ke nous avons ewe ensanble aweuch le deuantdit roi . disons e affermons le coustume iestre tele . lussaghe iestre tel e auoir este de si lonch tans de coi il nest point de memoire . si com*me* nostre sire li rois la dit deseure e afferme par cest p*re*sent escrit e proumetons par nos sairemens e par le foi ke nous deuons a nostre signeur le roi pour nous . pour nos oirs . e pour nos successeurs ke se oir descendoient de mo*n*signe*ur* Alixandre deuant noumet nous les tenriens . recheveriens e ariens pour drois oirs dou roiaume . Descoche . e pour nos loiaus signeurs sans nul contredit en tiel maniere . ke deuant est deuise . E quant a chou nous reno*n*chons generaument . e especiaume*n*t a toutes exceptions . actions cauillations de droit e de loy ke n*ous* poriens metre avant e alleghier pour iestre encontre ces choses u aucunes deles . Si supplions humilement par le teneur de ces p*re*sentes lettres a no saint pere lapostole ke il de se autorite daingne confermer toutes ces choses en n*ost*re absense sans autre requeste . E pour chou ke ces choses tant com*m*e est en nous soient fermeme*n*t tenues avons nous . aweuch le saiel n*ost*re chier signeur le roi deuant dit . pendus nos saiaus a ces p*re*sentes letres ki furent donnees lan de grasse mil*le* deu cens quatrevins e vn el mois de Decembre .

NOTE. [a] Robert bishop of Strathearn was Robert bishop of Dunblane.

ENDORSED. 1. Scriptum sigillandum sigillis domini regis et magnatum regni. 2. Lettres dou roi dEscoce et des barons dou mariage me damysele (two distinct but contemporary hands).

DESCRIPTION. 44.5 cm x 34.3 cm. Sealing: on narrow parchment tags, through single slits tucked into an elaborately designed fold, there appear the seals of the thirteen barons named above, of varying sizes, as well as the king's second great seal. With the exception of the seal of the bishop of St Andrews, which is in red wax, the magnates' seals are in white wax. The king's seal is in white wax, 10.0 cm in diameter, and is in near-perfect condition. There are casts of the obverse and reverse of this seal in NRS, RH 1/17, Drawer 2, nos 13, 14.

HAND. Scribe S.

SOURCE. Original. Archives de l'état à Namur, Chartes de Namur, no. 146.

PRINTED. *Edward I and the Throne of Scotland*, ii, 188–9; Reiffenberg, *Monuments*, i, 177–9; le Glay *Inventaire-sommaire*, i, pt 1, 31 (cal., in French).

COMMENT. There is a full transcript of this document in TNA, PRO 31/8/141/5 (Record Commission Transcripts, Series II: Transcripts of Documents in Different Archives and Libraries of the Low Countries). Volume 5 of this series includes transcriptions of the documents relating to the marriage of Prince Alexander and Marguerite of Flanders made in the nineteenth century by the state archivist of Belgium, M. Serrure. The transcriptions are, for the most part, accurate; Serrure accompanied each with a careful description of the seals and endorsements associated with each document. Photographs of the front and back of the deed may be found in NRS, RH 1/1/1. The dating of this document to c. 4 December is suggested by the fact that William de Mortagne lord of Rumes and Dossemer and Bernard dean of Messine, procurators for the count of Flanders, swore solemn oaths attesting the count's agreement to the terms of the dowry payments set out here and in no. 134 below, at Roxburgh on this date: see Archives départementales du nord, Lille, Chambre des comptes, B 403/2316, printed in Émile Varenberg, 'Épisodes des relations extérieures de la Flandre au Moyen-Age: trois filles de Gui de Dampierre', *Bulletin et annales de l'académie d'archéologie de Belgique*, 2è serie, 24:4 (1868), 625–7.

134 Announces that if the marriage between his son, Prince Alexander, and Marguerite daughter of Guy count of Flanders is completed as arranged [in no. 133, above], and Marguerite should die without heirs of their bodies before she has reached the age of twenty-three, he and his heirs shall remain bound to the count of Flanders in the amount of £5,500 sterling in compensation, payable at Berwick within three years of Marguerite's death. He agrees also to restore the sum of £11,000 which the count granted the couple in view of their marriage. If the count should die before Marguerite reaches the age of twenty-three, the compensation money is to be paid to his widow, Isabelle or, in the event of her death, to Marguerite's brothers and sisters. The compensation monies are to be paid in three annual rents of £2,000, £2,000 and £1,500, beginning on the day of Marguerite's death. If the full amount of the count's gift has not yet been remitted, the amount payable in compensation is to be adjusted accordingly. c. 4 December 1281.

Alixandres par le grasse de Dieu rois Descoche a tous chiaus ki ces p*re*sentes letres verront e oront . salut en n*ost*re Sign*eur* . Sache vostre vniu*er*sites ke . se mariaghes est fais e accomplis par sainte eglise entre Alixandre nostre ainsnet fil et no oir . e demisiele . Margheritain . ainsnee fille de noble homme . Guion . conte de Flandres e marchis de Namur kel a de noble dame Yssabiel se femme . fille au co*n*te de Lussenbourch e chele Margherite muire sains oir de leur deus chars . ainscois kele ait vint e deus ans passes . e aco*m*plis . nous e no successeur . sommes tenu e nous oblighons a rendre e paier . au conte deuant dit sil adont viuoit . cinch mile . e cinch cens l*ivres* desterlins . dedens t*ro*is ans . procainneme*n*t siuanz le mort de cheli Margheritain a Beruich en Escoche . en reco*m*pensation e en restor . de . onze mile . livres desterlins . ke li deuant dis quens donne a se fille e a mon fil . en aywe de leur mariaghe . Et sil auenoit chose ke del . conte defausist dedens le t*er*me de ces xxii . ans . nous e no successeur . soumes tenu a rendre . ces cinch mil . e cinch . cens l*ivres* desterlins a medame Yssabiel deuant dite . sele adont vit . v a ses oirs . ki li seroient demoure . seurs v freres g*er*mains de cheli Margheritain de ce cheli Yssabiel estoit defali . Et doiue*n*t ces cinch mile e cinch cens l*ivres* dest*er*lins estre paies a trois t*er*mes sest asauoir deus mile l*ivres* dest*er*lins dou jour ke chele Margherite morra en un an e a lautre en apries siuant entel meisme jour deus mile l*ivres* e au thierch an apries siuant en cel meisme jour mil e cinch cens l*ivres* dest*er*lins a Beruich en Escoche . Et sil auenoit chose ke chil onze mile l*ivres* ne fussent parpaiet au jour de le mort de cheli demisiele chou ki fauroit de cel paieme*n*t doit estre desconte de le somme de cinch mile e cinch cens l*ivres* deuant dis . Et de ces choses a tenir oblighons nous . nos oirs e nos successeurs de quanques nous poons par ces p*re*sentes lett*re*s e reno*n*cho*n*s quant a chou a toutes choses ki aidier nous poroient avenir encontre les choses deuant dites . Si vol*ons* e ot*ri*ons ke se cil denier nestoient paiet as t*er*mes deuant noumes ke li quens deuant dis u cil u chele acui chil denier seront estan prenghe sans injure e sans fourfait tant dou nous e de nos gens kil soufisse a plain paieme*n*t de celi deffaute . Et en tesmongnaghe e en seurte de ces choses fermeme*n*t tenir avons nous pendu nostre saiel a ces p*re*sentes letres ki furent donnees en lan de grasse . mil*le* . CC . q*ua*trevin . e vn . el mois de Decembre .

ENDORSED. Lettres le roi Descoce de rauoir le moitie dou mariage se me damisele morust deuant xxii ans passe (contemporary hand, the same as one of the endorsement writers above on no. 133 and below, nos 135, 140).

DESCRIPTION. 29.2 cm x 35.6 cm; fold 3.0 cm. Sealing: the king's second great seal, 10.0 cm diameter, in white wax, attached through two holes in the fold with braided double cords in crimson silk. The seal is in near-perfect condition.

HAND. Scribe S.
SOURCE. Original. Archives de l'état à Namur, Chartes de Namur, no. 149.
PRINTED. Reiffenberg, *Monuments*, i, 179–80; modern transcripts also in TNA, PRO 31/8/141/5 (Record Commission Transcripts, Series II).
COMMENT. There is a full transcript of this document in TNA, PRO 31/8/141/5 (Record Commission Transcripts, Series II: Transcripts of Documents in Different Archives and Libraries of the Low Countries); see above, Comments on no. 133 about this item. Photographs of the front and back of the deed may be found in NRS, RH 1/1/1. The count of Flanders agreed to the terms of the dowry through his procurators, William de Mortagne lord of Rumes and Dossemer and his chaplain, Bernard dean of Messine, who took oaths on his behalf at Roxburgh on 4 December 1281; see Archives départementales du nord, Lille, Chambre des comptes, B 403/2316.

135 Announces that if, after the marriage between his son, Alexander, and Marguerite daughter of Guy count of Flanders, it should happen that Marguerite survive her husband, she shall have a dowry of 1,300 merks sterling, payable in cash at Berwick and in addition, no later than 1 August after the wedding, the manor of Linlithgow in Lothian, worth a further 200 merks per annum. Simon Fraser undertakes an oath on the king's behalf to observe these terms; King Alexander further requests that the pope confirm these arrangements. Prince Alexander, for his part, swears an oath to take Marguerite to wife before the octaves of St Michael next and faithfully to observe this agreement, before the following witnesses: Bernard dean of Messine, William bishop of St Andrews, Donald earl of Mar, Alexander de Balliol, William de Soules and William de Mortagne, knight. c. 4 December 1281.

Alixandres par le grasse de Dieu rois Descoche a tous chiaus ki ces p*re*sentes letres verront e oront salut en no*st*re Signeur. Nous faisons asauoir a vostre vniu*er*site . ke pour chou ke Alixandres nos chiers fiex ainsnes e nos oirs e demisiele Margherite ainsnee fille de haut houme e noble Guion . conte de Flandres e marchis de Namur ke il a de noble dame . Yssabiel se femme fille au conte de Lussenbourch se doiuent asanbler par loial mariaghe nous ki desirons lacroissement de cheli demisiele volons e otroions boin*n*ement ke se chis mariaghes est p*ar*fais e chele Margherite sourviue nostre fil deuant dit . ke chele demisiele ait e prenghe en le vile de Beruich en Escoche a chiaus ki la seront en no liu cascun en tant com*m*e ele aura le vie el corps en[a] quelconques estat ke ele soit . treze cens mars desterlins en grant nombre . xiii . saus e iiii deniers pour le march . en non de doaire . u pour don de neuches . le p*ri*merain jour dauoust apres le dechies de chelui Alixandre . e aweuch chou le manoir de Linlithcu seant en no roiaume ou terroir de Loenois en le veskiet[b] de Saint Andriu . auquel manoir apartiengne*n*t deus cent mars dest*er*lins de rente cascun en . au deuant dit nombre e se tant ni auoit de rente chele Margherite doit auoir le deffaute aweuch ces treze cens mars au liu e au jour deuant dis tant kele ait q*ui*nze cens mars dest*er*lins par tout . Et est nos gres e no volontes ke chius Alixandres nos fiex . doe celi Margheritain de cel argent e de cel manoir . u doinst pour don de neuches le somme darghent e li manoir deseure noumet a cheli demisiele Margheritain . Et de chou faire donno*n*s nous autorite e plain pooir a celui Alixandre no fil . et nous meismes len doons e li donnons pour don de neuches tant com*m*e est en nous . Si proumetons pour nous pour nos oirs . e pour nos successeurs par no sairement . fait en no non . e pour nous . par Simon Fresel no cheualier . a cui nous donno*n*s plain pooir de jurer en nostre ame . ces deniers a rendre a cheli demisiele Margheritain . u a sen com*m*ant e le manoir laisier tenir en le maniere . deseure dite e ke jamais ne ferons ne ne pourchacerons a faire chose . coieme*n*t ne apiertemе*n*t . par coi chius doaires ne chius dons pour neuches soient enfraint . ne enpiriet en le greuanche de le demisiele deuant dite . Et pour toutes ces choses fermeme*n*t tenir . oblighons nous nos oirs e nos [successeurs e][c] tous les biens de no roiaume . en toutes les manieres ke nous poons par ces p*re*sentes letres saielees de no saiel . et renonchons quant a chou . a toutes choses ki a nous a nos oirs . e a nos successeurs porroient aidier a venir encontre ces choses [e][d] a cheli Margheritain greuer . Et supploions a no [saint pere][d] nostre signeur lapostole ke il toutes ces choses daingne confermer en nostre absence sans autre requeste . Apres est a sauoir ke jou Alixandres . ainsnes fiex e oirs . dou deuant dit roi Descoche ki ai entension e volente . de le deuant dite Margheritain prendre a femme e loial espeuse . doe celi Margheritain de ces deniers e dou manoir deseuredis . e doins a li pour dons de neuches en le p*re*sence de mon chier pere le roi . E proumeth par le foi de men cors [en le m]ain[d] . de mo*n*signeur Biernart doiien del eglise de Messines . par deuant reuere*n*t pere en Dieu . Willaume . evesque de Saint Andriu . Dounant[e] .conte de Mar[f] . Alixandre de Bailleul[g]. Willaume . de Soles[h] et no chier cousin Willaume de Mortaingne[i] . cheualiers . ke je celi Margheritain prenderai a femme . e a loial espeuse . i tost ke sainte eglise sasentira . par tel condition . ke toutes les choses ke pourparlees sont en ceste bessoigne . e les seurtes ke li quens doit faire au roi . des deniers e de le venue le[j] demisiele soient complies en le maniere ke parlet est . e se che nestoit fait dedens les octaues de saint Michiel[k] procainеme*n*t venant je weul . ke chele fianchale ne me lit de riens . Et pour ces choses deseure dites fe*r*mement a tenir ai je aweuch le saiel mo*n*signeur le roi . mon chier pere pendu men saiel a ces p*re*sentes lettres . ki furent donnees lan del grasse . mil*le* .CC . q*ua*trevins e vn el mois de Decembre .

NOTES. [a] Ou in B. [b] Eveskiet in B. [c] MS torn here; word supplied from B. [d] MS stained; words supplied from B. [e] Donant in B. [f] Ma' in B. [g] Bailluel in B. [h] Soles in B. [I] Mortaigne in B. [j] De le in B. [k] Mikiel in B.

ENDORSED. 1. Lettres le roi Descoce e monsigneur Alixandre son fil dou douaire me demysele (contemporary hand, the same as that of the second endorsement above on no. 133). 2. Lettres dassignacion du douaire que fait Alixandre roy Descoce et son filz pur les parties denomees a damme Margarite aineee fille du Signeur Guions conte de Flandres (sixteenth century) on the dorse of A; Copie par instrument dou douaire le fille de Flandres, qui eut à mari le fil dou roi d'Escoche (contemporary hand) on the dorse of B.

DESCRIPTION. 29.2 cm x 38.6 cm; fold 2.8 cm. The second great seal of Alexander III, in white wax, is attached to the left side of the document by means of a braided crimson silk cord passed through two holes in the fold; just over half of the seal survives. On the right side of the fold is the privy seal of Prince Alexander, similarly appended by a silk cord, in green wax, 3.0 cm in diameter. It depicts, on a shield within a rounded trefoil of six petals, a lion within a double tressure and a label. The legend reads SECRETV'. ALEX . FILII . REGIS . SCOCIE. There is a cast of this seal in NRS, RH 1/17, Drawer 56.

HAND. Scribe S.
SOURCE. Original. Archives de l'état à Namur, Chartes de Namur, no. 147 = A; Archives départementales du nord, Lille, Chambre des comptes, B 403/2323 (notarised copy dated 10 March 1284) = B; Archives nationales de France, MS K 531, no. 5A (copy, executed around the same time as B) = C. Transcribed here from A.
PRINTED. Reiffenberg, *Monuments*, i, 180–2 (A); Varenberg, 'Épisodes des relations extérieures de la Flandre au Moyen-Age', 627–30 (B); Glay, *Inventaire-sommaire*, i, pt 1, 31 (cal., in French); J. B. A. T. Teulet, *Inventaire chronologique des documents relatifs à l'histoire d'Ecosse conservés aux Archives du royaume à Paris* (Abbotsford Club, 1839), 3 (cal., in French).
COMMENT. The third transcript of the document, dated c. February 1300 (Text C), was made for Marguerite's brother, John I count of Namur, after her second marriage in July 1286 to Reynaud I count of Gueldres. It was enrolled with several other documents relating to this marriage; see Archives nationales de France, MS K 531, n. 14 (calendared in Teulet, *Inventaire*, 3). There is a full transcript of A in TNA, PRO 31/8/141/5 (Record Commission Transcripts, Series II: Transcripts of Documents in Different Archives and Libraries of the Low Countries); see above, Comments on no. 133 about this item. Photographs of the front and back of the deed may be found in NRS, RH 1/1/1. The bundle of documents of which the text of C constitutes one item includes also the confirmation of Pope Honorius IV that King Alexander requested. Prince Alexander's identification of William de Mortagne as his 'dear cousin' suggests that the two men were close. They were, in fact, related by marriage: the prince's great-grandfather, Enguerrand III of Coucy, had been the half-brother of William's mother, Yolande. On 8 October 1285 Pope Honorius addressed a letter to Marguerite, assuring her that the dowry of 1,300 merks from the fermes of Berwick and Linlithgow would duly be delivered to her (Theiner, *Monumenta*, no. 297). Several years later, however, arrears on the dowry were still outstanding, and in August 1293 representatives of her father appeared at John Balliol's Stirling parliament seeking payment of the sums still owed him (*RPS*, 1293/8/3).

136

Writes to Edward I king of England informing him that owing to troubling matters of concern to him and his realm, he has sent Alexander earl of Buchan, his constable and justiciar of Scotia, to the remote parts of his islands, for which reason the earl is not able to come to him as required. Requests that Edward excuse the earl's absence and his inability to perform the aid in Wales that he owes for the lands which he holds within England. Scone, 1 July a.r. 33 [1282].

Excellentissimo principi et f*ra*tri suo k*arissi*mo E . Dei gr*at*ia regi Angl*ie* illustri d*omi*no Ibernie et duci Aquitannie Alex*ander* eadem gr*at*ia rex Scott*orum* sal*utem* . et sincere dileccionis plenitudinem . Excelle*n*cie v*est*re . tenore p*re*sencium significam*us* . quod p*ro*pt*er* quedam ardua negocia . nos et regnu*m* nost*ru*m tangencia misimu*s* Alexandru*m* Cumyn comitem de Buchan const*abularium* et justi*ciarium* nost*ru*m ex boreali p*ar*te maris Scoc*ie* vsq*ue* ad p*ar*tes remotas insular*um* n*ost*rar*um* . propt*er* q*uo*d . ad p*re*claram magnificencie v*est*re presenciam hac vice accedere non potest .[a] Q*ua*re excellenciam v*est*ram rogamus attente . q*ua*tinus n*ost*ror*um* precaminum int*er*uentu absenciam ip*s*ius comitis in hac p*ar*te habere velitis excusatam . desicut auxiliu*m* quod vobis debet r*ati*one t*er*rar*um* q*ua*s de vobis tenet infra regnu*m* v*est*ru*m* paratu*m* sit ad eundu*m* in Walliam p*ro* v*est*re libito vol*un*tatis . vt intelleximu*s* . T*este* . me ipso ap*u*d Scon' p*ri*mo die Julii anno . r*egni* . n*ostri* . xxxiii°.

NOTES. [a] Poteat in printed version.
DESCRIPTION. 18.5 cm x 6.6 cm. Sealing: no evidence of a tag, tongue or seal.
HAND. Scribe O.
SOURCE. Original. TNA, Special Collections: Ancient Correspondence of the Chancery and the Exchequer, PRO SC 1/20/158.
PRINTED. *Foedera*, I, ii, 610; *Nat. MSS. Scotland*, i, no. 64 (facs.); *CDS*, ii, no. 215 (cal.).

137 Writes to Edward I king of England informing him that Alexander de Balliol of Cavers, knight, is occupied with the affairs of John, son of the late David earl of Atholl, whose lands and goods within Scotland have been destroyed and alienated by enemies, so he is unable to present himself to King Edward as required. Requests that Edward excuse Alexander de Balliol the service that he owes in his army. Kinross, 12 July a.r. 34 [1282].

Excellentissimo principi et fr*at*ri suo in *Christ*o k*arissi*mo d*omi*no . E . Dei gr*at*ia . regi Anglie illustri d*omi*no Ibern*ie* et duci Aquitan*nie* . Alex*ander* eadem gr*at*ia rex Scott*orum* . salutem . et felices ad vota successus cum i*n*cremento gl*or*ie et honoris . Cum Alex*ander* de Balliolo de Cauirs miles circa reformacionem status t*er*rarum et bonor*um* Joh*ann*is de Atholya filii quondam Dauid comitis de Atholia militis . i*n*fra regnu*m* nostrum que p*er* quosdam i*n*imicos suos maliciose ac nequiter deuastantur et alienantur vt i*n*telleximu*s* sic multipliciter occupat*us* . p*ro*pt*er* quod . excellencie v*est*re ad p*re*sens se p*re*sentare non poterit vt desiderat . serenitatem v*est*ram pro eodem affectuose requirimus et rogamus . quatin*us* cum s*er*uiciu*m* suu*m* q*uo*d vobis debet i*n* exc*er*citu v*est*ro ad p*re*sens mittat ut dicitur . ips*i*us absenciam in hac p*ar*te habere dignemini excusatam p*re*cum n*ost*rar*um* int*er*uentu . T*este* . me ips*o* apud Kynros xii° . die Julii ann*o* . r*egni* . n*ostri* . xxxiiii° .

DESCRIPTION. 19.1 cm x 6.6 cm. Sealing: formerly sealed on a tongue cut from right to left across the bottom of the deed, now torn away.
HAND. Scribe O.
SOURCE. Original. TNA, Special Collections: Ancient Correspondence of the Chancery and the Exchequer, PRO SC 1/20/159.
PRINTED. *Foedera*, I, ii, 644; *CDS*, ii, no. 219 (cal.).

138 Writes to Edward I king of England informing him that upon receiving his letter complaining of injuries done to the miners of Alston by Alexander's men, he has commanded his bailiffs of Tynedale to inform him on the matter; if found to be as Edward has represented, he will make fitting amends. Durris, 23 August a.r. 34 [1282].

Excellentissimo principi . et fr*at*ri suo . p*re*cordialissimo . d*omi*no . Edwardo . Dei gr*at*ia . regi Anglie illustri . d*omi*no . Hybern*ie* . et duci Aq*ui*tan*nie* . Alex*ander* eadem gr*at*ia . rex . Scott*orum* . salut*em* . et prosp*er*os ad vota successus . Contenta in l*itter*is v*est*ris nup*er* a v*est*ra nobilitate nob*is* missis[a] sup*er* iniuriis et gr*a*uaminib*us* minerariis v*est*ris de Aldinisto*un* . p*er* homines n*ost*ros vt dicebit*ur* illatis . intellexim*us* ad plenu*m* . et statim misim*us* l*itter*as n*ost*ras balliuis n*ost*ris Tyndalie . vt nob*is* sup*er* hoc significent veritate*m* . qua comp*er*ta . si ita inuentu*m* fuerit vt nob*is* significastis . competentes emendas d*ic*tis minerariis v*est*ris inde fieri faciem*us* . vt rogastis . et q*ua*tenus de iure d*ict*e . emende fu*er*int faciende . statum v*estr*um que*m* D*omin*us prosperum custodiat vna cum beneplacitis v*est*ris nob*is* si placet \ frequenter/ significetis . Teste me ip*s*o apud Durres' . xxiii° die Augusti . ann*o* . reg*ni* n*ost*ri . xxx°iiii° .

NOTES. [a] Altered from misis.
DESCRIPTION. 19.8 cm x 5.1 cm. Sealing: no evidence of a tag, tongue or seal.
HAND. Scribe P.
SOURCE. Original. TNA, Special Collections: Ancient Correspondence of the Chancery and the Exchequer, PRO SC 1/20/160.
PRINTED. *CDS*, ii, no. 224 (cal.).

139 Announces that Ada de Cassingray, daughter of the late William de Cassingray, on the Sunday before the feast of St Margaret the Virgin 1282, at Clunie, resigned to him the whole third part of the land of Cassingray (Fife), which she held of him by hereditary right as an heir of the late William in order that Nicholas de Haye, knight, might be infeft of the same. Accordingly, on the same day at the same place, at the urging of the said Ada and Nicholas and their friends he has infeft the said Nicholas in the same portion of land and received his homage for it. To be held in feu and heritage, with the common pasture on the muir of Kellie that pertains to the said portion of land, rendering as much forinsec service as pertains to such an amount of land in Kellieshire. Also grants that Nicholas may freely grind the corn from his own house at the mill of Kellie, but that his men must pay multure, as the charter of the king's grandfather, William, bears witness. Newbattle, 4 October a.r. 34 [1282].

. Alex*ander* Dei gratia rex Scott*orum* . omnibus probis hominibus tocius t*er*re sue clericis et laicis . sal*ut*em . Cum Eda de Glasgyngrey filia quondam Will*elm*i de Glasgyngrey die D*omini*ca prox*ima* ante festum beate Margarete virginis . anno D*omi*ni . M° .CC°. octoges*imo* . s*ecun*do . in capella n*ost*ra de Clony . nobis p*er* fustum et bac*ul*um resignau*er*it . totam t*er*tiam p*ar*tem t*er*re de Glasgyngrey . quam ip*s*a Eda de nobis iure hereditario tenuit tanq*uam* vna heredum p*redic*ti quondam Will*elm*i de Glasgyngrey . ad infeodand*um* Nich*ola*um de Haya militem de eadem t*er*ra cum p*er*tinenc*iis* . Sciatis nos ad instanciam p*redic*t*orum* Ede et Nicholai . ac amicor*um* suor*um* . eundem Nich*ola*um de dicta t*er*tia p*ar*te t*er*re de Glasgyngrey . d*ict*is . die . loco . et anno . infeodasse . et homagiu*m* suu*m* inde recepisse . Tenend*am* et habend*am* de nobis et heredibus n*ost*ris . eid*em* Nicholao et h*er*edibus suis . in feodo et h*er*editate . in t*er*ris . pratis . et pascuis . et cu*m* com*m*uni pastura de mora de Kellyn' . quanta p*er*tinet ad d*ict*am t*er*tiam p*ar*tem t*er*re p*re*nominate . libere integre et quiete . faciendo inde nobis forinsecum s*er*uiciu*m* quant*um* p*er*tinet ad tantam t*er*ram i*n* Kellynscyre . Concessimus et*iam* p*redic*to Nich*ola*o et heredibus suis . vt quieti sint de multura de domo sua p*ro*pria . ad mole*n*dinu*m* de Kellyn . set volumus q*uod* homines eor*um* dent multuram . s*ecun*d*um* q*uod* in carta felicis recordac*i*onis d*omi*ni Will*elm*i regis . aui n*ost*ri carissimi . plenius est expressum . Testibus . Jacobo senesc*allo* Scoc*ie* . Will*elm*o de S*anct*o Claro . Roberto de Cambrun' . Symone Fras*er* .

Pat*ri*cio de Graham . et Ricardo Fras*er* . apud Neubotyll' . quarto die Octobr*is* . anno regni n*ost*ri . t*ri*cesimo quarto[a] .

NOTES. [a]The last line ends with several bold forward strokes.
ENDORSED. Kasingray (fourteenth century).
DESCRIPTION. 22.6 cm x 12.7 cm; fold 2.8 cm. Sealing: on a parchment tag, 2.2 cm broad, through single slits, there appears a small fragment of the second great seal, in natural wax varnished brown. Only a small section of the central part of the seal is now visible.
HAND. Scribe G? This hand is found in only three other acts (above, nos 65, 66, 67, all dated 1267–8). It may well be the work of a different scribe, but it shares several characteristics with the earlier hand.
SOURCE. Original. NRS, Lindsay Papers, GD 203/2/3.
PRINTED. *HMC,* v, 624.

140 Announces that although the marriage arranged between his son, Prince Alexander, and Marguerite daughter of Guy count of Flanders and Isabella of Luxemburg, has not yet taken place as agreed in previous letters, no prejudice shall thereby result to Marguerite or the dowry set out there. Prince Alexander, on his own behalf, grants the same. Roxburgh, 11 November 1282.

Alisandres par le grase de Die rois Descoce a tous chiaus qui ces p*re*sentes lettres veront et oront . salut en nostre Segneur . Nous faisons asauoir a vostre vniu*er*site ke co*me* ensi soit ke nous auons eut convenences de mariage entre nous e noble hom*me* Guion . conte de Fla*n*d*re*s e marchis de Nam*ur* .dendroit no chier fil Alisandre . e no oir . e de demisiele Margerite . fille a noble hom*me* Guion conte de Fla*n*d*re*s e marchis de Nam*ur* . kil a de noble dame Ysabiel . sa fem*me* . fille au conte de Lusenbourc . e tiermes fu mis ke cis mariages deuoit est*re* fais deuens les octaues saint Mikael . ki fu en lan . M . et CC . quatrevins e deus . si com il apert en le lettre ke nous e no chier fils auons dounee a demisiele Margerite deuant dite saielee de nos saiaus e li mariages ne fust mie fais deuens ce tierme . nous volons ke demisiele Margerite ne soit de nient ariere pour le tierme passe . e ke nus p*re*judises ne li soit fais de sen douaire ne de sen don de noeces . e volons kille le teingne entirement ensi come il est deuises es lettres ke ille a de n*ous* et de Alisandre . no chier fil . tout en autretel point come se li mariages esyst estet fais deuens le tierme ki noume est . En tiesmo*n*gnage de ces p*re*sentes lett*re*s ke nous len avo*n*s donnoes saieles de n*ost*re p*ro*p*re* saiel . E iou Alisandres . fils e oirs a men chier se*n*gneur le roy Descoce loe gree et voel ke toutes ces coses deseure dittes ensi come mes chiers sires e peres les a deuisees . soient f*er*mes e estautes e bien tenues a demisiele Margerite . me chiere femme . e kille tie*n*gne sen douaire e sen don de noeces tout ensi kil fu deuise es lettres kille a de men chier se*n*gneur e pere . le roy Descoce . e de mi aussi ke se li mariages esyst eslet fais deuens le tierme ki mis y fu ensi ke deseure est dit . E p*ur* cou ki cu soit f*er*me cose e estaute e ke nus prejudises rien soit fais a demisiele Margerite me chire femme si ai iou pendut men saiel a ces p*re*sentes lettres avoec le saiel mon chier sengnur e pere le roy Descoce en conf*er*mance de toutes les deuises deseure dittes . Ces lettres furent faites a Rokebourc en lan de lincarnat*ion* nostre Segneur . M . CC . quatrevins e deus le ior saint Martin en Ivier.

ENDORSED. 1. Lettre de quitance dou marriage ki acarya (contemporary hand, the same as one of the endorsement writers in nos 133, 134, 135 above). 2. Lettres par lesquelles le roy Descoce consent que si le mariage ne se solempnisoit endedans le temps prefix que les donacions eussent a serfir leur effect comme si le heir feust fait endedens le temps (sixteenth century).

DESCRIPTION. 28.0 cm x 13.3 cm; fold 2.8 cm. The second great seal of Alexander III, in white wax, is attached to the left side of the document by means of two braided crimson silk cords passed through single slits; just over half of the seal survives. On the right side of the fold is the seal of Prince Alexander, similarly appended by means of silk cords, in green wax, 3.4 cm in diameter. It depicts, on a shield within a rounded sixfoil, a lion within a double tressure, the background field decorated with branches. The legend reads: S' ALEX . ILLUSTRIS REG SCOTORVM PRIMOGENITI. There is a cast of the seal in NRS, RH 1/17, Drawer 56.

HAND. Scribe S.

SOURCE. Original. Archives de l'état à Namur, Chartes de Namur, no. 157.

PRINTED. Reiffenberg, *Monuments*, i, 182–3.

COMMENT. There is a full transcript of A in TNA, PRO 31/8/141/5 (Record Commission Transcripts, Series II: Transcripts of Documents in Different Archives and Libraries of the Low Countries); see above, Comments at no. 133 about this item. The copyist, the Belgian archivist M. Serrure, appended to his transcription of this document a note (in French) stating that 'This same deed exists in another copy in the archives of Namur, Layette A. no. [blank] as a *vidimus* issued by the bishop of Thérouane, as follows: Nous, Henris par le grace de Dieu eveskes de Teruane faisons sauior a tous ke nous auons veu sains et entiers les lettres des nobles et excellent seigneur Alexandre par la grace de Diey roy dEscoce et mon seigneur Alexandre son ainet fil et oir, en le forme ci apres escrit Alex' par la grace etc. E nous Henris par le grace de Dieu eveskes de Terewane devant dit en temoignance et en conisance de toutes ces coises devant dites avons pendu nostre saiel a les presentes lettres ki furent donnees lan de grace mil CC quatrevins et trois le dimence devant lemiquareme el mois de march.' Serrure noted also that the bishop's seal, in brown wax, was appended to this copy; its current location is unknown.

141 Announces that he has received £5,096 3d in ready money from the hands of Henry Karwin, James Louchard and Gilles de Bruges, goldsmith, paid by Guy count of Flanders, by reason of the marriage of the king's son and heir, Alexander and Marguerite, daughter of the said count Guy, made to him as the first term's payment of Marguerite's dowry. Dunkeld, 25 December a.r. 34 [1282]

Alex*ander* Dei gratia rex Scott*orum* omnibus homini*bus* ad quos presentes littere p*er*uenerint sal*ute*m . Noue*ri*tis nos recepisse et in pecunia numerata habuisse per manus Henrici Karwyn . Jacobi Luchars' . et Egidii de Brugis aurifabri . quinq*ue* mill*e* libr*as* quarter viginti libr*as* . sexdecim libr*as* . et tres denarios sterlingor*um* de peccunie[a] sum*m*a in qua nobilis vir Gydo comes Flandrie et marchio de Namur' nobis r*ati*one maritagii Alexandri filii n*os*tri k*arissi*mi primogeniti et Margarete . filie comitis predi*ct*i tenebatur . de t*er*mino p*ri*me solucionis . nobis faciende . In cuius rei testimoniu*m* p*re*sentibus sigillum n*ost*rum iussimus apponi . Dat*um* ap*u*d Du*n*keldin . xxv^{o} . die Decembr*is* . anno regni n*ost*ri t*ri*cesimo quarto .

NOTES. [a] Sic, pecunie.

ENDORSED. [Littera regis] Alexandri Scothorum quod recepta a comiti Guydone V^{m} libras lxxxxvi libras iid sterl' de summa quod idem comes debebat sibe dare p[ro] matrimonio filii ipsius regis et filie comitis (contemporary hand).

DESCRIPTION. 23.5 cm x 6.6 cm, L x 4.7 cm, R. Sealing: On a tongue of 2.5 cm breadth, cut from the right side of the parchment piece, there is appended the king's second great seal, 7.5 cm in diameter, in white wax. About one-third of the seal is broken off around the edges; the rest is in good condition.

HAND. Scribe T.

SOURCE. Original. Archives départementales du nord, Lille, Chambre des comptes, B 403/2530.

PRINTED. Uredius, *Genealogia,* Probationes, pars prima, 98; pars secunda, 69; le Glay *Inventaire-sommaire,* i, pt 1, 31 (cal., in French).

142 Writes to Guy count of Flanders requesting that he assign £50 in the king's name to Baldwin de Mortagne, knight, out of the money that the count withheld from the first payment of his daughter's dowry. Berwick, 14 February a.r. 34 [1283].

Alexander Dei gratia rex Scottorum nobili viro et caro amico suo Gydoni comiti Flandrie et marchioni de Namur' . salutem et amorem sincerum . Sciatis quod volumus quod Baldewyno de Mortaing' militi consanguineo nostro dilecto soluantur quinquaginta libre sterlingorum de denariis in quibus nobis tenemini de prima solucione nobis per vos facienda . Quare vos rogamus quatinus dictas quinquaginta libras dicto Baldewyno adueniente termino solucionis primo faciende . nomine nostro liberari faciatis . Et nos dictas quinquaginta libras vobis in dicta solucione nobis per vos facienda faciemus allocari . In cuius rei testomonium has nostras litteras vobis mittimus patentes. Teste . me ipso apud Berwyc' . xiiii° . die Februarii anno regni nostri tricesimo quarto .

ENDORSED. Littera regis Alexandri Scotthorum de solucione facienda Baldewino de Mauritania milite de . L. libras sterlingorum ad mandatum ipsius regis et in defaltacionem eorum quod sibi debebantura comite Guydone preter matrimonium inter filium ipsius regis et filiam comitis (contemporary hand).

DESCRIPTION. 18.0 cm x 8.2 cm, L x 4.7 cm, R. On a tongue of 2.1 cm broad, cut from the right side of the parchment piece, there is appended the king's second great seal, 7.5 cm diameter., in yellow wax. About one-third of the seal is broken off around the edges; the rest is in good condition.

HAND. Scribe T.

SOURCE. Original. Archives départementales du nord, Lille, Chambre des comptes, B 403/2543.

PRINTED. Le Glay, *Inventaire-sommaire,* i, pt 1, 36 (cal., in French).

143 Writes to Guy count of Flanders requesting that he release, from the balance of the first payment of his daughter's dowry, the sum of £200 to his merchants, Henry Karwin and Alexander de Newcastle-on-Tyne, sent to France on his business. Scone, 20 February a.r. 34 [1283].

Alexander Dei gratia rex Scottorum nobili viro et amico suo karissimo Gydoni comiti Flandrie et marchioni de Namur' . salutem et sincere dilecionis affectam . Amiciciam vestram rogamus attente quatinus Henrico de Carwy et Alexandro dicto de Novo Castro super Tynam mercatoribus nostris latoribus presencium quos pro negociis nostris ad partes Francie transmittimus ducentas libras sterlingorum de denariis in quibus nobis tenemini de residuo solucionis primi termini nobis facte per vos liberari faciatis ex parte nostra . Et dictas ducentas libras vobis faciemus allocari . In cuius rei testimonium presentibus sigillum nostrum fecimus apponi . Datum apud Scon' vicesimo die Februarii anno regni nostri tricesimo quarto.

ENDORSED. Littera Alexandri regis Scothorum per quas rogat comitem Guydonem vt faciat deliberari CC libras sterlingorum quiquisdam nuncios suis quos misit in Francia de denariis in quibus ipse comes eidem regi tenetur de residuo solucio primi termini (contemporary hand).
DESCRIPTION. 20.5 cm x 7.0 cm, L x 4.2 cm, R. On a tongue of 2.5 cm broad, cut from the right side of the parchment piece, there is appended the king's second great seal, 9.5 cm diameter, in yellow wax. A small portion of the seal is broken off around the edges; the rest is in very good condition.
HAND. Scribe T.
SOURCE. Original. Archives départementales du nord, Lille, Chambre des comptes, B 403/2545.
PRINTED. Uredius, *Genealogia*, pars secunda, 69; le Glay, *Inventaire-sommaire*, i, pt 1, 36 (cal., in French).
COMMENT. Photographs of the front and back of the deed may be found in NRS, RH 1/1/1.

144 Writes to Edward I king of England requesting his favour on behalf of William de Soules, knight, who is prosecuting a plea before King Edward's justiciars in England concerning the advowson of the church of Stanfordham (Northumberland). Scone, 28 March a.r. 34 [1283].

Magnifico principi et f*rat*ri suo in *Christ*o k*arissi*mo d*omi*no . E . Dei *grat*ia regi Angl*ie* illustri d*omi*no Ibernie et duci Aquitan*n*ie Alex*ander* eadem *grat*ia rex Scott*orum* sal*ut*em cum dilecione sincera pro Will*elm*o de Soulis milite . caro et speciali n*ost*ro excellencie v*est*re p*re*ces porrigimus sp*ec*iales quatinus eidem Will*elm*o u*e*l actornatis suis in loquela quam prosequit*ur* coram justiciariis v*est*ris in Anglia sup*er* aduocac*i*one eccl*es*ie de Stamfordham . eidem Will*elm*o u*e*l d*ic*tis actornatis suis s*ecun*d*um* Deum et iusticiam vos velitis exhibere fauorabiles et benignos p*er* quod celsitudini v*est*re ob fauorem et iusticiam tam caro nostro inpensam teneamur ad grates et g*rat*ias sp*eci*ales . T*este* . me ips*o* ap*u*d Scon' . xxviii^{o} die Marcii ann*o* . r*egni* . n*ostri* . xxxiiii^{o} .

DESCRIPTION. 20.1 cm x 5.1 cm. Sealing: no evidence of a tag, tongue or seal.
HAND. Scribe O.
SOURCE. Original. TNA, Chancery Miscellanea, PRO C 47/22/5/22.
PRINTED. *CDS,* ii, no. 233 (cal.); *L & I,* vol. xlix, 187 (note).

145 Writes to Edward I king of England informing him that the bailiffs of his liberties of Tynedale and Penrith tell him that Edward's bailiffs, Master Henry of Newark archdeacon of Richmond and Thomas de Normanville, knight, are troubling and making claims on these liberties on account of the aid recently imposed in England. Admits that they may be doing so out of ignorance of his rights, but requests that Edward command them to desist. Stirling, 7 June a.r. 34 [1283].

Magnifico ac egregio principi . et f*rat*ri suo in *Christ*o k*arissi*mo . d*omi*no Edwardo Dei g*rat*ia . regi Angl*ie* illustri . d*omi*no Hibern*ie* . et duci Aquitan*nie* . Alex*ander* eadem g*rat*ia rex Scott*orum* . sal*ut*em . et amorem sinceru*m* cu*m* semp*er*[a] parata ad beneplacita voluntate . Cum ad plenu*m* confidamus v*est*ri g*rat*ia . q*uod* voluntatis v*est*re non est . quod aliqua p*er* quoscumque de v*est*ris fiant *contra* nos et libertates n*ost*ras . que fieri non debent . nec sunt unquam retroactis[a] temporibus[a] vsitata . et intellex*er*imus p*er* balliuos n*ost*ros libertatu*m* n*ost*raru*m* Thyndallie et de Penerith' cum pertinenciis quod . balliui v*est*ri . magi*st*er Henricus de Neuwerk archidiaconus Richemu*n*die . et Thomas de Normanwil' miles . qui forte libertates n*ost*ras p*re*dictas ad plen*um* non norunt[a] . occasione auxilii i*n* Anglia de nouo i*m*positi p*re*di*c*tas lib*er*tates[b] n*ost*ras molestare et calu*m*pniare incipient . Regiam maiestatem v*est*ram ad q*uam* recurrimus in agendis n*ost*ris co*n*fide*n*ter \ v*est*ri gr*at*ia / tenore p*re*sencium requirim*us* dep*re*cantes . q*ua*tin*us* p*re*di*c*tis . H . et T . v*est*ris si placet velitis dare litt*er*is in p*re*ceptis . vt p*re*dictas libertates n*ost*ras sicut s*em*p*er* hactenus esse consueueru*n*t et debent . ab om*n*i exacc*i*one hui*us*mo*d*i liberas esse p*er*mittentes . a p*redic*tis molestac*i*one et calu*m*pnia desistant om*nin*o . De bonis et honorib*us* p*er* beniuolenciam vestram ad n*ost*ram instanciam vt audiuim*us* v*est*ri gr*at*ia Ingerramo de Gynis militi consang*ui*neo n*ost*ro p*er* vos factis . celsitudini v*est*re k*ariss*ime . grates referim*us* speciales valeat et vigeat vestra \cara/ fraternitas p*er* t*em*po*r*a diuturna . Dat*um* ap*u*d Striuelyn . vii° . die Junii anno . r*egni* . n*ostri* . xxxiiii° .

NOTES. [a] These words are written over an erasure. [b] The preceding three words are cramped and crammed into a small space.
DESCRIPTION. 21.1 cm x 9.1 cm. Sealing: no evidence of a tag, tongue or seal.
HAND. Scribe O.
SOURCE. Original. TNA, Special Collections: Ancient Correspondence of the Chancery and the Exchequer, PRO SC 1/20/161.
PRINTED. *CDS*, ii, no. 241 (cal.). The tax of a fifteenth was introduced in the English parliament of 1275. See also below, no. 170.

146 Writes to Edward I king of England thanking him for offering solace after the death of his son in the person of brother John of St Germain of the Dominican order, and for having regard for their kinship and friendship. Reminds him that although death has now carried off all of his blood in Scotland, much good may yet come to pass through the child of his daughter, Edward's niece, the late queen of Norway, who is now his heir apparent. Asks that Edward give credence without question to his envoy, Andrew abbot of Coupar, and that he send news back by the same messenger. Edinburgh, 20 April a.r. 35 [1284].

Magnifico p*r*incipi d*om*ino . E . D*e*i gr*at*ia regi Anglor*um* illustri d*omi*no Hib*erni*e et duci Aquit*anni*e fr*at*ri suo dilectissimo suus Alexander eadem gracia rex [Scottorum] salutem et o[mne quod] est optimum cum dil*ecc*i*o*ne sincera et parata ad b*ene*placita voluntate . Quamuis fidelis amic*us* a dileccione [amici sui recedere non everit] et excellencie v*est*re constanciam ob plura . beneficia debeam*us* p*er* multam experienciam [non immerito commendare] . de eo t*am*[en ad presens quod post tristissimas et intollerabiles] angustias et euent*us* quos sensim*us* et sentim*us* de morte filii n*ost*ri dilectissimi nepotis v*est*ri cari p*er* fratrem Joh*ann*em de sanc*t*o Germano de ordine [fratrum minorum] desolacionis solaciu*m* non modicu*m* p*r*opinastis mandantes . q*uod* licet sang*ui*nem v*est*rum in p*ar*tib*us* [nostris mors taliter] sustulerit sorte sua nos tamen [manemus][a] i*n*dissolubilis amoris vinculo dante

Domino n*os*tro p*er*petuo colligati . celsitudini v*es*tre k*arissi*me per ceteris curialitatibus et b*e*neficiis ad g*ra*tes [tradendas?] nos [tenemur?][a] ob [san]guinis reu*er*enciam ad v*es*tram si placet memoriam reducentes q*uod* ex sang*ui*ne v*es*tro scilicet ex filia nepte[b] v*es*tre filie n*os*tre k*arissi*me q*uo*ndam bone memorie regine Norwag*ie* que nu*n*c est apparens h*er*es n*os*tra diuina p*ro*uidente clemencia . multa bona poterunt prouenire que [ ][c] . fedus indissolubile inter vos et nos *contra*ctum tanq*uam* int*er* fideles et co*n*stantes nisi morte tamen nu*nquam* dissolueret*ur* sicut firmit*er con*fidim*us* et tenem*us* . Hinc est quod magnificenciam v*es*tram dilectissimam specialit*er* dep*re*camur quatin*us* hiis que religiosus vir Andre*as* abbas de Cupr*o* et [ ][d] v*es*tre dilectissime [ ][d] dignemini fidem indubitam adhibere. mandantes nob*is* cum fiducia p*er* eundem v*es*tre [benigne?][c] [Valeat excellencia vestra] per tempora longiora . [Teste meipso apud Castrum] Puellar*um* xx° die . April*is* anno regni n*ostri* xxx° quinto.

NOTES. Letters in brackets supplied from printed version. Examination of the letter under ultraviolet light and, later, with the assistance of digital software yielded a few words that were illegible to Stones. [a] There is a small gap in the MS here. [b] Sic, nepote. [c] Two–three words illegible. [d] Ten–eleven words illegible.

DESCRIPTION. 24.9 cm x 7.9 cm. Sealing: no evidence of a tag, tongue or seal. Much of the surface of the document is badly stained and illegible, even under ultraviolet light.

HAND. Scribe O.

SOURCE. Original. TNA, Special Collections: Ancient Correspondence of the Chancery and the Exchequer, PRO SC 1/20/162.

PRINTED. Stones, *Anglo-Scottish Relations,* no. 13; *CDS*, ii, no. 250 (cal.).

147 Writes to Edward I king of England concerning John de Masun, who claims that King Alexander owes him for purchases of wines and in consequence of whose numerous appeals, Edward has twice written him on John's behalf. Alexander has now learned that when Weland, the clerk of his chamber, appointed the Tuesday after the feast of St Luke at Haddington for payment of [some] merchants, John came with his claim. Weland told him to produce letters of agreement between him and King Alexander's council, duly sealed, upon which he would be paid without further delay. When John declined to do so Weland sought advice from his associates and other merchants, who counselled that unless John first accounted, and then on payment delivered up the letters, he neither could nor ought safely to pay him. John therefore withdrew, having through his own fault received only partial payment. He requests that Edward enjoin John to come to Scotland and to account reasonably with his men, so that he may receive without delay what is owed him and what Edward's letters have sought. Dundee, 18 May a.r. 35 [1284].

Serenissimo p*r*incipi f*ra*tri suo k*arissi*mo d*omi*no Edwardo D*e*i g*ra*tia regi Angl*ie* illust*ri* d*omi*no Hibe*rnie* et duci Aquitan*nie* Alex*ander* eadem g*ra*tia rex Scott*orum* sal*u*tem . et vere ac sincere dilecc*i*onis semp*er* augm*en*tum . Sup*er* eo q*uo*d Joh*ann*es Mazun celsitudine*m* v*es*tram sup*er* q*uo*dam debito q*uo*d sibi deberi asserit . pro vinis captis ad s*er*uiciu*m* nos*tru*m ab eodem . cu*m* necesse no*n* esset . vos pluries interpellauerit . per quod litteras vestras iam bis misistis nobis pro ipso . veritatem vobis sicut pro certo didicimus a fidelibus nostris et iuratis . constare facimus per presentes . Quod cum Welandus clericus camere nostre loco camerarii nostri constitutus . diem Martis post festum beati Luce Ewangeliste apud Hadingtun ad pagamentum faciendum diuersis mercatoribus pro rebus captis ab eis statuisset et assignasset . dictus Johannes Mazun petens debitum suum pro vinis suis comparuit ibidem in presencia plurimorum . cui respondens dictus Welandus dixit quod idem Johannes certam conuencionem fecerat cum quibusdam de nostro consilio super qua conuencione dictus Johannes litteras habuit sigillatas quibus ostensis eidem sine vlteriori dilacione incontinenti solui faceret quod debebat . Quo Johanne nolente dictam conuencionem neque litteras ostendere supradictas . dictus Welandus petiit consilium a sociis et mercatoribus quid super huiusmodi secundum rationem foret faciendam . qui consuluerunt quod nisi dictus Johannes prius computaret et deinde pagamento suo recepto litteras resignaret . ei quicquam soluere tute non potuit nec debebat . Et sic dicto Johanne recedente parte pagamenti sui recepta parte non recepta . culpa sua remansit negocium inperfectum . Quam ob rem si placet precipiatis eidem Johanni quod personaliter accedat ad partes nostras tracturandum cum hominibus nostris et rationabiliter computarendum cum ipsis sicut alias eidem Johanni mandari precipimus . et semper voluimus . vt quicquid ei debetur recipiat . quod ei plene siue more dispendio solui faciemus . et eo multo libencius quod pro ipso nobis vestras litteras destinastis . Teste me ipso apud Dunde . x°viij° die Maii anno regni nostri xxx° quinto .

DESCRIPTION. 22.6 cm x 8.4 cm. Sealing: no evidence of a tag, tongue or seal.
HAND. Scribe O.
SOURCE. Original. TNA, Chancery Miscellanea, PRO C 47/22/3/3.
PRINTED. *CDS*, ii, no. 252 (cal.); *L & I*, vol. xlix, 187 (note).

148 Writes to the sheriff of Lanark and his bailies of Rutherglen, informing them that he has given and by this deed granted in perpetuity 100s annually from Rutherglen to the priest who, at the king's presentation, shall celebrate solemn masses and other divine offices at the altar of St Kentigern in Glasgow Cathedral, for him, his ancestors and heirs. Commands and instructs them to ensure that the priest receives the said 100s annually. Forfar, 28 May a.r. 35 [1284].

[ ]lexander[a] Dei gracia[b] rex Scottorum. vicecomiti de Lanark' et balliuis suis de Rutherglen'[c] qui pro tempore fuerint. salutem . Sciatis nos dedisse. et hoc presenti scripto nostro concessisse pro nobis et heredibus nostris inperpetuum[d] presbitero qui in cathedrali ecclesia Glasguen'[e] ad altare beati[f] Kentegerni[g] pro nobis antecessoribus et dictis heredibus nostris missarum solemnia et alia diuina officia perpetuo celebraturus esse[h]. ad presentacionem[i] nostram centum solidos sterlingorum recipiendos apud Rutherglen[j] per manus vestras singulis annis inperpetuum[d] . Quare vobis mandamus et precipimus. quatinus dicto presbitero dictos centum solidos. singulis annis habere faciatis. Videlicet. medietatem ad festum

Pentecost*en* et alia*m* medietate*m* ad festu*m* b*eati*[f] Martini in yeme[k] . Et nos d*ict*os centu*m* solid*os* vob*is* in compotis v*est*ris faciem*us* plenius allocari. Testibus Will*elm*o de Soulis. justic*iario* . Laodon*ie*. Will*elm*o de Brechy*n*·[l] et Galf*ri*do de Moubr*ay*[m]. militibus apud Forfar'[n] . xxviii°. die Maii. anno regni n*ost*ri tricesimo q*ui*nto[o].

NOTES. [a] Blank space left for initial A, which is missing. Text B spells the king's name out in full in bold, enlarged letters, possibly recreating scribal embellishment in the original deed. [b] Gratia in B. [c] Rutherglen in B. [d] In perpetuum in B. [e] Glas[se] in B. [f] Letter 'B' only in B. [g] An annotator of Text B has written into the margin here 'intecessoribus'. [h] Celebraturus est in B. [i] Presentationem in B. [j] Rethirglen in B. [k] Hyeme in B. [l] 'Pretzy' in B. [m] Mubray in B. [n] B omits the place date. [o] Regnal year omitted in B.

RUBRIC. 1. Carta centum solidorum de Roglen' pro rege ministranti soluendorum (A). 2. Carta Alexandri regis III quatinus centum solidos de Rutherglen capellano celebranturo in ecclesia cathedralis Glasg' (B).

SOURCE. SCA, MS. JB 1, no. 4, Liber ruber ecclesiae, fos. xlii[r-v] = A; Glasgow University Library, MS. Gen. 198, fo. 269 = B.

PRINTED. *Glasgow Registrum*, i, no. 235; Hamilton, *Lanark and Renfrew*, 223.

COMMENT. For a note about the sources, see above, Comment to no. 108. The author of Text B claims to have made his transcription from the original deed, to which was appended the king's (second) great seal. He described it (in Latin) as follows: 'To this charter is appended the great seal of Scotland, in white wax, much worn, showing on one side the king as an equestrian figure and on the other (the king) sitting on his throne, his right arm bent, holding a sceptre, and on his head a crown.' Cosmo Innes, editor of the Maitland Club version of the Glasgow cartulary, noted the seal briefly but did not describe it (*Glasgow Registrum*, i, cxxv, note c). Alexander's brieve is noted briefly also (in an English summary) in Glasgow University Library, MS. Gen. 1245, Item 1, fo. 259. A late transcript appears at NRS, RH 2/2/5.

149 Grants and by this charter confirms to the brethren of the Knights Hospitallers of Jerusalem all their possessions, hospitals and alms, whether these be churches or worldly possessions, to be held as freely as the charter of his father, King Alexander II, bears witness. Grants also that the brethren's men both within and beyond Rutherglen be free of all toll and custom; further grants them all fines levied before the burgh's bailies there. The brethren are to be quit of fines of any kind in return for a payment of one ell of white scarlet [cloth]. All the above named possessions are to be held in pure and perpetual alms. Scone, 17 June a.r. 35 [1284].

Alexander[a] Dei gracia rex Scotorum omnibus probis hominibus tocius terre sue clericis et laicis salutem . Sciatis presentes et futuri nos concessisse et hac presenti carta nostra confirmasse Deo et fratribus hospitalis Jerusalem omnes donaciones terrarum et hospitalium et elemosinarum que eis racionabiliter facte sunt tam in ecclesiis quam in aliis rebus et possessionibus mundanis. Volumus eciam et firmiter precipimus vt predicti fratres omnes possessiones et elimosinas suas habeant et teneant adeo libere et quiete sicut carta clare memorie domini regis Alexandri patris nostri super hiis et aliis libertatibus dictis fratribus confecta proportat et testatur. Volumus eciam et concedimus omnibus hominibus predictorum fratrum et qui de eisdem quicquid tenent in burgo aut extra burgum vt quieti sint ab omni tholoneo et ab omnibus aliis consuetudinibus in omnibus empcionibus et vendicionibus mundanis qualitercunque contingents. Et si coram nobis uel aliquibus balliuis nostris super aliquo defectu fuerint amerciati prefata amerciamenta sancto Johanni et dictis fratribus concessimus imperpetuum. Et si idem fratres aliquomodo fuerint amerciati sint quieti pro vna vlna albi scarleti. Volumus insuper et concedimus vt dicti fratres omnia prescripta habeant et teneant in liberam puram et perpetuam elemosinam. Testibus Malis comite de Stratherne Donaldo comite de Mar Jacobo senescallo Scocie. Apud Scone decimo septimo die mensis Junii anno regni nostri tricesimo quinto.

NOTE. [a] In capital letters.
SOURCE. NRS, Great Seal Register, C 2/12, no. 51.
PRINTED. *Templaria*, pt. ii, 2–3; *RMS*, ii, no. 1791 (cal.).
COMMENT. The deed is cited in a transumpt of King James IV dated 19 October 1488. The latter lists grants made to Hospitallers and Templars by several of his predecessors, including a confirmation of his father, James III, which itself confirmed earlier grants of kings Malcolm IV and Alexander III to the Hospitallers of Torphichen. James III's charter also cites the charters of his royal predecessors.

150 Writes to Edward I king of England sending him good wishes and, by the bearers, a present of four falcons, one white and three grey. Haddington 'in Scocia', 26 June a.r. 35 [1284].

Serenissimo n*ec*non et excellenti p*r*incipi d*omi*no Edwardo D*ei* gr*at*ia regi Angl*ie* illust*ri* d*omi*no Hib*ernie* et duci Aquitan*nie* dil*ec*tissimo fratri suo . suus Alex*ander* eadem gr*at*ia rex Scott*orum* . sal*ut*em . et intime ac sincere dilecc*i*onis s*e*mp*er* augmentu*m* . De statu v*est*ro nobis k*aris*simo et v*est*ror*u*m s*e*mp*er* affectantes scire et intellig*er*e felices euent*us* . celsitudinem v*est*ram tenore p*re*senciu*m* dep*re*camur et [iam?][a] ad solaciu*m* n*ost*rum maximu*m* nob*is* rumores significare velitis ylaritatem v*est*ram et v*est*ror*um* co*n*tinentes . Et quia firmit*er* credim*us* v*est*ri gr*at*ia et tenemus q*uod* quocie*n*s de statu n*ost*ro vob*is* p*ro*spera reseruantur . effecti estis leciores . scire velitis q*uod* in rece*n*ssi[b] p*re*senciu*m* a nob*is* b*e*n*e*dicto D*omi*no eram*us* in statu co*m*petenti . mittim*us* vobis p*er* latores p*re*senciu*m* quatuor gerfalcones vnu*m* album et tres griseos vtina*m* optimi sint et valeant vt vellem*us* . si aliqua penes nos vob*is* placu*er*int . nob*is* si placet significare poteritis co*n*fident*er* val*ea*t . semper . T*este* me ip*s*o ap*u*d Hadi*n*gtu*n* in Scoc*ia* . xx^{o}vi^{to} . die Junii anno . r*egni* . n*ostri* . xxx^{o} quinto .

NOTES. [a] MS faded here, one word missing. [b] Sic, recensum.
DESCRIPTION. 20.3 cm x 5.1 cm. Sealing: formerly sealed on a tongue cut from right to left across the bottom of the deed, now torn away.
HAND. Scribe O.
SOURCE. Original. TNA, Special Collections: Ancient Correspondence of the Chancery and the Exchequer, PRO SC 1/20/163.
PRINTED. *CDS*, ii, no. 253 (cal.).

151 Writes to Edward I king of England informing him that Gerard de Orlac', merchant, has been arrested and brought to London at the unlawful suit of certain merchants of Cahors (in Gascony). As Gerard has certain matters to relate to Alexander on behalf of his son-in-law, the king of Norway, he requests that, on receipt of good sureties to return to London, Edward show favour by having him released, so that he may report what he has to say. Edinburgh, 27 June a.r. 35 [1284].

Magnifico principi fratri suo karissimo domino . E . Dei gratia regi Anglorum illustri domino Hibernie et duci Aquitannie . Alexander eadem gratia rex Scottorum salutem . et glorie et honore augmentum . Pro Gerardo de Orlac' mercatore qui ad instanciam quorundam mercatorum de Caurs' ipsum iniuste prosequentium arrestatus est vt dicitur Lundon' . et qui nobis aliqua habet exponere vt intelleximus ex parte cari filii nostri domini regis Norwagie . celsitudini vestre preces porrigimus speciales attencius deprecantes quatinus percipere velitis quod dictus Gerardus recepta prius ab eo bona securitate ad partes Lundon' reuert[endi] et de se conquerentibus iuste ibidem vel alibi pro voluntate vestra respondendi et iuri parendi ad nos venire possit . dicturus nobis si qua [ ][a] dicere ex parte dicti regis Norwagie . Tamen inde si placet facientes . vt nuncio suo si quod habet nobis exposito preces nostras sibi [ ][b] de ipso conquerentibus in partibus vbi arrestatus est . exhibeatur iusticie complementum . Valeat semper . Teste . me ipso apud Edinburg' xx°vii° die Junii anno regni[c] tricesimo quinto .

NOTES. Words in brackets are supplied by conjecture. [a] One word illegible owing to staining. [b] Three–four words illegible. [c] Word nostri omitted here.

DESCRIPTION. 21.6 cm x 5.8 cm. Sealing: formerly sealed on a tongue cut from right to left across the bottom of the deed, now torn away. The right half of the document is stained.

HAND. Scribe O.

SOURCE. Original. TNA, Special Collections: Ancient Correspondence of the Chancery and the Exchequer, PRO SC 1/20/164.

PRINTED. *CDS*, v, pt. 2, no. 50 (cal.).

152 Gives, grants and by this charter confirms to the monks of Newbattle abbey the land of Easter Craig of Gorgie (Midlothian), for a pittance to be paid annually on the feast of St James, on which day they shall celebrate mass for his ancestors, children and heirs. The said land was formerly held by Thomas son of William de Lamberton, who resigned and quitclaimed it into the king's hands on the vigil of the Blessed Apostles Peter and Paul, at Edinburgh before Patrick de Graham, knight, William de Kinghorn, then constable of the said castle, and Ranulf of the king's wardrobe. To be held in pure and perpetual alms. Stirling, 1 July a.r. 35 [1284].

Alexander Dei gratia rex Scottorum. omnibus probis hominibus tocius terre sue. salutem. Cum Thomas filius Willelmi de Lambirton'. in vigilia beatorum apostolorum Petri et Pauli. apud Castrum Puellarum. in presencia nostra constitutur. coram Patricio de Graham milite. Willelmo de Kynggorn tunc constabulario dicti castri nostri. et Ranulpho de gardropa[a] nostra. totum ius et clamium. quod habuit vel habere potuit in terra de. Estircrag. de Gorgyn. cum pertinenciis pro se et heredibus suis in perpetuum nobis per fustum et baculum reddiderit resignauerit. et quietum clamauerit non coactus sua bona et spontanea voluntate. Sciant presentes et futuri nos pro anime nostre salute et pro animabus regum antecessorum nostrorum. Puerorum. et heredum nostrorum dedisse . concessisse et hac presenti carta nostra confirmasse. Deo et ecclesie beate Marie de Neu'. et monachis ibidem Deo seruientibus. et seruituris ad vnam pitanciam singulis annis faciendam[b] habendam die beati Jacobi ap*ost*oli illa*m* te*rram* de Estircrag de Gorgyn cu*m* iustis p*er*tinenc*ii*s suis p*er* r*ec*tas suas di*ui*sas. et eade*m* die b*eat*i Iacobi celeb*ra*bunt missas *pro* nob*is*. An*te*cessorib*us*. Pueris. et h*er*edib*us* n*ost*ris in p*er*pet*uum* . Tenenda*m* et h*abe*ndam p*redict*is mo*n*ach*is*. de nob*is*. et h*er*edib*us* n*ost*ris in puram et p*er*pet*uam* ele*mos*in*am*. adeo libere. quiete. plenar*ie* et honorifice. sicut aliq*ua* elemosina de nob*is* *con*cessa. i*n* regno n*ost*ro liberi*us* et q*u*iec*ius* iuste tenet*ur* et possidetur ext*ra* regale. cu*m* lib*er*tatibus et aysiame*n*tis ad d*ict*am t*er*ram p*er*tine*n*tib*us*. Testib*us*. Waltero comite de Meneteth. Patricio de Grah*am* Andr*ea* de Morauia. Joh*ann*e de Kynros. Walt*er*o de Lynddessay. militib*us* p*ri*mo die Julii. anno reg*ni* nostri. t*ri*cesimo quinto ap*ud* Str*i*uelyn.

NOTES. [a] Sic, garderoba. [b] Word underlined in MS; perhaps because it was mistaken or superfluous.

RUBRIC. At bottom of folio: Ista donac*io* t*er*re de le Crag' inportat pitta*n*cia*m* facie*n*dam die b*eat*i Jacobi an*n*uati*m* (fourteenth century).

SOURCE. NRS, Adv. MS. 34.4.13, Chartulary of Newbattle Abbey, fos x^{r-v}.

PRINTED. *Newbattle Registrum*, no. 41.

153

Gives, grants and by this charter confirms to his clerk, Master Ralph de Dundee, a half ploughgate in the territory of Rait (Perthshire). The said land was formerly held by Robert Wischard, clerk, son of the late Utring called 'Castball', who resigned and quitclaimed it, for default of service, into the king's hands at Dundee on the Wednesday next after the feast of the translation of St Thomas in the year 1284, before several magnates of the realm. To be held in feu and heritage for an annual render of one pound of pepper and for performing the forinsec service owed from that land. Dundee, 11 July a.r. 36 [1284].

Alex*ander* Dei gratia rex Scottorum omnibus probis hominibus tocius terrae sue salutem. Sciatis nos dedisse concessisse et hac presenti carta nostra confirmasse magistro Radulpho de Dunde clerico nostro illam dimidiam carucatam terre cum pertinentiis in territorio de Rath quam Robertus Wyscard clericus filius quondam Utringi dicti Castball de nobis tenuit et ob defectum seruicii quod nobis inde debuit nobis die Mercurii proxima post festum translationis sancti Thome martiris anno Domini milles*imo* ducentesimo octogesimo quarto coram quibusdam magnatibus nostris apud Dunde per fustum et baculum reddidit et quietam clamauit et totum ius suum quod in dicta terra habuit vel habere potuit pro se et hominibus suis in perpetuum resignavit. Tenendam et habend*am* eidem magistro Radulpho et heredibus suis de nobis et heredibus nostris in feodo et hereditate libere et quiete reddendo inde annuatim nobis et heredibus nostris unam libram piperis ad Pentecosten et faciendo inde nobis et heredibus nostris forinsecum servicium quantum pertinet ad dictam terram. Testibus Douenaldo comite de Mar, Nicholao de Haya, Jacobo de Ramesey et Patricio de Abirnithyn militibus. Apud Dunde undecimo die Julii anno regni nostri tricesimo sexto.

RUBRIC. The copyist added the following heading to his transcript, perhaps from an original endorsement: Carta regis Alexandri clerico suo super dimidia carucata terre in territorio de Rath' concessa.

SOURCE. NLS, Adv. MS. 34.3.25, fo. 149, an eighteenth-century transcript by Walter Macfarlane of the original then in the possession of William Robertson of Ladykirk. The original has not been traced.
PRINTED. *Highland Papers*, ii, 124.
COMMENT. A deed of Bishop John of Dunkeld datable to the last decade of the twelfth century notes that Rait (Rathoc) was 'the *capud* of the *comitatus* of Atholl' (*Scone Liber*, no. 55). That status is in turn confirmed by the identification of Rait in a late twelfth-century legal compilation as the site within the mormaership of Atholl where, customarily, accusations of theft, homicide and other violent offence were heard and determined (see A. Taylor, '*Leges Scocie* and the Lawcodes of David I, William the Lion and Alexander II', *SHR*, 88 (2009), 223, 274). Its importance as an ancient legal site is probably the reason why Edward I deliberately included it on his circuit around the conquered kingdom in 1296. See Stevenson, *Documents*, ii, 29. A modern transcript appears in NLS, Adv. MS. 34.3.25, fo. 149.

154 Commands the sheriff and bailies of Elgin to pay annually to the Friars Preachers of Elgin from the fermes of their bailliaries, two chalders of grain, two of barley and one of malt, which he has given them for their sustenance in perpetuity. Kintore, 29 March a.r. 36 [1285].

Alexander Dei g*rat*ia[a] rex Scottorum vicecomiti et balliuis[b] de Elgyne[c] salutem. Mandamus vobis et precipimus q*ua*t*in*us de firmis ballie vestre de Elgyne[d] .fratribus predicatoribus eiusdem loci persoluatis singulis annis. ad festum sancti Martini in yeme[e] duas c[eldras][f] frumenti. duas c[eldras] ordei et unam c[eldram] brasei[g]. quas. eis ad sustentationem eor*u*m inperpetuum[h] percipiendas dedimus. Et nos dictas duas c[eldras] frumenti et duas c[eldras] ordei[i] necnon et unam c[eldram] brasei[g] vobis in compotis vestris faciemus singulis an*n*is allocari. per l*itte*ras eoru*n*d*e*m fratrum de recepto. Testibus Alexandro Comynne[j] comite de Buchane'. justiciario et constabulario Scoc*ie* Donaldo comite de Marr[k] Ingeramo de Gynes[l] . Reginaldo le Chyne[m] militibus. Apud Kyntor[n] xxix[oo]die Marcii anno regni n*os*tri tricesomo sexto.

NOTES. [a] In B the first three words appear in large print. [b] Balluius suis in B. [c] Elgyn' in B. [d] Elgin in B. [e] Hieme in B. [f] Word used here in the original supplied from B. Text A uses only the initial c in all instances where the word appears. [g] Brasii in B. [h] Perpetue in B. [i] Duas celdras ordei et duas celdras frumenti in B. [j] Comyn' in B. [k] Mar in B. [l] Gynis in B. [m] Chen patre in B. [n] Kyntore in B. [o] Vicesimo nono in B.
RUBRIC. Carta illustris regis Alexandri (sixteenth century).
SOURCE. NRS, Great Seal Register, C 2/1, no. 149 = A; NLS, Adv. MS. 34.7.2, Register of Writs concerning the Hospital of Maison Dieu and the Dominican friary at Elgin, fos 30^{r}–31^{v} = B. The latter is a register dated 1548 of 'authenticated' copies of writs concerning the hospital of Maison Dieu and the Dominican friary of Elgin. Alexander III's grant is cited in an inspeximus of King David II dated 15 April 1369. Transcribed here from A.
PRINTED. *RRS*, vi, no. 436; *RMS*, i, no. 245; *RMS*, iv, no. 638 (cal.).

155 Writes to Edward I king of England expressing his pleasure to hear of his good health in the letter brought by Ingram de Gynes and thanking him for the assistance that he has given Ingram in his affairs. Aboyne, 1 April a.r. 36 [1285].

Egregio principi f*ra*tri suo in *Christo* do*min*o k*ariss*imo Edwardo Dei g*rat*ia regi Angl*ie* illust*ri* do*min*o Hib*ernie* et duci Aq*ui*tan*nie* Alex*ander* eadem gr*at*ia [rex Scottorum] . sal*ut*em . cum om*n*imodis gl*or*ie et honoris i*n*crementis . Littere q*ua*s p*er* Inge*r*amum de Ginis caru*m* co*n*sangu*i*neu*m* nos*t*rum ves*t*ra nob*is* [destinata] serenitas sup*er* continencia status ves*t*ri iocu*n*da quam *con*tinue tam scire q*ua*m audire cu*m* animi n*os*tri solacio ac recrea*ci*one peroptamus . nos ad gaudii fulcimentu*m* suscitaru*n*t . Quocirca dilecc*i*oni ves*t*re k*arissi*me tenore p*re*senciu*m* significam*us* p*er* p*re*sentes q*uod* te*m*po*r*e co*n*fecc*i*onis p*re*senciu*m* sospitate debita gaudebam*us* D*omi*no be*ne*dicto . id idem de vob*is* scire desiderantes indefinent*er* . Et quia p*er* d*ic*tum Inge*r*amum didicim*us* ad plenu*m* q*uod* amore n*os*tri negocia sua iuxta votu*m* p*re*cepistis expediri . Excellencie ves*t*re non im*m*erito ad g*ra*tes assurgim*us* speciales . p*ar*ati semp*er* p*ro* viribus ves*t*ra be*ne*placita vt tenemur adimplere . Valeat magnificencia ves*t*ra p*er* te*m*po*r*a longena . Teste me ip*s*o ap*u*d Obeyn . p*ri*mo die Ap*ri*lis anno reg*n*i nostri xxx^{o}vi^{to} .

NOTES. Words in brackets are conjectural; MS is stained in places.
DESCRIPTION. 23.4 cm x 6.1 cm. Sealing: formerly sealed on a tongue cut from right to left across the bottom of the deed, now torn away. Parts of the document are stained.
HAND. Scribe O.
SOURCE. Original. TNA, Special Collections: Ancient Correspondence of the Chancery and the Exchequer, PRO SC 1/20/165.
PRINTED. *CDS*, ii, no. 267 (cal.).
COMMENT. The assistance that Alexander requested related to the inheritance of Ingram's wife, Christina de Lindsay. She was the heiress of William de Lindsay of Lamberton (d. 1283), a significant land holder both in England and Scotland. In the spring of 1284 King Edward instructed his chancellor to convene an inquest to assess Lindsay's estate (TNA, PRO SC 1/9/91). Alexander's request of a year later still suggests that Edward's 'assistance' was rather long in coming.

157 Gives, grants and by this charter confirms to the church and canons of Whithorn the advowson of the church of the Holy Trinity at Ramsay, in Man, for the upkeep of divine service to St Ninian and for the table of the religious of Whithorn. To be held in pure and perpetual free alms. Glenluce, 24 May a.r. 36 [1285].

Om*n*ibus *Christ*i fidelib*us* p*re*sentes l*ite*ras visur*is* vell[a] auditur*is* Alexander Dei g*ra*tia rex Scotorum sal*ut*em in D*omi*no sempite*rnam*. Nove*ri*tis nos diuine caritat*is* intuitu et pro salute nostra ac liberum[b] nostror*um* antecessor*um* et successor*um* nostrorum at*que* o*mn*ium fideliu*m* defu*n*ctor*um* dedisse co*n*cessisse et hac p*re*senti carta nostra co*n*firmasse Deo et b*eat*o Niniano co*n*fessori ecc*les*ie Candidecase in Galualia et cano*nicis* ibide*m* Deo seruientib*us* et s*er*uitu*r*is in pura*m* et pe*r*petua*m* elemosina*m* ius aduocation*is* ecc*les*ie sancte \Trinitat*is*/ apud Ramsayth i*n* Man*n*ia cu*m* o*mn*ib*us* libertatib*us* et iustis pe*r*tinentiis suis ad sustentacione*m* diuini seruitii ibide*m* sancto pred*ic*ti ac religio*sorum* d*ic*ti monasterii ad me*n*sa*m* eorundem liber*e* et quiete plenarie et honorifice in om*n*ib*us* . Testibus Johan*n*e Cumin de Buchan' Ricardo Kynard. Pat*r*icio de Barklay Andrea de Morrania et Dauide de Torthorruld' militib*us* apud Glenluss' vicesi*mo* q*ua*rto die Maii an*n*o regni n*os*tri t*r*icesimo sexto.

NOTES. [a] Sic, vel. [b] Sic, liberorum.
RUBRIC. The following heading, written in an early sixteenth-century hand, appears before the entry: Donac*i*o ecc*les*ie s*anc*te Trinit*atis* apud Ramsay p*er* Alexandru*m* rege*m*.

SOURCE. San Marino, CA, Huntington Library, MS EL 993, item 9, a transumpt of 1504, which reproduces several extracts from the (now lost) priory register.
PRINTED. Stringer, *Reformed Church*, 48–9, no. 9; Talbot, *Priory of Whithern*, App., no. 9 (with several errors); *HMC*, xi, App., pt. 8, 150 (note).
COMMENT. The diplomatic of the act is unusual: its clause of address suggests a scribe 'unfamiliar with the usages of the Scottish chancery' and, as Keith Stringer has suggested, it may well have been executed at Whithorn and submitted to the chancery at a later date for authentication with the royal seal (Stringer, *Reformed Church*, 49).

158 Takes the abbot and monks of Balmerino, their lands, their men, their possessions and the possessions of their men, movable and immovable, under his firm peace and protection, strictly forbidding anyone from causing any harm or injury to them, on pain of his full forfeiture; also grants that no one may take poinds from them or their men for anything other than their own debts, except in his burghs. Commands his justices, sheriffs, provosts and their bailies to compel all those in their burghs or bailiaries who owe a debt to the religious to pay them without delay. Dundee, 17 June a.r. 36 [1285].

Alex*ander*[a] Dei gr*at*ia rex Scott*orum* om*n*ib*us* probi*s* ho*mini*bus toci*us* te*rr*e sue sal*utem*. Sciat*is* nos viros religiosos abb*at*em et conue*n*tu*m* de Balm*ury*nach. te*rr*as suas. ho*m*ines suos. et vniue*rs*as eoru*m* possessiones ac om*n*ia bona sua et ho*m*inu*m* suor*um* mobilia et im*m*obilia sub fi*r*ma pace et p*ro*tect*io*ne n*ost*ra iuste suscepisse. Quare firmiter p*ro*hibem*us* ne quis eis malu*m*. Molestia*m*. iniuria*m*. seu g*ra*uamen inferre p*re*sumat iniuste super n*ost*ram plenaria*m* forisfacturam . Concessim*us* ecia*m* eisd*em* religiosis q*uod* nullus in regno n*ost*ro capiat namos[b] vel ho*min*um suor*um* nisi p*ro* debitis p*ro*p*ri*is exceptis burgis n*ost*ris. Mandam*us* insup*er* et p*re*cipimus om*n*ib*us* vicecomitib*us* et balliuis n*ost*ris quatin*us* om*n*es illos qui in balliis vestris debita debent d*ic*tis religiosis ad eade*m* debita eis iuste et sine dilacione redde*n*da p*ro*ut ide*m*[c] religiosi v*e*l eor*um* cert*us* attornat*us* lator p*re*senc*ium* d*ic*ta debita sibi deberi racionabi*li*ter p*ro*bare pot*er*int[d] iuste co*m*pellatis ita q*uod in*[e] \pro/ defectu v*est*ro sup*er* hoc[f] querimoniam de cet*er*o audiamus. Test*ibus* Gilberto de Vnfraivile comite de Ang*us*. Nich*olao* de Haya. Walter*o* de Lindesay et Joh*ann*e de Haia militib*us* ap*ud* Dunde. q*uin*to dec*imo* k*alendas* Julii anno r*egni* nostri. xxx° sexto.

NOTES. [a] Initial A rubricated. [b] The word nostros is crossed out here. [c] Sic, iidem. [d] Poterint compellatis in printed version. [e] Sic, quod. [f] Large blank space here in MS.
RUBRIC. De protectione Regis et ut nulle capiat namos eorum (fourteenth century).
SOURCE. NLS, Adv. MS. 34.5.3, Chartulary of Balmerino Abbey, fo. 19v.
PRINTED. *Balmerino Liber*, no. 53.

159 Grants to the burgesses of Kinghorn and more generally announces that, for the improvement of the burgh, they should have a market every Thursday, to be held as freely as burgesses and their communities elsewhere in the kingdom enjoy their markets. Largo, 26 June a.r. 36 [1285].

Alexander Dei gracia rex Scottorum omnibus probis hominibus tocius terre sue salutem. Sciatis nos pro vtilitate et melioracione burgi nostri de Kyngorne concessisse burgensibus et communitati eiusdem loci forum infra dictum burgum omni die Jovis. Tenendum et habendum adeo libere quiete et honorifice sicut aliqui alii burgenses et communitates infra regnum nostrum habent in burgis suis diebus eis concessis empcionibus et vendicionibus vtendo et hoc omnibus quorum interest significamus. In cuius rei testimonium hac literas nostras sibi fieri fecimus patentes. Testibus Nicholao de Haya, Andrea de Morauia, David de Westona[a] militibus. Apud Largauch xxvi^{to}[b] die Junii anno regni nostri xxxvj^{to}[c].

NOTES. [a] The printed version has the (very unlikely) Lvestona. [b] Vicesimo sexto in the printed version. [c] Tricesimo sexto in the printed version.

RUBRIC. Carta communitatis burgi de Kyngorn.

SOURCE. NRS, Great Seal Register, C 2/1, no. 87. The grant is cited in an inspection, with additional grants, of King David II dated 2 July 1364.

PRINTED. *RMS*, i, no. 183; *RRS*, vi, 353 (note).

COMMENT. There is a sixteenth-century transcript in BL, MS. Harl. 4693, fo. 4^{r}. The following note is appended to the transcript: 'Confirmacio cartae Alexandri 3tii per regem Dauidem 2^{d}um facta burgensibus burgi de Kingorne ut pro utilitate et melioratione dicti burgi habeant forum omni die Jovis. Carta Alexandri regis est de data apud Largauch 6 Junii anno regni sui 36. Testes fuerunt Nicolaus de Haya et Andreas de Morrauia. Confirmacio est de data apud Perth 2 Julii anno regni nostri 29. Testes fuerunt Patricius episcopus Brechinensis cancellarius nostri Villielmus comes de Douglass etc'. A modern transcript appears in NLS, Adv. MS. 34.3.25, fos 109–10.

160 Writes to Edward I king of England, informing him that he is sending his envoys, William de Soules, justiciar of Lothian and butler of Scotland, Simon Fraser and Richard de Straiton, requesting that he give them credence. 'Tuly mac Argentuly', 10 August a.r. 37 [1285].

Magnifico p*r*incipi f*ra*tri suo in *Christo* k*arissi*mo d*omi*no Edwardo Dei g*rat*ia regi Angl*ie* illust*ri* d*omi*no Hib*er*n*ie* et duci Aq*ui*tan*nie* . Alex*ander* eadem g*rat*ia rex Scott*orum* sal*ute*m . et mutue dil*ecc*i*o*nis *con*tinuu*m* incrementu*m* . Redeuntes ad nos dil*ecti* et fideles n*os*t*ri* Will*elmu*s de Soulys justici*arius* Laodonie et buticularius Scoc*ie* Simon Fraser' et Ricardus de St*ra*tun latores p*re*senciu*m* nobis statu*m* ves*t*ru*m* in eoru*m* recessu a vob*is* p*ro*sperum fore et iocundu*m* nu*n*ciarunt q*uo*d nob*is* iuxt*a* cotidianu*m* desideriu*m* n*ost*r*u*m ad animi n*ost*ri cedit solaciu*m* et ylaritatem . excellencie v*est*re significa*n*tes p*er* presentes . q*uod* uos et regina*m* v*est*ra*m* *in* recessu eoru*n*dem a nob*is* b*e*n*e*dicto D*omi*no . bona sospitate vigebamus . Et quia eosdem nu*n*cios n*ost*ros ad vos duximus it*er*ato mittendos . celsitudinem v*est*ram requirim*us* et rogam*us* attente . q*ua*tin*us* hiis que vob*is* dix*er*int ex p*ar*te n*ost*ra fide*m* adhib*er*e dignemini indubitatam sup*er* eisdem v*est*re b*e*n*e*placita volu*n*tatis nob*is* p*er* eosdem remandantes . Test*e* me ip*s*o ap*u*d Tuly mac Argentuly . x^{o} die Aug*us*ti . anno r*egni* . n*ostri* . xxx^{o}vii^{o} .

DESCRIPTION. 20.3 cm x 5.8 cm. Sealing: no evidence of a tag, tongue or seal.

HAND. Scribe O.

SOURCE. Original, TNA, Special Collections: Ancient Correspondence of the Chancery and the Exchequer, PRO SC 1/20/166.

PRINTED. *CDS*, ii, no. 272 (cal.).

COMMENT. The identification of the place date of this act is problematic; it is clearly corrupt and may reflect the inability of its author, Scribe O, to handle Gaelic names with ease. If, as seems likely, underlying part of the name is the Gaelic element *tulach* (hill), it may represent sites as far apart as Ardentilly (Perthshire), Arndilly (on the river Spey in Moray) or even Ardentinny (on Loch Long, Argyll). The personal element *mac*, however, remains inexplicable.

161 Writes to Edward I king of England offering surety and requesting that he write to the sheriff of Northumberland to give safe-conduct to John [de Masun?] so that he may be brought to King Alexander without delay. If the said John returns to Scotland he will better be able to account with his creditors ... and with the men who are bound to him [including the chamberlain?]. Edinburgh, 25 October a.r. 37 [1285].

Magnifico principi domino [Edwardo Dei gratia rex Anglie illustri domino Hibernie et duci Aquitanie Alexander eadem gratia rex] Scottorum salutem . [ ][a] cendo et de securitate sua [ ][b] nobis aut eis [ ][c] ciam precipere velitis [ ][c] ri faciem*us* iniusto p*er* vestras [ ][c] per [ ][d] conduratur [ ][e] predicta indilate . nobis et nos [ ][d] securitatem si facerit non poterimus . Idem Joh*ann*es [ ][f] in secura [ ][g] tatur sine mora . Et si dictus Joh*ann*es [2 words][h] ad p*re*ces n*ost*ras . nullus novit communicare cum cre[ ][i] eis reddere quod debet [ ][d] regno nostro idem Joh*ann*i in aliquo teneantur et camerarius [ ][a] Teste me ipso apud Castr*um* Puellar*um* xxv° die O*cto*bris . ann*o* . r*egni* . nostri .xxx°vii°.

NOTES. Words in brackets are conjectural. [a] Twelve–thirteen words illegible. [b] Fourteen–fifteen words illegible. [c] Fifteen–sixteen words illegible. [d] Three–four words illegible. [e] Ten–eleven words illegible. [f] One word illegible. [g] Four–five words illegible. [h] Two words illegible. [i] Seven–eight words illegible.

DESCRIPTION. 24.4 cm x 7.6 cm. Sealing: formerly sealed on a tongue cut from right to left across the bottom of the deed, now torn away. The document is badly damaged, defaced with a large stain, several holes and the top section torn away completely. Most sections remain illegible even under ultraviolet light and with the assistance of digital software.

HAND. Scribe O.

SOURCE. Original. TNA, Special Collections: Ancient Correspondence of the Chancery and the Exchequer, PRO SC 1/20/167.

PRINTED. *CDS*, v, pt, 2, no. 51 (cal.).

162 Grants and by this charter confirms to Patrick de Graham, knight, the gift that Malise earl of Strathearn made him of the land of Foswell in Strathearn. To be held heritably, as Malise's charter bears witness, saving the king's service. Scone, 13 November a.r. 37 [1285].

Alex*ander* Dei g*rat*ia rex Scotto*rum* om*n*ibus probis hominib*us* tocius t*er*re sue sal*utem* . Sciatis nos concessisse et hac p*re*senti carta n*ost*ra confirmasse dona*cio*nem illam quam Malisius comes de Strath-erin fecit domino Pat*ri*cio de Graham militi de t*er*ra de Foschall' . in Stratherin hereditar*ie* . Tenend*am* et habend*am* dicto Patricio de d*ict*o comite hereditar*ie* s*ecund*um q*uod* carta ips*i*us Malisii comitis exinde *con*fecta plenius iuste testat*ur* et proportat . saluo s*er*uicio n*ost*ro . Testibus Alex*andro* Cumyn comite de Buch*an* *con*st*abulario* et just*iciario* Scoc*ie* . Douenaldo comite de Mar' . Gilberto de Umfra-muill' comite de Anegus . Jacobo senescallo Scoc*ie* . Joh*ann*e Cumyn Willelmo de Morauia, Reginaldo le Chen patre et Pat*ri*cio de Berkeley militib*us* Apud Scon' . xiii° . die Novembr*is* anno regni n*ost*ri t*ri*cesimo septimo .

ENDORSED. 1. Confirmacio donacionis comitis de Strathern' de terra de Fossakel (contemporary). 2. King Allex'r confirmacioun of Malise erle of Stratherne's chartour geven to Pa: Lord Graeme of Foswall 13 Nov 37 yeir of his regne (sixteenth century).
DESCRIPTION. 20.6 cm x 9.1 cm; fold 3.3 cm. Sealing: formerly sealed on a tag, 1.3 cm broad, through single slits. The seal is missing.
HAND. Scribe U.
SOURCE. NRS, Montrose Muniments, GD 220/1/A/1/3/7.
PRINTED. *HMC*, ii, 166, no. 13.
COMMENT. This charter is one of three relating to the Graham family's late-thirteenth-century claims to Foswell as tenants of the earls of Strathearn, and the only one of the three that is genuine. NRS, GD 220/1/A 1/3/5 purports to be a charter by which King Alexander III confirmed to David de Graham the gift that Malise earl of Strathearn had made him of the lands of Kincardine, Coul, Cloan, Foswell, Pairney and Bardrill (all in Perthshire); it is dated at Selkirk, 28 June a.r. 22 (1271). While there remains attached to its parchment tongue a small fragment of wax, the latter is so defaced as to be illegible. More suspiciously still, the parchment surface of the document appears to have been scraped clean before being reused; hardly a practice one might expect in the royal writing office or a nobleman of the status of the Grahams. Some years ago, an attempt was made to photograph the document using ultra-sensitive plates in the hope of revealing the script that appears to underlie the present text. No such script was positively identified either with the light or using digital software. Altogether, the peculiarities of the document suggest that it is of dubious authenticity. Equally peculiar is NRS, GD 220/1/A/1/3/6. It is purportedly a second charter of Alexander III confirming Earl Malise's grant of the above-named estates to David de Graham, identical in its contents but with a new date of issue, Scone, 13 November a.r. 37 (1285), long after David's death around 1272. The seal and tag are both missing, and it is in the same hand as the spurious act of 1271. David de Graham did, in fact, hold these estates by grant of Malise II earl of Strathearn (C. J. Neville, *Native Lordship in Medieval Scotland: The Earldoms of Strathearn and Lennox, c. 1140–1365* [Dublin, 2005], 50n.); he obtained them when he married the earl's daughter. Title to the estates may have been challenged following his death, with King Alexander willing to confirm – and perhaps assume warrandice for – Foswell. The spurious acts may, on the other hand, have been much later fabrications.

163 Gives, grants and by this charter confirms to the burgh of Lanark all its rights, liberties and privileges with all the liberties and privileges that the king's burghs customarily enjoy. Strictly prohibits anyone within the sheriffdom of Lanark from purchasing wool, hides or any other merchandise, carrying on any commerce or making broadcloth, cut or dyed, other than the burgesses of Lanark; similarly, no merchant in the sheriffdom may purchase any merchandise other than from them on pain of his full forfeiture. If any foreign merchant is found purchasing wool or any other merchandise from anyone other than the burgesses the sheriff is to seize him and hold his goods until the king releases them. Reminds the burgesses and all who do business with them that they should contribute to the king's aid. All who bring wood or timber for the maintenance of the burgh are to have the king's firm peace, and no one should presume to poind or harm them as they travel on the highway going into or leaving the town, under pain of his full forfeiture. Grants finally that the burgesses of Lanark have all the rights of commonty in the lands pertaining to the burgh as their predecessors have customarily enjoyed. Scone, 15 November a.r. 27 [1285].

Alexander Dei gr*at*ia rex Scotorum om*n*ib*us* probis hom*in*ibus tocius terre sue[a] salute*m*. Sciatis nos dedisse concessisse et hac carta n*ost*ra co*n*firmasse burgo n*ost*ro de Lan*ar*k et burgen*sibus* n*ost*ris in eode*m* burgo n*ost*ro manentes[b] o*mn*ia iura libertates. et p*ri*uilegia que uel quas predicti[c] burgen*ses* n*ost*ri temporibus n*ost*ris siue alicui*us* ant*e*cessoru*m* n*o*strorum tempore hactenus habuerunt et possiderunt seu habere debuerunt vnacu*m* om*n*ibus libertatibus burgi adeo libere sicut alii burgi n*ost*ri communiter infra regnu*m* n*ost*rum de nobis liberius et quietius tenentur et possidentur. Prohibemus eciam ne quis infra viceco*m*itatu*m* n*o*strum de Lanark emeret[d] lanas vel coria vel aliquam[e] aliam mercaturam exerceat[f] vel pannum latum aut[g] tinctum aut tonsum faciat preter burgen*ses* n*ost*ri de Lanark. Item ne aliquis alius mercator infra dict*u*m viceco*m*itatu*m* n*ost*rum vel in burgo nostro de Lanark aliqua*m* mercaturam emerat[h] nisi a d*ict*is burgen*sibus* de Lanark super n*ost*ram [plenariam][i] forisfactura*m*. Si quis alienus mercator inue*n*tus fuerit [infra][i] d*ict*um viceco*m*itatum n*ost*rum de Lanark emens lanas corea vel aliqua*m* mercatura*m* aliam consimilem exerceat[j] cu*m* bonis suis capiatur et teneatur donec de eo n*ost*ram fecerimus volu*n*tate*m*. Volum*us* et p*r*ecipimus q*uod* o*m*nes mane*n*tes in d*icto*[e] burgo n*ost*ro de Lanark cu*m* d*ict*is burgen*sibus* n*ost*ris com*m*unicantes contribuant ad auxiliu*m* n*o*strum cu*m* eisdem burgen*sibus* n*ost*ris de Lanark. Et quod o*m*nes qui ligna aut mere*m*iu*m* attrah*entes*[k] ad d*ict*um burgu*m* n*ost*rum[e] de Lan*ar*k sustentandum n*ost*ram firma*m* pacem haberent[l] ita q*uod* nullus eos namare presumat seu i*n*iuste grauare in via n*ost*ra regia eundo ad d*ict*am villam de Lan*ar*k vel redeundo ab eadem sup*er* n*ost*ram plenaria*m* forisfactura*m*. Concedimus insup*er* q*uod* dicti burgen*ses* n*ost*ri de Lanark adeo libere habeant et possideant o*mn*ia sua com*m*unia et commune*m* pastura*m* sua*m* in moris petariis mossis et maresiis et i*n* om*n*ibus aliis asiamentis ad d*ict*am villam de Lanark iuste spectan*tibus* sicut in aliquo te*m*pore d*ict*i burgen*ses* n*ost*ri vel aliquis an*te*cessorum suoru*m* p*er* suas rectas diuisas et metas hactenus iuste habuerunt et possiderunt et eisd*em* vsi sunt vs*que* ad hec te*m*pora. Testibus Alex*andr*o Cumyn[m] comite de Buchane constab*ulario* et justic*iario* Scotie Henrico[n] comite de Stratherin[o]. Dovenaldo[p] comite de Marche[q], Jacobo senescallo Scocie, Reginaldo de Chen patre, Symone[r] Fras*er* et Patricio de Grahame militibus apud Scon' decimo qui*n*to die Nove*m*bris anno regni *nostri* tricesimo septimo[s].

NOTES. [a] B adds clericis et laicis. [b] Manentibus in B. [c] Iidem in B. [d] Emat in B. [e] Omitted in B. [f] Exerceant in B. [g] Et in B. [h] Emat in B. [i] MS torn here, supplied from B. [j] Exerciat in B. [k] Attrahunt in B. [l] Habeant in B. [m] Cummyn in B. [n] A and B; both are mistakes for Malisio. [o] Stratherne in B. [p] Tovenaldo (sic) in *RMS*. [q] A and B; both are mistakes for Mar. [r] Simone in B. [s] Trigesimoseptimo in B.

SOURCE. NRS, Acts of the Lords of Council and Session, CS 6/13, fos 85^{v}–86^{r} = A; Great Seal Register, C 2/27, no. 216 = B. Transcribed here from A.

PRINTED. *Lanark Recs.*, 308–9; *RMS*, iii, no. 2308 (cal.).

164 Grants and gives to Richard de Straiton part of the king's forest of Clunie in feu and heritage and in free forest, for £4 13s 4d annually. 1266 x 1273.

Alexander Dei *gra*tia rex Scotorum om*n*ibus probis hominibus tocius regni sui clericis et laicis salutem. Noverit vniuersitas vestra nos c*on*cessisse et dedisse dilecto et fideli n*ost*ro Ricardo de Straton' militi illam partem terre foreste n*ost*re del Clune quequidam pars vocatur Drosclune de la Straton' iacente*m* ex p*ar*te boriali et occidentali claus*ura* parci nostri et torrentis de Strat*on* et vsque ad moram que vocatur Idulany. Tenend*am* et habend*am* dicto Ricardo et heredibus suis de nobis et heredibus nostris in feodo et hereditate in libera foresta in om*n*ibus aliis libertatibus com*m*oditatibus ad dictam terram p*er*tinentibus seu p*er*tinere valentibus reddendo inde an*n*uatim quatuor libras tresdecim solidos et quatuor denarios. In cuius rei testimonium p*rese*ntibus sigillum nostrum precipimus apponi. Hiis testibus Will*el*mo Wissard cancellario Thoma Ra*n*ulphi camerario Alexandro comite de Buchane justiciario Reginaldo le Chene vicecomite de Kincardine et multis aliis.

RUBRIC. The heading reads: King Alexander the third; to Richard de Stratone knight charter of that part of the royal forest of Clune which is called Drosclune de la Stratone.
SOURCE. NRS, RD 1/8 fos. 220r-v, a register of deeds compiled between 26 March 1565 and 17 February 1566.
COMMENT. There is much that is unusual in this deed, not least the dispositive clause and the detailed description of the imparcation of the forest of Clunie. Both may be the consequences of scribal error committed when the original deed was copied. The witness clause, however, is consistent with a date of 1266 x 1273, and Richard de Straiton is reliably attested in the period 1276–85 (above, nos 97, 110, 128, 160 and possibly no. 116; below, no. 282). 'Drosclune' is Disclune in Kincardineshire; 'Idulany' may be Adielinn in Angus, also located within the boundaries of the medieval forest of Clunie. A modern transcript appears in NRS, RH 1/1/1.

165 Grants and by this charter confirms to the monks of Lindores the gift that Henry de Hastings, knight, made them of the whole of his toun of Flinders in Garioch, in exchange for the second teinds that, by gift of Henry's grandfather, Earl David of Huntingdon, they have customarily taken from his lands beyond the Mounth. To be held in perpetuity, as Henry's charter bears witness, saving the king's service. 1264 x 1269.

Alexander[a] Dei *gra*tia rex Scott*orum* om*n*ib*us* p*ro*bis hominib*us* toci*us* t*er*re sue sal*u*t*em*. Sciatis nos co*n*cessisse et hac p*re*senti carta n*ost*ra *confir*masse donat*i*o*n*em illa*m* q*uam* Henric*us* de Hastinges miles fecit D*e*o et ecc*lesi*e s*anc*t*e* Marie et s*anct*i Andre[b] de Lundors et monachis ibide*m* D*e*o seruientib*us*. et in p*er*petuu*m* seruitur*is* de tota villa sua de. Flandres' i*n* Garuiach p*er* rectas diuisas suas quas h*ab*uit t*em*por*e* eiusdem donac*io*nis sue. i*n* escambiu*m* sec*un*dar*um* decimaru*m* q*uas* consueuerunt p*er*cip*ere* de t*er*ris suis ult*ra* le Moneth de dono comitis. D*aui*d. aui sui. Tenend*a* et h*abe*nd*a* eisde*m* monachis et eor*um* successorib*us* i*n* p*er*petuu*m* de d*ic*to Henr*ico* et h*er*edib*us* suis cu*m* om*n*ib*us*. iurib*us* aisiam*ent*is et p*er*tinenciis ad ip*s*am villa*m* iuste spectantib*us* adeo lib*er*e. quiete. plenarie et honorifice. sicut carta ip*s*ius Henr*ici* eisdem monachis exinde *con*fecta pleni*us* iuste testatur. saluo seruicio n*ost*ro. Test*ibus* etc .

NOTES. [a] Initial A written outside the margin. [b] Sic.

RUBRIC. De confirmacione de Flandris (fourteenth century).

SOURCE. Caprington Castle, Kilmarnock, Lindores Cartulary, fos. 82^{v}–83^{r}.

PRINTED. *Lindores Cart.*, no. 119.

COMMENT. Henry de Hastings was knighted in 1264 (*Close Rolls, 1261–64*, 306); he died in 1269. The charter is roughly contemporary with another of King Alexander's confirmations to Lindores, dated 29 August 1261 (above, no. 33), which also concerns second teinds.

166

Gives, grants and by this charter confirms to William de Badby the whole land of Manor (Peeblesshire), resigned and quitclaimed by Nicholas Corbet, knight, into the king's hands at Kinclaven on Sunday the morrow of St Mark the Evangelist, 1271 by means of sealed letters, which were then enrolled in the royal chapel. To be held in feu and heritage by the same boundaries it had on the day when King David was alive and dead, together with the homage and services of all the free tenants there, excepting those on the land which King Malcolm, brother of King William, gave to the late Norman the huntsman, with soke and sake, gallows and pit, toll, team and infangenthief, for the service of one knight. If William should die without a legitimate heir, then his bastard son, John, is to hold the land by the same terms, and if John should die without legitimate issue, then the land is to revert to the king. 26 April 1271 x 29 March 1286.

Alexander Dei gratia rex Scotorum omnibus probis hominibus totius terre[a] salutem. Sciant presentes et futuri nos dedisse concessisse et hac presenti carta nostra confirmasse Willelmo de Baddeby pro homagio et servitio suo totam terram de Meners cum pertinentiis quam Nicolaus Corbet miles nobis reddidit et resignauit per suas litteras patentes sigillatas sigillo suo et sigillis multorum aliorum baronum nostrorum quas in capella nostra inrotularia fecimus die Dominica in crastino sancti Martini[b] evangeliste anno gratie 1271[c] apud Kynchecheuyn et quiete clamauit pro se et heredibus suis in perpetuum totum ius et clameum quod ipsi habuerunt in eadem terra vel habere poterunt in futurum. Tenendam et habendam eidem Willelmo et heredibus suis de corpore suo legittime exeuntibus de nobis et heredibus nostris in feodo et hereditate in bosco et plano in prato et pascuis in moris et maresiis in stagnis molendinis et aquis per rectas diuisas suas[d] habuit die quo rex David fuit viuus et mortuus cum homagio et servitiis libere tenentium eiusdem terre excepta terra quondam Normanni venatoris quam rex Malcolmus frater regis Willelmi aui nostri ei dedit ita libere et quiete plenarie et honorifice cum socco et sacca cum furca et fossa cum tol et tem et infangandhef[e] sicut alii barones nostri terras[f] suas de nobis liberius et quietius plenius et honorificentius tenent et possident. Faciendo inde nobis et heredibus nostris seruitium vnius militis. Et si contingat quod idem Willelmus absque legittimo herede de corpore suo in fata decedat volumus et concedimus quod Johannes filius eius bastardus teneat et habeat sibi et legittimis heredibus suis de corpore suo exeuntibus predictam terram de Meners cum suis pertinentiis in feodo et hereditate pro homagio et servitio suo de nobis et heredibus nostris adeo libere quiete plenarie et honorifice per seruitium vnius militis sicut superius est expressum. Et si contingat predictum Jhoannem[g] vel aliquem heredum predicti Willelmi vel predicti Johannis legittime procreatum absque legittimo herede de corpore suo in fata decedere volumus quod predicta terra de Meneris cum omnibus pertinentiis suis ad nos et heredes nostros libere et sine contradictione aliqua reuertatur. Teste etc.

NOTES. [a]Word sue missing in copy, reinserted into printed version. [b]*Sic* for Marci. The printed version opts for (the surely correct) Marci here, celebrated 25 April. [c] Millesimo ducentesimo septuagesimo primo in the printed version. [d]Word quas missing in MS. [e] Sic, corrected to infangandthef in printed version. [f]Word nostras crossed out in MS. [g] Sic, Johannem. Spelled as such in MS, though whether this reproduces an error in the lost roll or a mistake on the part of the copyist is uncertain.
RUBRIC. Carta Willelmi de Baddeby. The MS copy includes several marginal comments inserted opposite specific passages in the document, i.e. at line 5: Inrotulato in capella Regis; at line 13: Normannus venator; at line 14: Rex Malcolmus frater Regis Willelmi aui Regis Dauid; at line 19: successio bastardi per talliam. Whether these comments are those of the copyist or were written into the original roll in error is uncertain.
SOURCE. NLS, Adv. MS. 34.2.1b, 'Haddington Manuscript', fo. 117[r].
PRINTED. *RMS*, i, App., no. 95.
COMMENT. This deed represents a rare survival of a text from the many rolls of letters patent, remembrances and other materials from the Scottish chancery lost at sea in 1633. Thomas Hamilton, later first earl of Haddington, copied some of these materials. The reconstructed texts that form the so-called 'lost rolls' of the Great Seal are discussed in *RMS*, i, vi–viii and, more comprehensively, in *RRS*, v, 215–48. William's descendant, Alexander, forfeited the barony when he went over to the English side, and in 1309 Robert I granted half of it to Adam Marshall (ibid., v, no. 60). Alexander later came into Robert's peace, but his attempts to reclaim the other half of the barony failed; see NLS, Adv. MS. 34. 2. 1b, fo. 117[v]; *RRS*, v, 19; *RPS*, A1323/7/4; *RMS*, i, App., no. 96. The absence of a witness list makes it impossible to date the grant more precisely than the period between the session of the king's council to which it makes reference and the end of King Alexander's reign.

167 Announces that the dean and chapter of Aberdeen shall suffer no prejudice by reason of the king's presentation of Master Andrew de Grandtully, his clerk, to the church of Fordyce during the vacancy of the see. The dean and chapter shall fully enjoy the right to make the next presentation following the withdrawal or death of the said Master Andrew. Kintore, 8 July 1272 x 7 July 1273 (a.r. 24).

Alexander Dei gracia rex Scott*orum* om*nibus* p*ro*bis hom*in*ibus suis ad quos p*re*sentes l*itt*ere p*er*uen*er*int. sal*utem*. Sciatis q*uod* nolim*us* q*uod* aliquod fiat p*re*iudiciu*m* decano et capi*tu*lo Ab*er*donen' p*er* p*re*senta*cio*nem n*ost*ram q*uam* fecim*us* t*em*p*or*e vacaci*on*is eccl*es*ie Ab*er*donen' de magi*st*ro Andrea de Gare*n*tuly cl*er*ico n*ost*ro ad eccl*es*iam de Fordys que spectat ad p*re*dictos decanu*m* et capitul*u*m pleno iure q*uo*minu*s* plene et lib*er*e gaudeant. iure suo et possessione sua in ecc*les*ia memorata post cessione*m* vel decessu*m* ip*s*ius mag*ist*ri Andree. In cui*us* rei testi*moni*um has l*itt*eras n*ost*ras fieri fecim*us* patentes. Test*ibus* Alex*andr*o Comyn' comite de Buchane justic*iario* Scoc*ie*. Hugone de Ab*er*nethy et Joh*anne* de Malevile apud Kyntor. anno regni nostri. xxiiii[to] .

RUBRIC. Protestacio facta per dominum regem sede vacante (sixteenth century).
SOURCE. NLS, Adv. MS. 16.1.10, Register of the Cathedral Church and Bishopric of Aberdeen, fo. 20[r].
PRINTED. *Aberdeen Registrum*, i, 29–30.
COMMENT. See Dowden, *Bishops*, 106–7 concerning the vacancy of the see.

168 Gives and grants by this charter to John de Swinburne ten merks annually from his chamber for the rest of his life, to be paid by the hand of the king's bailiff of Tynedale, as the charter that he has bears witness. After 20 March 1274 x 19 March 1286.

Alex*ander* Dei gratia rex Scott*orum* omnibus ad quos littere presenti peruenerint salutem. Cum nuper dedisse et concessisse per cartam nostram dilecto et fideli nostro Johanni de Swynburn' decem marcas annuas et [im]perpetuo de camera nostra percipiendas nos ad instanciam et supplicacionem ipsius Johnannis de Swynburn' [mandamus?] quod illas decem macas annuas de cetero recipiat et habet omnibus diebus uite sue [ ][a] Tyndal' per manus balliui nostri eiusdem qui pro tempore fuerit [ ][a] [secumdum tenorem] cartam [ ][a] entes. In cuius rei testimonium has litteras nostras [fieri fecimus patentes. Testibus] [ ][b] Willelmo de Sancto Claro Simone Fraser et [ ] [a].

NOTES. The document is damaged; words in brackets are conjectural. [a] Two words illegible. [b] Three–four words illegible.
SOURCE. TNA, PRO C 145/66/24/1.
PRINTED. *Cal. Inqu. Misc.*, i, no. 2032.
COMMENT. The letters are cited in the record of an inquest held at Lanercost on 12 February 1307 where, in support of his claim to have ten merks yearly of all the fermes of Tynedale and reasonable estovers for his manor of Haughton in all the woods belonging to the manor of Wark in Tynedale, John de Swinburne presented copies of two charters of King Alexander III, one dated at Roxburgh on 20 March 1274 (see above, no. 88), the second at some other time, presumably, but not certainly, later. The text of the second charter is now almost completely obliterated, though the terminology that is legible suggests that the chancery clerk copied it into the record of this inquest from an authentic deed. The inquest itself was probably held in response to John's petition to Edward I, which is recorded in TNA, PRO SC 8/279/13920; *PROME*, ii, 539.

169 Gives, grants and by this charter confirms to the abbot and monks of Scone a fishery of one net in the fishery called 'Gerny' (Cairney?), once known as the king's net, in the river Tay. To be held in pure and perpetual alms. 21 January 1264 x 26 February 1275.

[ ]lexander[a] Dei gracia rex Scottorum o*mn*ibus probis homi*ni*b*us* tocius terre sue sal*ute*m. Sciatis nos ad honorem Dei et beate virginis mat*ris* eius beati Michaelis et o*mni*um s*anct*orum et pro salute a*ni*m*e* mee Margarete cohort*is* mee predil*ec*te lib*er*orum predecessor*um* et successorum meorum dedisse concessisse et hac p*rese*nti carta mea

confirmasse in puram et perpetuam elemosinam religiosis viris abb*ati* et *con*uentui de Scona Deo *ser*uientib*us* et s*er*uituris in perpetuu*m* piscariam vnius ret*is* in piscaria que vocatur Gern*u*y super[b] aquam de Tay que ret*e* regis ant*ea* vocabatur. cum tali itin*er*e ad eand*em* piscariam et reditu ab ead*em* quale racionab*i*liter ante habere consueuerunt. Tenend*as* et habend*as* dictis abbati et *co*nue*n*tui in perpetuum adeo libere quiete et honorifice sicut alie elemosine mee de me libere et quiete iuste tenentur et possidentur . Testibus.

NOTES. There are some beautifully executed drawings in the margins and around some letters. [a] Space for initial A left blank. [b] MS repeats super.

SOURCE. NLS, Adv. MS. 34.3.28, Chartulary of Scone Abbey, fo. 14v.

PRINTED. *Scone Liber*, no. 107.

COMMENT. It is unusual to find the singular possessive pronoun among the charters of Alexander III (anime *mee*). The explanation may be that the scribe was using as a model a similar grant by an earlier king. This occurred also in no. 102 above, where the use of the singular reflects close copying from earlier deeds to Dunfermline. The absence of a witness list makes it difficult to date the charter more precisely than the period between the birth of Prince Alexander and the death of Queen Margaret. 'Gernuy' may be Cairnie, near the Tay in St Madoes parish, Perthshire.

170 Writes to Edward I king of England informing him that he is told that Sir Ralph de Dacre and William de Hyrlan, clerk, collectors of the fifteenth in Cumberland, have collected the tax from his manors there. Reminds Edward that he holds his manors freely, and that all issue, commodities, escheats and aids that are raised from the men of his manor should remain to him and his heirs, as is shown in the agreements made between their ancestors concerning these manors. He therefore requests that these liberties continue to be observed and that Edward command his assessors to cease making demands on the men of his manor. 3 May, post 1275 x 19 March 1286.

[Exce]llentissimo principi ac f*ra*tri suo in *Christ*o k*ariss*imo . domino . Edwardo . D*ei* g*ra*tia reg*i* Angl*ie* . d*omi*no Hib*er*nie . et duci Aq[uitannie] A . ead*em* g*ra*tia rex Scoc*ie* . sal*ute*m . [Dominus] Ranulf*us* de Daker' et Will*elmus* de Hyrlan' . cl*er*icus . taxatores quindecimi infra comitatum Cumberl' de hominib*us* man*er*ior*um* n*ost*ror*um* [ ][a] comitatus quindecimu*m* o*mn*ium bonoru*m* suor*um* exigant vt intelleximus . Et nos eadem man*er*ia . ita liber*e* tenem*us* . q*uod* om*n*es p*ro*uentus . com*m*oditates . escaeta . et auxilia . q*ue* de ho*min*ibus p*redictorum* man*er*ior*um* n*ost*ror*um* em*er*g*ere* pot*er*unt . nob*is* et heredib*us* n*ost*ris remaneant .vt pat*et* in *conuencion*ibus inter p*ro*genitos n*ost*ros de eisd*em* man*er*iis . f*act*is . Et licet huiusmod*i* exacc*i*ones et g*ra*tie . alias temp*o*-*r*ib*us* retr*o*actis vob*is* et p*ro*genitis v*est*ris fuerint p*er* c*ommuni*tatem Anglie . co*n*cesse . t*am*en tenentes n*ost*ri p*redictorum* man*er*ior*um* . de huiusmod*i* exacc*i*onib*us* et graciis . semp*er* quieti remanserunt . n*ec* hui*usmod*i ab ip*s*is aliq*uo* tempore t*ra*nsacto petebatur . Propt*er* quod diligentissimam f*rater*nitatem v*est*ram affectuose exoramus . quatin*us* amore n*ost*ri . lib*er*tates n*ost*ras . p*redict*orum man*er*ior*um* p*er* p*ro*genitos v*est*ros nob*is* concessas . et usq*ue* huc integ*ra*l*i*t*er* vsitatas omnib*us* temp*o*rib*us* retr*o*actis . temp*o*r*e* v*est*ro si placet nob*is* integras et illesas . concedere et cons*er*uare velitis . mandantes si placet . p*redict*is taxatorib*us* q*uod* ab hui*usmodi* exacc*i*onib*us* de hominib*us* no*st*ris p*re*d*ict*orum man*e*rioru*m* desistant. Valeat f*rate*rnitas vestra semp*er* in D*omi*no.

NOTE. The top left corner of the MS is torn away; words in brackets supplied, where possible, by conjecture. [a] One word illegible.
DESCRIPTION. 22.1 cm x 6.4 cm. Sealing: no evidence of a tag, tongue or seal.
HAND. Scribe P.
SOURCE. Original. TNA, Special Collections: Ancient Correspondence of the Chancery and the Exchequer, PRO SC 1/20/168.
PRINTED. *CDS*, v, no. 38 (cal.).
COMMENT. TNA, PRO C 47/22/9/15 records three letters of King Edward I to Alexander that touch on this and other matters relating to the Scottish king's lands in England. The rights and privileges that Alexander III claimed within his English lands became a matter of contention with Henry III in the 1260s, and continued to trouble relations between the crowns well into the reign of Edward I. This petition forms part of a substantial body of material relating to the question. The introduction of a tax of a fifteenth at the October 1275 parliament offers a *terminus post quem* for this letter; a *terminus ante quem* is more difficult to establish. Edward I's ministers continued to challenge Alexander's rights and privileges for the rest of the latter's reign.

171 Grants and by this charter confirms to the canons of Whithorn the gift that his eldest son, Alexander lord of Man, made them of the lands of Ballacgniba and Dalmarown, the church of St Ronan and the chapel of St Ninian at Ballacgniba in Man. To be held in pure and perpetual alms, as Alexander's charter, authenticated with his father's seal, bears witness. 2 July 1266 x 28 January 1284, possibly 1275 x 1281.

Alexander Dei g*ra*tia rex Scotor*um* om*n*ib*us* probis homi*n*ibus totius t*er*re sue salute*m*. Sciatis nos co*n*cessisse et p*rese*nti carta nostra co*n*firmasse donatio*n*em illa*m* qua*m* Alexander filius noster p*ri*mogenit*us* domin*us* Man*n*ie fecit Deo et b*ea*to Niniano et cano*n*ic*is* Premonstratens*is* apud Candida*m*casam [a] s*er*uie*n*tibus et i*m*pe*r*petuu*m* seruitur*is* de t*err*is de Ballacgniba et de Dalhamer cu*m* p*er*tinenciis et de eccl*e*sia sancti Runami et de capella sancti Niniani de Ballacgniba in Man*n*ia . Tenendas et habendas eisdem cano*n*ic*is* et successorib*us* suis i*mper*petuu*m* de d*ict*o Alexandro filio nostro et heredibus suis in libera*m* pura*m* et pe*r*petua*m* elemosina*m* cum om*n*ibus suis iustis p*er*tinenciis libertatib*us* et asiame*nt*is adeo libere quiete plenarie et hono*ri*fice sicut carta predi*ct*i Alexandri eisde*m* cano*n*ic*is* exinde confecta et sigillo nostro sigillata pro eo q*uod* ipsi i*n* mi*n*ori etate constitut*us* no*n*dum sigillu*m* habet pleni*us* iuste testatur. Testib*us* etc .

NOTES. [a] Word Deo missing here.
RUBRIC. The following heading, written in an early sixteenth-century hand, appears before the entry: Confirmac*io* Alexandri eius pat*ri*s sup*er* d*ic*ta donac*io*ne. Alexander's grant appears in the preceding entry.
SOURCE. San Marino, CA, Huntington Library, MS EL 993, item 5, a transumpt of 1504, which reproduces several extracts from the (now lost) priory register.
PRINTED. Stringer, *Reformed Church*, 47–8, no. 7; Talbot, *Priory of Whithern*, App., no. 7; *HMC*, xi, App., pt. 8, 150 (note).
COMMENT. The lands of Ballacgniba lie in Greeba, near Crosby, Isle of Man; they were probably coterminous with the later barony of St Trinian. Dalhamer, elsewhere referred to as Balhamer, is Ballaharry. The grant dates to the period between the sealing of the Treaty of Perth (2 July 1266), when Magnus king of Norway ceded Man to the Scottish crown, and the death of Prince Alexander lord of Man in January 1284. A more

precise dating might place it between 1275, when Alexander III sent an army against the Manxmen and more firmly established Scottish rule there, and 1281. In this grant Prince Alexander is not yet old enough to have a seal, but he had acquired one by December 1281, when negotiations began for his marriage (see above, no. 135).

172 Commands the bailie of Man to permit the prior and canons of Whithorn to collect the issues from their church and lands in Man without any hindrance. 2 July 1266 x 19 March 1286.

Alexander Dei *gra*tia rex Scotorum. balliuo Mannie qui pro t*em*p*o*re fu*er*it fideli suo salute*m*. Ma*n*damus tibi et precipimus firmit*er* quatinus permittas p*ri*orem et cano*n*icos Candidecase qui pro tempore fuerint abducer*e* fructus et alia bona p*ro*uidencia de eccl*es*ia sua et t*er*ris suis quas habent in Man*n*ia sine impedime*n*to tuo vell[a] s*er*uie*n*ciu*m* tuor*um* ita q*uod* com*m*odum suum libere facere habeant de eisde*m*. In cui*us* rei testimo*n*i*um* etc .

NOTE. [a] Sic, vel.
RUBRIC. The following heading appears before the entry: Mandamus [sic] d*omi*ni reg*is* Alexandri balli*v*o Man*n*ie.
SOURCE. San Marino, CA, Huntington Library, MS EL 993, item 6, a transumpt of 1504, which reproduces several extracts from the (now lost) priory register.
PRINTED. Stringer, *Reformed Church*, 48, no. 8; Talbot, *Priory of Whithern*, App., no. 8 (with several errors); *HMC*, xi, App., pt. 8, 150 (note).
COMMENT. The lack of a witness list makes it difficult to date the document more precisely than the period between 1266, when King Magnus IV ceded the Isle of Man to the Scottish crown, and the king's death.

173 Grants and by this charter confirms the agreement made between the monks of Kelso abbey and the mayor, provosts and community of Berwick concerning a seventh part of the mills of Berwick, as is contained in the writings of both parties. 13 July 1249 x 16 November 1278.

Alex*ander*[a] Dei *gra*tia rex Scott*orum*. om*n*ib*us* p*ro*bis ho*min*ib*us* toci*us* t*er*re sue sal*utem*. Sciatis nos co*n*cessisse et p*re*senti carta co*nfir*masse co*n*uenc*io*nem f*ac*tam int*er* d*omi*nos abb*a*tem et co*n*uentu*m* de Kalchow ex p*ar*te vna. et maiore*m*. p*re*positos. ac com*m*una*m* de Berewyc' ex alt*er*a. sup*er* tota septima p*ar*te molendinor*um* de eade*m* villa. Tenenda et h*abe*nda*dic*tis maiori. et p*re*positis ac com*m*une[b]de Berewic' ac om*n*ib*us* suis successorib*us* de d*ic*tis abb*a*te et co*n*uentu et suis successorib*us* adeo lib*er*e. q*u*iete. plenarie. et honorifice sic*ut* in sc*ri*ptis eor*um* exinde co*n*fectis ex vt*raque* p*ar*te pleni*us* iuste co*n*tinet*ur*. Test*ibus*.

NOTES. [a] Red initial. [b] Communie in printed version, erroneously.
RUBRIC. Co*n*firm*atio* reg*is*. Al*exandri* super co*n*ue*n*c*ione* int*er* nos et com*m*uni*am* Berwyci. de septi*m*a p*ar*te molendinor*um* (in red) (fourteenth century).
SOURCE. NLS, Adv. MS 34.5.1, Chartulary of Kelso Abbey, fo. 21r (incomplete).
PRINTED. *Kelso Liber*, i, no. 38; *Rot. Scot.*, i, 268.
COMMENT. This document appears in Scoular, *Handlist* as no. 307. It more properly belongs to the reign of Alexander III and should be paired with no. 284 below, to which it is related. In the parliament that Edward I held in Berwick in the autumn of 1305 the abbot and convent submitted a petition requesting resumption of the payment of various rents they claimed in Berwick and Perth, namely '20 merks annually, which they used to receive from the mills of Berwick, and 40s annually, which they used to receive from the farms of the town of Berwick' (and, in addition, 40 shillings annually from the

fermes of Perth). The king commanded that the abbot appear before the guardian and chamberlain of Scotland with written proof of his claims, 'and justice will be done to them according to what used to be done in the time of King Alexander' (TNA, PRO SC 9/12, m.11; *PROME*, ii, 139). The monks failed to convince the king's officials on this occasion, and the revenues were in fact not returned to them until the 1330s, when an inquest ordered by King Edward III confirmed that the monks had the revenues by gift of King Alexander III (*Rot. Scot.*, i, 268).

174 Grants and by this charter confirms to the abbot and convent of Lindores the grant that his father, King Alexander II, made them, that is, that the monks should have in pure and perpetual alms all the lands that they have had and held since the original foundation of their house, together with all the liberties to which they have been accustomed, quit of aids, armies, and other forinsec services. Strictly prohibits anyone from causing them injury or harm in violation of this grant, on pain of his full forfeiture. 13 July 1249 x 19 March 1286, probably early.

Alex*ander* D*e*i gr*at*ia rex Scott*orum*. om*n*ib*us* p*ro*bis ho*min*ib*us* toci*us* t*er*re sue sal*utem*. Sciant p*re*sentes et futuri nos co*n*cessisse et hac carta n*ost*ra co*n*firmasse abb*at*i et co*n*uentui de Lundors co*n*cessionem illam q*ua*m d*omin*us. A. bone memorie illustr*i*s rex pat*er* nost*er* fecit eisdem. videlicet. vt h*abe*ant et teneant i*n* lib*er*am pura*m* et p*er*petua*m* elemosina*m* om*ne*s terras suas quas h*abuer*unt et tenu*eru*nt a p*ri*ma fundac*io*ne dom*us* sue de Lundors cu*m* o*m*nib*us* lib*er*tatib*us* quib*us* uti co*n*sueu*eru*nt. et q*uod* quieti sint de auxiliis. ex*er*citibus et aliis forinsecis seruiciis de p*redic*tis t*er*ris. Q*uare* fi*r*mit*er* p*ro*hibem*us*. ne quis co*ntra* ha*n*c co*n*cession*em* nostrum. eos i*n*iuste uexare p*re*sumat super n*ost*ram plenariam forisfacturam. Test*ibus*. etc.

RUBRIC. Item de confirmacione.
SOURCE. Caprington Castle, Kilmarnock, Lindores Cartulary, fo. 83[r].
PRINTED. *Lindores Cart.*, no. 121.
COMMENT. The absence of a witness list makes it difficult to date this grant. The broad protection that it offers suggests that it was issued soon after the king's inauguration, when it was not unusual for religious houses to seek confirmation of their possessions.

175 Commands his justiciars, sheriffs and all his bailies to permit the abbot and convent of Lindores abbey to enjoy the liberties which they had in the time of Alexander [II] and to desist from unlawfully disturbing them. 13 July 1249 x 19 March 1286, probably early.

Alex*ander* D*e*i gr*at*ia rex Scott*orum*. justiciariis. vicecomitib*us* et om*n*ib*us* aliis bailliuis[a] tocius t*er*re sue ad quos p*re*sentes litt*er*e p*er*ue*n*erint sal*utem*. Mandam*us* uos et p*re*cipimus. q*ua*tin*us* p*er*mittatis abb*at*em et co*n*uentu*m* de Lundors gaud*er*e eisde*m* lib*er*tatib*us* quibus t*em*pore inclite recordait*i*onis[a] d*omi*ni regis Alex*andri* p*at*ris n*ost*ri et n*ost*ro hactenus iuste gauisi su*n*t et pacifice nec ips*o*s s*uper* eisdem libertatib*us* aliquo modo vexetis i*n*iuste. p*er* q*uod* ab eis iustam querimoniam audiamus. Test*ibus* etc .

NOTE. [a] Sic.
RUBRIC. De mandato reg*is* Alexandri (fourteenth century).
SOURCE. Caprington Castle, Kilmarnock, Lindores Cartulary, fo. 83[v].
PRINTED. *Lindores Cart.*, no. 122.
COMMENT. For dating, see above, no. 174.

LOST ACTS CERTAINLY OR PROBABLY THE SUBJECT OF WRITTEN RECORD

176 Commands an inquest at the instance of Henry de Ulverston, who has brought suit against Waldeve Kokes in respect of land in the territory of Nether Ayton (Berwickshire) [1249 x 1260].

SOURCE. Fraser, *Keir*, 197–8.
COMMENT. Notice of the act survives in a concord dated c. 1260, in which Bertram son of Henry de Ulverston quitclaimed to his kinsman, Waldeve Kokes, two oxgangs in Nether Ayton. Bertram had pursued title to the lands against Waldeve in a suit initiated 'by the king's letters', that is, by means of a brieve of right, probably directed to the prior of Coldingham, in whose court the case was heard and settled. See H. L. MacQueen, 'The Brieve of Right Re-visited', in R. Eales and D. Sullivan (eds), *The Political Context of Law: Proceedings of the Seventh British Legal History Conference, Canterbury 1985* (London, 1987), 22. While the witness list of the charter does not allow for a more precise dating than 1249 x 1260, Norman Reid and Geoffrey Barrow have suggested that the document (and the brieve to which it makes reference) were issued closer to the earlier date. Reid and Barrow, *Sheriffs*, 7n.

177 Confirms a grant by Neil earl of Carrick and his wife to the monks of Saddell abbey [13 June 1250 x 1256].

SOURCE. *RMS*, ii, no. 3170.
COMMENT. In 1508 King James IV issued to the bishop of Lismore a comprehensive confirmation of several charters granted in favour of the monks of Saddell; these included a royal confirmation of the couple's gift of lands in Carrick. Neil succeeded to the earldom on the death of his father in June 1250; he died in 1256.

178 Commands the sheriff of Roxburgh to hold an inquest concerning the lands in Roxburghshire of the deceased Simon de Lede [1250 x 1260, 14 September].

SOURCE. *CDS*, iv, App. i, no. 3; *CDS*, iv, no. 1756 (NRS, Documents transferred from the Public Record Office, London, RH 5/39).
COMMENT. Notice of this brieve occurs in the record of a report copied into the English rolls of chancery during the reign of Edward I. The original inquest was held in Roxburgh 'in accordance with the king's mandate'; it sought to determine the terms by which Simon held his lands of Sir Malcolm de Moravia of Drumsagard.

179 Certifies a bond by which King Henry III undertakes to pay, within four years of Easter next coming, the sum of 5,000 merks of silver for the dowry of his daughter Margaret, lately wed to King Alexander. York [1251, 26–27 December].

SOURCE. BL, MS Stowe 551, fos. 15–16.
COMMENT. This MS consists of a series of notes and transcripts compiled in the later eighteenth century by the archivist and collector Thomas Astle as a companion volume to his transcription of medieval Scottish deeds (BL, MS Stowe 551). The original bond now appears to be lost, but Astle, who claimed to have seen it, noted that on 27 December Alexander commanded his bailies to certify it. Henry's chancery clerks enrolled the bond on the same day; see *CPR, 1247–58*, 121–2. The dowry was never paid in full.

180 Commands a perambulation of the marches between Cleish and 'Crambeth' (Kinross-shire) [1252].

SOURCE. NRS, Papers of the Lindsay Family of Dowhill, GD 254/1.
COMMENT. The brieve of perambulation is cited in the text of a formal agreement concerning these boundaries made in 1252 between Duncan and Patrick, brothers, together with their wives Ela and Christina, sisters, on the one part, and Gilbert de Cleish, knight, on the other. A transumpt of this agreement, dated 29 November 1459, appears in GD 254/5. The place name Crambeth is obsolete and is now represented by Dowhill, in Cleish parish, Kinross-shire.

181 Writes to Pope Innocent IV seeking the privilege of unction [ante 1253].

SOURCE. *Summa aurea D. Henrici Cardinalis Hostiensis ... D. Nicolai Superantij summarijs ac adnotationibus illustrata ...* (Lyon, 1548), fo. 35^v.
COMMENT. Notice of this letter occurs in Book I, Chapter XV of Hostiensis's treatise, in the context of a discussion of the nature and significance of unction. The canonist notes that traditionally secular rulers receive unction at the hands of their metropolitan bishops. In realms where no such tradition currently exists, rulers must apply to the pope for the privilege of receiving unction. The king of Aragon did this, Hostiensis observes, 'and the king of Scotland daily pursues the pope for the privilege'. The Summa had been completed by c. 1253.

182 Commands an inquest at the instance of Emma, daughter and heir of deceased Gilbert de Smeaton, who has sued Dunfermline abbey in respect of the land of Smeaton (East Lothian) [ante 1253, 17 December].

SOURCE. Above, no. 18. The king's letters constitute one of the earliest examples of the brieve of mortancestry in Scotland. See MacQueen, *Common Law*, 167, 169, 172.

183 Commands Alexander Comyn earl of Buchan justiciar of Scotia to perambulate the lands of Conon and Tillyhiot (both in Angus), the boundaries of which are in dispute between the monks of Arbroath abbey and Sir Peter de Maule lord of Panmure and his wife Christine [c. 1254, ante 22 June].

SOURCE. *Arbroath Liber*, i, no. 366.
COMMENT. The brieve is mentioned in the text of a formal agreement reached between the parties after the perambulation, held on 22 June 1254.

184 Writes to King Henry III concerning a forthcoming meeting. Wark [1255, c. 8 September].

SOURCE. Above, no. 22.
COMMENT. Notice of this letter survives in two English patent roll entries, both dated 23 September 1255, that make reference to 'the king of Scotland's letter respecting the forthcoming convention, made with the K. of England at Wark'. Both note that the letter was then in the custody of Master John Mansel. The letter must have been written around 8 September, when Henry held a meeting with the young king and queen to begin negotiations for the governance of Scotland under a new council. See also Stones, *Anglo-Scottish Relations*, no. 10; *CDS*, i, nos 2017, 2019; *CPR, 1247–58*, 426. As of 14 May 1259 the letter had not yet been returned to Alexander. It was mentioned in a message that Henry III sent to the young king on that date concerning various matters, including Alexander's enthronement and recent developments in the kingdom of Man. In respect of the letter, 'which the K. of Scotland wishes restored', Henry wrote that, preoccupied as he was with rebellion in Wales and the affairs of Sicily, he could do nothing at the moment. See *CCR, 1256–1259*, 477; *CDS*, i, no. 2157.

185 Confirms to the Knights Hospitaller all their possessions and free customs. Kinghorn [8 July 1255 x 7 July 1256, a.r. 7].

SOURCE. BL, Harl. MS 4693, fo. 26r.
COMMENT. This MS was compiled in the early seventeenth century by Sir James Balfour of Denmilne and Kinnaird, Lyon King of Arms. It contains abstracts and copies of several early Scottish charters, many now lost.

186 Commands Alexander Comyn earl of Buchan justiciar of Scotia to hold an inquest to determine whether Dunfermline abbey owes suit to the sheriff court of Perth for the lands of Fordie, Couttie, Bendochy, Little Keithock, Inchturfin and Dummernech (all in Perthshire) [1255].

SOURCE. Below, no. 187.

187 Grants remission to the monks of Dunfermline abbey from the obligation to render suit to the sheriff court of Perth for the lands of Fordie, Couttie, Bendochy, Little Keithick, Inchturfin and Dummernech (Perthshire). Holyrood [13 January 1256, a.r. 7].

SOURCE. *RPS*, 1256/1; *Dunfermline Registrum*, no. 85.
COMMENT. The king's quitclaim is mentioned in an inquest convened before Alexander Comyn earl of Buchan justiciar of Scotia. The previous year, David de Lochore sheriff of Perth had imposed a fine of four merks on the abbot and monks of Dunfermline for failing to make suit of the shrieval court in respect of the lands noted above, held in chief of the king. The monks complained to the king; he ordered an inquest and a jury of barons duly convened to determine 'whether the said suit ought to happen concerning these lands or not'. On 13 January 1256, in a meeting (colloquium) of the king and his council at Holyrood, Gilbert de Hay reported the jurors' findings.

188 Confirms to the nuns of Coldstream Alexander de Synton's grant of the land of Todrig [1256 x 1274, possibly 1266 x 1270].

SOURCE. *Coldstream Chartulary*, no. 25.
COMMENT. Notice of the king's act occurs in the text of Alexander de Synton's grant, which notes that the nuns are to hold the land 'as the first charter of infeftment and the king's charter regarding the elemosinary status of the land bear witness'. For the dating, see W. W. Scott, *Syllabus of Scottish Cartularies: Coldstream,* at http://www.arts.gla.ac.uk/scottishstudies/charters/Coldstream_rev.pdf.

189 Grants to William de Swinburne various sums of money [1257 x 1286, probably 1259 x 1272].

SOURCE. *APS*, i, 116.
COMMENT. Notice of the grant(s) occurs in the list of rolls, memoranda and other documents sent to England at the command of Edward I in 1292, in an entry that records four letters by Swinburne attesting receipt of £100, £40, £40 and £100, 'which the king of Scots assigned him'. The payments may have been made in relation to his duties (1259–72) as treasurer of Queen Margaret, but they may also reflect his status as the recipient of many other favours on the part of the king. His career is examined in detail in Holford and Stringer, *Border Liberties* 255–6, 258–60, 264–5.

190 Grants to Margaret queen of Scotland, in support of her chamber, the manor of Sowerby in Cumberland [ante 1257, 9 April].

SOURCE. *CPR, 1247–58*, 548; *CDS*, i, no. 2081.
COMMENT. Notice of this grant survives in a confirmation of Henry III dated 9 April 1257. It represented some or part of the land that Alexander settled on his new wife at the time of their marriage.

191 Commands that an inquest be held concerning the manor of Haughton, the land called 'The Huntland' and the manor of Williamston in the fee of Knarsdale, all in the liberty of Tynedale [ante 1257, 16 April].

SOURCE. NCS, Swinburne (Capheaton) Estate Papers, ZSW/1/12.
COMMENT. The brieve has not survived, but the inquest convened pursuant to the king's command is preserved in a final concord made between William de Swinburne and Reginald Prat before royal justices on the date noted above. See also above, no. 25.

192 Commands the bailiff of Tynedale to permit the justices of the king of England to hold an eyre within the liberty [1257, ante June].

SOURCE. Above, no. 25.
COMMENT. The eyre was held at Nunwick in April; the roll recording its business is now lost.

193 Instructs his envoys, the abbot of Jedburgh and William de Hay, to request that Henry III send prudent and discreet magnates to the colloquium that he is planning to convene at Stirling [ante 1258, 25 March].

SOURCE. *CDS*, i, no. 2114; *Close Rolls 1256–1259*, 300.
COMMENT. Alexander's message is noted in a letter of Henry III addressed to Sir Robert de Neville, dated as above, ordering him to assist the young king. The colloquium is discussed briefly in *RPS*, A1258/1.

194 Instructs his envoys, the provost of St Andrews and Thomas de Normanville, to discuss with King Henry III his plans for a forthcoming colloquium [ante 1258, 13 May].

SOURCE. *CDS*, i, no. 2126; *Close Rolls 1256–1259*, 310.
COMMENT. The envoys are identified in a letter of Henry III to Alexander dated as above. The colloquium is discussed briefly in *RPS*, A1258/1.

195 Writes letters of credence on behalf of the abbot of Dunfermline and William de Hay, envoys to Henry III king of England [ante 1258, 27 April].

SOURCE. *CCR, 1256–59*, 329; *CDS*, i, no. 2133.
COMMENT. The letters are mentioned in a message of Henry III addressed to Alexander, dated as above, in which Henry names the Scottish envoys.

196 Grants to John of Acre the dower lands of Alexander II's widow, Marie de Coucy [c. 1258].

SOURCE. *APS*, i, 115.
COMMENT. Notice of this grant survives in the list of rolls, remembrances and other documents taken by Edward I from Scotland in 1292. Marie de Coucy married John de Brienne king of Acre between the autumn of 1256 and the early summer of 1257; it is likely that King Alexander III confirmed the couple's title to the lands as soon as he had reached his age of majority.

197 Grants to William de Swinburne, the king's clerk, that he and his heirs may take estovers in the wood of Haughton (in Tynedale) [22 March 1258, a.r. 9].

SOURCE. Bodleian Library, Oxford, Dodsworth MS XLV, fo. 89^v (cal.). This volume, dated 1638, is one of an extensive series of transcriptions compiled by the antiquary Roger Dodsworth. It consists of Latin-language summaries and some full transcriptions of several charters then in the possession of Sir William Widdrington of Widdrington. This collection is now lost.
PRINTED. Dodsworth's summary of this charter was published in *Northumb. and Durham Deeds*, 242.

198 Grants to John de Halton the manor of Sewing Shields (in Tynedale), for an annual payment of half a merk [1258 x 1266].

SOURCE. Palgrave, *Docs. Hist. Scot.*, i, 3, 9; *CDS*, ii, no. 319.
COMMENT. The grant is noted in the record of an extent dated late 1286 or early 1287 in which Edward I's escheator north of Trent, Sir Thomas de Normanville, assessed the value of the lands in England of which Alexander III had died seised. It is noted again in the record of the inquisition *post mortem* held after Halton's death in 1287. The grant was made before 1266: the sessions that began at Wark in November 1279 make mention of Halton's manor house and park there (Hartshorne, *Feudal and Military Antiquities*, App., xxxiii–xxxiv). Halton was a wealthy land holder in Northumberland; clearly, Alexander III's gift represented the king's wish to draw him into the royal affinity. See *NCH*, x, 390–1.

199 Petitions Edward I for a settlement concerning his rights in the manor of Wheatley, Nottinghamshire as heir of his aunt Margaret, widow of Hubert de Burgh [1258 x 1275].

SOURCE. TNA, Chancery Miscellanea, PRO C 47/22/3/14.
PRINTED. *CDS*, ii, no. 63 (cal.).
COMMENT. This is a little roll, much defaced, compiled by a clerk of the English chancery, of various matters that were pending between the king of Scots and the king of England on the death of Henry III in November 1272. It was probably compiled in preparation for the visit of Alexander III to Westminster to attend Edward's coronation in the summer of 1274. Alexander III acquired an interest in the dower lands of his aunt Margaret, sister of Alexander II, when she died in 1258, predeceased by her only child Margaret. Wheatley lay in the honour of Tickhill. Appended to Alexander's petition is a partial record of the legal process that identified Margaret's heirs. Edward's response to this petition was terse: he ordered that Alexander produce a written record in support of his claim. The latter ought to have been able to do so: an inventory of muniments stored in the treasury compiled in 1282 included a *processus super Qwetley habitus coram iusticiarios Anglie* (*APS*, i, 109). See also above, no. 39.

200 Grants to Robert de Bellingham and William de Bellingham jointly the ferme of the mill of Bellingham (in Tynedale) and the profits of justice arising from the lands of Bellingham and Hesleyside for an annual rent of £10 [1258 x 1275].

SOURCE. TNA, Justices in Eyre, of Assize, of Oyer and Terminer, and of the Peace, etc.: Rolls and Files, PRO JUST 1/657, mm 4–4d; Palgrave, *Docs. Hist. Scot.*, i, 9.
COMMENT. William and Robert appear to have been brothers; the former was King Alexander's forester in Tynedale and the recipient of other gifts. In 1293 John de Widdrington appeared before justices in eyre presiding at Wark, claiming that the Bellinghams had unlawfully exercised commonty on his holdings in Bellingham. In their defence Robert and William produced a charter of Alexander III which they proceeded to read aloud. This act granted them the feu ferme of the mill and the profits of justice

as noted above 'to be held in perpetuity for an annual *reddendo* of £10'. They testified further that for as long as the king had been alive they had enjoyed common rights in all the lands of the manor. John replied with a formidable and extraordinary attack on the admissibility of a Scots royal charter within the kingdom of England. Eventually, the parties agreed to concord. The grant, which was noted also in the extent of the lands of the king of Scotland in England carried out after Alexander III's death, cannot be dated more precisely than 1258 x 1275. See also *NCH*, xv, 235–6.

201 Grants to William de Bellingham a messuage and ten acres of arable land in Bellingham [1258 x 1275].

SOURCE. TNA, Justices in Eyre, of Assize, of Oyer and Terminer, and of the Peace, etc.: Rolls and Files, PRO, JUST 1/657, mm 2, 4d.
COMMENT. The king's grant became the subject of litigation at the eyre sessions convened at Wark in 1293. Geoffrey son of Simon claimed that he had been unlawfully disseised of the lands; in his defence, William stated that King Alexander 'gave, granted and by his charter confirmed' the lands to William, stipulating that he pay a *reddendo* of 10d for each acre. William's title to the lands was challenged a second time at the same sessions, this time by John de Widdrington, who sought to prevent William from claiming commonty over his substantial holdings of moorland, pasture and woods. William again produced in evidence a charter of King Alexander III. The lands were here identified as having been formerly in the possession of William son of Orme. Bellingham stated that he held them of the king 'for homage and service'. The charter won Bellingham secure title to the estate; he then came to a concord with Widdrington. Alexander's grant cannot be more accurately dated than 1258 x 1279; at the eyre sessions that began in Wark in the latter year Bellingham informed the presiding justices that he and his ancestors had held two-thirds of the manor of Bellingham of the kings of Scotland and their predecessors 'from time beyond memory', in return for performing the duties of foresters of Tynedale. See Hartshorne, *Feudal and Military Antiquities* App., xxviii–xxix; *NCH*, xv, 236–7.

202 Grants to his clerk Adam de Liberatione the lands of Pettinain (Lanarkshire) for the service of two archers and one serjeant, with grooms and hounds [ante 1259, 1 May].

SOURCE. *APS*, i, 98; *CDS*, i, no. 2175 (NRS, Documents transferred from the Public Record Office, London, RH 5/41); *Records of Lanark*, 341.
COMMENT. The gift is cited in the record of an inquest held on the date above before the sheriff and bailies of Lanark, probably at the petition of Adam, who claimed that the charter granting him the lands was being 'detained unjustly'. The jurors confirmed Adam's claim and noted further that his daughter, Isabella, was then in possession of the disputed charter.

203 Commands the sheriff and bailies of Lanark to hold an inquest concerning title to the land of Pettinain (Lanarkshire) by Adam de Liberacione [ante 1259, 1 May].

SOURCE. Above, no. 202.
COMMENT. The brieve is mentioned in an inquest concerning title to this land convened at Lanark on the above date.

204 Sends John de Dundemor to King Henry III of England to discuss the monies that Henry owes him [ante 1259, 14 May].

SOURCE. *CDS*, i, no. 2157; *Close Rolls, 1256–1259*, 477.
COMMENT. In a letter addressed to King Alexander on the above date, Henry III 'acknowledges the messages delivered by his envoy'.

205 Commands Andrew, attorned clerk of the justiciar, to summon an inquest concerning the land of 'Polnegulan' in Lennox [ante 1259, 18 December].

SOURCE. *APS*, i, 99; *CDS*, i, no. 2174 (NRS, Documents transferred from the Public Record Office, London, RH 5/21).
COMMENT. The letters are mentioned in an inquest into the descent of these lands held at Dumbarton on the date noted above. 'Polnegulan' is now lost.

206 Writes to Pope Alexander IV requesting the appointment of a provincial minister for the Franciscan friars of Scotland [c. 1260].

SOURCE. *Ad Bullarium Franciscanum ... Supplementum studio et labore Fr. Flaminii Annibali de Latera ... dispositum, praeviis animadversionibus in notas eiusdem Sbaraleae illustratum*, ed. F. M. Annibali (Rome, 1780), 140; W. M. Bryce, *The Scottish Grey Friars* (2 vols, Edinburgh, 1909), i, 9–10, ii, 275.
COMMENT. The petition is mentioned in a letter of 1260 addressed to the king. Here, the pope acknowledged the support and advice that the friars might offer the king 'in his tender years' and commanded the appointment. Together, however, the chapter general of the order and King Henry III delayed the appointment until 1278. See W. Mackay Mackenzie, 'A Prelude to the War of Independence', *SHR*, 27 (1948), 110.

207 Confirms Germanus as prior of Coldingham [c. 1260].

SOURCE. *Durham Annals and Documents of the Thirteenth Century*, ed. F. Barlow (Surtees Soc., 1945), nos 38, 43, 44.
COMMENT. Letters patent addressed to King Alexander III by Prior Hugh of Durham requesting confirmation of the appointment are recorded in contemporary Durham priory formularies. Germanus duly succeeded to the office c. 1260 (Watt and Shead, *Heads of Religious Houses,* 31).

208 Grant of a licence to Peter de Insula to strengthen his mill-dam at Chipchase (Northumberland) [1 July 1260, a.r. 11].

SOURCE. Bodleian Library, Oxford, MS. Dodsworth XLIX, fo. 8^v^, described above at no. 197. This volume, dated 1639, is one of a series of transcriptions compiled by the antiquary Roger Dodsworth. It consists of Latin-language summaries of several charters then in the possession of Cuthbert Heron of Chipchase. This collection is now lost.
PRINTED. Dodsworth's summary of this charter was published in *Northumb. and Durham Deeds*, 110, and in *NCH*, iv, 333n.
COMMENT. In 1287, Peter's son Robert obtained from Edward I a new licence to build a dam on the water of Wark at Chipchase. See Palgrave, *Docs. Hist. Scot.*, i, 9.

209 Writes to the justiciar of Lothian concerning an action of novel dissasine sued against John Scot of Reston for the land of Reston (Berwickshire) [ante 6 March 1261].

SOURCE. *Coldingham Correspondence*, no. 1.
COMMENT. Notice of a 'pair' of royal letters survives in a mandate dated as above, by which Hugh de Berkley justiciar of Lothian commanded William Badby constable of Berwick to levy the sum of £10 from John's land. It is likely that the 'pair' refers to both a brieve of dissasine and summons to the defender to appear in court; see MacQueen, *Common Law*, 162n.

210 Commands William de Douglas, John de Lamberton and Richard de Bickerton, knights, to perambulate and deliver to Aymer de Maxwell land in the feu of Pencaitland [ante 24 March 1261].

SOURCE. *CDS*, iv, App. i, no. 4; *CDS*, i, no. 2675 (NRS, Documents transferred from the Public Record Office, London, RH 5/31).
COMMENT. The letter is preserved in a memorandum deposited in the English Exchequer during the reign of Edward I. The document notes that as of the date noted above, and in response to 'letters patent' of Alexander III, the lands in question were duly delivered to Maxwell.

211 Writes to Henry III of England attesting receipt of part of the £1,000 which Henry promised to pay to him at the fair of St Botulph in 1261 in respect of his marriage to Henry's daughter, Margaret [post 28 July 1261].

SOURCE. *Cal. Liberate Rolls, 1260–67*, 52; *CPR, 1258–1266*, 170.
COMMENT. Notice of this letter survives in an entry in the liberate rolls for 28 July 1261, in which Henry commanded the treasurer and chamberlain of the exchequer to pay 125 merks to William de Swinburne, treasurer of Queen Margaret. See also below, no. 212.

212 Writes another letter to Henry III attesting receipt of the balance of £1,000, as in no. 211 above [post 28 July 1261].

SOURCE. *Cal. Liberate Rolls, 1260–67*, 52; *CPR, 1258–1266*, 170. The second letter is noted in a marginal entry in the liberate rolls.

213 Writes to King Henry III of England acknowledging receipt of 500 merks owed in respect of his marriage to Queen Margaret, paid to Alexander steward of Scotland [ante 17 March 1262].

SOURCE. *Cal. Liberate Rolls, 1260–67*, 79.
COMMENT. Notice of the letter survives in a writ from Henry III to his treasurer and chamberlains dated 17 March 1262, which notes that the payment was to be made to Alexander steward of Scotland. See also *Foedera*, I, i, 417, dated 23 March, a letter of Henry III to Alexander III, noting that 'we have satisfied our beloved Alexander the steward, in your name, concerning this five hundred merks according to your request'. The payment, Henry claimed, meant that 'we now have no more money remaining in our hands', and he went on to request, politely but quite firmly, that Alexander 'not take it ill that for the present' no more dowry money would be forthcoming. He set terms for the payment of two further instalments in September 1262 and Easter 1263; in fact, the dowry was never paid in full. See also *Close Rolls 1261–1264*, 117.

214 Confirms Gilbert de Ruthven's quitclaim of the lands of Fowlis Easter (Perthshire) to William de Mortimer [ante 31 March 1262].

SOURCE. NRS, Papers of the Maule Family, Earls of Dalhousie, GD 45/27/100.
COMMENT. The text of Ruthven's quitclaim notes that the king ordered the act formally enrolled in chancery at the request of the beneficiary.

215 Confirms a grant by King Alexander II to the burgesses of Peebles of the peat moss of Waddenshope [ante 7 October 1262].

SOURCE. Above, no. 40.
COMMENT. The king's confirmation is noted in a brieve dated as above commanding an inquest to determine whether Robert Cruik deforced the burgesses of Peebles of the peat moss of Waddenshope (Peeblesshire).

216 Commands Alexander Comyn earl of Buchan justiciar of Scotia to hold an inquest to determine whether Ewan thane of 'Ratthen' held the land of Meft (Moray) in chief of the king [ante 27 November 1262].

SOURCE. *APS*, i, 101 (NRS, Documents transferred from the Public Record Office, London, RH 5/27).

COMMENT. Notice of this brieve survives in an inquest held at Inverness on the above date. The text of the quitclaim notes that, at William's request, the king ordered the act formally enrolled in chancery. The thanage of 'Ratthen' or 'Rathenec' lay between Elgin and the river Spey; it now survives in the name Rapenache Manor, near Meft in Moray. This was the same land that Alexander Comyn of Buchan later sought to secure from Edward I (below, no. 313).

217 Founds a church dedicated to the Holy Cross at Peebles [1262?].

SOURCE. *Chron. Fordun*, i, 299; *Scotichronicon*, v, 335.

COMMENT. *Chron. Fordun*, i, Annal 54, describes the discovery of a 'stately and venerable' cross at Peebles in the spring of 1262 (though it is misdated here, and again by Bower, to 1261) and, not long afterwards, of a stone urn containing the ashes and bones of a man, believed by some to be a late third-century martyr, and by others to be a 'Bishop Nicholas'. Miraculous occurrences soon followed: 'Wherefore the king, by the advice of the bishop of Glasgow, had a handsome church made there, to the honour of God and the Holy Cross.' The nature of the relics and the foundation date of the eponymous church of the Holy Cross at Peebles much preoccupied antiquarians; see F. A. Greenhill, 'Notes on Scottish Incised Slabs (II)', *PSAS*, 80 (1948), 50–61, and J. S. Richardson, 'Note on the Cross Kirk at Peebles', ibid., 61–66. Richardson's conclusion is that there was an interval of perhaps six to seven years between the discovery of the cross and relics and the building of the new church. Easson expresses doubts about the foundation (see *MRHS*, 109–10), but Penman accepts it as genuine (M. Penman,'Royal Piety in Thirteenth-Century Scotland: the Religion and Religiosity of Alexander II (1214–49) and Alexander III (1249–86)', in J. Burton, P. Schofield and B. Weiler (eds), *Thirteenth Century England XII: Proceedings of the Gregynog Conference, 2007* [Woodbridge, 2009], 24–5). In 1327 the church is referred to as a monastic house staffed by members of the Trinitarian order; the master was then receiving an annual fee of £7 from the exchequer (*ER*, i, 71). While the foundation of the church or monastic house did not with certainty generate a written deed, such an act is proposed here, for it would have been highly unusual for the king to endow a new foundation without a formal record. The firing of the church by an English army in 1549 destroyed a good part of the fabric of the church and probably also its archives.

218 Writes letters presenting his chaplain, Richard, to the church of Covington (Lanark) [ante 29 September 1262].

SOURCE. *CDS*, i, no. 2676 (NRS, Documents transferred from the Public Record Office, London, RH 5/32).

COMMENT. The letters are mentioned in an inquest convened at Michaelmas by the dean of Christianity of Lanark on the occasion of a double presentation to the church of Covington. The incumbent, Adam de Quarentely, who had been appointed by Alexander II's queen, Marie de Coucy, challenged King Alexander's nomination.

219 Grants the lands of Menstrie and Sauchie (Stirlingshire) to Gillespie Campbell [1262–3].

SOURCE. *ER*, i, xlv, 24.

COMMENT. The grant is mentioned in an account rendered by the sheriff of Stirling in 1263 for £40 received from these estates, which had been 'given to Gillespic Campbell'. See also Boardman, *Campbells*, 29n.

220 Grants letters remitting two amercements, one incurred by the master of the Knights Hospitallers of Torphichen, the other by John le Blund [ante 1263].

SOURCE. *ER*, i, 26.
COMMENT. Notice of these letters occurs in the account submitted by Roger de Mowbray sheriff of Linlithgow for the year 1263. The nature of the transgressions is unknown.

221 Commands Sir Alexander Uvieth sheriff of Lanark to hold an inquest to determine if Henry de Wiston was a minor when he granted the lands of Sornfallow, 'Hefshunt' and 'Drumgran' (all in Lanarkshire) to Hugh de Moravia, knight [ante 5 March 1263].

SOURCE. *CDS*, i, no. 2677 (NRS, RH 5/33).
COMMENT. An inquest was held on the above date in pursuance of this brieve, when the jurors returned that, while Henry had been of age, he had not been vested or seised of the lands when, out of 'violence and fear, and [while] in prison', he granted them to de Moravia. 'Hefshunt' is now lost; 'Drumgran' is probably Dungavel in the modern parish of Wiston and Roberton.

222 Writes to King Henry III of England accrediting his envoy Ralph, who is charged with discussing various matters [13 March x 19 July 1261].

SOURCE. *Close Rolls, 1261–64*, 295–6.
COMMENT. The clerical envoy was probably Ralph de Dundee. Alexander's letter may be dated soon after the death of Henry III's treasurer, John of Caux, whose demise earlier in March Henry III blamed for his inability to address Alexander's concerns, and before 19 July of that same year, by which time John's successor had already vacated the office (*Handbook of British Chronology*, 104). The matters for discussion included debts of Henry III to the king, Alexander's rights in the lands of Penrith (Cumberland) and the disposition of the estate of Alexander's recently deceased aunt, Margaret, sister of Alexander II (d. 1258). These matters remained outstanding for the rest of Henry III's reign and well beyond; see, for example, above, no. 199).

223 Grants letters of safe conduct in favour of the envoys of King Haakon IV of Norway [August–September 1263].

SOURCE. *Regesta Norvegica, vol. I: 822–1263*, ed. E. Gunnes (Bergen, 1989), no. 1013.
COMMENT. The document is mentioned in a letter of King Haakon, where it is referred to as a brieve (*brev*). One of the envoys may have been a nobleman named 'Kolbein the knight'; more certainly on the king's mission to Scotland was Henry bishop of Orkney (*Icelandic Sagas*, ed. W. Dasent [4 vols, London, 1887–94], iv, 353–4; *Hákonar Saga and a Fragment of Magnús Saga*, ed. G. Vigfusson [RS, 1887], 340). They may have been charged with carrying to Scotland the letter from the Norwegian magnates noted in *Scotichronicon*, v, 341, 463. The movements of envoys and messengers between Scotland and Norway between the autumn of 1263 and the sealing of the Treaty of Perth in July 1266 are disentangled in R. I. Lustog, 'The Treaty of Perth: A Re-examination', *SHR* 58 (1979), 37–9. Each of the missions from Scotland required letters of accreditation and/or safe conduct, and although these are mentioned indirectly, only a handful may be verified. See also below, no. 231.

224 Commands the burgesses of Ayr to hold the castle of Ayr and to take measures for its protection [1263].

SOURCE. *ER*, i, 6.
COMMENT. Notice of this brieve occurs in the account of William earl of Menteith sheriff of Ayr for the year 1264. The mobilisation was part of the provision made throughout western Scotland in preparation for the invasion of King Haakon IV of Norway.

225 Writes letters granting unspecified powers, probably in the north, to the earl of Buchan and Alan Durward at the time of the advent of the king of Norway [probably 1263].

SOURCE. *ER*, i, 19–20.
COMMENT. Notice of these letters occurs in the account rendered by Lawrence Grant sheriff of Inverness in 1264. Here Grant noted a series of fines imposed by Comyn and Durward, acting on the authority of letters patent of the king of Scots. As in no. 223 above, the king issued the order in preparation for an attack by King Haakon IV of Norway.

226 Commands William earl of Mar chamberlain of Scotland to lead 200 serjeants to the Isles [1263].

SOURCE. *ER*, i, 11.
COMMENT. Notice of this brieve occurs in the account rendered by William earl of Mar chamberlain of Scotland for the year 1264. The command was issued in preparation for an attack by King Haakon IV of Norway.

227 Commands eight serjeants to remain at Blervie castle (Moray) at the time of the coming of the king of Norway [probably 1263].

SOURCE. *ER*, i, 18.
COMMENT. Notice of this brieve survives in an account later submitted to the exchequer by Alexander Comyn earl of Buchan for expenditures of 104s relating to the victualling of the king's men for a period of six months.

228 Grants to Gilbert de Kinross the land of Culthill (Perthshire), worth £20, for his lifetime [probably 1263].

SOURCE. *ER*, i, 34, 51.
COMMENT. Noted in accounts rendered by the sheriff of Kinross in 1263 and 1290, where the estate is named as 'Cuthylgrudyn'. The second entry notes that the estate was given to Gilbert 'by the king's charter'.

229 Grants to Robert Hod 40s annually and a suit of clothing [ante 1264].

SOURCE. *ER*, i, 12.
COMMENT. Noted in the account rendered by Andrew de Garioch sheriff of Aberdeen for the year 1264. The money was given *per cartam domini regis*, the clothing 'by gift of the king'.

230 Grants to William de Swinburne, for his laudable services, the lands of Haughton Strother (in Tynedale) for an annual reddendo of 10s. Scone [10 February 1264, a.r. 15].

SOURCE. Bodleian Library, Oxford, MS Dodsworth XLV, fo. 47^v; BL, MS Lansdowne 326, fo. 132^r. These volumes, dated 1638–9, belong to a series of transcriptions compiled by the antiquary Roger Dodsworth. Each consists of Latin-language summaries and, occasionally, full transcriptions of several dozen charters then in the possession of various Northumberland families; this document was included among the muniments of the Swinburnes of Capheaton. Some of the Swinburne documents are now on deposit with the NCS; many more, including this one, are now lost.
PRINTED. The MS Dodsworth XLV summary of this charter was published in *Northumb. and Durham Deeds*, 199.
COMMENT. Alexander III made a second grant of this property to Swinburne in 1273, 'at the instance of Margaret, our beloved consort', augmenting its value by granting him

the privilege of free forest in the lands, and replacing the render of 10d with a blenche ferme. See above, no. 84.

231 Grants letters of safe conduct in favour of an envoy of Magnus king of Man [1264].

SOURCE. *Chron. Fordun*, i, 300; *Scotichronicon*, v, 349.
COMMENT. Fordun and Bower both relate that in the summer of 1264, although he refused to grant the truce that Magnus Olafsson had requested, Alexander III provided the latter's envoy with a safe conduct to return to the island.

232 Writes to the bishop of Sodor assuring him that he will not attack the Isle of Man for the time being [c. 1264].

SOURCE. *APS*, i, 112.
COMMENT. Notice of the letter and its contents survive in a list of muniments taken from the treasury at Edinburgh castle in 1292 and deposited in Berwick by order of King Edward I.

233 Grants letters remitting their amercements to various (unspecified) persons, levied in the sheriffdom of Fife [1264].

SOURCE. *ER*, i, 4.
COMMENT. Notice of these letters occurs in the account submitted by David de Lochore sheriff of Fife for the year 1264.

234 Commands the sheriff of Forfar to pay to Augustine the tailor six and a half merks for cloth and fur lining, purchased at the fair of Dundee for the king's use [1264].

SOURCE. *ER*, i, 8.
COMMENT. Notice of this act occurs in the account rendered by E (*sic*, Robert) Mowat sheriff of Forfar for the year 1264, where the king's mandate is cited.

235 Commands the sheriff of Forfar to give forty cows to the king's sister, Marjorie [1264].

SOURCE. *ER*, i, 26.
COMMENT. Notice of this deed occurs in the account rendered by W. (*sic*, Robert) Mowat sheriff of Forfar for the year 1264. The cows were levied on the authority of letters issued by the earl of Buchan justiciar of Scotia, acting in turn on the king's mandate.

236 Commands the justiciar of Lothian to deliver sasine of the grange belonging to Ewen thane of Kettins (Angus) to Simon de Kinross, royal clerk [1264].

SOURCE. *ER*, i, 10.
COMMENT. Notice of this brieve occurs in the account rendered by Stephen Fleming justiciar of Lothian, listing revenues and expenses since his last accounting.

237 Grants letters remitting four amercements incurred by Eymer de Maxwell [ante 1265].

SOURCE. *ER*, i, 32.
COMMENT. The letters are noted in the account rendered by William de St Clair sheriff of Haddington for the year 1265. The fines amounted to 64s 10d.

238 Writes letters granting a respite, until the feast of St Peter next, to the thane of Forteviot in respect of 20 merks owed to the king [ante 1266].

SOURCE. *ER*, i, 18.
COMMENT. The letters are noted in the account rendered by John Cameron sheriff of Perth for the year 1266.

239 Grants letter of remission, on account of poverty, of a fine of £32, incurred by four men who, under pledge, failed to produce an indictment before the justiciar on the appointed day [ante 1266].

SOURCE. *ER*, i, 34.
COMMENT. Noted in the account rendered by Andrew de Garioch sheriff of Aberdeen for the year 1266.

240 Confirms a grant by Malcolm earl of Fife to his son, Mac Duff, of the tenements of Rires and Creich (Fife) [ante 1266].

SOURCE. *RPS*, 1293/2/2–3; *APS*, i, 445.
COMMENT. Notice of this confirmation occurs in a record of pleas heard in the parliament held at Scone in February 1293, when MacDuff appeared before the king to explain why he had occupied the lands. He answered that his late father, Earl Malcolm II, had given him the estates and that King Alexander had confirmed the gift. He then 'displayed the aforesaid charter and confirmation of the lord King Alexander'. MacDuff's title to the lands nonetheless remained in dispute several years after Alexander's death; see TNA, Special Collections: Parliament Rolls, Exchequer Series, PRO SC 9/7, mm 1–2 (*PROME*, i, 616–23).

241 Grants to Godred MacMores the office of king's bailie in the Isle of Man [post 1266].

SOURCE. *Chron. Lanercost* (Stevenson), 64.
COMMENT. Godred is identified as one of four men appointed in succession to the office after King Magnus's surrender of the kingdom of Man. See also below, nos 242, 243, 246.

242 Grants to Alan fitz Count the office of king's bailie in the Isle of Man [post 1266].

SOURCE. *Chron. Lanercost* (Stevenson), 64.
COMMENT. See above, no. 241.

243 Grants to Maurice Okarefair [Acarsan] the office of king's bailie in the Isle of Man [post 1266].

SOURCE. *Chron. Lanercost* (Stevenson), 64.
COMMENT. See above, no. 241. Acarsan acted as justiciar in litigation between the prior of St Bees and the abbot of Rushen in 1301; see below, no. 245.

244 Commands an inquest at the instance of the abbot of Rushen in a plea against the prior of St Bees concerning tenements in Dhoon Glen and Ballellin in the Isle of Man [post 1266].

SOURCE. Below, no. 245.
COMMENT. The brieve led to an inquest before Maurice Acarsan, the justiciar assigned to determine the matter.

245 Grants to the abbey of Rushen some lands on the Isle of Man [post 1266].

SOURCE. *Register of the Priory of St Bees*, ed. J. Wilson (Surtees Society, 1915), no. 497.
COMMENT. Notice of this grant survives in the record of a dispute between the prior of St Bees and the abbot of Rushen concerning title to one messuage, three tofts, 60 acres of land and 60 acres of moor in Dhoon Glen and Ballellin, heard on 19 June 1301 before justices of the bishop of Durham after the prior had purchased a writ of novel disseisin. The prior argued that the abbot had disseised him of the lands; the abbot presented the counter claim that King Alexander III had gifted them to his predecessor – presumably soon after the Treaty of Perth of 1266 – but he could produce no charter of infeftment in support of his case. The litigants eventually sought licence to concord, with the prior securing title to Ballellin and the abbot to Dhoon Glen. The settlement strongly suggests that the claims of Rushen abbey were legitimate. The place names are identified in W. Cubbon, 'Saynt Maholde and Saynt Michell: Notes on Christian's Barony, Maughold', *Proceedings of the Isle of Man Natural History and Antiquarian Society*, new ser. 2 (1926), 447–55.

246 Grants to Reginald, the king's chaplain, the office of king's bailie in the Isle of Man [post 1266].

SOURCE. *Chron. Lanercost* (Stevenson), 64.
COMMENT. See above, no. 241.

247 Confirms to Juliana wife of Ralph de 'Bracstayden' the grant of land in Stichill that Joan de Morville made her. Cadzow [3 August 1267, a.r. 19].

SOURCE. NRS, J. Maitland Thomson Collection, GD 212/2/33, p. 4 (rev.).
COMMENT. Reference to a confirmation by 'King Alexander' is made in Maitland Thomson's notes on a nineteenth-century inventory of Kenmure Estate papers, where it is described as one item among several in 'Bundle 51'. The original charter is now lost. If the dating of that original is accurate, the document must be an act of Alexander III, rather than of his father, for on 4 August a.r. 19 Alexander II is known to have been far away from Cadzow, at Selkirk (Scoular, *Handlist*, no. 178). The identity of this Joan de Morville is not certain. Although two women by this name are attested in the mid-thirteenth century among the nobility of Westmorland and Cumberland in England, this otherwise unknown Joan would seem more appropriately to belong to the branch of the family whose members held lands in Lauderdale. The identities of Joan's beneficiary, Juliana, and her husband are equally problematic, but it may be significant that the two English Joans were related by marriage to the family of Ranulf, one of the ancestors of the Randolph family. This Ranulf may be the same Ralph, husband of Juliana, named above. The need to affirm title to lands situated in Stichill as late as 1267 was the consequence of a protracted dispute concerning the estate that first pitted Thomas son of Ranulph against the prior of Durham in the 1230s (see P. C. Ferguson, *Medieval Papal Representatives in Scotland: Legates, Nuncios, and Judges-delegate, 1125–1286* [Stair Society, 1997], 28–90).

248 Petitions Edward I for wardship of the lands of Sir Henry de Hastings lying within the liberty of the earldom of Huntingdon, as freely as his predecessors exercised this prerogative by their charters [1269 x 1274].

SOURCE. TNA, Chancery Miscellanea, PRO C 47/22/3/14.
PRINTED. *CDS*, ii, no. 63 (cal.).
COMMENT. This is a little roll, much defaced, compiled by a clerk of the English chancery, of various matters that were pending between the king of Scots and the king of England on the death of Henry III in November 1272. It was probably compiled in preparation for the visit of Alexander III to Westminster to attend Edward's coronation

in the summer of 1274. The subject to which this petition alludes dates it to the period between 1269, when Hastings died, and the summer of 1274. Edward's response was terse: he ordered that Alexander produce the charters in support of the claim.

249 Issues letters of outlawry against William Wysman, otherwise known as William Seliman [1269 x 1279].

SOURCE. TNA, Justices in Eyre, of Assize, of Oyer and Terminer, and of the Peace, etc.: Rolls and Files, PRO JUST 1/649, m. 11, printed in Hartshorne, *Feudal and Military Antiquities*, App., lvi.
COMMENT. Jurors summoned to attend the eyre session convened to hear crown pleas at Wark in Tynedale in November 1279 testified that in the king's letters of outlawry the suspect's surname had been mistakenly identified as Wysman, rather than Seliman. The accusation of homicide originally brought against him must have been made since the last visitation of the eyre in 1269; since then he had been committed to prison and set free on recognisance, then absconded.

250 Writes to King Henry III, requiring him to redress the injuries done to the king and his men of Penrith by Roger de Lancaster and others [ante 1 November 1270].

SOURCE. TNA, Chancery Miscellanea, PRO C 47/12/1/4; *CPR, 1266–72*, 585.
COMMENT. Notice of this letter occurs in an inquest held on the above date pursuant to a commission of oyer and terminer directed to Robert de Neville, John de Oketon and Geoffrey de Neville, justices of the king of England. The commission was appointed after Henry admitted that he had 'many times been required by Alexander king of Scotland to redress the transgressions, injuries, losses and grievances' done to him and his men of Penrith. See also above, no. 86.

251 Grants to Ranulf de Haughton a messuage, 224 acres of arable land, 4 acres of wood and 4 acres of meadow in Haughton [1270 x 1275].

SOURCE. TNA, Justices in Eyre, of Assize, of Oyer and Terminer, and of the Peace, etc.: Rolls and Files, PRO JUST 1/657, m. 3.
COMMENT. Title to the lands was the subject of litigation at the eyre convened at Wark in 1293. Ranulf de Haughton died childless in 1275, by which time he had sold or leased most of his lands to John de Swinburne. Ralph's nearest heirs, his sister and nephew, sought a share of the estate. The act is datable to the early 1270s, when several similar transactions occurred. See *NCH*, xv, 203–4 and above, no. 93.

252 Makes an agreement with the prior of Carlisle concerning the boundaries of their respective lands in Penrith and Sowerby (Cumberland) [1270s?].

SOURCE. *APS*, i, 108.
COMMENT. This deed, labelled as an 'amicable composition', is listed among the inventory of muniments and writings stored in the treasury in Edinburgh that was compiled in September 1282, where it was included under the heading *Negotia tangentia Angliam*. See also above, no. 86 and the next three entries below, which also relate to administrative and legal wrangles involving these manors.

253 Writes to Adam de Crookdake concerning his common rights in the manor of Sowerby (Cumberland) [1270s?].

SOURCE. *APS*, i, 109.
COMMENT. This letter is listed among the inventory of muniments and writings stored in the treasury in Edinburgh that was compiled in September 1282, where it was included under the heading *Negotia tangentia Angliam*. It probably dates to the 1270s,

when King Alexander was involved in considerable debate with Edward I over common rights in many of his English manors. Adam de Crookdake went on to become an attorney and, eventually, an eyre justice.

254 Writes to Geoffrey son of Ivo concerning his common rights in the manor of Sowerby (Cumberland) [1270s?].

SOURCE. *APS*, i, 109.
COMMENT. This letter, together with the preceding two entries, is listed among the inventory of muniments and writings stored in the treasury in Edinburgh that was compiled in September 1282, where it was included under the heading *Negotia tangentia Angliam*. It, too, probably dates to the 1270s, when King Alexander was involved in considerable debate with Edward I over common rights in many of his English manors. Geoffrey son of Ivo, a Cumberland man, was a member of an inquest held at Carlisle before the escheator in September 1274 (*CDS*, ii, no. 24).

255 Grants to his tenants of Sowerby and Penrith (Cumberland) various rights in the waste lands beyond the forest of Inglewood [1270s?].

SOURCE. TNA, Special Collections: Ancient Petitions, PRO SC 8/2/65.
COMMENT. The grant is mentioned in a series of petitions submitted by the men of Sowerby and Penrith to Edward II in parliament soon after the latter's succession. The two manors had been part of the Scottish king's endowment in England and, like those other estates, were seized into Edward I's hands after Alexander III's death and eventually granted to the bishop of Durham. The new regime soon proved onerous, and in three letters of this four-petition document the tenants seek restoration of privileges that they had customarily enjoyed in Inglewood forest as tenants of the Scottish crown. A fourth petition notes that Alexander III had extended some of these privileges to the waste lands that lay beyond the area demarcated as forest. Edward II's response was a promise to examine the tenants' claims.

256 Confirms to the monks of Coupar Angus abbey the gift that Sir Hugh de Abernethy made them of 2 acres of arable land in his territory of Lour, in the 'Unflate', on the north side next to the public road leading to Forfar, saving the king's service. Witnesses: Richard[a] bishop of Man, John de Hay, Alexander Fraser, William Olifard, William Bisset, Coupar Angus. Kinclaven [24 March 1271].

NOTE. [a] *Coupar Angus Rental* has Rinaldo (Reginaldo), no doubt a mistake for Richard.
SOURCE. *Coupar Angus Rental*, i, no. 45, printed from NLS Adv. MS 33.2.9, fo. 14, sixteenth-century extracts by Sir James Balfour from the lost register of the abbey.
COMMENT. This document appears in Scoular, *Alexander II* as no. 373 on the basis of the entry in the rental, which assigns to it the date of 24 March in the twenty-second year of that king's reign (1236). It more properly belongs to the reign of Alexander III, who granted the lands of Lour (Angus) to Sir Hugh in 1265 (see above, no. 55). Hugh made his gift to the monks at Kinclaven c. 1271, not in 1273, as the entry in the lost register notes (at no. 44); Alexander himself dated another of his acts in the same place just a month later (above, no. 76).

257 Grants his assent to the election of a bishop to the see of St Andrews, according to the custom of the realm [ante 1271, 3 June].

SOURCE. *Moray Registrum*, no. 261.
COMMENT. The king's 'assent' is noted in a letter from the prior and chapter of St Andrews to Pope Gregory X, dated as above. The letter notes that after the death of Bishop Gamelin the canons petitioned and obtained Alexander III's permission to proceed.

258 Commands Malcolm earl of Lennox, at the instance of John Wardrop and his wife, Mary, to do justice concerning disputed title to the lands of Cochno, Edinbarnet, Finnich, Ballagan and Drumcruin (all in Lennox) [1271].

SOURCE. *Paisley Registrum*, 180.
COMMENT. The brieve is noted in the record of a hearing convened in the earl's court to settle a long-simmering dispute between the monks of Paisley and members of the earl's kindred concerning lands belonging to the church of Kilpatrick. The dispute is discussed in C. J. Neville, *Native Lordship in Medieval Scotland: The Earldoms of Strathearn and Lennox, c.1140–1365* (Dublin, 2005), 145–8.

259 Grants to Duncan de Forbes the lands of Forbes and Kearn (Aberdeenshire) in free barony [8 July 1271 x 7 July 1272, a.r. 23].

SOURCE. NRS, Lord Forbes collection, GD 52/1447.
COMMENT. Noted in an early modern memorandum compiled by John Lord Forbes that discusses the antiquity of the Forbes family. The memorandum notes further that the estates are to be held in free barony *cum socco et sacca furca et fossa*, and assigns the date a.r. 23 (1271–2), to it. In 1695 the Lord Clerk Register, Sir John Skene, claimed to have seen the same charter among the muniments belonging to Lord Forbes; he dated it then to 'anno 28', apparently a misreading of 'anno 23' (*SP*, iv, 43; Macfarlane, *Genealogical Collections*, ii, 209). In the first edition of his *De verborum significatione* (1597), Skene once again mentioned the king's grant and claimed that the 'charter is yet extant' (Sir John Skene, *De verborum significatione*, *sub* the entry entitled *Liberum Tenementum*, in *The lauues and actes of Parliament, maid be King Iames the First, and his successours kinges of Scotland* [Edinburgh, 1597]). The original charter remains untraced.

260 Petitions Edward I for compensation for lands within the forest of Morton (Cumberland), enclosed by Edward's ministers in violation of the customary rights of his tenants there [1271 x 1274].

SOURCE. TNA, Chancery Miscellanea, PRO C 47/22/3/14.
PRINTED. *CDS*, ii, no. 63 (cal.).
COMMENT. This is a little roll, much defaced, compiled by a clerk of the English chancery, of various matters that were pending between the king of Scots and the king of England on the death of Henry III in November 1272. It was probably compiled in preparation for the visit of Alexander III to Westminster to attend Edward's coronation in the summer of 1274. Although tension between the crowns about the prerogatives of the kings of Scotland within the Cumberland estates designated as forest arose as early as 1268 (and, indeed, troubled the later years of the reign of Alexander II), encroachments on the customary rights of the tenants in this part of the estate flared up afresh in 1271–2. They were the subject of a lengthy and detailed inquest recorded in TNA, PRO C 47/12/1/4, 5 which included a new perambulation of the lands in question. This brought no respite to the dispute, and although Edward conceded that the enclosure had taken place, tensions continued in this part of the border region; see, for example, TNA, PRO JUST 130B, m. 9; JUST 1/132, mm 1, 7, 17d, 27, 32d; JUST 1/133, mm 1, 17d, 28d, 29, 29d.

261 Commands the sheriff to hold an inquest in the full court of the county of Roxburgh to settle a dispute between the hospital of Soutra and Walter de Moravia, knight [ante 19 January 1272].

SOURCE. Above, no. 86.
COMMENT. The inquest was summoned on the date noted above 'pursuant to the king's mandate'.

262 Petitions Edward I for 100s *per diem*, a gift customarily made to the king of Scotland on his visits to the English court [c. 1274, ante 28 December].

SOURCE. TNA, Chancery Miscellanea, PRO C 47/22/3/14.
PRINTED. *CDS*, ii, no. 63 (cal.).
COMMENT. This is a little roll, much defaced, compiled by a clerk of the English chancery, of various matters that were pending between the king of Scots and the king of England on the death of Henry III in November 1272. It was probably compiled in preparation for the visit of Alexander III to Westminster to attend Edward's coronation in the summer of 1274. In recent years such expenses had, in fact, been accounted for in the English Exchequer: see, for example, *HN*, III, iii, 284. Edward's answer to this request, however, was decidedly curt: he noted that Alexander did not come at the command of the English king, but rather to do his duty (*devoir*) to him. He did, in the end, assign him the gift, in the shape of a payment of £175. See *CDS*, ii, no. 37; *Feodera*, I, ii, 520.

263 Writes to King Edward I on receipt of a fee from him [1274–5].

SOURCE. TNA, Exchequer: Treasury of the Receipt: Miscellaneous Books, PRO E 36/268.
PRINTED. Palgrave, *Antient Kalendars*, i, 134.
COMMENT. The original letter has not been traced. It was, however, cited in an inventory of exchequer records compiled by Bishop Stapledon c. 1323, which referred to 'certain letters (patent) of Alexander king of Scotland, together with letters from divers merchants requesting sums of money from Edward king of England, [delivered to] Geoffrey de Neubaud, former keeper of the bishopric of Durham'. Neubaud and John de Luvetot acted as keepers of the bishopric between August and December 1274. The letters probably relate to the king's visit to England that same autumn, and probably to the fee requested above in no. 262.

264 Grants to Hugh, son and heir of Gilbert de Grindon, land in Huntland (Tynedale), in exchange for the manor of Grindon [1274 x 1282].

SOURCE. *PROME*, i, 194, 209–10, and App. no. 91 (TNA, Chancery: Vetus Codex, PRO C 153/1, mm 125^r, 143^v–144^r; TNA, PRO, Special Collections: Ancient Petitions, SC 8/218/10861B); *Cal. Inqu. Misc.*, i, no. 2021. This document, and the several that follow, cannot be dated more precisely than 1274 x 1286.
COMMENT. The tortuous story of the attempts by both Grindon and his rival, William de St Clair, to secure title to these and other Tynedale lands (below, nos 265–8) is unravelled in Holford and Stringer, *Border Liberties*, 256–5.

265 Commands the bailiff of Wark in Tynedale to seize the lands of Grindon into the king's hands [1274 x 1282].

SOURCE. *PROME*, ii, 451, 496, 513–14 (TNA, Chancery: Vetus Codex, PRO C 153/1, mm 125, 138, 143d-144).
COMMENT. See above, no. 264. Two early fourteenth-century petitions submitted to the English parliament (TNA, Special Collections: Ancient Petitions, PRO SC 8/218/10861A and B) further reveal that King Alexander purchased the estate from the lord of Grindon.

266 Gives £26 of land in Langwathby and Sowerby (Cumberland) to Hugh de Grindon [1274 x 1282].

SOURCE. *PROME*, ii, 496, 513–14 (TNA, Chancery: Vetus Codex, PRO C 153/1, mm 138, 143d-144; TNA, Special Collections: Ancient Petitions, PRO SC 8/218/10861B).

COMMENT. A charter (*carta*) gifting the land of 'Langwathby and 40 librates of land in Penrith' is listed in the inventory of September 1282 of 'muniments and writings' deposited in the king's treasury in Edinburgh (*APS*, i, 108). The inventory document and this grant were almost certainly related to the contest between William de St Clair and Hugh de Grindon noted above in no. 264.

267 Commands the bailiff of Penrith to put Hugh de Grindon in possession of lands in Langwathby and Sowerby (Cumberland) [1274 x 1282].

SOURCE. *PROME*, i, 209–10, App., no. 91 (TNA, Chancery: Vetus Codex, PRO C 153/1, mm 143^{v}–144^{r}; TNA, Special Collections: Ancient Petitions, PRO SC 8/218/10861B).
COMMENT. This brieve and the next are related to the troubles that William de St Clair experienced in his attempt to secure title to the £40 of land that Alexander III had granted him in no. 264, above.

268 Grants £40 of land in Scotland to William de St Clair [1274 x 1282].

SOURCE. *PROME*, ii, 451, 496, 513–14 (TNA, Chancery: Vetus Codex, PRO C 153/1, mm 125, 138, 143d-144; TNA, Special Collections: Ancient Petitions, PRO SC 8/218/10861B).
COMMENT. Noted in a petition that Hugh de Grindon submitted to King Edward I of England in parliament in 1307. The grant cannot be dated more precisely than 1274 x 1282. See also *PROM*E, ii, 451, 474.

269 Grants to Alexander de Ros the ferme of the mill of Grindon (Tynedale), to be held for an annual payment of 4 merks [1274 x 1286].

SOURCE. Palgrave, *Docs. Hist. Scot.*, i, 4, 11.
COMMENT. The grant is noted in the record of an extent dated late 1286 or early 1287 that assessed the value of the lands in England of which Alexander III had died seised. Thomas de Normanville, Edward I's escheator north of Trent, returned that in 1286 the mill had returned £16 8s (over a period of eight months); the following year it brought in only £2 13s 4d. Ros was a significant land holder both within and beyond the liberty of Tynedale. His title to the mill and the charter by which Alexander III had infeft him were noted again in a petition submitted to Edward I's 1307 parliament at Carlisle by Ros's son. See TNA, PRO SC 8/281/10861B; TNA, Chancery: Vetus Codex, PRO C 153/1, mm 138, 143d. The grant cannot be dated more accurately than 1274 x 1286, the former representing the date when Ros succeeded to his father's Tynedale estates.

270 Grants 22 merks annually to Eymer de Hadden for land in Hadden (Roxburghshire) [1274 x 1286].

SOURCE. *PROME*, ii, 160–1; *CDS*, iv, no. 1815 (TNA, Special Collections: Parliament Rolls, Exchequer Series, PRO SC 9/12, m. 13d).
COMMENT. Notice of this grant survives in a petition that Hadden presented to Edward I in the autumn parliament of 1305, in which he noted that Alexander III had paid him the fee through the hands of the sheriff of Roxburgh. Edward's response was to demand that Eymer bring his claim before the lieutenant of Scotland, and there present his 'charter or other muniment'.

271 Writes, together with his wife, Queen Margaret, eight letters patent concerning debts owed and paid to various merchants [probably ante 1275].

SOURCE. *APS*, i, 116.
COMMENT. Notice of these letters occurs in the list of rolls, memoranda and other

documents sent to England at the command of Edward I in 1292. One of the items was 'a box containing eight documents' described as above; the entry notes also that the merchants had acknowledged payment of the sums owed them.

272 Commands the sheriff, bailies and provosts of Dumbarton not to trouble the men of the bishop of Glasgow going to and returning from Argyll with their merchandise. Edinburgh 18 June 1275, a.r. 26].

SOURCE. *RRS*, v, no. 359 (note); *RMS*, ix, no. 601 (note); Strathclyde Regional Council Archives, Glasgow, MS D-TC 1/1, 1–2, no. 2.
COMMENT. Notice of this document occurs in a royal confirmation by Charles I, dated 16 October 1636, of several charters concerning the privileges of the burgesses of Glasgow, printed in *Charters and Other Documents relating to the City of Glasgow*, ed. J. D. Marwick and R. Renwick (2 vols in 3, SBRS, 1894), I, ii, no. 12, as well as in a (now lost) deed of confirmation issued by Robert I. The inventory offers some information about the latter, identifying it as 'a chartor dated 15 November 1329 approveing and rectifeing ane chartor granted be King Alexander his predecessor last deceist [which was King Alexander the 3rd] dated at Maiden Castle the 18 day of June and of the said King Alexander his rigne the 26 yeir [which wes the year of God 1275] which is preported verbatim in the said King Roberts chartor and beirs the said King Alexander to direct his chartor to the shirreff baillies and proveists of Dumbarton and to say to hem theirby that they knew weill how his majestie had granted to the bishop of Glasgow that his men of Glasgow might goe to and returne from Argyll with their merchandize frielie and without any impediment and berans the same wes granted be his majestie to the said bishop before the foundation of the brugh of Dunbarton commanding therfor that if they had taken ony thing from the said bishop his men that without delay they wold make restitutione and that non should vex or trouble them against this concession wpon his majesties heighest displasure'. The passage makes it difficult to distinguish the text of the deed of 1275 from that of the confirmation of 1329, but in form and content the act of 1275 closely resembles the terminology found in several other of Alexander III's brieves of protection.

273 Petitions Edward I for compensation for lands within the park of Plumpton (Cumberland), unlawfully enclosed by Edward's ministers [c. 1275].

SOURCE. TNA, Chancery Miscellanea, PRO C 47/22/3/14.
PRINTED. *CDS*, ii, no. 63 (cal.).
COMMENT. This is a little roll, much defaced, compiled by a clerk of the English chancery, of various matters that were pending between the king of Scots and the king of England on the death of Henry III in November 1272. It was probably compiled in preparation for the visit of Alexander III to Westminster to attend Edward's coronation in the summer of 1274. Although tension between the crowns about the prerogatives of the kings of Scotland within the Cumberland estates designated as forest arose as early as 1268 (and, indeed, troubled the later years of the reign of Alexander II), encroachments on Plumpton in particular began in earnest in the summer of 1274. See *CDS*, i, nos 2487, 2540; *CDS*, ii, no. 17.

274 Petitions Edward I on behalf of the burgesses of Berwick, who seek a confirmation of the charter granted to them by Henry III [c. 1275].

SOURCE. TNA, Chancery Miscellanea, PRO C 47/22/3/14.
PRINTED. *CDS*, ii, no. 63 (cal.).
COMMENT. This is a little roll, much defaced, compiled by a clerk of the English chancery, of various matters that were pending between the king of Scots and the king of England on the death of Henry III in November 1272. It was probably compiled in preparation for the visit of Alexander III to Westminster to attend Edward's coronation

in the summer of 1274; the following year three new petitions were added to it (see also below, nos 275, 278). King Henry III's charter to the burgesses, dated 6 November 1260, extended royal protection to them within England in matters of debt and poinding (*Cal. Charter Rolls, 1257–1300*, 32). Edward's response to Alexander's petition was noncommittal: he undertook only to do 'what is fitting'.

275 Petitions Edward I on behalf of a burgess of Leith, who was poinded in the port of Hull by two men of York at the behest of Sir John Comyn [c. 1275].

SOURCE. TNA, Chancery Miscellanea, PRO C 47/22/3/14.
PRINTED. *CDS*, ii, no. 63 (cal.).
COMMENT. This is a little roll, much defaced, compiled by a clerk of the English chancery, of various matters that were pending between the king of Scots and the king of England on the death of Henry III in November 1272. It was probably compiled in preparation for the visit of Alexander III to Westminster to attend Edward's coronation in the summer of 1274. This petition cannot be precisely dated, but the action taken against the (unnamed) merchant of Leith, in which he claimed to have lost £100, was probably a consequence of a ruling by Comyn in his capacity as justiciar of Galloway, an office he held in 1275 (Barrow, *Kingdom of the Scots*, 86). Edward's response to this petition was favourable: he ordered that the man be delivered 'as this seems just'.

276 Writes to the canons of the priory of Rushen abbey (Man), informing them that the election by which they and the people of Man promoted Abbot Gilbert to the see of Man and the Isles was canonically unlawful. Informs them that he has installed his own candidate, Master Mark, in the see [1275].

SOURCE. *Chronicles of the Reigns of Stephen, Henry II., and Richard I.*, ed. R. Howlett (4 vols, London, 1884–9), ii, 569; *Chronica regum Manniae et Insularum: The Chronicle of Man and the Sudreys from the Manuscript Codex in the British Museum*, ed. P. A. Munch, rev. A. Goss (Manx Society Publications, 1974), 117.
COMMENT. 'Master Mark' was Mark de Galloway; King Alexander further identifies him as a brother of the royal bailie of Man. In order to assure Mark's secure hold on the see, the king immediately sent him to Norway for consecration. See below, no. 277.

277 Writes to John II archbishop of Nidaros, concerning Mark bishop of Man and the Isles [1275].

SOURCE. *Chronicles of the Reigns of Stephen*, ed. Howlett, ii, 569; *Chronica regum Manniae et Insularum: The Chronicle of Man and the Sudreys from the Manuscript Codex in the British Museum*, ed. Munch, rev. Goss, 250.
COMMENT. The chroniclers state that immediately after installing Mark de Galloway on the episcopal throne King Alexander sent him to the metropolitan archbishop in Norway 'with a letter from himself, together with other letters which he had been able to extort from the clergy'. The continuator of the chronicle of William de Newburgh wrote even as these events were occurring, and admitted that he did not know what happened thereafter (*Chronicles of the Reigns of Stephen*, ed. Howlett, ii, 569). The author of the *Manx Chronicle*, however, reveals that Mark duly made his way to Archbishop John at Tönsberg, where he was consecrated ('*Íslenzkir annálar*', in *Sturlunga Saga including the Islendinga Saga of Lawman Sturla Thordsson and Other Works*, ed. G. Vigfusson [2 vols, Oxford, 1878], ii, 381).

278 Petitions Edward I on behalf of Alexander MacDougall of Argyll, whose ship and goods to the value of 160 merks were recently captured at Bristol. He requests the release of the ship [c. 1275].

SOURCE. TNA, Chancery Miscellanea, PRO C 47/22/3/14.
PRINTED. *CDS*, ii, no. 63 (cal.).
COMMENT. This is a little roll, much defaced, compiled by a clerk of the English chancery, of various matters that were pending between the king of Scots and the king of England on the death of Henry III in November 1272. It was probably compiled in preparation for the visit of Alexander III to Westminster to attend Edward's coronation in the summer of 1274. This petition is no doubt related to the incident that was the subject of a later letter from Alexander III to Edward I (above, no. 92). Alexander MacDougall was active at sea on behalf of his king in the autumn of 1275, when he led an expedition to the Isle of Man. Edward's response was favourable: his clerk added to the roll the words: 'granted, as it seems right'.

279 Establishes a chapel dedicated to St Laurence (Forres) in honour of his late queen, Margaret, and assigns to it 6 merks annually in alms for prayers for her soul [post 1275].

SOURCE. *PROME*, ii, 160; *CDS*, iv, no. 1815 (TNA, Special Collections: Parliament Rolls, Exchequer Series, PRO SC 9/12, m. 13).
COMMENT. The charter is mentioned in a petition presented to Edward I in the autumn parliament of 1305, when Adam the chaplain of Moray requested payment of the fee. Edward's response was to order him to show written evidence of the gift to the lieutenant and chamberlain of Scotland.

280 Commands his bailiff and eschaetor in Tynedale, John Tecket, to seize the lands of John Comyn (I) of Badenoch, deceased [c. 1277].

SOURCE. TNA, Justices in Eyre, of Assize, of Oyer and Terminer, and of the Peace, etc.: Rolls and Files, PRO JUST 1 /649, m. 2d, printed in Hartshorne, *Feudal and Military Antiquities*, App., xii; PRO JUST 1/657, m. 2d.
COMMENT. This brieve is mentioned, first, in an action of novel disseisin concerning the lands of Thornton that John Comyn son of John Comyn I of Badenoch brought against his brother, John II of Badenoch, before justices in eyre at Wark in the autumn of 1279, and again in the record of the eyre that sat at Wark in 1293. Comyn's sons subsequently disputed title to the lands; see also below, no. 281.

281 Commands his bailiff and escheator in Tynedale, John Tecket, to deliver to John Comyn (II) of Badenoch, son of John Comyn (I) of Badenoch, the estates that his father held in Tynedale [c. 1277].

SOURCE. TNA, Justices in Eyre, of Assize, of Oyer and Terminer, and of the Peace, etc.: Rolls and Files, PRO JUST 1/649, m. 2d, printed in Hartshorne, *Feudal and Military Antiquities*, App., xii.
COMMENT. This brieve is mentioned in an action of novel disseisin concerning the lands of Thornton that John Comyn Junior son of John Comyn I of Badenoch brought against his brother, John II of Badenoch, before justices in eyre at Wark in the autumn of 1279. The defendant testified that he took possession of his father's inheritance in accordance with a brieve that Alexander III had directed to Tecket. The latter confirmed this testimony.

282 Confirms a quitclaim by John de Strachan, performed in the chamber of the lord king, of the lands of Beath Waldeve (Fife), with all men and cottars dwelling on the same with their posterity, and with all pertinents and rights with which he held said land of the king. Edinburgh [post 1278, 21 May x 4 September].

SOURCE. *Dunfermline Registrum*, no. 86.
COMMENT. Strachan, son and heir of the late Sir Ralph de Strachan, quitclaimed

the lands into the hands of Alexander III between the dates noted above before an assembly that included Sir William de St Clair, sheriff of Edinburgh; the chamberlain, Sir John de Lindsay; Sir Richard de Straiton; Patrick de Lamberton, clerk; Master John de Musselburgh, clerk; Master William de Cramond, clerk; Sir William Bisset; William, clerk of the constable of Edinburgh castle; and several other 'trustworthy persons'. At Strachan's request the king appended his seal to the deed of quitclaim.

283 Writes letters authorising Robert Bruce earl of Carrick to swear homage to Edward I on his behalf for the lands and tenements that he holds in England [ante 1278, October].

SOURCE. Stones, *Anglo-Scottish Relations,* no. 12(b).
COMMENT. Bruce made mention of Alexander's authorisation in the oath that he swore to Edward I in the Michaelmas parliament convened at Westminster in October 1278. It was no doubt in relation to the homage matter that Edward I instructed a clerk of his chancery to prepare letters under the great seal of England; see *Calendar of Chancery Warrants preserved in the Public Record Office* (London, 1927), 4.

284 Grants the ferme of the burgh of Berwick to the mayor and community thereof [post 1278].

SOURCE. *Cal. Inqu. Misc.,* ii, no. 1601.
COMMENT. The grant is noted in an inquest held on 22 February 1338 before Walter de Weston chamberlain of Berwick, when the mayor, bailies and common clerk of the burgh sought arrears of the fees and robe owed them by virtue of their offices. They claimed that until the time of James (*sic*, read John) de Lindsay, that is 1278–81, they had received their fees from the hands of the chamberlain of Scotland; 'afterwards, King Alexander granted the town to farm to the mayor and commonalty, the said fees being allowed therein'.

285 Grants to Geoffrey de Sebergham rights of common pasture in Sowerby (Cumberland), to be held heritably [20 November 1278 x 19 November 1279].

SOURCE. *Thomas Denton, A Perambulation of Cumberland 1687–1688*, ed. A. Winchester and M. Wane (Surtees Society and Cumberland and Westmorland Antiquarians and Archaeological Society, 2003), 246; but see also *APS*, I, 108.
COMMENT. Notice of the grant survives in the text of Denton's lengthy description of Cumberland, Westmorland and the Isle of Man (a manuscript now preserved as Cumbria Record Office D/Lons/L12/4/2/2), undertaken at the behest of Sir John Lowther, MP for Westmorland. The entries offer brief histories of the landowners of the county's manors based on medieval source materials that were then extant. Denton claimed that this charter of Alexander III's was dated '7° Ed'; the editors of the *Perambulation* suggest that his local information is highly trustworthy, given Denton's knowledge of the region and his experience with legal records, including charters (ibid., 19–20). He may nonetheless have confused Geoffrey with a Walter de Sebergham, who is noted in the inventory of 1282 as having made an amicable concord with 'the king of Scots' (*APS*, i, 108). A dating of 1278 x 1279 would place this grant firmly in the context of ongoing discussions between Alexander and Edward I about the rights that the king of Scotland claimed within his Cumberland possessions.

286 Grants to Walter the baker and Hawys, his spouse, a tenement land in the burgh of Perth [ante 1279].

SOURCE. *Inchaffray Charters*, no. 110.
COMMENT. The king's grant is noted in the record of a formal agreement between the abbot of Inchaffray and the couple, after both parties laid claim to a tenement formerly in the possession of Nicholas Pape. Walter and Hawys argued that their right to the land was implicit in 'letters of their lord the king'. The agreement required that they renounce their claim in return for a cash payment.

287 Grants to William bishop of St Andrews permission to make a testament to dispose of his spiritual and worldly goods [ante 1279, 28 May].

SOURCE. *APS*, i, 116.
COMMENT. Notice of this letter (*littera*) occurs on a list of memoranda, rolls and other documents sent to London in 1292 at the command of Edward I. The lost deed may refer to the reign of Alexander II and the death of Bishop William Malveisin of St Andrews in 1238, but on balance probably belongs to the reign of Alexander III; it is so identified in Watt, *Graduates*, 594. William Wishart bishop of St Andrews (d. 28 May 1279) was notorious both for his licentiousness and his acquisition of private property. Watt has traced the descent of title to some of his lands to his illegitimate children (ibid., 590, 594). A written testament will have ensured Bishop William's opportunity to dispose of his private possessions.

288 Appends his seal to an extract from the roll of the fines issued at an earlier eyre session, levied for unlawful entry into the lands of Ouston in Tynedale [ante November 1279].

SOURCE. TNA, Justices in Eyre, of Assize, of Oyer and Terminer, and of the Peace, etc.: Rolls and Files, PRO JUST 1/649, m. 3.
COMMENT. Notice of this fine appears in the record of the eyre which visited Tynedale in 1279, when a litigant produced the estreat in support of claim to Ouston. The sessions of 1279 were held at Wark between November 1279 and January 1280; the 'earlier eyre' was probably that of 1257, convened at Nunwick. See also below, no. 292.

289 Leases pasture land in Hesleyside (Tynedale) to William de Bellingham [ante November 1279].

SOURCE. TNA, Justices in Eyre, of Assize, of Oyer and Terminer, and of the Peace, etc.: Rolls and Files, PRO JUST 1/649, m. 4.
COMMENT. The arrangement is noted in the record of the eyre which began its visit of Tynedale in 1279, when two of the king's tenants brought writs of novel disseisin against Bellingham. The latter defended his title by explaining that the king had earlier converted the land from free forest. The sessions at Wark began in November 1279 and concluded in January 1280.

290 Grants the wardship of Alexander son and heir of Sir David de Lindsay of Barnweil to John Comyn of Badenoch [ante November 1279].

SOURCE. TNA, Justices in Eyre, of Assize, of Oyer and Terminer, and of the Peace, etc.: Rolls and Files, PRO JUST 1/649 m. 11d, printed in Hartshorne, *Feudal and Military Antiquities*, App., lvii.
COMMENT. The gift is noted among the list of heirs and heiresses compiled for Alexander III at the eyre of Wark in Tynedale which began in 1279. Alexander de Lindsay's father, Sir David, had been active in royal service, including as chamberlain, until his death in 1279 while on crusade.

291 Grants to the monks of Arbroath abbey an annual gift of £9 6s 8d from the fermes of his demesne lands in Fife, which the monks pay annually to the prior and convent of St Thomas the Martyr of Canterbury [post 12 November 1279].

SOURCE. *Rot. Scot.*, i, 39.
COMMENT. Notice of this grant appears in a writ of Edward I dated 6 March 1297. Here the king commands John de Warenne keeper of Scotland to ensure that the sheriffs of Forfar and Fife render to the monks of Arbroath the annual sum of £14 6s 8d to which they are entitled by virtue of 'divers charters of Alexander late king of Scots'.

Alexander, it continues, made these gifts for the pious purposes set out in said charters, but the sheriffs of Forfar and Fife have been unlawfully withholding the sums. (The monks did, indeed, petition Edward in 1297 for restitution of the fermes: see TNA, PRO SC 8/34.) In one of these 'divers charters', no. 127 above, Alexander granted the monks of Arbroath 100s (£5) from the fermes of his manor of Forfar and requested that the gift be sent to Canterbury for the feeding of thirteen paupers; the balance of the £14 6s 8d, that is, the £9 6s 8d of this lost act, were obviously assigned at some later date from royal demesne lands in Fife. The gift was also the subject of another letter, below, no. 300.

292 Appends his seal to an estreat from the feet of fines relating to the eyre lately held at Wark in Tynedale [post January 1280].

SOURCE. *APS*, i, 116.
COMMENT. Notice of the sealed extract appears in a list of memoranda, rolls and other documents sent to London in 1292 at the command of Edward I. The Wark eyre ended in January 1280.

293 Confirms a grant by Humphrey de Bohun earl of Hereford to John, his son, of the lands of Ratho and Bathgate [ante 1281, 25 July].

SOURCE. *APS*, i, 116.
COMMENT. Notice of this confirmation occurs on a list of memoranda, rolls and other documents sent to London in 1292 at the command of Edward I. The list includes 'letters of King Alexander confirming Humphrey [III] de Bohun's gift to his son of all his lands in Lothian'; these were Ratho and Bathgate. John subsequently sold both to the king for the very considerable sum of £989 (and perhaps more) and they became, in turn, part of the wedding gift that Alexander bestowed on his daughter-in-law, Marguerite of Flanders, on her marriage to Prince Alexander.

294 Commands his bailiffs of Tynedale to inform him about alleged injuries to the miners of Edward I, king of England, at Alston [1282, c. 23 August].

SOURCE. Above, no. 138.
COMMENT. The mandate is noted in a letter to King Edward I dated as above.

295 Grants to William de Swinburne free warren in his demesne lands of Haughton, Haughton Strother, Williamston, Slaggyford, Capel Shaws and Staward, in the liberty of Tynedale [28 September 1282, a.r. 34].

SOURCE. BL, Lansdowne MS 326, fo. 133^{v}; Bodleian Library, Oxford, MS Dodsworth XLV, fo. 48^{v}.
COMMENT. These volumes, dated 1638–9, belong to a large series of transcriptions compiled by the antiquary Roger Dodsworth. Each consists of Latin-language summaries and, occasionally, full transcriptions of several dozen charters then in the possession of various Northumberland families; this document was included among the muniments of the Swinburnes of Capheaton. Some of the Swinburne documents are now on deposit with the Northumberland Collections Service; many more, including this one, are now lost.
PRINTED. Dodsworth's summary of this charter was published in *Northumb. and Durham Deeds*, 203.
SOURCE. TNA, Justices in Eyre, of Assize, of Oyer and Terminer, and of the Peace, etc.: Rolls and Files, PRO JUST 1/657, m 9d; BL, Lansdowne MS 326, fo. 133 (*Northumb. and Durham Deeds*, 203).

COMMENT. This would appear to be a third royal charter relating to Swinburne's lands in Northumberland: no. 230 above represents an initial grant, made in 1264, no. 84 above a reissue, with greater privileges, dating to 1273. Swinburne's widow, Margaret, presented either this charter or its 1273 version in evidence at an inquest before justices in eyre at Wark in 1293. See above, Comments at no. 84.

296 Commands Thomas de Charteris, Ralph de Bosco and William de Dumfries to undertake an inventory of muniments and writings stored in the Treasury in Edinburgh [1282, ante 29 September].

SOURCE. *APS*, i, 10.
COMMENT. The inventory that the king's agents compiled runs for several pages in the printed text of *APS*, i. It offers a valuable – if frustrating – glimpse of the richness of the archives that Edward I carried off to England the following decade. The inventory is discussed above, 37–9.

297 Writes to Baldwin de Mortagne, knight, granting him £50 sterling, to be deducted from the sum owed to the king by the count of Flanders [December 1282 x February 1283].

SOURCE. Original. Archives départementales du nord, Lille, Chambre des comptes, B 403/3088 (Stevenson, *Documents*, i, 118–19).
COMMENT. Reference to the grant occurs in a letter of Baldwin dated 2 October 1289, in which the latter acknowledged receipt of the amount, 'which sum the most high and most powerful lord the king of Scotland gave me'. The sums owed by the count of Flanders relate to the marriage of Prince Alexander to Marguerite. For the dating, see above, nos 141 and 142.

298 Writes his last testament, including therein a bequest of £100 to Elena de Prenderlathe, for her service to the queen of Norway [ante 9 April 1283].

SOURCE. *Cal. Inqu. Misc.*, i, no. 1936; *CDS*, ii, no. 1596; iv, no. 1761, App., no. 6.
COMMENT. Notice of this gift occurs in the record of an inquest *post mortem* held on 30 September 1304 in Northumberland into the lands of the late Elena de Prenderlathe. The death of his daughter Margaret on the date noted above rendered obsolete the elaborate arrangements for the succession set out in 1281 (above, no. 133). The princess's demise may have prompted Alexander to write a first draft of his will; alternatively, the death of his daughter on the date noted above may have led him to amend his will so as to include the bequest.

299 Writes to King Edward I requesting favour for Ingram de Gynes in the settlement of title to lands formerly in the possession of William de Lindsay [1283, ante 17 April].

SOURCE. TNA, Special Collections: Ancient Correspondence of the Chancery and the Exchequer, PRO SC 1/9/91 (*CDS*, v, no. 47).
COMMENT. Ingram de Gynes married Christina, daughter and heiress of Sir William de Lindsay, in May 1283; meanwhile, on 17 April the chancellor of England had written to the keeper of the rolls indicating that King Edward I had approved the marriage. Alexander III later wrote to Edward thanking him for his favour; see above, no. 155.

300 Writes to the prior and chapter of Canterbury cathedral concerning his gift of money to feed thirteen paupers every Tuesday [ante 7 August 1283].

SOURCE. Canterbury Cathedral Archives, CCA-DCc-Register/B, fo. 304^v.

COMMENT. A letter of Prior Thomas Ringmer of Canterbury to Alexander III dated 7 August 1283 mentions the recent visit of G. monk of Arbroath bearing letters from the king on this subject. See also above, nos 127 and 291.

301 Writes letters acknowledging a debt to John de Masun, merchant, of £172 for 500 casks of wine [ante 1284].

SOURCE. Stevenson, *Documents*, i, 73 (TNA, Chancery Miscellanea, PRO C 47/22/1/44).
COMMENT. Notice of the king's 'divers letters' occurs in the record of an inquest dated 3 February 1289, by which Edward I assisted Masun to secure the monies owed him from the executors of the late king's estate.

302 Writes to King Edward I acknowledging an ongoing debt to the merchant John de Masun [c. 1284, post 17 May].

SOURCE. *CDS*, ii, no. 264 (TNA, Chancery Miscellanea, PRO C 47/22/9/9).
COMMENT. Reference to King Alexander III's letter is made in a petition that Masun submitted to King Edward I c. 1284, which noted that Edward had written to Alexander 'three times' requesting that the debt be settled. Alexander replied favourably, 'desiring that the writer should come to him and he should be satisfied'. Masun further complained that when he sought to recover his money, the king of Scotland's men threw him in prison and 'snatched from his hand' the obligatory letter. See also above, nos 147 and 301, and below, no. 319.

303 Grants to Reginald de Haughton, son of Ranulf de Haughton, a moiety of the manor of 'Wiggelsmere' (Tynedale) [ante 1285, 13 July].

SOURCE. NCS, Swinburne (Capheaton) Estate Records, ZSW 1/43; *HN*, III, i, 19.
COMMENT. The grant is mentioned in a deed dated Edinburgh 13 July 1285 by which John Comyn quitclaimed to William de Swinburne all his rights in a moiety of the lands of 'Wigglesmere' (now Greenlee Lough). It stipulated that the land was henceforth to be held of Ranulf de Haughton 'as the charter and instruments granted by King Alexander to Reginald de Haughton bear witness'. For another grant to Ranulf de Haughton, see above, no. 251.

LOST ACTS OF UNDETERMINED DATE CERTAINLY OR PROBABLY THE SUBJECT OF WRITTEN RECORD

(arranged alphabetically by principal beneficiary)

I. ACTS IN FAVOUR OF LAY BENEFICIARIES

304 Confirms to Alexander son of Colin son of Carimer of Cupar the charter by which the latter's kinsman, Richard de Kilmaron, gave him the land called Woodflat in 'Kinmult', 'otherwise known as Lillockisfeyld' (Lillock, Fife).

SOURCE. NRS, RH 1/2/681 (a photocopy of the original among the papers of the Maitland family earls of Lauderdale at Thirlestane Castle); see also *APS*, i, 110.

COMMENT. Richard's gift and his request for its confirmation are the subjects of an unusual petition addressed to Alexander III. Here, Richard requested that the king confirm the grant of the land called 'Woddeflatter' in 'Kinmult', otherwise known as 'Lillockisfeyld' (Lilac or Lillock, Fife), that he had made to Alexander son of Colin son of Carimer. 'Kinmult' is now the Mount; 'Lillockisfeyld' is now Lilac or Lillock, in Monimail parish, Fife. The charter is listed in an inventory of now lost thirteenth-century muniments compiled for Edward I in 1292; in the printed version the place name is misidentified as Kinmuck (Aberdeenshire).

305 Grants to John de Badby the lands of Manor (Peeblesshire).

SOURCE. *RMS*, i, App. II, no. 594.

COMMENT. The grant is mentioned in a fragmentary copy of a great seal roll, now lost. It is perhaps a regrant to John as heir of William de Badby, to whom King Alexander gifted the land after it was quitclaimed by Nicholas Corbet. See above, no. 166.

306 Grants to Robert Cameron of Ballerno a fee of 20 merks annually.

SOURCE. *Rot. Scot.*, i, 14.

COMMENT. Notice of this grant occurs in a writ of Edward I dated 16 December 1292 directing the bailies of Inverness to make payment to the beneficiary of the ferme owed him 'of the gift of the late King Alexander of good memory'. See also below, no. 310.

307 Grants to John de Carberry land worth 10 merks per annum in Stirling from the ferme of that town, for the term of his life.

SOURCE. *PROME*, ii, 228 (TNA, Special Collections: Parliament Rolls, Exchequer Series, PRO SC 9/12, m. 12d).

COMMENT. The grant is cited in a petition presented by Carberry to Edward I in the autumn parliament of 1305. Here, Carberry requested return of the rent 'which he had of the gift and grant of King Alexander for the term of his life', and which he had lost to William Olifard in the recent war. Edward agreed only to have the chamberlain of Scotland hold an inquest into the matter to determine 'what is just'.

308 Grants to Thomas de Charteris and Lady Joanna de Vescy half the barony of Wilton (Roxburghshire), which the said Joanna had resigned to the king, to be held for the service of one quarter of a knight.

SOURCE. Stevenson, *Documents*, ii, 463–4; *CDS*, ii, no. 1435.
COMMENT. Notice of this charter occurs in the record of a chancery inquest dated 2 January 1303 into the lands of William de Charteris. The jurors reported that Lady Joanna had been seised of half the barony and that she had quitclaimed her lands into the hands of King Alexander, who had then 'infeft Sir Thomas de Charteris and her jointly'. They added that while they knew there had been a 'muniment' of some kind attesting this grant they did not know its tenor. Finally, they noted that Sir Thomas had died the previous November as 'a king's enemy', but that his son, William, had recently come into the peace of Edward I.

309 Grants to Reginald le Cheyne, senior, knight, some land near the Crummock burn (Ayrshire).

SOURCE. *Scone Liber*, no. 146.
COMMENT. The grant is noted in a charter of Reginald le Cheyne the younger that gifted the lands to the monks of Scone abbey. Here, Reginald noted that King Alexander had granted to his father, Reginald senior, the land lying north of the burn and east of a manor formerly in the possession of Alexander Comyn earl of Buchan.

310 Grants to Reginald le Cheyne, junior, on the occasion of his knighting, a £20 yearly fee from the royal chamber until he should later be provided with land of that value.

SOURCE. *PROME*, ii, 135, 250; *CDS*, ii, no. 1737 (TNA, Special Collections: Parliament Rolls, Exchequer Series, PRO SC 9/12 m. 10; TNA, Special Collections: Ancient Petitions, PRO SC 8/9/438).
COMMENT. Alexander III's grant is cited in a petition that Reginald presented to King Edward I in the autumn parliament of 1305. Here, he recounted that he had been in receipt of the pension before King John had given him title to lands near Elgin. King Edward ordered that Cheyne's charter be examined and that the records of the Scottish exchequer be searched for evidence that the pension had been paid. See also *Rot. Scot.*, i, 14, a writ of King Edward dated 16 December 1292 directing the bailies of Inverness to make payment to Cheyne of the ferme owed him 'by gift of the late King Alexander of good memory'.

311 Grants to Thomas de Clenhill, knight, a fee of 20 merks annually.

SOURCE. *Rot. Scot.*, i, 15.
COMMENT. Notice of the grant occurs in a writ of Edward I dated 3 January 1292 directing the sheriff of Fife to make an overdue payment to the beneficiary, who was accustomed to receive the fee 'by gift of the late King Alexander'.

312 Exchanges with Alexander (Comyn) earl of Buchan title to Comyn lands lying near the river Tay.

SOURCE. *Scone Liber*, no. 146.
COMMENT. The exchange is mentioned in a charter of Reginald le Cheyne, junior, in favour of the monks of Scone abbey, which notes that the exchange involved lands located near Drumoig (Fife) next to the river Tay.

313 Grants to Alexander Comyn earl of Buchan a yearly fee of £20, to be taken from the Wardrobe or by way of a nominal rent for land in 'Rafran' (Rathen?) (Moray), until provided with land to that amount.

SOURCE. TNA, Special Collections: Ancient Petitions, PRO SC 8/93/4650.
COMMENT. The grant is cited in a much defaced petition presented to King Edward I sometime between 1286 and Comyn's death in 1289. This appears to consist of

several requests for payment, both of debts left outstanding at Alexander III's death and for services rendered in the aftermath of the king's demise. Edward I's responses to Comyn's petitions are, by contrast, legible: in answer to the request for land in 'Rafran' he indicated that he would 'take counsel' on the matter, but only after Comyn had shown him Alexander III's charter. Comyn's son, Alexander, was still petitioning Edward I for restoration of this grant in 1305, but the king's response was as evasive as it had been two decades earlier: this time, he indicated that 'the king is not advised to grant his rents'. See *CDS*, ii, no. 1617; *PROME*, ii, 162, 261 (TNA, PRO SC 9/12, m. 13d; SC 8/99/4934). For the earlier history of the lands of 'Rafran' see above, no. 216.

314 Grants to Duugal the ferryman a fee to maintain two boats on the river Spey.

SOURCE. *PROME*, ii, 160; *CDS*, iv, no. 1815 (TNA, Special Collections: Parliament Rolls, Exchequer Series, PRO SC 9/12, m. 13).
COMMENT. The grant is mentioned in a petition that Duugal presented to Edward I in the autumn parliament of 1305 in which he noted that he held a charter of King Alexander III bearing witness to the gift. Edward's response was to order him to prove the claim by showing the deed to the lieutenant and chamberlain of Scotland.

315 Grants to John de Enfield a void plot in Berwick, rendering 60d to the abbot and convent of Kelso and 16d to the abbot and convent of Melrose.

SOURCE. TNA, Chancery: Miscellaneous Inquisitions, PRO C 145/63/5; *Cal. Inqu. Misc.*, i, no. 1928.
COMMENT. Alexander III's grant is mentioned briefly in the text of an inquest convened in Berwick in the summer of 1304 at the command of Edward I. Edward had renewed John's title to the tenement sometime before then, but now apparently sought to compel the tenant to pay rent for it. John successfully defended the terms under which he held the plot, noting that it had not before owed rent of any kind to the king of Scotland.

316 Grants the sum of £18 annually to Ralph de Hadden for certain damages which he suffered in the border lands.

SOURCE. *Rot. Scot.*, i, 13.
COMMENT. Notice of this grant occurs in a writ of Edward I dated at Roxburgh on 10 December 1292 addressed to John de Twynham, fermer of the burgh of Dumfries. The writ notes that King Alexander had approved and paid the petitioner's claim for compensation from these revenues.

317 Grants to John the surgeon an annual fee of 8 merks sterling from the rents of the thanage of Tannadice (Angus), in return for one pair of gilt spurs annually, to be rendered at the fair of Dundee.

SOURCE. *RRS*, v, no. 111.
COMMENT. Notice of Alexander III's gift occurs in a charter of Robert I dated 26 December 1316 confirming the rent to John's heir William de Walterston.

318 Grants to Simon de Lennox the office of serjeant in the earldom of Lennox.

SOURCE. TNA, Chancery Files, Tower and Rolls Chapel Series, Cancelled Letters Patent, PRO C 266/434; TNA, Chancery: Petty Bag Office: Writ Files, PRO C202/H/4, no. 34.
PRINTED. *CDS*, v, no. 369 (cal.).
COMMENT. Notice of the grant survives in the draft of a letter patent of Edward I dated 20 April 1304. Here, the king notes that he has granted to Gilbert son of Simon of Lennox 'the serjeanty (*seriantie*) of the county of Lennox that Alexander of good

memory, late king of Scotland, gave to Gilbert's father'. Simon's father Gilbert may be the Gille Brigte MacAbsolon who appears frequently as a witness to the acts of the native earls of Lennox in the middle years of the thirteenth century.

319 Bond to John de Masun, merchant, for the sum of £2197 8s sterling owed for wines.

SOURCE. *Rot. Scot.*, i, 17.
COMMENT. Notice of the bond appears in the cancelled draft of a letter sent from Edward I to John Balliol, dated Kirkby, 8 April 1293, ordering Balliol to make good the sums owed to Masun by the late king.

320 Grants to David de Torthorald, knight, an annual fee of £12 sterling.

SOURCE. NRS, List of Documents Transferred from the Public Record Office, London, RH 5/120 (Stevenson, *Documents*, i, 39–40).
COMMENT. Notice of the king's charter is made in a brieve from the Guardians of Scotland to Alexander de Balliol chamberlain of Scotland directing him to pay the sum to Sir David according to the terms of Alexander III's 'charter'. See Simpson, *Handlist*, no. 287.

321 Grants to Sir Ingram de Umfravill and Isabel his spouse 100 merks of land in tenancy, namely, 40 merks of land in the earldom of Carrick, and £40 from the king's chamber.

SOURCE. *RPS*, 1293/2/15.
COMMENT. Notice of this grant survives in a record of the pleas heard in the parliament held at Scone in February 1293, when the couple claimed the revenues 'by gift of the late king'.

322 Assigns the office of keeper of the royal park at Wark (Tynedale), with a fee of 1½d per diem.

SOURCE. Palgrave, *Docs. Hist. Scot.*, i, 5, 11.
COMMENT. The appointment is noted in the record of an extent dated late 1286 or early 1287 in which Edward I's escheator north of Trent, Sir Thomas de Normanville, assessed the value of the lands in England of which Alexander III had died seised. In 1287 the fee cost the crown £2 5s 6d.

2. ACTS IN FAVOUR OF ECCLESIASTICAL BENEFICIARIES

323 Grants to the Friars Preacher of Ayr land in the same burgh worth 21s for enlarging their cemetery.

SOURCE. *Ayr Friars Chrs*, no. 10.
COMMENT. The grant is mentioned in a gift of this same rent, together with other lands and goods, that Juliana de Pont made to the Dominicans of Ayr around 1340. Here, she relates that the annual rent was held by her 'predecessors', including her father, Adam burgess of Ayr, who had been given it by 'King Alexander' (more likely Alexander III than his father), but that some time later, at the king's request, Adam agreed to exchange the land for an annual rent of the same value from Alloway, so that the friars might enlarge the grounds of their cemetery.

324 Gives annual gifts of money and wax to the Friars Minor of Berwick, Roxburgh, Haddington, Dumfries and Dundee.

SOURCE. TNA, Chancery Miscellanea, PRO C 47/22/2/32–34; Stevenson, *Docs. Hist. Scot.*, ii, nos 84–6.

COMMENT. The gifts are noted in a report of 1297 compiled by Hugh de Cressingham, then treasurer of Scotland. The inquest was held at the behest of Edward I, who commanded a search of the rolls then in the treasurer's possession for evidence of the friars' claims to these gifts. Although there is some doubt about the extent to which the Franciscans had acquired substantial property in Scotland before 1296, these gifts appear to be genuine. See the discussion in *MRHS*, 125–7.

325 Grants 100s annually to the prior of Carlisle.

SOURCE. *ER*, i, 37–8.
COMMENT. Mention of this grant appears in the account submitted by Andrew de Moravia sheriff of Ayrshire for the year 1298.

326 Writes letters presenting Bogo de Clare to the rectory of Simonburn (Northumberland).

SOURCE. TNA, Justices in Eyre, of Assize, of Oyer and Terminer, and of the Peace, etc.: Rolls and Files, PRO JUST 1/657, m. 9d.
COMMENT. At the eyre sessions convened at Wark in 1293, in answer to the customary articles concerning vacant churches and churches in the king's gift, jurors reported that 'the church of Simonburn is in the gift of the king. Bogo de Clare holds it as a gift of Alexander late king of Scotland; it is worth 400 merks per annum'. For other references to Bogo de Clare's tenure of the office, see *Fasti Dunelmenses*, ed. D. S. Boutflower (Surtees Society, 1927), 26, 148; *NCH*, xv, 186.

327 Confirms to the monks of Coupar Angus abbey Sir Hugh de Abernethy's grant of the advowson of the church of Meathie (Angus).

SOURCE. *Coupar Angus Chrs*, i, no. 112.
COMMENT. Notice of this grant occurs in an inspeximus (dated soon after 1328) of a charter of William de Lamberton bishop of St Andrews. The text of the episcopal charter states that Sir Hugh's son and heir, Sir Alexander, and King Alexander III each confirmed the gift. Hugh's grant is no longer extant. A charter datable to 1297 x 1304 (*Coupar Angus Chrs*, no. 65) and a confirmation of King Robert I issued in 1308 (*RRS*, v, no. 3) note that Sir Alexander de Abernethy was the donor of the church of Meathie, but there seems little reason to doubt either that Sir Hugh was the initial benefactor or that the king should subsequently have confirmed his gift.

328 Writes letters presenting William Flamberd to the church of Carlatton, in the diocese of Carlisle.

SOURCE. TNA, Justices in Eyre, of Assize, of Oyer and Terminer, and of the Peace, etc.: Rolls and Files, PRO JUST 1/137, m. 13; *Reg. Halton*, i, 163; Stevenson, *Documents*, i, 359.
COMMENT. The king's right of presentation is noted in the records of the justices itinerant who visited Cumberland in 1293, where jurors reported that among the escheats then in the hands of King Edward was the church of Carlatton, at that time occupied by Flamberd 'by the gift of King Alexander'. The Scottish king's right of presentation was noted again some years later in the record of an inquest convened on 2 October 1300 at the command of John de Halton bishop of Carlisle, after Anthony Bek bishop of Durham sought to present Robert de London to the vacant church. The jurors returned that Alexander III had made the last presentation.

329 Grants to the Friars Preachers of Perth, in free alms, exemption from multure at the king's mills of Perth for five chalders of wheat and ten chalders of bere and the privilege of 'roumfre' for their grain.

SOURCE. *RRS*, v, no. 228.
COMMENT. Notice of this grant occurs in a confirmation of King Robert I dated 26 April 1323, which reviewed the terms of the original gift. For the term 'roumfre', see *DOST*, *q.v.*

330 Grants to the nuns of St Leonard's, Perth, an annual rent of 60s in Perth.

SOURCE. Stevenson, *Documents*, ii, 92.
COMMENT. Notice of this grant occurs in a petition presented to King Edward I in the parliament held at Berwick in the late summer of 1296. Here, the prioress noted that her house had been 'infeft and seised' of the sum by gift of the late king.

UNATTRIBUTABLE ACTS: ALEXANDER II OR ALEXANDER III

Grants to the dean and chapter of Aberdeen the patronage of the church of Logie Buchan (Aberdeenshire). (Very doubtful)

SOURCE. *Calendar of Scottish Supplications to Rome, iv: 1433–1447*, ed. A. I. Dunlop and D. MacLauchlan (Glasgow, 1983), no. 231.
COMMENT. The authenticity of this act seems most uncertain. According to the known history of the church, it passed to the cathedral chapter of Aberdeen by grant of King David II; I. B. Cowan, *The Parishes of Medieval Scotland* (SRS, 1967), 136–7; *RRS*, vi, no. 277.

Grants to the house of Dominican friars of Aberdeen twenty-six merks annually out of the fermes, customs and mills of Aberdeen.

SOURCE. *RMS*, ii, no. 1311.
COMMENT. This grant by 'King Alexander' is noted in a general confirmation of the friars' possessions and privileges granted by James III on 30 September 1477. The foundation of the friary is traditionally assigned to Alexander II (*MRHS*, 116), but this gift may have been made by Alexander III.

Grants to the abbot and monks of Arbroath abbey four merks at Easter from the fermes of Kinghorn (Fife) for lighting the great altar.

SOURCE. BL, MS Additional 33245, fos. 140^{v}–141^{r} (new foliation).

Grants to the house of Dominican friars of Berwick forty merks yearly.

SOURCE. *ER*, i, 208.
COMMENT. According to a late source, the friary was founded by Alexander II, and it certainly existed by 1241 (*MRHS*, 116). Nevertheless this annual was perhaps assigned by Alexander III.

Grants to Fearn abbey various privileges, including freedom from royal exactions.

SOURCE. NAS, J. and F. Anderson Collection, GD297/196; see *OPS*, ii, II, 435.
COMMENT. The Premonstratensian house of Fearn, the early history of which is most obscure, may have been founded by Farquhar earl of Ross in 1221 × c.1227 (*MRHS*, 101). The source here is a confirmation of William, fifth earl of Ross, dated 5 March 1355/6, which refers to the liberties conferred on the abbey by the charters of 'King Alexander'. Both king Alexanders may have been meant.

Grants or confirms to Haddington priory (unspecified) property or properties.

SOURCE. *RMS*, ii, no. 610.

Issues a brieve (*breve domini regis*) at the request of Henry the clerk in an action against Balmerino abbey for land in Perth which he claimed to hold of the bishop of Dunkeld.

SOURCE. *Balmerino Liber*, no. 30.

COMMENT. Since the source, recording that Henry abandoned his claim in the burgh court of Perth, cannot be dated more closely than the mid-thirteenth century, this brieve may have been sued out of either king's chancery. Henry was the son and heir of Laurence, son of Guy who, by '1231' – with Henry's consent – had sold to Balmerino the land he held of Bishop Gilbert of Dunkeld in a street leading to the Inch of Perth (ibid., nos 25–6). According to MacQueen, *Common Law*, 202, this act was almost certainly a brieve *de recto in burgo*.

Confirms to Holystone priory (Northumberland) an annual rent of eight merks payable at Easter out of the burgh ferme of Berwick which was granted to the nuns by King David I in exchange for land in Roxburgh.

SOURCE. *CDS*, iv, no. 991; see TNA, PRO, SC 8/184/9190, translated in *NCH*, xv, 459-60 (where 'seven marks' is given in error).
COMMENT. See *David I Chrs*, no. 245.

Issues a brieve (*per litteras regias*) at the request of Mariota daughter of Samuel in an action against William (of Bondington) bishop of Glasgow for the land of Stobo, which was heard before Gilbert Fraser, sheriff of of Traquair (i.e., Peebles).

SOURCE. *Glasgow Registrum*, i, no. 130.
COMMENT. The source – Mariota's charter whereby she resigned to Bishop William her claims to Stobo in return for an (unspecified) annual rent – is misdated 1233 × 9 January 1234 in Reid and Barrow, *Sheriffs*, 32. It is witnessed by Richard chancellor of Glasgow, and the correct date-limits are April 1249 × 1258 (cf. Watt and Murray, *Fasti*, 208). For Bishop William's contemporary grant to Mariota of ten merks yearly from the revenues of his manor of Eddleston (Peeblesshire), see *Glasgow Registrum*, i, no. 172. According to MacQueen, *Common Law*, 171–2, this act was possibly a brieve of mortancestry.

Confirms to the burgesses of Nairn their rights and privileges.

SOURCE. *RMS*, v, no. 1700.

Grants to the inhabitants of Rosemarkie the privileges of a burgh, including freedom from all forinsec service, aids and other burdens.

SOURCE. *RMS*, v, no. 2212.
COMMENT. See Pryde, *Burghs*, 41.

Grants (to an unspecified beneficiary) a charter concerning Kinmuck (in Keithhall and Kinkell, Aberdeenshire).

SOURCE. *APS*, i, 110.

INDEX OF PERSONS AND PLACES

In general conformity with previously published volumes in the *Regesta Regum Scottorum* series the following conventions are used. Christian names are given in a modern form where this exists, ignoring the original 'de'. Patronymics are indexed uder the Christian name of the son; medieval patronymics recorded as Fitz or Mac are treated similarly. The letter W appearing before a number means that the person appears as a witness on that page, but more than one occurrence is not noted. Counties are identified by their pre-1974 names. The authority for the location of sites is normally the several series of maps (25-inch, 6-inch, 1-inch), hard copy or electronic, published by the Ordnance Survey. The spelling of place names normally follows that found in the OS maps, with variants as they appear in the documents listed after the National Grid number. Where appropriate, medieval variants are assigned a separate entry with a cross-reference to the modern form.

Abercrombie [NO5102], Abyrcrombin, chapel at, 134, 136
Aberdeen, Abberden', Abbirdern', Aberden', Abirden, Abirdene, Abredenne, 18, 35, 60
  bishop of, 20, 51n, 70, 71, 72, 73, 78, 138, 139, 166, 167; *see also* Benham, Hugh; Cheyne, Henry; Ralph; Ramsay, Peter
  burgesses of, 24, 124, 132; men of, 132
  burgh of, 89, 124
  cathedral church of, 70, 71; chapter of, 138, 139, 234; dean and chapter of, 195, 196, 234
  customs of, 234
  Dominican friars of, 234
  fermes of, 234
  mills of, 234
  see of, 20, 71, 195, 196
  sheriff of, 70, 71, 211, 213; *see also* Garioch, Andrew
  sheriffdom of, 70, 71
Aberdeenshire, 27, 81
Abernethy [NO1816], Abberneythyn', Abbernyth', Abernethyn', Abernithyn', Abernyth', Abirnith', Abirnethy, Abirnethyen, Abirnethyn, Abirnith', Abirnithin, Abrinithyn', 97
Abernethy, Hugh, 34, 57, 86, 216, 232. W 80, 91, 92, 93, 96, 97, 106, 107, 108, 110, 111, 113, 139, 152, 196; son of *see* Alexander
  Patrick, knight, W 185
  William, 86
Abirbrothoc *see* Arbroath
Aboyne [NO5298], Obeyne, acts dated at, 107, 108, 187
  church of, 138, 139
Acarsan, Maurice, 213
Acquitannia *see* Aquitannia
Acre, John, king of, 204
Adam, abbot of Melrose, 24
Adam, burgess of Ayr, 231
Adam, chaplain, 222
Adam, earl of Carrick, 103. W 104, 105
Adielinn [NO3571], Idulany, muir of, 193
Adilstanfurd *see* Athelstaneford
Adkar, hill called (lost, near Kedlock Hill, NO3718), 59, 60
Ælric, Master, mason, 134, 136
Æthelred, Etheldred, son of King Malcolm III, 133, 134, 135, 136
Agnes, daughter of Simon, 83
Airdmanston *see* Hermiston
Airth, Erth, Bernard, 114
Alan, master of a Scottish ship, 127
Alan of the chamber (*de camera*), 147
Aldstel *see* Calot Shad
Alexander IV, Pope, 73, 207
Alexander I, king of Scots (1107–24), 33, 133, 134, 135, 136
Alexander II, king of Scots (1214–49), 3, 4, 12, 13, 21, 22, 23, 28, 32, 35, 43, 51n, 58, 62, 70, 71, 72, 73, 74, 85, 86, 87, 88, 89, 90, 91, 92, 94, 110, 117, 122, 123, 127, 134, 136, 137, 138, 182, 200, 208, 209, 210, 214, 215, 216, 220, 224, 231, 234
  sister of *see* Margaret, widow of Hubert de Burgh
  widow of, 20, 209; *see also* Coucy, Marie
Alexander III, king of Scots (1249–86), v, vi, 1, 3, 4, 5, 6, 7, 8, 9, 10, 11, 12, 13, 14, 15, 16, 17, 18, 19, 20, 21, 22, 23, 24, 25, 26, 27, 28, 29, 30, 31, 32, 33, 34, 35, 36, 37, 38, 40, 42, 43, 49n, 51n, 52n, 54n, 57, 58,

59, 60, 61, 62, 63, 64, 65, 66, 67, 69, 70, 71, 72, 74, 75, 76, 77, 78, 79, 80, 81, 82, 83, 84, 85, 86, 87, 88, 89, 90, 91, 92, 93, 94, 95, 96, 97, 98, 99, 100, 101, 102, 103, 104, 105, 106, 107, 108, 109, 110, 111, 112, 113, 114, 116, 117, 118, 119, 120, 121, 122, 123, 124, 125, 126, 127, 128, 129, 130, 131, 132, 134, 136, 137, 138, 139, 140, 141, 142, 143, 144, 145, 146, 147, 148, 149, 150, 151, 152, 153, 154, 155, 156, 157, 160, 164, 165, 166, 167, 168, 169, 170, 171, 172, 173, 174, 175, 176, 177, 178, 179, 180, 181, 182, 183, 184, 185, 186, 187, 188, 189, 190, 191, 192, 193, 194, 195, 196, 197, 198, 199, 200, 201, 202, 204, 205, 206, 207, 208, 209, 210, 213, 214, 215, 216, 217, 218, 219, 220, 221, 222, 223, 224, 225, 226, 228, 229, 230, 231, 232, 233, 234
bailies of, 140, 154, 173, 182, 183, 188, 200, 201, 213, 214, 215, 219
chamber of, 149, 181, 196, 229, 231
chancellor of, 153
chancery of *see* Scotland, chancery of
chaplain of, 138, 139, 209, 214
children of, 16, 23, 54n, 131, 148, 149, 150, 179, 180, 184, 185, 187, 196; *see also* Alexander; David; Margaret
clerks of, 185, 195, 196, 205, 206, 212; *see also* Dundee, Master Ralph; Grandtully, Master Andrew; Liberacione, Adam; Simon; Swinburne, William; Wischard, Robert
council, counsellors of, 5, 67, 68, 71, 72, 112, 157, 159, 160, 164, 165, 166, 185, 195, 202
daughter of *see* Margaret, daughter of Alexander III
death of, 9, 14, 15, 124, 165–8, 206, 213, 216, 229, 230
enthronement of, 202
envoys of, 75, 81, 82, 89, 90, 100, 115, 129, 131, 136, 143, 146, 148, 149, 150, 151, 152, 153, 159, 164, 177, 179, 188, 189, 204, 206, 210
fermes belonging to, 156, 157, 205, 206, 228
heirs of, 158, 162
justiciars of, 200
knighting of, 16
letters of, 71, 72, 74, 83, 115–17, 122–4, 127, 128, 129, 131, 140–1, 143–4, 173, 175–6, 178, 181, 186, 201, 202, 207, 208, 209, 210, 211, 212, 213, 218, 219, 222, 223, 225, 226, 227
majority of, 204
manors of, 197, 198
marriage of, 3, 11, 16, 208
men of, 151, 173
mills belonging to, 156, 232
minority of, 5, 4, 12, 13, 20, 23, 26, 28–9, 30, 31, 32
officials of, 140
park belonging to, 193
provender under, 147
regnal years of, 3, 5, 14, 182
seal of, v, 9, 12, 13, 14, 19, 20, 25, 26, 27, 30–4, 35, 51n, 52n, 53n, 57, 58, 61, 63, 64, 66, 73, 75, 76, 77, 80, 83, 84, 87, 90, 91, 93, 94, 95, 96, 97, 99, 104, 105, 106, 107, 108, 109, 110, 111, 112, 113, 114, 117, 118, 120, 122, 123, 124, 129, 130, 131, 132, 140, 141, 143, 145, 146, 147, 149, 150, 152, 156, 157, 165, 168, 169, 171, 173, 174, 175, 176, 177, 178, 179, 180, 181, 182, 188, 189, 191, 193, 195, 198, 223, 224, 225, 228
servant of, 156
sheriffs of, 154, 188, 200
sister of *see* Marjorie
sons of *see* David; Alexander
tenant of, 153
testament of, 226
visits to England, 205, 214, 217, 218, 220, 221, 222
wardrobe under, 147, 184
wife of *see* Margaret, wife of Alexander III
writing chapel of, 3, 7, 10, 28, 29, 80, 106, 110, 114, 174, 194; *see also* Scotland, chancery of
Alexander, knight, son of Hugh Abernethy, 232
Alexander, merchant of Newcastle-upon-Tyne, 178
Alexander of the chapel, 23
Alexander, Prince, son of Alexander III, 4, 19, 23, 26, 38, 50, 52n, 157, 160, 197, 199
death of, 54n, 179, 180
letters of, 17, 26, 51n, 175–6
lord of Man, 198
marriage of, 13, 14, 25, 165–72, 175–6, 225
oath by, 170–1
putative heirs of, 165–9
seal of, 171, 175, 176
Alexander, son of Alexander Comyn earl of Buchan, 230
Alexander, son of Colin son of Carimer, 18, 50n, 228
Alexander, son of David Lindsay, 224
Alloway [NS3318], 231

Alston (Cumberland), Aldinistoun, 173, 225
Alwin, son of Alwin Mes, 86, 87
Andrew, abbot of Coupar Angus, 154, 179, 180
Andrew, bishop of Caithness, 134, 136
Andrew, son of Nicholas, 100, 101, 102, 103. W 104
Angus, Anegos, Anegus, 49n
  earl of, W 112, 125, 141, 153, 159, 164, 188, 190; *see also* Umfraville, Gilbert
Anjou, Andegavia, 75
Annabella, sister of Malise II earl of Strathearn, 21
Annan, Anandia, John, king's chaplain, 138, 139
Annandale, val de Anand, valle Anandie, 37
  lord of *see* Bruce, Robert V
  lordship of, 112
Aquitaine, Aquitania, Acquitannia, Aquitannia, Aquytania, Aquytannia, Aquytanya
  duke of, 75, 82, 83, 84, 85, 115, 123, 126, 127, 128, 129, 131, 139, 140, 142, 143, 146, 147, 148, 150, 151, 152, 153, 172, 173, 178, 179, 180, 183, 184, 186, 189, 190, 197; *see also* Edward I; Henry III
Aragon, king of, 202
Arbroath [NO6341], Aberbr', Abirbrothoc, Abirbrothoc', Abyrbrothoc, 35
  abbey of (Tironensian), 154
  abbot of, 35, 125, 126, 154, 234. W 137, 138, 154; *see also* Bernard; William
  convent of, 125, 126
  men of, 125; *see also* Tarves
  monks of, 154, 202, 224, 225, 227, 234
Ardentilly, Perthshire, 190
Ardentinny [NS1887], 190
Argyll, Argadia, Ergathyl', 134, 136, 220
  Alexander of, 127, 221, 222; men of, 127
  Ewen of, 74
Arndilly [NJ2848], 190
Arufinn, Elan, W 160, 164
Ashkirk, Haschirch', Henry, 68, 69
Asketin, Assketin, 100, 101, 102, 103. W 104; *see also* Norway, chancellor of
Astle, Thomas, 95, 201
Athelstaneford [NT5377], Adilstanfurd, Elstanford, Elstaneford', 63
Atholl, Athole, Atholya, earl of, 173. W 97; son of, 173; *see also* Strathbogie, David;
  earldom and mormaership of, 186
Auchensoul [NX2693], Ackinsauhil', 77, 78
Augustine, tailor, 212
Aumale, Albermarl', count of, 74; *see also* Forz, William
Avenel, Auenel', Roger, 87
Ayr [NS3421], Ar, 35, 79, 80, 130
  burgesses of, 79, 80, 210
  burgh of, 231
  castle of, 210
  cemetery in, 231
  fair at, 79–80
  Friars Preacher of, 231
  sheriff of, 232
Ayr, river, Ar', 94, 95
Aytoun, W. E., 154, 156

Badby, Alexander, 195
  John, 194–5, 228
  William, 194, 195, 207, 228
Badenoch, lord of, 222, 224; *see also* Comyn, John I; Comyn, John II
Bailleul *see* Balliol
Baillieland Burn [NS 2161], Bayllolfislandys, 141, 142
Balchrystie [NO4602], Balcristyn, 133, 135
Balconathin *see* Balgonie
Balfour, James, of Denmilne and Kinnaird, Lord Lyon, 60, 203, 216
Balgonie [NO1917], Balconathin', 64
Balhamer *see* Ballaharry
Ballacgniba (now lost, near Crosby, SC3080, Isle of Man), 198
Ballagan [NS5879], 217
Ballaharry [SC3280), Balhamer, Dalhamer, Isle of Man, 198
Ballellin [SC4587], Isle of Man, 213, 214
Ballerno [NO2830], 228
Balliol, Bailleul, Bayllol, Bayol', Alexander, of Cavers, knight, 166, 167, 170, 171, 173, 231. W 113
  Devorguilla, Deruorguilla, 141, 142; demesne of, 141
  Edward, 17
  Guy, W 91, 94
  John, 66, 72. W 63
  John, king of Scots *see* John, king of Scots
Balmerino [NO3524], Balmurynach
  abbey of (Cistercian), 21, 234; men and possessions of, 188
  abbot of, 165, 188; *see also* Perisby, William
  monks of, 21, 79, 188
Balwearie [NT2590], Belecherin, 133, 135
Banff, sheriff of, 70, 71
Bardrill [NN9108], 191
Barklay *see* Berkeley
Barmuir [NS4428], Barmor, 99

Barnego [NS7838], Brengoen', 60, 61
Barnweil [NS4130], 224
Bathgate [NS9869], 165, 225
Bayllolfislandys *see* Baillieland Burn
Bayol *see* Balliol
Beath [NT1590], Beth, 133, 135
Beath Waldeve, Beth Waldef', Beethwaldef, 146, 147, 222
Beaton, Beton, Roger, Master, 143
Bedrule, Rulebethok', barony of, 150, 151; *see also* Comyn, John I
Bek, Anthony, 125, 232
Belecherin *see* Balwearie
Belgium, 168
Belhelvie [NJ9417], 165
Bellingham (Tynedale), ferme of the mill of, 205, 206
manor of, 206
Bellingham, Robert, 205
William, 205, 206, 224
Bendochy [N2041], 203
Benham, Hugh, 166, 167
Bergen (Norway), Bergys', Bergens', Berngen', 157, 158, 160, 161, 163
Peter, bishop of, W 104
Berkeley, Berclay, Berkel', Berklay
Hugh, 77, 207. W 92, 94, 95, 97, 100, 107, 109, 112, 113, 125, 128, 130, 141
Humphrey (Winfred), 58, 59
Patrick, knight, W 109, 154, 155, 187, 190
Richenda, daughter of Humphrey, 58, 59
Bernard, abbot of Arbroath, 35
Bernard, dean of Messine, 168, 170, 171
Bernard, Burnard, Sir Richard, of Fairnington, 65, 66
Bernardus *see* Bjarne, Master
Bernerius *see* Bjarne
Bernham, David, W 65
Berwick, Berewic, Berewyc', Beruic, Beruich, Berwyc', Berwych', Berewyc, Berewyc', Berewyk, 50n, 131, 158, 159, 161, 162, 165, 168, 169, 170, 199, 212
act dated at, 177
bailies of, 223
burgesses of, 220, 221
chamberlain of, 223; *see also* Weston, Walter
common clerk of, 223
community of, 199, 223
constable of, 207; *see also* Badby, William
dwelling in, 18, 133, 135
fermes of, 172, 199, 223, 235
Friars Minor of, 231, 232, 234
inhabitants of, 131, 140
land in, 230
mayor of, 199, 223
mills of, 156, 157, 199
parliament at, 165, 199, 233
provosts of, 199
sheriff of, 157
tract of land in *see* Calot Shad
Beton *see* Beaton
Beverley, Beuerl', minster, 74
provost of 74; *see also* Mansel, John
Bickerton, Bygertun', Bykerton', Bykirtun', Richard, knight, 76, 105, 106, 111, 207
Bigod, Hugh, 74
Richard, 74
Birmanstone *see* Hermiston
Bishop Nicholas, 209
Bisset, Biset, Bisetht, Byset', Byseth', Bysseth, Robert, W 132
Walter, W 59, 61
William, knight, 147. W 99, 110, 113, 117, 119, 124, 137, 138, 153, 216, 223
Bjarkey, Berkrey (Norway), barony of, 165
Bjarkey, Bjarne, 159, 164
Bjarne, knight, 157, 159, 160, 164; *see also* Erlingsson, Bjarne
Bjarne, Master, 157, 160; *see also* Lodinsson, Bjarne
Blervie [NJ0757], castle of, 211
Blund, John le, 210. W 68, 70, 72
Bohun, Humphrey, 225
son of, 225
Bolgin *see* Wester Bogie
Bologna, 27, 28
Boltby, Bolteby, Nicholas, 115–16
Bondington, William, 28, 66, 72, 235. W 65
Bosco, Ralph, 20, 28, 37, 226
Botulph, St, fair of, 208
feast of, 82
Bower, Walter, 209, 211
Boynds [NJ7822], Bondes, 81
Brackenwrae [NY3586], Bracanwra, 109
Brackland [NN6408], Brocule, Broculy, 108
Bracstayden, Ralph, 214
Braid [NT2470], Bradd', 144
Brechin [NO6059], Brechin', Brechyn', Breskin, Brethyn, Breyham', act dated at, 129
bishop of, 131, 166, 167, 189; *see also* Comyn, William, of Kilconquhar; Crachin, William; Patrick
Brechin, William, knight, 72, 73. W 63, 76, 87, 154, 159, 164, 182
Brengoen *see* Barnego
Brienne, John *see* Acre, king of
Bristol (England), Bristov, 127, 221, 222
bailiffs of, 127

Britain, British Isles, 4, 7, 30
British Museum, 95
Broculy *see* Brackland
Broomhill [NO2013], Pardusin, 133, 134
Broun, Brun', David, knight, 117. W 118
Broxmouth [NT6976], Brokismuthe, 87, 88
Bruce, Bruis, Brus, Bruys, family, 35
 Robert V, 27, 72–3, 74, 81, 99, 112
 Robert VI, earl of Carrick, 143, 166, 167, 223. W 125, 147
Bruges, Brug, Gilles de, 176
Buchan, Bocham', Bochan', Bouchan', Bouscan, Buch', Buchan', Buchane, Buchwan'
 earl of, 86, 87, 140, 202, 203, 209, 211, 212, 229. W 63, 66, 68, 70, 72, 74, 75, 77, 79, 87, 89–90, 96, 97, 99, 104, 105, 112, 119, 121, 125, 126, 139, 147, 152, 159, 164, 166, 167, 172, 186, 190, 192, 193, 196; *see also* Comyn, Alexander
 John Comyn of, knight, W 187
Burnard *see* Bernard
Burntisland [NT2385], 133, 135; *see also* Kinghorn
Byseth *see* Bisset

Cadzow [NS7152], Cadihow', Cadyhou, 34, 214
Cadzow, William, 72, 74
Cahors (France), Caurs', merchants of, 183, 184
Cairn Table [NS7524], Carnetabell', Carentabel, 94, 95, 99
Cairnie [NO1920] *see* Gernuy
Caithness, Catinens, bishop of, 134, 136; *see also* Andrew
Calcov *see* Kelso
Calder Comitis *see* Earl's Calder
Caledoun, Caldouer *see* Earl's Calder
Callander, parish of, 108
Callendar, Kalentyr', Alwin, 68, 69
Calot Shad [NU0052], Aldstel, 133, 135, 137
Cambrun *see* Cameron, Cambrun'
Cambuskenneth [NS8093], Cambuskin', abbey of (Augustinian)
 abbot of, W 68; *see also* Richard
Cameron, Cambrun', John, 213
 Robert, 228. W 124, 174
Campbell, Cambel', Gillespie, W 98–9, 209
Campbell, Lord Frederick, 95
Campsie, Camsi, Finlay, 114
 daughters of, 114
Candida Casa *see* Whithorn
Canterbury (England), Cantuaria, church of St Thomas of, 154, 224–5
 chapter of, 226–7
 prior of, 226, 227; *see also* Ringmer, Thomas
Capel Shaws (Tynedale), 225
Capheaton (Northumberland), 211, 225
Carberry [NT3570], Crebarrin, 133, 135
Carberry, John, 228
Cardoness, Kerdener; Bertram, W 141
Cardross [NS3477], 35
Carham (Northumberland), Karham, 74
Carlatton (Cumberland), church of, 232
Carlisle (Cumberland), 219
 bishop of, 232; *see also* Halton, John
 diocese of, 232
 prior of, 215, 232
Carnoto *see* Charteris
Carrick, Carr', Carric', Carrik', Carryk, Karrik', Karryk, 20, 68, 69, 149, 201
 bailies of, 77, 78, 130
 earl of, 68, 69, 72, 73, 103, 130, 143, 166, 167, 223. W 104, 105, 125, 147, 201; *see also* Adam; Bruce, Robert VI; Duncan; Neil
 earldom of, 201, 231
 men of, 130
Carrick, Hector, 77–8
 John, 77–8
 Roland, 130
Carron, river (?Keryne) (Stirlingshire), 118, 119
Carwy *see* Karwin
Caskieben [NJ8312], Caskyben', 81
Cassingray [NO4707], Glasgyngrey, 174, 175
Cassingray, Ada, 174
 William, 174
Castle, Castilkayroch', Richard, 85
Castlehill of Manor *see* Manor
Castrum Oliverus *see* Oliver Castle
Castrum Puellarum *see* Edinburgh
Catalonia, ship from, 18
Catcune [NT3560], Cattekon, 153
Catscleugh [NS8180], Cattiscloch', 68, 69
Caurs *see* Cahors
Caux, John, 210
Cavers [NT5516], Cauirs, lord of *see* Balliol, Alexander, 113, 173
Charles I, king of England (1625–49), 220
Charteris, Master Thomas, 20, 28, 29, 37, 54n, 131, 226, 228–9
 William, 229
Cheam, John, bishop of Glasgow, W 91, 97, 106
Cheyne, Chen, Chen', Henry, bishop of Aberdeen, 19, 71
 Reginald senior, knight, 229. W 87, 107, 108, 110, 118, 121, 124, 126,

127, 152, 155, 186, 190, 192, 193
Reginald the younger, knight, 229
Chipchase (Northumberland), 207
Christine, daughter of Bernard Fraser, knight, 117–18; *see also* Mowbray, Roger
Christine, daughter of Simon, 83
Cistercians, 24
Clackmannan, Clacman', Clacmanan'
feu of, 86, 87, 137
county of, 134, 136
toun of, 134, 136
Clare, Bogo, 232
Richard, earl of Gloucester and Hereford, 74
William, 74
Claricia, daughter of Willim Lenn, 77
Cleish [NT0898], 202
Cleish, Gilbert, knight, 202
Clement, bishop of Dunblane, 72. W 68, 69
Clenhill, Thomas, knight, 229. W 137, 138
Cleth' *see* Keith
Clifton [NT1070], Cliftun', 68, 69
Cloan [NN9711], 191
Clunie [NO1043], Clune, Cluny, 36, 174
forest of, 21, 193
Coalston [NT5171], Cumbircolstoun', 117
Cochno [NS4974], 217
Colban, earl of Fife, 19. W 107, 108
Coldingham [NT9066]
convent of, 130
priory of (Benedictine)
prior of, 9, 130, 201
Coldinghamshire, Coldynghamchyr', Coldinghamscyr', 130, 131
Coldstream [NT8439], Caldestrem' Kaldestrem'
nuns of, 10–11, 90, 113, 203
priory of (Cistercian nunnery), 90
Colinton *see* Hailes
Collessie [NO2813], Cullesin', church of, 91
Comyn, Comin, Commins, Comyne, Comynne, Coumins, Cumin, Cummyn, Cummynge, Cumyn' Cumyng', Cvmyn, Cvmyn'
Alexander, earl of Buchan, 78, 86, 87, 140, 166, 167, 172, 202, 203, 208, 211, 212, 229–30. W 63, 66, 68, 70, 72, 79, 87, 89–90, 96, 97, 99, 104, 105, 112, 119, 121, 125, 126, 139, 147, 152, 159, 164, 186, 190, 192, 193, 196; lands of, 229; son of, 230 *see also* Alexander; wife of, 140
David, 66, 67
family, 27
Fergus, 86 W, 89
John I, Lord of Badenoch, knight, 72, 75, 87, 150, 151, 221, 222, 224. W 90, 92, 111, 112, 115, 118, 121; son of, 222
John II, Lord of Badenoch, knight, 166, 167, 222. W 117, 130, 144, 159, 164, 187, 190
Walter, earl of Menteith, W 57, 63, 65, 66, 68, 69, 70, 72, 77
William, of Kilconquhar, bishop of Brechin, 166, 167
William of Kilbride, W 91, 93, 119, 124, 125, 132, 147, 151, 152, 153
Conisbrough, Cunyburg, Cunygburg', William, knight, 109
Conon [NO5744], 202
Conveth, Cuneueth' *see* Laurencekirk
Corbet, Corbeth, Corbetth, Nicholas, knight, 87, 88, 194. W 94, 106, 228
his wife, 87–8
Corbridge, Correbrig', Alexander, clerk, 23. W 68
Coucy, lord of *see* Enguerrand III
Marie, wife of Alexander II, queen of Scots, 30, 204, 209
Coul [NN9711], 191
Coultra [NO 3523]
Coumins *see* Comyn
Coupar Angus [NO2239], (Cistercian) Cupro Monachorum
abbey of, 216, 232
abbot of, 154, 179, 180; *see also* Andrew
act dated at, 154
monks of, 232
register and rental of, 216
Couttie [NO2141], 203
Covington [NS9739], church of, 209
Crachin, William, 131
Crag' *see* Easter Craiglockart
Craigie [NO1122], Cragy, Cragyn, Crengyn, 62
fermers of, 98
Crail [NO6107], Karal, 137
acts dated at, 59
Cralyng superior *see* Upper Crailing
Crambeth (now Dowhill), barony of, 202
Cramenane *see* Cremannan
Cramond, William, clerk of the wardrobe, 147. W 223
Crauchie [NT5678], Crauchot', 118
Crebarrin *see* Carberry
Creich [NO3321], 213
Cremannan [NS5489], Cramenane, 118, 119
Cressingham, Hugh, 232
Cristiana, wife of Walter Lindsay, then Walter Percy, 126
Crookdake, Adam, 215–16
Cruik, Cruik', Robert, 85, 86, 208

Crummock burn [NS3554], 229
Culdees (Celedei), 133, 135
Culer, William, W 141
Culthill [NO0941], Cuthylgrudyn, 211
Cultmalundie, Easter and Wester [NO0422], Culltmelyndeys, Cultemelyndis, 149, 150
Cumberland, Cumberland', Cumberlaund, Cumerl' (England), 16, 19, 111, 122, 123, 151, 197, 214, 216, 217, 220, 223, 232
bailiff of, 85, 111; *see also* Castle, Richard
sheriff of, 84
Cumin *see* Comyn
Cuneueth *see* Laurencekirk
Cunningham, Cuningham', Cunyngham (Ayrshire), 20, 68, 69, 141
Cupar [NO3714], Cupro, Cuper, Cupir', Cupyr, 18, 228
acts dated at, 137, 138, 143
monks of, 60
Cuthbert, St, 156
feast of, 71, 72
shrine of, 33, 123
Cuthylgrudyn, 211

Dacre, Dakre, Ralph, 197
Dalcove [NT6432], Dalcoue, 68, 69, 87, 88
Dalhamer *see* Ballaharry
Dallas, Dolays, William, knight, 23, 152
Dalquhairn [NX8979], Dalkarn', forest of, 66
Daltulich [NH9848], Daltely, 107
Dampierre, Guy, count of Flanders, marquis of Namur, 12, 14, 25, 26, 165–70, 172, 175, 176–8
daughter of *see* Marguerite, wife of Alexander
wife of *see* Isabelle, countess of Flanders
Darybald, Robert, 76, 105–6
David I, king of Scots (1124–53), 4, 10, 67, 71, 107, 133, 134, 135, 136, 194, 195, 235
David II, king of Scots (1329–71), 12, 22, 71, 119, 186, 189, 234
chancellor of *see* Patrick, bishop of Brechin
David, earl of Huntingdon, 81, 193, 194
David, son of King Alexander III, 38
Dee, river (Aberdeenshire), 20
Denton, Thomas, 223
Devon, river, Douane (Fife), 89
Dhoon Glen [SC4586], Isle of Man, 213, 214
Dillon, John, 142
Disclune [NO6070], Drosclune de la Straton, 193
Dod, William, 154, 155
Dodsworth, Roger, 76, 106, 125, 128, 205, 207, 211, 225
Dodyngston *see* Duddingston
Dolaysmykel' *see* Meikle Dallas
Dollar [NS9698], Dolar', Doler, 137, 138
Dominicans, 186, 231, 232, 234
Donald, earl of Mar, 166, 167, 170, 171. W 119, 126, 159, 164, 183, 185, 186, 190
Donbarr *see* Dunbar
Donnekans *see* Duncan
Dossemer, lord of *see* Mortagne
Dougal, Dufgall, brother of Maldouen, earl of Lennox
Douglas, Duueglas', Andrew, 132
William, knight, 72, 132, 207
Douglas, Douglass', earl of, 189; *see also* William, earl of Douglas
Dounans *see* Donald
Dowhill, barony of, 202
Drem [NT5179], Drem', 63
church of, 63
Dremmesfeld (lost, near Drem, NT5179)
bondmen of, 63
demesne of, 63
Dronley [NO3435], Drunlav, 62, 63
Drosclune de la Straton *see* Disclune
Drumbernin *see* Dunbarney
Drumcruin (now obsolete, in Lennox), 217
Drumoig [NO 4325], 229
Drumsagard, lordship of, 201
Duddingston, Dodyngston, Thomas, 144
Dumbarnie [NO4403], Drumbernin, 133, 135
Dumbarrow [NO1119], 137
Dumbarton, Dumbarton', Dunbartan, Dunbertan, Dunbretan, 57, 114, 207
bailie of, 114, 220; *see also* Stewart, Walter
burgh of, 220
fermes of, 65
provosts of, 65, 220
sheriff of, 114, 220; *see also* Stewart, Walter
Dumfries [NX9676], Dumfes', Dunf', acts dated at, 113, 151
fermes of burgh of, 230
Friars Minor of, 231, 232
Dumfries, William, 14, 20, 25, 27, 28, 37, 38, 39, 226
Dummernech (now lost), 203
Dunbar [NT6778], Donbar, Donbarr', Dumbar', Dunbar', Dunbarr', earl of, 72, 73, 74, 113, 159, 164, 166, 167. W 61, 75, 76, 79, 88, 91, 92, 95, 97, 99, 104, 106, 111, 128, 141, 144, 147, 150, 151; *see also* Patrick

Dunbarney [NO1118], 137
Dunbartonshire, 35
Dunblane, Dumblan', Dunblan', bishop of, 72, 143, 149, 154, 166, 167, 168. W 68, 69, 91, 97, 152, 153; *see also* Clement; Prebenda, Robert; William
Duncan II, king of Scots (1094), 133, 134, 135, 136
Duncan, brother of Patrick, 202
  Ela, wife of, 202
Duncan, earl of Carrick, 68, 69
Duncan III, earl of Fife, 166, 167. W 159, 164
Dundaff [NS7484], Dundaf', 68, 69, 70
Dundaff, lord of *see* Graham David
Dundee, Dunde, 34, 185
  acts dated at, 34, 181, 185, 188
  fair of, 212, 230
  Friars Minor of, 231, 232
Dundee, Master Ralph, 27, 185, 210
Dundemore, Dundemar, Dundemor, Dundemor', Henry, knight, W 137, 138
  John, 72, 74, 206. W 81, 93
Dunduff, [NT0891], Dunduf', 70
Duneglas *see* Douglas
Dunfermline, Dunf', Dunfermel', Dunfermeline, Dunfermelyn, Dunfermelyn', Dumfermleine, 53n, 133, 134, 135, 136, 197
  abbey and convent of (Benedictine), 28, 67, 68, 70, 114, 115, 133, 135, 202, 203; brethren of, 134, 136; lands of, 133, 134, 135, 136; men and possessions of, 114, 133, 134, 135, 136
  abbey church of St Margaret of, 133, 134, 135, 136; *see also* Holy Trinity, church of; high altar of, 133, 134, 135, 136
  abbot of, 9, 28, 31, 67, 68, 70, 72, 107, 114, 134, 136, 204; *see also* Kenleith, Robert; Simon
  act dated at, 155
  burgh of, 133, 135
  ferme of, 133, 135
  dwelling in, 133, 135
  mill of, 133, 135
  men of, 70
  monks of, 7, 8, 137, 138, 146, 147, 203
  royal demesne in, 133, 135
  toft in, 134, 136
Dungavel [NS6537], Drumgran, 210
Dunipace [NS8-83], 36
Dunkeld [NO0242], Dunkelden', Dunkeldin, Dunkeldyn, Dunkeldyn', 53n
  abbot of, 133, 135
  act dated at, 176
  bishop of, 72–3, 186, 234, 235. W 58, 64, 91, 97, 112; *see also* Gilbert; Inverkeithing, Richard; John
  canon of, 37
  church in, 134, 136
  dean of, 75; *see also* Stuteville, Robert
Dunstan, archbishop, St, feast of, 146
Dunure [NS2515], 130
Durham (England), 17, 33, 123, 124
  act dated at, 124
  bishop of, 125, 131, 140, 216, 232; *see also* Bek, Anthony; justices of, 214
  bishopric of, 218
  prior and priory of, 207, 214; *see also* Hugh, prior of Durham
Durris [NO7796], Durres', Durrys', acts dated at, 36, 79, 151, 174
Durward, Hostiarius, Alan, 31, 211. W 58, 63, 72, 73, 76, 78, 97, 105, 107, 108, 110
Duugal, ferryman, 230

Earl's Calder, barony of, Caledouer, Caledoun, 68, 69
  feu of, 132
Easson, David, 209
East Douglas, Est' Douglas (now lost, in Stirlingshire), 118, 119
East Kilbride [NS6254], Killebrid', lady of *see* Valognes, Isabella
East Linton [NT5977], Lyueryngham', 117, 118
East Lothian, 53n
East Meadow, Estmedu, 65, 66
Easter Craiglockart [NT2370], 144; *see also* Easter Craig of Gorgie
Easter Craig of Gorgie [NT2372], Estcrag' de Gorgyn, Estircrag de Gorgyn, Estircrag de Gorgyne, 144, 184, 185
Easter Douglas Water [NN0207], 'Est' Douglas', Duueglas, *Dubhghlais*, 118, 119
Ebor' *see* Yorkshire
Eckford, barony of, Ecfurde, 121, 122
Eddleston [NT2447], 235
Edgar, king of Scots (1097–1107), 133, 134, 135, 136
Edgar, Edger', Walter, 149, 150
  Patrick, knight, 149
Edinbarnet [NW5174], 217
Edinburgh, Castrum Puellarum, Edinburg, Edinburg', Edenburg', Edor', Edynburg', Maiden Castle, 5, 34, 86, 87, 117, 146, 154, 156, 184, 212, 215, 216, 219
  acts dated at, 35, 57, 64, 65, 70, 71, 89, 90, 100, 111, 148, 149, 153, 180, 184, 190, 220, 222
  castle and constable, 15, 25, 147, 184,

212, 223, 226; *see also* Kinghorn, William; ferme of, 134, 136
dwelling in, 133, 135
sheriff of, 147, 223; *see also* St Clair, William
sheriffdom of, 144
toft in, 134, 136
Edward I, king of England (1272–1307), 11, 12, 16, 17, 19, 23, 26, 27, 28, 33, 36, 38, 51n, 54n, 71, 121, 125, 126, 127, 128, 129, 131, 139, 140, 142, 143, 144, 146, 147, 148, 149, 150, 151, 152, 153, 165, 172, 173, 178, 179, 180, 181, 183, 184, 186, 187, 189, 190, 196, 197, 199, 201, 203, 204, 208, 209, 212, 214, 215, 216, 217, 218, 219, 220, 221, 222, 223, 224, 225, 226, 227, 228, 229, 230, 232, 233
bailiffs of, 148, 178, 179; *see also* Newark, Henry; Normanville, Thomas
children of, 148, 150, 151, 153
coronation of, 205, 214, 217, 218, 220, 221, 222
court of, 149, 150
escheator of, 205, 219, 231
letters of, 128, 129, 139, 140, 143, 150, 173, 179, 180, 181, 186, 187, 190, 198, 227, 230, 231
ministers of, 217, 220
wife of, 148, 150, 151
Edward II, king of England (1307–27), 216
Edward III, king of England (1327–77), 200
Eglisdisdane, Eglysdissentyn [NN6706], now lost, 108
Eilean Fraoch, Frechelan, 105
castle of, 105
Eleanor, queen of England, 33, 82, 84, 122, 123, 124
Elena, wife of Bernard Airth, 114
Elgin [NJ2163], Elgyn', Elgyne, 80, 209, 229
acts dated at, 36, 110, 127
bailies of, 186
burgesses of, 23, 109, 110
burgh of, 109, 110; fermes of, 186
Dominican friary in, 186
Friars Preachers of, 186
hospital in, 186
king's garden at, 80
sheriff of, 80, 186; *see also* Montfort, Alexander
Elizabeth, wife of Alexander Comyn, 140, 141
Elstaneford *see* Athelstaneford
Emfrayvyl *see* Umfraville
Emma, daughter of Gilbert Smeaton, 67–8
Enfield, John, 230
Engelwod' *see* Inglewood
England, 6, 12, 26, 27, 32, 34, 37, 38, 71, 72, 197, 198, 208, 218, 219, 220, 221, 223
army of, 209
chamberlain of, 208
chancellor of, 226
chancery of, 3, 5, 12, 13, 16, 17, 74, 140, 144, 201, 205, 214, 217, 218, 220, 221, 222, 223, 229
community of, 197
crown of, 12, 16, 20, 120, 131, 140, 198, 217, 220, 231
exchequer of, 16, 208, 218
great seal of, 223
justices of, 178
kingdom of, 11, 102, 140, 155, 172, 178, 179, 187, 206
kings of, 23, 38, 54n, 197, 214, 217, 218, 220, 221, 222, 225; *see also* Charles I; Edward I; Edward II; Edward III; Henry III; John
laws of, 115, 116
marshal of, 74; *see also* Bigod, Richard
parliaments in, 50n, 165, 179
queen of *see* Eleanor
treasurer of, 208, 210; *see also* Caux, John
Enguerrand III, lord of Coucy, 172
Eric II, king of Norway, 25, 37, 105, 157, 158–65, 183, 184
chamber of, 158, 161
children of, 158, 161, 162
envoys and representatives of, 157–64
mother of, 159, 164
wife of *see* Margaret, daughter of Alexander III
Erlingsson, Bjarne, 165
Errol, Erole, Eroll, feu of (Perthshire), 60
Erth *see* Airth
Escoche *see* Scotland
Eskendy, Eskendi, Simon, 147
Estcrag' de Gorgyn *see* Easter Craiglockart
Eslington, Exlington', Exlingtun', John, 76, 105, 106
Etheldred *see* Æthelred
Europe, 4, 14, 15, 25, 27, 31, 32
Eva, wife of Malcolm son of Duncan, sister of Maldouen, earl of Lennox, 60, 61
Ewan, thane of Kettins, 212

Fairnington [NT6428], Farningdun, east meadow of (Estmedu), 65, 66
Richard Bernard of, knight, 65, 66
Farne Island (Northumberland), Farneland, monks of, 156; *see also* Henry
Farquhar, earl of Ross, 234

Fearn [NH8377], abbey of (Premonstratensian), 234
Fenton, Fentoun, John, W 115
Fergus, justiciar of Scotia, 70, 71
Fetters [NO3510], Fothros, 133, 135
Fife, Fif', Fiffich, Fyf, Fyf', Fyfe, 18, 60, 61, 72, 133, 134, 135, 136, 137, 138, 143, 224, 225
  bailie of, 113; *see also* Lascelles, Richard
  earl of 19, 68, 69, 72, 73, 166, 167, 213. W 89, 92, 98, 107, 108, 159, 164; *see also* Colban; Duncan III; Malcolm
  earldom of, 19
  royal demesne land in, 225
  sheriff of, 113, 212, 224, 225, 229; *see also* Lascelles, Richard; Lochore, David
  sheriffdom of, 212
Fiffich *see* Fife
Finnich Malise [NS4895], Finnich, 217
Fintray, Fyntre, Fyntreth, feu of (Aberdeenshire), 61, 62
fitz Count, Alan, 213
Flamberd, William, 232
Flanders, Flandres, 5, 13, 14, 25, 26, 37, 38
  count of, 226; *see also* Dampierre, Guy
  procurators of, 168; *see also* Bernard, dean of Messine; Mortagne, William
Flinders [NJ5928], Flandres', 193, 194
Flotterton, Hugh, 18
Fod [NT1288], Foeth, 133, 135
Forbes [NJ3612], 217
Forbes, Duncan, 217
  Lord John, 217
Fordell [NT1485], Fordale, mill of, 154, 155
Fordie [NO0841], 203
Fordun, Fordun', John, 52n, 211
  parson of, 74; *see also* Swinburne, William
Fordyce [NJ5563], Fordys, church of, 27, 195, 196
Forfar, Forfar', 36, 216
  acts dated at, 5, 34, 87, 139, 182
  bailies of, 83
  manor of, 154, 225
  sheriff of, 83, 212, 224, 225; *see also* Monte Alto, Roger; Mowat, Robert
Forres [NJ0358], 36
Forteviot, thane of, 213
Forth, river, Forth', mare Scocie, mare Scottie, 35, 78, 88, 89, 118, 119, 133, 134, 135, 136
Fortune, [NT5379], Fortun', 118
  hospital of, 118
Forveleth, Forueleth, daughter of Finlay Campsie, 114; *see also* Monorgan, Norrin
Forz, de Fortibus, William, count of Aumale, 74
Foswell, [NN9710], Foschall', Fossakel, Foswall, 21, 190, 191
Fothrif, Fotheref', Fotherif', Fotheryf', 216
  parish of, 133, 135
  province of, 133, 134, 135, 136
Fothros *see* Fetters
Fowlis Easter [NO3233], 208
France, king of, 38
  kingdom of, 26, 102, 177, 178
  royal house of, 30
Franciscans, 157, 150, 179, 207, 231–2
Fraoch Eilan *see* Eilean Fraoch
Fraser, Fraser', Frauser, Fresel, Fresiel, Alexander, W 216
  Gilbert, 235
  Master William, 26, 28, 54n. W 137, 147, 153
  Richard, knight, 146. W 113, 117, 118, 175
  Simon, knight, 91, 165, 166, 167, 170, 171, 189. W 95, 109, 117, 118, 125, 130, 132, 139, 144, 147, 150, 151, 152, 153, 155, 156, 174, 192, 196
Frechelan *see* Eilean Fraoch
Friars Minor *see* Franciscans
Friars Preacher *see* Dominicans
Fyn, son of Gunter, W 104
Fynnovhyn Burn, Fynnovhne (now lost, in Stirlinghire), 118, 119
Fyf' *see* Fife
Fyntre, Fyntreth *see* Fintray

G., monk of Arbroath, 227
Galbraith, Galbrath', William, 68, 69
Galdenoch [NX1861], Godenech, 99
Gall Water (now lost, in Stirlingshire), 118, 119
Galloway, Galualia, Galwachia, Galwath', Galwathya, 187
  justiciar of, 221. W 94; *see also* Comyn, John I; Maxwell, Eymer
Galloway, Alan of, 141, 142; heirs of, 141
  Mark of, 221; *see also* Mark, Master
Gamelin, Gamellin, Master, 28, 31, 37, 54n, 72, 216. W 68, 87, 89, 91, 92, 97, 104, 106; *see also* St Andrews, bishop of
  familia of, 28
Garioch, Garuiach, 81, 193, 194
Garioch, Andrew, 211, 213
Gartly, Andrew, 27
Gatmilk *see* Goatmilk
Geddewurth *see* Jedburgh
Gellet, Gelland, shire of, 133, 135
Geoffrey, brother of Richard, 68, 69
Geoffrey, son of Ivo, 216
Geoffrey, son of Simon, 206

Germanus, prior of Coldingham, 207
Gernuy, fishery at, on River Tay, 196, 197
Giffard, Hugh, 72, 73. W 75
 James, 110
Gilbert, abbot of Rushen, 221
Gilbert, bishop of Dunkeld, 235
Gilbert, earl of Angus *see* Umfraville, Gilbert
Gilbert, son of Simon de Lennox, 230, 231; *see also* Mac Absolon, Gille Brigte
Ginis *see* Gynes
Girvan [NX1897], Innirgarvan', 68, 69
Glasgow, Glas', Glascu, Glasg', Glasgu, Glasgw, 35, 54n, 142, 154
 bishop of, 9, 28, 66, 72, 121, 122, 141, 150, 151, 166, 167, 209, 235. W 57, 61, 65, 91, 97, 104, 106, 152, 153, 220; *see also* Bondington, William; Cheam, John; Wishart, Robert; Wishart, William; men of, 220
 burgesses of, 220
 cathedral church of St Kentigern (St Mungo), 66, 141, 151, 182; altar of, 181; cartulary of, 182; muniments of, 142; priest of, 181
 chancellor of, 235; *see also* Richard
 chapter of, 65, 141
 Friars Preachers of, 65
 see of, 27, 112
Glasgyngrey *see* Cassingray
Glaskhel (lost, near Clachan of Campsie, NS6179), 60, 61
Glencarny, Glencharnich, Glenkerny, Glennegerni, Gilbert, junior, 107, 108
 wife of, 107, 108
Gloucester, earl of, 74; *see also* Clare, Richard
Goatmilk, Gatmilk, shire of, 133, 135
Godenech *see* Galdenoch
Godfrey, Master, 159, 164
Gordon, John, 142
Gourlay, Hugh, 72
 William, 72
Grace of God (Gracia Dei), religious house called, 117, 118
Graham, Graeme, Graham', Gram', David, knight, 9, 21, 51n, 52n, 68, 69, 70, 72, 191. W 68; wife of, 191
 family, 21, 24, 51n, 191
 Henry, 68, 69. W 78
 Patrick, knight, 21, 24, 149, 184, 190. W 124, 132, 147, 152, 153, 175, 185, 192
Grandtully [NN9152], Garentuly, Master Andrew, 195, 196
Grant, Lawrence, 211
Great Cumbrae Island (N. Ayrshire), Lochcumberay, act dated at, 126
Great Sea (Magni Haff'), 100, 101, 102
Greater Inveresk (now Barbachlaw, NT3671), Inuiresk maiorem, 133, 135
Greeba [SC3080], Isle of Man, Ballacgniba, 198
Grey, John, 74
Grindon (Tynedale), Grindon, ferme of, 219
 manor of, 218
 mill of, 219
Grindon, Gilbert, 218
 Hugh, 218, 219
Guardians of Scotland, v, 15, 16, 29, 50n, 231
Gurle *see* Gourlay
Gueldres, count of *see* Reynaud I
Guy, Guidon, count of Flanders *see* Dampierre, Guy
Gynes, Genes, Ginis, Gynis, Ingram, knight, 179, 186, 187, 226. W 126, 186
 wife of *see* Lindsay, Christina

Haakon IV, king of Norway, 210, 211
Hadden [NT7936], 219
Hadden, Hawden, Eymer, 219
 Ralph, 230
 William, W 61
Haddington [NT5173], Hadigton', Hadington', Hadingtoun', Hadingtun, Hadyngton', Hadyntun', 63, 180, 181
 acts dated at, 35, 60, 113, 117, 118, 125, 141, 150, 183
 burgess of, 117; *see also* Wyppot, William
 dwelling in, 133, 135
 earl of *see* Hamilton, Thomas
 fair of, 144
 Friars Minor of, 231, 232
 priory of (Cistercian nunnery), 63, 234
 sheriff of, 212; *see also* St Clair, William
Haddington, David, W 59
Hailes (now Colinton) [NT2268], Hales, 133, 135
Haliburton, Halibirton', Henry, W 109
Halton, John, 205
Halton, John, bishop of Carlisle, 232
Hamilton, Thomas, 195
Haschirch *see* Ashkirk
Hastings, Henry, knight, 193, 194, 214, 215
Haughton (Tynedale), Haludon, Haluton', Halutoun', Haluchton', Hauton', 76, 105, 106, 120, 121, 127, 128, 196, 204, 215, 225
 wood of, 205, 215

Haughton, Ranulf, 127, 128, 215, 227
son of *see* Reginald
Haughton Strother (Tynedale), Haluton-strother', 120, 121, 211, 225
Hawden *see* Hadden
Hawys, wife of Walter the baker, 223
Hay, Haia, Haya, Augustine, 154, 156
Gilbert, 60, 72, 203. W 57, 58, 60, 62–3, 72–3, 121
John, knight, W 98, 188, 216
Nicholas, knight, 10, 174. W 156, 185, 188, 189
William, 60, 62, 204 W, 59; *see also* Mar, earl of
Hector, son of Hector Carrick, 77–8
Hefshunt (now lost, in Lanarkshire?), 210
Henry III, king of England, 3, 11, 12, 16, 17, 71–3, 74, 75, 78, 81, 82, 83, 84, 85, 115, 116, 117, 122, 123, 124, 198, 201, 202, 205, 206, 207, 208, 210, 214, 215, 217, 218, 220, 221, 222
counsellors of, 74
court of, 85
daughter of, queen of Scotland *see* Margaret
letters of, 74, 204, 206, 207, 208
wife of *see* Eleanor
writ of, 208
Henry, abbot of Kelso, W 88
Henry, bishop of Orkney, 210
Henry, bishop of Thérouanne, 176
Henry, earl of Northumberland, 4
Henry, earl of Strathearn *see* Malise II, earl of Strathearn
Henry, monk of Farne Island, 156
Henry, son of Laurence son of Guy, clerk, 234, 235
Hereford, earl of, 74, 225; *see also* Bohun, Humphrey; Clare, Richard
Hermiston [NT1770], Airdmanston, Hirdmaniston', Hirdmanyston', Hyrdmannistoun', Hyrdmanston', 132
Hermiston, John, W 59, 60, 62, 64
Heron, Cuthbert, 207
Hesleyside (Tynedale), 205, 224
Heton, barony of, 121, 122
Hibernia *see* Ireland
Hilary, St, feast of, 115, 116
Hillington [NS5164], Hyliniston', 68, 69
Hillington, Philip, 68–9
Hindlaw, Huntelaw (Tynedale), 127, 128
Hirdmanyston *see* Hermiston
Hod, Robert, 211
Hok, John, 76, 105, 106
Holy Cross, church of, Peebles, 209
Holm Cultram (Cumberland), Holmcultran, abbot and convent of, 155
Holy Spirit, 160
Holy Trinity, 14, 100, 102, 134
church of; at Dunfermline, 133, 134, 135, 136, 137, 138; *see also* St Margaret of Scotland; at Dunkeld, 134, 136; at Ramsay, isle of Man, 7, 187; at Soutra, 88, 92
feast of, 86, 124, 139, 142
Holy Trinity and the Captives, order of, 117, 118
Holyrood (Edinburgh), 203
abbey (Augustinian), 117
act dated at, 203
canons of, 117
Holystone (Northumberland), priory of (Augustinian), 235
Honorius IV, Pope, 172
Horndean [NT9049], Horneden', 110
Hospitallers, military order of, 203
brethren and hospital of, 182, 183; *see also* Torphichen; master of the order of, 210
Hostiarius *see* Durward
Hostiensis, 202
Houston [NT5678], Huwystun', 117, 118
manor of, 117, 118
Hugh, prior of Durham, 207
Hugh, son of Gilbert Grindon, 218
Hugh, son of Waltheof, 58, 59
Hugh, suitor of the barony of Upper Crailing, 121, 122
Hull (England), port of, 221
Humfrancuile *see* Umfraville
Humshaugh, Homisale, Homishaule (Tynedale), 127, 128
Huntingdon, earl of, 81, 193, 194; *see also* David
earldom of, 214
Huntland, the, Le Huntland' (Tynedale), 76, 105, 106, 204, 218
Hutton, Matthew, 95
Huwystun *see* Houston
Hybernia *see* Ireland
Hyliniston' *see* Hillington
Hyrdmannistoun *see* Hermiston
Hyrlan, William, clerk, 197

Ibernia *see* Ireland
Idulany *see* Adielinn
Inchaffray, abbot of, 223
Inchcolm [NT1982], Insula Sancti Columbe, monastery and canons of (Augustinian), 154, 155
Inchturfin (now lost), 203
Inglewood Forest, Engelwod', Inglewode (Cumberland), 16, 124, 216
bailiffs of, 123
justices of, 122, 123
steward of, 123, 124; *see also* Lancaster, Roger; Leyburne, William

sub-bailiff of, 111; *see also* Bickerton, Richard
Innernethy [NO1817], Innarnethy, Innernith', Innernithyn', 57, 58
Innes, Cosmo, 19, 142, 154, 182
Innirgarvan' *see* Girvan
Innocent IV, Pope, 202
Insula, Peter, 207
Inuirese Minorem *see* Little Inverese
Inveresk [NT3472], Inueresk, church of, 133, 135
Invergirvan *see* Girvan
Inverkeithing [NT1382], Innerkethin, Innerkethin', Inuirkethin, Inuyrkethine, burgesses of, 89, 154, 155; *see also* Matilda, wife of William Dod
ferry at, 134, 136
Inverkeithing, Richard, 28, 54n, 72, 73. W 58, 91, 97; *see also* Dunkeld, bishop of
Inverleith [NT2475], Inuerlech, Inyrlech, 156
mill of, 156
Inverness [NH6646], Inuerness', Inuernis, Inuernys, Invernes, 58, 209
acts dated at, 36, 78
bailies of, 228, 229
burgesses of, 10
Friars Preachers of, 126; house belonging to, 126
sheriff of, 211; *see also* Grant, Lawrence
Inverurie, Inuerury, parish of, 81
Inyaney (now lost, in Kirkden parish, Angus), 83
Ireland, Hibernia, Hybernia, Hybernya, Ibernia, Ybernia, lord of, 75, 82, 83, 84, 85, 115, 123, 126, 127, 128, 129, 131, 139, 140, 142, 143, 146, 147, 148, 150, 151, 152, 153, 172, 172, 173, 178, 179, 180, 183, 184, 186, 189, 190, 197; *see also* Edward I; Henry III
Irongray, parish of *see* Kirkpatrick-Irongray
Isaac, son of Gauton, W 159, 164
Isabel, wife of Ingram Umfraville, 231
Isabella, daughter of Adam de Liberacione, 21
Isabelle, countess of Flanders, daughter of the count of Luxemburg, 165–6, 167, 168, 169, 170, 175

James, St, apostle, feast of, 95, 157, 185
James III, king of Scots (1460–88), 183, 234
James IV, king of Scots (1488–1513), 183, 201
James V, king of Scots (1513–42), 127
James, Jambis, Richard, 121, 122
Jedburgh [NT6520], Geddewuth', Jeddewrth'
abbot of, 72, 204
acts dated at, 36, 106
Jerusalem, 138, 182
John the Baptist, St, feasts relating to, 79, 80, 100, 102, 103, 107, 157, 160
John, king of England (1198–1216), 38, 54n
John, king of Scots (1292–6), v, 6, 29–30, 33, 38, 125, 172, 229, 231
John II, archbishop of Nidaros, 221
John, bishop of Dunkeld, 186
John, chamberlain, 70, 71
John, count of Namur, 172
John, heir of William Walterston, 230
John, prior of St Andrews, W 137, 138
John, son of Finn, W 159, 164
John, son of Humphrey de Bohun, 225
John, son of the earl of Atholl, 173
John, surgeon, 230
Juliana wife of Ralph de 'Bracstayden', 214

Kalchow *see* Kelso
Kaldestrem' *see* Coldsream
Kalentyr' *see* Callendar
Karal *see* Crail
Karham *see* Carham
Karric *see* Carrick
Karruch *see* Carrick
Karwin, Karwyn, Henry, 176, 177
Kasingray *see* Cassingray
Kathlac *see* Kedlock
Kearn [NJ5126], 217
Kedlock [NO3819], Kathlac, Kathlath, 59
Keith [NT4564], Cleth', 133, 135
Keith, Keth, John, W 117
Kellie [NO5105], Kellyn, church of, 134, 136
mill of, 174
muir of, 174
Kellieshire, Kellynscyre, 174
men of, 174
Kelnasydhe *see* Kilsyth
Kelso [NT7233], Kalchow, Kelch', Kelchou, Kelchou', Kelsou, 107
abbey of Holy Trinity of, 199 (Tironensian)
abbot of, 29, 72, 107, 200, 230 W, 88; *see also* Henry
acts dated at, 110, 111, 122
convent of, 230
monks of, 29, 107, 199
Kenleith, Robert, 23, 28, 31, 54n
Kennedy, James, of Dunure, 130
John, 130
Kentigern, St, 141, 150, 151, 181
Kerd, Gilfolan, 127

Kerdener *see* Cardoness
Keryn', Keryne (now lost, in Stirlingshire), 118, 119
Kettins [NO2439], thane of *see* Ewen
Kilbride, Kelbride, Kelbryd', Kelebrid, Kellebride, Kilbryd, Kirbrid, Kylbrid', Kylbryde, William Comyn, lord of, W 91, 93, 124, 125, 132, 147, 151, 152, 153; *see also* East Kilbride
Kildrummy, 18
Kilmaron [NO 3516], Richard, 18, 228
Kilpatrick [NS4672], church of, 217
Kilsyth [NS7178], Kelnasydhe, 61
Kilwinning, Kilwynyn', act dated at, 78
Kincaid, [NS6476], Kincaith', Kyncath', 68, 69
Kincardine [NN9411], 191
Kincardine [NJ6000], Kyncard', Kyncardin, Kyncardyn, Kyncardyn', 36
  acts dated at, 36, 63, 132, 141
  sheriff of, 193; *see also* Cheyne, Reginald
Kincardineshire, 21, 193
Kinclaven [NO1537], Kynchecheuyn, Kynclewyn', 194, 216
  act dated at, 114
Kinghorn [NT2786], Kynggorn, Kyngorn', Kyngorne, 133, 135, 137, 189
  acts dated at, 62, 202
  burgesses of, 188, 189
  burgh of, 188, 189
  fermes of, 234
Kinghorn, William, 184
Kinmuck [NJ 8119], 228, 235
Kinmult *see* the Mount
Kinnaber [NO 7261], 51n
Kinnaird, James Balfour of, Lord Lyon, 60
  Richard, knight, W 187
Kinnear, Kinner, Kyner, feu of (Fife), 79
Kinnear [NO4023] Kyn', Kyner', Kynner', Kynher'
  John, 59
  Matthew, 59
  Simon, son of Simon of, 59, 79
Kinninmonth [NT2199], Kynman, John, 60
Kinross, Kynros' [NO1103], acts dated at, 36, 81, 117, 173
  sheriff of, 211
Kinross, Gilbert, 211
  John, knight, W 185
  Simon, 212
Kintore [NJ7916], Kyntor', acts dated at, 36, 119, 124, 186, 196
Kintyre, Kentyr, 134, 136
Kirkby (Cumberland), 231
Kirkcaldy, Kercaledin, shire of, 133, 134
Kirkcudbright, Adam, 38
Kirkpatrick, Kirkepatric, feu of (now Kirkpatrick-Irongray, Kirkudbrightshire), 66
Kirkton, Kyrketon, Alexander, knight, 143
  Richard, 111
Knaresdale, Knarisdal', Knarisdall', fee of (Tynedale), 76, 105, 106, 204
Knights of the Hospital of St John of Jerusalem *see* Hospitallers
Knights of the Temple of Solomon in Jerusalem *see* Templars
Kokes, Waldeve, 201
Kolbein the knight, 210
le Krag' *see* Easter Craiglockart
Kyle (in Cunningham), Kale, Kule, 95, 96, 99
  free forest of, 96
Kynard' *see* Kinnaird
Kynchecheuyn *see* Kinclaven
Kyngorn' *see* Kinghorn
Kynman *see* Kinninmonth
Kynros *see* Kinross
Kynsitus (also Brunolus), son of John, W 104–5
Kyntor' *see* Kintore

Lacy, Edmund, 74
Lamberton, Lamberton', Lambertoun, Lambirton', Lambirtun', Lambyrton', Lammerton', Lemerton, 187
  Alexander, knight, 144
  John, knight, W 89, 91, 92, 93, 94, 95, 98, 121, 132, 137, 138, 207
  Malcolm, 144
  Patrick, clerk of the livery, 147. W 223
  William, bishop of St Andrews, 232
  William, 144; son of *see* Thomas
Lammermuir, Lambirmor, region of, 133, 134, 135, 136
Lanark [NS8843], Lanark', act dated at, 86
  bailies of, 206
  burgesses of, 191, 192
  burgh of, 191, 192
  dean of Christianity of, 209
  inhabitants of, 7
  sheriff of, 181, 206, 210; *see also* Uvieth, Alexander
  sheriffdom of, 191, 192
Lancaster, Roger, 124, 215
Lanercost (Cumberland), 196
Langholm [NY3684], Langholm', 109
Langley, Langeley (Tynedale), manor of, 115, 116
Langwathby (Cumberland), 218, 219
Largo[NO4103], Largauch, act dated at, 189
Largs [NS2059], Larges', 141, 142
  battle of, 165
Larkhall [NS7551], 93

Lascelles, Lasceles', Ralph, W 113
Lauderdale, 214
Lauer *see* Pitliver
Laurence, St, 222
Laurencekirk [NO7171], Cuneueth', 58, 59
Lede, Simon, 201
Leith [NT2776], burgess of, 221
Lenn, William, 77
Lennel [NT8540], Laynell, Laynhal', Laynhale, 113
  Southtoun (Suthtun, Suthtun') of, 113
Lennox, Leuenax, Leuenax', 207
  earl of, 68–9, 114, 118, 119, 216, 231; *see also* Maldouen; Malcolm I; court of, 217; kindred of, 217
  earldom of, 68, 69, 230
Lennox, Simon of, 230–1
  son of *see* Gilbert
Lesellyn, Leselly', Simon, 147
Lesmahagow [NS8139], Lemahag', monks of, 93
  prior of, 9, 93
  priory of (Tironensian), 93
Lessuden, Lessedwyn', Thomas, 118
Lethgaven, Letgauen, Lethgauen' (possibly Lediken, NJ6528), 81
Lethmacdunegil, Lethmacduuegil *see* Mastertown
Leven, river, Leuen, Leuene (Fife), 57, 89
Leybourne, Layburn, William, 122, 123, 124
Leys, Hay family of, 60
Liberacione, Adam, 206
Lillock, Lilac [NO3317], Lillockisfeyld, 18, 228
Lindores [NO2418], Lundor, Lundoris, Lundors, 99
  abbey and convent of (Tironensian), 61, 62, 81, 91, 96, 98, 193, 194, 200
  abbot of, 9, 61, 62, 81, 91, 96, 98, 200
  act dated at, 96
  church of St Andrew and St Mary at, 193
  forest of, 96
  lands belonging to, 96
  monks of, 193
Lindores, John, clerk, 81, 82
Lindsay, Lindes', Lindesay, Lyndes', Lynddessay
  Christina, 187, 226
  David, knight, 72, 73, 224; son of, 224
  John, 146, 147, 223. W 98, 147, 151, 157, 223
  Walter, knight, 78, 79, 126. W 111, 185, 188
  William, of Lamberton, 187, 226
Linlithgow [NT0077], Linchitchu, Linlithcu, Linlithqv, Linlitqv, 64, 65
  acts dated at, 65, 92
  bailies of, 64, 65
  collectors of fermes of, 64
  dwelling in, 133, 135
  fermes of, 172
  manor of, 170
  ploughgate in, 133, 135
  provosts of, 5
  sheriff of, 64, 65, 210; *see also* Mowbray, Roger
Lismore, bishop of, 201
Little Inveresk, Inuerese Minorem (lost, probably near Barbauchlaw, NT3671), 133, 134
Little Keithick [NO1938], 203
Loch Awe, 105
Loch Lomond (Stirlingshire), 118, 119
Loch Long, 190
Lochore [NT1796], Louchoir, Louchor', Louthor'
  David, knight, 72, 203, 212. W 62, 70, 137, 138, 139, 147
Lochcumberay *see* Great Cumbrae Island
Lockhart, Loccard, Stephen, knight, 144
Lodinsson, Bjarne, 165; *see also* Bjarne, Master
Loenois *see* Lothian
Logie, Logyn', Thomas, 147
Logie Buchan [NJ9829], church of, 234
London (England), Lundon', 183, 184, 224, 225
London, Robert, 134, 136, 232
Lonsdale, Vlnesdal', Ralph, 84
Lord Clerk Register, 217; *see also* Skene, Sir John
Lothian, Laudonie, Loenesse, Loenois, 21, 170, 225
  justiciar of 76, 77, 92, 94, 95, 97, 100, 107, 109, 112, 113, 125, 155, 156, 159, 164, 182, 189, 207, 212; *see also* Berkeley, Hugh; Fleming, Stephen; Moray, Walter; Soules, William
  clerk of, 207
Louchard, Luchars', James, 176
Louchor, Louthor *see* Lochore
Louis, son of the king of France, 38
Lour [NO4746], Lowr, Lowres, Lur', 96, 97, 216
Lowther, Sir John, 223
Luke, St, feast of, 180, 181
Lundors *see* Lindores
Lupel, Robert, knight, 159, 164
Luscar [NT0589], Luscher, 133, 134
Lusignan, Lezign', Geoffrey, 74
Luvetot, John, 218
Luxemburg, Lusenbourc, Lussenbourch *see* Isabelle, countess of Flanders

Lvestona *see* Weston
Lyon King of Arms, 60, 203
Lysours, Lysurs', William, 86
Lyueryngham *see* East Linton

MacAbsolon, Gille Brigte
MacDougall, Alexander, of Argyll, 221, 222
MacDuff of Fife, 213
Macfarlane, Walter, 119, 186
Machan [NS7650], Machan', act dated at, 93
Machudri, John, 68, 69
MacMores, Godred, 213
MacNachdan, Gilchrist, 105
Macusuuell, Maccusuuell *see* Maxwell
Magnus IV, king of Norway and king of Man, 100–4, 105, 198, 212, 213
Maid of Norway *see* Margaret
Mailer [NO1020], Maler, 62; *see also* St Magdalen's
Makerstoun, [NT6317], Malkaruyston', 87, 88
Malcolm III, king of Scots (1058–93), 35, 133, 134, 135, 136
Malcolm IV, king of Scots (1153–65), 7, 15, 48n, 71, 133, 134, 135, 136, 183, 194, 195
Malcolm II, earl of Fife, 60, 68, 69, 72, 73, 213. W 89, 92, 98
  son of *see* MacDuff of Fife
Malcolm I, earl of Lennox, 118, 119, 217
Malcolm, son of Duncan, 60–1; *see also* Fife, earl of
  Eva, his wife, 60–1
Malcolm, son of the earl of Lennox, 68, 69
Maldouen, Maldoueny, earl of Lennox, 60, 61, 68, 69
  brother of, 114
Maler *see* Mailer
Malevile *see* Melville
Malhen *see* St Magdalen's
Malise II, earl of Strathearn, 21, 24, 72, 73, 50n, 91. W 76, 97
  daughter of, 191
  sister of *see* Annabella
Malise III, earl of Strathearn, 190, 191. W 105, 159, 164, 166, 167, 183, 192
Malusens *see* Malise
Malveisin, William, 224
Man and the Isles, Mannia, 4, 14, 19, 52n, 100–4, 159, 160, 163, 164, 187, 198, 202, 212, 213, 214, 221, 222, 223; *see also* Sudrey islands
  bailies of, 213, 214; *see also* Acarsan, Maurice; fitz Count, Alan; MacMores, Godred; Reginald, chaplain; brother of one of, 221
  bishop of, 100, 102; *see also* Gilbert; Mark, Master; Richard
  instruments relating to, 100–4, 159, 163
  king of, 212
  lord of *see* Alexander, Prince
  lordship of, 198
  men of, 199
  people of, 221
  see of, 221
Manor [NT6632], Meners, 194, 195, 228
  barony of, 195
Mansel, Maunsell', Master John, 74, 202; *see also* Beverley, provost of
Manuel, priory of (Cistercian nunnery), 65
  nuns of, 65
Mar, Ma', Mar', Marche, Mare, Marr, Marr'
  earl of, 34, 62, 65, 75, 86, 87, 166, 167, 211 W; 65, 66, 67, 68, 70, 72, 77, 86, 87, 89, 90, 91, 92, 96, 97, 98, 100, 104, 105, 112, 125, 126, 159, 164, 166, 167, 170, 171, 183, 185, 186, 190, 192; *see also* Donald; Hay, William; William
Margaret, daughter of Alexander III, queen of Norway, 23, 25, 27, 37, 51n, 105, 157–65, 179, 180, 226; children of, 158, 161, 162, 164
Margaret, daughter of Simon, 83
Margaret, Maid of Norway, 53n, 165
Margaret, St, wife of Malcolm III, queen of Scots, 28, 35, 146, 133, 134, 135, 136
Margaret, sister of Alexander II, lady of Tickhill, 85
Margaret, widow of Hubert de Burgh, 205, 210
  Margaret, daughter of, 205
Margaret, widow of William Swinburne, 226
Margaret, wife of Alexander III, queen of Scots, 3, 4, 16, 17, 28, 71, 72, 75, 82, 83, 120, 121, 137, 196, 201, 202, 203, 204, 208, 211, 219, 222
  chamber of, 203
  death of, 38, 197
  treasurer of, 203, 208; *see also* Swinburne, William
Margaret, wife of Nicholas Corbet, 87, 88
Margaret, wife of Gilbert Glencarny, junior, sister of John Prat, 107
Marguerite, wife of Prince Alexander, 13, 14, 25, 38, 165–71, 172, 175–7, 226
  brother of *see* John I, count of Namur
  dowry of, 19, 26, 168–9, 170–1, 172, 175–7, 225
  second husband of, 172; *see also* Reynaud I, count of Gueldres
Marion, daughter of Simon, 83

Mariota, daughter of Samuel, 235
Marjorie, sister of Alexander III, 212
Mark, evangelist, St, feast of, 194
Mark, Master, 221; *see also* Galloway, Mark of
Marown Old Church, Isle of Man [SC 3178], 98
Marshall, Marecallus, Mariscallus, Adam, 195
Richard, W 57, 67
Martin in Winter, St, feast of, 65, 109, 125, 175, 182, 186
Martin V, Pope, 166, 167, 168, 170, 171
Mary, St, feast relating to, 112
Mary, countess of Menteith, 108
Mary, wife of Eymer Maxwell, 72
Mary, wife of John Wardrop, 114, 217
Masterton, Maistertun', William, 147
Mastertown [NT1284], Lethmacdunegil, 134, 136, 137
Masun, Mazun, John, 180–1, ?190, 227, 231
Matilda, wife of William Dod, 154, 155
Matthew, abbot of Melrose, W 67
Matthew, brother of John Kin[near], 59
Matthew, cleric of Tillicoultry, 87
Mauchline [NS4927], Machelyn', Mauchlyn', Mauhelyn', 94, 95, 99
Maule, Peter, knight, 202
Christine, wife of, 202
Maurice, Friar Minor of Norway, 157, 160
Maurice, son of Galbraith, 68, 69
Mauritania *see* Mortagne
May, priory of (Augustinian), 17
Maxwel, Mackisuuell', Macusuuell', Makeswell, Makyswell', Maxwell', Maxwelle
Aylmer, Eymer, knight 72, 74, 85, 86, 207, 208, 212 W, 61, 66, 67, 78, 94
Herbert, 109
Meathie [NO4646], church of, 232
Meft [NJ2763], 80, 209
Megotta, daughter of Margaret lady of Tickhill, 85
Meikle Dallas [NJ1152], Dolaysmykel', 152
Meiners *see* Menzies
Mel, Mele, Gunter, W 104
Melach Burn (now lost, in Stirlingshire), 118
Meldrum, Megeldrom, Melgedrum, Alexander, 147
Patrick, W 155
Melrose [NT5434], Melros, Melros', 88
abbey and convent of St Mary (Cistercian), 24, 53n, 65, 66, 94, 95, 99, 230; lands of, 110, 111; men of, 99, 110, 111
abbot of, 9, 24, 65, 66, 87, 88, 94, 95, 230. W 67; *see also* Adam; Matthew
acts dated at, 87, 88, 91, 93
monks of, 10, 87, 88, 92, 93, 94, 95, 99, 110, 111
refectory of, 88
Melville, John, W 196
Meners, 70; *see also* Manor
Menmuir [NO5364], 165
Menstrie [NS8496], 209
Menteith, Menh' h, Menech', Meneteth', Meneth', Menethet, Menetht, Menetye, Menteth, Mentethe, Menthet, Minethey, countess of, 108; *see also* Mary
earl of, 108. W 60, 63, 65, 66, 68, 69, 70, 72, 75, 77, 87, 97, 114, 125, 154, 159, 164, 185; *see also* Comyn, Walter; Stewart, Walter (d. 1293/4)
earldom of, 19
Menteith, William, W 57
Menzies, Meiners', Meners, Merness', Meygners, Meyneris, Meyners, Meyner, Meyns
David, W 60
Robert, chamberlain, 72. W 57, 58, 60, 61, 62, 63, 64, 72, 73, 75, 103, 104, 106
Merchiston [NT2472], Merhammeston, 144
Mertoun [NT6232], Merton', 68, 69
Mes, Alwin, 86, 87
Messine, dean of *see* Bernard
Meyners *see* Menzies
Michael, St, 196
feast of, 84, 171, 175
Midhow, Midhoue (Tynedale), 127, 128
Minnauer (lost, possibly Menzion, NT0923), 68, 69, 70
Moncreiffe [NO1121], Muncref', Muncreff, 64
Moncreiffe, Matthew, 64
Moniabrock [NS3563], Moniabrocd', church of, 61
Monimail parish, 228
Monorgan, Monorgund, Norrin, 114
wife of, 114
Monte Alto, Montealto
Bernard, W 95, 109, 110, 113, 119, 121, 153, 157
Roger, 74, 83
William, W 88, 89, 110, 121
Montfort, Monte Forti, Alexander, brother of John, 63
Alexander, 80
John, brother of Alexander, 63
Montrose [NO7159], Monros', 50n
act dated at, 83
castle of, 83
Montrose, duke of, 21

Moray, Moravia, 23, 107, 152
bishop of, 27, 152
chaplain of, 222
Moray, Morrauia, Moravia, Moreuya, Moreve, Morruia, Alexander, knight, 138. W 107, 108, 110
Andrew, knight, 232. W 185, 187, 189
Hugh, knight, 210
Malcolm, knight, 138
Malcolm (knight), lord of Drumsagard, 201
Walter, knight, 121, 122, 217. W 67, 72, 73, 76, 90, 95, 111, 141; ancestors of, 122; men of, 122
William, knight, 147, 166, 167. W 151, 190
Morham, Adam, 75
Mortagne, Mauritania, Mortaing', Mortaingne
Baldwin, knight, 177, 226
William, knight, lord of Rumes, 168, 170, 171, 172; mother of *see* Yolande
Mortimer, William, 208
Morton (Cumberland), forest of, 217
Morville, Joan, 214
the Mount [NO3316] (in Monimail parish), 18, 228
Mounth, the, Moneth', 11, 58, 81, 193, 194
Mowat, Bernard, 165
Robert, 212
Mowbray, Moubray, Mubray, Mumbray, Munbray, Cristiana, 117, 118
Geoffrey, knight, W 152, 182
Roger, 64, 68, 69, 72, 73, 84, 117, 118, 210. W 90
Mugdock [NS5577], Mucraw, 68, 69
Muncref *see* Moncreiffe
Musselburgh, Muskelb', feu of (East Lothian), 67
Musselburgh, Muxilburg', Master John, clerk of the provender, 147. W 223

Nairn [NH8856], burgesses of, 235
Namur (Belgium), archives of, 176
marquis of *see* Dampierre, Guy
Namur, count of *see* John I
Neil, earl of Carrick, 72, 73, 130, 201
wife of, 201
Ness, river (Inverness-shire), Nys, 126
Nether Ayton [NT9362], 201
Neubaud, Geoffrey, 218
Neuwerk *see* Newark
Nevay [NO3243], Neuith', 96, 97
Nevay, Henry, knight, 96, 97
Neville, Geoffrey, 123, 215
Robert, knight, 204, 215
Newark, Neuwerk Henry, 178, 179
Newbattle [NT3366], Neu', Neubotell', Neubotil, Neubotyll', Newbotill, Newebolt', Neweboltle
abbot of, 72
acts dated at, 66, 92, 115, 175
church and monks of 184
Roger, abbot of, W 58
Newburgh [NO2318], Novus Burgus, 98, 99
fair at, 98
Newburgh, William, 221
Newburn [NO4503], Nithebren, 133, 135
Newcastle-upon-Tyne, Nova Castro, 177
Nicholas, baker, 156
Nidaros (Norway), archbishop of, 221; *see also* John
Ninian, St, 198
Norfolk, Norf', earl of, 74; *see also* Bigod, Richard
Norhamshire (Northumberland), 140
Norman, huntsman of the king, 194, 195
Normandy, Normannia, 75
Normanville, Normanuill, Normanwil, Thomas, knight, 72, 178, 179, 204, 205, 219, 231
North Tynedale, barony of (Northumberland), North Tindall, North Tindall', 115, 116
liberty of, 115, 116
Northumberland, Northumbrie, 16, 19, 28, 115–16, 125, 128, 205, 211, 225, 226
earl of *see* Henry
jury from, 131
sheriff of, 115, 116, 131, 190
Norway, Noruuagia, Norvagia, Norvwagia, 37, 54n, 157–65, 210, 211, 221
bailie of the king of, 101, 102
chancellor of, 100, 101, 102, 104, 157, 160; *see also* Asketin; Bjarne, Master
customs of, 158, 161
diplomatic documents relating to, 165
envoys from, 103, 157–64, 165, 210
kingdom of, 103, 104, 105, 160
kings of, 13, 14, 25, 37, 100, 103, 104, 105, 157–65, 183, 184, 198, 210, 211; *see also* Eric II; Haakon IV; Magnus IV
lands in, 157, 158, 160, 162
laws and customs of, 158, 161, 162
magnates of, 100, 102, 157, 159, 160, 164, 210; *see also* Andrew, son of Nicholas
Maid of *see* Margaret
money of, 157, 160
proctors of, 157–65
queen of, 159, 164, 179–80, 226; *see also* Margaret, daughter of Alexander III

Nunwick (Tynedale), Nunewyc', Nunewych', 106, 120, 121, 204, 224

Obeyne *see* Aboyne
Okarefair *see* Acarsan
Oketon, William, 215
Olafsson, Magnus, 212
Olifard, David, 122
  Walter, knight, 122
  William, 228. W 216
Oliver Castle, barony of, Castrum Oliuerus, 68, 69
Orkney, Orchaden', Orchadia, 159, 162, 163
  bishop of, 100, 101, 102, 157, 160, 210; *see also* Henry; Peter
  church of St Magnus of, 100, 102
Orlac, Gerald, 183, 184
Our Lady *see* Virgin Mary
Ouston (Tynedale), 224

Pairney [NN9713], 191
Paisley [NS4864]
  abbot of, 9, 57
  convent of (Benedictine), 57
  monks of, 217
Panmure, lord of *see* Maule, Peter
  lordship of, 202
Pape, Nicholas, 223
Pardusin *see* Broomhill
Paris (France), 28, 142
Park, Parco, John, W 81, 98
Paslet *see* Paisley
Patrick, bishop of Brechin, W 189
Patrick, brother of Duncan, 202
  Christina, wife of, 202
Patrick III, earl of Dunbar, 68, 69, 72, 73, 113. W 61, 75, 76, 79, 88, 91, 92, 95, 97, 99, 104, 106, 111, 125, 141, 144, 147, 150, 151, 159, 164, 166, 167
  Patrick, son of, 159, 164; *see also* Patrick IV, earl of Dunbar
Paul, St, feasts relating to, 184
Peebles [NT2540], Peblis, 29, 209
  bailies of, 86, 87
  burgesses of, 86, 87, 208
  mill of, 91, 92
  sheriff of, 85, 86; *see also* Maxwell, Eymer
Peeblesshire, 70
Pencaitland [NT4468], feu of, 207
Penick, [NH9155], Pethenac, 133, 135
Penrith (Cumberland), Penerith', Penreth, liberty of, 111, 179, 215, 219
  bailiff of, 219
  tenants of, 216
Percy, Percey, Walter, 126
Perisby, Hugh, W 156
  William, 165
Perth, Pert', Perth', 35, 77, 199, 233, 234
  acts dated at, 77, 97, 100, 104
  burgh of, 29, 62, 77, 89, 98, 107, 223
  burgh court of, 235
  castle of, 133, 135; chapel of, 133, 135
  church of, 133, 135
  dwelling in, 33, 135
  fermes of, 98, 107, 200
  fishery in, 134, 136
  Friars Preacher of, 62, 98, 232; church of, 100, 101, 103
  Inch of, 235
  mills of, 232
  provosts of, 62, 98, 106
  sheriff of, 213. W 62, 203; *see also* Cameron, John; Lochore, David
  sheriff court of, 203
  treaty sealed at, 101, 102, 105, 198, 210, 214
Perthshire, 21, 34
Peter, St, feasts relating to, 100, 157, 158, 160, 161, 184, 213
Peter, bishop of Bergen, W 105
Peter, bishop of Orkney, 157, 160
Pethenac *see* Penick
Pethglassyn *see* Pitglassie
Petioceher *see* Pitteuchar
Petnarcha *see* Urquhart
Petri, Andrew, W 160, 164
Pettinain [NS9542], 206
Phale' (now lost, in Stirlingshire), 118, 119
Philippa, daughter of Adam Tynedall, 115, 116
Picardy, 14, 25, 52n
Pitbauchlie [NT1086], Petbachlakin, 133, 134
Pitcairn [NN8850], Petcarn, Petcarn'
  John, 57, 58
Pitconmark [NT2392], Petconmarthin, Petcomarthy, 133, 135, 137
Pitcorthie [NT1086], Petcorthin, 133, 134
Pitglassie, Edward, W 137
Pitliver [NT0685], Lauer, 133, 134
Pitteuchar [NT2899], Petioceher, 133, 135, 137
Plessis, Plessetis, John, 74
Plumpton (Cumberland), park of, 220
Polnegulan (now lost, in Lennox), 207
Polwarth, Poulwrth', Adam, 68, 69
Pont, Juliana, 231
  father of *see* Adam, burgess of Ayr
Porghyl *see* Tourgill
Prat, Prast, Prat', Prath', John, knight, 107
  Reginald, 76, 105, 106, 204
Prebenda, Robert, 143, 149, 152, 153, 166, 167, 168. W 91, 97
Prenderlathe, Elena, 226

Pretzy' *see* Brechin
Primrose [NT1084], Primros, 133, 135
Prony *see* Pairney

Quarentely, Adam, 218
Quincy, Quency, Quency', Qwyncy, Roger, 68, 69, 76, 77, 91
ancestors of, 91
heirs of, 140, 141; *see also* Elizabeth, wife of Alexander Comyn; Zouche, Helen; lands of, 140, 141

Rabbayne, Elias, 74
Rafran *see* Rathen
Rait [NO2327], Rath, Rathoc, 185, 186
Ralph, bishop of Abderdeen, 138, 139
Ralph, envoy *see* Dundee, Master Ralph
Ralph of the wardrobe, 184
Ramsay, Ramsayth (Isle of Man), 8, 187
Ramsay, Rames', Ramesey, Rameshey, Rammes', Ramsayth', James, knight, W 185
John, 147
Peter, 70, 71, 72, 73; *see also* Aberdeen, bishop of
William, 72, 73
Randin of the wardrobe, 147
Randolph, Ranulph, Ranulph', Raulf', family, 214
Thomas, 110, 131, 214. W 100, 109, 124, 141, 156, 157, 193
Ranulf family, 214
Rapenache Manor [NK0060], Rafran', Rathen, Ratthenec [NJ2764], 209
act dated at, 80
Rath *see* Rait
Rathenec *see* Rapenache Manor
Ratho [NT1471], 165, 225
Rathoc *see* Rait
Ratthen [NK0060], Rafran, Rathenec, 209, 230
Reading, abbey of (Cluniac), 18
Reginald, chaplain, 214
Reginald, clerk, 146
Reginald, land holder in Fife, 59
Reginald, son of Ranulf Haughton, 227
Reston [NT8862], 207
Rethirglen *see* Rutherglen
Revel family, 21
Reynaud I, count of Gueldres, 172
Richard, abbot of Cambuskenneth, W 68
Richard, almoner of the Order of Knights Templar, 72
Richard, bishop of Man, W 216
Richard, brother of Geoffrey, 68, 69
Richard, chancellor of Glasgow cathedral, 235
Richard, chaplain, 209
Richard, suitor of the barony of Heton, 121, 122
Richenda (Rychenda), daughter of Winfred (Humphrey) Berkeley, 58, 59
Richmond (Yorkshire), Richemund, archdeacon of *see* Newark, Henry
Rihill, Rihill', Rihille, Reginald, clerk, 27, 151, 152, 153
Rinaldus *see* Richard, bishop of Man
Ringmer, Thomas, 227
Ripley, Rypeley, William, 152
Rires [NO4604], 213
Robert I, king of Scots (1306–29), 7, 10, 11, 12, 13, 25, 32, 33, 34, 35, 50n, 54n, 89, 92, 105, 119, 195, 220, 230, 232, 233
Robert III, king of Scots (1390–1406), 90
Robert, bishop of Dunblane *see* Prebenda, Robert
Robert, bishop of Glasgow *see* Wishart, Robert
Robert, son of Adam Bassenthwaite, 84
Robertson, William, of Ladykirk, 186
Roger, priest, 133, 135
Roglen' *see* Rutherglen
Romer, court of, 102
Ros, Alexander, 219; son of, 219
Robert, 38, 54n, 72, 219. W 57, 62, 64, 66, 67, 68, 70
Rosemarkie [NH7357], inhabitants of, 235
Roslin [NT2763], Roskelyn, Roskelyn', 154
Roslin, Henry, 153
Ross, earl of, 234; *see also* Farquhar; William
Rothiemay [NJ5448], 165
Roxburgh [NT6930], Rokburc', Rokebourc, Rokeburg', Rokesburg', Rokisburc', Rokisburch', Rokisburg, Roxbrugh, Roxburg', Roxburghe, 143, 157, 170, 235
acts dated at, 13, 25, 26, 35, 60, 61, 67, 72, 73, 75, 91, 121, 122, 125, 128, 129, 143, 147, 160, 165, 168, 175, 196, 230
bailie of, 110; *see also* Randolph, Thomas
court held at, 121, 122, 217
dwelling in, 133, 135
fortress of, 60
Friars Minor of, 231, 232
sheriff of, 110, 201, 217, 219; *see also* Randolph, Thomas
sheriffdom of, 121, 122
Roxburghshire, 122, 201
Rulebethok' *see* Bedrule
Rulehaugh (now obsolete, near Old Fodderlee, NT6014), Rulehalch', 150, 151
Rumes, lord of *see* Mortagne
Rushen [SC3497], abbey of (Cistercian), 214, 221

abbot of, of, 213, 214, 221; *see also* Gilbert
canons of, 221
Rutherford, Rutyrford', Nicholas, 86
Rutherglen [NS5862], Rethirglen, Rutherglen, 181, 182
bailies of, 181
burgh of, 182
Ruthven, Rothewen', Gilbert, knight, 149, 150, 208
Rye Water, Dalry, 142
Ryedale, Ryesdale (Ayrshire), 141
Rypeley *see* Ripley

St Andrews, Sanctus Andreas, Saint Andriu, 31, 54n, 133, 135
acts dated at, 70
archdeacon of, 72 W, 81; *see also* Wishart, William
bishop of, 9, 26, 28, 31, 37, 62, 65, 72, 143, 149, 166, 167, 168, 170, 171, 216, 224, 232. W 68, 87, 89, 91, 92, 97, 104 106, 147; *see also* Bernham, David; Fraser, William; Gamelin; Lamberton, William; Malveisin, William; Wardlaw, Henry; Wishart, William
canons of, 59, 60, 216
chapter of, 216
prior of, 216. W 137, 138; *see also* John
priory of (Augustinian), 59, 60, 137
provost of, 204
see of, 216
St Bees (Cumberland), prior of, 213, 214
St Clair, Sancto Claro, Sancto Cleir, Saint Cler, William, knight, 19, 26, 146, 153, 156, 166, 167, 212, 218, 219. W 81, 89, 115, 124, 132, 139, 144, 147, 150, 151, 152, 155, 174, 196, 223
St Germain, Sancto Germano, John, 179, 180
St James Compostela, 16, 78, 79
St Lazarus, brethren of, 59
St Leonard's, priory of (Augustinian nunnery), 233
prioress of, 233
St Maddoes (Perthshire), parish of, 197
St Magdalen's, Malhen, Malhena (now lost, near Craigie, NO1122), fermers of, 98
St Trinian, barony of, 198
Saddell [NR7832], abbey and monks of, 201
Saluain, John, W 68
Santiago *see* St James Compostela
Sauchie [NS7888], 209
Schen *see* Cheyne
Scone, Scon', Schon', 35, 36, 112
abbey of (Augustinian), 33
abbot of, 154, 196, 197; *see also* Thomas
acts dated at, 34, 51n, 58, 62, 63, 90, 97, 98, 99, 105, 107, 112, 120, 121, 131, 155, 172, 178, 183, 191, 192, 211
monks of, 196, 197, 229
moot hill of, 35
parliament held at, 213, 231
priory and convent of, 35, 77
Scotia, Scocie, justiciar of, 11, 58, 63, 68, 70, 71, 72, 73, 76, 78, 86, 87, 89, 90, 96, 97, 99, 105, 112, 121, 125, 126, 155, 172, 186, 190, 192, 193, 196, 202, 203, 208, 212; *see also* Comyn, Alexander; Durward, Alan; Fergus; Stewart, Walter (d. 1246)
Scotland, Escoce, Escoche, Scocie, Scotie, 6, 7, 8, 12, 14, 17, 19, 24, 25, 26, 27, 32, 33, 35, 38, 54n, 128, 142, 158, 160, 204, 210, 232
arms of, 30, 32
bailies of, 123, 128
barons of, 134, 165–78, 194, 195
bishops of, 134
burgesses of, 189
burghs of, 98, 109–10, 111, 114, 124, 188, 189, 191, 192
butler of, 189; *see also* Soules, William
chamberlain of, 27, 28, 60, 61, 62, 63, 64, 65, 66, 67, 68, 70, 71, 78, 80, 89, 90, 91, 92, 96, 97, 98, 100, 105, 124, 131, 146, 147, 157, 180, 181, 190, 193, 211, 223, 224, 231; *see also* Balliol, Alexander; John; Lindsay, John; Maxwell, Eymer; Meyners, Robert; Randolph, Thomas; William, earl of Mar
chancellor of, 6, 15, 18, 23, 25, 26, 27, 28, 29, 31, 32, 33, 34, 35, 37, 86, 137, 147, 189, 193; *see also* Fraser, William; Kenleith, Robert; Parick, bishop of Brechin; Wishart, William
chancery of, 3, 4, 5, 6, 7, 8, 9, 10, 12, 13, 14, 15, 16, 17, 19, 20, 22–30, 33, 34, 36, 37, 119, 188, 195, 196, 208, 209, 235
clergy of, 100, 133, 134
communities of, 189
constable of, 68, 69, 76, 77, 91, 126, 139, 155, 172, 186, 190, 192; *see also* Comyn, Alexander; Quincy, Roger
crown of, 4, 6, 12, 27, 28, 29, 31, 38, 120, 124, 131, 198, 199, 216, 217, 220
diplomatic documents relating to, 165
earls of, 134

English chamberlain of, 200, 222, 228, 230
English guardian of, 200
English lands of, 12, 19, 33, 36, 123, 124, 125, 131, 139, 155, 178, 179, 197, 198, 203, 204, 205, 206, 215, 216, 217, 218, 219, 220, 223, 231; *see also* Langwathby; Penrith; Sowerby; Tynedale; men of, 123
English lieutenant of, 219, 222, 230
English treasurer of, 232
exchequer of, 15, 17, 20, 29, 36, 37, 108, 209, 211, 228
great seal of, 12, 13, 14, 26, 27, 31, 32, 33, 58, 61, 63, 64, 90, 93, 94, 96, 97, 110, 111, 112, 113, 118, 124, 131, 132, 147, 157, 168, 169, 171, 175, 176, 177, 178, 182, 228
guardians of *see* Guardians of Scotland
keeper of, 224; *see also* Warenne, John
kingdom of, 8, 9, 13, 24, 27, 34, 35, 39, 71, 72, 74, 100, 102, 104, 118, 119, 126, 127, 128, 140, 155, 158, 160, 161, 162, 164, 165–8, 170, 171, 180, 181, 183, 187, 190, 191, 192, 219
kings of, v, 3,4, 6, 8, 10, 15, 17, 18, 19, 22, 23, 25, 26, 27, 29, 30, 32, 33, 34, 35, 36, 38, 54n, 74, 79, 80, 90, 91, 92, 93, 94, 103, 106, 118, 126, 131, 133, 134, 135, 136, 146, 158, 162, 165, 166, 168, 169, 176, 191, 192, 197, 202, 206, 214, 217, 218, 220, 221, 222, 230; *see also* Alexander I; Alexander II; Alexander III; David I; David II; Duncan II; Edgar; James III; James IV; James V; John; Malcolm III; Malcolm IV; Robert I; Robert III; William I; cain of, 133, 135; court of, 134, 136; demesne of 133, 134, 135, 136, 137, 224, 225; fermers of, 89, 154; heirs of, 158, 161, 162, 165–8; kitchens of, 137; pleas belonging to, 133, 135; profits belonging to, 133, 135; teinds belonging to, 133, 135
justiciars of, 128
laws and customs of, 100, 102, 128, 158, 162, 165, 166, 216
lieges of, 127
magnates of, 100, 129, 185
merchants of, 128, 177
men of, 131, 133, 134, 135, 136, 140
parliament of, 172
people of, 133, 134
queens of, 71, 72, 73, 75, 79, 80, 137; *see also* Margaret
religious of, 155
servants of, 125
sheriffs of, 128
steward of, 86, 87, 97, 99, 129, 159, 164, 174, 183, 190, 192, 208; *see also* Walter, son of Alan; Stewart, Alexander; Stewart, James
succession to the throne of, 8, 13–14, 20, 26, 38, 39, 158, 162, 164, 165, 166, 226
treasury of, 14, 19, 24, 36, 205, 212, 215, 219, 226
Scot, John, 207
Scots College, Paris, 142
Scotston [NO7373], Scottistun', 59
Scottish Sea, 78, 88, 89; *see also* Forth, river
Scurry, fishery called, 126
Sebergham, Geoffrey, 223
  Walter, 223
Segan, Thomas, 60
Sehynne' *see* Shian
Seisil, Seysil, Soysit, Thomas, 141–2
Seliman, William *alias* William Wysman, 215
Selkirk [NT4728], Selek', Selkirk', Selekirk', Selekyrke, 88, 214
  acts dated at, 79, 88, 94, 130, 150, 191 (spurious)
Serrure, M., 168, 176
Sewing Shields (Tynedale), 205
Shetland Islands (insule Yhetlandie), 100, 102
Shian [NS5589], Sehymmie, Sehynne', 118, 119
Sicily, 202
Simon, abbot of Dunfermline, W 107
Simon, doorkeeper of Montrose Castle, 83
Simon, son of Simon Kinnear, 59, 60
Simonburn (Northumberland) [NY8773], rectory of, 232
Sinclair *see* St Clair
Siward, Syward, Richard, W 113
Skene, Sir John, 217
Slaggyford, Slaggingford', Slaghingford' (Tynedale), 76, 105, 106, 225
Slindon, Auduenus, W 160, 164
Smailholm [NT6436], Smalham, 122
Smeaton [NT3569], Smetheby, Smithetun', Smythetun', 67, 68, 133, 135, 202
Smeaton, Gilbert, 202
  Emma, daughter of, 202
Sodor, bishop of, 212
Soles *see* Soules
Solomon, King, 138
Somerville, Someruill', William, W 106
Sornfallow [NS9233], 210
Soules, Soles, Soulis, Sulys, Nicholas, 72. W 68, 70

William, knight, 147, 166, 167, 170, 171, 178, 189. W 155, 156, 159, 164, 182
South Tynedale, barony of (Nothumberland), Soth Tindall, SuthTyndall', 115, 116
Southtown of Lennel, 113
Soutra [NT4558], Soltr', hospital of Holy Trinity, 89, 91, 122, 217
attorneys of, 122
brethren of, 11, 88, 89, 91, 92, 99, 100, 121, 122
church of, 92
master of hospital of, 11, 91, 99, 100, 121, 122; men of, 100
Sowerby (Cumberland), 203, 218, 219, 223
manor of, 215, 216
tenants of, 216
Spango [NS2374], Spangok', 68, 69
Sparetunt, John, burgess of Perth, 77
Spey, river (Moray), 20, 80, 190, 209, 230
Stanfordham (Northumberland), Stamfordham, 178
Stapledon, Walter, 218
Stavanger, Stauangren', Torgils, bishop of, 104
Staward, Staworth, Staworth', Staworthe' (Tynedale), 115, 116, 225
Stewart (*senescallus*)
Alexander, 68, 69, 72, 73, 94, 95, 99, 208. W 57, 61, 65, 68, 79, 121, 129, 130, 159, 164; his wife and family, 94, 95
James, knight, W 130, 174, 183, 190, 192
Walter (d. 1246), 86, 87
Walter (d. 1293/4), 108, 114, 134, 136. W 97, 125, 154, 159, 164, 185
Stichill [NT7138], 214
Stirling, Striuelin, Striuelyn, Striuelyn', Strivelyne, 36, 67, 133, 135
acts dated at, 36, 68, 76, 83, 84, 99, 129, 130, 132, 152, 179, 185
churches in, 133, 135
colloquium at, 204
dwelling in, 133, 135
fermes of, 228
parliament at, 172
sheriff of, 87, 209; *see also* Avenel, Richard
Stirlingshire, 21
Stobo [NT1837], 235
Strachan, Strathechyn', Strathetheyn', John, 146, 147, 222, 223
Ralph, knight, 146, 222
Stradierne *see* Strathearn
Straiton [NS3804], Straton, Stratona, Stratun
water called, 193
Straiton, Stratun, Strattun, Richard, knight, 21, 143, 146, ?147, 189, 193. W 130, 155, 223
Strathblane [NS5679], Stratblachan', 68, 69
Strathbogie, David, knight, 173. W 97; *see also* Atholl, earl of
son of, 173
Strathearn, Stradierne, Stratherin, Strathern', Stratherne, 190
bishop of *see* Dunblane, bishop of
earl of, 24, 51n, 72, 73, 166, 167, 190, 191. W 76, 97, 159, 164, 183, 192; *see also* Malise II; Malise III
Strathgryfe [NS3370], Stratgrif', 68, 69
Stratun *see* Straiton
Stuteville, Stutevill, Robert, 75
Suannoch, daughter of Simon, 83
Sudrey Islands, insule Sodoren', Sodorensium, 100
Sules *see* Soules
Swinburne, Swynburn, Swyneburn, Swyneburn', Swynneburne, family, 211, 225
John, knight, 17, 125, 127, 128, 151, 152, 153, 196, 215
William, 27, 31, 74, 75, 76, 77, 82, 105, 106, 115, 117, 117, 119, 121, 203, 204, 205, 208, 211, 225, 26
widow of, 121, 225; *see also* Margaret
Surrey, Surr', earl of, 74; *see also* Warenne, John
Sybil, wife of Alexander I, queen of Scotland, 133, 134, 135, 136
Synton, Alexander, 203

Tannadice [NO4758], Thanethes', 97
fermes of, 48n, 97
thanage of, 230
Tarves [NJ8631], Taruays, Tarvays, 125, 126
Tay, river, Thaei, Thay, 133, 134, 135, 136, 196, 197, 229
Tecket, John, 222
Templars, military order of, 72, 138, 139, 183
Teviot, river, Teuyoth, 150, 151
Thérouanne (France), Terewane, Teruane, bishop of, 176; *see also* Henry
Thomas, apostle, St, feast of, 67
Thomas, martyr, St, 154; *see also* Canterbury
feast of, 185
Thomas, abbot of Scone, 154
Thomas, son of Randolph, 72. W 57, 70
Thomas, son of William Lamberton, 184
Thomson, J. Maitland, 34, 37, 52n, 90, 115, 214
Thornton (Tynedale), 222

Tickhill, honour of (Nottinghamshire), 85, 205
Tillicoultry [NS9197], Tillicultre, Tulicultry, Tulleclutre, Tulyculter, 7, 34, 86, 87
Matthew, cleric of, 87
Tilliol, Tilloloy, Peter, knight, 83
Tiron, Tyron (France), 107
Todrig [NT4220], 203
Tönsberg (Norway), 221
Torgils, Thorgils, bishop of Stavanger, 105. W 104
Torphichen, 183, 210
Torthorald, David, knight, 231. W 187
Tourgill [NS2264], Torhgil, Torkgill, 141, 142
Tours, Turribus, Eustace, W 87, 88, 96, 107, 108
Tower burn (Dunfermline), 133, 135
Traquair [NT3334], Tracquar', Traquayr', Traueqr', Trecquar', Treqwar', Treuequayr, Treuequayr', Trouequayr', Trouequer
acts dated at, 79, 80, 82, 84, 85, 95, 144, 146, 148, 153
bailies of, 91
mill of, 92
sheriff of, 91, 235; *see also* Fraser, Gilbert; Fraser, Simon
Trent, river (England), 123, 219, 231
Trondheim, Nithdroen', Nithdrosen, church of, 100, 102
Tillyhiot [NO5543], 202
Tuly mac Argentuly (now lost), act dated at, 189, 190
Tweed, river, Tuede, 87, 88, 131, 140
Twynham, John, 230
Tyne, river, Tyna (Northumberland), 76
Tynedale (Northumberland), Thyndall, Tindall', Tyndal', Tyndall', liberty of, 12, 19, 27, 76, 105, 106, 116, 119, 121, 125, 129, 179, 196, 204, 205, 211, 215, 218, 219, 224, 225, 231; *see also* North Tynedale; South Tynedale
bailiffs of, 11, 119, 120, 173, 178, 196, 204, 218, 222, 225; *see also* Swinburne, William; Tecket, John
escheator of, 222; *see also* Tecket, John
forester of *see* Bellingham, William

Ulverston, Bertram, 201
Henry, 201
Umfraville, Humfrauill', Humfrauyle, Umframuill', Vmfranuill', Vnfraivile, Gilbert, W 112, 125, 141, 153, 159, 164, 188, 190
Ingram, knight, 148, 149, 231; wife of, 149, 231; *see also* Isabel
Robert, 148, 149
Upper Crailing, barony of, Cralyng' superior, 121, 122
Urquhart [NO1908], Petnarcha, 133, 134
Utring called 'Castball' *see* Wischard, Robert
Uvieth, Vuiet, Alexander, knight, 72, 210

Val de Anand *see* Annandale
Valences, Valenc', William, 74
Vallibus *see* Vaux
Valognes, Valloniis, Richard, W 113
Isabella, 66
Varia Capella (Stirlingshire), lands in the parish of, 68, 69
Vaux (Vallibus), Alexander, W 113
John, W 57, 60, 61, 62, 63, 64, 72
Vescy, Eustace, 38, 54n
Joanna, 228, 229
Vieuxpont, Veteri Ponte, Nicholas, W 156
Virgin Mary *see* Mary, St
feasts relating to, 112, 157, 160, 174
Vivenus, knight, W 159, 164
brother of *see* Bjarne, knight
Vlnesdal' *see* Lonsdale
Vmfranuill' *see* Umfraville
Vnfraivile *see* Umfraville
Vuiet *see* Uviet

Waddenshope, [NT2636], Waltanishop', peatmoss of, 85, 86, 208
Walchope, Walchoup', Alan, 147
Walerand, Robert, 74
Wales, Wallia, 172, 202
Waleys, Richard, tenant of Alexander Stewart, 99
Walter, baker, 223
spouse of, 223
Walter, earl of Menteith *see* Stewart, Walter
Walter, son of Alan, 86, 87; *see also* Stewart, Walter (d. 1246)
Walterston, William, 230
heir of, 230; *see also* John
Waltheof, Hugh, son of, 58
Wardlaw, Henry, 62
Wardrop, de Wardroba, John, 114, 217
wife of *see* Mary
Warenne, John, earl of Surrey, 74, 224
Wark(Tynedale), Werk', 74, 76, 121, 128, 202, 205, 206, 215, 218, 222, 224, 225, 226, 232
manor of, 196
royal park at, 231
Warwick, Warr', earl of, 74; *see also* Plessis, John
Wauchop [NT5908], Waluchop
Weland, clerk, 180, 181
Wester Beath (now obsolete, in Beath parish, Fife), Beeth Occidental, Beth' Occidental, 138

Wester Bogie [NT2493], 'Bolgin', 133, 134
Wester Kinghorn *see* Burntisland
Western Isles, 172, 211
Westminster, 17, 18, 205, 214, 218, 220, 221, 222, 223
Westmorland, Westmerland, 151, 214, 223
Weston, Andrew, knight, W 189
  Walter, 223
Wheatley (Nottinghamshire), Wetely, 85, 205
Whithorn, Candidacasa, church and canons of, 8, 52n, 187, 188, 198
  prior of, 9
  priory of (Premonstratensian), 4
Widdrington (Northumberland), 205
Widdrington, John, 205, 206
  William, 128, 205
Wigglesmere (now Greenlee Lough, Northumberland), 227
William I, king of Scots (1165–1214), 3, 7, 15, 35, 38, 48n, 51n, 54n, 61, 89, 92, 134, 136, 152, 156, 157, 174, 194, 195
William, abbot of Arbroath, 154. W 137, 138
William, archdeacon of St Andrews, W 81; *see also* St Andrews, bishop of
William, bishop of Brechin *see* Comyn, William; Crachin, William
William, bishop of Dunblane, 154
William, bishop of St Andrews *see* Fraser, William; Malveisin, William; Wishart, William
William, chaplain, 23
William, clerk, 147
William, earl of Douglas (temp. David II), W 189
William, earl of Mar, 34, 62, 86–7, 211. W 65, 66, 67, 68, 70, 72, 77, 86, 87, 89, 90, 91, 92, 96, 97, 98, 100, 104, 105, 112, 125; *see also* Hay, William
William earl of Ross, 234
William, son of Orme, 206
William the chaplain, clerk, 23, 72. W 68
Williamston, villa Willelmi (now lost, in Culsalmond, Garioch), 81
Williamston (Tynedale), Wyllamestun', Williamiston', 76, 105, 106, 204, 225
Wilton [NT5015], barony of, 228, 229
Winchester, Winton', Wynton', earl of, 68, 69, 76, 77, 91, 140; *see also* Quincy, Roger.
Wischard, Robert, 185
Wishart, Whischard, Whischard', Wischard', Wissard, Wyscard', Wyschard', 74
  John, 72, 74
  Robert, 121, 122, 141, 151, 166, 167. W 147, 152, 153
  William, Master, 27, 28, 54n, 72, 74, 86, 143, 149, 166, 167, 168, 170, 171, 224. W 57, 61, 65, 81, 147, 193
Wiston, Henry, 210
Wiston and Roberton, parish of (Lanarkshire), 210
Woodflat [NO3316], Woddeflatter (now lost, in Monimail parish), 18, 228
Woolmet [NT3169], Wymeth, 133, 135
Wrangham [NJ6331], 81
Wymes *see* Wemyss
Wymeth *see* Woolmet
Wyntoun, Andrew, 19
Wyppot, Willam, 117
Wyrfaut, Roger, 58
Wysman, William *alias* William Seliman, 215

Ybernia *see* Ireland
Yhetland *see* Shetland
Yolande, mother of William Mortagne, 172
York (England), act dated at, 201
  men of, 221
Yorkshire, Ebor', 151
Yssabiel *see* Isabelle

Zouche, Zuche, Helen, 140, 141

INDEX OF SUBJECTS

abbeys, 8, 18, 20, 21, 24, 28, 35, 53n, 67, 87, 88, 94, 95, 98, 117, 125, 133, 134, 146, 154, 155, 184, 199, 200, 201, 202, 203, 214, 216, 221, 224, 229, 232, 234
abbots, 4, 9, 24, 28, 29, 31, 35, 57, 58, 61, 62, 65, 66, 67, 68, 70, 72, 81, 88, 91, 94, 95, 96, 98, 99, 106, 107, 108–9, 114, 115, 125 126, 133, 134, 135, 136, 137, 138, 154, 155, 165, 179, 188, 196, 197, 199, 200, 203, 204, 213, 214, 221, 223, 230, 234
accounts, 15, 29, 36, 108, 180, 190, 209, 210, 211, 212, 213, 218, 232
accusations (*calumpniae*), 104, 130, 134, 135, 136, 179, 186, 215
acre(s), 59, 60, 63, 134, 137, 141, 206, 214, 215 216; *see also iugum*
administration, royal, 4, 11, 18, 19, 20, 28, 29, 30, 34, 35, 215
advowson(s), 8, 61, 100, 112, 178, 187, 232
agister, 120
aid(s), 120, 121, 124, 125, 129, 172, 178, 179, 191, 192, 197, 200, 235
allowances, 10
alms, 86, 137, 156, 182, 222; *see also* alms (*in elemosina*), tenure in
alms (*elemosina*), tenure in, 59, 60, 66, 67, 88, 91, 92, 94, 95, 97, 106, 107, 113, 117, 118, 126, 136, 137, 138, 141, 147, 150, 151, 156, 182, 183, 184, 185, 187, 196, 197, 198, 200, 203, 232
altars, 133, 134, 135, 136, 181, 234
amends, 18, 71, 112, 173
amercements, 99, 122, 123, 182, 183, 210, 212
animals, 7, 92, 93, 135; *see also* beasts; livestock
annuities, 10, 29
anointing, 30
appanage, 19
appurtenances *see* pertinents
arable, 206, 215, 216
archbishop(s), 146, 221
archers, 206
archives, 9, 15, 16, 19, 20, 21, 22, 29, 39, 54n, 142, 176, 209, 226
arms, royal, 30, 32
armour, 17
army, 173, 199, 200, 209
arrears, 172, 223
arrest, 127, 131, 183, 184
assigns, 59, 69, 76, 100, 102, 103, 106, 109, 121, 144, 149, 162, 163
assizes, 57, 120
attestation (bear witness, witnessing), 2, 5, 7, 11, 12, 13, 14, 57, 59, 60, 61, 62, 63, 64, 65, 66, 77, 79, 81, 87, 88, 91, 92, 93, 95, 99, 107, 108, 109, 113, 117, 118, 132, 138, 141, 149, 151, 168, 193, 203, 208, 214, 229, 235
attestor(s), 4, 8, 81; *see also* witnesses
attorneys, 4, 17, 65, 89, 115, 122, 178, 188, 207, 216
authentication, 12, 19, 20, 30–1, 32, 54n, 90, 188, 198
authenticity, 20, 21, 22, 51n, 89, 92, 134, 136, 186, 191, 196, 234

bailiaries, 65, 90, 110, 114, 186, 188
bailies, bailiffs, 10, 11, 18, 58, 64, 65, 72, 73, 77, 78, 83, 85, 86, 90, 91, 101, 102, 110, 111, 113, 114, 115, 116, 119, 120, 122, 123, 127, 128, 130, 140, 141, 148, 154, 173, 178, 179, 181, 182, 186, 188, 196, 199, 200, 201, 204, 206, 213, 214, 218, 219, 220, 221, 222, 223, 225, 228, 229
baker, 156, 223
barley, 186
barons, 12, 13, 38, 71, 72, 73, 74, 100, 101, 102, 104, 127, 133, 134, 160, 165, 166, 167, 168, 194, 195, 203; *see also* magnates
barony, 68, 69, 115, 116, 121, 122, 195, 198, 228, 229
  tenure in, 86, 87, 96, 115, 116, 152, 153, 194, 195, 217
bastardy, 195
beasts, 93, 133, 135
benefice(s), 27, 38, 112, 154
bequest, 226
bere, 232
Berne Manuscript, 49n
Bible, 25, 30, 103, 160, 164
bishop(s), 4, 8, 9, 20, 26, 27, 28, 31, 37, 51n, 57, 61, 62, 64, 65, 66, 68, 69, 70, 71, 72, 73, 78, 87, 89, 91, 92, 97, 98, 100, 101, 102, 104, 106, 121, 122, 125, 131, 133, 134, 136, 138, 140, 141, 143, 145, 147, 149, 151,

152, 153, 154, 157, 160, 166, 167, 168, 170, 171, 176, 186, 189, 201, 202, 209, 210, 212, 214, 216, 218, 220, 221, 224, 232, 234, 235
bishopric(s), 20, 27, 71, 100, 112, 134, 195, 196, 218; *see also* see(s), episcopal
blenche ferme, 212
boat(s), 89, 230; *see also* ferry; ship(s)
bond(s), 201, 231
bondmen, 63, 122, 134, 136; *see also* serfs
border, Anglo-Scottish, 17, 124, 131, 140, 144, 217, 230; *see also* marches, Anglo-Scottish
boundaries, 57, 59, 60, 61, 63, 64, 69, 76, 77, 87, 89, 99, 105, 106, 107, 108, 118, 135, 136, 137, 144, 151, 152, 185, 192, 193, 194, 202, 215; *see also* marches
bovate(s) *see* oxgang(s)
breach of peace, 10, 11, 101
bridge(s), 134, 136
brieves, 7, 9, 10–12, 15, 16, 24, 27, 70, 71, 77, 78, 80, 83, 85, 86, 108, 109, 110, 113, 114, 120, 182, 201, 202, 204, 206, 207, 208, 209, 210, 211, 212, 213, 214, 217, 219, 220, 222, 231, 234, 235
  of mortancestry, 11, 67, 202, 235
  of novel dissasine, 207, 214, 222
  of perambulation, 202, 207, 208
  of protection, 10–11, 24, 61, 74, 90, 93, 111, 114–15, 132, 155, 188, 200, 220; *see also* peace, king's; protection
  of right, 201, 235
brieve-charter, 10, 11, 16
broadcloth, 191, 192
bulls, papal, 15, 29, 37
burgesses, 7, 10, 18, 23, 24, 58, 77, 79, 80, 85, 86, 89, 109, 110, 117, 124, 132, 154, 155, 188, 189, 191, 192, 208, 210, 220, 221, 231, 235
burghs, 7, 29, 34, 35, 58, 62, 64, 65, 77, 89, 90, 98, 106, 107, 133, 135, 188, 189, 191, 192, 223, 230, 231, 235
burial, 134, 136
burn, 118, 142, 229; *see also* stream
butler, of Scotland, 189

cain, 106, 107, 133, 134, 135, 136
calendar(s), 1, 16, 40, 42, 43, 172
calumpniae *see* accusations
caparisons, 32
captain, 127
captions, 79, 80
caput, 115–16
carts, 92, 93
cartularies, 1, 21, 40, 41, 51n, 77, 119, 142, 154, 182; *see also* registers
carucate *see* ploughgate
castle(s), 15, 25, 68, 69, 72, 73, 83, 105, 133, 134, 135, 136, 157, 159, 161, 184, 185, 210, 211, 212, 220, 223, 228
cemetery, 231
ceremonies, 5, 7, 8, 16, 23, 32, 33, 34
chalders, 91, 92, 98, 156, 186, 232
chamber, king's, 125, 146, 147, 149, 158, 161, 180, 181, 196, 203, 222, 229, 231
chamberlain, of Berwick, 223
  of England, 208
  of Scotland, 27, 28, 60, 61, 62, 63, 64, 65, 66, 67, 68, 70, 71, 78, 80, 89, 90, 92, 96, 97, 98, 100, 105, 110, 124, 131, 146, 147, 157, 180, 181, 190, 193, 200, 211, 220, 222, 223, 224, 228, 230, 231
chancellor, of England, 187, 226
  of Norway, 100, 101, 102, 103, 104, 157, 160, 165
  of Scotland, 6, 15, 18, 23, 25, 26, 27, 28, 31, 33, 34, 35, 37, 81, 86, 131, 137, 147, 153, 189, 193
chancery, English, 3,5, 12, 13, 16, 17, 74, 140, 144, 201, 205, 214, 217, 218, 220, 221, 222, 223, 229
  Flemish, 5, 14, 25, 26, 52n
  French, 26
  of Melrose abbey, 24
  rolls of, 15, 16, 20, 28, 29, 37, 38, 74, 106, 140, 194, 195, 201, 202, 203, 204, 205, 208, 209, 214, 217, 218, 219, 220, 221, 222, 224, 225, 226, 228, 232
  Scottish, 3, 4, 5, 6, 7, 8, 9,10, 12, 13, 14, 15, 16, 17, 19, 20, 22–30, 33, 34, 36, 37, 119, 188, 195, 196, 208, 209, 235; *see also* chapel, royal; writing office
chapel(s), 133, 134, 135, 138, 139, 198, 222
  royal, 3, 10, 15, 23, 24, 28, 29, 80, 106, 107, 110, 114, 174, 194, 195; *see also* chancery, Scottish; writing office
chaplain(s), 23, 68, 72, 138, 139, 170, 182, 209, 214, 222
chapters, cathedral, 65, 138, 139, 141, 142, 195, 196, 207, 216, 226, 234
charter(s), 1, 3, 4, 5, 6, 7, 8, 9, 10, 11, 15, 16, 19, 20, 21, 22, 23, 24, 27, 29, 34, 35, 37, 38, 41, 48n, 51n, 52n, 57, 58, 59, 60, 61, 62, 63, 64, 65, 66, 67, 68, 69, 71, 75, 76, 77, 79, 80, 81, 86, 87, 88, 89, 90, 91, 92, 94, 95, 96, 97, 98, 99, 105, 106, 107, 108, 109, 110, 111, 113, 117, 118, 119, 120, 121, 124, 125, 126,

127, 128, 130, 131, 132, 134, 137, 138, 139, 141, 142, 144, 146, 147, 149, 150, 151, 152, 153, 154, 155, 156, 157, 160, 174, 182, 183, 184, 185, 186, 187, 189, 190, 191, 192, 193, 194, 195, 196, 197, 198, 199, 200, 201, 203, 205, 206, 207, 211, 213, 214, 215, 217, 219, 220, 221, 222, 223, 224, 225, 226, 227, 228, 229, 230, 231, 232, 234, 235; *see also* instruments; muniments; writ-charters

chiefs of kindred, 130; *see also kenkynoll*

children, 23, 54n, 75, 115, 116, 131, 148, 149, 150, 151, 153, 157, 158, 161, 162, 163, 165, 166, 167, 184, 185, 196, 224

chirograph, 14, 104, 160, 164, 165

Christmas, 16, 122, 125

chroniclers, 19, 53n, 209, 212, 221

chronicles, 19, 53n, 221

church(es), 8, 27, 61, 62, 63, 66, 71, 77, 91, 92, 100, 101, 102, 103, 126, 133, 134, 135, 138, 139, 141, 150, 178, 181, 182, 187, 195, 196, 198, 199, 209, 217, 232, 234

  presentation to, 27, 138, 181, 195, 196, 209, 232

churchyard, 126

clauses, 3, 5, 10, 11, 13, 14, 25, 26, 87, 142

  dating, 3, 5, 12, 14, 20, 34, 35, 40, 42, 71, 235; *see also* place names

  dispositive, 7, 8, 9, 10, 11, 40, 47n, 193

  holding, tenurial, 8, 21, 128

  narrative, 8

  of address, 3, 4, 8, 22, 188 ; *see also fideli homines*; *probi homines*

  of invocation, 8

  of notification, 3, 4, 14, 25, 26

  of salutation, 3

  sealing, 13, 14, 26; *see also* authentication

  testing, of attestation, 4, 5, 7, 11, 12, 13, 14, 20, 42, 48n, 193; *see also* witness lists

  see also attestation; royal style

Clerk of the Rolls, 28, 29, 37

clerk(s), 3, 4, 5, 13, 20, 23, 27, 28, 29, 37, 42, 68, 74, 81, 82, 87, 119, 121, 131, 133, 144, 145, 146, 147, 151, 153, 180, 181, 185, 195, 196, 197, 201, 205, 206, 207, 210, 212, 214, 217, 218, 220, 221, 222, 223, 234; *see also* scribes

close rolls, English, 16

cloth, 18, 156, 182, 191, 192, 212

clothing, 211, 212; *see also* robes

coffer(s), 15, 37

collation, 138; *see also* presentation

collector of fermes, 64

  of fifteenth, 197

colloquium, 34, 203, 204; *see also* parliament, Scottish

commodities, 197

common law, English, 151

  Scottish, 11, 92, 93; *see also* law, of Scotland

common pasture, 58, 59, 85, 86, 174, 192, 223; *see also* pasture

commonty, 111, 191, 192, 205, 206, 216, 223

compensation, 154, 168, 169, 217, 220, 230

composition, 215; *see also* concord

concord, 14, 24, 71, 76, 100, 106, 201, 204, 206, 214, 223; *see also* convention

confirmations, 3, 7, 8–10, 15, 16, 18–19, 21, 23, 24, 26, 27, 29, 31, 38, 41, 51n, 52n, 57, 58, 59, 60, 61, 62, 63, 64, 65, 66, 67, 68, 69, 70, 71, 76, 77, 79, 80, 81, 85, 86, 87, 88, 89, 91, 92, 94, 95, 96, 97, 98, 99, 104, 105, 106, 107, 108, 109, 110, 113, 117, 121, 124, 125, 126, 127, 128, 130, 132, 133, 134, 136, 137, 138, 139, 140, 141, 142, 144, 146, 149, 150, 151, 152, 153, 154, 155, 156, 161, 166, 170, 172, 182, 183, 184, 185, 186, 187, 189, 190, 191, 192, 193, 194, 196, 197, 198, 199, 200, 201, 203, 204, 206, 207, 208, 213, 214, 216, 220, 222, 225, 228, 230, 232, 233, 234, 235

constable, of Berwick, 207

  of Edinburgh castle, 147, 184, 223

  of Scotland, 76, 77, 91, 126, 139, 155, 159, 164, 172, 186, 190, 192

convent(s), 11, 57, 61, 62, 65, 66, 67, 68, 70, 77, 81, 91, 94, 95, 96, 98, 99, 108, 109, 114, 115, 125, 126, 130, 154, 155, 188, 197, 199, 200, 224, 230

convention, 123, 160, 181, 197, 199; *see also* concord

conversi, 155

conveyance, 3, 5, 6, 8, 10, 15, 16, 23, 29, 34, 47n

corn, 88, 98, 122, 156, 174

coronation, 30, 31, 32, 157, 160, 205, 214, 217, 218, 220, 221, 222

coroner, 120

correspondence, 7, 11, 17, 37

cottars, 60, 63, 222

council, royal, of England, 122–3

  of Scotland, 5, 7, 10, 12, 13, 19, 27, 34, 57, 67, 68, 71, 72, 73, 74, 86, 87, 112, 136, 137, 145, 147, 157, 159, 160, 164, 165, 166, 167, 168, 180, 181, 185, 195, 202, 203

count(s), 12, 14, 25, 112, 165, 166, 167, 168, 169, 170, 171, 172, 175, 176, 177, 213, 226
countess, 108
court, royal, of England, 16, 27, 85, 128, 149, 150, 218
 of Scotland, 4, 9, 10, 11, 23, 28, 29, 34, 35, 134, 136
 of the count of Flanders, 26
court(s), 10
 burgh, 235
 county, 121, 122, 128
 justiciar's, 24, 207
 of King's Bench, 17
 of the abbot of Dunfermline, 134, 135
 of the earl of Lennox, 217
 of the prior of Coldingham, 201
 sheriff, 203, 217
 see also suit of court
cows, 212
croft(s), 134, 136
crops, 133, 135
crown pleas, 29, 133, 215
crusade, 224
cumelahe, 135; *see also* serfs
customs (*consuetudines*) 4, 8, 10, 13, 14, 16, 25, 26, 27, 40, 57, 64, 79, 80, 81, 89, 90, 92, 93, 100, 102, 104, 116, 119, 121, 122, 124, 128, 133, 137, 139, 141, 144, 151, 152, 156, 158, 161, 162, 165, 166, 179, 182, 186, 191, 193, 200, 203, 216, 217, 218, 229, 232; *see also* laws; usages
customs (imposts), 89, 182, 234

damage(s), 101, 102, 140, 158, 159, 160, 162, 163, 164, 230
dean(s), 65, 75, 168, 170, 195, 209, 234
debts, 11, 12, 58, 65, 70, 73, 75, 83, 90, 114, 115, 132, 172, 180, 181, 188, 206, 210, 219, 221, 227, 230
deer, 133, 135
default of service, 8, 34, 86, 96, 185
demesne, 63, 88, 89, 97, 99, 100, 102, 120, 121, 133, 134, 135, 137, 141, 224, 225
diploma(s), 5, 8
diplomacy, 11, 14, 15, 23, 37, 124, 165
diplomatics, 1, 3–6, 7, 8, 12, 15, 17, 25, 26, 37, 188
dispute(s), 17, 21, 27, 33, 112, 115, 121, 124, 202, 206, 213, 214, 217, 222
dissasine, 11, 207
disseisin, 19, 206, 214, 222, 224
distraint, 58, 123
 of knighthood, 78
divine office, 181, 187; *see also* mass
donation, 18; *see also* gift(s)
doorkeeper (*janitor*), 83
dower, 10, 85, 158, 204, 205
dowry, 19, 82, 83, 157, 158, 159, 160, 161, 162, 163, 164, 165, 168, 170, 171, 172, 175, 176, 177, 201, 208; *see also* tocher
drengage, 19
dwelling(s), 133, 135; *see also* house(s)

earl(s), 4, 12, 19, 21, 24, 34, 51n, 60, 61, 62, 63, 65, 66, 67, 68, 69, 70, 72, 73, 74, 75, 76, 77, 78, 79, 80, 81, 86, 87, 88, 89, 90, 91, 92, 95, 96, 97, 98, 99, 100, 101, 103, 104, 105, 106, 107, 108, 111, 113, 114, 116, 118, 119, 120, 121, 125, 126, 128, 130, 132, 134, 139, 140, 141, 143, 144, 147, 149, 150, 151, 152, 153, 154, 155, 159, 164, 166, 170, 172, 173, 183, 185, 186, 188, 189, 190, 191, 192, 193, 194, 195, 196, 201, 202, 203, 209, 210, 211, 212, 213, 217, 223, 225, 229, 234
easements, 59, 60, 61, 63, 64, 107, 108, 109, 113, 117, 126, 138, 141, 144, 153, 155, 185, 192, 194, 198
Easter, 91, 92, 148, 201, 208, 234, 235
embassies, 26, 27
encroachments, 36, 124, 217, 220
endorsement(s), 25, 40, 42, 58, 63, 64, 65, 66, 70, 75, 76, 77, 82, 87, 93, 94, 95, 96, 97, 99, 106, 107, 108, 111, 112, 113, 118, 120, 121, 124, 131, 132, 142, 150, 154, 157, 165, 168, 169, 171, 175, 176, 177, 178, 185, 191
English language, 40, 41
engrossment, 13, 15, 19, 29, 51n
enthronement, 66, 202
entry, 57, 87, 224
envoys, 17, 25, 26, 27, 37, 75, 88, 89, 100, 101, 103, 122, 123, 129, 131, 134, 136, 139, 140, 142, 143, 144, 145, 146, 147, 148, 149, 150, 151, 152, 157, 158, 159, 160, 162, 164, 165, 177, 178, 179, 184, 189, 204, 206, 210, 212; *see also* messengers
escheator, 120, 205, 216, 219, 222, 231
escheats, 81, 97, 99, 122, 197, 232
estovers, 196, 205
estreat, 224, 225
exchange (*excambium*) 29, 60, 81, 137, 193, 194, 218, 229, 231, 235
exchequer, English, 16, 208, 218
 Scottish, 15, 17, 20, 29, 36, 37, 108, 209, 210, 211, 212, 213, 229
executor(s), 227
exit, 57, 87, 88
expenses, 158, 159, 162, 163, 212, 218
extent(s), 20, 66, 83, 119, 120, 205, 206, 219, 231, 232
eyre, 16, 19, 50n, 76, 112, 119, 121, 128,

131, 204, 205, 206, 215, 216, 222, 224, 225, 226, 232

fairs, 79, 80, 82, 124, 144, 208, 212, 230; *see also* market
familia see household
falcons, 36, 183
fat, 133, 134, 135, 136
fee (land), 76, 105, 204; *see also* feu
fee (money), 209, 218, 219, 222, 228, 229, 230, 231
fence(s), 111
fermers, 65, 88, 89, 92, 97, 98, 110, 157, 230
fermes, farms, 29, 49n, 62, 63, 64, 65, 71, 85, 92, 97, 98, 106, 107, 117, 119, 120, 133, 134, 136, 154, 156, 157, 161, 186, 196, 199, 205, 212, 219, 223, 224, 225, 228, 229, 234, 235
ferry, 134, 136; *see also* boat(s); ship(s)
ferryman, 230
feu, 60, 61, 66, 67, 79, 86, 92, 132, 137, 207
feu and heritage, tenure in, 57, 59, 60, 61, 63, 68, 69, 86, 87, 96, 97, 107, 108, 118, 119, 130, 144, 152, 153, 162, 163, 174, 185, 193, 194, 195
feudal incidents, 121
feuferme, 109, 117, 205
fideli homines, 72, 75, 77, 78, 80, 83, 84, 86, 87, 97, 110, 111, 114, 116, 119, 120, 121, 122, 124, 127, 129, 131, 139, 142, 143, 145, 146, 149, 151, 153, 180, 181, 187, 189, 193, 196, 199
fifteenth, tax of, 179, 197–8
final agreement, 157, 160; *see also* concord
fine(s), 99, 122–3, 159, 182, 183, 203, 211, 212, 213, 224, 225; *see also* amercements
fire, 133, 135
fish, 133, 135
fish net(s), 133, 135, 196, 197
fishery, 57, 87, 88, 126, 133–6, 196, 197
fishpond, 57, 58
forest, 10, 16, 21, 33, 36, 61, 62, 66, 86, 87, 95, 96, 111, 118, 119, 120, 121, 122, 123, 124, 130, 133, 135, 136, 193, 205, 212, 216, 217, 220, 224; *see also* park(s); wood(s)
forester(s), 71, 73, 120, 205, 206
forfeiture, 11, 48n, 49n, 58, 61, 62, 64, 65, 70, 74, 75, 79, 80, 86, 87, 89, 90, 91, 92, 93, 95, 96, 99, 100, 102, 111, 114, 115, 118, 119, 130, 132, 134, 135, 136, 155, 168, 188, 191, 192, 195, 200
forgeries *see* spurious acts
forinsec service, 137, 146–7, 174, 185, 200, 235; *see also* military service
formularies, 10, 11, 49n, 207
franchise(s), 27, 112
free warren 121, 130, 131, 225
French language, 4, 14, 25, 26, 27, 42, 51n, 52n, 112, 166, 167, 168, 169, 170, 171, 172, 175, 176, 177, 178
friars, 62, 65, 98, 100, 126, 157, 186, 207, 231, 232, 234
friend(s), 19, 27, 88, 101, 112, 142, 145, 174, 177, 179
friendship, 12, 102, 139, 140, 143, 145, 177, 179, 215, 223
fugitives, 11, 99–100, 101, 133, 134, 135
fur, 212

Gaelic language, 58, 108, 119, 189–90
gallows, 86, 87, 96, 97, 128, 152, 153, 194, 195, 217; *see also* pit and gallows
garden, 80
gauge, 18
gift(s), 3, 7, 8, 9, 17, 18, 20, 23, 27, 34, 36, 41, 49n, 52n, 57, 58, 59, 60, 62, 63, 64, 66, 68, 70, 71, 76, 77, 79, 81, 87, 88, 91, 94, 99, 105, 107, 108, 109, 113, 117, 125, 127, 130, 132, 133, 134, 135, 136, 137, 138, 141, 149, 150, 154, 157, 158, 161, 169, 185, 187, 190, 191, 193, 198, 200, 201, 205, 206, 211, 213, 214, 216, 218, 219, 222, 224, 225, 226, 228, 229, 230, 231, 232, 233
gloves, 120, 121
gold, 133, 135
goldsmith, 176
goods, 65, 100, 101, 102, 110, 127, 128, 136, 154, 155, 158, 162, 173, 191, 192, 193, 221, 224, 231
  immovable, 90, 93, 110, 111, 114, 132, 155, 188
  movable, 90, 93, 110, 111, 114, 132, 155, 188
  see also possessions
gospels *see* Bible
grain, 137, 156, 186, 232
grange, 212
grooms, 206
guild, 23, 109, 110

hand, chancery, 24
hand, court, 24
hands, scribal, 22–5, 32, 37, 40, 42, 51n, 58, 61, 62, 63, 64, 65, 66, 70, 71, 74, 75, 76, 77, 78, 79, 80, 82, 83, 84, 85, 86, 87, 91, 93, 94, 95, 96, 97, 98, 99, 104, 105, 106, 107, 108, 109, 110, 111, 112, 113, 117, 118, 120, 121, 124, 126, 127, 129, 130, 131, 132, 139, 140, 141, 143, 145, 146, 147, 148, 149, 150, 152, 153, 157, 165, 168, 169, 170, 171, 172,

173, 174, 175, 176, 177, 178, 179, 180, 181, 183, 184, 187, 189, 190, 191, 198
harm, 61, 74, 90, 92, 93, 104, 114, 125, 132, 148, 151, 155, 173, 188, 191, 192, 200; *see also* injury
harness, 17
heirs, heiresses, 4, 14, 19, 67, 68, 72, 73, 83, 86, 87, 94, 95, 96, 97, 100, 101, 102, 103, 105, 108, 109, 112, 114, 115, 116, 118, 119, 121, 130, 140, 141, 146, 148, 157–63, 165, 166, 167, 168, 169, 170, 171, 174, 175, 176, 179–80, 181, 184, 187, 195, 197, 202, 205, 215, 218, 223, 224, 226, 228, 230, 232, 235
heraldic devices, 30–4, 58, 66, 171, 176, 182; *see also* seal (*sigillus*)
herbage, 120, 121
heritable tenure, 85, 86, 102, 112, 116, 138, 140, 146, 148, 174, 190, 223
hides, 133, 134, 135, 136, 191, 192
highway, king's, 126, 191, 192
holding clause, 8, 57, 59, 60, 61, 62, 63, 64, 66, 68, 69, 76, 77, 79, 80, 81, 86, 87, 88, 91, 94, 95, 96, 97, 99, 100, 102, 105, 106, 107, 108, 109, 113, 117, 118, 119, 120, 121, 128, 130, 132, 135, 137, 138, 139, 141, 144, 146, 147, 149, 150, 151, 152, 153, 154, 155, 156, 159, 161, 174, 182, 184, 185, 187, 189, 190, 193, 194, 196, 197, 198, 199, 206, 217, 219, 223, 227, 228
Holy Trinity and Captives, order of, 117, 118
homage, 10, 33, 100, 102, 131, 174, 223
homage and service tenure, 57, 63, 64, 76, 77, 87, 96, 97, 106, 144, 152, 153, 194, 195, 206
homicide, 186, 215
horse, 32; *see also* mares
hospices, 78
hospital, 11, 88, 89, 91, 92, 98, 99, 118, 121, 182, 186, 203, 210, 217
hospitality, 10, 105; *see also* wayting
hostages, 101, 104, 160, 164
hounds, 206
house(s), 18, 35, 205; *see also* dwelling(s); religious house(s)
household, 24, 28, 30, 37, 63, 156, 174
  royal, 6, 17, 18, 19, 21, 23, 27, 157, 158
hunting, 7, 36, 62, 86, 95, 96, 118, 130
huntsman, 194
hybrid instruments, 5, 7, 10, 11

improvement of burghs, 80, 109, 110, 188, 189
inauguration, 33, 35, 200
indenture(s), 12, 25, 50n
indictment, 213
infangentheof, 86, 87, 96, 97 152, 153, 194, 195
infeftment, 5, 7, 8, 10, 15, 34, 68, 69, 137, 152, 174, 203, 214, 233
inheritance, 9, 18, 100, 166, 187, 222
injury, 61, 74, 90, 92, 93, 100, 101, 102, 111, 114, 132, 140, 151, 155, 168, 169, 173, 188, 200, 215, 225; *see also* harm
inquest(s), 10, 18, 19, 20, 29, 66, 77, 78, 80, 83, 85, 86, 108, 110, 113, 114, 120, 121, 122, 125, 128, 140, 187, 196, 200, 201, 202, 203, 204, 205, 206, 207, 208, 209, 210, 213, 215, 216, 217, 223, 226, 227, 228, 229, 230, 232
inquisition(s) *post mortem*, 83, 125, 205, 226
insignia, royal, 30, 32, 171, 176
inspeximus, 90, 92, 119, 154, 186, 232
instruments, 3, 5, 8, 10, 11, 15, 16, 24, 35, 48n, 74, 92, 93, 139, 147, 159, 162, 163, 227; *see also* letters; muniments
interest(s), landed, 19, 85, 165, 205
interest (money), 159, 162, 163, 164
inventories of muniments, 15, 16, 19, 20, 25, 28, 29, 37–9, 50n, 205, 214, 215, 216, 218, 219, 220, 223, 226, 228
iron, 133, 135
islands, 19, 100, 101, 102, 103, 104, 105, 126, 155, 156, 157, 158, 159, 160, 161, 162, 163, 172, 198, 199, 207, 211, 212, 213, 214, 221, 222, 223, 235
itinerant justices, 76, 106, 119, 123, 151, 232; *see also* eyre; justices, English
iugum, 134, 136, 137

jewels, jewellery, 15
juries, jurors, 115, 116, 120, 131, 203, 206, 210, 215, 229, 232
justices (English), 16, 19, 76, 106, 119–20, 121, 122, 123, 128, 131, 151, 178, 204, 205, 206, 214, 215, 222, 226, 232
justiciar(s) (Scottish), 11, 24, 29, 41, 89, 90, 110, 111, 114, 115, 128, 188, 200, 213
  of Galloway, 94, 221
  of Lothian, 76, 77, 92, 94, 95, 100, 107, 109, 112, 113, 125, 155, 156, 159, 164, 182, 189, 207, 212
  of Scotia, 11, 58, 63, 68, 70, 71, 77, 79, 80, 86, 87, 89, 90, 96, 97, 99, 105, 112, 121, 125, 126, 155, 172, 186, 190, 192, 193, 196, 202, 203, 207, 209, 212

Keeper of the Rolls, 15, 20, 226
kenkynoll, 130
kindred, 130, 217
King's Bench, 17
kitchens, royal, 137
knight service *see* military service
knighthood, 78
knighting, 16, 194, 229
knights, 4, 10, 23, 24, 32, 52n, 64, 65, 66, 76, 77, 78, 83, 86, 87, 89, 96, 97, 98, 105, 106, 107, 108, 109, 117, 118, 121, 122, 127, 128, 137, 138, 141, 142, 144, 145, 146, 148, 149, 151, 152, 153, 156, 159, 164, 166, 167, 170, 171, 173, 174, 177, 178, 179, 182, 184, 185, 186, 187, 188, 189, 190, 191, 192, 193, 194, 195, 197, 201, 202, 203, 204, 205, 207, 210, 214, 216, 217, 221, 222, 223, 224, 226, 228, 229, 231, 232

labour services, 134, 136
laboureres, 11
lambs, 134, 136
Latin language, 14, 26, 27, 30, 41, 76, 106, 125, 128, 165, 182, 205, 207, 211, 225
law(s), canon, 27, 221
  civilian, 14–15
  of England, 115, 140, 151, 205, 206, 220, 224
  of Norway, 158, 161, 162
  of Scotland, 3, 8, 9, 10, 11, 16, 57, 71, 72, 85, 92, 93, 99, 100, 102, 110, 112, 128, 140, 141, 158, 161, 162, 165, 166, 167, 168, 200, 215, 225
  of the forest, 16
  of the marches, 12, 139
  see also assizes; customs; usages
lawyer(s), 10
legend (sigillographic), 30, 31, 32, 33, 93, 94, 96, 171, 176
legislation, 11
letters (missives), 10, 11, 12, 13, 14, 15, 17, 18, 23, 24, 25, 26, 27, 33, 37, 38–9, 54n, 57, 65, 67, 71, 72, 74, 82, 83, 84, 90, 92, 103, 105, 114, 115, 116, 117, 120, 124, 127, 128, 129, 131, 132, 139, 140, 141, 142, 143, 144, 145, 149, 150, 151, 161, 166, 172, 173, 175, 176, 177, 178, 179, 180, 181, 186, 187, 194, 196, 198, 200, 201, 202, 203, 204, 206, 207, 208, 209, 210, 211, 212, 213, 215, 216, 218, 219, 221, 222, 223, 224, 225, 226, 227, 231, 235
  close, 7, 13, 24, 123, 124
  judicial, 10–11
  of accreditation, 210
  of credence, 143, 204
  of mortancestry, 67, 202
  of outlawry, 215
  of presentation, 209, 232
  of protection, 74, 93, 132
  of quittance, 101, 102
  of receipt, 101, 176
  of remission, 210, 212, 213
  of respite, 213
  of safe conduct, 190, 210, 212
  patent, 7, 13, 14, 15, 16, 42n, 49n, 51n, 65, 74, 79, 82, 89, 91, 92, 97, 105, 107, 111, 115, 116, 120, 125, 144, 154, 157, 164, 189, 194, 196, 207, 208, 211, 218, 219, 230
liberate rolls, English, 208
liberties (freedoms), 79, 59, 60, 61, 63, 64, 80, 89, 90, 94, 95, 97, 98, 99, 100, 104, 107, 108, 109, 113, 116, 117, 118, 120, 124, 126, 136, 138, 139, 141, 143, 144, 150, 153, 155, 179, 182, 185, 187, 191, 192, 193, 197, 198, 200, 234
liberty (franchise), 62, 96, 102, 115, 116, 129, 178, 179, 197, 204, 214, 219, 225
licence, 7, 8, 38, 41, 57, 62, 77, 86, 87, 89, 95, 96, 118, 119, 130, 155, 164, 207
liege men, 18, 100, 102, 127, 146
lieutenant of Scotland, 219, 222, 230
lighting of altars, churches, 62, 134, 136, 234
litigation, 8, 9, 10, 15, 29, 85, 124, 206, 213, 215
livery, 147
livestock, 133, 135; *see also* animals; beasts
lodgings, 78
lost acts, 1, 6, 16–20, 43, 201–33

magnates, 5, 9, 13, 14, 31, 34, 57, 67, 71, 72, 73, 75, 86, 100, 112, 129, 159, 160, 161, 162, 163, 164, 168, 185, 204, 210; *see also* barons
malt, 98, 133, 135, 137, 186
manor(s), 35, 76, 78, 80, 105, 115, 116, 117, 118, 122, 123, 154, 160, 161, 170, 171, 196, 197, 198, 203, 204, 205, 206, 209, 215, 216, 218, 223, 225, 227, 229, 235
mantle, 32, 33
marches, 87, 88, 108, 202; *see also* boundaries
  Anglo-Scottish, 72, 80, 139, 140, 148
mares, 134, 135, 136
market, 3, 98, 124, 188, 189; *see also* fair
marquis, 165, 166, 169, 170, 175, 176
marriage, 3, 11, 13, 14, 16, 17, 19, 21, 25, 26, 37, 38, 82, 97, 105, 120, 121, 126, 157–65, 165–72, 175–6, 199, 201, 204, 208, 214, 225, 226
marshal, of England, 74

marshes, 69, 87, 95, 152, 192, 194
mason, 134, 136
mass, 181, 182, 184, 185; *see also* divine office
meadow(s), 65, 66, 69, 87, 93, 95, 119, 120, 134, 135, 136, 152, 153, 174, 194, 215
memoranda, 17, 74, 203, 208, 217, 219, 224, 225
merchandise, 89, 155, 191, 192, 220
merchant(s), 17, 109, 128, 177, 180, 181, 183, 184, 191, 192, 218, 219, 220, 221, 227, 231
mercy, royal, 16, 21, 72, 101, 104
merklands, 149, 160, 161
merks, 17, 38, 67, 68, 77, 82, 101, 102, 103, 105, 106, 107, 125, 157, 158, 159, 160, 161, 162, 163, 165, 170, 172, 196, 199, 201, 203, 208, 212, 213, 219, 221, 222, 228, 229, 230, 231, 232, 234, 235
messengers, 142, 179, 210; *see also* envoys
messuage, 77, 206, 214, 215
Michaelmas, 84, 170, 209, 223
military orders, 72, 138, 182, 183, 203, 210
military service, 8, 16, 34, 57, 59, 60, 61, 62, 63, 64, 65, 66, 68, 76, 77, 79, 81, 86, 87, 88, 96, 99, 100, 106, 107, 108, 113, 118, 121, 144, 152, 153, 172, 173, 185, 190, 193, 194, 195, 206, 216, 228; *see also* forinsec service
mill(s), 69, 87, 91, 92, 95, 127, 128, 133, 135, 152, 153, 154, 155, 156, 157, 174, 194, 199, 205, 219, 234
milldam, 207
miners, 173, 225
ministers, 89, 123, 140, 198, 207, 217, 220
miracle(s), 209
monasteries, 53n, 67, 68, 94, 98, 146, 154, 155, 187, 209
money, money rents, 22, 34, 49n, 69, 77, 78, 92, 102, 103, 109, 133, 134, 135, 136, 137, 152, 157, 158, 159, 160, 161, 162, 163, 164, 165, 168, 169, 170, 176, 177, 178, 181, 182, 193, 196, 199, 200, 201, 203, 205, 206, 207, 208, 209, 211, 212, 213, 218, 219, 221, 222, 223, 224, 225, 226, 227, 228, 229, 230, 231, 232, 233, 234, 235; *see also* gold; renders; rent(s); sterling silver
monks, 7, 8, 10, 21, 29, 60, 79, 87, 88, 92, 93, 94, 95, 99, 106, 107, 110, 111, 117, 134, 136, 137, 138, 146, 147, 154, 156, 157, 184, 185, 188, 193, 194, 196, 199, 200, 201, 202, 203, 216, 217, 224, 225, 227, 229, 232, 234
moot hill, 35
mormaership, 186
mort d'ancestor, 19
mortancestry *see* brieve(s), of mortancestry
moss, 85, 192, 208
muir(s), 59, 69, 76, 87, 95, 99, 133, 134, 152, 165, 174, 192, 194, 206, 214
multure, 156, 174, 232
muniments, vi, 21, 25, 28, 29, 38, 50n, 60, 71, 111, 128, 139, 142, 203, 205, 211, 212, 215, 216, 217, 219, 225, 226, 228, 229

negotiations, 20, 37, 38, 72, 74, 84, 129, 130, 139, 140, 145, 150, 172, 177, 181, 187, 199, 202, 215, 216
neyfs, 11, 86, 87, 99, 100; *see also* *cumelahe*, serfs
notarial deeds, 3, 58
notifications, 3, 4, 13–14, 25, 26, 106
notitiae, 15, 16, 18; *see also* lost acts
novel dissasine, 207
novel disseisin, 19, 214, 222, 224
nun(s), 10, 11, 63, 64, 65, 90, 113, 114, 203, 233, 234, 235
nunnery, 63
nuptials *see* marriage

oath(s), 26, 54n, 72, 73, 101, 103, 104, 120, 122, 159, 164, 166, 167, 168, 170, 171, 180, 181, 223
oatmeal, 91, 92, 137
oblations, 133, 135, 138; *see also* prayer(s)
officials, 4, 6, 10, 11, 19, 33, 36, 71, 83, 130, 140, 200
oxgang(s), 59, 60, 63, 141, 201
outlaw(s), 16, 215
oyer and terminer, 176, 215

parchment, 1, 7, 12, 13, 14, 22, 24, 33, 37, 40, 41, 51n, 64, 70, 83, 111, 113, 165, 168, 175, 176, 177, 178, 191
pardon, royal, 16, 112; *see also* mercy; remission
parish(es), 50n, 61, 67, 81, 108, 133, 135, 142, 197, 202, 210, 228
parish church, 126
park(s), 36, 193, 205, 220, 231
parliament, English, 17, 18, 50n, 165, 179, 198, 199, 216, 218, 219, 222, 223, 228, 229, 230, 233
  Scottish, 18, 21, 33, 172, 213, 231; *see also* colloquium
parson, 74
passage, legal right of, 93, 134, 136
pasture, 87, 92, 94, 95, 119, 120, 135, 141, 152, 153, 174, 194, 206, 224, 223, 224; *see also* common pasture
patent rolls, English, 16, 74, 143

paths, 95
patronage, 24, 149, 234
paupers, 154, 213, 225, 226
payments, 10, 11, 12, 14, 15, 26, 38, 67, 70, 71, 82, 83, 88, 98, 103, 105, 111, 125, 157, 158, 159, 161, 165, 168, 169, 172, 176, 177, 180, 181, 182, 184, 196, 199, 201, 203, 205, 208, 218, 219, 220, 222, 223, 228, 229, 230
peace, king's, 10, 11, 61, 74, 75, 90, 93, 100, 101, 102, 104, 111, 114, 116, 126, 132, 133, 134, 149, 155, 188, 191, 195, 229
peat moss, 85, 86, 192, 208
pension(s), 17, 101, 103, 104, 149, 229
Pentecost, feast of, 64, 65, 121, 125, 154, 157, 161, 181, 182, 185
perambulation, 16, 19, 115, 116, 117, 202, 207, 217
perpetual vicar(s), 138, 139
pertinents, 18, 57, 59, 60, 61, 63, 64, 67, 68, 69, 76, 80, 86, 87, 89, 91, 94, 95, 96, 97, 100, 102, 106, 107, 108, 109, 112, 113, 116, 117, 118, 119, 122, 123, 124, 132, 134, 135, 136, 138, 139, 141, 142, 144, 146, 149, 151, 152, 153, 154, 155, 156, 162, 163, 164, 174, 179, 184, 185, 187, 191, 193, 194, 195, 198, 222
petition(s), 12, 17, 18, 19, 50n, 71, 75, 116, 125, 148, 165, 196, 198, 199, 205, 206, 207, 214, 215, 216, 217, 218, 219, 220, 221, 222, 225, 227, 228, 229, 230, 233
pilgrim(s), 134, 136
pilgrimage, 16, 33, 78, 123, 124
piracy, 127, 159; *see also* plunder
pirates, 18, 128, 163
pit and gallows, 86, 87, 96, 97, 152, 153, 194, 217; *see also* gallows
pittance, 94, 184, 185
place dates *see* clauses, dating
place names, vi, 3, 34, 40, 70, 119, 142, 202, 214, 228
plains, 69, 95, 103, 152, 153, 194
plaints, 20
pleas, 20, 29, 75, 81, 99, 102, 112, 122, 123, 133, 135, 140, 178, 213, 215, 231; *see also* suit(s)
pledges, 58, 67, 68, 70, 75, 88, 90, 114, 115, 132, 159, 162, 164, 213
plough(s), 88, 89, 122
ploughgate(s), 60, 61, 109, 133, 135, 185
ploughland, 63
plunder, 18, 110, 128
plunderer(s), 101, 104
poind(s), poinding, 10, 11, 58, 70, 74, 75, 90, 114, 132, 133, 188, 191, 221
pond(s), 57, 58, 69, 87, 95, 152, 153, 194
pope(s), 19, 30, 31, 73, 101, 103, 166, 167, 168, 170, 171, 172, 202, 207, 216
possessions, 8, 9, 11, 17, 27, 61, 65, 71, 74, 90, 93, 110, 111, 114, 132, 133, 134, 182, 188, 200, 203, 223, 224, 234; *see also* goods
prayer(s), 33, 222
prebend, 27
prerogative(s), 16, 128, 131, 140, 214, 217, 220
presentation, 27, 98, 138, 139, 181, 182, 195, 209, 232
priest(s), 133, 135, 181
prince(s), 4, 13, 14, 17, 18, 19, 25, 26, 32, 38, 51n, 52n, 54n, 71, 72, 73, 75, 78, 81, 82, 83, 84, 85, 101, 115, 126, 127, 128, 129, 131, 139, 140, 142, 143, 145, 146, 147, 148, 149, 150, 151, 153, 160, 164, 165, 166, 168, 170, 171, 172, 173, 175, 178, 179, 180, 183, 184, 186, 189, 190, 197, 198, 199, 225
princess(es), 11, 16, 17, 19, 27, 37, 51n, 82, 105, 157, 226
prior(s), 4, 9, 93, 130, 137, 138, 154, 199, 201, 207, 213, 214, 215, 216, 224, 226, 227, 232
prioress, 233
priories, 4, 19, 35, 59, 60, 188, 198, 199, 207, 221, 234, 235
prises *see* captions
prison, 210, 215, 227
privilege(s), 7, 8, 9, 11, 17, 18, 20, 23, 28, 30, 31, 41, 71, 120, 124, 167, 191, 198, 202, 212, 216, 220, 226, 232, 234, 235
probi homines, *prudes homes*, 3, 4, 8, 57, 58, 59, 60, 61, 62, 63, 66, 67, 69, 70, 74, 76, 77, 78, 79, 80, 81, 83, 86, 88, 89, 90, 91, 92, 93, 94, 95, 96, 97, 98, 99, 105, 106, 107, 108, 109, 110, 113, 114, 115, 117, 118, 119, 121, 124, 125, 126, 128, 130, 132, 136, 137, 138, 141, 144, 146, 149, 151, 152, 153, 154, 155, 156, 174, 182, 184, 185, 188, 190, 192, 193, 194, 195, 196, 198, 199, 200
procurators, 107, 159, 160, 161, 162, 164, 165, 168, 170
profits, 70, 71, 81, 133, 135, 205, 206
prohibitions, 7, 10, 11, 61, 62, 70, 74, 80, 86, 87, 89, 91, 92, 93, 95, 96, 114, 118, 119, 130, 132, 135, 155, 188, 191, 192, 200
promise(s), 13, 72, 73, 82, 157, 158, 159, 160, 162, 163, 208, 216
protection, royal, 10, 24, 61, 74, 90, 93, 111, 114, 132, 134, 155, 188, 200, 220, 221
provender, 137, 147

provost(s), 11, 62, 64, 65, 74, 78, 89, 90, 98, 106, 110, 111, 114, 115, 188, 199, 204, 220

quatrefoils, 32
queens, 4, 12, 28, 38, 71, 72, 73, 75, 79, 80, 82, 84, 120, 121, 122, 123, 124, 133, 134, 135, 136, 137, 146, 148, 150, 151, 157, 159, 160, 161, 164, 179, 180, 189, 197, 202, 203, 207, 208, 209, 219, 222, 226
quitclaim, 5, 7, 28, 64, 67, 68, 86, 87, 96, 99, 100, 144, 146, 153, 156, 160, 184, 185, 194, 201, 203, 208, 209, 222, 223, 227, 228, 229; *see also* resignation of land

rams, 134, 136
ratification, 20, 72, 138, 139, 159, 161, 162, 163, 164, 165
recognisance, 215
recognitions, 20, 120
rectory, 232
refectory, 88
Reformation, Scottish, 142
regarder, 120
Register of the Great Seal, 127, 186, 195
registers, 4, 20, 71, 186, 188, 198, 199, 216; *see also* cartularies
registers of deeds, 21, 193
relics, 15, 209
relief, 120, 121
religious house(s), 35, 91, 100, 117, 122, 200
remission, 101, 104, 203, 210, 212, 213; *see also* mercy; pardon
render(s), 49
  in gloves, 120, 121
  in money, 109, 193, 206, 211; *see also* money rents
  in pepper, 144, 185
  in spurs, 230
  see also rent(s)
renders, military *see* forinsec service; military service
rent(s), 34, 65, 77, 102, 134, 136, 157, 159, 161, 163, 169, 170, 199, 205, 228, 230, 231, 233; *see also* render(s)
rental, 51n, 71, 216
resignation of land, 7, 34, 67, 86, 96, 100, 102, 103, 104, 144, 146, 153, 156, 174, 181, 184, 185, 194, 228, 235; *see also* quitclaim
reversion, 194, 195
revocation, 22
rights (jurisdictional), 10, 11, 19, 27, 33, 36, 41, 67, 70, 71, 74, 77, 80, 86, 89, 94, 98, 99, 100, 110, 112, 120, 124, 128, 130, 133, 135, 136, 137, 146, 147, 158, 159, 174, 178, 191, 195, 198, 210, 215, 216, 217, 222, 223, 227, 232
rivers, 20, 35, 57, 80, 87, 89, 94, 109, 126, 131, 140, 151, 190, 196, 209, 229, 230; *see also* waters
roads, 216, 235; *see also* highway
robes, 125, 223; *see also* clothing
rod, 8; *see also* staff and baton
rod of office, 30
rolls, 15, 172
  chancery, 15, 20, 28, 29, 37, 50n, 106, 194, 195, 201, 203, 204, 205, 208, 209, 214, 217, 218, 219, 220, 221, 222, 224, 225, 226, 232
  charter, 74
  exchequer, 15, 37, 224
  Great Seal, 228
  liberate, 208
  parliament, 17
  patent, 16, 74, 143, 202
roumfre, 232–3
royal style, 3
rubrics, rubrication, 40, 79, 93, 107, 138, 142, 188

safe conduct, 190, 210, 212
sake, 86, 87, 96, 152, 153, 194, 217
sailors, 155
sale, 9, 29, 65, 66, 182, 189, 235
salt, 133, 135
sasine, 71, 106, 139, 212; *see also* seisin
sceptre(s), 30, 32, 33, 182
schedules, 15, 74
'Scottish King's Household' (treatise), 6, 29–30, 33, 34, 52n
scribe(s), 3, 4, 5, 6, 7, 9, 10, 11, 12, 13, 14, 22, 23, 24, 25, 27, 32, 40, 41, 42, 51n, 52n, 58, 61, 63, 64, 65, 66, 70, 75, 76, 77, 78, 79, 80, 82, 83, 84, 85, 86, 87, 91, 93, 94, 95, 96, 97, 99, 105, 106, 107, 108, 109, 110, 111, 112, 113, 117, 118, 119, 120, 121, 124, 126, 127, 129, 130, 131, 132, 140, 141, 142, 143, 145, 146, 147, 148, 149, 150, 152, 153, 157, 165, 168, 170, 172, 173, 174, 175, 176, 177, 178, 179, 180, 181, 182, 183, 184, 187, 188, 189, 190, 191, 193, 197, 198
sea, 78, 88, 89, 100, 127, 128, 155, 165, 172, 195, 222
seal (*selichus*), 133, 135
seal (*sigillus*), great, of Scotland, 12, 13, 14, 26, 27, 31, 32, 33, 58, 61, 63, 64, 90, 93, 94, 96, 97, 110, 111, 112, 113, 118, 124, 131, 132, 147, 157, 168, 169, 171, 175, 176, 177, 178, 182, 228
  great, of England, 223
  of Alexander III, v, 9, 12, 13, 14, 19,

20, 25, 26, 27, 30–4, 35, 51n, 52n, 53n, 57, 58, 61, 63, 64, 66, 73, 75, 76, 77, 80, 83, 84, 87, 90, 91, 93, 94, 95, 96, 97, 99, 104, 105, 106, 107, 108, 109, 110, 111, 112, 113, 114, 117, 118, 120, 122, 123, 124, 129, 130, 131, 132, 140, 141, 143, 145, 146, 147, 149, 150, 152, 156, 157, 165, 168, 169, 171, 173, 174, 175, 176, 177, 178, 179, 180, 181, 182, 188, 189, 191, 193, 195, 198, 223, 224, 225, 228
of Prince Alexander, 14, 26, 52n, 171, 175, 176, 198, 199
of others, 25, 26, 33, 34, 78, 86, 104, 109, 110, 114, 165, 168, 176, 194
of the king of England, 223
personal, 12
privy, 12, 30–1, 33–4, 53n, 123, 124, 147, 171
secret, 30, 33, 147, 171
small, 12, 26, 30–2, 33, 53n, 58, 66, 76
seal cast(s), 53n, 171, 176
seal fragments, 12, 32, 51n, 58, 61, 63, 64, 93, 94, 97, 110, 113, 126, 132, 175, 191
seal matrix, 25, 26
seal tags, 30, 51n, 58, 61, 63, 64, 65, 66, 70, 76, 77, 80, 83, 84, 87, 91, 93, 94, 95, 96, 97, 99, 105, 106, 107, 108, 109, 110, 112, 113, 117, 118, 121, 124, 129, 130, 131, 132, 140, 141, 143, 145, 146, 147, 149, 150, 152, 157, 165, 168, 173, 174, 175, 178, 179, 180, 181, 189, 191, 198
seal tongues, 12, 13, 27, 30, 33, 51n, 65, 75, 78, 79, 80, 82, 83, 84, 85, 86, 109, 110, 111, 113, 117, 120, 124, 126, 127, 129, 130, 131, 140, 141, 143, 145, 146, 147, 148, 149, 150, 152, 153, 173, 174, 176, 177, 178, 179, 180, 181, 183, 184, 187, 189, 190, 191, 198
see(s), apostolic, 101
episcopal, 102, 112, 134, 195, 196, 216, 221
seisin, 19, 77, 124; *see also* sasine
serfs, 11, 133, 134; *see also cumelahe*
serjeant(s), 206, 211, 230, 231
servants, 6, 17, 21, 28, 35, 125, 155, 156, 199
service, king's, 8, 34, 57, 59, 60, 61, 64, 65, 66, 68, 76, 77, 79, 81, 87, 88, 89, 100, 102, 106, 107, 108, 109, 113, 118, 144, 149, 154, 190, 193, 195, 216; *see also* default of service; forinsec service; homage and service tenure; military service
settlement, 19, 20, 38, 82, 140, 205, 214, 226
sheriff(s), 11, 58, 62, 64, 65, 70, 71, 78, 80, 83, 84, 85, 86, 87, 89, 90, 91, 108, 110, 113, 114, 115, 116, 120, 128, 131, 144, 146, 147, 154, 156, 157, 181, 186, 188, 190, 191, 193, 200, 201, 203, 206, 209, 210, 211, 212, 213, 217, 219, 220, 223, 224, 225, 229, 232, 235
sheriff court, 203
sheriffdom(s), 70, 144, 191, 192, 202
shield(s), 30, 32, 171, 176
ship(s), 18, 89, 101, 106, 125, 127, 128, 136, 155, 165, 221; *see also* boat(s); ferry
shipwreck, 101, 104
shires, 133, 134, 135
shrine, 33, 123
silken cords, 14, 169, 171, 176
silver *see* sterling silver
soke, 86, 87, 96, 97, 152, 153, 154, 194, 217
souls, 66, 73, 88, 91, 101, 103, 104, 117, 136, 141, 145, 154, 164, 184, 187, 189, 196, 197, 222
spurious acts, 20–1, 51n, 52n, 105, 191
staff and baton, resignation by, 8, 67, 87, 96, 144, 146, 153, 156, 174, 184, 185
sterling silver, 17, 77, 82, 97, 101, 102, 103, 107, 125, 154, 156, 157, 160, 162, 163, 168, 169, 170, 176, 177, 178, 181, 201, 226, 230, 231
steward, 57, 61, 65, 68, 69, 72, 73, 79, 80, 86, 87, 94, 95, 97, 99, 108, 121, 122, 123, 124, 125, 129, 130, 134, 154, 159, 164, 174, 183, 190, 192, 208
stream, 57, 63, 119, 131, 140; *see also* burn
sub-bailiff, 111
suit(s), 19, 58, 67, 79, 84, 85, 123, 183, 201
suit of court, 99, 120, 127, 128, 203
sur double queue, 12, 13, 14
sureties, 183, 184; *see also* pledges
surgeon, 230
sword(s), 30, 32, 33

tag(s), 30, 51n, 58, 61, 63, 64, 66, 70, 76, 77, 80, 83, 84, 87, 91, 93, 94, 95, 96, 97, 99, 105, 106, 107, 108, 109, 110, 112, 113, 117, 118, 121, 124, 129, 130, 131, 132, 140, 141, 143, 145, 146, 147, 149, 150, 152, 157, 165, 168, 173, 174, 175, 178, 179, 180, 181, 189, 191, 198
tailor, 212
tallow, 133, 134, 135, 136
tax, 179, 197, 198
team, 86, 87, 96, 97, 152, 153, 194, 195
teinds, 20, 51n, 70, 71, 81, 133, 134, 135, 136, 138, 152, 193, 194

tenant(s), 5, 7, 8, 9, 10, 16, 19, 22, 23, 29, 34, 99, 115, 116, 128, 156, 191, 194, 216, 217, 224, 230
tenement(s), 50, 99, 117, 118, 128, 140, 141, 213, 223, 230
tenure, 9, 10, 19
terce, 19
testament, 224, 226
testimony, 4, 222
testing clause, 4, 5, 7, 11, 14, 42, 48n; *see also* witness list(s)
thanages, 70, 71, 80, 81, 209, 230
thane, 209, 212, 213
theft, 186
throne, 4, 20, 26, 30, 32, 58, 66, 165, 182, 202, 211
throne, succession to, 8, 13, 14, 20, 26, 58, 162, 164, 165–8
timber, 7, 10, 61, 86, 87, 95, 96, 118, 119, 130, 191, 192; *see also* wood
tocher, 14, 21, 26, 157, 165, 172; *see also* dowry
toft(s), 59, 63, 134, 136, 214
toll(s) (fiscal), 89, 99, 134, 182
toll (jurisdiction), 86, 87, 96, 97, 152, 153, 194, 195
transumpts, 49n, 58, 62, 65, 67, 98, 155, 183, 188, 198, 199, 202
treasurer, 28, 203, 208, 210, 232
treasury, 15, 20, 25, 37, 112, 205, 212, 215, 216, 219, 226
treaties, 13, 14–15, 29, 37, 38, 39, 100–5, 157, 198, 210, 214
trefoils, 32, 33, 171
tressure, double, 30, 32, 171, 176
Trinitarian order, 209
tronage, 18
truce, 212

unattributable acts, 22, 43, 234–5
unction, 32, 202
universities, 14, 27, 28
usages, 16, 93, 139, 179, 188, 197; *see also* customs

vacancy, 27, 112, 139, 195, 196, 232
venison, 120, 121, 135
verderer, 120
vert, 120, 121
vicar, 138
vicarage, 138, 139
victualling, 211
voucher to warrant, 21, 31; *see also* warrandice

war, 20, 71, 159, 163, 228
wardship, 19, 97, 112, 121, 214, 224
wardrobe, 114, 147, 184, 185, 229
warrandice, 9, 21, 31, 191
warrant for payment, 15
warren *see* free warren
waste, 173, 216
water(s), 57, 69, 87, 89, 95, 108, 109, 118, 119, 126, 133, 135, 142, 152, 163, 194, 197, 207
wax, 24, 30, 51n, 58, 61, 62, 63, 64, 66, 76, 93, 94, 96, 97, 98, 110, 111, 112, 113, 124, 131, 132, 156, 157, 168, 169, 171, 175, 176, 177, 178, 182, 191, 231
wayting, 10; *see also* hospitality
whales, 134, 136
wheat, 232
widow(s), 10, 13, 67, 121, 161, 169, 204, 205, 226
widowhood, 118, 141
wife, 3, 4, 25, 75, 80, 107, 108, 114, 117, 118, 126, 140, 149, 150, 154, 155, 165, 166, 167, 169, 170, 171, 175, 187, 201, 202, 204, 214, 217, 219
wine, 18, 180, 181, 227, 231
witness lists, 3, 4, 5, 7, 11, 21, 23, 34, 42, 88, 96, 142, 195, 197, 199, 200, 201; *see also* clauses, of attestation
witnesses, 5, 8, 11, 81, 170, 216, 231
witnessing *see* attestation
wood *see* timber
woods, 61, 62, 69, 87, 95, 96, 128, 152, 153, 194, 196, 205, 206, 215; *see also* forest; park(s)
wool, 191, 192
writ(s), 10, 19, 27, 186, 208, 214, 224, 228, 229, 230
writ-charters, 6, 7, 15, 41
writing office, 3, 7, 12, 20, 24, 25, 37, 51n, 191; *see also* chancery, Scottish; chapel, royal
wyverns, 33

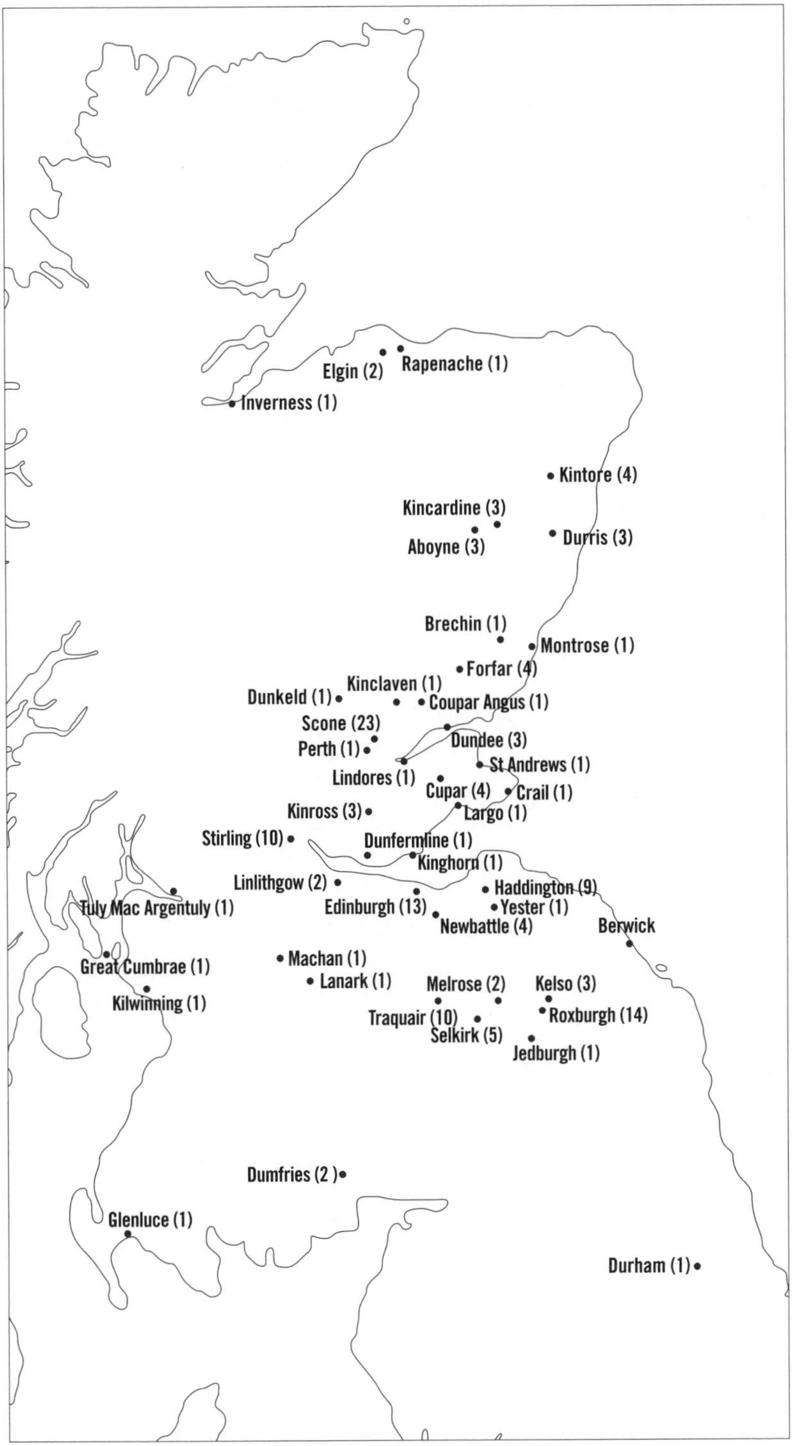

Map of Scotland showing the places at which Alexander III's acts were issued (number of acts at each place in parenthesis)